CONTENTS

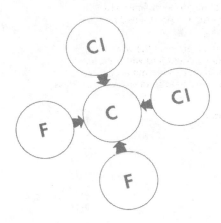

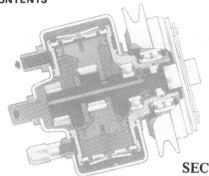

SECTION 2 SYSTEM DIAGNOSIS

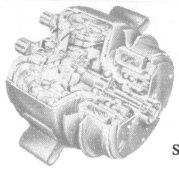

SECTION 3 SERVICE PROCEDURES

AUTOMOTIVE AIR CONDITIONING

6th Edition
Boyce H. Dwiggins

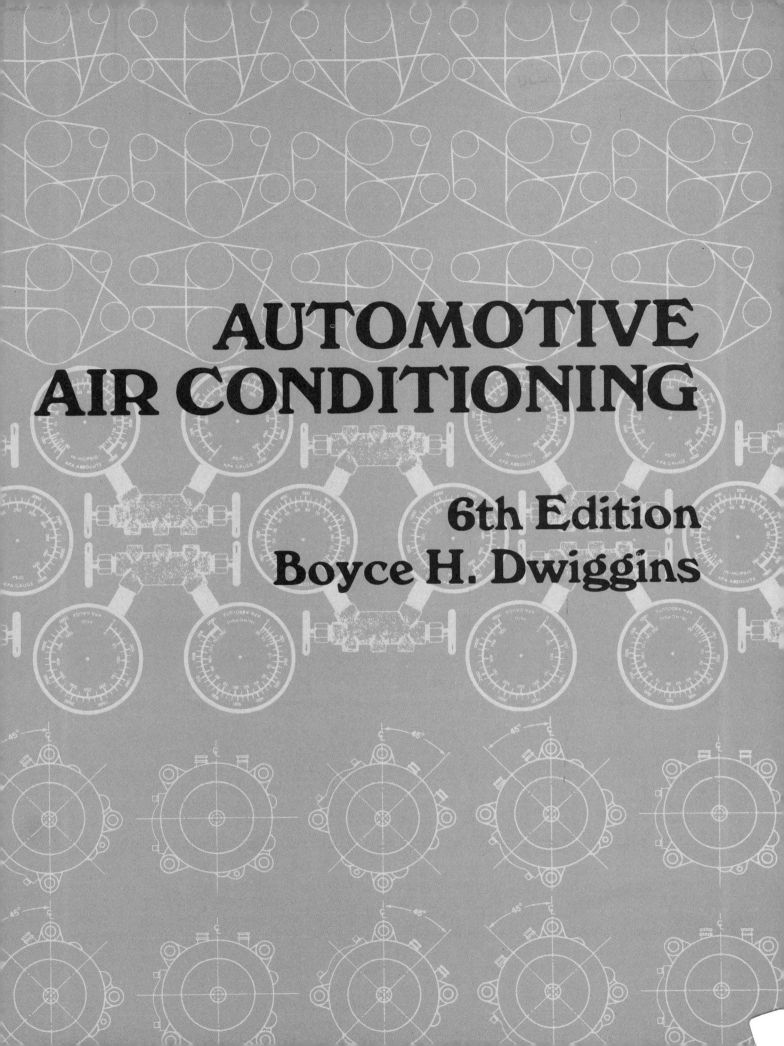

NOTICE TO THE READER

Photos of V-5 compressor and accumulator/dehydrator courtesy of Harrison Radiator Division of General Motors Corporation, Lockport, NY.

Photo of thermostatic expansion valve courtesy of Eaton Corporation, Controls Division, Carol Stream, IL.

Photo of manifold gauge set courtesy of Robinair Division, Sealed Power Corp., Montpelier, OH.

Delmar Staff

Associate Editor: Joan Gill
Managing Editor: Barbara A. Christie
Production Editor: Ruth East
Publications Coordinator: Karen Seebald

For information, address Delmar Publishers Inc.
2 Computer Drive West, Box 15-015
Albany, New York 12212

10 9 8 7 6 5 4 3

Printed in the United States of America
Published simultaneously in Canada
by Nelson Canada,
A division of The Thomson Corporation

Library of Congress Cataloging-in-Publication Data

Dwiggins, Boyce H.
    Automotive air conditioning.

    Includes index.
    1. Automobiles—Air conditioning. 2. Automobiles—
Air conditioning—Maintenance and repair. I. Title.
TL271.5.D9   1988   629.2'77   87-27196
ISBN 0-8273-3081-2 (soft)
ISBN 0-8273-3082-0 (instr. guide)

PREFACE

Automotive Air Conditioning, 6th Edition, continues in the best selling tradition established in 1967 by the first edition. The most up-to-date automotive air conditioning technology has been included: electronic temperature controls, new domestic and foreign compressors, and CCOT and FFOT clutch systems.

The information given in this text is a balanced introduction to automotive air conditioning. The student will develop a basic understanding of the theory, diagnostic practices, and service procedures essential to air conditioning. At the same time, the student will develop habits of sound practice and good judgment in the performance of all air-conditioning procedures. The instructional units can be regarded as entry level for those who apply immediately the basic skills developed in the class and shop. The units are preparatory for those who plan continued study in advanced phases of refrigeration and air conditioning, including systems not related to automotive applications.

The text contains three basic sections. Section 1 is arranged in the natural order of dependence of one principle, law, or set of conditions upon another. The material within a unit follows an organized pattern which helps the student to see relationships. Section 2 guides the student in the performance of system diagnostic procedures. This is accomplished by stressing diagnosis through the use of a manifold and gauge set. Sixteen color plates are included for interpretation of various system functions and malfunctions. Section 3 presents step-by-step instructions for the application of specific service procedures. A Glossary is provided to aid in identifying component parts and phrases relevant to automotive air conditioning.

It is suggested that each topic in this text be considered as an assignment to be carried out by the student.

An Instructor's Guide provides solutions to all of the objective questions and problems. Suggested answers are given wherever there may be variations in the responses given by the students. Lesson plans are provided for each unit of the text.

ABOUT THE AUTHOR

Boyce H. Dwiggins organized one of the first courses in vocational education for Automotive Air Conditioning. This course has run continuously since 1965. He was in charge of automotive classes as a county-level administrator and was a consultant for the writing of educational specifications for a five-shop automotive complex in an area vocational center.

Mr. Dwiggins has served as an examiner, administering the "Automotive Excellence" test for the International Garage Owner's Association (IGOA) for the certification of auto mechanics. He was invited to serve with a committee of the National Institute for Automotive Service Excellence (NIASE) to write the certification test for automotive air conditioning.

Mr. Dwiggins holds patents on teaching devices and copyrights on teaching material in the automotive and refrigeration fields. He has conducted workshops for automotive and refrigeration teachers throughout the eastern United States. He is currently Department Head of the Industrial Department of a vocational-technical center in Florida.

ACKNOWLEDGMENTS

This text would not have been possible without the generous cooperation of the many manufacturers of automotive air-conditioning equipment and components. Their contributions over the past twenty-one years, since the first edition, have been most helpful in providing the latest information available.

Chrysler Motors Corporation

Controls Company of America

Everhot Products Company

Ford Motor Company

General Electric Company

General Motors Corporation:
   Buick Motor Division, Cadillac Motor Car Division, Chevrolet Motor Division, Delco Radio Division, Oldsmobile Division

Mapco

John E. Mitchell Company, Inc.

Murray Corporation

Robinair Manufacturing Company

Sankyo

Sears, Roebuck and Company

Tecumseh Products Company

Thermal Industries

T.I.F. Instruments, Inc.

Uniweld Products, Inc.

Warner Electric Brake and Clutch Company

York Corporation, Subsidiary of Borg-Warner Corporation

Thanks to the instructors who reviewed the revised manuscript.

Larry Adams, Portland Community College, Portland, Oregon

Edward Hester, Cedar Valley College, Lancaster, Texas

George Knebel, Northwestern Business College, Lima, Ohio

Mr. Gaff, ITT Technical Institute, Chelsea, Massachusetts

Thanks is expressed to Mr. Richard G. Herd, former Associate, Vocational-Industrial Education, State of New York, for his initial assistance and encouragement, and to Mr. Earl Pescatore, Automotive Specialist, Sheridan Vocational-Technical Center, Hollywood, Florida, for his critical review.

A special thanks to Mr. Steve Wylie and the staff of Mr. Tom's Automotive, Pompano Beach, Florida, for their front-line technical assistance.

Last, but by no means least, thanks to the team at Delmar Publishers Inc. for steering this text through all six editions.

. . . . . and, to Edward and Judith, this book is dedicated.

B. H. Dwiggins

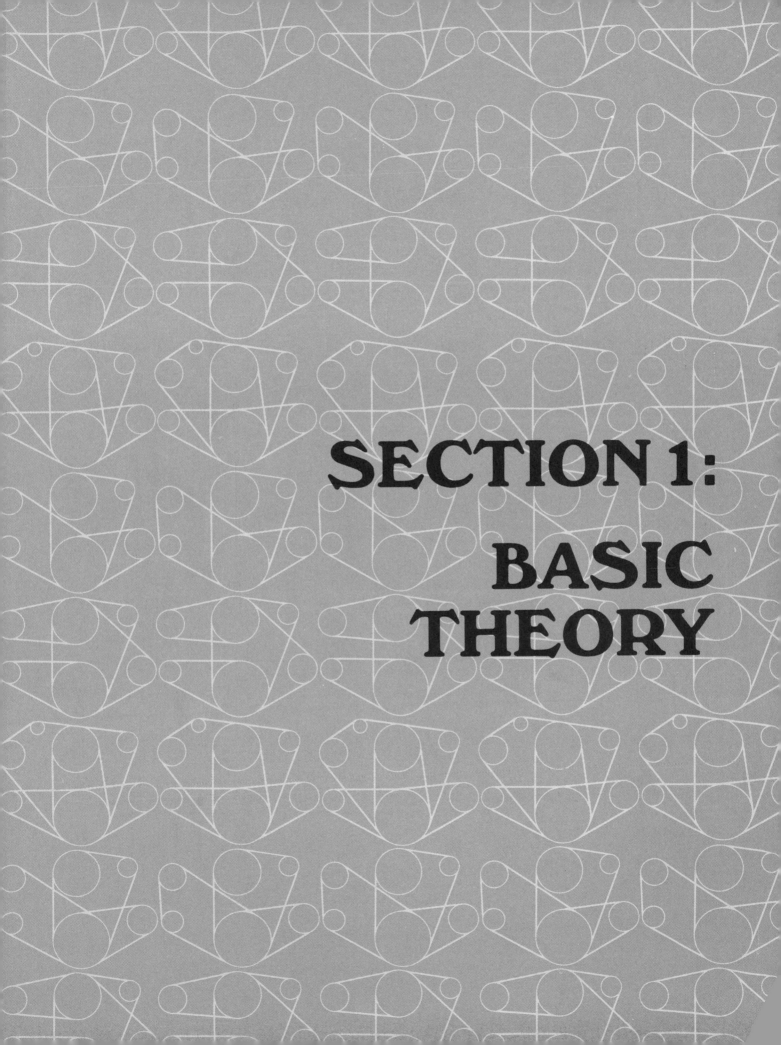

SECTION 1:

BASIC THEORY

UNIT 1:

Introduction

Refrigeration and air conditioning are not discoveries of the twentieth century. Simple forms of refrigeration and air conditioning were in use twelve thousand years ago. Although these early systems were crude by today's standards, they served the same purpose as modern units.

Many aspects of modern life were made possible only after sophisticated air-conditioning systems were developed. Numerous vital components associated with the United States space program could not have been manufactured without the use of air conditioning. For example, many precision mechanical and electrical parts must be manufactured and assembled under very strict tolerances. These tolerances require the control of temperature and humidity within a range of a few degrees. For example, this microprocessor chip, only about 1/16 inch (1.59 mm) square, is a miniaturized electronic circuit etched into a base of silicon. It was manufactured in a temperature/humidity-controlled en-

vironment made possible by modern refrigeration techniques, figure 1-1.

Automotive air conditioning was available in 1940, but it did not become popular until 1960. Since that time, interest in air conditioning has increased yearly. Air conditioning is now one of the most popular selections in the entire list of automotive accessories.

In 1962, slightly more than eleven percent of all cars sold were equipped with air conditioners. This percent accounted for 756 781 units, including both factory-installed systems and those added after the purchase of the automobile. Just five years later, in 1967, the total number of installed air-conditioning units rose to 3 546 255. At the present time, nearly eighty percent of all automobiles sold are equipped with air-conditioning units. It is expected that the usage of these units will remain at approximately eighty percent. This means that eighty cars out of every one hundred cars on the road will be

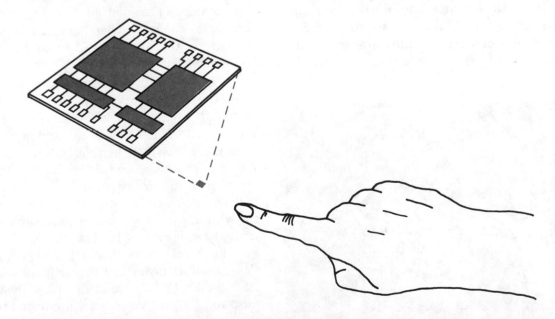

Fig. 1-1 This microprocessor, only about 1/16-inch (1.59-mm) square is a miniaturized electronic circuit etched into a base of silicon. It was manufactured in a temperature/humidity controlled environment made possible by modern refrigeration techniques.

equipped with factory-installed or add-on air conditioning. When air conditioning was first used in automobiles, it was considered a luxury. Its usefulness soon made air conditioning a necessity.

At this point, the definition of air conditioning should be reviewed before tracing its history and its application to the automobile. *Air conditioning* is the process by which air is cooled, cleaned, and circulated. In addition, the quantity and quality of the conditioned air are controlled. This means that the temperature, humidity, and volume of air are controlled in any given situation. Under ideal conditions, air conditioning can be expected to accomplish all of these tasks at the same time. The student should recognize that the air-conditioning process includes the process of refrigeration (cooling by removing heat).

HISTORICAL DEVELOPMENT OF AIR CONDITIONING

Refrigeration, as we know it today, is less than eighty-five years old. Some of its principles, however, were known as long as ten thousand years before Christ.

The Egyptians developed a method for removing the heat from the Pharaoh's palace. The walls of the palace were constructed of huge stone blocks, each weighing over a thousand tons. Every night, three thousand slaves dismantled the walls and moved the stones to the Sahara Desert. Since the temperature in the desert is cool during the night, the stones gave up the heat they had absorbed during the day. Before daybreak the slaves moved the stones back to the palace site and reassembled the walls, figure 1-2. As a result of this crude form of refrigeration, it is thought that the Pharaoh enjoyed temperatures of about 80°F (26.6°C) inside the palace while the temperature outside soared to about 130°F (54.4°C). Three thousand men worked all night to do a job that modern refrigeration easily handles. Although the work effort is less today, the same principle of refrigeration is applied to present systems as was applied in the Pharaoh's time. That is, heat is removed from one space and is transferred to another space.

Shortly after the beginning of the twentieth century, T. C. Northcott, of Luray, Virginia, became the first man known to history to have a home with central heating and air conditioning. A heating and ventilating engineer, Northcott built his house on a hill above the famous Caverns of Luray. Because of his work, he knew that air filtered through limestone was free of dust and pollen. This fact was important because both Northcott and his family suffered from hay fever.

Some distance behind his house he drilled a five-foot (1.5 meters) shaft through the ceiling of the cavern. He installed a forty-two-inch (1.07 meters) fan in the shaft to pull eight thousand cubic feet (2 265 cubic meters) of air per minute through the shaft. He then constructed a shed over the shaft and from this built a duct system to the house. The duct was divided into two chambers, one above the other. The upper chamber carried air from the cavern and was heated by the sun. This chamber provided air to warm the house on cool days. The lower chamber carried cool air from the cavern; this air was used to cool the house on warm days.

The humidity (moisture content) of the air from the cavern was controlled in a chamber in Northcott's basement where air from both ducts was mixed. The warmer air contained a greater amount of moisture than the cooler air. Northcott was able to direct conditioned air from the mixing chamber of the air system to any or all of the rooms in his house through a network of smaller ducts. In the winter, the air was heated by steam coils located in the base of each of the branch ducts.

Each year more than 350 000 people visit the Caverns of Luray where the temperature is a constant 54°F (12.22°C) and the air is always free of dust and pollen. Visitors are impressed by the fact that in this residence, the ingenuity of one inventor provided central heating and air conditioning long before these conveniences were available on a large scale.

Fig. 1-2 Moving stones of Pharaoh's palace back in place

Domestic Refrigeration

Domestic refrigeration systems appeared first in 1910, even though ice has been made artificially since 1820. In 1896, the Sears, Roebuck and Company catalog offered several *refrigerators* for sale, figure 1-3. The refrigeration, however, was provided by ice. The icebox shown held twenty-five pounds of ice and was useful only for the short-term storage of foods. Incidentally, the selling price for this refrigerator was $5.65.

The first manually operated refrigerator was produced by J. L. Larsen in 1913. The Kelvinator Company produced the first automatic refrigerator

Fig. 1-3 Early *refrigerator* was actually an icebox (1896)

in 1918. The acceptance of this new refrigerator was slow. By 1920, only about two hundred units had been sold.

In 1926, the first hermetic (sealed) refrigerator was introduced by General Electric. The following year, Electrolux introduced an automatic absorption unit. A four-cubic foot refrigerator was introduced by Sears, Roebuck and Company in 1931. The refrigerator cabinet, figure 1-4, and the refrigeration unit were shipped separately and required assembly. The cost of this refrigerator was $137.50. In terms of the price per cubic foot, the 1931 refrigerator is comparable to the modern refrigerator.

Mobile Air Conditioning

The first automotive air-conditioning unit appeared on the market in 1927. True air conditioning was not to appear in cars for another thirteen years. However, air conditioning was advertised as an option in some cars in 1927. At that time, air conditioning meant only that the car could be equipped with a heater, a ventilation system, and a means of filtering the air.

In 1940, Packard offered the first method of cooling a car by means of refrigeration. Actually, Packard's first units were commercial air conditioners adapted for automotive use. Two years earlier, a few passenger buses had been air conditioned by the same method.

Accurate records were not kept in the early days of automotive air conditioning. However, it is known that before World War II there were between 3 000 and 4 000 units installed in Packards. Defense priorities for materials and manufacturing prevented the improvement of automotive air conditioning until the early 1950s. At that time, the demand for air-conditioned vehicles began in the Southwest.

Many large firms were able to report increased sales after air conditioning was installed in the cars of their salespeople. Many commercial vehicles are now air conditioned, including buses and taxicabs. Truckers realize larger profits because drivers who have air-conditioned cabs average more mileage than those who do not.

In 1967, all of the state police cars on the Florida Turnpike were air conditioned. Since then, law enforcement agencies across the nation have added air conditioning to their vehicles.

Mobile air conditioning is not only found in cars, trucks, and buses. In recent years, mobile air-conditioning application has been expanded for use in such farm equipment as tractors, harvesters, and thrashers. Additionally, mobile air-conditioning systems have been developed for use in other off-the-road equipment, such as backhoes, bulldozers, graders, and so on.

Actually, mobile air conditioning may be found in almost any kind of domestic, farm or commercial equipment that requires an onboard operator.

Yesterday and Today

From this brief history it can be seen that although forms of air conditioning and refrigeration were in use thousands of years ago, the period of rapid growth for the refrigeration industry has occurred in the past half century.

Atomic submarines are able to remain submerged indefinitely due, in part, to air conditioning. Modern medicine and delicate machine components are perfected in scientifically controlled atmospheres. Computer centers are able to function properly because they are kept within a specific range of temperature and humidity levels.

THE INDUSTRY

Automobile air conditioning today is no longer a luxury – it is a necessity. Millions of Americans enjoy the benefits it produces. Businesspeople are able to drive to appointments in comfort

$137⁵⁰

4 Cubic Feet Food Storage Capacity

For families of two to three. Actually 4.01 cubic feet of usable space. Shelf area 8.26 square feet. Outside dimensions, 51 in. high (including legs), 24½ in. wide, 20½ inches deep. Three ice cube trays, each containing ten ice cubes size 1⅛ inches long x 1½ in. wide x 1¼ in. deep. Mounted on legs 8 inches high. Insulation, two inches of Dry Zero. Shipping weight, 330 lbs. Not Prepaid.
23EM2240½—Cash Price ... **$137.50**
Easy Payment Price ... **$151.25**
Terms: $10 Down, $10 a month. Use Time Payment Order Blank in Back of Catalog.

Fig. 1-4 Early refrigerator (1931)

and arrive fresh and alert. People with allergies are able to travel without the fear of coming into contact with excessive dust and airborne pollen. Because of the extensive use of the automobile in America, automobile air conditioning is playing an important role in promoting the comfort, health, and safety of travelers throughout the land. Today eighty percent of all cars produced are equipped with air conditioners.

The number of cars, trucks, and recreational vehicles (RVs) equipped with air-conditioning systems has increased rapidly during the past thirty years.

It is easy to understand how automotive air conditioning has become the industry's most sought after product. In the South and Southwest, specialty auto repair shops base their entire trade on selling, installing, and servicing automotive air conditioners throughout the year.

COST OF OPERATION

It is the general opinion of many that the ever-increasing cost of fossil fuel will put an early end to the "luxury" of automotive air conditioning. The air-conditioning system does place an extra load on the engine. Any engine load requires fuel. Therefore, it seems apparent that the use of an air conditioner will reduce gasoline mileage. This is true, but only for stop-and-go driving.

At highway speeds, air-conditioned cars, with their windows closed and the air conditioning operating, actually average two to three percent better mileage than do nonair-conditioned cars. The aerodynamic design considerations of the car body are based upon having the windows closed. When the windows are closed, it seems that reduced wind resistance offsets the demand load of the air-conditioning system on the engine.

As EXXON published in its *Happy Motoring News*® (Vol. 19), "At 40 mph or faster you'll use more gasoline by driving with your windows open than you will by operating an air conditioner with all the windows closed. Open windows cause that much 'drag'."

The number of new car sales has decreased in recent years. However, the percent of new cars sold with air-conditioning systems has remained about the same. Aftermarket sales, service, and repairs on automotive air conditioners have actually increased to some extent. Car owners are simply keeping their cars longer, and in better repair.

THE SERVICE TECHNICIAN

How does all this affect the student of automotive air conditioning? As the popularity of air conditioning in vehicles increases, it is obvious that the need for installation, maintenance, and service technicians will also increase. Many shops that just a few years ago added air-conditioning service as a sideline, now find it to be their primary business.

The air-conditioning technician must have a thorough working knowledge and understanding of the operation and function of the circuits and controls of the automotive air conditioner. A good knowledge of the equipment, special tools, techniques, and skills of the trade is also essential.

Air conditioning has made it possible for the Space Age to become part of the twentieth century. What was fiction at the turn of the century is commonplace today. The service technician's contribution to the industry may help make today's fiction commonplace by the twenty-first century.

SAFETY

It must be recognized that the procedures used by technicians performing automotive service vary greatly. It is not possible to anticipate all ways or conditions under which service may be performed. Therefore, it is not possible to provide precautions for every conceivable hazard that may result. The following precautions, then, are basic and apply to any type automotive service.

1. Wear safety glasses or goggles for eye protection.
2. Set the parking brake. Place the gear select in *park* (automatic transmissions) or *neutral* (manual transmissions).
3. Be sure the ignition switch is in the OFF position, unless otherwise required for the procedure.
4. When required for the procedure, operate the engine *only* in a well-ventilated area.
5. Keep clear of all moving parts when the engine is running. Remove rings, watches, and loose-hanging jewelry. Avoid loose clothing. Tie long hair securely behind the head.
6. Keep hands, clothing, tools, and test leads away from the radiator cooling fan. Electric cooling fans can start without warning even when the ignition switch is in the OFF position.
7. Avoid contact with hot parts such as radiator, exhaust manifold, and high-side refrigeration lines.

Review

Select the appropriate answer from the choices given for the following questions.

1. How did moving the stones of the Pharaoh's palace into the desert help to keep the palace cool?

   a. The palace was given a chance to air out.
   b. The stones gave up heat in the desert during the day.
   c. The stones gave up heat in the desert during the night.
   d. The stones could be easily rotated for reassembly.

2. The first advertised air conditioning for a car was

   a. in 1940, by Packard.
   b. in 1927, consisting of a heater, a ventilation system, and a filter.
   c. in 1926, by General Electric.
   d. after the war, in the 1950s.

3. What is the greatest technical accomplishment to date, which was made possible, in part, by air conditioning?

   a. The space program
   b. Modern medicine
   c. Computer electronics
   d. All of the choices are perhaps equally as great

4. What percent of the total domestic car production will be equipped with air conditioning this year?

   a. About 80%
   b. Between 70% and 80%
   c. 70%, or less
   d. 90%, or more

5. Generally, at a speed of 40 mph or faster, less fuel will be used with the air conditioner

   a. off and the windows open.
   b. on and the windows closed.
   c. off and the windows closed.
   d. on and the windows open.

6. What underhood part(s) becomes hot when the engine is running?

   a. Radiator
   b. Exhaust manifold
   c. Radiator hoses
   d. All of the answers are correct.

7. Which underhood part(s) may start and run without warning?

   a. The heater blower motor
   b. The radiator fan clutch
   c. The electric radiator fan
   d. All of the answers are correct.

CONTINUED

8. When working under the hood of a car

    a. securely tie back long hair.
    b. avoid loose clothing.
    c. remove jewelry.
    d. All of the answers are correct.

9. Before working under the hood of a car,

    a. set the parking brake.
    b. place the automatic transmission in neutral.
    c. chock the rear wheels.
    d. All of the answers are correct.

10. Technician A says that the greatest underhood hazard is the belts. Technician B says that the greatest underhood hazard is fans and fan blades. Who is correct?

    a. Technician A
    b. Technician B
    c. Both technicians are correct.
    d. Neither technician is correct.

UNIT 2:

The Metric System

The metric system of units was first introduced in France in about 1790. The first system of metric units, called the CGS (centimeter-gram-second) system, was based on the centimeter (cm) as the unit of length, the gram (g) as the unit of mass, and the second (s) as the unit of time.

This system was used a little over one hundred years until, at the turn of the last century, a more practical set of metric units known as the MKS (meter-kilogram-second) system was developed. This system, based on the meter (m), kilogram (kg), and second (s), was used for about fifty years. In about 1950, the ampere (A) was added as the fourth unit. This made it possible to link electrical units with mechanical units. The name was then changed to the MKSA system.

SYSTEM OF UNITS
(SI METRICS)

Later, a system of metric units was established, based on the four MKSA units plus the kelvin (K) as the unit of temperature, the candela (cd) as the unit of luminous intensity, and the mole (mol) as the unit of substance.

Since the names of the previous system had been based on the first letter of designated units, this system might have been called the MKSAKCM system. Instead, it was decided to name this system the *Systeme International d'Unites* or, more commonly, the SI system of units (metrics).

Some liberty is taken with the system standards. The SI metric standard for a unit of temperature is the kelvin (K). The Kelvin Scale, used primarily for engineering, indicates that the freezing temperature of water (H_2O) at sea level is 273°K, and the boiling point is 373°K. The American Society of Heating, Refrigeration, and Air-Conditioning Engineers (ASHRAE) has adopted the Celsius (C) scale for practical technical application. On the Celsius scale, the freezing point of water at sea level is 0°C, and the boiling point is 100°C.

Decimal System

Metric units are based on the decimal system of measure. Fractions are not used in the metric system. One need only think in terms of *ten*. Multiples or submultiples of any unit are related to the unit by powers of ten. Compared to working with fractions, calculations in metrics are made quite rapidly. The chance of error is also greatly reduced. For these reasons, the SI metric system is simple to learn and use.

Division and Power

In the metric system, separation of numbers, when over four, is by the insertion of a space (actually a half-space) instead of the customary comma. Four-digit numbers such as 1,000, may be expressed as 1000 or 1 000; the space may or may not be used. However, the space is always used in numbers of more than four digits. For example, 10,000 becomes 10 000; 100,000 becomes 100 000; 1,000,000 becomes 1 000 000, and so on.

Another way of expressing metric numbers is by power. *Power* indicates how many times a prime number is multiplied by itself. For example, the number 100 may be expressed as 10^2 ($10 \times 10 = 100$); 1 000 may be expressed as 10^3 ($10 \times 10 \times 10 = 1 000$); 10 000 expressed as 10^4 ($10 \times 10 \times 10 \times 10 = 10 000$), and so on. Either way of expression, by whole number or by power, is acceptable.

Multiples and Submultiples

Powers of ten are referred to as *multiples* and *submultiples*. In metrics, these powers have both a prefix and a symbol. The chart of figure 2-1 includes the prefixes and symbols most commonly used.

Symbols

It is important to use symbols correctly so as not to change their meaning. When capital letters

Number	Power	Prefix	Symbol
1 000 000 000 000	10^{12}	tera	T
1 000 000 000	10^9	giga	G
1 000 000	10^6	mega	M
1 000	10^3	kilo	k
100	10^2	hecto	h
10	10^1	deka	da
0.1	10^{-1}	deci	d
0.01	10^{-2}	centi	c
0.001	10^{-3}	milli	m
0.000 001	10^{-6}	micro	μ
0.000 000 001	10^{-9}	nano	n
0.000 000 000 001	10^{-12}	pico	p

Fig. 2-1 Powers, prefixes, and symbols commonly used in metrics

are required, lowercase letters must not be used. For example, the capital letter M is the symbol for the prefix mega, whereas the lowercase letter m is the symbol for the prefix milli. There is a great difference between mg (milligrams) and Mg (megagrams). One mg is 1/1 000th of a gram, whereas one Mg is one million grams.

The common metric terms and symbols used by the automotive air-conditioning technician are found in the chart of figure 2-2.

The word *Celsius* (C) is often confused with the word *Centigrade* (C). The word Centigrade, often used to denote temperature, is used in some parts of the world to denote fractions of a right angle. For this reason, the word Celsius is used in the SI metric system.

It should be noted also that the lowercase letter m is used as the symbol for the unit *meter* as well as for the prefix *milli*. As illustrated in figure 2-2, when used in combination, mm becomes *millimeter* (1/1 000th of a meter). It is therefore very important that attention be given to the use of abbreviations and symbols in the metric system.

CONVERSIONS

Formulas have been developed for the rapid conversion of English-metric and metric-English units. The chart of figure 2-3 gives the formulas most commonly used by the automotive air-conditioning technician.

Fraction to Decimal Conversions

The decimal system must be used to convert English values to metric values. Therefore, any English fractional value must first be converted to

Term	Symbol
Celsius	C
centimeter	cm
gram	g
kilogram	kg
kilometer	km
kilopascal	kPa
liter	L
meter	m
milliliter	mL
millimeter	mm

Fig. 2-2 Common metric terms and symbols

METRIC TO ENGLISH		
Multiply	**By**	**To Get**
Celsius (°C)	1.8 (+32)	Fahrenheit (°F)
gram (g)	0.035 3	ounce (oz)
kilogram (kg)	2.205	pound (lb)
kilometer (km)	0.621 4	mile (mi)
kilopascal (kPa)	0.145	lb/in^2 (psi)
liter (L)	0.264 2	gallon (gal)
meter (m)	3.281	foot (ft)
milliliter (mL)	0.033 8	ounce (oz)
millimeter (mm)	0.039 4	inch (in)

ENGLISH TO METRIC		
Fahrenheit (°F)	(–32) 0.556	Celsius (°C)
foot (ft)	0.304 8	meter (m)
fluidounce (fl oz)	29.57	milliliter (mL)
gallon (gal)	3.785	liter (L)
inch (in)	25.4	millimeter (mm)
mile (mi)	1.609	kilometer (km)
ounce (oz)	28.349 5	gram (g)
pound (lb)	0.453 6	kilogram (kg)
lb/in^2 (psi)	6.895	kilopascal (kPa)

Fig. 2-3 Metric to English and English to metric conversion factors

an English decimal. This is easily accomplished by dividing the numerator by the denominator. The *numerator* is the number above the line; the *denominator* is the number below the line.

Whole numbers remain whole numbers. The whole number is separated from the fraction by a decimal. For example, 1 and 1/2 becomes 1.5; 1 and (1 ÷ 2) = 1.5. A decimal is placed after the whole number and the fraction is converted to a decimal.

Those who use a calculator will find the decimal system most welcome. Calculators may also be used easily to convert fractions to decimals as well. Remember to hold decimal equivalents to three or four places. The fraction 5/64, for example, converts to 0.078 125 on a calculator. The four-place decimal of 0.078 1 or three-place decimal of 0.078 should be sufficient.

Popular conversions for fractions of an inch, in 1/16th fractional inch, are given in figure 2-4. If the decimal is of a fraction only and does not contain a whole number, the decimal should be preceded by a zero. The decimal conversion for 1/4 is 0.25, not simply .25, indicating that there is no whole number.

COMMON METRICS

The automotive air-conditioning technician will be concerned with only a few of the metric system conversions. These units include weight, measure, temperature, and pressure.

Fraction	Decimal
1/16	0.062 5
1/8	0.125
3/16	0.187 5
1/4	0.25
5/16	0.312 5
3/8	0.375
7/16	0.437 5
1/2	0.5
9/16	0.562 5
5/8	0.625
11/16	0.687 5
3/4	0.75
13/16	0.812 5
7/8	0.875
15/16	0.937 5

Fig. 2-4 Decimal conversions for fractions of an inch (in 1/16th fractional inch)

Weight

The customary ounce (oz) is the gram (g) in the metric system. One ounce is equal to 28.349 5 grams. The standard "pound" Refrigerant 12 actually contains 14 ounces or 396.893 grams. Due to the metric system, this packaging may change to contain 400 grams which is just a little more than 14 ounces (14.108 oz).

The customary pound (lb) becomes the kilogram (kg) in the metric system. One pound is equal to 0.453 6 kilogram. The standard 15-lb cylinder of Refrigerant 12, containing 6.804 kg, may be repackaged to contain, say, 7 kg.

Again, to convert ounces to grams, multiply by 28.349 5; to convert grams to ounces, multiply by 0.035 3. To convert pounds to kilograms, multiply by 0.453 6; to convert kilograms to pounds, multiply by 2.205. One fluidounce (fl oz) is equal to 29.573 milliliters (mL).

Measure

The customary inch (in) becomes the millimeter (mm) in the metric system. One inch is equal to 25.4 millimeters. The customary foot (ft) becomes the meter (m). One foot is equal to 0.304 8 meter.

To convert inches to millimeters, multiply by 25.4; to convert millimeters to inches, multiply by 0.039 4. To convert feet to meters, multiply by 0.304 8; to convert meters to feet, multiply by 3.281.

If it is desirable to convert inches to meters, multiply the decimal equivalent of inches to feet, in the chart of figure 2-5, by the factor 0.304 8. For example, 1 inch is equal to 0.025 4 meter (0.083 3 × 0.304 8 = 0.025 4 meter).

Inch	Decimal Equivalent
1	0.083 3
2	0.166 6
3	0.25
4	0.333 2
5	0.416 6
6	0.5
7	0.583 1
8	0.666 4
9	0.75
10	0.833
11	0.916 3

Fig. 2-5 Decimal equivalent of inches to feet

Temperature

In the English system, the normal body temperature is 98.6°F. The equivalent to this in the metric system is 37°C. At sea level, the freezing point of water (H_2O) is 32°F or 0°C, and the boiling point is 212°F or 100°C.

To convert Fahrenheit (F) to Celsius (C), *first* subtract 32 *then* multiply by 0.555 6. To convert Celsius (C) to Fahrenheit (F), *first* multiply by 1.8 *then* add 32.

Pressure

The customary pounds per square inch (psi), pounds per square inch gauge (psig), and pounds per square inch absolute (psia) become kilopascal (kPa) in the metric system. One pound per square inch is equal to 6.895 kPa. One kPa equals 0.145 pound per square inch.

Early confusion when using the metric system led many sources to take the stand that the conversion from psi was to kilograms per square centimeter (kg/cm^2). To set the record straight and to avoid confusion, ASHRAE has endorsed the American Standard Metric Practice Standards (IEEE 268-1979 and ASTM 380-79), as supplied by the U.S. Department of Commerce, National Bureau of Standards. The following are excerpts from those standards.

3.4.6 PRESSURE AND VACUUM — Gauge pressure is absolute pressure minus ambient pressure (usually atmospheric pressure). Both gauge pressure and absolute pressure are properly expressed in pascals, using SI prefixes

English Series				Metric Series			
Size	Diameter		Threads Per Inch	Size	Diameter		Threads Per Inch (prox)
	in	mm			in	mm	
#8	0.164	4.165	32 or 36				
#10	0.190	4.636	24 or 32				
1/4	0.250	6.350	20 or 28	M6.3	0.248	6.299	25
				M7	0.275	6.985	25
5/16	0.312	7.924	18 or 24	M8	0.315	8.001	20 or 25
3/8	0.375	9.525	16 or 24				
				M10	0.393	9.982	17 or 20
7/16	0.437	11.099	14 or 20				
				M12	0.472	11.988	14.5 or 20
1/2	0.500	12.700	13 or 20				
9/16	0.562	14.274	12 or 18	M14	0.551	13.995	12.5 or 17
5/8	0.625	15.875	11 or 18				
				M16	0.630	16.002	12.5 or 17
				M18	0.700	17.780	10 or 17
3/4	0.750	19.050	10 or 16				
				M20	0.787	19.989	10 or 17
				M22	0.866	21.996	10 or 17
7/8	0.875	24.765	9 or 14				
				M24	0.945	24.003	8.5 or 12.5
1	1.000	25.400	8 or 14				
				M27	1.063	27.000	8.5 or 12.5

Fig. 2-6 Comparison of English and metric fasteners.

as appropriate. Absolute pressure is never negative. Gauge pressure is positive if above ambient pressure and negative if below. Pressure below ambient is often called vacuum; whenever the term *vacuum* is applied to a numerical measure it should be made clear whether negative gauge pressure or absolute pressure is meant. See 3.5.5 for methods of designating gauge pressure and absolute pressure.

3.5.5. ATTACHMENTS TO UNIT SYMBOLS — . . . . . no

attempt should be made to construct SI equivalents of the abbreviations "psia" and "psig," so often used to distinguish between absolute and gauge pressure. If the context leaves any doubt as to which is meant, the word *pressure* must be qualified appropriately. For example:

> . . . at a gauge pressure of 13 kPa
>
> or
>
> . . . at an absolute pressure of 13 kPa

Where space is limited, such as on gauges, nameplates, graph labels, and in table headings, the use of a modifier in parentheses, such as "kPa (gauge)" or "kPa (absolute)," is permitted.

METRIC REFERENCES IN THIS TEXT

So there is no doubt, all references to the metric system of pressure throughout this text will be for *gauge pressure* based at sea level ambient unless otherwise noted.

When applicable and practical, the metric equivalent of all English terms will be given in parentheses. For example, "The boiling point of water at atmospheric pressure is 212°F (100°C) and the freezing point is 32°F (0°C)."

For those English units that will not convert to a standard metric unit no parenthetical notation will be made. For example, "Remove the six 1/4-inch capscrews holding the seal plate." The chart of figure 2-6 compares English and metric fasteners from #8 (English) through M27 (metric). Note that there is no metric fastener that will replace an English fastener.

Review

Convert the following fractions to decimals.

1. 1/10 = _____
2. 1/25 = _____
3. 5/32 = _____
4. 3/8 = _____
5. 1/3 = _____
6. 3/64 = _____

Convert the following temperature scales.

7. 42°F = _____°C
8. 100°C = _____°F
9. 200°F = _____°C

Convert the following measures of distance.

10. 10 ft = _____ m
11. 254 mm = _____ in
12. 10 mi = _____ km

Convert the following weights.

13. 5 lb = _____ kg
14. 250 g = _____ oz
15. 27 oz = _____ g

Convert the following liquid measures.

16. 10 L = _____ gal
17. 40 gal = _____ L
18. 3 gal = _____ L

Convert the following pressure values.

19. 68.95 kPa = _____ psi
20. 110 psi = _____ kPa

UNIT 3:

Body Comfort

The normal temperature of the adult human body is 98.6°F (37°C). This temperature is sometimes called subsurface or deep-tissue temperature as opposed to surface or skin temperature. An understanding of the process by which the body maintains its temperature is helpful to the student because it explains how air conditioning helps keep the body comfortable.

THE BODY PRODUCES HEAT

All food taken into the body contains heat in the form of calories. The large or great calorie is used to express the heat value of food. The large calorie is the amount of heat required to raise one kilogram of water one degree Celsius. In addition, 252 calories equal one British thermal unit. One British thermal unit (Btu) equals the amount of heat needed to raise the temperature of one pound of water one degree Fahrenheit, figure 3-1. Metrically, one calorie of heat is required to raise the temperature of one gram of water one degree Celsius.

As calories are taken into the body, they are converted into energy and stored for future use. The conversion process generates heat. All body movements use up the stored energy and, in doing so, add to the heat generated by the conversion process.

The body consistently produces more heat than it requires. Therefore, for body comfort, all of the excess heat produced must be given off by the body.

THE BODY REJECTS HEAT

The constant removal of body heat takes place through three natural processes which all occur at the same time. As shown in figure 3-2, these processes are:

- convection
- radiation
- evaporation

Convection

The *convection* process of removing heat is based on two phenomena:

- Heat flows from a hot surface to a surface containing less heat. For example, heat flows from the body to the air surrounding the body when the air temperature is less than the skin temperature.
- Heat rises. This is evident by watching the smoke from a burning cigarette, or the steam from boiling water.

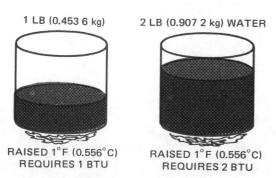

1 LB (0.453 6 kg)   2 LB (0.907 2 kg) WATER

RAISED 1°F (0.556°C)   RAISED 1°F (0.556°C)
REQUIRES 1 BTU   REQUIRES 2 BTU

Fig. 3-1 Effect of weight on Btu

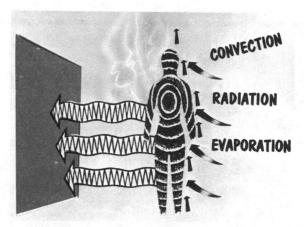

Fig. 3-2 Processes by which heat is removed from the body

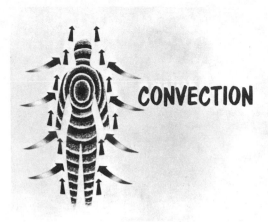

Fig. 3-3 Heat loss by convection

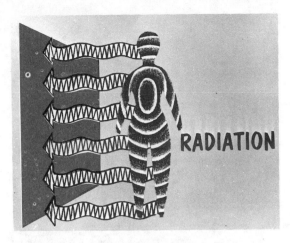

Fig. 3-4 Heat loss by radiation

When these two phenomena are applied to the body process of removing heat, the following occurs:

• The body gives off heat to the surrounding air (which has a lower temperature).
• The surrounding air becomes warmer and moves upward.
• As the warmer air moves upward, air containing less heat takes its place. The convection cycle is then completed. See figure 3-3.

Radiation

Radiation is the process which moves heat from a heat source to an object by means of heat rays, figure 3-4. This principle is based on the phenomenon that heat moves from a hot surface to a surface containing less heat. Radiation takes place independently of convection. The process of radiation does not require air movement to complete the heat transfer. This process is not affected by air temperature, although it is affected by the temperature of the surrounding surfaces.

The body quickly experiences the effects of sun radiation when it moves from a shady to a sunny area.

Evaporation

Evaporation is the process by which moisture becomes a vapor, figure 3-5. As moisture vaporizes from a warm surface, it removes heat and thus cools the surface. This process takes place constantly on the surface of the body. Moisture is given off through the pores of the skin. As the moisture evaporates, it removes heat from the body.

Fig. 3-5 Heat loss by evaporation

Perspiration appearing as drops of moisture on the body indicates that the body is producing more heat than can be removed by convection, radiation, and normal evaporation.

CONDITIONS THAT AFFECT BODY COMFORT

The three main factors that affect body comfort are temperature, relative humidity, and air movement, figure 3-6.

Temperature

Cool air increases the rate of convection; warm air slows it down. Cool air lowers the temperature of the surrounding surfaces. Therefore, the rate of radiation increases. Since warm air raises the surrounding surface temperature, the radiation rate decreases. In general, cool air increases the rate of evaporation and warm air slows it down. The evaporation rate also depends

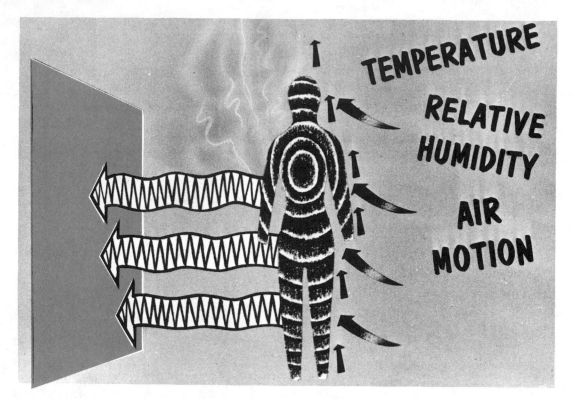

Fig. 3-6 Conditions which affect body comfort

upon the amount of moisture already in the air and the amount of air movement.

Humidity

Moisture in the air is measured in terms of humidity. For example, 50% relative humidity means that the air contains half the amount of moisture that it is capable of holding at a given temperature.

A low relative humidity permits heat to be taken away from the body by evaporation. Because low humidity means the air is relatively *dry*, it can readily absorb moisture. A high relative humidity has the opposite effect. The evaporation process slows down in humid conditions; thus, the speed at which heat can be removed by evaporation decreases. An acceptable comfort range for the human body is 72° to 80°F (22.2°C to 26.6°C) at 45% to 50% relative humidity.

Air Movement

Another factor which affects the ability of the body to give off heat is the movement of air around the body. As the air movement increases, the following processes occur.

- The evaporation process of removing body heat speeds up because moisture in the air near the body is carried away at a faster rate.
- The convection process increases because the layer of warm air surrounding the body is carried away more rapidly.
- The radiation process increases because the heat on the surrounding surfaces is removed at a faster rate. As a result, heat radiates from the body at a faster rate.

As the air movement decreases, the processes of evaporation, convection, and radiation decrease.

Review

Select the appropriate answer from the choices given for the following questions.

1. What is the normal body temperature?

   a. 96.7°F (35.9°C)   c. 96.8°F (36.0°C)
   b. 97.6°F (36.4°C)   d. 98.6°F (37.0°C)

2. How many calories are there in one Btu?

   a. 525   c. 252
   b. 522   d. 225

3. What is the relative humidity when the air holds one-fourth of all the moisture it can hold?

   a. 25%   c. 75%
   b. 50%   d. 100%

4. The temperature and humidity comfort range for the human body is

   a. 72°F–80°F (22.2°C–26.6°C) at 45%–50% humidity.
   b. 72°F–80°F (22.2°C–26.6°C) at 50%–55% humidity.
   c. 68°F–70°F (20.0°C–21.1°C) at 45%–50% humidity.
   d. 68°F–70°F (20.0°C–21.1°C) at 50%–55% humidity.

5. The human body gives off heat by

   a. evaporation.   c. radiation.
   b. convection.   d. All of these are correct answers.

6. Why do humans perspire?

7. The body receives heat in two ways. Describe one way.

8. A group of people in an enclosed room causes the temperature of the room to increase. Explain why this happens.

9. Describe the process of heat transfer by radiation.

10. What effect does cool air have on the process of heat transfer by convection?

UNIT 4:

Matter

The effects of heat energy within an air-conditioning system must be understood by the technician. Thus, the topics which follow deal with matter, heat, pressure, and the principles of refrigeration. These physical laws are basic to an understanding of air-conditioning systems.

Matter is defined as anything that occupies space and has weight. All things are composed of matter and are found in one of three forms: solid, liquid, or gas, figure 4-1. As an example, consider one of the more common substances, water. Water in its natural form is liquid. If enough of its natural heat is removed, it turns to ice, a solid. If heat is added to water and its temperature is raised enough, it boils and vaporizes, changing to gas (steam).

Although various procedures can be applied to matter to cause it to change from one state to another, most objects and things are usually thought of in their natural state.

For example, water, as a liquid, flows and cannot take a shape of its own. Therefore, water assumes the shape of the container in which it is placed. In a container, water exerts an outward and downward force. The greatest force of the water is toward the bottom, lessening toward the top of the container.

As another example, steam or gas dissipates into the surrounding air if it is not contained. When placed in a sealed or enclosed container, gas exerts pressure in all directions with equal force.

When water occurs in the solid state as ice, it holds a certain shape and size. Ice exerts force in a downward direction only.

THE STRUCTURE OF MATTER

The structure of matter is shown in figure 4-2. All matter, regardless of its state, is composed of small parts (particles) called *molecules*. Each molecule of matter is actually the smallest particle of a material which retains all the properties of the original material. For example, if a grain of salt is divided in two, and each subsequent particle is divided again (and the process is continued until the grain is divided as finely as possible), the smallest stable particle having all the properties of salt is a molecule of salt. The word *stable* means that a molecule is satisfied to remain as it is.

Although the molecule may seem to be the smallest possible division, each molecule is in itself made up of even smaller particles of matter. These particles are known as *atoms*. When compared with the molecule, the atoms within a molecule are not always stable. Instead, atoms tend to join with atoms of other substances to form new and different molecules and substances.

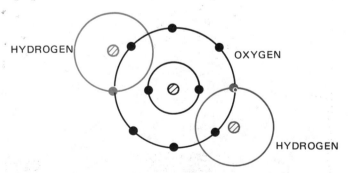

Fig. 4-2 The structure of matter. Two hydrogen (H) atoms combined with one oxygen (O) atom results in one molecule of water (H_2O).

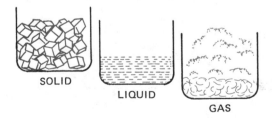

SOLID

LIQUID

GAS

Fig. 4-1 Three basic states of matter

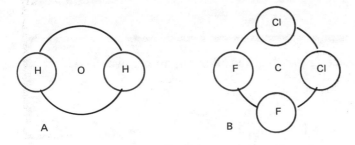

Fig. 4-3 Combined atoms produce different molecules of matter. A: Two hydrogen (H) atoms and one oxygen (O) atom produces water (H_2O). B: Two fluorine (F) atoms, two chlorine (Cl) atoms, and one carbon (C) atom produces Refrigerant-12.

The speed freedom (or position) and the number of molecules determines: the state of the material, the temperature of the material, and the effect the material has on other parts or mechanisms of which it may be a part.

ARRANGEMENT AND MOVEMENT OF MOLECULES

A given material consists of millions and millions of molecules which are all alike. Different materials have different molecules. The characteristics and properties of different materials depend on the nature and arrangement of the molecules. In turn, the behavior of each molecule largely depends on the material (substance) of which the molecule is composed, figure 4-3.

Regardless of the state of a material, the molecules within the material are continuously moving. This movement is called *kinetic* energy because it is an energy of motion. The addition of heat energy to a material increases the kinetic energy of the molecules of the material. In solids, the motion of the molecules is in the form of vibration. That is, the particles never move far from a fixed position. In figure 4-4, note how the addition of heat energy affects the motion of the molecules of water in each of its three states.

When heat energy is added to or removed from a material, a change in the state of the material occurs. Heat, then, is the factor that governs the movement of the molecules making up the substance. The removal of heat causes the molecular action to slow down: liquids solidify and gases become liquids. The addition of heat causes the molecular action to speed up: liquids boil and solids become liquids.

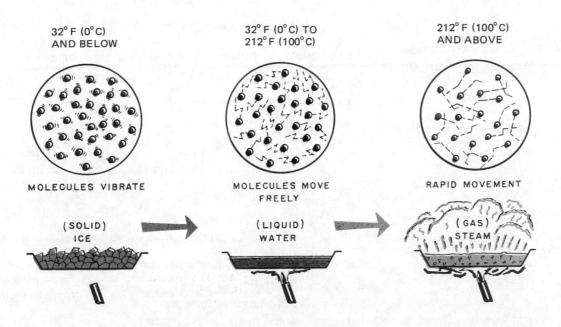

Fig. 4-4 Freedom of molecules in basic states of matter

Review

Select the appropriate answer from the choices given for the following questions.

1. The three states of matter are

   a. solid, liquid, and gas.
   b. liquid, gas, and vapor.

   c. solid, gas, and vapor.
   d. fluid, liquid, and gas.

2. What are examples of the three states of matter?

   a. Steel, water, and air
   b. Ice, water, and steam
   c. Rock, ocean, and cloud
   d. All of these choices are examples of the three states of matter.

3. A solid exerts pressure in

   a. all directions equally.
   b. one direction (down).

   c. two directions (out and down).
   d. three directions (up, out, and down).

4. Atoms tend to join with other atoms of a different substance to form

   a. stronger atoms.
   b. a different substance.
   c. a stable molecule.
   d. All of these choices are correct answers.

5. Energy in motion is known as

   a. static energy.
   b. kinetic energy.

   c. fixed energy.
   d. free energy.

6. When heat is removed from a substance, it changes from a

   a. liquid to a solid.
   b. liquid to a gas.

   c. solid to a liquid.
   d. solid to a gas.

7. In which direction does matter in the gaseous state exert pressure?

   a. In all directions with equal force
   b. In a downward direction only
   c. In an outward and downward direction
   d. In all directions with greatest pressure downward

8. Steam is water in the

   a. liquid state.
   b. gaseous state.

   c. solid state.
   d. All of these choices are correct answers.

9. How can water be changed from a liquid to a steam?

   a. By removing heat
   b. By removing or adding heat

   c. By adding heat
   d. Liquid is not changed to steam

10. How does the movement of molecules differ between water and steam?

    a. Molecules move more rapidly in water than in steam.
    b. Molecules move more rapidly in steam than in water.
    c. Molecules move at about the same speed in steam and water.
    d. Molecules move freely in water but not in steam.

UNIT 5:

Heat

The word heat may be defined in many ways. The definition best suited for refrigeration service is that *heat* is a form of energy which can be transferred from one place to another. This transfer, however, cannot take place unless there is a difference in temperature between the two objects in which transfer is to take place.

Everything in nature contains heat. Some things contain more heat than others — but all contain heat. Heat cannot be created or destroyed, but it can be moved from one place to another or from one form of energy to another form of energy. Heat energy travels in one direction only: from a warmer object to a cooler object. This transfer of heat takes place in one of three ways: by conduction, convection, or radiation.

Conduction means that heat is being transferred through a solid. For example, when food is frying in a pan, heat from the burner is conducted through the pan and to the food.

Convection means that heat transfer is taking place as a result of the circulation of a fluid. The automobile cooling system is a good example of convection cooling. The coolant (a mixture of water and antifreeze) in the cooling system removes the heat created by the engine by carrying it from

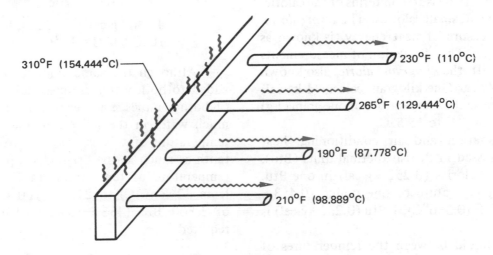

310°F (154.444°C)

230°F (110°C)

265°F (129.444°C)

190°F (87.778°C)

210°F (98.889°C)

Fig. 5-1 Metals differ in conductivity of heat

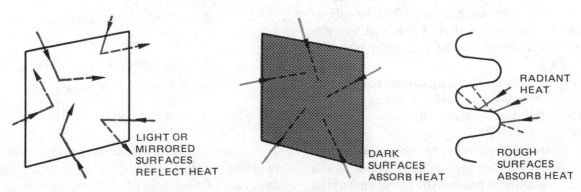

LIGHT OR
MIRRORED
SURFACES
REFLECT HEAT

DARK
SURFACES
ABSORB HEAT

RADIANT
HEAT

ROUGH
SURFACES
ABSORB HEAT

Fig. 5-2 Reflection, transmission and absorption of heat rays

the engine block to the radiator. The heat is then dissipated into the surrounding air.

Radiation means that heat is being transmitted through a medium and the medium does not become hot. An example of this situation is the way in which people acquire sunburns at the beach. That is, part of the heat from the sun is transmitted to the skin through the air.

SENSIBLE HEAT

Sensible heat is any heat that can be felt and that can be measured on a thermometer.

One example of sensible heat is the heat in the surrounding air. This air is called *ambient air.* The temperature of this air is called the *ambient temperature.* When this temperature drops ten or fifteen degrees, one feels cool. An increase in the temperature causes one to feel warmer.

MEASUREMENT OF HEAT

Heat energy is measured in terms of the calorie. There are large and small calories. The *gram calorie,* the smallest measure of heat energy, is known as the *small calorie.* This discussion of measurements is concerned with the *kilogram calorie,* also known as the *large calorie.* One kilogram calorie (1 kg-cal) is required to raise the temperature of one gram (1 g) of water from 14.5°C to 15.5°C.

In refrigeration and air conditioning, heat energy is expressed in British thermal units (Btu). There are 252 calories (0.252 kg-cal) in one Btu. To raise the temperature of one pound (0.453 6 kg) of water 1°F (0.556°C), 1 Btu (0.252 kg-cal) is required.

Water is liquid between the temperatures of 32°F (0°C) and 212°F (100°C). This is a range of 180°F (100°C) and is called the *subcooled liquid range* for water. For each Btu (0.252 kg-cal) of heat added to one pound (0.453 6 kg) of water in this range, the temperature of the water increases 1°F (0.556°C).

Thus, if 180 Btu (45.36 kg-cal) of heat energy are added to one pound (0.453 6 kg) of water at 32°F (0°C), the temperature of the water is increased to 212°F (100°C).

To obtain the final value of the water temperature, divide the Btu (or kg-cal) being added to the water by the number of pounds (or kilograms) of the water. This value is then added to the original temperature (°F or °C) to obtain the new temperature.

Btu ÷ pounds (lb) = H (heat)
H + original temperature = new temperature

Thus, by adding 180 Btu (45.36 kg-cal) to one pound (0.453 6 kg) of water at 32°F (0°C), the result is:

English
180 Btu ÷ 1 lb = 180°F
180°F + 32°F = 212°F

Metric
45.36 kg-cal ÷ 0.453 6 kg = 100°C
100°C + 0°C = 100°C

Now, if 180 Btu (45.36 kg-cal) of heat energy are added to ten pounds (4.536 kg) of water at 32°F (0°C), the temperature of the water is raised to only 50°F (10°C), as follows:

English
180 Btu ÷ 10 lb = 18°F
18°F + 32°F = 50°F

Metric
45.36 kg-cal ÷ 4.536 kg = 10°C
10°C + 0°C = 10°C

Although the same amount of heat energy is added to both water samples and the temperature of both samples is increased, there is ten times as much water in the second sample. Therefore, the temperature of this sample is increased only one-tenth as much as the original sample. To raise the temperature of ten pounds (4.536 kg) of water from 32°F (0°C) to 212°F (100°C), the addition of 1 800 Btu (453.6 kg-cal) of heat energy is required:

English
1 800 Btu ÷ 10 lb = 180°F
180°F + 32°F = 212°F

Metric
453.6 kg-cal ÷ 4.536 kg = 100°C
100°C + 0°C = 100°C

LATENT HEAT

Latent heat is the term applied to the heat required to cause a change of state of matter. This heat cannot be recorded on a thermometer, and it cannot be felt. The British thermal unit (Btu) is used as the standard measure for latent heat.

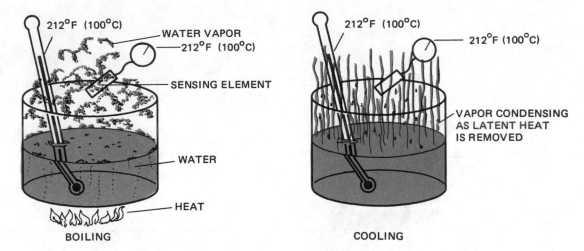

Fig. 5-3 Effect of latent heat

It was shown previously that a change of state occurs when a solid changes to a liquid or a liquid changes to a gas or vice versa. Water at atmospheric pressure between 32°F (0°C) and 212°F (100°C) is called *subcooled liquid*. Water at 212°F (100°C) is called *saturated liquid*. That is, water at 212°F (100°C) contains all of the heat it can hold and still remain a liquid. Any additional heat will cause the water to vaporize.

To change the state of one pound (0.453 6 kg) of water at 212°F (100°C) to one pound (0.453 6 kg) of steam at 212°F (100°C) requires an amount of heat equal to 970 Btu (244.44 kg-cal). This heat is called the *latent heat of vaporization*. Remember that this latent heat cannot be measured on a thermometer and does not cause a change in the temperature of the water.

In addition, steam at 212°F (100°C) gives up 970 Btu (244.44 kg-cal) of heat per pound (0.453 6 kg) as it condenses into water at 212°F (100°C). The heat released in this process is called the *latent heat of condensation*.

The additional removal of heat at the rate of 1 Btu (0.252 kg-cal) per pound (0.453 6 kg) lowers the temperature of the water. This temperature decrease can be measured on the thermometer until 32°F (0°C) is reached. (A later section of this unit covers the use of thermometers to make heat measurements.)

At 32°F (0°C), all of the heat that can be removed from the water without causing a change of state is removed. The heat that must be removed so that one pound (0.453 6 kg) of water at 32°F (0°C) can be changed to one pound (0.453 6 kg) of ice is 144 Btu (35.288 kg-cal). This value of heat energy is called the *latent heat of fusion*.

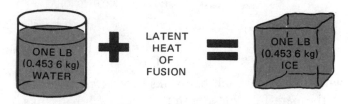

Fig. 5-4 Change from liquid to solid state

This principle governing the addition and removal of heat energy is the basis for refrigeration and air conditioning. A refrigerant is selected for its ability to absorb and to give up large quantities of heat rapidly.

Figure 5-5 illustrates the relative values of the latent heat of fusion and the latent heat of vaporization for water.

SPECIFIC HEAT

Every element or compound has its own heat characteristics. Every substance has a different capacity for accepting and emitting heat.

The capacity to accept (absorb) or emit (expel) heat is known as the *specific heat* or *thermal heat* of a substance. *Specific heat* is defined as the amount of heat that must be absorbed by a material if it is to undergo a temperature change of 1°F (0.556°C).

The following experiment can be performed with three small balls, each made of a different substance, such as copper, steel, and glass. Heat the balls in a container of hot oil until they all reach the same temperature. Now, place each of the three balls on a slab of paraffin and observe

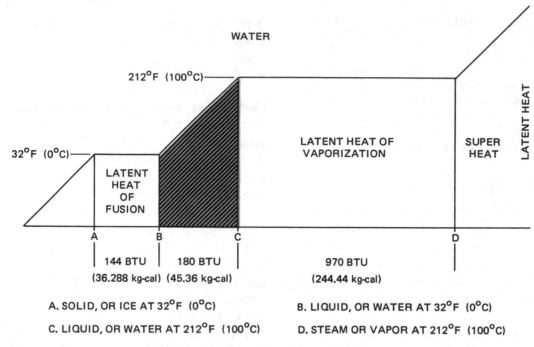

WATER

Fig. 5-5 Latent and sensible heat values for water

A. SOLID, OR ICE AT 32°F (0°C)

B. LIQUID, OR WATER AT 32°F (0°C)

C. LIQUID, OR WATER AT 212°F (100°C)

D. STEAM OR VAPOR AT 212°F (100°C)

what happens. Each ball sinks to a different depth in the paraffin. The depth to which each ball sinks depends on the amount of heat emitted. This experiment illustrates that different materials, at the same temperature, absorb and emit different amounts of heat.

A scale is used to show the relationship of the abilities of various substances to absorb or emit heat. Water (H_2O) is used as a standard to which other substances are compared. The value of water is given as 1 or 1.000. When compared to water, most substances require less heat per unit of weight to cause an increase in their temperature. Two

exceptions to this statement are ammonia (NH_3) with a specific heat of 1.100, and hydrogen (H) with a specific heat of 3.410.

For example, since the specific heat of glass is 0.194, it requires less than 1/5 the number of Btu to raise its temperature as required for an equal amount of water. The specific heat of copper (Cu) is 0.093. This means that just under 1/11th the value in Btu is required to raise the temperature of copper as required for an equal amount of water.

When a comparison is made between glass and water or copper and water, it can be seen that only 0.194 and 0.093 times as much heat energy is re-

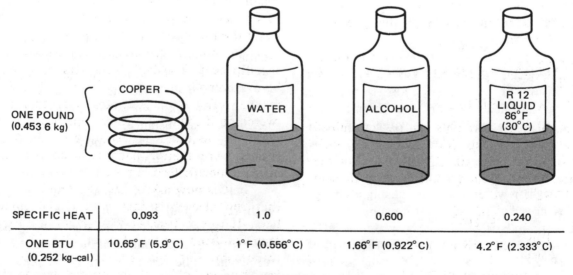

	COPPER	WATER	ALCOHOL	R 12 LIQUID 86°F (30°C)
ONE POUND (0.453 6 kg)				
SPECIFIC HEAT	0.093	1.0	0.600	0.240
ONE BTU (0.252 kg–cal)	10.65°F (5.9°C)	1°F (0.556°C)	1.66°F (0.922°C)	4.2°F (2.333°C)

Fig. 5-6 Specific heat values

Air	0.240	Nitrogen	0.240
Alcohol	0.600	Oxygen	0.220
Aluminum	0.230	Rubber	0.481
Brass	0.086	Silver	0.055
Carbon dioxide	0.200	Steel	0.118
Carbon tetrachloride .	0.200	Tin	0.045
Gasoline	0.700	Water, fresh . . .	1.000
Lead	0.031	Water, sea	0.940

Fig. 5-7 Specific heat values of selected solids, liquids, and gases

quired to change the temperature of these materials $1°F$ ($0.556°C$). This is true because materials vary in their ability to absorb, emit, and exchange heat. Thus, if equal amounts of copper, steel, glass, or any other substance are heated through equal changes of temperature, each material will absorb a different amount of heat.

Since it is known that the specific heat of water is 1.000, and that one Btu (0.252 kg-cal) is required to raise the water temperature $1°F$ ($0.556°C$) per pound (0.453 6 kg), there is a simple way of determining how many degrees (F or C) per unit of weight other materials can be raised.

$$\frac{1\ 000}{\text{Specific Gravity}} \div \frac{\text{Weight}}{\text{Heat Energy}} = \frac{\text{Temperature}}{\text{Change}}$$

For example, the specific heat of aluminum (Al) is 0.230. By applying the previous formula, it is found that one Btu (0.252 kg-cal) raises the temperature of one pound (0.453 6 kg) of aluminum $4.35°F$ ($2.42°C$).

English

$$\frac{1.00}{0.230} \times \frac{1\ \text{lb}}{1\ \text{Btu}} = 4.347\ 83 \div 1 = 4.347\ 83°F$$

(round off to $4.35°F$)

Metric

$$\frac{1.00}{0.230} \times \frac{0.453\ 6\ \text{kg}}{0.252\ \text{kg-cal}} = 4.347\ 83 \div 1.8 = 2.415\ 45°C$$

(round off to $2.42°C$)

Values for other materials can be determined in the same manner. Thus, for lead with a specific heat of 0.031, one Btu (0.252 kg-cal) raises the temperature of one pound (0.453 6 kg) of lead $32.25°F$ ($17.92°C$):

English

$$\frac{1.00}{0.031} \times \frac{1\ \text{lb}}{1\ \text{Btu}} = 32.258\ 1 \div 1 = 32.258\ 1°F$$

(round off to $32.26°F$)

Metric

$$\frac{1.00}{0.031} \times \frac{0.453\ 6\ \text{kg}}{0.252\ \text{kg-cal}} = 32.258\ 1 \div 1.8 = 17.921\ 1°C$$

(round off to $17.92°C$)

A certain type of specific heat is called a *heat load*. When dealing with automobiles, the heat load is an important factor in the efficiency of air-conditioning systems. Items to be considered in determining the heat load include the color of the automobile, the amount of glass area, and the number of passengers.

When determining the refrigeration requirements for a particular application, the specific heats of all materials involved must be considered in the heat load. For example, in a refrigerated truck body, the specific heat of the product being cooled is an important factor, as is the amount of insulation and the type of material in the body. The number of times the doors are opened and closed as well as the length of time the product is to be refrigerated are also important factors.

COLD — THE ABSENCE OF HEAT

What is meant by the word cold? *Cold* is the absence of heat. If cold is to be understood, then the student must first understand what heat is. *Heat* is energy and it is present in all things. Heat cannot be contained. The molecular structure of all things is changed into one of three forms by heat.

Heat is molecular movement. For example, Unit 4 showed that water is liquid between $32°F$ ($0°C$) and $212°F$ ($100°C$). If heat is added to water at $212°F$ ($100°C$), its molecular movement is increased. As a result, water vaporizes and turns to steam. When heat is removed from water at $32°F$ ($0°C$), its molecular movement is decreased. The water then solidifies and turns to ice.

All matter generates heat which is called specific heat. The body generates heat that must be overcome if one is to feel cool. The food stored in the refrigerator generates heat that must be overcome if the food is to be kept at a safe temperature as required for short-term or long-term storage. Any matter that is to be cooled must first have its specific heat removed or overcome.

If it is now asked, "What is cold?" it appears that the answer is that cold is the absence of heat. If this is true, at what point is all the heat removed from matter? Ice, at $32°F$ ($0°C$), is said to be cold. But solid carbon dioxide (CO_2), or dry ice, is even colder at its normal temperature of

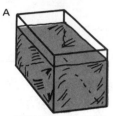
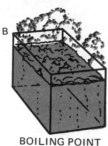

FREEZING POINT

0°C (CELSIUS)
492°R (RANKINE)
273°K (KELVIN)
32°F (FAHRENHEIT)

BOILING POINT

100°C (CELSIUS)
672°R (RANKINE)
373°K (KELVIN)
212°F (FAHRENHEIT)

Fig. 5-8 Fixed reference points on temperature scales for water

−109.3°F (−165.8°C). Dry ice is so cold that if it is touched, one has the sensation of being burned. However, it cannot be said that dry ice is cold either because it still contains a large amount of heat as measured in Btu.

Absolute cold, then, is the absence of all heat. Complete absence of heat does not occur until the temperature of −459.67°F (−273.16°C) is reached. All temperature above this value contains heat. For example, −459°F still contains 0.67°F of heat; −273°C still contains 0.16°C of heat.

Absolute cold, like other absolutes, has not yet been achieved by scientists. A Dutch physicist, Wander de Haas, working at the University of Leiden (Holland), achieved a temperature of 0.004 4°C above absolute zero. In 1957, Dr. Arthur Spohr, working at the U.S. Naval Research Laboratory, achieved a temperature of less than one-millionth of a degree kelvin (K) above absolute zero (0.000 001°K). The Kelvin scale, used in physics, uses 0°K for absolute cold, 273°K as the freezing point for water, and 373°K as its boiling point.

In summary then, cold is the absence of heat energy. According to current scientific theory, absolute zero is the point at which all molecular movement stops. Since molecular movement causes heat energy, it follows that if there is no movement there is no heat.

THERMOMETERS

Long ago, it was recognized that it was desirable to have a device to measure the temperature of matter to determine how much heat the object or matter contained. Such a device became known as a *thermometer*.

About 1585, Galileo Galilei constructed a crude water thermometer. Although this thermometer was very inaccurate, the principles stated by Galileo in the construction of his device helped other scientists to design more accurate instruments.

More than one hundred years later, in 1714, Gabriel D. Fahrenheit constructed a thermometer using a column of mercury. From the time of Galileo and until Fahrenheit's experiments, temperature-measuring devices used tubes of alcohol and other substances as indicators.

Fahrenheit realized that even though many thermometers had been made, none of these devices had been constructed to a standard scale. Recognizing the need for a standard scale, Fahrenheit decided that a zero should be placed on the tube to indicate the absence of heat. He then reasoned that all values above zero were relative and contained so many units of heat.

Fahrenheit then decided that it was necessary to take his tube of mercury to be calibrated to the coldest location that could be found in the world. After talking with sailors, he decided that Iceland was the ideal place to make his measurements.

Once in Iceland, he waited until he was told that "This is the coldest day we have seen." He then made a mark on his glass tube to indicate zero, the absence of heat. He waited until it became warmer and noted that as the ice melted, his mercury column expanded 32/1 000th of its original volume. This measurement was repeated several times and each time the same expansion of the mercury column occurred. Fahrenheit designated this point as 32°.

He also noted that normal body temperature was 98.6°, and that when water boiled his column of mercury expanded to 212/1 000th of its original volume.

Fahrenheit's thermometer was accepted as the standard and was the most widely used device for many years. There are, however, three other scales in use today.

While Fahrenheit was working on his thermometer, Anders Celsius, a Swedish astronomer, proposed the centigrade thermometer. On this thermometer he designated the temperature of melting ice as 0° and the boiling point of water as 100°. This scale, now known as the Celsius scale, is used in metric measurement.

In 1848, at the age of 24, W.T. Kelvin (Lord Kelvin) proposed the absolute scale of temperature, which still bears his name. The Kelvin scale is used

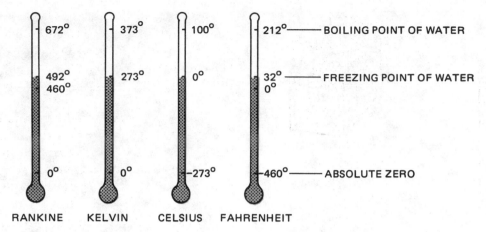

Fig. 5-9 Kinds of temperature scales

in scientific work. A comparison of the various temperature scales is given in figure 5-9.

The Rankine scale thermometer is named after its inventor W.J.M. Rankine, a Scottish engineer. On the Rankine scale, the freezing point of water is 492°R and its boiling point is 672°R.

Kelvin temperature equivalents are obtained by adding 273° to the Celsius temperature; the Celsius equivalent is obtained by subtracting 273° from the kelvin temperature.

Rankine temperature equivalents are obtained by adding 460° to the Fahrenheit temperature; the Fahrenheit equivalent is obtained by subtracting 460° from the Rankine temperature.

Several types of thermometers are available to the service technician, figure 5-10. The most popular style is the stem/dial thermometer. This thermometer has an all metal stem and an easy-to-read dial.

In general, the accuracy of this type of thermometer is ±1% throughout the entire indicated temperature scale. Several ranges are available: 0°F to 220°F and −40°F to +160°F. The latter range is the most popular for use with air-conditioning systems. Both ranges can be used on either the high side of a refrigeration system, figure 5-11, or on the low side of the system, figure 5-12.

Thermometers are also available with the metric scale or with both English and metric scales.

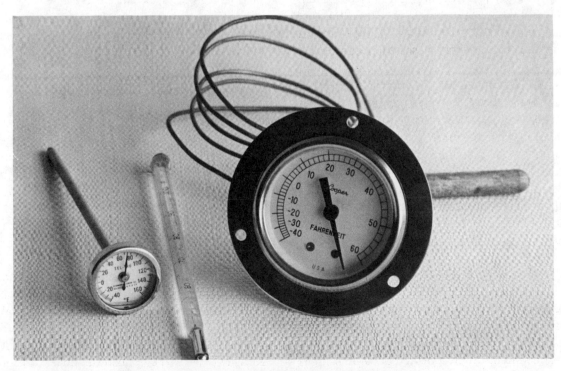

Fig. 5-10 Three types of thermometers

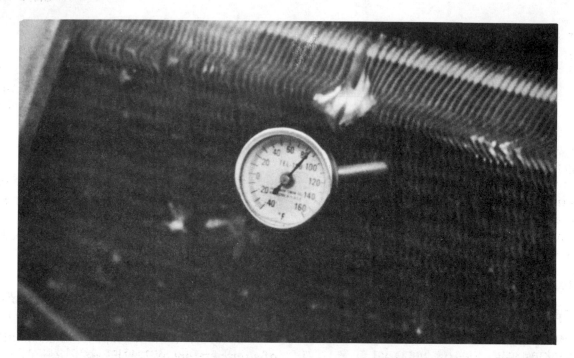

Fig. 5-11 Thermometer used to check condenser temperature

Fig. 5-12 Thermometer used to check evaporator temperature

A popular scale range for a metric thermometer is −10°C to +110°C. This scale is approximately equal to the English scale of 14°F to 230°F.

TEMPERATURE CONVERSION

Most of the servicing work on air conditioners and refrigeration systems deals with temperature values on the Fahrenheit scale. However, the conversion to the metric system means that the student should be able to work with the Celsius scale as well. On many occasions, the student will be required to make conversions between the Fahrenheit and Celsius scales.

The conversions are quite simple.

For example, to change a Celsius reading to Fahrenheit:

- Multiply the Celsius reading by 1.8
- Add 32°

Assume that it is necessary to convert a temperature of 115°C to the Fahrenheit equivalent.

First, multiply the value by 1.8:

$$115°C \times 1.8 = 207°$$

Then add 32:

$$207° + 32° = 239°F$$

Thus,

$$115°C = 239°F$$

As another example, consider the boiling point of water at 100°C or 212°F. Given the value of 100°C, it can be proved that the Fahrenheit equivalent is indeed 212°F.

$$100°C \times 1.8 = 180°$$
$$180° + 32° = 212°F$$

To change a Fahrenheit reading to the Celsius equivalent, the Fahrenheit value is first reduced by 32° and then is multiplied by 0.556.

Thus, to change a Fahrenheit reading to Celsius:

- subtract 32°
- multiply by 0.556

By applying these steps the Celsius equivalent of a temperature of 221°F can be found.

$$221°F − 32° = 189°$$
$$189° \times 0.556 = 105°C$$

This formula can be proved just as in the previous case by converting the boiling point of water on the Fahrenheit scale, 212°F, to its Celsius equivalent.

$$212°F − 32° = 180°$$
$$180° \times 0.556 = 100°C$$

Review

HEAT

Select the appropriate answer from the choices given.

1. What is the smallest measure of heat energy?

    a. Btu (0.252 kg-cal)
    b. Gram calorie
    c. Kilogram calorie
    d. One gram

2. What is the boiling point of water at sea level?

    a. 212°F (100°C)
    b. 198.6°F (92.55°C)
    c. 121°F (85°C)
    d. 189.6°F (123.11°C)

3. If 180 Btu (45.36 kg-cal) are added to eight pounds (3.628 8 kg) of water at 35°F (1.667°C), what is the new temperature?

    a. 215°F (101.67°C)
    b. 145°F (62.78°C)
    c. 57.5°F (14.17°C)
    d. 75.5°F (24.17°C)

4. If ten Btu (2.52 kg-cal) are removed from one pound of water (0.453 6 kg) at 35°F (1.667°C), what is the new temperature?

    a. 25°F (−3.89°C)
    b. 32°F (0°C)
    c. 45°F (7.22°C)
    d. 35°F (1.667°C)

CONTINUED

5. What is absolute cold?
   a. −459.67°F (−273.16°C)   c. The absence of heat
   b. Absolute zero   d. All are correct answers

Briefly answer each of the following questions.

6. Define sensible heat.

7. What is meant by the term ambient temperature?

8. What is latent heat?

9. Explain the process of heat transfer by convection.

10. If 160 Btu (40.32 kg-cal) of heat energy are added to five pounds (2.268 kg) of water at 77°F (25°C), what is the new temperature? Show the formula and figures used to arrive at the answer.

THERMOMETERS

Briefly answer each of the following questions. Show the formulas used for determining the temperature conversions and show all calculations.

11. Change 25°C to Fahrenheit.

12. Change 40°C to Fahrenheit.

13. Change 0°C to Fahrenheit.

14. Change 59°F to Celsius.

15. Change 113°F to Celsius.

16. Change 32°F to Celsius.

17. Name four temperature scales in use today.

18. Of the four scales now used, which one is most commonly used in air-conditioning work?

19. How did Fahrenheit determine that the freezing point of water was 32° on his scale?

20. What is normal body temperature on the Fahrenheit scale? On the Celsius scale?

UNIT 6:

Pressure

To understand air conditioning one must understand pressure. The best example of the action of pressure and what it means is shown by the air (gas) envelope around the earth (see Unit 4). This gas consists primarily of oxygen, 21% by volume. and nitrogen, 78% by volume, figure 6-1. The remaining 1% consists of several other gases. This combination of gases is called the *atmosphere*. It extends nearly six hundred miles (965.6 km) above the earth and is held in place by the gravitational pull of the earth.

ATMOSPHERIC PRESSURE

The six-hundred mile (965.6-km) belt of gas surrounding the earth exerts a pressure that is measured in pounds per square inch (psi) in the English system or kilopascals (kPa) in the metric system. For a one-square-inch (6.452-cm^2) area the pressure of the 600-mile (965.6-km) column of gas is 14.69 psia (101.287 kPa absolute). This figure, rounded off to 14.7 psia (101.4 kPa absolute), is known as *atmospheric pressure.*

PRESSURE MEASUREMENT

Service manuals provided by manufacturers often refer to the normal pressure of an air-conditioning system as psi or psig. In some cases, this pressure is also referred to as psia. However, there is a considerable difference among the actual meanings of the three abbreviated terms.

The abbreviation for pounds per square inch is psi. This term refers to the amount of pressure per square inch and does not consider or compensate for atmospheric pressure. In general, the phrase,

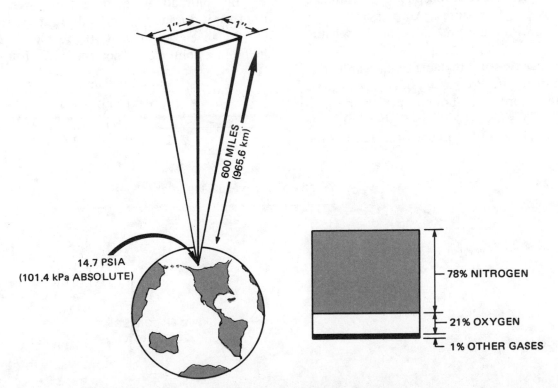

Fig. 6-1 Atmospheric pressure

"The low-side gauge should read 28 psi," really means 28 psig (193.06 kPa).

Pounds per square inch gauge, abbreviated psig, is the amount of pressure in pounds per square inch indicated on a gauge that is adjusted to atmospheric pressure at sea level. Zero pressure on a gauge so adjusted compensates for the atmospheric pressure at sea level of 14.696 psi, usually rounded off to 14.7 psi (101.356 kPa rounded off to 101.4 kPa).

Pounds per square inch absolute, abbreviated psia, refers to the amount of pressure measured from absolute zero. This value equals the gauge pressure plus 14.7 psi (101.4 kPa absolute). Thus, a gauge calibrated in psia reads 14.7 psi (101.4 kPa absolute) without being connected to a pressure source.

As an example, assume that two gauges are connected to the same test port of an air conditioner. One gauge is calibrated in psig and reads 28 psi (193.06 kPa) of pressure (zero reference). The other gauge is calibrated in psia and reads approximately 42.7 psia (294.416 kPa absolute). That is, 28 psi + 14.7 psi = 42.7 psia, or 193.06 kPa + 101.356 kPa = 294.416 kPa absolute.

TEMPERATURE AND PRESSURE

All pressures above atmospheric pressure are referred to as gauge pressures. All pressures below atmospheric pressure are said to be in the vacuum range.

Zero gauge pressure remains zero regardless of what the altitude is. Pressures above atmospheric pressure are recorded as pounds per square inch gauge or psig. Pressures below atmospheric pressure are recorded as inches of mercury or inHg (in is the abbreviation for inch and Hg is the abbreviation or the chemical symbol for mercury).

At sea level (where the atmospheric pressure is equal to 14.7 psi or 101.4 kPa), the boiling point of water is 212°F (100°C). At any point higher than sea level, the atmospheric pressure is lower and so is the boiling point of water. The point at which water boils decreases at the rate of 1.1°F (0.61°C) per thousand feet (304.8 m) of altitude. To find the boiling point of water at any given altitude, multiply the altitude (in thousands of feet or meters) by 1.1 for °F or by 0.61 for °C. The result of this operation is then subtracted from 212°F (100°C) to obtain the new boiling point.

For example, in an airplane flying at a height of 12 000 feet (3 657.6 m), water boils at about 198.8°F (92.7°C).

English

12 000 ft ÷ 1 000 = 12
12 × 1.1° = 13.2°
212°F – 13.2°F = 198.8°F

Metric

3 657.6 m ÷ 304.8 = 12
12 × 0.61° = 7.32°
100°C – 7.32°C = 92.7°C

In Colorado, water boils at a lower temperature than it does in the flatlands or at sea level.

At an elevation of 8 900 feet (2 712.72 m), the boiling point can be determined as follows:

English

8 900 ft ÷ 1 000 = 8.9
8.9 × 1.1° = 9.8°
212°F – 9.8°F = 202.2°F

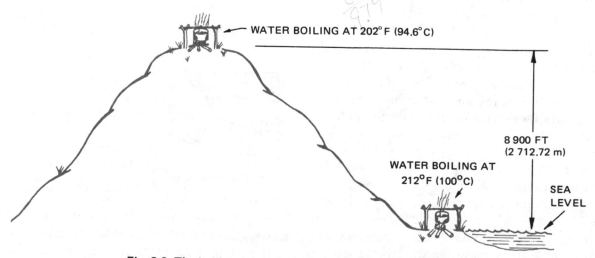

Fig. 6-2 The boiling point of water at an elevation of 8 900 feet

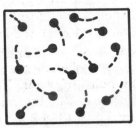

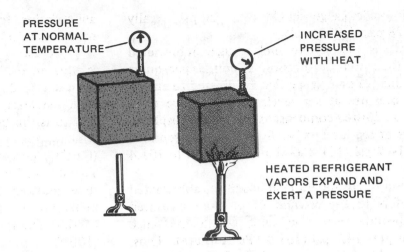

PRESSURE AT NORMAL TEMPERATURE

INCREASED PRESSURE WITH HEAT

VAPOR MOLECULES MOVE RAPIDLY, ARE FAR APART, HAVE COMPLETE FREEDOM, AND ARE IN MOTION CONTINUOUSLY

HEATED REFRIGERANT VAPORS EXPAND AND EXERT A PRESSURE

Fig. 6-3 Temperature rise affects movement and pressure

Metric

$$2\,712.72 \text{ m} \div 304.8 = 8.9$$
$$8.9 \times 0.61° = 5.4°$$
$$100°C - 5.4°C = 94.6°C$$

Thus, the boiling point of water at this elevation is about 202°F (94.6°C).

It should be noted that the small error in the comparisons of temperatures (converting Fahrenheit to Celsius or Celsius to Fahrenheit) is due to the conversion factors of 1.1°F and 0.61°C per thousand feet or 304.8 meters. If both of these factors are extended to four or five decimal places, the error is reduced.

It should also be noted that water boils when it contains all the heat it can for a given condition. Thus, when water boils at a lower temperature, it contains less heat; when it boils at a high temperature, it contains more heat.

If the boiling point of water is affected by a pressure drop, it is reasonable to assume that a pressure increase also affects the boiling point of water.

This principle is often put to use when food is prepared in a pressure cooker. The boiling point of the water is increased because the pressure is increased. As the water changes from a liquid to steam, a pressure is created because the vapor cannot escape from the sealed pot. As a result, the vapor is superheated to a higher temperature. The food cooks much faster because it is exposed to a greater temperature and pressure.

The automobile cooling system is another example where the temperature is increased by increasing pressure. Some system manufacturers have been able to increase the working pressure of a cooling system to 16 psi (110.3 kPa) of pressure

or more. With each psi (6.895 kPa) of pressure increase, the boiling point of the water (or coolant) is increased about 2.53°F (1.4°C).

A cooling system having a pressure cap rated at 7 psi (48.2 kPa) causes an increase in the boiling point of the coolant by 17.7°F (9.8°C). The new boiling point of the coolant (with the pressure cap in place) is found in the following manner:

English

Multiply the rating of the cap, in psi, by 2.53, then add 212°F

$$7 \text{ psi} \times 2.53°F = 17.7°F$$
$$17.7°F + 212°F = 229.7°F$$

Metric

Multiply the rating of the cap, in kPa, by 0.20, then add 100°C

$$48.2 \text{ kPa} \times 0.2°C = 9.6°C$$
$$9.6°C + 100°C = 109.6°C$$

The boiling point of the coolant in a system containing a 12-psi (82.7-kPa) cap can be found in the same manner:

English

$$12 \text{ psi} \times 2.53°F = 30.3°F$$
$$30.3°F + 212°F = 242.3°F$$

Metric

$$82.7 \text{ kPa} \times 0.2°C = 16.5°C$$
$$16.5°C + 100°C = 116.5°C$$

Assume that an apparatus is known to hold the temperature of a coolant to 260°F (126.6°C). It is desired to pressurize the system. The size of the pressure cap may be determined by subtracting the normal boiling point of water from the desired temperature. This result is then divided by 2.53°F to find psi in the English system, or divided by 0.2°C to find kPa in the metric system. In this case, a 19-psi (131-kPa) pressure cap is required.

English

$$260°F - 212°F = 48°F$$
$$48°F \div 2.53°F = 18.9 \text{ psi}$$

Metric

$$126.6°C - 100°C = 26.6°C$$
$$26.6°C \div 0.2°C = 133 \text{ kPa}$$

If water boils at a higher temperature when pressure is applied to it and at a lower temperature when the pressure is reduced, it is obvious that the temperature can be controlled to a greater degree of accuracy if the pressure is controlled.

Review

Select the appropriate answer for the choices given.

1. What is the atmospheric pressure at sea level?
   a. 0 psia (0 kPa)
   b. 14.7 psig (101.4 kPa)
   c. Either a or b is correct
   d. Neither a nor b is correct

2. What is the chemical symbol for mercury?
   a. θ
   b. ''
   c. E
   d. Hg

3. How is the chemical symbol for mercury used in air-conditioning or refrigeration service?
   a. To indicate pressure
   b. To indicate vacuum
   c. For the boiling point of water
   d. For the condensing point of refrigerant

4. The new boiling point of water at an elevation of 8 500 feet (2 590.8 m) is
   a. 202.7°F (203°F) (95°C).
   b. 201.25°F (201°F) (93.88°C)
   c. 221.3°F (221°F) (105°C).
   d. 221.75°F (222°F) (105.55°C).

5. What is the new boiling point of water at a pressure of 2 psig (13.8 kPa)?
   a. 212°F (100°C)
   b. 217°F (103°C)
   c. 223°F (106°C)
   d. 230°F (110°C)

Briefly answer each of the following questions.

6. Define pressure.

7. What is the chief advantage of a pressurized cooling system in a car?

8. How does driving a car at high altitudes affect the water temperature in a pressurized cooling system?

9. Define the term psig.

10. To prevent water, as a coolant in the car cooling system, from boiling at an operating temperature of 257°F (125°C), what is the pressure rating of the pressure cap? Show the formula used in arriving at the answer.

UNIT 7:

Principles of Refrigeration

AIR CONDITIONING

When one hears the term air conditioning, usually the first thing that comes to mind is cold fresh air. Actually, a true air-conditioning system automatically controls the temperature, humidity, purity, and circulation of the air. In automotive applications, air conditioning is any system that cools and dehumidifies the air inside the passenger compartment of an automobile or truck.

THE MECHANICAL
REFRIGERATION SYSTEM

The mechanical refrigeration system installed in a modern vehicle uses a special refrigerant to absorb heat inside the evaporator. To do this, the refrigerant changes from a liquid to a vapor. Since the evaporator is located inside the passenger compartment, air blown over the fins of the evaporator is directed to the passengers for their comfort.

It is necessary to remove the heat absorbed by the refrigerant from the inside of the evaporator. One possible method of removing this heat is to expel the heat-laden refrigerant vapor to the outside air. However, this is an expensive procedure. The preferred method is to reclaim the refrigerant for reuse in the system. The heat alone is removed and expelled to the outside air.

The process of reclaiming the refrigerant begins at the compressor. The function of the compressor is to pressurize the heat-laden vapor until its pressure and temperature are much greater than that of the outside air. The compressor also pumps the vapor to the condenser. At the condenser, the vapor gives up its heat and changes back to a liquid. The condenser is located outside the passenger compartment. Since the air passing over the condenser is much cooler than the vapor inside the condenser, the vapor gives up much of its heat and changes back to a liquid. The liquid refrigerant then passes

from the condenser to the receiver/drier where it is stored until it is needed again by the evaporator.

This example of a mechanical refrigeration system demonstrates three basic laws of refrigeration which are the basis of all natural and mechanical refrigeration systems.

LAW I
To refrigerate is to remove heat. The absence of heat is cold. Heat is ever present.

Law I is illustrated by the refrigeration system of an automobile. Heat is removed from the passenger compartment of the automobile. In so doing, the temperature is lowered. The absence of heat is cold.

LAW II
Heat is ready to flow or pass to anything that has less heat. Nothing can stop the flow of heat; it can only be slowed down. Heat cannot be contained no matter how much insulation is used.

Law II is demonstrated by the special refrigerant in the evaporator. In this instance, heat is ready to flow to anything that contains less heat.

LAW III
If a change of state is to take place there must be a transfer of heat. If a liquid is to change to a gas, it must take on heat. The heat is carried off in a vapor. If a vapor is to change into a liquid it must give up heat. The heat is given up to a less hot surface or medium.

Law III is shown by the liquid refrigerant in the evaporator. That is, as the refrigerant takes on heat, it changes to a vapor. The heat is carried off to be expelled outside the car.

TON OF REFRIGERATION

For many years, refrigeration units were rated in horsepower (hp). The *horsepower* is a theoretical unit of energy. One horsepower is the amount of energy required to raise 33 000 pounds (1 497 kg) one foot (305 mm) in one minute.

These early refrigeration units had ratings of 1/4 hp, 1/2 hp, 3/4 hp, and 1 hp. Such a rating, however, was a very inaccurate method of describing the output of an air-conditioning unit since the horsepower value referred only to the compressor size.

Another term used to describe the capacity of an air-conditioning system is the *ton*. A ton of refrigeration is generally considered to be equivalent to one horsepower. An air-conditioning unit with a rating of 1/2 hp is also said to have half a ton of refrigeration.

The value of a ton of refrigeration in Btu/hr can be determined if the latent heat of fusion for water is known. The amount of heat required to cause a change in state of one pound of ice at 32°F to one pound of water at 32°F is 144 Btu.

In applying this value, it must be remembered that a ton of matter (water) contains 2 000 pounds. Since 144 Btu are required to change one pound of solid water (ice) to a liquid, the equivalent value for one ton can be found by multiplying the amount of energy required to change one pound by 2 000 pounds.

144 Btu × 2 000 lb = 288 000 Btu

This value is the amount of heat energy (in Btu) required to change the state of one ton of ice to one ton of liquid in twenty-four hours. To determine the Btu/hr for a ton of refrigeration, divide 288 000 by 24.

144 Btu × 2 000 lb = 288 000 Btu
288 000 Btu ÷ 24 hr = 12 000 Btu/hr

One ton of refrigeration is thus equivalent to 12 000 Btu/hr. Most air-conditioning units now sold have a Btu rating. When a manufacturer lists an air-conditioning unit as a one-ton unit, the Btu

rating must also be listed. For example, a 3/4-ton unit should have a rating of 9 000 Btu. This practice is followed to prevent units of lower capacity being sold as one-ton units.

144 Btu × 2 000 lb = 288 000 Btu
288 000 Btu × 3/4 ton = 216 000 Btu
216 000 Btu ÷ 24 hr = 9 000 Btu/hr

Thus, each quarter ton of refrigeration is equivalent to 3 000 Btu.

What is the rating, in tons, for an 11 000-Btu/hr unit? Since the value of 11 000 Btu is close to that of a one-ton unit, the hp or ton rating of this unit is also established at one. The same reasoning also applies to a 13 000-Btu/hr unit so that it too is called a one-ton unit.

In a similar fashion, assume that machine (A) is rated at 10 525 Btu/hr and machine (B) is rated at 13 475 Btu/hr. Since both of these values are closer to 1 hp than they are to the next fractional horsepower (1/4 horsepower), they both are rated as 1 hp. Actually, the two machines are almost a quarter of a horsepower apart in their ratings.

Machine A	10 525 Btu/hr
Machine B	13 475 Btu/hr
Difference	2 950 Btu/hr

It is easy to see that there is a wide range in the Btu/hr value of an air-conditioning unit rated at 1 ton. The consumer should be aware of this range when considering the purchase of refrigeration equipment of any size.

Automotive air conditioners are rated at well over a ton of refrigeration. Because of the tremendous heat load in the car, a unit rated at 8 000 to 10 000 Btu does a very poor job of keeping the average modern car cool.

For example, General Motors rates its factory-installed units at a full 1 3/4 tons, or about 21 000 Btu. This value is the same amount of cooling that is required to cool the average two-bedroom house. Of course, a house is well insulated and does not have as great a problem of heat loss by radiation as the automobile experiences.

Review

Answer each of the following questions.

1. What is a ton of refrigeration?

   a. 288 000 Btu/hr
   b. 144 000 Btu/hr

   c. 12 000 Btu/hr
   d. 24 000 Btu/hr

2. What is a horsepower of refrigeration?

   a. 10 525–13 475 Btu/hr
   b. 288 000 Btu/hr

   c. 2 950 Btu/hr
   d. Horsepower rating is not used

3. Why are modern air-conditioning units rated in terms of Btu/hr rather than by ton or horsepower?

   a. The ton or horsepower rating is not accurate.
   b. The Btu/hr rating gives a true indication of cooling capacity.
   c. Either of the answers, a or b, is correct.
   d. There is no difference in Btu/hr, ton, or horsepower ratings.

4. The Btu/hr rating of a one-ton air conditioner can range between what values?

   a. 11 000–13 000 Btu/hr
   b. 10 000–14 000 Btu/hr
   c. 10 525–13 475 Btu/hr
   d. There is no range. One ton is 12 000 Btu/hr.

5. What is the cooling capacity of an air conditioner in the average car?

   a. 18 000 Btu/hr
   b. 21 000 Btu/hr

   c. 24 000 Btu/hr
   d. There is no "average."

6. The absence of _____ is cold.

   a. heat
   b. all heat

   c. molecular movement
   d. All answers are correct

7. Heat is ready to flow to anything that has less _____ .

   a. resistance
   b. substance

   c. heat
   d. All answers are correct

8. As refrigerant takes on heat it changes to a _____ .

   a. liquid
   b. vapor

   c. solid
   d. heated mass

9. Heat is dissipated in the outside air by the _____ .

   a. evaporator
   b. condenser

   c. receiver
   d. radiator

10. As refrigerant gives up its heat it changes to a _____ .

   a. liquid
   b. vapor

   c. solid
   d. cooled mass

UNIT 8:

Refrigerant and Refrigeration Oil

The term *refrigerant* refers to the fluid used in a refrigeration system to produce cold by removing heat. For automotive refrigeration systems, Refrigerant 12 is used. It has the highest safety factor of any refrigerant available that is capable of withstanding high pressures and temperatures without deteriorating or decomposing.

Nature has not provided a perfect refrigerant. Thus it was necessary to devise a compound for automotive use. A fluorinated hydrocarbon known as carbon tetrachloride was selected since it met the requirements most closely with only a few minor changes.

Carbon tetrachloride (popularly known as carbon-tet), consists of one atom of carbon (C) and four atoms of chlorine (C1). The chemical symbol for this compound is $CC1_4$. To change carbon tetrachloride into a suitable refrigerant, two of the chlorine atoms are removed and two atoms of fluorine (F) are introduced in their place. The new compound, known as dichlorodifluoromethane, is Refrigerant 12. It has many applications in various types of refrigeration systems. The chemical symbol for Refrigerant 12 is $CC1_2F_2$. This means that one molecule of the refrigerant contains one atom of carbon, two atoms of chlorine, and two atoms of fluorine.

Refrigerant 12 is ideal for automotive use because of its relatively low operating pressures, as compared to other refrigerants. Its stability at high and low operating temperatures is also desirable. Refrigerant 12 (commonly abbreviated R-12) does not react with most metals such as iron, aluminum, copper, or steel. However, liquid R-12 may cause discoloration of chrome and stainless steel if large quantities are allowed to strike these surfaces.

R-12 is soluble in oil and does not react with rubber. Some synthetic rubber compositions, however, may deteriorate if used as refrigerant hose. Only synthetic rubber hose, such as Buna 'N', designated for refrigeration service should be used.

R-12 does not affect the taste, odor, or color of water or food. In normal use it is not harmful to animal or plant life. At the present time, however, pending federal legislation is considering restricting the sale of R-12 — perhaps by a form of rationing. The concern is due to some scientific investigation which claims that expended R-12 is contaminating the ozone. In spite of the most sophisticated statistical analyses of actual ozone measurements, none has detected ozone depletion, however.

Refrigerant 12 is odorless in concentrates of less than 20%. In greater concentrations, it can be detected by the faint odor of its original compound, carbon tetrachloride.

TEMPERATURE AND PRESSURE RELATIONSHIP OF REFRIGERANT 12

One of the characteristics of Refrigerant 12 which makes it a suitable refrigerant for automotive use is the fact that the temperature (on the Fahrenheit scale) and English system pressure values in the 20 to 80 psig range are very close.

The table in figure 8-2 shows that there is only

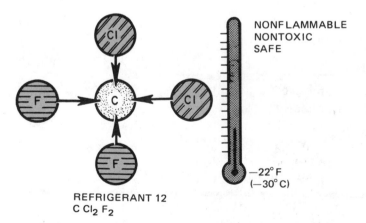

NONFLAMMABLE
NONTOXIC
SAFE

—22° F
(—30° C)

REFRIGERANT 12
C Cl₂ F₂

Fig. 8-1 Composition, boiling point, and properties of Refrigerant 12

Temp. °F	Press. psig	Temp. °F	Press. psig	Temp. °F	Press. psig	Temp. °F	Press. psig	Temp. °F	Press. psig
0	9.1	35	32.5	60	57.7	85	91.7	110	136.0
2	10.1	36	33.4	61	58.9	86	93.2	111	138.0
4	11.2	37	34.3	62	60.0	87	94.8	112	140.1
6	12.3	38	35.1	63	61.3	88	96.4	113	142.1
8	13.4	39	36.0	64	62.5	89	98.0	114	144.2
10	14.6	40	36.9	65	63.7	90	99.6	115	146.3
12	15.8	41	37.9	66	64.9	91	101.3	116	148.4
14	17.1	42	38.8	67	66.2	92	103.0	117	151.2
16	18.3	43	39.7	68	67.5	93	104.6	118	152.7
18	19.7	44	40.7	69	68.8	94	106.3	119	154.9
20	21.0	45	41.7	70	70.1	95	108.1	120	157.1
21	21.7	46	42.6	71	71.4	96	109.8	121	159.3
22	22.4	47	43.6	72	72.8	97	111.5	122	161.5
23	23.1	48	44.6	73	74.2	98	113.3	123	163.8
24	23.8	49	45.6	74	75.5	99	115.1	124	166.1
25	24.6	50	46.6	75	76.9	100	116.9	125	168.4
26	25.3	51	47.8	76	78.3	101	118.8	126	170.7
27	26.1	52	48.7	77	79.2	102	120.6	127	173.1
28	26.8	53	49.8	78	81.1	103	122.4	128	175.4
29	27.6	54	50.9	79	82.5	104	124.3	129	177.8
30	28.4	55	52.0	80	84.0	105	126.2	130	182.2
31	29.2	56	53.1	81	85.5	106	128.1	131	182.6
32	30.0	57	55.4	82	87.0	107	130.0	132	185.1
33	30.9	58	56.6	83	88.5	108	132.1	133	187.6
34	31.7	59	57.1	84	90.1	109	135.1	134	190.1

Fig. 8-2 Temperature-pressure chart for Refrigerant 12 (English system)

a slight variation between the temperature and pressure values of the refrigerant in this range. (The metric equivalent of this table is given in figure 8-3.) These variations can be detected by sensitive thermometers and pressure gauges. In this range, the assumption is made that for every pound of pressure recorded, the temperature is the same. For example, figure 8-2 indicates that for a pressure of 23.1 psig, the temperature is 23°F. This value is the temperature of the refrigerant itself. It is not the temperature of the outside surface of the container or the air passing over it.

The objective in automotive air conditioning is to allow the evaporator to reach its coldest point without icing. Since ice forms at 32°F (0°C), the fins and cooling coils of the evaporator must not be allowed to reach a colder temperature. Because of the temperature rise through the walls of the cooling fins and coils, the temperature of the refrigerant may be several degrees cooler than that of the air passing through the evaporator.

For example, a pressure gauge reading of 28 psig (193.06 kPa) means that the temperature of the refrigerant in the evaporator is about 30°F (-1.1°C). Because of the temperature rise through the fins and coils, the air passing over the coil is about 34°F or 35°F (1.1°C or 1.7°C).

HANDLING REFRIGERANT

Liquid refrigerant should be properly stored and used since it can cause blindness if it splashes into the eyes. In addition, if refrigerant is allowed to contact the skin, frostbite may result.

A refrigerant container should never be exposed to excessive heat or be allowed to come into contact with a heating device. The increase in refrigerant pressure inside the container as a result of heating can become great enough to cause the container to explode.

If refrigerant is allowed to come into contact with an open flame or heated metal, a poisonous gas is created. Anyone breathing this gas becomes violently ill. *Remember — refrigerant is not a toy.*

EVAPORATOR TEMPERATURE °C	EVAPORATOR PRESSURE GAUGE READING KILOPASCAL		AMBIENT TEMPERATURE °C	HIGH PRESSURE GAUGE READING KILOPASCAL (GAUGE)
	(GAUGE)	(ABSOLUTE)		
-16	73.4	174.7	16	737.7
-15	81.0	182.3	17	759.8
-14	87.8	189.1	18	784.6
-13	94.8	196.1	19	810.2
-12	100.6	201.9	20	841.2
-11	108.9	210.2	21	868.7
-10	117.9	219.2	22	901.8
- 9	124.5	225.8	23	932.2
- 8	133.9	235.2	24	970.8
- 7	140.3	241.6	25	1 020.5
- 6	149.6	250.9	26	1 075.6
- 5	159.2	260.5	27	1 111.5
- 4	167.4	268.7	28	1 143.2
- 3	183.2	268.7	29	1 174.9
- 2	186.9	288.2	30	1 206.6
- 1	195.8	288.2	31	1 241.1
0	206.8	308.1	32	1 267.3
1	218.5	319.8	33	1 294.8
2	227.8	329.1	34	1 319.7
3	238.7	340.0	35	1 344.5
4	249.4	350.7	36	1 413.5
5	261.3	362.6	37	1 468.6
6	273.7	375.0	38	1 527.9
7	287.5	388.8	39	1 577.5
8	296.6	397.9	40	1 627.2
9	303.3	404.6	42	1 737.5
10	321.5	422.8	45	1 854.7

Fig. 8-3 Temperature-pressure chart for Refrigerant 12 (metric system)

It should be handled only by a trained refrigeration service technician.

The term *Freon* is commonly used to refer to Refrigerant 12. Freon and Freon 12 are registered trademarks of E.I. duPont de Nemours and Company. These terms should be applied only to refrigerant manufactured or packaged by this company or by a processing plant licensed by duPont.

Refrigerant 12 is also packaged in the United States under several other brand names, such as Genatron 12, Isotron 12, and Ucon 12.

R-12 is commonly packaged in 14-ounce (396.9 g) cans, figure 8-4, which are called "pound" cans. This refrigerant is also available in 2-pound (0.907 2-kg) and 2-1/2 pound (1.134-kg) cans. These cans use a special adapter as a means of transferring the refrigerant to the system. No attempt should be made to remove the refrigerant by other means.

R-12 is also available in 10-, 12-, 15-, and 30-pound (4.536-, 5.443-, 6.804-, and 13.61-kg)

disposable cylinders. It is also available in 25- and 145-pound (11.34- and 65.772-kg) deposit cylinders. R-12 is also sold to manufacturers and large-quantity users in 2 000-pound (907-kg) cylinders, tank trucks, and railroad tank cars.

The pound cans of refrigerant are the most popular because of their convenience and the ease of measuring the proper amount of refrigerant into a system. However, bulk packaging of refrigerant (in cylinders or tanks) generally is the least expensive method of buying refrigerant.

R-12 drums and cylinders are painted white for easy identification. However, there is no standard system of refrigerant color codes. Some manufacturers may use different colors to designate the same refrigerant. Therefore, it is suggested that the contents of a cylinder be identified before the refrigerant is introduced into the system. Do not rely on the color of the container as a means of identification.

Fig. 8-4 Typical "pound" can of Refrigerant 12 actually contains 14 ounces (397 grams)

SPECIAL SAFETY PRECAUTIONS

Because it is important that the student be aware of the hazards involved in the use of Refrigerant 12, the following safety procedures must be observed.

Recall that Refrigerant 12 is:

- odorless
- undetectable in small quantities
- colorless
- nonstaining

However, R-12 is *dangerous* because of the damage it can do if it strikes the human eye or comes into contact with the skin. Since the evaporation temperature of R-12 is –21.6°F (–29.9°C), suitable eye protection should be worn by anyone handling R-12 to protect the eyes from splashing refrigerant. If R-12 does enter the eye, freezing of the eye can occur with resultant blindness. The

following procedure is suggested if R-12 enters the eye(s).

1. Do not rub the eye.
2. Splash large quantities of cool water into the eye to increase the temperature.
3. Tape a sterile eye patch in place to prevent dirt from entering the eye.
4. Go immediately to a doctor or hospital for professional care.
5. *Do not attempt self-treatment.*

If liquid R-12 strikes the skin, frostbite can occur. The same procedure outlined for emergency eye care can be used to combat the effects of R-12 contact with the skin. Refrigerant 12 in air is harmless unless it is released in a confined space. Under this condition, Refrigerant 12 displaces oxygen in the air and may cause drowsiness or unconsciousness. However, the automobile owner and the service technician need not be concerned about the safety of the automotive air-conditioning system because of the small capacity of the unit as compared to the large capacity of the car interior.

Refrigerant 12 must not be allowed to come into contact with an open flame or a very hot metal. Many texts, including previous editions of *Automotive Air Conditioning*, state that fluorocarbon refrigerants, such as Refrigerant 12, produce phosgene gas when exposed to hot metal or an open flame. The proper name for phosgene is carbonyl chloride ($COCl_2$).

Tests made by Underwiters' Laboratory, Inc. (UL) in 1933 indicated that R-12 produced this highly toxic gas during decomposition. Tests in recent years, using advanced technology equipment, prove that phosgene is not produced in this manner. Decomposition does, however, result in the formation of carbonyl fluoride (COF_2) and carbonyl chlorofluoride ($COClF$) with small amounts of free chlorine (Cl_2).

Though 20 to 50 times less toxic than phosgene, the decomposed gases of R-12 must be avoided. At high concentrations, the lack of oxygen (O), which results in asphyxiation, is the real hazard. A primary rule, then, is to *avoid breathing these fumes or any others.* The human body requires oxygen in the quantity found in noncontaminated air. Diluting air with any foreign gas can reduce the available oxygen to a level that may be *harmful* or, in some cases, *fatal.*

The following rules also must be observed when handling R-12 and other similar refrigerants.

Fig. 8-5 Typical emergency eyewash station

1. Above 130°F (54.44°C), liquid refrigerant completely fills a container and hydrostatic pressure builds up rapidly with each degree of temperature rise. To provide for some margin of safety, *never heat a refrigerant cylinder above 125°F (51.66°C) or allow it to reach this temperature.*

NOTE: It is the practice of some service technicians to place containers of Refrigerant 12 into a pan of warm water as an aid in speeding up the charging process. *This practice is not recommended, and especially not for the inexperienced.* Even the "pros" are sometimes injured with this procedure.

Fig. 8-6 Typical emergency eyewash fountain

2. *Never apply a direct flame to a refrigerant cylinder or container. Never place an electrical resistance heater near or in direct contact with a container of refrigerant.*

3. *Do not abuse a refrigerant cylinder or container.* To avoid damage, use an approved valve wrench for opening and closing the valves. Secure all cylinders in an upright position for storing and withdrawing refrigerant.

4. *Do not handle refrigerant without suitable eye protection.*

5. *Do not discharge refrigerant into an enclosed area having an open flame.*

6. When purging a system, discharge the refrigerant slowly.

7. *Do not discharge Refrigerant 12 into a confined space.* Discharge refrigerant only in a well-ventilated area.

8. For an automotive refrigeration system, do not introduce anything but pure Refrigerant 12 and approved refrigerant oil into the system.

REFRIGERATION OIL

The moving parts of a compressor assembly must be lubricated to prevent damage during operation. Oil is used on these moving parts and on the seals and gaskets as well. In addition, a small amount of oil is added to the refrigerant which circulates through the system. This refrigerant/oil combination maintains the thermostatic expansion valve in the proper operating condition.

The oil which must be used in an automobile air-conditioning system is a nonfoaming sulfur-free grade specifically formulated for use in certain types of air-conditioning systems. This special oil is known as *refrigeration oil,* figure 8-7, and it is available in several grades and types. The grade and type to be used is determined by the compressor manufacturer. To replace oil that may be lost due to a refrigerant leak, *pressurized oil,* figure 8-8, is available in disposable cans. This particular container contains 2 fluidounces (59 milliliters) of oil and a like measure of Refrigerant 12. The Refrigerant 12 provides the necessary pressure required to force the oil into the system.

Refrigeration oil is clear to light yellow in color. Any impurities will cause the oil to range in color from brown to black. Another characteristic of refrigeration oil is that it is practically odorless. Thus, a strong odor of oil in the system indicates that the oil is impure. Impure oil must be removed and replaced with clean, fresh oil. The receiver/drier

Fig. 8-7 Refrigeration oil in one-gallon (3.785-L) container

Fig. 8-8 Refrigerant oil charge for adding oil to system

should also be replaced and a good pumpdown performed before the system is recharged.

THE CLASSIFICATION OF REFRIGERATION OIL

The classification of refrigeration oil is based on three factors: viscosity, compatibility with refrigerants, and pour point.

Viscosity

The *viscosity rating* for a fluid is based on the time, in seconds, required for a measured quantity of the fluid to pass through a calibrated orifice when the temperature of the fluid is 100°F (37.8°C). The resistance to flow of any liquid is judged by the viscosity rating of the fluid. The higher the viscosity number, the thicker the liquid.

The fluorocarbon group of refrigerants (R-12 is included in this group) requires oil with a viscosity of about 300 for air-conditioner service. Some air conditioners, however, can use an oil with a viscosity rating as high as 1 000.

The *Saybolt Universal Viscosity* (SUV) is defined as the time, in seconds, required for sixty cubic centimeters of oil, at 100°F (37.8°C), to flow through a standard Saybolt orifice.

Compatibility

Refrigeration oil must be compatible with the refrigerant used in the system. This means that the oil must be capable of existing (remaining an oil) when mixed with the refrigerant. In other words, the oil is not changed or separated by chemical interaction with the refrigerant.

The compatibility of a refrigeration oil with a refrigerant is determined by a test called a *floc test F*. This test is performed by placing a mixture containing 90% oil and 10% refrigerant in a sealed glass tube. The mixture is then slowly cooled until a waxy substance appears. The temperature at which this substance forms is recorded as the *floc point*.

Pour Point

The temperature at which an oil will just flow is its *pour point*. This temperature is recorded in degrees Fahrenheit. The pour point is a standard of the American Society for Testing Materials (ASTM).

SERVICING TIPS

The oil level of the compressor should be checked each time the air conditioner is serviced. Always check the manufacturer's recommendations before adding oil to the air-conditioning system. The procedures for adding oil to all compressors can be found under the heading of Service Procedures, Section 3, in this text.

When the oil is not being poured, the oil container must remain capped. Always be sure that the cap is in place and tightly secured. Oil absorbs moisture and moisture is damaging to the air conditioner.

SUMMARY

The properties of a good refrigeration oil are low wax content, good thermal and chemical stability, low viscosity, and a low pour point. A few simple rules are listed as follows for handling refrigeration oil:

DO
- Use only approved refrigeration oil.
- Make sure the cap is tight on the container when not in use.
- Replace oil if there is any doubt of its condition.
- Avoid contaminating the oil.

DO NOT
- Transfer oil from one container to another.
- Return used oil to the container.
- Leave the oil container uncapped.
- Use a grade of oil other than that recommended for the air conditioner.

Review

Circle the letter designating the answer of your choice.

1. What is the refrigerant temperature for a gauge reading of 21 psig?

    a. 19°F

    b. 20°F

    c. 21°F

    d. 22°F

2. If the refrigerant temperature is 24°F, what should the gauge pressure be?

    a. 23.9 psig

    b. 24.6 psig

    c. 25.3 psig

    d. 26.1 psig

3. What is the refrigerant temperature for a gauge reading of 36 psig?

    a. 38°F

    b. 39°F

    c. 40°F

    d. 41°F

4. If the refrigerant temperature is 34°F, what should the gauge pressure be?

    a. 30.9 psig

    b. 31.7 psig

    c. 32.5 psig

    d. 33.4 psig

5. Between what pressures are the temperature and pressure values of Refrigerant 12 very close (English values)?

    a. 20 psig and 80 psig

    b. 15 psig and 85 psig

    c. 25 psig and 85 psig

    d. 15 psig and 90 psig

6. To prevent ice formation on the fins and coils of the evaporator, the temperature should never be allowed to go below

    a. 28°F.

    b. 30°F.

    c. 32°F.

    d. 34°F.

7. Refrigerant in the liquid state, if allowed to strike the eye, can cause

    a. serious damage.

    b. blindness.

    c. discomfort.

    d. all of the answers are correct

8. If Refrigerant 12 comes into contact with an open flame, it causes

    a. an explosion.

    b. a harmful gas.

    c. the flame to become extinguished.

    d. instant vaporization.

9. Why should one *not* overheat a refrigerant container?

    a. It will explode

    b. It serves no purpose

    c. It ruins the refrigerant

    d. Refrigerant will not vaporize

10. What is the *most important* safety measure to observe if liquid refrigerant strikes the eye?

    a. Immediately summon the class to show them that accidents *do* happen.

    b. Keep the victim calm and assured that the accident is not serious.

    c. Reprimand the victim for being careless.

    d. Immediately splash large quantities of cool water into the eye.

UNIT 9:

The Refrigeration Circuit

This unit is concerned with the basic refrigeration circuit. The following description of the refrigeration part of the air-conditioning system is intended to familiarize the service technician with the general arrangement and function of the components in the system. A complete understanding of the overall operation of the system is necessary when working on air-conditioning units. Each component of the system will be examined in detail.

CAUTION: It should be emphasized again that eye protection is recommended when servicing air-conditioning units.

Study the schematic diagram of the components of the refrigeration system, figure 9-1. The compressor (B) pumps heat-laden refrigerant vapor from the evaporator (A). The refrigerant is compressed at (B) and then is sent, under high pressure, to the condenser (C) as a superheated vapor.

Since this vapor is much hotter than the surrounding air, it gives up its heat to the outside air flowing through the condenser fins.

As the refrigerant vapor gives up its heat, it changes to a liquid. The condensed liquid refrigerant is filtered, dried, and temporarily stored, under pressure, in the receiver/drier (D) until it is needed by the evaporator.

Liquid refrigerant is metered from the receiver/drier into the evaporator by the thermostatic expansion valve (E). This valve controls the flow of refrigerant in this part of the system. The pressure of the refrigerant is lowered by the expansion valve. As a result, the refrigerant begins to boil and change to a vapor. During this process, the refrigerant picks up heat from the warm air passing through the fins of the evaporator. Thus, the process repeats as this heat is transmitted first to the compressor, and then to the condenser for dissipation.

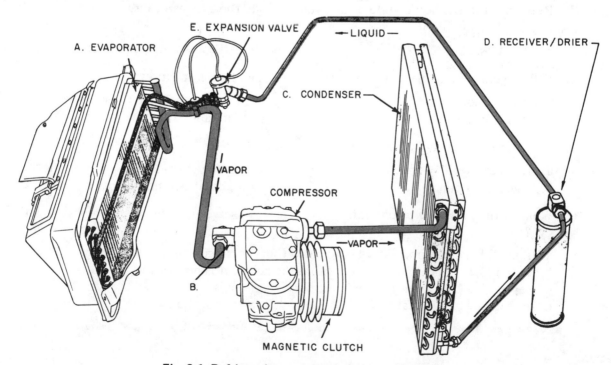

Fig. 9-1 Refrigeration system components (typical)

Fig. 9-2 Receiver/driers

In the following discussion, the sizes of the system hoses are given, as is the state of the refrigerant in the hoses and in the components. Although the hose sizes may vary in different systems, the state of the refrigerant at various points in all systems is the same.

RECEIVER/DRIER

The discussion of the refrigeration system components begins with the receiver/drier assembly, figures 9-2 and 9-3. This device stores the refrigerant until it is needed. The receiver/drier (or drier) is a cylindrical metal can with two fittings and, in most cases, a sight glass. The drier is located in the high-pressure side of the air-conditioning system. In general, the construction of the receiver/drier is such that refrigerant vapor and liquid are separated to insure that 100% liquid is fed to the thermostatic

expansion valve. The assembly can be divided into two parts: the receiver and the drier.

The receiver section of the tank is a storage compartment. This section holds the proper amount of extra refrigerant required by the system to insure proper operation. The receiver insures that a steady flow of liquid refrigerant can be supplied to the thermostatic expansion valve.

The drier section of the tank is simply a bag of desiccant, such as silica gel, that can absorb and hold a small quantity of moisture.

A screen is placed in the receiver/drier to catch and prevent the circulation of any debris that may be in the system. Although this screen cannot be serviced, two other filtering screens in the system can be cleaned or replaced if necessary. These screens are located in the thermostatic expansion valve inlet and the compressor inlet.

The refrigerant then moves through a rubber hose called the liquid line to the evaporator metering device (thermostatic expansion valve or fixed orifice tube). The liquid line is usually 5/16 inch (7.9 mm) inside diamter (ID) though some may be 1/4 inch (6.3 mm) ID. In some installations, the liquid line is made of copper, steel, or aluminum. The liquid line can also be a combination of rubber and copper, steel, or aluminum. The refrigerant in the liquid line is high-pressure liquid, figure 9-4. The receiver/drier is covered in greater detail in Unit 15.

THERMOSTATIC EXPANSION VALVE

The thermostatic expansion valve, or TXV, figure 9-5, is located at the inlet side of the evaporator. This valve is the controlling device for the system and separates the high side of the system from the low side. A small restriction, or orifice, in the valve allows only a small amount of liquid refrigerant to pass through the valve into the evap-

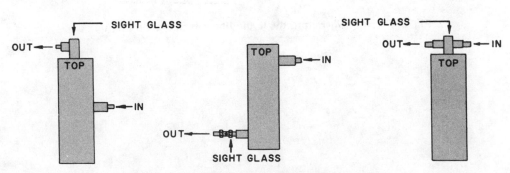

Fig. 9-3 Three types of receiver/drier assemblies

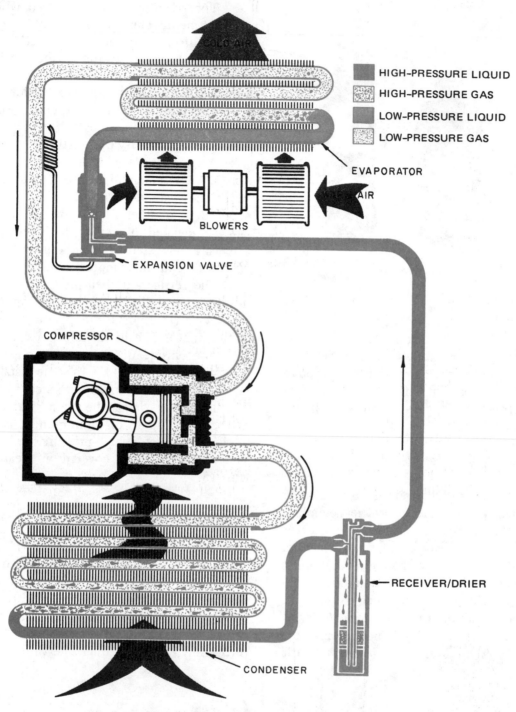

HIGH-PRESSURE LIQUID
HIGH-PRESSURE GAS
LOW-PRESSURE LIQUID
LOW-PRESSURE GAS

COLD AIR

EVAPORATOR

WARM AIR

BLOWERS

EXPANSION VALVE

COMPRESSOR

RECEIVER/DRIER

HOT AIR

CONDENSER

Fig. 9-4 The refrigerant in the liquid line is high-pressure liquid

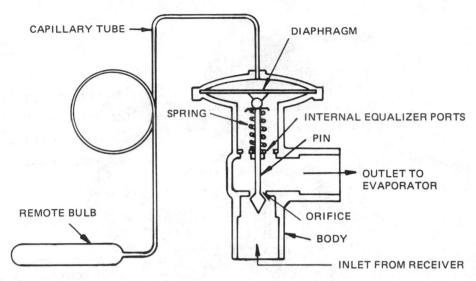

Fig. 9-5 Thermostatic expansion valve

orator from the drier. The amount of refrigerant passing through the valve depends upon the evaporator temperature. The orifice is about 0.008 ihch (0.2 mm) in diameter. A pin can be raised and lowered in the orifice to change the size of the opening (up to the 0.008-inch diameter). It is evident that only a small amount of refrigerant can enter even when the valve is wide open.

The refrigerant inside the thermostatic expansion valve, and immediately after it, is 100% liquid. A small amount of liquid refrigerant, known as *flash gas,* vaporizes immediately after passing

through the valve. All the liquid soon changes state, however. As soon as the liquid pressure drops, the liquid refrigerant begins to boil. As it continues to boil, it must absorb heat. This heat is removed from the air passing over the coils and fins of the evaporator. As a result, the air feels cool. Remember, the heat is being removed from the air; cold air is not being created.

The thermostatic expansion valve meters the proper amount of refrigerant into the evaporator. Refrigerant that is properly metered into the evaporator is 100% liquid just after the thermostatic expansion valve, except for the flash gas, and 100% vapor (gas) at the outlet, or tailpipe, of the evaporator. The expansion valve has a sensing element called a remote bulb or capillary bulb, figure 9-6. This bulb is attached to the evaporator tailpipe to sense outlet temperatures. In this manner, the expansion valve can regulate itself. The thermostatic expansion valve is covered in greater detail in Unit 16.

EVAPORATOR

The evaporator, figure 9-7, is the part of the refrigeration system where the refrigerant vaporizes as it picks up heat. Heat-laden air is forced through and past the fins and tubes of the evaporator. Heat from the air is picked up by the boiling refrigerant and is carried in the system to the condenser.

Factors which are important in the design of an evaporator include the size and length of the tubing, the number of fins, and the amount of air passing through and past the fins. The heat load is

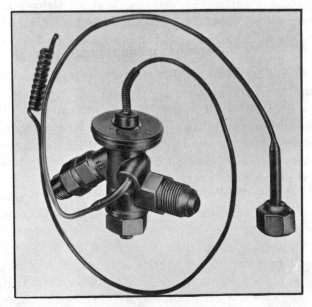

FLARE TYPE

Fig. 9-6 Externally equalized thermostatic expansion valve

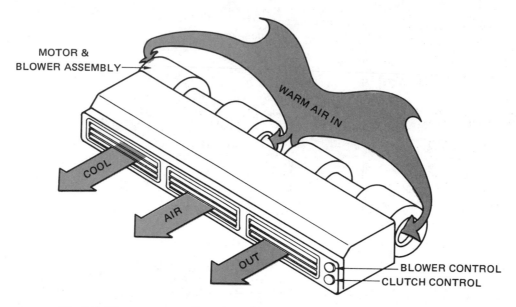

MOTOR &
BLOWER ASSEMBLY

WARM AIR IN

COOL

AIR

OUT

BLOWER CONTROL
CLUTCH CONTROL

Fig. 9-7 The evaporator (heat is picked up from the air inside the evaporator)

also an important consideration. *Heat load* refers to the amount of heat, in Btu, to be removed.

The evaporator may have two, three, or more rows of tubing as determined by the design to fit a specific housing and still be able to achieve the rated capacity in Btu. The refrigerant as it leaves the evaporator on its way to the compressor is low-pressure gas.

If too much refrigerant is metered into the evaporator, the unit floods. As a result, the unit does not cool because the pressure of the refrigerant is higher and it does not boil away as quickly. In addition, when the evaporator is filled with liquid refrigerant, the refrigerant cannot vaporize properly. This step is necessary if the refrigerant is to take on heat. A flooded evaporator allows an excess of liquid refrigerant to leave the evaporator, with the result that serious damage may be done to the next component, the compressor.

If too little refrigerant is metered into the evaporator, the system is said to be *starved*. Again, the unit does not cool because the refrigerant vaporizes or boils off too rapidly, long before it passes through the evaporator.

COMPRESSOR

The refrigerant compressor, figure 9-8, is a pump especially designed to raise the pressure of the refrigerant. According to the laws of physics, when a gas or vapor is compressed (pressure increased) its temperature is also increased propor-

tionately. When its pressure and temperature are increased, the refrigerant condenses more rapidly in the next component, the condenser.

Many different models of current production automotive air-conditioning compressors are found on today's cars. Additionally, many other models, now discontinued, are still in use. Automotive air-conditioning compressors, depending on design, have one, two, four, five, six, or ten cylinders (pistons).

Several different compressors may be found on some car lines. For example, American Motors may use a Sankyo, Tecumseh, York or Delco Air compressor, depending on application. Different models of a particular compressor may be found on some car lines. Mazda, for example, uses a Sankyo compressor either model 507 or 508, depending on application.

Regardless of manufacturer and model, all automotive compressors are of the same design; reciprocating piston. This means that the piston(s) moves in a linear motion, back and forth or up and down. The only exception is York's Vane Rotary compressor which was introduced, and discontinued, in the early 80s. Only about 50 000 of these compressors were produced with no appreciable application in the marketplace.

The following is a brief description of compressor operation. More detailed information is given in Unit 14, "Compressors." Service and repair procedures for the most popular compressors are given in Section 3 of this text.

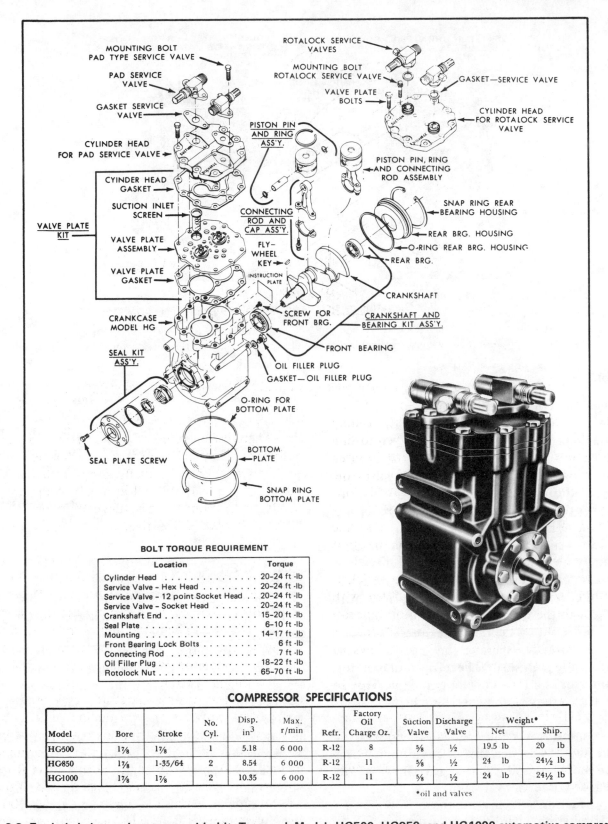

BOLT TORQUE REQUIREMENT

Location	Torque
Cylinder Head	20–24 ft -lb
Service Valve – Hex Head	20–24 ft -lb
Service Valve – 12 point Socket Head	20–24 ft -lb
Service Valve – Socket Head	20–24 ft -lb
Crankshaft End	15–20 ft -lb
Seal Plate	6–10 ft -lb
Mounting	14–17 ft -lb
Front Bearing Lock Bolts	6 ft -lb
Connecting Rod	7 ft -lb
Oil Filler Plug	18–22 ft -lb
Rotolock Nut	65–70 ft -lb

COMPRESSOR SPECIFICATIONS

Model	Bore	Stroke	No. Cyl.	Disp. in³	Max. r/min	Refr.	Factory Oil Charge Oz.	Suction Valve	Discharge Valve	Weight* Net	Weight* Ship.
HG500	1⅞	1⅞	1	5.18	6 000	R-12	8	⅝	½	19.5 lb	20 lb
HG850	1⅞	1-35/64	2	8.54	6 000	R-12	11	⅝	½	24 lb	24½ lb
HG1000	1⅞	1⅞	2	10.35	6 000	R-12	11	⅝	½	24 lb	24½ lb

*oil and valves

Fig. 9-8 Exploded view and parts assembly kit, Tecumseh Models HG500, HG850, and HG1000 automotive compressors

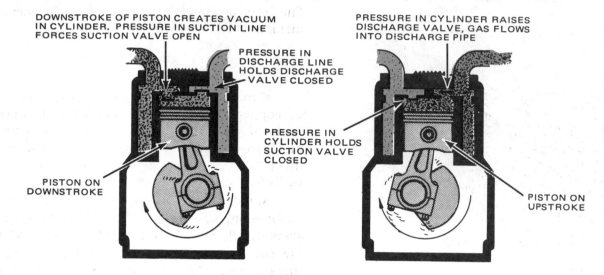

DOWNSTROKE OF PISTON CREATES VACUUM IN CYLINDER. PRESSURE IN SUCTION LINE FORCES SUCTION VALVE OPEN

PRESSURE IN CYLINDER RAISES DISCHARGE VALVE, GAS FLOWS INTO DISCHARGE PIPE

PRESSURE IN DISCHARGE LINE HOLDS DISCHARGE VALVE CLOSED

PRESSURE IN CYLINDER HOLDS SUCTION VALVE CLOSED

PISTON ON DOWNSTROKE

PISTON ON UPSTROKE

Fig. 9-9 Operating cycle of reciprocating compressor

Operation

Each piston of the compressor is equipped with a set of suction and discharge valves and valve plates. While one piston is on the intake stroke, the other is on the compression stroke, figure 9-9. The piston draws in refrigerant through the suction valve and forces it out through the discharge valve. When the piston is on the downstroke, or intake stroke, the discharge valve is held closed by the action of the piston and the higher pressure above it. At the same time, the suction reed valve is opened to allow low-pressure gas to enter. When the piston is on the upstroke, or compression stroke, refrigerant is forced through the discharge valve and the suction valve is held closed by the same pressure.

The compressor separates the low side of the system from the high side. The refrigerant entering the compressor is a low-pressure gas. When the refrigerant leaves the compressor, it is a high-pressure gas.

The compressor is equipped with service valves which are used to service the air-conditioning system. The manifold and gauge set is connected into the system at the service valve ports. All procedures such as evacuating and charging the system are carried out through the manifold and gauge set.

Refrigeration oil is stored in the *sump* of the compressor to keep the crankshaft, connecting rods, and other internal parts lubricated. A small amount of this oil circulates throughout the system with the refrigerant. Internal provisions allow this oil to return to the compressor.

The hose leaving the compressor contains high-pressure refrigerant vapor. The hose is made of synthetic rubber and is usually 13/32-inch (10.3 mm) inside diameter. This rubber hose often has extended preformed metal (steel or aluminum) ends with fittings. Known as the *hot gas discharge line,* it connects to the inlet of the condenser. It should be noted that the inlet of the condenser is always at the top — never at the bottom.

CONDENSER

The purpose of the condenser is the opposite of that of the evaporator. Refrigerant in the gaseous state liquefies or condenses in the condenser. To do so, the refrigerant must give up its heat in Btu. *Ram air,* or the air passing over the condenser, carries the heat away from the condenser and the gas condenses. The heat removed from the refrigerant (so that it can change to a liquid), is the same heat that was absorbed in the evaporator to change the refrigerant from a liquid to a gas.

The refrigerant is almost 100% gas when it enters the condenser. A very small amount of gas may liquefy in the hot-gas discharge line, but the amount is so small that it does not affect the operation of the system.

The refrigerant is not always 100% liquid when it leaves the condenser. Since only a certain amount of heat can be handled by the condenser at a given time, a small percentage of the refrigerant may leave the condenser in a gaseous state. Again,

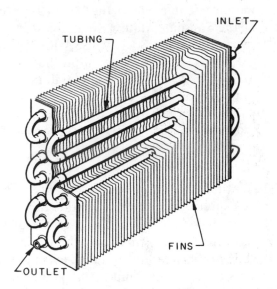

Fig. 9-10 Condenser

this condition does not affect the system operation since the next component is the receiver/drier.

As indicated previously, the inlet of the condenser must be at the top of the unit, figure 9-10. With the inlet in this position, the condensing refrigerant can flow to the bottom of the condenser where it is forced, under pressure, to the receiver/drier through the liquid line.

The refrigerant in the condenser is a combination of liquid and gas under high pressure. Extreme care must be exercised when servicing this component of the system.

From the condenser, the refrigerant continues to the receiver/drier through the liquid line. At this point, the cycle starts over again. The liquid line from the condenser can be either a rubber or a metal line in a variety of sizes.

HOSES

Refrigerant fluid and vapor hoses may be made of copper, steel, or aluminum. They are usually made of a synthetic rubber covered with a nylon braid for strength. The inner core is usually of Buna 'N', a synthetic rubber which is not affected by Refrigerant 12.

Standard hose sizes are given a number designation, such as #6, #8, #10, and #12. Size #6 is usually used for the liquid line, #8 or #10 as the hot gas discharge line, and #10 or #12 as the suction line. The chart of figure 9-11 gives the inside diameter (ID) and outside diameter (OD) of the two types of hoses used in automotive air-conditioning service.

THE ROTARY VANE AIR CYCLE (ROVAC) SYSTEM

Based on much the same principle that is used to provide cooling for the passenger compartment of commercial aircraft, an attempt is being made to develop a rotary vane air cycle (ROVAC) air-conditioning system that is suitable for automotive use. The ROVAC System, (a trade name) or a similar system, may someday replace the Refrigerant 12 vapor cycle system now in use. It should be noted that an air cycle system is an open system, as opposed to a vapor cycle system which is a closed system.

As an incentive for developers to find an alternate method of comfort cooling, thus eliminat-

Hose Size	Inside Diameter		Outside Diameter (OD)			
			Rubber Hose		Nylon Hose	
	English	Metric	English	Metric	English	Metric
#6	5/16 in	7.94 mm	3/4 in	19.05 mm	15/32 in[1]	11.9 mm[3]
#8	13/32 in	10.32 mm	59/64 in[1]	23.42 mm[3]	35/64 in[1]	13.89 mm[3]
#10	1/2 in	12.7 mm	1-1/32 in[2]	25.8 mm[4]	11/16 in[1]	17.46 mm[3]
#12	5/8 in	15.87 mm	1-5/32 in[2]	29.37 mm[4]	NA	NA

[1] ± 1/64 inch
[2] ± 1/32 inch
[3] ± 0.4 mm
[4] ± 0.8 mm

Fig. 9-11 Inside and outside diameters of rubber and nylon hose commonly used for automotive air-conditioning service.

ing fluorocarbon refrigerants, United States Government agencies, such as NASA, and the military have supported the ROVAC efforts. Though in development for more than twelve years, a practical system, from the standpoint of cost, has not yet been produced for automotive use.

Operation

As shown in figure 9-12, the compressor of the ROVAC system is called a *circulator*. The condenser is called a *primary heat exchanger* and the evaporator is called the *secondary heat exchanger*. A *collector* in the system serves in a similar manner as an accumulator in a conventional (vapor cycle) system; it separates liquid (hydrocarbon) from the vapor (air). Unlike an accumulator, however, the liquid is retained in the collector and is not metered back into the system by the circulator.

A small amount of liquid oil circulates in the system at all times to provide lubrication for the circulator. The other liquid, comprised of alcohol and hydrocarbons, is vaporized in the secondary heat exchanger as it picks up heat. Conversely, this vapor is changed back to a liquid in the primary heat exchanger as its heat is given up to the outside air.

Though promising, after years of research and development, the rotary vane air cycle system, for automotive application, in mid-1982 was set aside at ROVAC, at least for the time being. According to an announcement made at the May 1982 Conference of the Sunshine State Association-Refrigeration Service Engineers Society (SSA-RSES), the efforts of ROVAC will be centered on the production of a 2.5-ton system for residential and commercial applications. This decision, it seems, was made by Hill International Incorporated, which acquired controlling stock of ROVAC in early 1982.

SUMMARY

The entire refrigeration cycle exhibits several processes as the refrigerant changes state in various sections of the system. When the pressure of the refrigerant drops in the evaporator, the refrigerant boils. While boiling, the refrigerant picks up heat. The compressor raises the temperature and pressure of the refrigerant so that it condenses in the condenser. At this point, the refrigerant gives up the same heat (in Btu) that it picked up in the evaporator.

The thermostatic expansion valve controls the flow of refrigerant into the evaporator and thereby separates the high side of the system from the low side. The compressor increases gas pressure and separates the low side of the system from the high side. This is the basic air-conditioning circuit from which all of the other automotive refrigeration circuits are patterned. A good understanding of the simple circuit makes an understanding of the other circuits much easier.

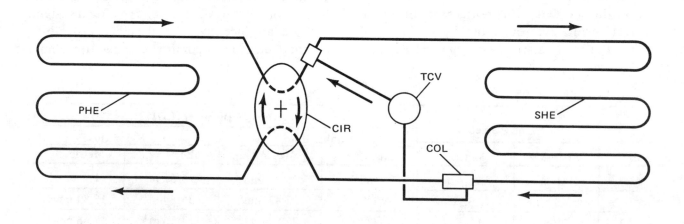

COL — Collector
CIR — Circulator
PHE — Primary Heat Exchanger

SHE — Secondary Heat Exchanger
TCV — Temperature Control Valve

Fig. 9-12 Typical mechanical schematic of a ROVAC system. This type of system is being developed for possible automotive application.

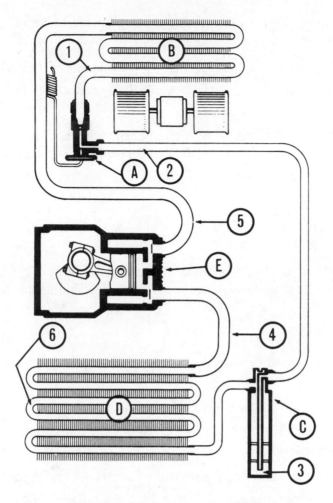

Fig. 9-13 The refrigeration system

Review

Refer to figure 9-13 to answer the following questions.

1. What component is shown as D?

   a. Evaporator
   b. Condenser

   c. Receiver/drier
   d. Thermostatic expansion valve

2. What component is shown as A?

   a. Evaporator
   b. Condenser

   c. Receiver/drier
   d. Thermostatic expansion valve

3. What component is shown as B?

   a. Evaporator
   b. Condenser

   c. Receiver/drier
   d. Thermostatic expansion valve

4. What component is shown as C?

   a. Evaporator
   b. Condenser

   c. Receiver/drier
   d. Thermostatic expansion valve

CONTINUED

5. What is the state of the refrigerant in line 4?

    a. High-pressure vapor   c. High-pressure liquid
    b. Low-pressure vapor   d. Low-pressure liquid

6. What is the state of the refrigerant as it leaves the evaporator, line 5?

    a. High-pressure vapor   c. High-pressure liquid
    b. Low-pressure vapor   d. Low-pressure liquid

7. What is the purpose of the compressor, component E? Technician A says it is to change the refrigerant vapor to a liquid. Technician B says it is to change the refrigerant liquid to a vapor.

    a. Technician A is correct.
    b. Technician B is correct.
    c. Either technician could be correct.
    d. Both technicians are wrong.

8. What is the state of the refrigerant as it immediately enters the evaporator, line 1? Technician A says it is all liquid with some flash gas. Technician B says it is all vapor due to flash gas.

    a. Technician A is correct.
    b. Technician B is correct.
    c. Either technician could be correct.
    d. Both technicians are wrong.

9. What is the purpose of the desiccant in the receiver/drier?

    a. To clean the refrigerant.   c. To dry the refrigerant.
    b. To strain the refrigerant.   d. All of the answers are correct.

10. Which is more serious, a flooded evaporator or a starved evaporator? Why?

    a. A flooded evaporator, because the refrigerant will not evaporate.
    b. A flooded evaporator, because liquid refrigerant may return to the compressor, damaging the compressor.
    c. A starved evaporator, because sufficient heat will not be absorbed in the evaporator.
    d. A starved evaporator, because refrigerant will be superheated on return to the compressor, damaging the compressor.

UNIT 10:

Moisture and Moisture Removal

For all practical purposes, refrigerant can be considered to be moisture free. The moisture content of new refrigerant should not exceed ten parts per million (10 ppm) of refrigerant.

If new refrigerant and refrigeration oil are used in a system, then any moisture found in the system must come from outside sources, such as a break in a line or from improperly fastened hoses or fittings on the installation.

Whenever a unit is removed from the system for repair or replacement, air is introduced into the system. As a result, there is always a danger of moisture entering the unit since air contains moisture. Refrigerant absorbs moisture readily when exposed to it. To keep the system as moisture free as possible, all air conditioners use a receiver/drier which contains a bag of desiccant such as silica gel, figure 10-1. Desiccants are able to absorb and hold a small quantity of moisture.

Any water introduced into the system in excess of the amount that the desiccant can handle is free in the system. Even one drop of free water cannot be controlled and causes irreparable damage to the internal parts of the air conditioner.

Moisture in concentrations greater than 20 ppm causes serious damage. To illustrate how small an amount 20 ppm is, one small drop of water in an air-conditioning system having a capacity of three pounds amounts to 40 ppm, or twice the amount that can be tolerated.

Refrigerant 12 reacts chemically with water to form hydrochloric acid. The heat generated in the system speeds up the acid-forming process. The greater the concentration of water in the system, the more concentrated is the corrosive acid formed.

The hydrochloric acid corrodes all of the metallic parts of the system, particularly those made of steel. Iron, copper, and aluminum parts are damaged by the acid as well. The corrosive process creates oxides which are released into the refrigerant as particles of metal which form a sludge. Further damage is caused when oxides plug the

screens in the thermostatic expansion valve, compressor inlet, and the drier itself.

One automotive air-conditioner manufacturer indicates that alcohol, or methanol, should be added to the system. This manufacturer states that a system freezeup can be avoided by adding 0.07

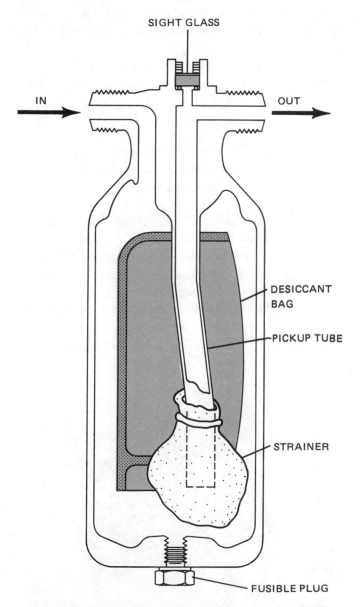

Fig. 10-1 Cutaway view of receiver/drier showing details

fluidounces (2.0 mL) of alcohol per pound (0.453 6 kg) of refrigerant. However, the addition of alcohol to the system can cause even greater damage since the drier seeks out alcohol even more than moisture in the system. Thus, the drier releases all of its moisture and absorbs the alcohol. This additional free moisture in the system can now cause more severe damage to the system components. Once a system is saturated with moisture, irreparable damage is done to the interior of the system. If the moisture condition is neglected long enough, pinholes caused by corrosion appear in the evaporator and condenser coils and in any metal tubing used in the system. Any affected parts must be replaced.

In addition, aluminum parts can become so corroded that the compressor is unserviceable. Valves and fittings can be damaged so severely that they are no longer usable.

Whenever there is evidence of moisture in a system, a thorough system cleanout is recommended. Such a cleanout should be followed by the installation of a new drier and a complete system pumpdown using a vacuum pump.

The air-conditioning technician can prevent the introduction of unwanted moisture and dirt into a system by following a few simple rules.

- When servicing the air conditioner, always install the drier last.
- When servicing the air-conditioner parts, always cap the open ends of hoses and fittings immediately.
- Never work around water, outside in the rain, or in very humid locations.

- Do not allow new refrigerant or refrigeration oil to become contaminated.
- Always keep the refrigeration oil container capped.
- Develop clean habits; do not allow dirt to enter the system.
- Keep all service tools free of grease and dirt.
- Never fill a unit without first insuring that air and moisture are removed.

MOISTURE REMOVAL

Many problems can arise due to excessive moisture in a refrigeration system. After any repair work, the system must be pumped down or evacuated to remove any moisture present. This section shows how a refrigeration system is pumped down and explains how a vacuum is used to remove moisture. Recall that a pressure below zero pounds gauge pressure (0 psig or 0 kPa gauge) is referred to in terms of inches of mercury (inHg) English or kilopascals absolute (kPa absolute) metric.

The removal of moisture from a system can cause serious problems for the service technician who is not equipped with the proper tools. A vacuum pump is a must for air-conditioning service. Although other methods can be used, the vacuum pump is still the most efficient means of moisture removal. Figures 10-2 and 10-3 show typical vacuum pumps in common use.

Moisture is removed in the air-conditioning system by creating a vacuum. In a vacuum, the moisture in the system boils. The pumping action of the vacuum pump then pulls the moisture in the form of a vapor from the system. When the pres-

Fig. 10-2 Standard vacuum pump

Fig. 10-3 Lightweight high-vacuum pump suitable for automotive air-conditioning service

sure is increased on the discharge side of the pump, the vapor again liquefies. This process usually occurs inside the pump.

It is possible to use the air-conditioning compressor to evacuate the system. However, this procedure is not recommended because a minimum of thirty minutes is required to remove the moisture at a compressor speed of about 1 750 r/min. The compressor is lubricated by refrigeration oil in its sump. An oil pump usually circulates the oil, some of which is picked up in the refrigerant vapor. Since the compressor may run dry of oil when operated as a vacuum pump, the compressor can become seriously damaged. Additionally, the vacuum pressures are exposed to atmospheric pressure above the discharge valve plate and most vapor moisture will again liquefy in the compressor discharge cavity (inside the compressor). Thus, if the automotive compressor is used to evacuate the system, the moisture-laden vapor is pulled out of the system and most of it is deposited inside the compressor. Nothing is gained in this procedure since the moisture is still inside the system.

The student should review Unit 6 for information relating to how a vacuum pump accomplishes moisture removal. Unit 6 covers temperature-pressure relationships and the boiling of water at a lower temperature at higher altitudes. A point to remember is that at higher altitudes the atmospheric pressure has a lower value than at sea level. A vacuum pump can simulate conditions at a higher altitude by mechanical means. A good vacuum pump is capable of evacuating a system to a pressure of 29.76 inHg (0.81 kPa absolute) or better. At this pressure, water boils at $40°F$ ($4.44°C$). In other words, if the ambient temperature is $40°F$ ($4.44°C$) or higher, the water boils out of the system.

Recall that at 0 inHg (101.3 kPa absolute) at sea level, water boils at $212°F$ ($100°C$). To find the boiling point of water in a vacuum (absolute pressure), use the table in figure 10-4 (English) or figure 10-5 (metric). Note that the boiling point of water is lowered only $112°F$ ($62.2°C$) to $100°F$ ($37.7°C$) as the pressure is decreased from 0 inHg (101.3 kPa absolute) at sea level to 28 inHg (0.98 kPa absolute). However, the boiling point drops by $120°F$ ($66.6°C$) as the pressure decreases from 28 inHg (0.98 kPa absolute) to 29.91 inHg (0.30 kPa absolute).

The degree of vacuum achieved and the amount of time the system is subjected to a vacuum determine the amount of moisture removed from the system.

System Vacuum Inches Mercury	Temperature °F Boiling Point
24.04	140
25.39	130
26.45	120
27.32	110
27.99	100
28.50	90
28.89	80
29.18	70
29.40	60
29.66	50
29.71	40
29.76	30
29.82	20
29.86	10
29.87	5
29.88	0
29.90	-10
29.91	-20

Fig. 10-4 Boiling point of water under a vacuum (English)

System Vacuum kilopascals absolute	Temperature °C Boiling Point
19.66	60.0
15.61	54.4
12.02	48.8
9.07	43.3
6.80	37.7
5.08	32.2
3.75	26.6
2.77	21.1
2.03	15.5
1.15	10.0
0.98	4.4
0.81	- 1.1
0.60	- 6.7
0.47	-12.2
0.44	-15.0
0.40	-17.8
0.33	-23.0
0.30	-28.8

Fig. 10-5 Boiling point of water under a vacuum (metric)

The recommended minimum pumping time is thirty minutes. If time allows, however, a four-hour pumpdown achieves better results.

The removal of moisture from a system can be compared to the boiling away (vaporization) of water in a saucepan. It is not enough to cause the water to boil; time must be allowed for the water to boil away.

MOISTURE REMOVAL AT HIGHER ALTITUDES

The information just given for moisture removal by a vacuum pump is true for normal atmospheric pressures at sea level, 14.7 psig (101.3 kPa absolute). It also holds true for higher pressures at higher altitudes if the boiling point is reduced to a point below the ambient temperature.

As indicated in Unit 6, moisture (water) boils at a lower temperature at higher altitudes. However, it must be pointed out that vacuum pump efficiency is reduced at higher altitudes.

For example, the altitude of Denver, Colorado is 5 280 feet (1 609 m) above sea level. Water boils at 206.2°F (96.78°C) at this altitude, but the maximum efficiency of a vacuum pump is reduced. A vacuum pump that can pump 29.92 inHg (0.27 kPa absolute) at sea level can only pump 25.44 inHg (15.44 kPa absolute) at this altitude. Note in figures 10-4 and 10-5 that water boils at about 130°F (54.4°C) at this pressure.

The English formula for determining vacuum pump efficiency at a given atmospheric pressure is:

$$\frac{\text{Atmospheric Pressure in Your Location}}{\text{Atmospheric Pressure at Sea Level}} \times \frac{\text{Pump Rated}}{\text{Efficiency}} = \frac{\text{Actual}}{\text{Efficiency}}$$

Assume that a vacuum pump has a rated efficiency of 29.92 inHg at sea level (0.27 kPa absolute) and that the atmospheric pressure at Denver is 12.5 psia (86.18 kPa absolute). To determine the actual efficiency at this location, the formula is:

$$\frac{12.5}{14.7} \times 29.92 = 25.44 \text{ inHg}$$

The metric formula for determining vacuum pump efficiency at a given atmospheric pressure is:

$$\frac{\text{Atmospheric Pressure at Sea Level} - \text{Atmospheric Pressure in Your Location} + \frac{\text{Original}}{\text{Efficiency}} = \frac{\text{Actual}}{\text{Efficiency}}}{}$$

Assuming the same conditions previously mentioned the formula is applied in the following manner:

$$101.32 - 86.18 + 0.27 = 15.41 \text{ kPa absolute}$$

In this example, the ambient temperature must be raised above 130°F (54.44°C) if the vacuum pump is to be efficient for moisture removal. To increase the ambient temperature under the hood, the automobile engine can be operated with the air conditioner turned off. The compressor, condenser, and some of the hoses may be heated sufficiently; however, some other parts, such as the evaporator and the receiver/drier, will not be greatly affected.

Another method of moisture removal is the *sweep* or *triple evacuation* method. Although this method cannot remove all of the moisture, it should be sufficient to reduce the moisture to a safe level if the system is otherwise sound and a new drier is installed.

TRIPLE EVACUATION METHOD

The basic steps in the triple evacuation method are given here. The procedures for connecting the manifold and gauge set into the system, operating the vacuum pump, and adding and purging refrigerant, are given in the Service Procedures section of this text.

Procedure

1. Connect a manifold and gauge set to the system. Insure that all hoses and connections are tight and secure.
2. Pump a vacuum to the highest efficiency for 15-20 minutes.
3. Break the vacuum by adding Refrigerant 12. Increase the pressure to 1-2 psig, (6.8-13.7 kPa).
4. Pump a vacuum to the highest efficiency for 15-20 minutes (second time).
5. Break the vacuum by adding Refrigerant 12. Increase the pressure to 1-2 psig (6.8-13.7 kPa).
6. Pump a vacuum to the highest efficiency for 25-30 minutes (third time).
7. The system is now ready for charging.

Review

Briefly answer each of the following questions.

1. What is the maximum moisture content allowable in new refrigerant?

    a. 5 ppm   c. 15 ppm
    b. 10 ppm   d. 20 ppm

2. What component part of the system attracts the most moisture?

    a. Compressor   c. Thermostatic expansion valve
    b. Receiver/drier   d. Condenser and/or evaporator

3. What acid is formed by the chemical combination of Refrigerant 12 and water?

    a. Sulfuric   c. Hydrochloric
    b. Citric   d. Hydrofluoric

4. The formation of this acid can be prevented by

    a. adding alcohol to the system.
    b. drying all parts before assembly.
    c. adding a second receiver/drier.
    d. insuring that the system is as dry as possible.

5. What symbol (English) is used to denote a vacuum pressure?

    a. psig   c. kPa absolute
    b. inHg   d. Any of these may be used

6. What "tool" is used to remove moisture from an automotive air-conditioning system? Technician A says that the system compressor may be used. Technician B says that a vacuum pump should be used.

    a. Technician A is correct.   c. Both technicians are correct.
    b. Technician B is correct.   d. Both technicians are wrong.

7. What is the minimum recommended length of time a vacuum pump should be used for moisture removal?

    a. 15 minutes   c. 1 hour
    b. 30 minutes   d. 4 hours

8. How does moisture enter the system?

    a. Through carelessness and neglect during repair or assembly
    b. Through moisture-laden air during routine servicing
    c. Through components that are damaged or unprotected
    d. All of the above are correct answers

9. Technician A says that vacuum pump efficiency is greatest at sea level; technician B says that altitude has no effect on efficiency. Who is correct?

    a. Technician A
    b. Technician B
    c. Neither is correct.

10. The pressure 0 inHg or 0 psig is equal to what pressure in the metric scale?

    a. 86.18 kPa absolute   c. 101.3 kPa absolute
    b. 86.18 kPa gauge   d. 101.3 kPa gauge

UNIT 11:

Service Valves

The service technician almost always must enter the air-conditioning system to perform diagnostic, testing, and service procedures. This is necessary to record the pressures within the system as an aid in determining a problem, if any. This unit deals with the *service valve,* a device that allows the service technician to enter the refrigeration system by mechanical means. The service valve, then, provides a means to connect the manifold and gauge set into the system. Unit 12 covers the gauges and manifold which are connected to the service valve and used in actual diagnostic and service procedures.

Most air-conditioning systems have two service valves: one on the low side of the system and one on the high side of the system, figure 11-1. Some General Motors, Chrysler, and Ford systems have three valves. The third valve, figure 11-2, is on the low side of the system.

Basically, there are two types of service valve: the Schrader (automatic) valve, figure 11-3, and the hand shutoff (manual) valve, figure 11-4. Though different in appearance and operation, they both serve the same purpose.

SCHRADER VALVE

The Schrader-type valve is, by far, the most popular service valve today. The Schrader-type service valve is very similar to a tire valve in appearance and operation. This valve, figure 11-5, has only two positions: *cracked* (open) and *back seated* (closed). The normal operating position of this valve is back seated. This valve is cracked or opened by a pin or bar in the end of the manifold hose, figure 11-6, or in a special hose adapter, figure 11-7. Whenever the hose or adapter is screwed onto the Schrader valve, system pressures are impressed on corresponding gauges.

It is important to note that hoses and/or adapters should not be connected to a Schrader fitting unless the valve is first connected to the gauge manifold. Conversely, hoses should not be disconnected from the gauge manifold while it is connected to a Schrader service valve. To do so will result in a loss of refrigerant and could cause personal injury.

The standard low-side Schrader valve fitting is 1/4-inch SAE. High-side valve fittings may be 1/4-inch SAE, although many may be smaller. The

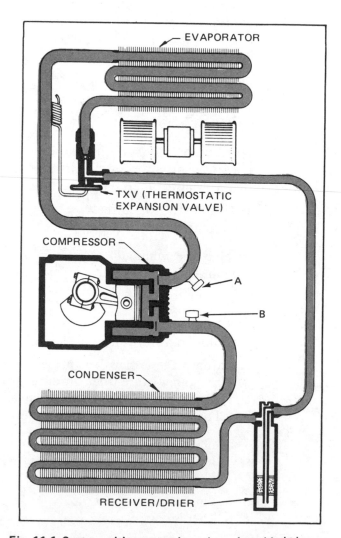

Fig. 11-1 System with two service valves: low side (A) evaporator oulet/compressor inlet, and high side (B) compressor outlet/condenser inlet.

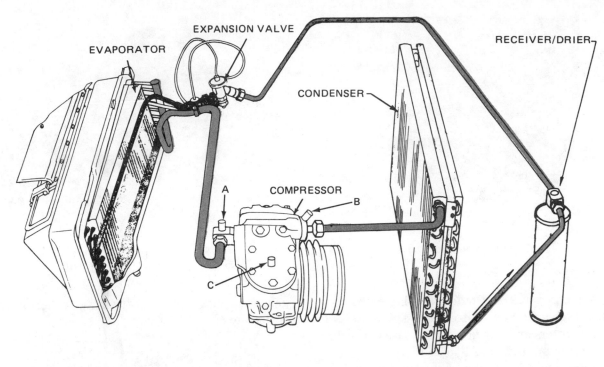

Fig. 11-2 System with three service valves: low side (A) evaporator outlet, high side (B) compressor outlet/condenser inlet, and a second low side (C) compressor inlet

Fig. 11-3 "Acorn" protective cap keeps dirt and moisture out of Schrader-type service valve and, at the same time, helps to prevent leaks

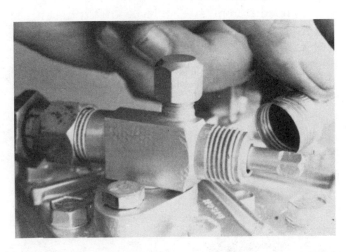

Fig. 11-4 Protective cover keeps dirt and moisture out of "stem" packing gland of manual-type service valve

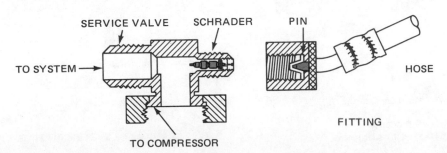

Fig. 11-5 Pin in fitting of service hose cracks (opens) the Schrader valve when hose is attached to service valve

Fig. 11-6 Pin in manifold hose

Fig. 11-7 Special hose adapter

smaller fitting requires a reducing adapter to connect the high-side hose into the system. Several types of adapters are shown in figure 11-8. Another fitting, often found in the high side of the system, is the quick connect/disconnect type, figure 11-9. This fitting also requires a special adapter to connect the high-side hose into the system.

The different size or type of fitting on the high-pressure side of the system helps to prevent reversing the hoses of the manifold and gauge set. Reversing the hoses would impress high-side system pressure on the low-side gauge and could affect

gauge accuracy, in addition to other problems which are covered later.

HAND SHUTOFF VALVE

The hand shutoff service valve is often referred to as a manual valve. Although it is not as common as in past years, it is still found on some systems. The hand shutoff valve has a 1/4-inch (square end) stem that is used for opening and closing. For these operations, some technicians use pliers or vise grips, but it is recommended that a service-valve

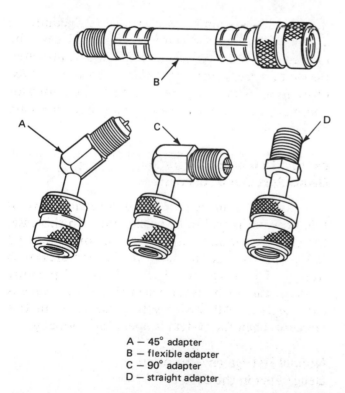

A — 45° adapter
B — flexible adapter
C — 90° adapter
D — straight adapter

Fig. 11-8 Adapters used to connect high-side gauge hose into the system

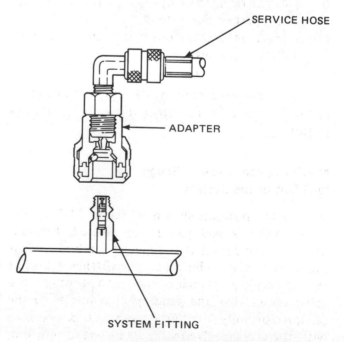

Fig. 11-9 Quick connect/disconnect fitting and adapter

Fig. 11-10 Service-valve wrench is used to back seat, "crack" (midposition), or front seat manual-type service valve

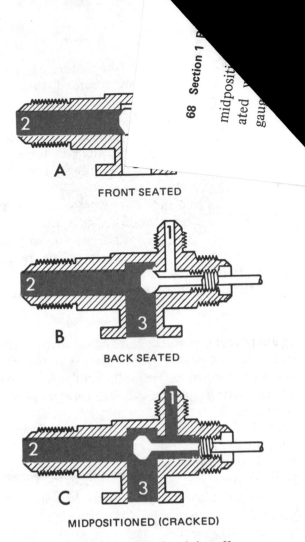

A — FRONT SEATED

B — BACK SEATED

C — MIDPOSITIONED (CRACKED)

Fig. 11-11 Service valves, hand shutoff type

wrench, figure 11-10, be used to position this type of valve.

The service valve is back seated when the stem is turned fully counterclockwise (ccw). It is cracked when the stem is turned one or two turns clockwise (cw) off the back-seated position. The valve is front seated when the stem is turned fully clockwise (cw).

The hand shutoff valve is a three-position device that can be used for the three functions shown in figure 11-11.

A. To shut off refrigerant flow; the gauge port is not part of the system
B. Normal refrigerant operation; the gauge port is not part of the system
C. Normal refrigerant operation; the gauge port is part of the system

The following sections describe each position and define the points at which refrigerant is allowed to flow.

No Refrigerant Flow — Gauge Port Out of the System

In the position shown in figure 11-11A, the service valve is said to be front seated. For this case, the refrigerant is trapped in the hose end of the service valve. The gauge port fitting is toward the atmosphere. Tracing the path through the valve shows that the gauge port connects to the compressor only. If the compressor is operated with the service valve in the front-seated position, and the gauge port is capped, the compressor will surely be damaged. This is because there is no area

into which to pump the compressed refrigerant. As a rule of thumb, the compressor should never be operated with the service valve(s) in the front-seated position, *except for detailed step-by-step service procedures* which may be used to test compressor volumetric efficiency. These service procedures are outlined in Section 3.

Normal Refrigerant Operation — Gauge Port Out of the System

As shown in figure 11-11B, a service valve in this position is said to be back seated. In this case, the compressor and hose outlet are connected and refrigerant is free to flow if the compressor is started. The gauge port is closed off and pressure readings cannot be taken when the service valve is back seated. All service valves should be in this position when the system is operating normally.

Normal Refrigerant Operation — Gauge Port in the System

When the service valve is in the position shown in figure 11-11C, it is said to be in the cracked or

on. In this case, the system can be oper-
while pressures are recorded through the
port openings.

Actually, in the cracked position the service
valve is not really midpositioned. The service valve
is cracked when the valve stem is turned from
one-half to one full turn clockwise (cw) off the
back-seated position.

The technician must always back seat the
valves before attempting to remove the gauge hose
from the service valves. Failure to do so results in
a loss of refrigerant. For example, figure 11-11C
shows that refrigerant is present at all outlets
when the service valve is in the cracked position.

SUMMARY

Service valves, regardless of type or style,
require little repair or maintenance. On occasion,
however, a service valve may leak. If the leak is
through the gauge port opening (either automatic
or manual type) a cap with a rubber insert may be
used. If the leak is severe or is around the service
stem (manual) it is recommended that the entire
service valve be replaced.

There is no rule of thumb as to where a service valve will be found in the system. On two-valve
systems, the low-side service valve may be found
anywhere from the evaporator outlet to the compressor inlet. On three-valve systems, one low-side
valve will be found before (upstream of) the suction pressure regulator device. The other low-side
service valve will be found after (downstream of)
the suction pressure regulator device.

On either two-valve or three-valve systems,
the high-side service valve will be found anywhere
from the compressor outlet to the condenser inlet
or anywhere from the condenser outlet to the
evaporator inlet.

Review

1. How many positions does the hand shutoff service valve have?
   a. One
   b. Two
   c. Three
   d. Four

2. How many positions does the Schrader-type service valve have?
   a. One
   b. Two
   c. Three
   d. Four

3. The low-side service valve will be found
   a. anywhere between the evaporator outlet and the compressor inlet.
   b. anywhere between the compressor outlet and the condenser inlet.
   c. at the compressor inlet.
   d. at the compressor outlet.

4. In what position is the service valve for normal operation?
   a. Front seated
   b. Midpositioned
   c. Back seated
   d. Unseated

5. What position of the hand shutoff service valve may cause compressor damage?
   a. Front seated
   b. Midpositioned
   c. Back seated
   d. Unseated

UNIT 12:

Manifold and Gauge Set

A basic tool for the air-conditioning service technician is the manifold and gauge set. Since system pressures accurately indicate total system performance, a means must be provided to make these measurements on any air-conditioning unit. The manifold and gauge set is essential in making these measurements. The servicing of most automotive air conditioners requires the use of a two-gauge manifold set, figure 12-1. Some systems, however, require a three-gauge set, figure 12-2, or one two-gauge set with a single gauge, figure 12-3.

For a two-gauge set, one gauge is used on the low (suction) side of the system. The other gauge is used on the high (discharge) side of the system. Systems requiring the use of a third gauge have a second low-side fitting which requires a low-pressure gauge.

MANIFOLD

The gauges are connected into the air-conditioning system through a manifold and high-pressure hoses. The manifold, figure 12-4, contains provisions for fittings to which gauges and hoses can be connected. In addition, two hand wheels are provided on the manifold for controlling the flow of refrigerant through the manifold.

The gauges are attached to the manifold by 1/8-in NPT (pipe) connections. Hoses connect to the manifold with 1/8-in NPT x 1/4-in SAE (flair) half-unions. (Later paragraphs in this unit describe the types of hoses used with the manifold.)

The low-side hose fitting is directly below the low-side gauge and the high-side hose fitting is below

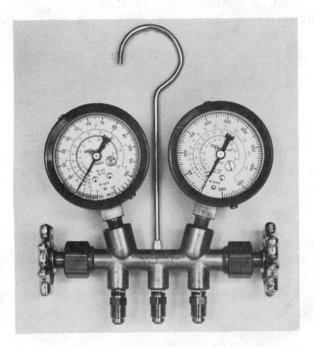

Fig. 12-1 Manifold and gauge set, side wheel

Fig. 12-2 Manifold and three-gauge set, front wheel

Fig. 12-3 Single-gauge compound gauge used for system diagnosis

Fig. 12-4 Manifold bar and hand wheels (hand valves)

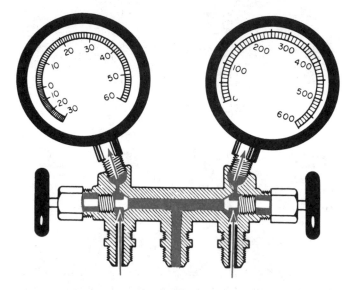

Fig. 12-5

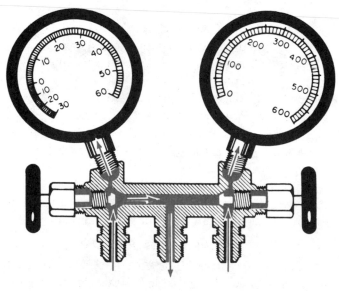

Fig. 12-6

the high-side gauge. The center hose fitting of the manifold is used for charging, evacuation, or any other service that is required.

Both the low and high sides of the manifold are provided with hand shutoff valves. When the hand valve is turned all the way to the right, in a clockwise (cw) direction, the manifold is closed. However, the gauge indicates the system pressure in the hose. Figure 12-5 shows both manifold hand valves in the closed position. For this condition, pressures can still be recorded on each gauge.

The hand valve is opened by turning it to the left or counterclockwise (ccw). When the hand valve is open, the system is opened to the center hose port of the manifold set. This condition is desirable only when refrigerant must be allowed to enter or leave the system.

If the low-side manifold hand valve is opened, figure 12-6, the passage is complete between the low-side port and the center port only. The low-side gauge indicates only the low-side pressure. The high side remains closed and the high-side gauge indicates only the high-side pressure.

Similarly, when only the high-side hand valve is opened, figure 12-7, the passage is complete between the high-side port and the center port. Again, the low-side and high-side gauges indicate only the pressure in their respective sides.

If both hand valves are opened, figure 12-8, both the low-side and high-side ports are open to the center port. However, the pressures indicated on the gauges are not accurate when both hand valves are opened. Some of the high-side pressure feeds through the manifold to the low-side gauge, with the result that the high-side pressure indication is decreased and the low-side pressure indication is increased, figure 12-8.

The manifold is used to perform nearly all of the air-conditioning system tests and diagnostic

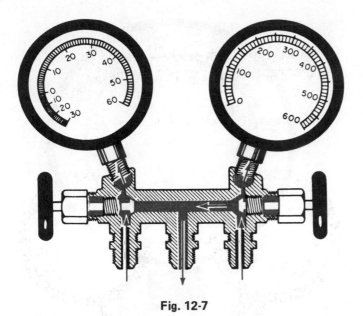

Fig. 12-7

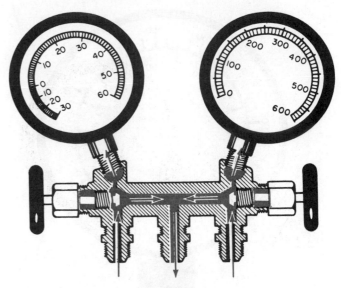

Fig. 12-8

procedures. Manifolds are available in a front valve type, a side valve type, and an offset valve type.

LOW-SIDE GAUGE (ENGLISH)

The English scaled gauge used on the low side of the system is called a *compound gauge,* figure 12-9. A compound gauge is designed to give both vacuum and pressure indications. This gauge is connected through the manifold and the high-pressure hose to the low side of the air-conditioning system.

The vacuum scale of a compound gauge generally is calibrated to show pressures from thirty inches of mercury (30 inHg) to zero inches of mercury (0 inHg). The pressure scale is calibrated to indicate pressures from zero pounds per square inch gauge (0 psig) to one hundred twenty pounds per square inch gauge (120 psig). The compound gauge is constructed so as to prevent any damage to the gauge if the pressure should reach a value as high as 250 psig. The gauge described in this paragraph is designated in the following manner:

30″–0–120 psi, with retard to 250 psi.

Pressures above 80 psig are rarely experienced in the low side of the system. However, such pressures may result if the manifold hoses are crossed so that the manifold gauges are connected backwards to the air-conditioning system. (Even experienced service technicians can make this type of error.)

LOW-SIDE GAUGE (METRIC)

The metric scaled gauge to be used on the low side of the system seems, at this time, to be rather

Fig. 12-9 Compound gauge

confusing. For below atmospheric pressure, some sources are using millimeters of mercury (mmHg), and kilograms per square centimeter (kg/cm^2) for above atmospheric pressure. As noted in Unit 2, these scales are incorrect.

Other sources are using negative kilopascal (–kPa) values (3.38 kPa = 1 inHg) for below atmospheric pressure, and positive kilopascal (+kPa) values (6.895 kPa = 1 psig) for above atmospheric pressure. According to IEEE Standard 268–1979, 3.4.6, "Absolute pressure is never negative." (See Unit 2.)

Therefore, it seems likely that the correct English/metric low-side gauge scale will be one of those shown in figure 12-10A or figure 12-10B. Figure 12-10A has a standard inHg/psig English scale and a kPa absolute metric scale. Figure 12-10B gives both metric and English scales as absolute.

It seems reasonable that the scale of figure 12-10A will be used, particularly if a kPa (gauge) scale is used as a high-side gauge. If, on the other hand, the high-side gauge is scaled kPa (absolute), the low-side gauge scale of figure 12-10B will be used.

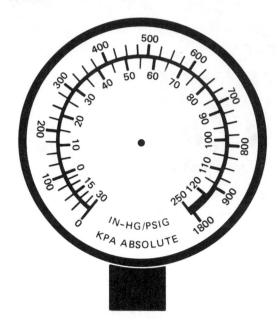

Fig. 12-10A Compound gauge showing psi (gauge) and kPa (absolute) pressure scales for comparison

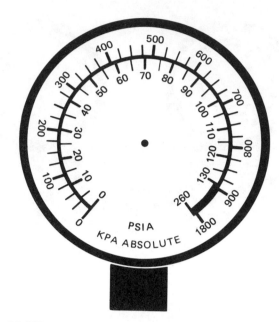

Fig. 12-10B Compound gauge scaled for absolute pressure

HIGH-SIDE GAUGE (ENGLISH)

The high-side gauge, figure 12-11, indicates the pressure in the high side of the system. Pressures in this area under normal conditions seldom exceed 250 psig. However, as a safety factor, it is recommended that the minimum scale indication of the gauge be 300 psig. A popular scale for the high-side gauge is 0-500 psig.

The high-side gauge is not calibrated as a compound gauge. Therefore, it cannot be damaged whenever the system is pulled into a vacuum.

Fig. 12-11 Pressure gauge

HIGH-SIDE GAUGE (METRIC)

High-side metric pressure gauges are being scaled, by some, at kilograms per square centimeter (kg/cm^2), using the literal translation (pounds = kilograms and square inches = square centimeters), whereby 1 psi equals 0.070 308 kg/cm^2. As noted in Unit 2, this scale is not correct according to SI metrics.

The correct conversion is to kilopascals (kPa), whereby 1 psi equals 6.895 kPa. Either of the high-side metric gauge scales of figure 12-12 is correct. Figure 12-12A is scaled kPa (gauge) and uses atmospheric pressure as zero reference. The pressure gauge in figure 12-12B shows psia and kPa absolute pressure scales for comparison. The low end of this gauge is at atmospheric pressure, or 14.696 psia (rounded off to 15 psia) English or 101.328 kPa absolute (rounded off to 100 kPa absolute) metric.

Since high-side pressure in an automotive air-conditioning system does not go below atmospheric, the gauge scale of figure 12-12A seems to be the logical choice. As for the low-side metric gauge scale — time will tell. The "standard" will, in time, become what the industry accepts.

GAUGE CALIBRATION AND SCALES

Many gauges are provided with calibration adjustment screws. A good gauge is reasonably accurate to about two percent of the total scale reading when it is calibrated so that the needle rests on zero when there is no applied pressure.

To calibrate a gauge, it is necessary to remove the glass or plastic cover and the retaining ring (bezel). A small screwdriver can then be used to turn the adjusting screw in either direction until

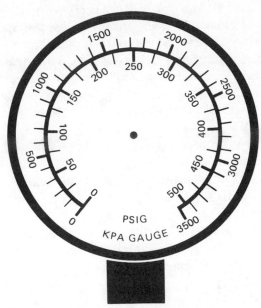

Fig. 12-12A Pressure gauge showing psi (gauge) and kPa (gauge) pressure scales for comparison

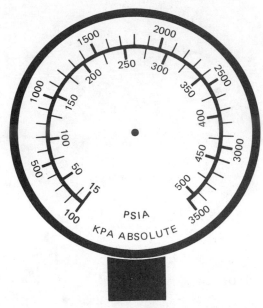

Fig. 12-12B Pressure gauge showing psi (absolute) and kPa (absolute) pressure scales for comparison

the pointer is lined up with the zero mark, figure 12-13. The adjusting screw must not be forced; to do so can damage the gauge.

Many gauges have inner scales which indicate the temperature-pressure relationship of three popular types of refrigerant: R-12, R-22, and R-502. The relationship of R-12 is outlined in Unit 8, and is considered again in Section 2 of this text. Refrigerants R-22 and R-502 are not used in automotive air conditioners primarily because of their higher operating pressures. R-22 is used in packaged and split air-conditioning and heat pump

systems. R-502 is used in lower-temperature applications, such as commercial ice makers.

HOSES

A charging hose, figure 12-14, is constructed to withstand working pressures in excess of 500 psi (344 8 kPa). Charging hoses may have a burst-pressure rating of up to 2 000 psi (13 790 kPa).

Hoses are available in several colors: white, yellow, red, and blue. Thus, a standard color code can be used when connecting the hoses. Blue is

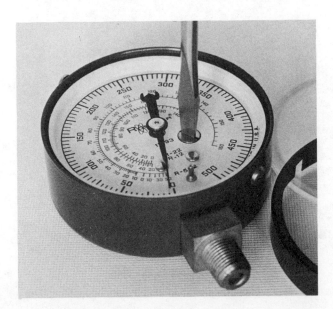

Fig. 12-13 Screwdriver used to recalibrate gauge to zero

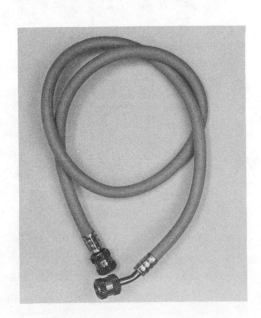

Fig. 12-14 Typical charging hose

Fig. 12-15 Special hose adapter

used on the low side, red is used on the high side, and white or yellow is used for the center port. The color-coded hoses lessen the chance of accidentally reversing the manifold connections to the air-conditioning system.

Hoses are usually purchased in standard lengths. Any length, however, may be obtained by special order. Standard lengths are 24 inches (610 mm), 36 inches (914 mm), 48 inches (1.22 m), 60 inches (1.52 m), 72 inches (1.83 m), 84 inches (2.13 m), 8 feet (2.44 m), and 12 feet (3.66 m). The standard and most frequently used hose is 36 inches (914 mm) in length. This length is sufficient for most automotive service needs.

The ends of standard charging hoses are designed to fit the 1/4-inch SAE (flare) fittings of the manifold set and compressor access ports. The hose fittings are equipped with replaceable nylon, neoprene, or rubber gasket inserts. These gaskets are always a potential source of leaks during evacuation and charging procedures and should be replaced periodically. Hoses are available with a built-in pin on one end, figure 12-15, for use on Schrader-type access ports. The hose end without the pin attaches to the manifold set. The hose end with the pin attaches to either the Schrader or hand shutoff-type service valve of the system. If the hose is not equipped with a pin, a Schrader-type adapter is available. If the pin (or adapter) is not used, gauge pressures cannot be determined and system servicing is not possible on systems equipped with Schrader valves.

THE THIRD GAUGE

As stated previously, some air conditioners require a third gauge for testing system pressures. This additional gauge is used on systems having some type of pressure control for the evaporator. Pressure controls are covered in Unit 19. The two low-side gauges are used to determine the pressure drop across the control device. Figure 12-16 shows the use of a three-gauge manifold. More information concerning the three-gauge manifold is given in Section 3, Service Procedures.

Fig. 12-16 Three-gauge manifold set used to check system pressures

Review

Select the appropriate answer from the choices given.

1. What English scale is required for the low-side (compound) gauge?
   a. 0–500 psig
   b. 30″–120/150 psig
   c. 0–300 psig
   d. 30″–120/250 psig

2. What is the recommended minimum scale of the English high-side (pressure) gauge?
   a. 0–500 psig
   b. 30″–120/150 psig
   c. 0–300 psig
   d. 30″–120/250 psig

3. What is the overall purpose of the manifold?
   a. To hold gauges and hoses
   b. To permit access to the system
   c. To permit system service
   d. All of these are correct.

4. When is the third gauge used?

   a. When checking pressure increase across a control
   b. When checking pressure drop across a control
   c. When checking pressure increase across the compressor
   d. When checking pressure drop across the compressor

5. When both of the manifold hand valves are closed,

   a. the low-side gauge shows the low-side pressure.
   b. the high-side gauge shows the high-side pressure.
   c. both gauges show the respective pressure of the low side and the high side of the system.
   d. both gauges indicate incorrect pressures.

6. A good gauge is reasonably accurate to about _____ percent of the total scale.

   a. one
   b. two
   c. three
   d. four

7. Which color is not generally provided for a color-coded hose set?
   a. Green
   b. Yellow
   c. Red
   d. Blue

8. Charging hoses should have a rated working pressure of
   a. 300 psi (2 068.5 kPa).
   b. 500 psi (3 447.5 kPa).
   c. 1 000 psi (6 895.0 kPa).
   d. 5 000 psi (34 475.0 kPa).

9. The proper English-metric conversion for pressure is
   a. 1 psi = 6.895 kPa.
   b. 1 inHg = 25.4 mmHg.
   c. 1 psi = 0.070 308 kg/cm^2.
   d. 1 inHg = 3.38 kPa.

10. The third gauge, when used, is a
    a. vacuum gauge.
    b. low-side gauge.
    c. high-side gauge.
    d. Any gauge may be used.

Leak Detectors

The methods of detecting leaks in an air-conditioning system range from using a soap solution to the use of an expensive self-contained electronic instrument.

The most popular detection instrument is the halide gas torch. Its popularity is due to its initial low cost, ease of handling, and simplicity of construction and operation.

HALIDE LEAK DETECTOR

The halide leak detector, figure 13-1, can detect a leak as slight as one pound (0.453 6 kg) in ten years. However, a great deal of practice and experience are required to be able to recognize such a slight leak.

The halide leak detector consists of two major parts: the detector unit and the gas cylinder. The gas cylinder is a nonrefillable pressure tank containing a gas such as propane. The detector unit consists of a valve (which controls the flow of gas to the burner), the burner (a chamber where the gas and air are mixed), and the search hose (a rubber tube through which air passes to the chamber).

Principle of Operation

Air is drawn through the search hose into the burner and the area of the copper reactor plate. When the gas and air mixture is ignited, the flow of gas is regulated until the flame burns about one-quarter inch above the opening in the reactor plate.

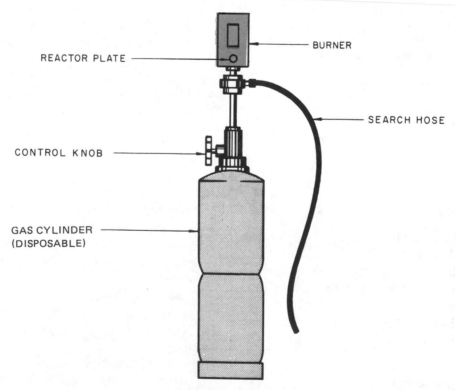

REACTOR PLATE

BURNER

SEARCH HOSE

CONTROL KNOB

GAS CYLINDER (DISPOSABLE)

Fig. 13-1 Halide leak detector

Fig. 13-2 Using soap solution as leak detector. Leak is revealed by bubbles.

This plate is heated by the flame to a red-hot temperature.

When the search hose comes into contact with leaking refrigerant, the refrigerant is drawn into the search tube and is brought to the reactor plate. As a result, the flame turns violet. In some cases, if the leak is severe enough, the flame is put out.

The proper use of the halide detector is covered elsewhere in this text. However, the following precautions in the use of this device cannot be stressed too often.

> CAUTION: A halide leak detector must be used in well-ventilated spaces only. *It must never be used in a place where explosives, such as gases, dust, or vapors, are present.* The vapors or fumes from the halide leak detector *must not be inhaled;* they may be poisonous.

Maintenance

Relatively little maintenance is required by the halide leak detector. On occasion, it may be necessary to replace the reactor plate (a part of the burner) to insure the proper operation of the unit.

Improper operation of the leak detector can result from an obstructed or collapsed search hose, or from dirt in the orifice or burner.

LEAK DETECTION USING A SOAP SOLUTION

A soap solution may be a more efficient method of locating small leaks. Since leaks often occur

in areas of limited access, a halide or electronic leak detector cannot be used to locate such leaks.

To perform the soap solution leak test, mix one-half cup of soap powder with water to form a thick solution which is just light enough to make suds with a small paintbrush. When this solution is applied to the area of a suspected leak, soap bubbles reveal the leak, figure 13-2.

In many instances, the leak in an air-conditioning system can be either a cold leak or a pressure leak. A cold leak occurs only when the unit is not at its operating temperature, such as in a car that is parked overnight. A pressure leak occurs at periods of high pressure within the system, such as when the automobile is slowly moving in heavy traffic on a very warm day.

LEAK DETECTION USING DYE

To locate either a cold leak or a pressure leak, it may be desirable to introduce a dye solution into the system. This dye is available in either yellow or red forms. The dye is safe for air-conditioning system use and does not affect the operation of the system.

When a leak cannot be detected in the shop, a dye solution is then added. After the automobile is driven a few days, the leak can be detected by the dye trace.

Once a dye is introduced into the system, it must remain there unless the complete system is cleaned out, the oil changed, and the drier replaced. The method of introducing dye into the system is covered in Section 3.

At least one manufacturer, E.I. duPont de Nemours and Company, produces Refrigerant 12 with a red dye. Called *Dytel®*, this refrigerant is charged into the system in the same manner as any other R-12, as covered in Section 3 of this text.

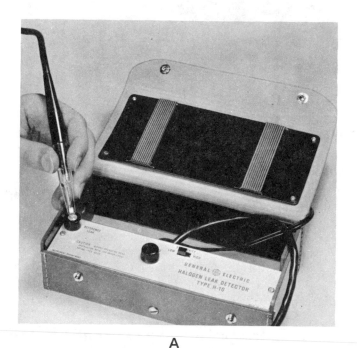

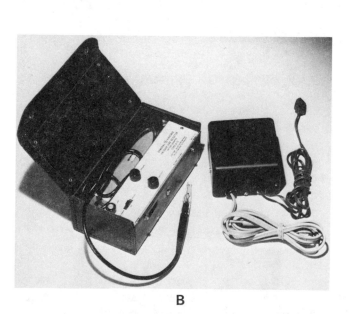

Fig. 13-3 Portable halogen leak detectors, 110–120 Vac (A) and battery powered, with charger (B).

ELECTRONIC LEAK DETECTORS

Electronic leak detectors are the most sensitive of all leak detection devices. The initial purchase price of an electronic leak detector is higher than that of a halide leak detector. In addition, this more sophisticated device requires more maintenance than the halide leak detector.

Electronic leak detectors are also known as halogen leak detectors. Such a device can detect a Refrigerant 12 rate of loss as slow as one-half ounce (14.1 g) per year. This value corresponds to one hundred parts of refrigerant to one million parts of air (100 ppm).

Two examples of the electronic leak detector are the General Electric Type H-10 and the Cordless Type H-11, figure 13-3. The H-10 detector operates on 120 volts (V), 60 hertz (Hz). The H-11 detector is a portable, cordless model that operates from a rechargeable battery. Both units are simple to operate and easy to maintain.

Another portable halogen leak detector is the model 5500 TIF manufactured by Thermal Industries, figure 13-4. This instrument is powered

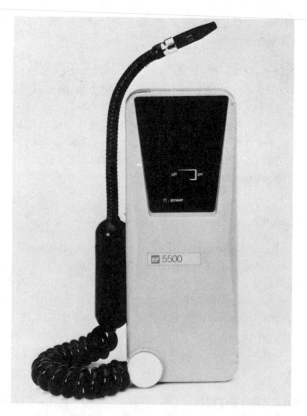

Fig. 13-4 Computerized electronic portable leak detector.

by two ordinary "C" cell flashlight batteries. Because the detector uses batteries, no warmup period is required. In addition, this instrument is capable of calibrating itself automatically "while in use."

Many other types of leak detectors are available. Space does not permit the description of each type of leak detector in this text. The student should contact local refrigeration suppliers for additional information on leak detectors.

Review

Answer each of the following questions.

1. How is soap solution added to the system for leak detection?

   a. Through the low side
   b. Through the high side
   c. Through either low or high side
   d. Soap solution is not added to the system

2. What is the sensitivity of the electronic (halogen) leak detector?

   a. 1/2 oz (14.1 g) per day
   b. 1/2 oz (14.1 g) per week
   c. 1/2 oz (14.1 g) per month
   d. 1/2 oz (14.1 g) per year

3. What precaution should be observed when using a halide or halogen leak detector?

   a. Use only in a well-ventilated area.
   b. Do not use in an explosive atmosphere.
   c. Do not inhale vapors (if any) given off by the leak detector.
   d. All of these are correct answers.

4. What type of leak warrants the use of a dye trace solution?

   a. A pressure leak
   b. A cold leak
   c. An internal leak
   d. A leak that cannot be detected by other means available

5. What method of leak detection is most popular?

   a. Halide
   b. Halogen
   c. Soap solution
   d. Dye trace

UNIT 14:

Compressors

At the present time, thirty-two different models of compressors are available for automotive air-conditioning application. Other models are on the drawing boards of compressor manufacturers, some of which will be developed and available for use in the near future.

The prime consideration and need for new compressor design is to reduce weight. Although weight is an important factor*, compressors must also be designed to be efficient and durable. The York Vane Rotary compressor was the first rotary compressor developed for automotive air-conditioning use.

FUNCTION

The compressor in the automotive air-conditioning system serves two important functions at the same time. One function is to create a low-pressure condition at the compressor inlet provisions to remove heat-laden refrigerant vapor from the evaporator. This low-pressure condition is essential to allow the refrigerant metering device (thermostatic expansion valve or fixed orifice tube, covered in Unit 16) to admit the proper amount of liquid refrigerant into the evaporator.

The second function of the compressor is to compress the low-pressure refrigerant vapor into a high-pressure vapor. This increased pressure raises the heat content of the refrigerant (see Unit 8). A high pressure with high heat content is essential if the refrigerant is to give up its heat in the condenser.

Failure of either function will result in a loss or reduction of circulation of the refrigerant within a system. Without proper refrigerant circulation in the system, the air conditioner will not function properly or may not function at all.

DESIGN

Many types of compressors are used in automotive air-conditioning systems. Regardless of the type, compressors are basically of the same design: reciprocating piston. *Reciprocating* means that the piston moves up and down, to and fro, or back and

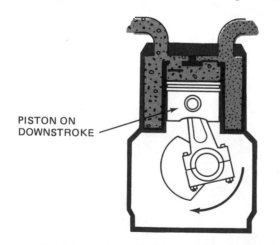
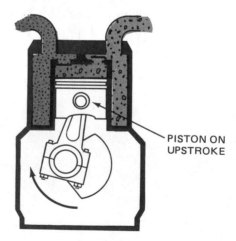

PISTON ON DOWNSTROKE

PISTON ON UPSTROKE

Fig. 14-1 Engine-driven clutch pulley drives crankshaft which, in turn, drives piston in compressor

*Overall vehicle weight is reduced by reducing the weight of individual components. A reduction in overall (gross) vehicle weight provides greater fuel economy, or, more miles per gallon (kilometers per liter) of gasoline.

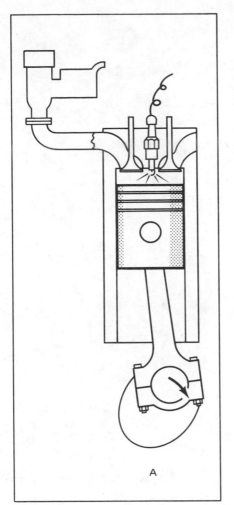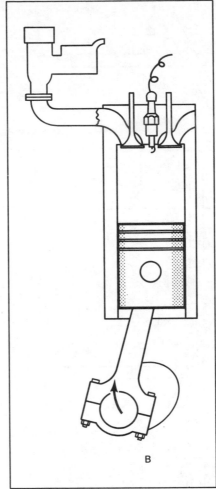

Fig. 14-2 The burning of air/fuel mixture (A) drives the piston which, in turn, rotates the crankshaft (B) in an engine

forth. Two basic methods of driving the piston are by *crankshaft* or *axial plate*. The axial plate is often called a *swash plate* or *wobble plate*.

Crankshaft

Driving the piston by crankshaft, figure 14-1, is an operation which is very similar to an automobile engine. The main difference is that a compressor crankshaft drives the piston, whereas in an engine the piston drives the crankshaft, figure 14-2. The compressor crankshaft is driven, directly or indirectly, off the engine crankshaft by means of pulleys and belts, figures 14-6 through 14-9.

Axial Plate

The other method of driving the piston is by axial plate, figure 14-3. The axial plate, pressed on

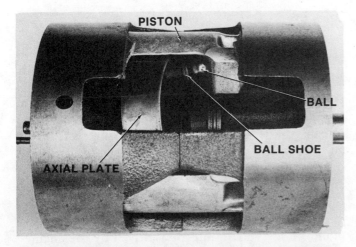

Fig. 14-3 Details of compressor axial plate, also referred to as swash plate.

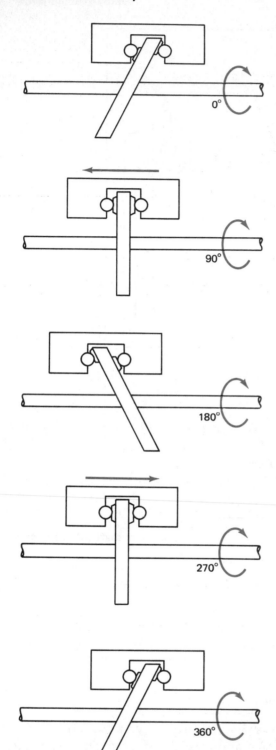

Fig. 14-4 One complete revolution of the crankshaft drives the piston from one end of its travel to the other by action of the axial plate which rotates with the crankshaft

Fig. 14-5 Clutch mounted on compressor

the main shaft, provides a reciprocation of the piston motion, figure 14-4. The axial plate is driven by the main shaft off the engine crankshaft, directly or indirectly, by means of pulleys and belts.

DRIVES

All automotive air-conditioning compressors have an electromagnetic clutch (Unit 17) attached to their crankshaft or main shaft, figure 14-5. This clutch provides a means of starting and stopping the compressor. Some compressors are driven by one or two belts off the engine crankshaft and have an idler pulley, figure 14-6, which is used to adjust belt tension. Some use an accessory device, such as an alternator or power-steering pump (pulley) as the belt adjustment provisions, figure 14-7.

Other compressors are driven off the water-pump pulley which, in turn, is driven by the engine crankshaft pulley, figure 14-8. In this application, the belt is tensioned by adjusting the compressor.

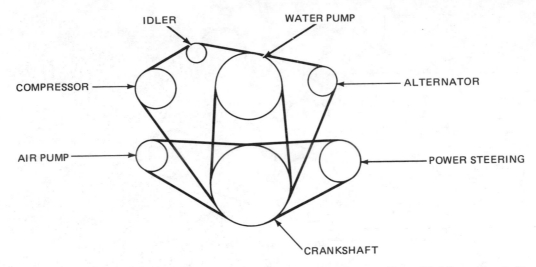

Fig. 14-6 Compressor driven off crankshaft pulley via water-pump pulley with idler pulley belt adjustment

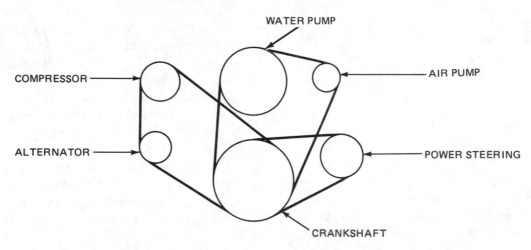

Fig. 14-7 Compressor driven off crankshaft pulley via alternator. Alternator adjustment provides belt tensioning.

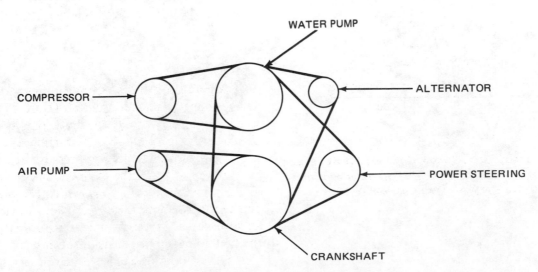

Fig. 14-8 Compressor is driven off water-pump pulley which is driven off the crankshaft pulley. Compressor belt tensioning is accomplished by positioning the compressor. Alternator adjustment provides water-pump belt tensioning.

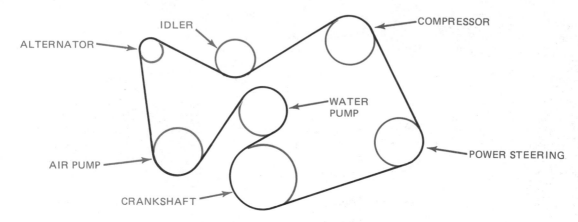

Fig. 14-9 Serpentine belt drive system.

Compressors are also driven off the crank-shaft by a single-belt drive, along with such other accessories as the power steering pump, air pump, alternator, and water pump. This system is known as a *serpentine drive,* figure 14-9. The belt, called V-rib or serpentine, is tensioned by a spring-loaded idler pulley which rides on the back (flat) side of the belt.

RECIPROCATING
OR PISTON-TYPE
COMPRESSORS

Automotive air-conditioning compressors, de-pending on design, have one, two, four, five, six, or ten pistons (cylinders). At least one domestic

manufacturer, Tecumseh, provides a single-cylinder compressor, figure 14-10. The two-cylinder, V-type compressor, figure 14-11, was manufactured by Chrysler Air-Temp until recent years. Two-cylinder, in-line compressors are currently manufactured by Nippondenso, figure 14-12, Tecumseh, figure 14-13, and York, figure 14-14.

Two-four cylinder, radial-design compressors are available: the R-4, figure 14-15, manufactured by Delco Air (Frigidaire), and the HR-980, figure 14-16, manufactured by Tecumseh.

Sankyo and Delco Air manufacture a five-cylinder compressor. The Sankyo compressor, figure 14-17, is a positive displacement compressor; the Delco Air V-5 compressor, figure 14-18, is of variable displacement design.

Fig. 14-10 Tecumseh single-cylinder compressor

Fig. 14-11 Chrysler Air-Temp two-cylinder compressor

Fig. 14-12 Nippondenso two-cylinder compressor

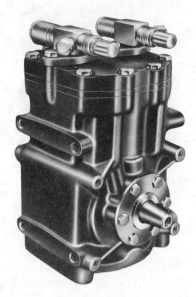

Fig. 14-13 Two-cylinder Tecumseh compressor

Three six-cylinder compressors are available: the Delco Air A-6, figure 14-19, the Delco Air DA-6, figure 14-20, and the Nippondenso, figure 14-21. These compressors are of the axial design.

A ten-cylinder compressor was introduced by Nippondenso in 1986. Known as model 10P-15, this compressor has the same general appearance as the six-cylinder compressor illustrated in figure 14-21.

Applications

Tecumseh's single-cylinder compressor is used on many aftermarket compact car applications, both domestic and import. Nippondenso's two-cylinder compressor is used on some import car lines. The Tecumseh and York two-cylinder compressors are often found on intermediate and full-size aftermarket applications, as well as on some

Fig. 14-14 Two cylinder York compressor

Fig. 14-15 Delco Air 4-cylinder compressor with clutch assembly

Fig. 14-16 Tecumseh HR-980 compressor.

Fig. 14-19 Delco Air 6-cylinder compressor with clutch assembly

Fig. 14-17 Sankyo 5-cylinder compressor with clutch assembly

Fig. 14-20 Delco Air DA-6 compressor.

Fig. 14-18 Delco Air V-5 compressor.

Fig. 14-21 Nippondenso 6-cylinder compressor

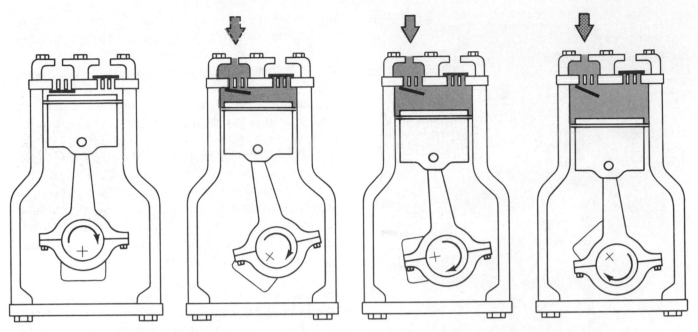

Fig. 14-22 Piston travel, top to bottom. Note position of suction and discharge valves.

American Motors and Ford car lines factory systems.

The Air-Temp two-cylinder, V-type compressor is found only on some Chrysler car lines. The manufacture of this compressor was discontinued by Air-Temp in early 1981. Although it is a very efficient and durable compressor, it is also heavy.

The four-cylinder compressor by Delco Air is standard equipment on some General Motors car lines, and also may be found on some American Motors, Checker, Mercedes-Benz, and Saab car lines. The Sankyo compressor may be found on American Motors, Dodge, Plymouth, BMW, Nissan/

Datsun, Fiat, Honda, Jeep, Mazda, Porsche, Subaru, Toyota, and Volkswagen car lines.

Delco Air 6-cylinder compressors may be found on General Motors, Checker, Ford, Lincoln, Mercury, Audi, Avanti, Jaguar, Mercedes-Benz, Peugeot, Rolls-Royce, and Volvo car lines.

The Nippondenso compressor is found on some Chrysler, Dodge, Ford, Lincoln, Mercury, and Plymouth car lines. At the present time, however, the Nippondenso 10-cylinder compressor is found only on some Ford and Mercury car lines.

Also, at the present time, the Delco Air vari-

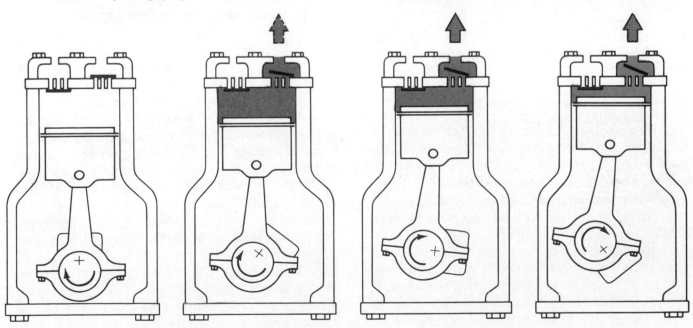

Fig. 14-23 Piston travel, bottom to top. Note position of suction and discharge valves.

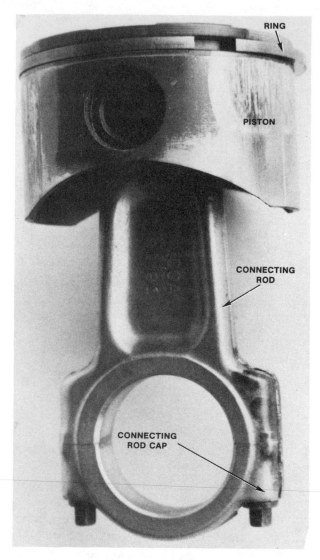

RING

PISTON

CONNECTING
ROD

CONNECTING
ROD CAP

Fig. 14-24 Typical piston fitted with ring

able displacement compressor, known as the V-5, is found only on some General Motors car lines.

Action (Reciprocating or Piston Type)

Low-pressure refrigerant vapor is compressed to high-pressure refrigerant vapor by action of the pistons and valve plates. For each piston, there is one intake (suction) valve and one outlet (discharge) valve mounted on a valve plate. For simplicity of understanding, a single-cylinder (piston) compressor will be discussed in this topic.

By action of the crankshaft, figure 14-22, the piston travels from the top of its stroke to the bottom of its stroke during the first half-revolution of the crankshaft. On the second half-revolution, the piston travels from the bottom of its stroke to the top of its stroke, figure 14-23. The first action,

top to bottom, is called the *intake* or *suction* stroke; the second action, bottom to top is called the *compression* or *discharge* stroke.

The piston is fitted with a piston ring, figure 14-24, to provide a seal between the piston and the cylinder wall. This seal helps provide a negative (low) pressure on the down or intake stroke, and a positive (high) pressure on the up or exhaust stroke.

During the intake stroke, figure 14-25, a low-pressure area is created atop the piston and below the intake and exhaust valves. The higher pressure atop the intake valve, from the evaporator, allows the intake valve to open to admit heat-laden refrigerant vapor into the cylinder chamber. The discharge valve is held closed during this time period. The much higher pressure atop this valve as opposed to the low pressure below it prevents it from opening during the intake stroke.

During the compression stroke, figure 14-26, a high-pressure area is created atop the piston and below the intake and exhaust valves. This pressure becomes much greater than that above the intake valve and closes that valve. At the same time, the pressure is somewhat greater than that above the exhaust valve. The pressure difference is great enough to cause the exhaust valve to open. This allows the compressed refrigerant vapor to be discharged from the compressor.

Piston action is repeated rapidly — once for each revolution of the crankshaft. At road speed, this action may be repeated 1 500 or more times each minute for each cylinder of the compressor.

YORK VANE ROTARY COMPRESSOR

York's vane rotary compressor, figure 14-27 provides the greatest cooling capacity per pound of compressor weight. It has no pistons and only one valve: a discharge valve. The discharge valve actually serves as a check valve to prevent high-pressure refrigerant vapor from entering the compressor through the discharge provisions during the off cycle, or when the compressor is not operating. The function of the rotary vane compressor (or vane rotary compressor, as it is called by York) is the same as that of the piston- or reciprocating-type compressor. Its operation, however, is entirely different.

The concept of rotary-type compressors for refrigeration service is not new. Two basic types of rotary vane compressors have been available for nonautomotive refrigeration use for many years. One type has vanes that rotate with the shaft; the

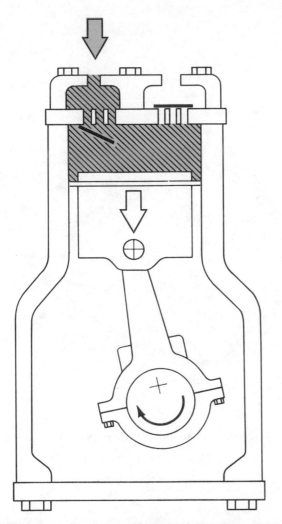

Fig. 14-25 Piston on downstroke (intake) pulls low-pressure refrigerant vapor into cylinder cavity. Note that intake (suction) valve is open and discharge valve is closed.

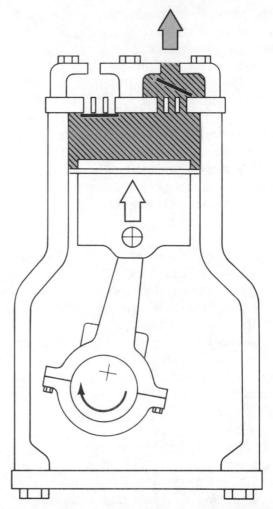

Fig. 14-26 Piston on upstroke (discharge) compresses refrigerant vapor and forces it out through the discharge valve. Note that the intake (suction) valve is closed and the discharge valve is open.

other type has stationary vanes. York's vane rotary compressor, for automotive air-conditioning service, is of the type with vanes that rotate with the shaft.

VARIABLE DISPLACEMENT COMPRESSORS

In 1985, Delco Air introduced a variable displacement compressor which was used that year on some models of all General Motors car lines. Designated as model V-5, this compressor can match any automotive air-conditioning load demand under all conditions. This is accomplished by varying the displacement of the compressor by changing the stroke of the pistons.

The five axially oriented pistons are driven by a variable-angle wobble plate. The angle of the

Fig. 14-27 York vane rotary compressor

wobble plate is changed by a bellows-activated control valve located in the rear head of the compressor. This control valve senses suction pressure, and controls the wobble plate angle based on crankcase-suction pressure differential.

When the air-conditioning demand is high, suction pressure will be above the control point, and the control valve will maintain a bleed from the compressor crankcase to the suction side. In this case, there is no crankcase-suction pressure differential, and the compressor will have maximum displacement. The wobble plate is at maximum angle providing greatest stroke (piston travel).

Conversely, when the air-conditioning demand is low and the suction pressure reaches the control point, the control valve will bleed discharge gas into the crankcase, and, in turn, close off a passage from the crankcase to the suction plenum.

The angle of the wobble plate is actually controlled by a force balance on the five pistons. Only a slight increase of the crankcase-suction pressure differential is required to create a force on the pistons sufficient to result in a movement of the wobble plate.

Temperature, then, is maintained by varying the capacity of the compressor; not by cycling the clutch ON and OFF. This action provides a more uniform method of temperature control and, at the same time, eliminates some of the noise problems associated with a cycling clutch system.

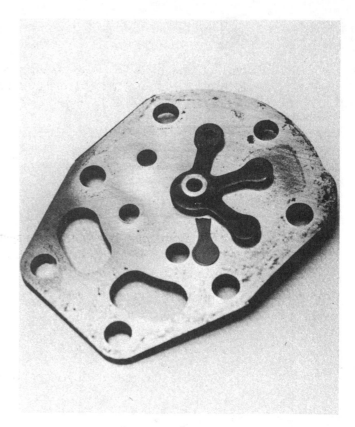

Fig. 14-28 Broken suction valve in valve plate assembly

DIAGNOSING PROBLEMS AND MAKING REPAIRS

Broken discharge valves in compressors, figure 14-28, are not an uncommon failure. Broken suction valves and piston rings are not as common, but lead to the same diagnosis. Broken valves and/or rings are easily diagnosed in one- and two-cylinder reciprocating compressors with the use of a manifold and gauge set. The first indication of failure is a higher-than-normal low-side (suction) pressure accompanied by a lower-than-normal high-side (head) pressure.

Valve and ring failures, however, are not as easily diagnosed in four-, five-, and six-cylinder compressors. The first indication of valve or ring failure in these compressors is that the belt(s) will not remain tightened. One defective discharge valve plate in a six-cylinder compressor sets up a vibration which, when not otherwise detected, literally shakes the belt(s) loose. This is true regardless of how well the adjustment provisions are tightened.

Many simple compressor repairs are usually a routine service provided by the automotive air-conditioning technician. These repairs include checking and adding oil, replacing the crankshaft seal, and replacing the valve plate assembly. More complex repairs are often "shopped out" to a specialty shop which has the facilities for semimass-rebuilding procedures. Because of the general high cost of labor, one-on-one compressor rebuilding is not usually economically feasible. The Service Procedures section of this text, Section 3, provides information for rebuilding procedures for those who desire to develop this skill.

Review

1. Service technician A says that a compressor pumps refrigerant as a vapor. Technician B says that a compressor pumps refrigerant as a liquid. Who is correct?

   a. Technician A
   b. Technician B
   c. Both technicians are correct.
   d. Both technicians are wrong.

2. At the present time, there is no _____ -cylinder compressor design.

   a. one
   b. two
   c. three
   d. four

3. The low-side gauge reads 55 psig (379 kPa) and the high-side gauge reads 130 psig (896 kPa). Technician A says that the system is low on refrigerant and probably has a leak. Technician B says that there is probably a blown head gasket or broken discharge valve.

   a. Technician A is correct.
   b. Technician B is correct.
   c. Either technician may be correct.
   d. Both technicians are wrong.

4. A variable displacement five-cylinder compressor is produced by

   a. Delco Air.
   b. Sankyo.
   c. Nippondenso.
   d. Air-Temp.

5. Current model General Motors car lines use a _____ -cylinder compressor.

   a. two
   b. four
   c. six
   d. eight

UNIT 15:

The Receiver/Dehydrator

The receiver/dehydrator (drier) is a very important part of an air-conditioning system. The load on the evaporator varies with temperature increases, increased humidity, or refrigerant losses due to small leaks. Thus, a storage area is necessary to hold extra refrigerant until it is needed by the evaporator. The receiver portion of the receiver/dehydrator unit serves as this storage area. Because of its function in storing liquid refrigerant, the use of a receiver means that it is not necessary to measure precisely the charge of refrigerant into the system. Several ounces (mL) over or under the recommended charge make little difference in system operation. In early air-conditioner units, a separate tank was often used as a receiver. In systems having a receiver tank, a separate dehydrator or drier is used. The drier is usually an in-line type and contains a filter and desiccant or drying material. A sight glass added at the outlet of the drier gives the service technician a means of observing the refrigerant flow in the system. Figure 15-1 illustrates the locations of the receiver/drier in the

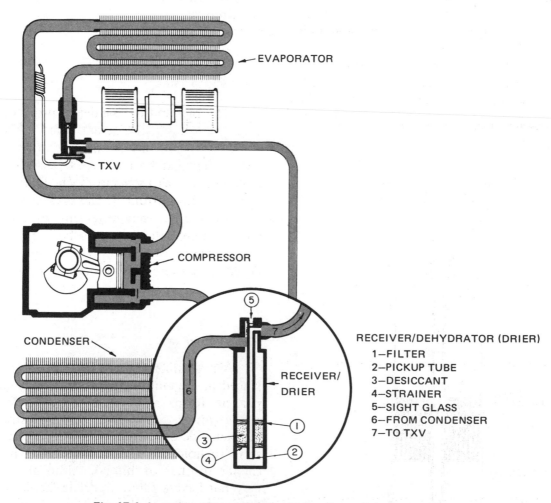

RECEIVER/DEHYDRATOR (DRIER)
1—FILTER
2—PICKUP TUBE
3—DESICCANT
4—STRAINER
5—SIGHT GLASS
6—FROM CONDENSER
7—TO TXV

EVAPORATOR

TXV

COMPRESSOR

CONDENSER

RECEIVER/DRIER

Fig. 15-1 Location of receiver/drier in the air-conditioning system

system and also indicates the components of the device.

RECEIVER/DRIER COMPONENTS

The Desiccant

A desiccant is a solid substance which can remove moisture from a gas, liquid, or solid. The desiccant commonly used in the drier is silica gel, molecular sieve, or Mobil-Gel®. The desiccant may be placed between two screens (which also act as strainers) within the receiver, figure 15-2, or it may be placed in a metal mesh bag and suspended from a metal spring. In some cases, the bag of desiccant is simply placed in the tank and is not held in place. It is not uncommon to shake a drier tank and hear the desiccant move. This sound does not mean that the receiver/drier is damaged (depending upon the type of receiver/drier).

The capacity of the desiccant for absorbing moisture depends upon the volume and type of desiccant used. For example, five cubic inches (81.94 cm^3) of silica gel can absorb and hold about 100 drops of water at 150°F (65.56°C).

Packaged additives claimed to prevent excessive system moisture from freezing are available in "one-shot" package form. This additive is nothing more than a type of alcohol. As discussed in Unit 10, some desiccants have a greater affinity for alcohol than for water, and release moisture to the system in order to absorb the alcohol. Other desiccants are rapidly deteriorated by alcohol. Although this additive probably does prevent system freeze-up, it is not recommended for automotive air conditioners.

The Filter

Most driers contain filters through which the refrigerant must pass before it leaves the tank. The filtering material prevents desiccant dust and other solids from being carried with the refrigerant into the air-conditioning system. Some driers have two filters, one on each side of the desiccant. The refrigerant must pass through both filters and the desiccant before leaving the receiver tank. Some driers do not have a filter and rely on the strainer to catch all foreign particles that otherwise would pass into the receiver/drier and from there into the system proper.

The Pickup Tube

The pickup tube is a device provided to insure that 100% liquid refrigerant is fed to the thermostatic expansion valve. Since the refrigerant entering the tank can be a mixture of gas and liquid, the tank also acts as a separator. The liquid refrigerant drops to the bottom of the tank and the gaseous part of the refrigerant remains at the top. The pickup tube extends to the bottom of the tank, thus insuring that a constant supply of gas-free liquid is delivered to the thermostatic expansion valve.

The Strainer

The strainer is made of fine wire mesh and is placed in the tank to aid in removing impurities (in particle form) as refrigerant passes through the receiver/drier. Some tanks have two strainers, one on each side of the desiccant. These strainers also serve to hold the desiccant in place (in a manner similar to that of filters). Although some driers may not have a filter, all driers should have one or more strainers. Refrigerant must pass through either filter(s) or strainer(s) before leaving the receiver tank.

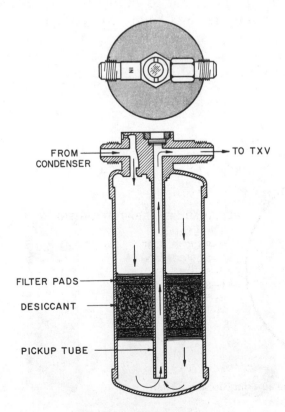

FROM CONDENSER

TO TXV

FILTER PADS

DESICCANT

PICKUP TUBE

Fig. 15-2 Receiver/drier

The Sight Glass

The sight glass is used to visually observe the flow of refrigerant in the system, and to determine if the system is undercharged. The sight glass may be located in the liquid or outlet side of the receiver/drier or it may be found at any point in the liquid line. From these locations, the service technician can readily observe the state of the refrigerant within the system. When the system is operating properly, a steady stream of liquid free of bubbles can be observed in the glass. The presence of bubbles or foam often indicates a system malfunction or a loss of refrigerant.

Using the sight glass to determine refrigerant charge is only valid if the ambient temperature is above 70°F (21.1°C). It is normal for continuous bubbles to appear in the sight glass on a cool day. If the sight glass is generally clear and the air conditioner is operating satisfactorily, occasional bubbles do not indicate a shortage of refrigerant. This condition may occur when the heat load changes and/or the compressor cycles OFF and ON.

It should be noted, however, that some systems do not have a sight glass. In such cases, system conditions must be determined with the manifold and gauge set.

HOW THE RECEIVER/DRIER FUNCTIONS

The location of the receiver/drier has a direct bearing on its ability to absorb and hold moisture. As indicated previously, five cubic inches (81.94 cm³) of silica gel desiccant can hold 100 drops of moisture at 150°F (65.56°C). As the temperature increases, the ability of the desiccant to hold moisture decreases. Thus, the ability of a desiccant to hold moisture is indirectly proportional to the surrounding temperature.

One manufacturer recommends the addition of alcohol to the air-conditioning system. However, the presence of alcohol in the system also decreases the drier's capacity to hold moisture. Although the alcohol prevents any moisture in the system from freezing, the presence of alcohol is detrimental in the long run. It is extremely important to remove the moisture because it reacts with Refrigerant 12 to form hydrochloric acid. Since this acid attacks all metal parts, the thermostatic expansion valve, compressor valve plates, and service valves will be damaged if moisture is allowed to remain in the system.

When the air-conditioning system is operating in the late evening and early morning hours when the outside temperatures are lower, the drier holds the moisture and prevents it from circulating in the system. Temperature increases during the day also cause the temperature of the desiccant to increase. When the desiccant reaches its saturation point, some of its moisture is released into the system.

As little as one droplet of moisture can collect inside the thermostatic expansion valve and change to ice in the valve orifice. This ice then blocks the flow of refrigerant and the cooling action stops.

Evidence of moisture in the system is not easy to detect in the shop procedures because it takes some time for the droplets to form and turn to ice. Diagnosis of this condition is made easier if the customer has this complaint:

"The air conditioner works fine for about fifteen minutes or so, but then it just quits. It even puts out hot air. I can turn it off for a few minutes, then turn it on, and it works fine for another ten to fifteen minutes."

This complaint is a common one and results from the addition of moisture or moisture-laden air to the air-conditioning system through careless installation or servicing procedures. In addition, this condition may be due to an improper pump-down for moisture removal before charging. To correct the condition, a new drier must be installed and the system must be pumped as long as possible to remove excess moisture before recharging.

Fig. 15-3 Receiver/driers

If the screens and/or strainers in the receiver/drier become clogged, refrigerant flow will be restricted. Normally, there is no noticeable pressure drop through the receiver/drier. A restriction can result in a considerable pressure drop between the inlet and outlet of the receiver/drier. This condition can easily be detected by feeling both lines. If the outlet line is cooler than the inlet line, the receiver/drier is clogged and must be replaced. Both inlet and outlet lines should be the same temperature (warm) in a properly operating system.

INSTALLATION AND SERVICING

The receiver/drier, figure 15-3, is usually located under the hood of the car. The drier should be placed where it can be kept as cool as possible. At least one independent manufacturer mounts the drier in the evaporator where it is always surrounded by the cool air of the evaporator.

Inlet and outlet fittings of receiver/driers may be 3/8-inch SAE flare, 5/16-inch barb, O-ring, or block type. Also, receiver/driers may have specially formed inlet and outlet tubing before the fitting provisions. As a rule of thumb, it is recommended to replace a receiver/drier with an exact duplicate.

Manufacturers' recommendations should be followed when mounting a drier. For proper operation, the vertical-type drier must be mounted so that it does not incline more than 15°. The inlet of the drier must be connected to the condenser outlet.

The word IN is generally stamped on the inlet side of the drier. If the inlet is not stamped, an arrow indicating the direction of refrigerant flow should be visible. The service technician must remember that the refrigerant flows from the condenser bottom toward the thermostatic expansion valve inlet. By connecting the drier in reverse, insufficient cooling can result.

As a result of improper handling or shipping, the internal parts of the drier may become dislodged and cause a partial restriction within the drier. This condition is indicated by a marked temperature change between the inlet and the outlet of the tank. If the restriction is great enough, frosting occurs at the drier outlet.

If the pickup tube is broken because of rough handling, abnormal flashing of the gas occurs in the liquid line. This is the same indication that is evident due to a low charge of refrigerant. In either case, a new drier must be installed.

When installing or servicing an air-conditioning system, the drier should be the last part connected to the system. Care should be exercised to prevent moisture and moisture-laden air from entering the system and the drier.

Do not uncap the drier until the unit is ready for installation. Remember: the desiccant attracts moisture from the surrounding air.

To remove moisture, it is essential to perform a complete evacuation of the system with an approved vacuum pump. This procedure is covered in Section 3 of this text.

Whenever a refrigeration system is opened for service, foreign matter can enter the system. Dirt and moisture or other noncondensible materials cause the quality of the refrigerant to deteriorate.

The corrosion of all metal parts due to hydrochloric acid (formed from the reaction of moisture and refrigerant) causes small metal particles to slough off the affected components. These particles can stop the flow of refrigerant in the system by clogging the screens that are placed in the system to remove such impurities.

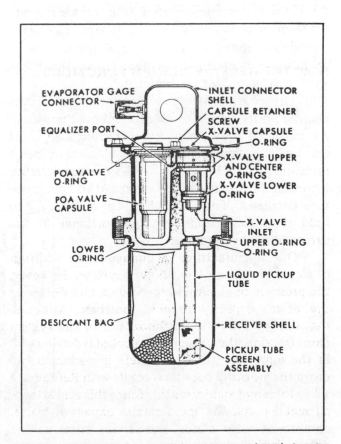

Fig. 15-4 Cutaway view of valves-in-receiver (VIR) showing detail of components

Screens are located in the inlet of the thermostatic expansion valve, the inlet of the compressor, and in the receiver/drier. All but the screen in the drier can be cleaned or replaced. If the screen in the drier becomes clogged, the entire receiver/drier unit must be replaced.

For a number of years, many factory-installed systems included the receiver and drier as part of an assembly called *valves-in-receiver* (VIR), figure 15-4. However, for the past ten years, this device is found only on some Audi, Ford, Lincoln, Mercury, and Volvo car lines. The VIR is covered in more detail in Unit 15. Repair and testing procedures are given in Section 3 of this text.

ACCUMULATOR

Some air-conditioning installations contain a device that resembles a receiver/drier. This device is known as an *accumulator,* figure 15-5. The accumulator is provided to prevent liquid refrigerant from entering the compressor. The accumulator also serves as a tank to store excess liquid refrigerant and contains a desiccant.

Another name for the accumulator is the *suction accumulator* since it is located in the suction line of the system, figure 15-6. This device is used in systems that, under certain conditions, may have a flooded evaporator. The accumulator separates the liquid refrigerant from the vapor. In other words, it *accumulates* the liquid.

Fig. 15-5 Accumulator located at the outlet of the evaporator

Refrigerant enters the top of the accumulator and liquid refrigerant falls to the bottom of the tank. Gaseous refrigerant remains at the top of the tank and is moved to the compressor through the pickup tube. At the bottom of the tank, the pickup tube contains a small hole or orifice. This orifice allows a very small amount of trapped oil or liquid refrigerant to return to the compressor.

Recall that a compressor can be damaged by an excess of liquid since it is a *positive displacement pump* and is not designed to compress liquids. Since only a controlled amount of liquid is allowed to return to the compressor through the pickup tube orifice, the compressor is not damaged.

The characteristics and composition of the desiccant in the accumulator are the same as those

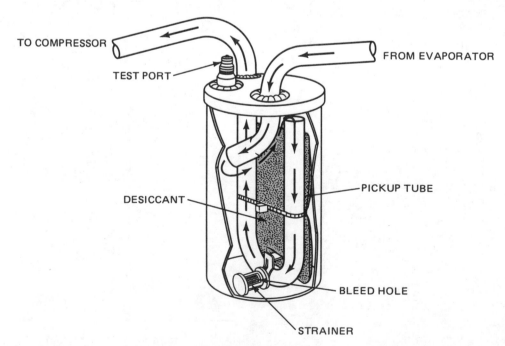

Fig. 15-6 Cutaway view of the accumulator. Note oil bleed hole to prevent oil from being trapped in accumulator.

for the receiver/drier. The accumulator cannot be serviced. If this device is found to be defective or *wet,* the entire unit must be replaced. Air-conditioning systems equipped with an accumulator have an expansion tube that serves as a metering device to the evaporator. If the expansion tube is clogged, it is again necessary to replace the accumulator. The expansion tube is covered in detail in Unit 16.

Review

Answer each of the following questions.

1. What is the purpose of the desiccant?

   a. To strain the refrigerant
   b. To filter the refrigerant

   c. To dry the refrigerant
   d. To meter the refrigerant

2. The sight glass is found

   a. in the inlet provisions of the receiver/drier.
   b. in the outlet provisions of the receiver/drier.
   c. anywhere in the line from the condenser outlet to the receiver/drier inlet (including the inlet).
   d. anywhere in the line from the receiver/drier outlet (including the outlet) to the thermostatic expansion valve inlet (including the inlet).

3. Technician A says that alcohol should be added to the air-conditioning system if there is excessive moisture. Technician B says that alcohol should be added to the system only when all other methods of system drying fail.

   a. Technician A is correct.
   b. Technician B is correct.
   c. Both technicians are wrong.

4. What is the purpose of the pickup tube?

   a. To pick up water vapor (to the desiccant)
   b. To pick up impurities (to the strainer or filter)
   c. To pick up liquid refrigerant (to the expansion valve)
   d. None of these answers is correct

5. At what angle of incline can a receiver/drier be mounted?

   a. 15 degrees
   b. 30 degrees

   c. 45 degrees
   d. 60 degrees

The Thermostatic Expansion Valve

The control of the proper amount of refrigerant entering the evaporator core, under varying heat load conditions, is the job of the metering device. This device is known as a *thermostatic expansion valve* (TXV or TEV), H-valve (also called block valve), or fixed orifice tube (also called expansion tube). The TXV or H-valve is usually found outside the evaporator case at the inlet provisions of the evaporator core. The fixed orifice tube (FOT) may be an intregal part of the inlet

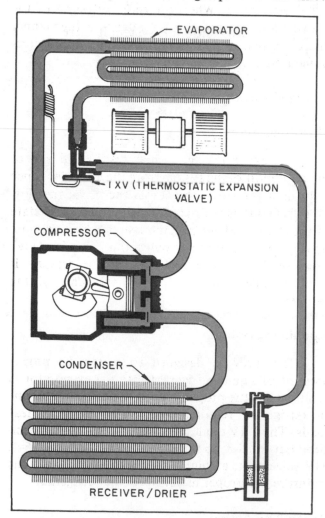

Fig. 16-1 Relation of the thermostatic expansion valve to the air-conditioning system

provisions of the evaporator, or it may be found inside the liquid line anywhere between the condenser outlet and the evaporator inlet. The TXV on some systems is found inside a device known as a valves-in-receiver (VIR) and, on other systems, it is part of a device called a combination valve or combo valve. These various metering devices are covered in this unit.

Two types of thermostatic expansion valves are in common use: the internally equalized valve and the externally equalized valve. Many factory-installed air conditioners use an externally equalized valve and aftermarket manufacturers commonly use an internally equalized valve. Figure 16-1 illustrates the typical location of the thermostatic expansion valve in the air-conditioning system.

OPERATION OF THE THERMOSTATIC EXPANSION VALVE

The diagram in figure 16-2 illustrates the construction of an expansion valve. The valve has an orifice with a needle-type valve and seat to provide variable metering. The needle is actuated by a diaphragm which is controlled by three forces:

- the evaporator pressure exerted on the bottom of the diaphragm which tends to keep the valve closed.
- the superheat spring pressure against the bottom of the needle valve which tends to keep the valve closed.
- the pressure of the inert liquid in the remote bulb or capillary tube against the top of the diaphragm which tends to open the valve.

Remote Bulb

Several types of inert liquid can be used in the remote bulb. However, for the moment, it is assumed that the fluid in the bulb is the same as that used in the system (Refrigerant 12). Because the

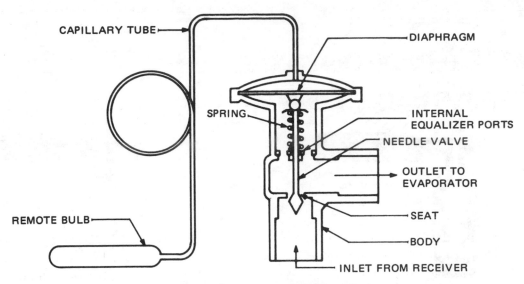

Fig. 16-2 Thermostatic expansion valve

same fluid or refrigerant is used, each exerts the same pressure, assuming that the temperature of each fluid is the same.

Under normal design considerations, the liquid refrigerant entering the evaporator boils by picking up heat and is in vapor (gas) form by the time it exits the evaporator coil. In fact, the refrigerant should be all vapor before reaching the end of the evaporator coil, and the vapor should become somewhat superheated. Although the superheated vapor is somewhat warmer than the temperature at which evaporation takes place, the pressure of the vapor is not changed. The remote bulb of the expansion valve is clamped onto the suction line. In this location, the bulb senses the warmer temperature of the evaporator outlet. The temperature of the inert fluid within the remote bulb increases, and its corresponding pressure is exerted on the diaphragm.

The increased pressure of the inert fluid exerted on the top of the diaphragm is greater than the combination of the evaporator pressure and the superheat spring pressure. As a result, the needle is moved away from the seat in the orifice. The needle valve opens until the superheat spring pressure and the evaporator pressure are great enough to balance the remote bulb pressure.

For example, when the needle valve is closed, it does not allow enough refrigerant to enter the evaporator. Thus, the evaporator pressure is low and the suction vapor is warm. This condition causes a positive pressure on top of the diaphragm and the needle valve opens.

When the needle valve is open, too much refrigerant is allowed to enter the evaporator. As a result, the evaporator pressure is high and the

suction vapor is cool. This condition creates a positive pressure under the diaphragm which closes the needle valve. When the three pressures of the thermostatic expansion valve balance in the manner just described, the evaporator remains fully operational under all load conditions.

The TXV has three main functions: it throttles, modulates, and controls.

Throttling Action

The expansion valve separates the high side of the air-conditioning system from the low side. Since there is a pressure drop across the valve, the flow of refrigerant is restricted, or throttled. The state of the refrigerant entering the valve is a high-pressure liquid. The refrigerant leaving the valve is a low-pressure liquid. A drop in refrigerant pressure is accomplished without changing the state of the refrigerant.

Modulating Action

The TXV is designed to meter the proper amount of liquid refrigerant into the evaporator as required for the proper cooling action. The amount of refrigerant required varies with different heat loads. The TXV modulates from the wide-open position, figure 16-3, to the closed position, figure 16-4. The valve seeks a point between these two positions to insure the proper metering of the refrigerant.

Controlling Action

The expansion valve is designed to change the amount of liquid refrigerant metered into the evaporator in response to load or heat changes. As the

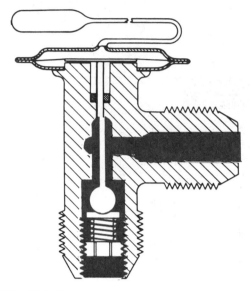

Fig. 16-3 Open thermostatic expansion valve

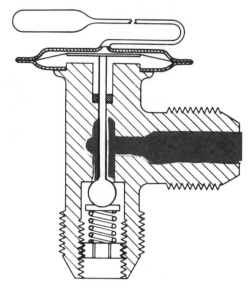

Fig. 16-4 Closed thermostatic expansion valve

load increases, more refrigerant is required by the evaporator. As the load is decreased, the valve closes and less refrigerant is metered into the evaporator core. This controlling action of the thermostatic expansion valve maintains proper refrigerant metering into the evaporator under varying heat-load conditions.

Superheat

The liquid refrigerant delivered to the evaporator coil usually completely vaporizes, or evaporates, before it reaches the coil outlet. Since it is known that the liquid refrigerant boils (vaporizes) at a low temperature (approximately $-21.6°$F or $-29.8°$C, at sea-level pressure), it can be seen that the vapor remains cold, even after all of the liquid is evaporated.

The cold vapor flowing through the remainder of the coil continues to absorb heat and becomes superheated. In other words, the temperature of the refrigerant is increased above the point at which it evaporates or vaporizes.

For example, an evaporator operating at a suction pressure of 28.5 psig (196.5 kPa) has a saturated liquid temperature of $30°$F ($-1.1°$C), according to the temperature-pressure chart in figure 16-5. As the refrigerant vaporizes (due to the absorption of heat from the evaporator), the temperature of the vapor rises until the temperature at the coil outlet, or tailpipe, reaches $35°$F ($1.67°$C). Thus, the difference between the inlet and the outlet temperatures is $5°$F ($2.7°$C).

This difference in temperature is known as *superheat*. All expansion valves are adjusted at the factory to operate under the superheat conditions present in the particular type of unit for which they are designed. When an expansion valve is being replaced, it is important to use a valve having the proper superheat range and the proper size. Although many thermostatic expansion valves look the same, they differ greatly in their applications.

TEMPERATURE-PRESSURE CHART

(Evaporator temperature range)

TEMPERATURE		PRESSURE	
°F	°C	psig	kPa
20	−6.6	21	144.7
22	−5.5	22.4	154.4
24	−4.4	23.8	164.1
26	−3.3	25.3	174.4
28	−2.2	26.8	184.7
30	−1.1	28.5	196.5
32	0	30	206.8
34	+1.1	31.7	218.5
36	+2.2	33.4	230.2
38	+3.3	35.1	242
40	+4.4	36.9	254.4

Fig. 16-5 Temperature-pressure chart, TXV range

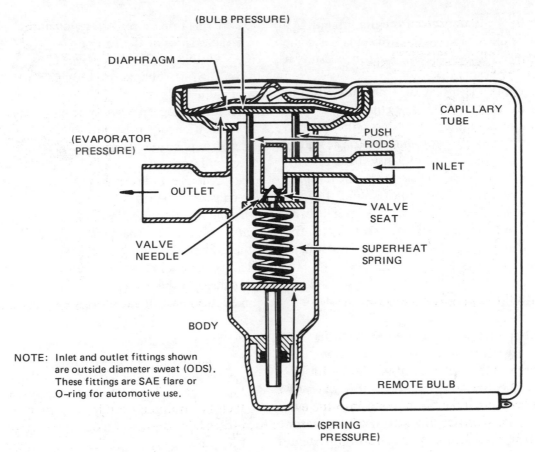

(BULB PRESSURE)

DIAPHRAGM

CAPILLARY TUBE

(EVAPORATOR PRESSURE)

PUSH RODS

INLET

OUTLET

VALVE SEAT

VALVE NEEDLE

SUPERHEAT SPRING

BODY

NOTE: Inlet and outlet fittings shown are outside diameter sweat (ODS). These fittings are SAE flare or O-ring for automotive use.

REMOTE BULB

(SPRING PRESSURE)

Fig. 16-6 Typical thermostatic expansion valve

THE THERMOSTATIC EXPANSION VALVE AS A CONTROL DEVICE

The thermostatic expansion valve consists of seven major parts, as shown in figure 16-6:

- valve body
- valve seat
- valve diaphragm
- push rod(s)
- valve stem and needle
- superheat spring with adjuster
- capillary tube with remote bulb

As indicated previously, the remote bulb is fastened to the outlet, or tailpipe, of the evaporator. The bulb senses tailpipe temperatures and activates the diaphragm in the valve through the capillary tube. In this manner, the proper amount of refrigerant is metered into the evaporator core.

For example, a high evaporator tailpipe temperature means that the evaporator is *starved* for refrigerant. This condition is indicated by an increase in the superheated vapor leaving the evap-

orator. As a result, the low-side pressure gauge indicates lower-than-normal readings.

The increased heat at the tailpipe causes an increase in the pressure exerted on the diaphragm by the expanding gases in the remote bulb through the capillary tube. The diaphragm, in turn, forces the push rods down against the valve stem and the needle valve, which is then pushed off its seat. In this way, more refrigerant is metered into the evaporator.

When the tailpipe temperature is low, there is less pressure on the remote bulb, capillary tube, and diaphragm, with the result that the needle valve is seated. In this case, the flow of refrigerant into the evaporator is restricted.

EQUALIZERS

It was stated previously that thermostatic expansion valves are either internally or externally equalized. The term *equalized* refers to provisions made for exerting evaporator pressure under the diaphragm. In an internally equalized valve there is a drilled passage from the evaporator side of the needle valve to the underside of the diaphragm. An externally equalized valve functions in the same manner, but can pick up the evaporator pressure at the outlet of the evaporator.

To overcome the effect of a pressure drop in larger evaporators, the externally equalized TXV is used. The external equalizer tube is connected to the tailpipe of the evaporator and runs to the underside of the diaphragm in the expansion valve. This arrangement balances the pressure of the tailpipe through the expansion valve remote bulb. The use of an external equalizer eliminates the effect of the pressure drop across the evaporator coil. Thus, the superheat settings depend only on the adjustment of the spring tension.

FIXED ORIFICE TUBE

A number of terms are used to identify the fixed orifice tube (FOT), such as expansion tube (ET), cycling clutch orifice tube (CCOT), and cycling clutch fixed orifice tube (CCFOT). By any name, this device replaces the thermostatic expansion valve to meter refrigerant into the evaporator in many factory-installed systems. It is found on some car lines in the inlet provisions of the evaporator. On other car lines, the FOT is found in the liquid line between the condenser outlet and the evaporator inlet. The old and new style expansion tubes, figure 16-7, are not interchangeable. The refrigerant entering the evaporator is controlled by the fixed orifice tube in a manner which is

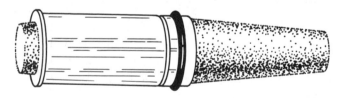

A OLD STYLE

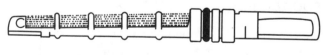

B NEW STYLE

Fig. 16-7 Old- and new-style expansion tube. The two styles are not interchangeable.

based on a pressure difference and the subcooling characteristics of the refrigerant.

Unlike the thermostatic expansion valve, the fixed orifice tube has no moving parts. The tube is not adjustable and its failure is usually a result of becoming clogged. Attempting to clean a clogged fixed orifice tube usually proves to be most difficult, if not impossible. It is best to replace the tube and accumulator.

An air-conditioning system equipped with an expansion tube does not have a receiver/drier. The drying agent for the system is found in an *accumulator*. The accumulator is located at the outlet of the evaporator. Accumulators are discussed in Unit 15. Testing and replacement procedures for the expansion tube are given in the Service Procedures in Section 3 of this text.

Screen

The thermostatic expansion valve is equipped with a screen in the inlet side of the valve, figure 16-8. This screen can be cleaned if it becomes clogged. If the screen requires cleaning, the receiver/dehydrator should be replaced. If the screen is too obstructed for cleaning, a new screen (and receiver/dehydrator) should be installed. The screen *must not be omitted* from the system.

The inlet of early series fixed orifice tubes (FOT) does not contain a screen. A screen was included in later series beginning in 1976. In either case, if the screen or tube becomes clogged, replacement is suggested. In addition, the accumulator should also be replaced to prevent a recurrence of the clogged FOT.

SUMMARY

If the expansion valve is removed from the air-conditioning system for cleaning or other service, it should be bench checked before it is reinstalled. Section 3 of this text, Service Procedures, covers the method of bench checking the TXV for efficiency. This procedure saves time as well as refrigerant which otherwise is lost through a defective valve.

Automotive expansion valves are provided with flare or O-ring fittings on each side. The comparison between the fittings is shown in figure 16-9. Although the valves shown may have the same ratings, they cannot be interchanged because the two types of fittings do not mate.

The previous descriptions of the thermostatic

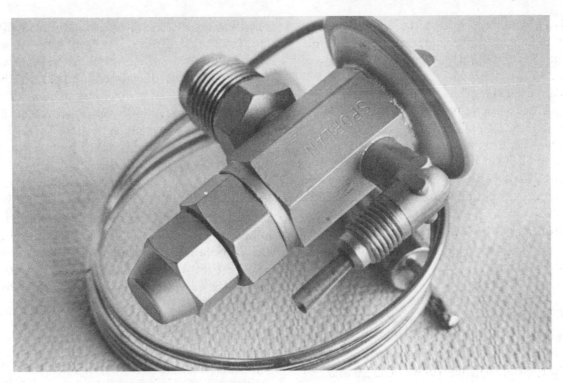

Fig. 16-8 Screen located at the inlet of the thermostatic expansion valve

expansion valve and the expansion tube make it clear that these devices are more sensitive to foreign materials than are any other parts of the air-conditioning system. This fact makes it essential to keep the system as free as possible of contaminants during service procedures.

To prevent the vital parts of the expansion valve from sticking or becoming corroded, the air conditioner should be operated for short periods during the months that normal operation is not practical. In this manner, the internal parts of the TXV, as well as the compressor, are lubricated and are kept operating freely. It must be noted, however, that some air-conditioning systems are equipped with a low ambient temperature switch and cannot be operated during cold weather. If this is the case, periodic operation of the system during cold weather is impossible.

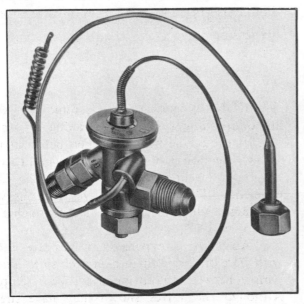 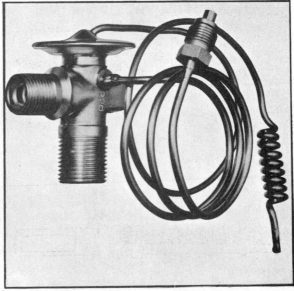

FLARE TYPE   O—RING TYPE

Fig. 16-9 Externally equalized thermostatic expansion valve

Fig. 16-10 Typical evaporator equalizer valves-in-receiver (EEVIR or VIR).

VALVES-IN-RECEIVER (VIR)

On some car lines a capsulized thermostatic expansion valve (TXV) is found in a device known as a *valves-in-receiver* (VIR) or, a later version, *evaporator equalizer valves-in-receiver* (EEVIR), figure 16-10. The VIR or EEVIR also contain the receiver with desiccant and a capsulized suction pressure regulator known as a *positive operated suction throttling valve* (POASTV) or, more simply, a POA valve.

A description of the VIR and an explanation of its operation is given in Unit 19. The TXV is capsulized and is placed inside the VIR assembly with the POA valve. Its function and purpose is similar to that of the standard TXV: to meter the proper amount of refrigerant into the evaporator under varying heat load conditions. Testing and service procedures of the VIR and its associated components are given in Section 3.

COMBINATION VALVE

The *combination valve,* also called *combo valve,* is found on some Ford car lines. The combo valve is similar in operation to the VIR in that it contains a thermostatic expansion valve (TXV) and a suction pressure regulator, known as a *suction throttling valve* (STV). The combo valve, figure 16-11, however, does not include a receiver or desiccant as does the VIR.

The TXV and STV assemblies of the combo valve may be serviced separately. The STV manifold housing separates from the TXV to gain access to the STV capsule. The TXV, which includes the low-side access service fitting, is serviced as a separate assembly.

It should be noted that the TXV of the combination valve has a much shorter capillary tube than does a standard TXV. Only one inch (25.4 mm) or so in length, there is no remote bulb to be secured to the evaporator outlet. Service and testing procedures are given in Section 3.

OTHER VALVE TYPES

In certain Chrysler car lines, the thermostatic expansion valve is called an *H-valve,* figure 16-12.

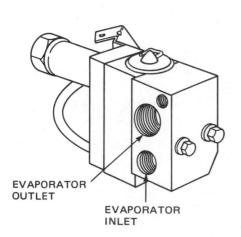

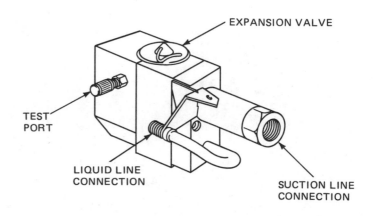

Fig. 16-11 Ford's suction throttling valve and expansion valve assembly (combination valve)

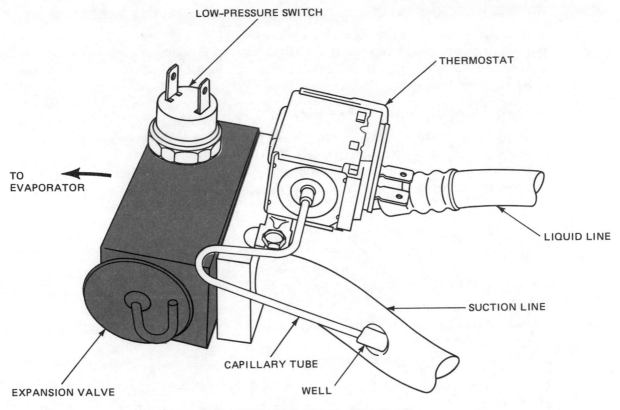

LOW–PRESSURE SWITCH

THERMOSTAT

TO EVAPORATOR

LIQUID LINE

SUCTION LINE

CAPILLARY TUBE

WELL

EXPANSION VALVE

Fig. 16-12 Chrysler's H-valve assembly

Some Ford car lines use a similar valve, called a *block valve*. Like the combination valve, the H-valve and the block valve do not have a capillary tube. Unlike the combination valve, however, the H-valve and the block valve do not have a suction pressure regulator as a part of their assembly. The suction pressure regulator in Chrysler air-conditioning systems equipped with the V-type compressor is found under the low-side compressor service valve assembly (covered in Unit 19).

The H-valve includes a low-pressure cutoff switch which may be serviced separately. The low-pressure cutoff switch, a part of the electrical circuit, interrupts current flow to the compressor clutch if high-side system pressure falls below a predetermined safe level. Operation of the cutoff switch is covered in Unit 17. Testing and service procedures for the H-valve and block valve are similar to those given for other types of thermostatic expansion valves.

Review

Select the appropriate answer from the choices given.

1. Which of the following is *not* a metering device?

    a. Thermostatic expansion valve
    b. Pressure modulator control

    c. Expansion tube
    d. TXV

2. Where is the remote bulb fastened?

    a. At the evaporator inlet
    b. At the TXV outlet

    c. At the tailpipe
    d. In the liquid line

3. Where is the screen located?

    a. At the inlet of the TXV
    b. At the outlet of the TXV

    c. In the center of the TXV
    d. There is no screen in the TXV

CONTINUED

4. Which of the following is a function of the thermostatic expansion valve?

    a. It controls the refrigerant flow into the evaporator.
    b. It controls the temperature of the refrigerant in the evaporator.
    c. It provides a dividing line restriction between the high and low sides of the system.
    d. All of these functions are performed by the TXV.

5. Where is the external equalizer tube fastened?

    a. Between the bottom of the diaphragm and the tailpipe of the evaporator
    b. Between the top of the diaphragm and the tailpipe of the evaporator
    c. Between the bottom of the diaphragm and the inlet of the evaporator
    d. Between the top of the diaphragm and the inlet of the evaporator

6. How is the expansion tube serviced?

    a. By replacement
    b. By cleaning the tube
    c. By cleaning the screen
    d. Expansion tubes require no service

7. Two types of thermostatic expansion valves (TXV) are

    a. SAE (flare) and O-ring.
    b. internally and externally equalized.
    c. metering and controlling.
    d. evaporator inlet and evaporator outlet.

8. Technician A says that the temperature difference between the inlet and the outlet of an evaporator is known as *subcooling*. Technician B says that this temperature difference is known as *superheat*.

    a. Technican A is correct.
    b. Technician B is correct.
    c. Both technicians are correct.
    d. Both technicians are wrong.

9. Technician A says that a thermostatic expansion valve system has a drying agent (desiccant) in the system. Technician B says that an expansion tube system has a drying agent (desiccant) in the system.

    a. Technician A is correct.
    b. Technician B is correct.
    c. Both technicians are correct.
    d. Both technicians are wrong.

10. When the evaporator is starved for refrigerant, what is the state (temperature and pressure) of the refrigerant leaving the evaporator?

    a. Higher-than-normal pressure; cooler-than-normal temperature
    b. Lower-than-normal pressure; cooler-than-normal temperature
    c. Higher-than-normal pressure; warmer-than-normal temperature
    d. Lower-than-normal pressure; warmer-than-normal temperature

UNIT 17:

Electrical Circuits

The basic automotive air-conditioning electrical circuit, such as that found on aftermarket systems, is a simple one, as shown in the schematic of figure 17-1. Generally, it consists of a fuse or circuit breaker, a master on/off/blower speed control, a thermostat, a blower motor, and a clutch coil.

Note in the schematic that only one wire is shown from the battery. The other side of the battery, as well as the blower motor and clutch coil, terminate to ground. The symbol used to indicate a ground connection is shown in figure 17-2.

The automobile chassis, body, and all metal parts are *common* (ground) in 12-volt, direct-current, negative-ground electrical systems. A separate ground wire is not required unless the car has fiberglass or other nonconducting body components.

The heater system utilizes the same fuse or circuit breaker and blower motor as those used for the air-conditioning system in most factory installed units. Additional electrical circuits associated with the cooling system are those which are used to warn of engine coolant underheating and/or overheating conditions. Such a warning device may be a *telltale* dash light or a dash gauge. Either device has a sending unit located in the engine coolant system.

FUSES AND CIRCUIT BREAKERS

A fuse or circuit breaker is used to protect the air-conditioning and/or heating components and wiring. These devices are usually rated at 20 to 30 amperes, depending upon the electrical system de-

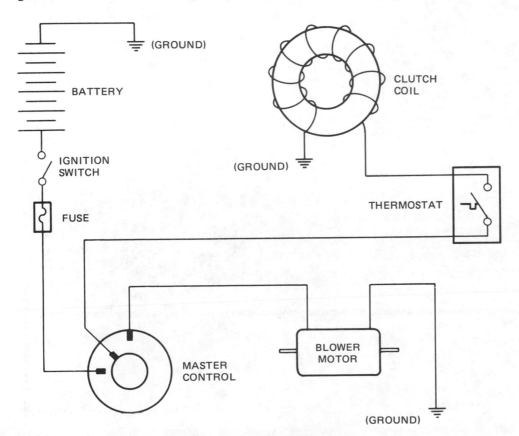

Fig. 17-1 Typical wiring schematic

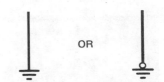

Fig. 17-2 Ground symbol indicates that the wire or device is grounded to the car body or frame

107

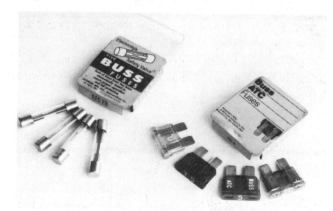

Fig. 17-3 Types of fuses used to protect automotive electrical circuits

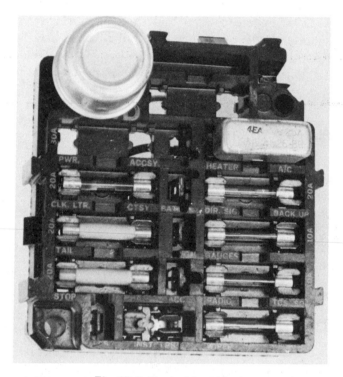

Fig. 17-4 Typical fuse block

sign. They should not be replaced with a unit of a higher rating.

Two types of fuses are currently found in domestic automobiles, figure 17-3. One type consists of a thin ribbon of flat wire enclosed in a glass tube with metal ends. The other type, also a thin ribbon of flat wire, is enclosed in a plastic case and has metal ends. One type may not be used to replace the other because of the difference in the metal ends which are used to secure the fuse in the fuseholder. The fuse is usually located in the main fuse block, figure 17-4. Occasionally, a glass-type fuse will be found in an in-line fuseholder, figure 17-5. The in-line fuseholder is often found on aftermarket accessory equipment, such as underdash air conditioners.

Excessive current *burns out* the fuse to interrupt its flow to the defective component. Fuses, like lightbulbs, sometimes fail due to age only. If, however, the replacement fuse "blows" soon after it is replaced, the cause of the problem must be corrected.

Circuit breakers are constructed of a bimetallic strip and a set of points (contacts), figure 17-6. Heat, caused by excessive current of a defective component, causes the bimetallic strip to bend. When the strip bends, the points open and current to the component is interrupted. With no current flow,

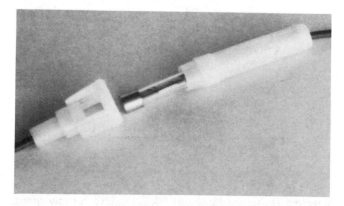

Fig. 17-5 In-line fuseholder with fuse for add-on accessories

Fig. 17-6 Typical circuit breaker with lugs for fuse block mounting

the bimetallic strip cools, and the points automatically reset (close). This action will continue until the cause of the problem is corrected or until the circuit breaker fails due to fatigue.

MASTER CONTROL

The master control generally includes the blower speed control provisions. The variable (infinite) speed control, also known as a *rheostat,* shown in figure 17-7, is popular with aftermarket systems. Also used are two-, three-, four-, and five-position blower speed controls, such as those shown in figure 17-8.

The four-speed control shown in figure 17-9 uses three internal resistors to provide motor speed

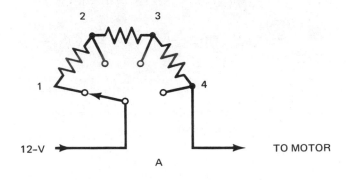

A

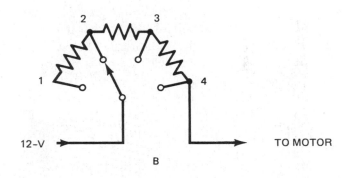

B

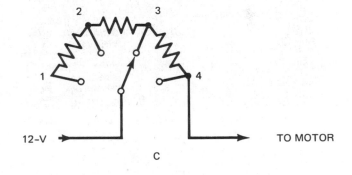

C

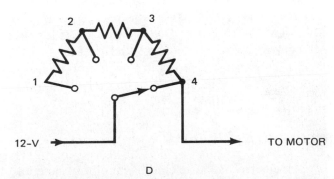

D

Fig. 17-9 Resistance in fan/blower circuit controls speed. Greatest resistance in circuit "A" provides for low speed. Less resistance in circuits "B" and "C" provides for medium speeds. No resistance in circuit "D" provides for high speed.

Fig. 17-7 Rheostat, a variable resistor used to provide infinite fan/blower-speed control

Fig. 17-8 Multiposition blower motor speed switch with dropping resistors (nichrome wire)

Fig. 17-10 Remote duct-mounted blower motor speed dropping resistors (nichrome wire)

Fig. 17-11 Multiposition switch used for fan or blower speed control with multitap motor or remote resistors

control. There is no OFF position; whenever the master switch is closed the blower motor will operate in its selected speed. Position "1" supplies current to the motor through all three resistors to provide low-speed operation. Position "2" supplies current to the motor through two resistors to provide medium-low speed. Current is supplied to the motor through one resistor in position "3" to provide medium-high blower speed. Position "4" supplies full battery voltage to the motor. With all resistors out of the circuit, full battery voltage provides high-speed operation of the blower motor.

Blower motor speed resistors may be remotely mounted, as shown in figure 17-10. Their operation is essentially the same as previously described. Regardless of where they are located, motor speed resistors are usually made of nichrome wire and are placed in the air conditioning and/or heater airstream for cooling.

Some three-, four-, and five-position blower control switches are not equipped with resistors, figure 17-11. These switches provide full battery voltage to any of several windings in the motor (see "Blower Motors" in this unit).

Generally, the blower motor speed control is also the master ON/OFF control as well. The blower switch in either ON position provides full battery voltage to the control thermostat. In this manner the compressor clutch will not energize unless the blower motor is running (see "Thermostat" next in this unit).

THERMOSTAT

An electromagnetic clutch is used on the compressors of most aftermarket units and on some factory-installed air conditioners to provide a means of temperature control. A device known as a *thermostat*, figure 17-12, controls the clutch. Located

REMOTE SENSING THERMOSTAT
(BELLOWS TYPE)

BIMETALLIC THERMOSTAT

Fig. 17-12 Thermostats

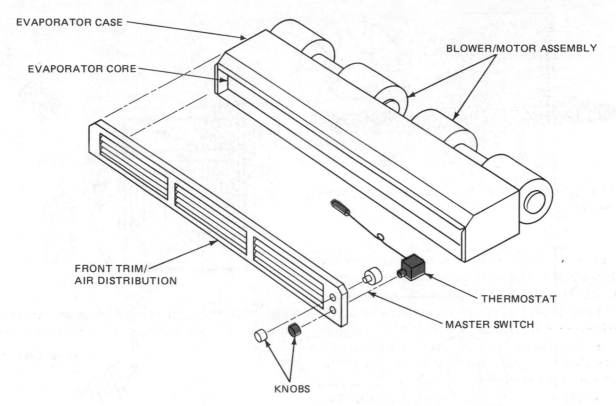

EVAPORATOR CASE

EVAPORATOR CORE

BLOWER/MOTOR ASSEMBLY

FRONT TRIM/
AIR DISTRIBUTION

THERMOSTAT

MASTER SWITCH

KNOBS

Fig. 17-13 Location of the thermostat in the underdash evaporator assembly

in the evaporator, figure 17-13, the thermostat is initially set by the driver to a predetermined temperature setting. The clutch cycles at this setting to control the average in-car temperature.

The thermostat is an electrical switch which is actuated by a change in temperature. It senses either evaporator core air temperature or the temperature of the refrigerant as it enters or leaves the evaporator (depending upon design). A temperature above that preselected closes a thermostatic switch and an electrical signal is sent to the clutch. The clutch is energized and the air conditioner will operate. Similarly, a temperature at or below that preselected will open the thermostatic switch to interrupt the electrical signal to the clutch. The clutch becomes deenergized, and the air conditioner will not operate.

Most thermostats have a positive OFF position so that the clutch can be turned off regardless of the temperature. In this way, the air-conditioner fans or blower can be used without a refrigerating effect.

Two types of thermostats are available for the control of the clutch: the bellows type and the bimetallic type. Both types of thermostats are temperature actuated. Although the principle of operation is different for each type of thermostat, they serve the same purpose in that they both control

the evaporator temperature by cycling the compressor on and off through the clutch.

BELLOWS-TYPE THERMOSTAT

A diagram of the construction of the bellows-type thermostat is shown in figure 17-14. A capillary tube connected to the thermostat is filled with a temperature-sensitive fluid or vapor. The capillary is attached to a bellows within the thermostat. This bellows, in turn, is attached to a swinging frame assembly. Two electrical contact points are provided. One contact is fastened to the swinging frame through an insulator and the other electrical contact is fastened to the body of the unit, again through an insulator.

Operation of the Bellows-Type Thermostat

When the gases inside the capillary tube expand, a pressure is exerted on the bellows. As a result of this pressure, the bellows closes the electrical contacts at a preselected temperature. Manual temperature control is provided by a shaft connected to the swinging frame and an external control knob. When the knob is turned in a clockwise direction, the spring tension is increased against the bellows. More pressure is required to overcome the

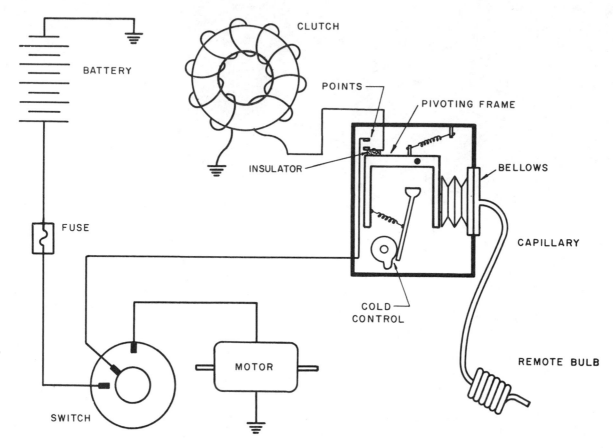

Fig. 17-14 The bellows-type thermostat

increased spring tension. The requirement for more pressure, of course, means that more heat is necessary. Since heat is being removed from the evaporator, this means that a lower temperature is required to *open* the points. On a temperature rise, the heat again exerts pressure on the bellows to *close* the points and allow for cooling.

Another spring within the thermostat regulates the temperature interval through which the points are open. This interval is usually a temperature rise of about 12°F (6.6°C) and gives sufficient time for the evaporator to defrost.

Most factory air-conditioning systems have a means to automatically cycle the clutch off at about 32°F (0°C). Some General Motors cycling clutch orifice tube (CCOT) systems use a preset thermostat to sense the temperature at the evaporator inlet. Some Chrysler H-valve equipped systems have a preset thermostat to sense the temperature at the evaporator outlet.

Many General Motors cycling clutch orifice tube (CCOT) and fixed orifice tube cycling clutch (FOTCC) systems use a pressure switch instead of a thermostat. The pressure switch, mounted on the accumulator, senses low-side pressure to cycle the

clutch off at about 30 psig (207 kPa). This pressure corresponds to a temperature of about 32°F (0°C).

Care must be exercised when handling a thermostat with a capillary tube. There should be no sharp bends or kinks in the capillary. When a bend must be made in the capillary, the bend is to be no sharper than one that can be formed around a finger.

For best results, the end of the capillary should be inserted into the evaporator core between the fins to a depth of about one inch (one millimeter). The capillary should not be inserted all the way through the fins because it will interfere with the blowers which are usually mounted behind the core.

If the capillary has lost its charge for any reason, the thermostat must be replaced. When there is no fluid in the capillary, the unit has no ON (cooling) cycle. The capillary cannot be recharged using standard tools.

BIMETALLIC-TYPE THERMOSTAT

The bimetallic-type thermostat is desirable as a replacement part on many aftermarket hang-on type air conditioners because of its lower cost. This thermostat does not have a capillary tube. The thermostat depends upon air passing over its bimetallic strips to maintain proper operation.

Operation of the Bimetallic-Type Thermostat

Manual temperature control with the bimetallic thermostat is achieved in the same manner as that described for the bellows-type thermostat. Cold air passing over the bimetallic leaf in the rear of the thermostat causes it to retract. By retracting it bows enough to open a set of points. As the temperature increases, the other leaf of the bimetallic element reacts to the heat and pulls the points back together. The OFF cycle range of this thermostat is also about 12°F (6.6°C) to allow for a sufficient defrost time.

The bimetallic thermostat is limited in application because it must be mounted inside the evaporator. In many instances, the bellows-type thermostat must be used, since its long capillary tube allows the thermostat to be placed some distance from the evaporator core.

SUMMARY

Most thermostats are adjustable. In addition, a means is provided for regulating the range between the opening and closing of the points. The adjustment in some thermostats is located under the control knob in the shaft; in other thermostats, the adjustment is located under a fiber cover on the body of the unit.

A thermostat lacking a setscrew can be considered to be a nonadjustable type. Malfunction of this type of thermostat requires replacement of the complete unit.

BLOWER MOTOR

Many styles and types of blower motors are available, depending upon their application, figure 17-15. Blower motors may have a single shaft or a double shaft. They may be flange mounted or they may have provisions for internal cooling. Regardless of the style or type, the blower motor drives one or two squirrel-cage blowers to move air across the evaporator and/or heater core, figure 17-16.

If motor speed control is provided by resistors, the motor will have only one winding, as shown in figure 17-17. Motor speed control may also be provided by multiwound motors, figure 17-18, as well. Resistance for speed control is provided by the motor windings and no external resistors are required.

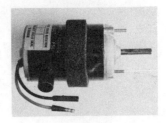
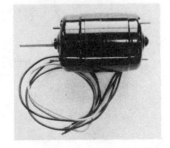

Fig. 17-15 Styles and types of blower motors depend upon their application. Generally, they are not interchangeable from one year/model car to another.

Automotive blower motors generally are not repairable. If found to be defective they must be replaced. Common causes of failure include worn bushings or brushes, or defective internal wiring. Before replacing a motor thought to be defective, however, always check to insure that the ground wire is secure, since most blower housings are constructed of nonconductive materials.

It must be noted that some replacement motors are reversible (REV) whereas many are not. It is important to note whether the defective motor turns clockwise (cw) or counterclockwise (ccw) facing the shaft end of the motor. The replacement motor selected should turn in the same direction. Other abbreviations relating to blower motors include DBL for double shaft, and THD for threaded shaft end(s).

ELECTROMAGNETIC CLUTCH

Automotive air-conditioner manufacturers use an electromagnetic clutch as a means of disengaging the compressor when it is not needed. For example, the compressor is disengaged when a defrost cycle is indicated in the evaporator or when the air conditioner is not being used.

Basically, all clutches operate on the principle of magnetic attraction. There are two general types of clutches: those with a stationary field and those with a rotating field.

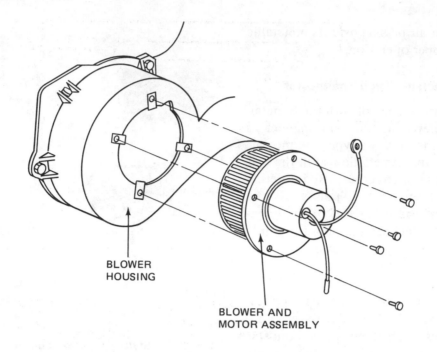

BLOWER
HOUSING

BLOWER AND
MOTOR ASSEMBLY

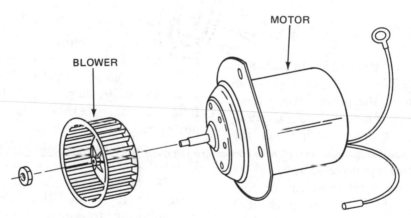

MOTOR

BLOWER

Fig. 17-16 Squirrel-cage blower, attached to the blower motor, is found inside the blower housing. The direction of rotation of the motor is important, depending upon blower housing design, to insure airflow.

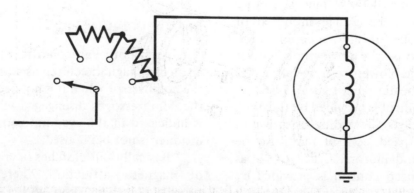

Fig. 17-17 Resistors in switch provide for low, medium and high fan/blower speed. Switch is shown in the OFF position.

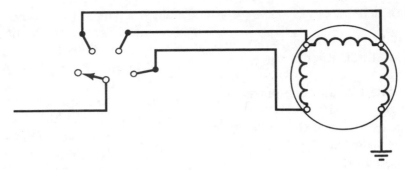

Fig. 17-18 Multiwound motor provides internal resistance required for low, medium, and high fan/blower speed. Switch is shown in the OFF position.

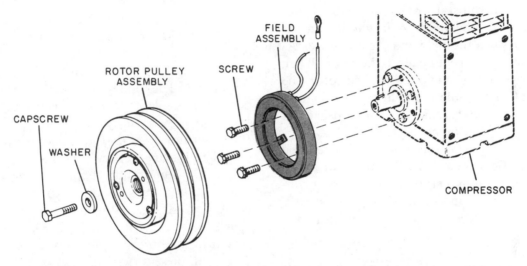

Fig. 17-19 Typical seal-mounted clutch field. Three screws are removed from the seal plate and replaced with screws supplied with the field to secure it to the compressor.

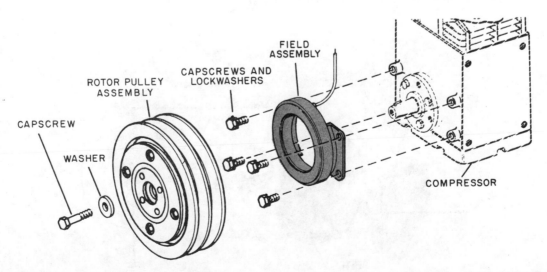

Fig. 17-20 Typical boss-mounted clutch field. The clutch field is secured to the compressor body with four screws furnished with it. The seal plate is not disturbed with this type of field.

The Stationary Field Clutch

The stationary field clutch is more desirable than the rotating field clutch for use since it has fewer parts to wear out.

The field is mounted to the compressor by mechanical means, figures 17-19 and 17-20, depending upon the type of field and the compressor supplied. The rotor is held on the armature by means of a bearing and snap rings. The armature is mounted on the compressor crankshaft.

When there is no current to the field, a magnetic force is not applied to the clutch. The rotor is free to turn on the armature which remains stationary on the crankshaft.

When the thermostat or switch is closed, current is applied to the field. A magnetic force is established between the field and the armature. As a result, the armature is pulled into the rotor. When the armature becomes engaged with the rotor, the complete unit turns while the field remains stationary. The compressor crankshaft then begins to turn and the refrigeration cycle starts.

When the switch or thermostat is opened, the current to the field is cut off. The armature disengages from the rotor and stops while the rotor continues to turn. The pumping action of the compressor is stopped until current is again applied to the field.

The Rotating Field Clutch

The rotating field clutch operates in the same manner as the stationary field clutch, with the exception of the field placement. In this case, the field is a part of the rotor and turns with the rotor. Current is applied to the field by means of brushes which are mounted on the compressor.

Current applied to the field through the brushes sets up a magnetic field which pulls the armature into contact with the rotor. The complete unit, consisting of the armature, rotor, and field, turns and causes the compressor to turn.

In both types of clutches, slots are machined in the armature and rotor to aid in concentrating the magnetic field and increasing the attraction between them.

Since the clutch engages and disengages at high speeds, as required for the proper temperature control, it is understandable that considerable scoring occurs on the armature and rotor surfaces. Such scoring is allowable and should not be a cause for concern.

The spacing between the coil and the pulley is important. The pulley should be as close to the coil as possible to achieve better magnetic flux travel. However, the pulley should not be so close that the rotor drags on the coil housing.

The spacing between the rotor and the armature is also important. If this spacing is too close, the armature drags on the rotor when the unit is turned off. If the rotor and armature are too far apart, there will be a poor contact between the armature and rotor when the unit is turned on. Either of these situations results in serious clutch malfunctions.

The spacing of the rotor and armature should be such that when the clutch is off, there is no drag. Also, when the clutch is turned on, the

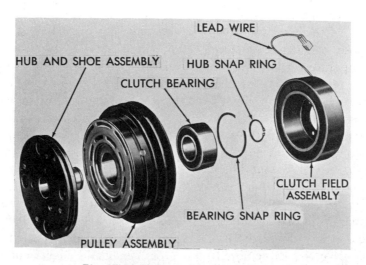

Fig. 17-21 Warner clutch plate type

proper spacing insures that no slippage will occur (except for the moment when the clutch is first engaged).

PRESSURE CUTOFF SWITCH

Many systems have a low- or high-pressure cutoff switch in the clutch circuit. These normally closed (NC) switches are sensitive to system pressure and open in the event of abnormal pressure. This interrupts current to the clutch coil to stop compressor action.

The low-pressure cutoff switch is found in the system anywhere between the evaporator inlet and the compressor inlet. In the event of an abnormally low pressure of, say, 5 psi (34.4 kPa) the switch will open to stop the compressor. This prevents further reduction of system pressure and protects the system from the possible entrance of air and/or moisture, as would be the case with a low-side leak.

The high-pressure cutoff switch is found in the system anywhere between the compressor outlet and the evaporator inlet. In the event of an abnormally high pressure of, say, 300 psi (2 068.5 kPa) this switch will open to stop compressor action. This prevents system damage and/or rupture that may be caused by further increase in pressure.

COMPRESSOR DISCHARGE PRESSURE SWITCH

Many factory systems use a compressor discharge pressure switch to disengage the compressor clutch electrical circuit. The action of this switch stops the compressor if the refrigerant charge is not adequate, say, due to a leak, to provide sufficient circulation within the system. The compressor discharge pressure switch is also called a no-charge switch and ambient low-temperature switch, or a low-pressure cutoff switch. The switch is designed to open electrically to shut off the compressor when high-side system pressure drops below 37 psig (255 kPa). This switch also performs the secondary function of an outside ambient air temperature sensor. When outside ambient air temperature falls below 25°F (−3.9°C) the reduced corresponding refrigerant pressure keeps the switch open.

The compressor discharge pressure switch, located in the high-pressure discharge line from the compressor or receiver/drier, cannot be repaired. If it fails in service it must be replaced with a new

unit. Its function is to protect the compressor, and it should not be bypassed with a jumper wire.

FACTORY-INSTALLED WIRING

The electrical schematic of figure 17-22 is only one of hundreds showing the wiring of factory-installed air-conditioning (cooling and heating) systems. When servicing these systems, it is necessary to consult the appropriate service manual for specific information and schematics. It should be noted that many factory-installed systems do not use a thermostat for temperature control. Many systems use an evaporator pressure control and/or a blend of hot and cool air to achieve the desired temperature. For further information, see "Pressure Controls" in Unit 19, and "Automatic Temperature Controls" in Unit 20.

COOLANT TEMPERATURE WARNING SYSTEM

The air-conditioning system, when operating, places a high demand on the engine since the condenser is mounted ahead (in front) of the radiator. Air available to remove unwanted heat from the engine coolant in the radiator is heat laden from having first passed through the condenser.

Often, a malfunctioning air conditioner will affect engine coolant temperature. Conversely, an overheated engine will affect air-conditioning performance. To monitor engine coolant condition, a dash light or a dash gauge is used.

Lamps

There are two types of engine coolant lamp systems (commonly called *telltale* or *idiot lights*): the one-lamp system and the two-lamp system. The one-lamp system, figure 17-23, warns that the engine has overheated and that immediate attention is required. The two-lamp system has one lamp to indicate *cold*, and one lamp to indicate *hot*, figure 17-24.

In the two-lamp system, the *cold* switch is closed until the engine coolant temperature reaches its normal operating temperature, usually about 180°F (82.2°C). In the one- and two-lamp systems, the *hot* contacts of the sending unit close when engine coolant temperature reaches about 250°F (121.1°C). The actual temperature at which this switch closes depends upon the engine design.

Pressurized engine cooling systems are covered in Unit 22. The disadvantage of the *telltale* light

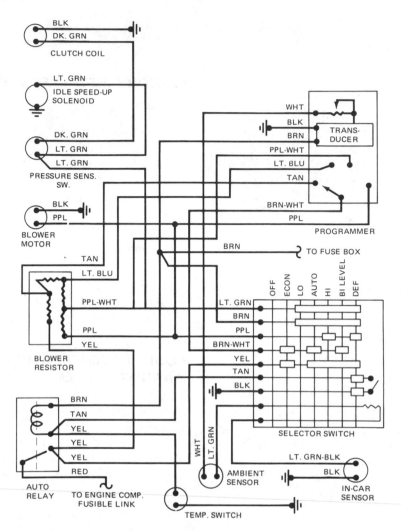

Fig. 17-22 Typical electrical schematic of factory-installed air-conditioning system

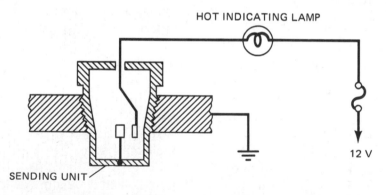

Fig. 17-23 One-lamp (hot) engine temperature indicator circuit

system is obvious — the *hot* lamp does not light until *after there is a problem*. This probably is why the *telltale* light is sometimes referred to as an *idiot light*.

Gauge

The coolant temperature gauge system, figure 17-25, consists of two parts: the dash (gauge) unit

and the engine (sending) unit. The sending unit contains a sintered material having the characteristics of changing resistance in relation to its temperature. This material, sealed in a metal bulb, is screwed into a coolant passage of the engine. It has a high resistance when cold, and a low resistance when hot.

The varying resistance of the sending unit regulates the amount of current passing through

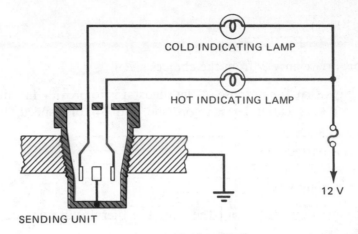

Fig. 17-24 Two-lamp (cold and hot) engine temperature indicator circuit

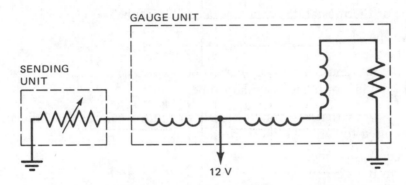

Fig. 17-25 Typical temperature gauge (GM system) schematic

the coil of the dash gauge and, in turn, moves the pointer accordingly.

Constant Voltage Regulator

Some gauge systems operate at full battery voltage of 12 volts, while others operate at a reduced voltage. The latter system incorporates into its circuit a constant voltage regulator (CVR), figure 17-26. Of bimetallic construction, the CVR contacts open and close at a frequency necessary to provide an *average* output of about 5 volts.

It should be noted that one CVR can be used to regulate the voltage for more than one gauge. In addition to the temperature gauge, the CVR can regulate voltage for the oil pressure and gas gauge as well. As a rule of thumb, if all gauges read incorrectly, the CVR is probably defective; if only one gauge reads incorrectly, either that gauge or its sending unit is probably defective.

Fig. 17-26 Constant voltage regulator for dash instruments

Review

Select the appropriate answer from the choices given.

1. Technician A says that the purpose of the rheostat is to provide infinite fan speed control. Technician B says its purpose is to provide 2-, 3-, 4-, or 5-speed fan control.

   a. Technician A is correct.
   b. Technician B is correct.
   c. Both technicians are correct.
   d. Both technicians are wrong.

2. What is the temperature rise from the time the thermostat contacts open until they reclose?

   a. About 4°F (2.2°C)   c. About 12°F (6.6°C)
   b. About 8°F (4.4°C)   d. About 16°F (8.8°C)

3. Which type of thermostat does not have a capillary tube?

   a. Bellows type
   b. Bimetallic type
   c. Both types in a and b have a capillary tube
   d. Neither type in a or b has a capillary tube

4. Technician A says that resistors are used to reduce voltage. Technician B says that resistors are used to control blower speed.

   a. Technician A is correct.
   b. Technician B is correct.
   c. Both technicians are correct.
   d. Both technicians are wrong.

5. What supplies current to the clutch field coil?

   a. The thermostat   c. The battery
   b. The master switch   d. All answers are correct

6. What type of clutch uses a brush set?

   a. Stationary field-type   c. Clutches do not use brush sets.
   b. Rotating field-type   d. All clutches use brush sets.

7. The *hot* dash lamp lights when engine coolant temperature reaches approximately

   a. 180°F (82.2°C).   c. 250°F (121.1°C).
   b. 212°F (100°C).   d. 280°F (137.7°C).

8. Some dash gauge systems use a constant voltage regulator to provide a voltage of about

   a. 3 volts.   c. 7 volts.
   b. 5 volts.   d. 9 volts.

CONTINUED

9. Technician A says that the blower motor often has a ground wire bonded to body metal. Technician B says that the clutch coil often has a ground wire bonded to body metal.

   a. Technician A is correct.
   b. Technician B is correct.
   c. Both technicians are correct.
   d. Both technicians are wrong.

10. How many resistors are required for a four-speed blower control?

   a. One   c. Three
   b. Two   d. Four

UNIT 18:

Vacuum Circuits

To understand vacuum circuits, it is first essential that the term *vacuum* be defined and understood. One definition, given by a leading encyclopedia, describes a *vacuum* as a portion of space that is *entirely* devoid of matter. Since all things contain matter in some form, it would seem that there is no such thing as a vacuum.

For all practical purposes, however, a vacuum must be thought of as a portion of space that is *partially* devoid of matter. For a better understanding, consider that a vacuum is a space in which pressure is *below* atmospheric pressure. A good example of a vacuum is demonstrated by a person drinking through a straw, figure 18-1. As the per-

Inches of Mercury (inHg)	Pounds Per Square Inch Absolute (psia)	Kilopascals Absolute (kPa absolute)
28.98	0.5	3.45
27.96	1.0	6.89
26.94	1.5	10.34
25.92	2.0	13.79
24.90	2.5	17.24
23.88	3.0	20.68
22.86	3.5	24.13
21.83	4.0	27.58
20.81	4.5	30.03
19.79	5.0	34.47
18.77	5.5	37.92
17.75	6.0	41.37
16.73	6.5	44.82
18.71	7.0	48.26
14.69	7.5	51.71
13.67	8.0	55.16
12.65	8.5	58.61
11.63	9.0	62.05
10.61	9.5	65.50
9.59	10.0	68.95
8.57	10.5	72.40
7.54	11.0	75.84
6.52	11.5	79.29
5.50	12.0	82.74
4.48	12.5	86.19
3.46	13.0	89.63
2.44	13.5	93.08
1.42	14.0	96.53
0.40	14.5	99.98
	15.0	103.42

Fig. 18-1 Sipping liquid through a straw produces a lower-than-atmospheric pressure (vacuum) at "A." The higher (atmospheric) pressure, "B," forces the liquid through the straw, due to a difference in pressure.

Fig. 18-2 Comparison of inches of mercury (inHg) to pounds per square inch absolute (psia) and kilopascals absolute (kPa absolute)

son sucks on the straw, a slight vacuum is created in the straw. Atmospheric pressure, which is greater than the vacuum pressure, is exerted against the liquid to force it up the straw.

Atmospheric pressure, at sea level, is 14.696 psia (101.328 kPa absolute). For all practical purposes, this value is usually rounded off to 14.7 psia (101.4 kPa absolute). At sea level, then, a pressure of 14 psia (96.5 kPa absolute) *is a vacuum.* Traditionally, English system vacuum pressure values are given in *inches of mercury* (inHg), as covered in Units 6 and 10.

Most automotive manufacturers' manuals give vacuum value requirements and specifications using the term *inches* only. In this unit, reference to vacuum values will be given in the English and metric absolute scales of pressure (see Unit 2). The conversion chart of figure 18-2 may be used as an aid for comparison of *inches* to *psia* and *kPa absolute.*

VACUUM-OPERATED DEVICES

Most vacuum-operated devices, such as *heater coolant valves* and *mode doors,* are activated with a *vacuum pot,* also called *vacuum motor* or *vacuum power unit.* The exertion (force) of atmospheric pressure on one side of a diaphragm causes the diaphragm to move toward the lower (vacuum) pressure side, figure 18-3. This moves the device to be controlled through a lever, arm, or rod linkage.

Dual-chamber vacuum pots (motors) operate below atmospheric pressure, based on pressure differential from one side to the other. A higher pressure on either side will move the diaphragm to the side with less pressure, figure 18-4. This provides a *push* or *pull* effect of the vacuum pot.

VACUUM SOURCE

The automobile engine, when running, provides a ready source of vacuum. This source is usually off the intake manifold and is routed to the various components through small-diameter synthetic rubber hoses. The engine vacuum supply varies from 0 in (14.69 psia or 101.3 kPa absolute) to 20 in (4.89 psia or 33.7 kPa absolute), or more, depending upon certain engine conditions. The reason for this vacuum variation is not important in this discussion. It is important, however, to be aware that engine vacuum *does* vary.

Because of this vacuum variation *reserve tanks* and *check valves* are used. These devices provide the means to maintain maximum vacuum values to properly operate air-conditioning and heater vacuum controls, figure 18-5. It should be noted that more than one reserve tank and/or check valve may be found in the air-conditioning and heating system vacuum circuit.

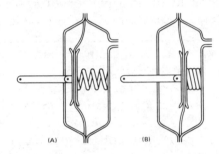

Fig. 18-3 Typical vacuum pot (motor) operation. (A) no vacuum applied and (B) full vacuum applied.

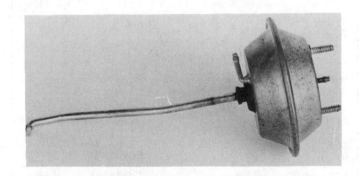

Fig. 18-4 Typical dual chamber vacuum motor (pot)

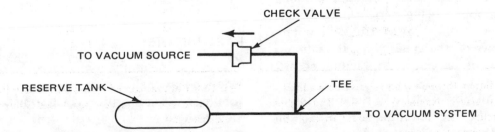

Fig. 18-5 Reserve tank provides vacuum source during periods of low- or no-engine vacuum. Check valve prevents vacuum loss back to the source during this period.

Fig. 18-6 Vacuum reserve tank

Fig. 18-7 Typical vacuum check valve

Reserve Tank

Reserve vacuum tanks are manufactured in a variety of sizes and shapes. Those most commonly used resemble a large juice can, figure 18-6. These tanks require no maintenance, but sometimes develop pin-hole size leaks due to rust or corrosion. When a tank is suspected of leaking, it may be removed from the car and pressurized to about 5 psig (34.4 kPa gauge). It is then leak-tested with a soap solution or by immersion in a tank of water. After releasing the pressure, the hole may be repaired by first cleaning the area to the bare metal with a wire brush or sandpaper, and then applying an epoxy or fiberglass material.

Check Valve

Many types and styles of check valve are used in the air-conditioning and heater vacuum circuit. Essentially, a check valve, figure 18-7, allows flow in one direction and checks (blocks) the flow in the opposite direction. A check valve is easily tested. Remove the suspected valve from the car and connect it, in series, to a vacuum pump and vacuum or compound gauge, figure 18-8. The direction of flow should be *away* from the pump. If a vacuum shows on the gauge when the pump is running the valve is closed; if no vacuum shows, the valve is defective.

Next turn the check valve so the direction of flow is *toward* the vacuum pump. If a vacuum now shows on the gauge when the pump is running, the valve is defective; if no vacuum shows, the valve is closing properly. A defective check valve must

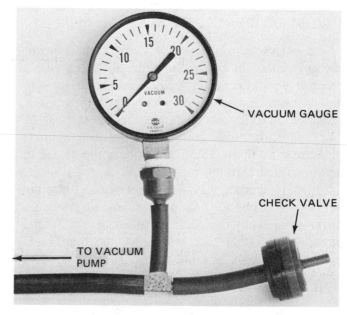

Fig. 18-8 Typical setup to test a check valve

be replaced since repairs are not usually possible or practical.

RESTRICTOR

Some vacuum systems have a *restrictor* to provide a delay or slow operation of a device. Restrictors have a small orifice which sometimes becomes clogged with lint or other airborne debris. Attempts to clean a restrictor usually prove unsuccessful, and replacement is suggested. To test a restrictor simply use a vacuum pump and gauge setup as pre-

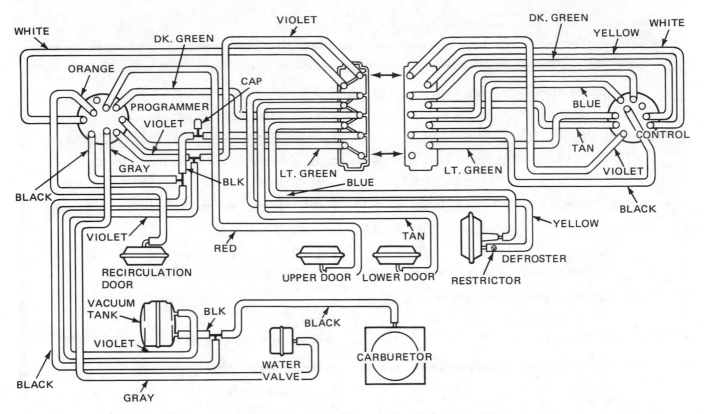

Fig. 18-9 Typical vacuum schematic of factory-installed air-conditioning system

viously described. The gauge should show a vacuum with the pump running and the restrictor connected in *either* or *both* directions.

VACUUM SYSTEM DIAGRAMS

The vacuum system diagram of figure 18-9 must be considered as typical since there are hundreds of vacuum systems used. For this reason, manufacturers' vacuum system diagrams for a specific year/model car must be followed. Basically,

the vacuum system is used to open, close, or position the heater coolant valve and mode doors to achieve a desired preselected temperature level. Operation of these components is covered in Unit 23.

A description of the various vacuum-operated devices associated with the air-conditioning and heating system is given in Unit 21. It should be noted that not all systems have all of the devices discussed. Appropriate manufacturers' vacuum system diagrams must be studied to determine which devices are used in any given circuit.

Review

Select the appropriate answer from the choices given.

1. Which of the following is a vacuum pressure?

   a. 18 psia (124.1 kPa absolute)
   b. 16 psia (110.3 kPa absolute)

   c. Both a and b are vacuum pressures
   d. Neither a nor b is a vacuum pressure

2. From the chart of figure 18-2, what is the proper conversion for 19 inches of mercury?

   a. 5.87 psia (40.51 kPa absolute)
   b. 5.62 psia (38.74 kPa absolute)

   c. 5.37 psia (37.13 kPa absolute)
   d. 5.12 psia (35.30 kPa absolute)

3. Which of the following *is not* affected by atmospheric pressure?

   a. Single-chamber pot (motor)
   b. Dual-chamber pot (motor)

   c. Both a and b are affected
   d. Neither a nor b is affected

4. Which of the following may be repaired?

   a. Vacuum reserve tank
   b. Restrictor valve

   c. Check valve
   d. None of these may be repaired

5. Which of the following *will not* allow vacuum flow in either direction?

   a. Reserve tank
   b. Check valve

   c. Restrictive valve
   d. Vacuum motor

UNIT 19:

Pressure Controls

Within the range of 20 psig (137.9 kPa) and 80 psig (551.6 kPa), the temperature of Refrigerant 12 has a close relationship to its pressure. This relationship is illustrated further in Section 2 of this text, System Diagnosis.

Liquid refrigerant is metered into the evaporator by the thermostatic expansion valve. The amount of refrigerant required is regulated by the heat load on the evaporator. As the heat load decreases, there is a corresponding decrease in the amount of refrigerant that is metered into the evaporator by the expansion valve. In this discussion of pressure controls, the student should recall that water droplets which accumulate on the evaporator freeze when the temperature drops below 32°F (0°C).

SUCTION PRESSURE REGULATORS

The suction pressure regulator controls the pressure of the refrigerant in the evaporator by preventing the pressure from falling below a predetermined range, usually 22 psig (151.6 kPa) to 30 psig (206.8 kPa) (depending on system design). If a setting of 30 psig (206.8 kPa) is assumed, the suction pressure regulator allows evaporator pressures of about 30 psi (206.8 kPa) to be released to the compressor. The control holds all pressures up to 30 psi (206.8 kPa). In this manner, the evaporator can maintain a constant pressure of 30 psig (206.8 kPa).

The operation of the evaporator in this manner is based on the assumption that the thermostatic expansion valve, suction regulator, and compressor are operating properly, figure 19-1. If, for example, the TXV is flooding the evaporator, the pressure in the evaporator rises above 30 psig (206.8 kPa), figure 19-2. This condition can be corrected by replacing the TXV, or by correcting any other problem that may be causing the flooding condition.

Flow through any type of suction pressure regulator is never completely stopped. A bypass is included so that a small amount of refrigerant and refrigeration oil can circulate through the system. This provision helps to eliminate the danger of compressor damage when a malfunction in the suction regulator causes it to close.

EVAPORATOR PRESSURE REGULATOR

The evaporator pressure regulator (EPR) valve is a fully automatic suction pressure control device that is used in certain Chrysler Corporation automotive air-conditioning systems. The EPR valve is located inside the compressor and is just under the suction side service valve, figure 19-3 on page 130.

The EPR valve, figure 19-4 on page 130, maintains the evaporator pressure, and thus its temperature, at a point just above freezing. As a result, any evaporator condensate cannot freeze during the normal operation of the evaporator. The pressure in the evaporator is maintained between 22 psig (151.6 kPa) and 26 psig (179.2 kPa) by the action of the EPR valve. If the EPR valve is operating properly, the compressor inlet pressure should be about 15 psig (103.4 kPa). However, this pressure can be higher or lower, depending on the evaporator heat load.

An EPR valve balance is maintained between the control spring pressure and the evaporator refrigerant pressure. A diaphragm seals the chamber and prevents refrigerant leaks. An increase of evaporator pressure against the diaphragm overcomes the control spring tension and moves the valve away from the seated position. As a result, there is an increase in the refrigerant flow from the evaporator to the compressor.

A decrease in evaporator pressure allows the control spring to move the valve toward the seat. The refrigerant flowing from the evaporator is restricted and the evaporator pressure increases until

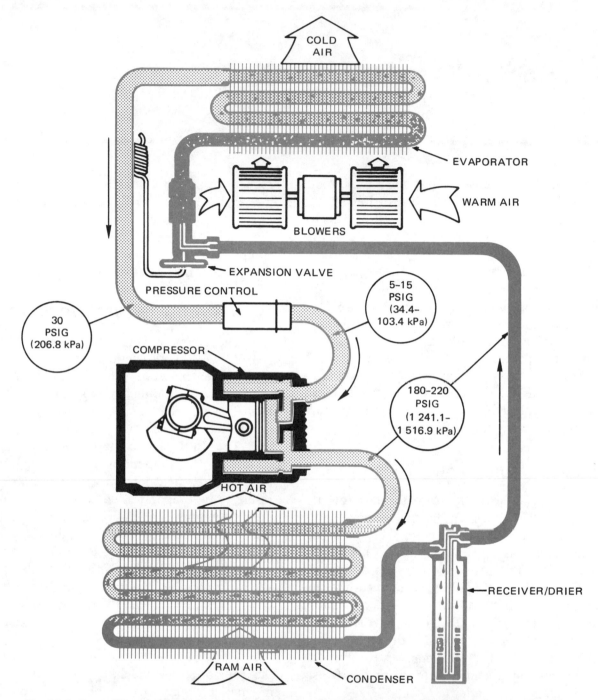

Fig. 19-1 Controlling action of the pressure control with the proper expansion valve metering

it reaches a value sufficient to reopen the EPR valve.

The opening and closing of the EPR valve continues until a balance is reached between the evaporator pressure and the spring tension. The valve then remains in a constant position until the evaporator heat load or the compressor speed changes and a new balance of pressures is required.

Although the EPR valve is located within the compressor on the suction side, it is not necessary to disassemble the compressor if the valve must be replaced. The EPR valve can be changed without removing the compressor from the engine compartment. Since the valve cannot be adjusted, any malfunction requires unit replacement.

An oil passage which runs inside the compressor between the suction line and the compressor crankcase also runs through the EPR valve. Since oil is carried out of the compressor in the refrigerant, the oil passage permits the oil to be returned to the crankcase, regardless of the condition of the

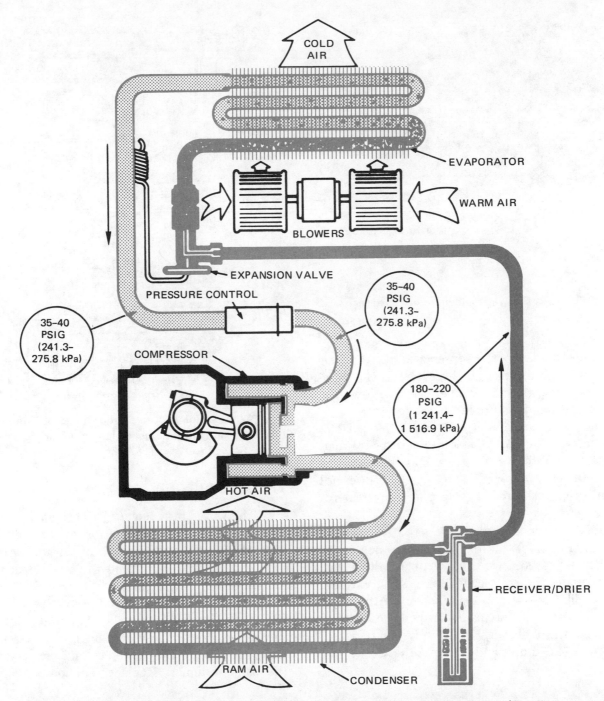

Fig. 19-2 Loss of controlling action of pressure control due to improper expansion valve metering (flooding evaporator)

EPR valve. In addition, the oil passage pressurizes the crankcase and prevents the crankcase pressure from dropping below the normal atmospheric pressure. If this pressure does drop into the vacuum range, atmospheric pressure can enter the system through the crankshaft seal assembly. The moisture content of the incoming air can contaminate the system. Another condition that can result from the addition of air at atmospheric pressure is higher-than-normal head pressures.

SUCTION THROTTLING VALVE

The suction throttling valve (STV) is a flow control device found at the evaporator outlet of some automotive air-conditioning systems, figure 19-5.

Its purpose is to maintain evaporator pressure at a predetermined level. This type of valve provides control with a much greater accuracy than is obtainable with many other types of controls. The

Fig. 19-3 EPR valve and oil return passage

STV holds the evaporator pressure to ±0.5 psig (±3.4 kPa). This means that there is at most a variation of one psig (6.895 kPa) between the low pressure and the high pressure in the evaporator.

The valve contains a *pilot valve* that enables it to achieve as close to absolute zero pressure as possible. The absolute pilot serves as the opposing force to the evaporator pressure. The STV does not rely on spring pressures or atmospheric pressure for its operation.

The inlet end of the valve has a test port to which the low-side manifold gauge is connected for testing, figure 19-6. Two other fittings on the valve accommodate the oil bleed line and the external equalizer line of the expansion valve. If the pilot-operated valve is not adjusted properly or is defective, the entire valve assembly must be replaced, since it is a sealed unit and cannot be serviced.

Fig. 19-4 EPR valve located under the low-side (suction) service valve

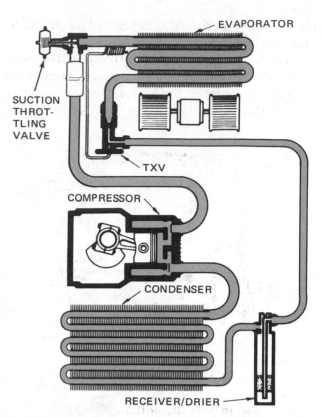

Fig. 19-5 Location of the pilot-operated absolute suction throttling valve in the air-conditioning system

VALVES-IN-RECEIVER

The valves in receiver (VIR) assembly, figures 19-7 and 19-8, is a combination of three different components: the thermostatic expansion valve, the suction throttling valve, and the receiver/dehydrator (including a sight glass).

Early series are called simply valves-in-receiver (VIR) and later series are called evaporator equalizer valves-in-receiver (EEVIR). Both are essentially the same device; they operate and are serviced in the same manner. Replacement parts or repair

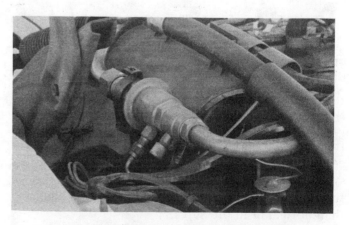

Fig. 19-6 Test port for manifold gauge on STV

kits are available for field repair following procedures outlined in Section 3 of this text.

The VIR assembly is mounted near the evaporator. Both the inlet and the outlet fittings of the evaporator connect to the VIR, as well as the liquid line and the suction line. The VIR is designed to

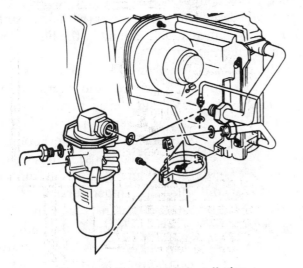

Fig. 19-7 Typical VIR installation

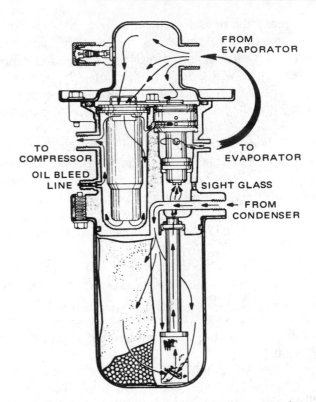

Fig. 19-8 Cutaway section of valves-in-receiver (VIR) showing detail of components and direction of refrigerant flow

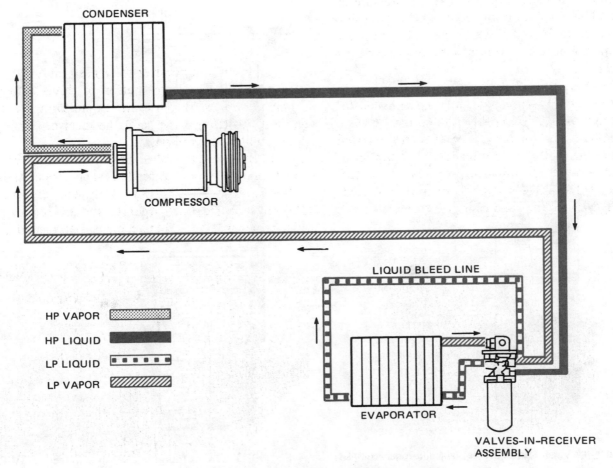

Fig. 19-9 System schematic with valves-in-receiver

eliminate the need for the equalizer external capillary and the TXV remote bulb. The diaphragm end of the TXV is exposed directly to refrigerant vapor entering the VIR from the outlet of the evaporator. The provision for external equalizing consists of a small hole (orifice) drilled in the housing wall between the STV and the TXV.

The desiccant is contained in the receiver shell and is replaceable. A liquid pickup tube containing a filter screen extends to the bottom of the shell. The filter traps impurities and prevents them from circulating through the system. A replaceable sight glass is located in the VIR housing at the inlet of the TXV.

The components of the VIR function in the same manner as similar separate system components. Because the VIR components are mounted in a common housing, their appearance is somewhat different from that of the individual units covered previously.

Figure 19-9 is a system schematic showing the valves-in-receiver assembly. Figures 19-10 and 19-11 describe the TXV and STV respectively as found in the VIR assembly.

COMBINATION VALVE

The *combination valve*, also called *combo valve*, used on some Ford car lines, is mounted at or near the inlet and outlet provisions of the evaporator. It is similar in function and operation to the valves-in-receiver (VIR). Unlike the VIR, however, the combo valve does not include the receiver and desiccant. The receiver (with desiccant) in a Ford system is usually found in the liquid line near the condenser outlet.

The combo valve, figure 19-12, separates into two sections for each service: the thermostatic expansion valve (TXV) and the suction throttling valve (STV). The TXV is covered in Unit 16. The STV operates in a manner similar to the evaporator pressure regulator (EPR). Its purpose is to regulate or control evaporator pressure at a predetermined level, thereby controlling its temperature.

The primary cause of failure is that the STV becomes stuck in the open position. This condition would be noted by a lower-than-normal evaporator

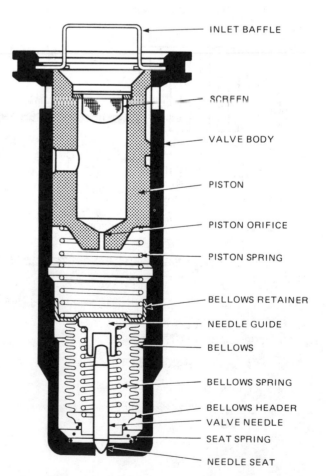

Legend for left figure:
DIAPHRAGM COVER
CHARCOAL
FILTER
RETAINER
POWER DIAPHRAGM
EQUALIZER PORT
DIAPHRAGM DISC
SEAL RETAINER RING
OPERATING PIN SEAL
OPERATING PIN
VALVE OUTLET PORT
VALVE SEAT
SPRING GUIDE
BLEED PORT
VALVE BODY
SPRING
NUT
VALVE INLET

Legend for right figure:
INLET BAFFLE
SCREEN
VALVE BODY
PISTON
PISTON ORIFICE
PISTON SPRING
BELLOWS RETAINER
NEEDLE GUIDE
BELLOWS
BELLOWS SPRING
BELLOWS HEADER
VALVE NEEDLE
SEAT SPRING
NEEDLE SEAT

Fig. 19-10 TXV as found in the valves-in-receiver (VIR) assembly

Fig. 19-11 STV as found in the valves-in-receiver (VIR) assembly.

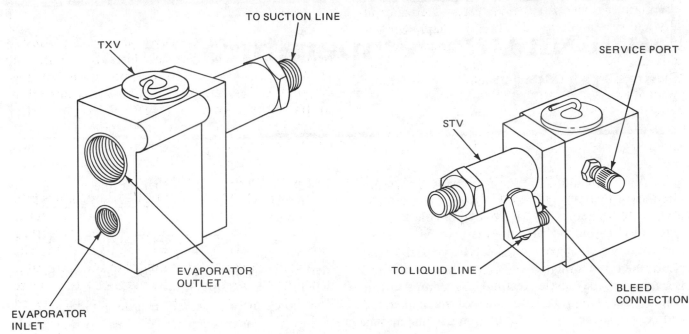

Fig. 19-12 Combination (combo) valve details

(low-side) pressure as measured at the access port of the TXV. In this case, the pressure taken at the compressor suction port service valve would be the same or nearly the same as that taken at the TXV. If the system is operating properly, a slight to considerable pressure drop between these two ports will be noted, depending upon evaporator load conditions.

Review

Select the appropriate answer from the choices given.

1. The evaporator pressure range for systems with an EPR valve, if operating properly, should be:

   a. 20–25 psig (137.9–172.3 kPa).   c. 29–30 psig (199.9–206.8 kPa).
   b. 22–26 psig (151.6–179.2 kPa).   d. exactly 30 psig (206.8 kPa).

2. The EPR valve is located

   a. at the compressor inlet.   c. at the evaporator inlet.
   b. at the compressor outlet.   d. at the evaporator outlet.

3. In a system equipped with any type of suction pressure regulator, an evaporator pressure of 36 psig (248.2 kPa) probably indicates

   a. a defective pressure regulator.   c. the system is operating properly.
   b. a defective expansion valve.   d. the system is low in refrigerant.

4. One design feature of the VIR is the elimination of the need for

   a. a TXV equalizer tube.   c. the drier desiccant.
   b. a sight glass.   d. All of these are correct.

5. What component is found in the VIR that is not found in the combo valve?

   a. The TXV   c. The suction pressure regulator
   b. The desiccant   d. All are found in both valves.

UNIT 20:

Automatic Temperature Controls

Many different types of semiautomatic and automatic temperature control systems are found in use today; so many, it is not possible to cover each system individually in this text. Systems are modified or changed from year to year and from car model to car model.

Since diagnostic testing procedures differ, typical testing procedures are not recommended. For example, test point *12* of one car line may be test point *10* or *14* of another car line. The *shorting* of the wrong test point could destroy an expensive component.

Some components are so sensitive that the 1.5-volt battery used in an analog ohmmeter may destroy it. A digital ohmmeter, then, must be used whenever a manufacturer's specifications suggest that component resistance measurements be taken. Some components and circuits are so sensitive to

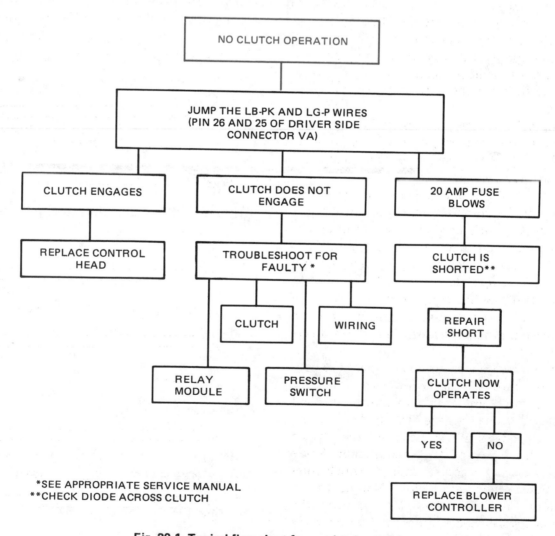

*SEE APPROPRIATE SERVICE MANUAL
**CHECK DIODE ACROSS CLUTCH

Fig. 20-1 Typical flow chart for no clutch operation.

outside influence, however, that some schematics are labeled "do not measure resistance." Heed this caution when it is noted to avoid unnecessary damage to delicate electronic components.

Though the systems differ in many respects, all are designed to provide in-car temperature and humidity conditions at a preset level (within system limitations), regardless of the temperature conditions outside the car.

The temperature control also functions to hold the relative humidity within the car to a healthful level and to prevent window fogging.

For example, if the desired temperature is 75°F (23.89°C), the automatic control system will maintain an in-car environment of 75°F (23.89°C) at 45 to 55 percent humidity, regardless of the outside weather conditions.

In even the hottest weather, a properly operating system can rapidly cool the automobile interior to the predetermined temperature (75°F or 23.89°C). The degree of cooling then cycles to maintain the desired temperature level. In mild weather conditions, the passenger compartment can be held to this same predetermined temperature (75°F or 23.89°C) without resetting or changing the control.

During cold weather, the system rapidly heats the passenger compartment to the predetermined 75°F (23.89°C) level, and then automatically maintains this temperature level.

The intent of this unit is to give an overall understanding of the components of the various systems, not to cover any particular system in detail These components include, but are not limited to, *coolant temperature sensor, in-car temperature sensor, outside temperature sensor, high-side temperature switch, low-side temperature switch, low-pressure switch, vehicle speed sensor, throttle position sensor, sunload sensor,* and *power steering cutout switch.*

Many automotive electronic temperature control systems have self-diagnostic test provisions whereby an on-board microprocessor-controlled subsystem will display a code. This code (number, letter, or alphanumeric) is displayed to tell the technician the cause of the malfunction. Some systems also display a code to indicate which computer detected the malfunction. Manufacturers' specifications must be followed to identify the malfunction display codes, since they differ from car to car. For example, in some General Motors car lines ".7.0" will be displayed to indicate no malfunction if "no trouble" codes are stored in the

Fig. 20-2 Typical thermistor.

computer. On some Ford car lines the "no trouble" code is "888."

It is also possible for the air-conditioning system to malfunction even though self-check testing indicates there are no problems. It is then necessary to follow a manufacturer's step-by-step procedures to troubleshoot and check the system. Again, typical diagnostic procedures are not practical because of the many different types of systems now found in service. For example, figure 20-1 illustrates diagnostic procedures for "no

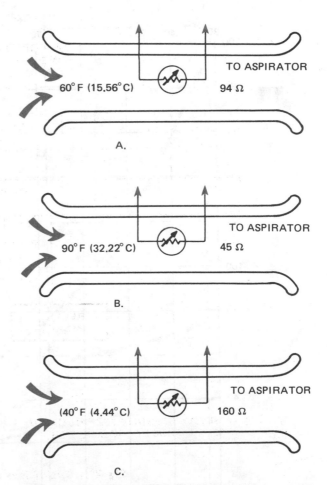

Fig. 20-3 The resistance of a thermistor changes as temperature changes.

clutch operation" for a particular year/model car. This procedure may not be applicable for that same car in another model year or for other similar cars in that same model year.

SENSORS

Although they may vary in physical appearance, sensors all have the same general operating characteristics. That is, they are extremely sensitive to slight changes in temperature. The change in resistance value of each sensor is inversely proportional to a temperature change. For example, when the temperature decreases, the resistance of the sensor increases; and, when the temperature increases, the sensor resistance decreases.

The sensor is actually a resistor whose resistance value is determined by its temperature. This type of resistor is called a *thermistor*, figure 20-2. While the theory of thermistor operation is not covered in this text, the student should be able to gain a good understanding of thermistor operation from the following description and figure 20-3, A through C.

In figure 20-3A, one thermistor is installed in a duct. With air at a temperature of 60°F (15.56°C) passing through the duct, the resistance value of the thermistor is 94 ohms. Refer to the thermistor value chart given in figure 20-4. If the temperature in the duct is 90°F (32.22°C), figure 20-3B, then the resistance of the thermistor decreases to about 45 ohms. If, however, the temperature is decreased

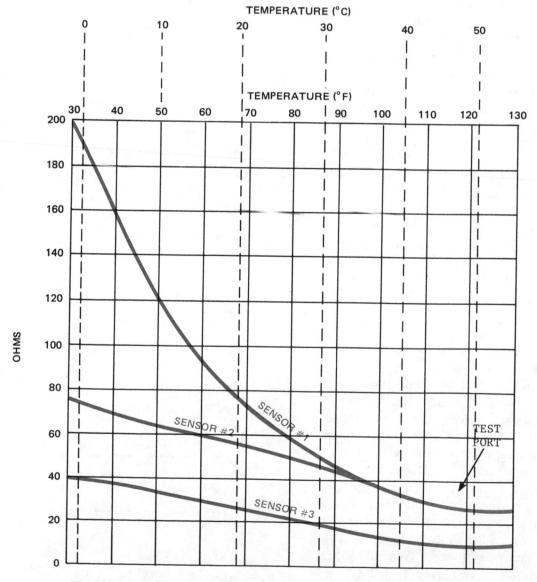

Fig. 20-4 Typical resistance values of thermistors (sensors) at various temperatures.

to 40°F (4.44°C), the thermistor resistance is increased to 160 ohms, figure 20-3C.

Figure 20-4 is a graph of individual sensor values at various temperatures. Compare the chart with the examples given to this point. Note that each sensor has a different value for a particular temperature.

ELECTRONIC TEMPERATURE CONTROL SYSTEMS

Many types of electronic temperature control systems are in use. The flow charts of figures 20-5 and 20-6 illustrate two typical systems. The following information relates to many of the components found in an electronic temperature control system. Not all components, however, are found in all systems.

CONTROL PANEL

The control panel is found in the instrument panel at a convenient location for both driver and front-seat passenger access. Any of three types of control panel may be found: manual, figure 20-7; push button, figure 20-8; or touch pad, figure 20-9. All serve the same purpose; to provide operator input control for the air-conditioning and heating system. Some control panels have features that other panels do not have, such as provisions to display in-car and outside air temperature in English or metric units.

Provisions are made on the control panel for operator selection of an in-car temperature between 65°F (47.2°C) and 85°F (56.6°C) in one-degree increments. Some have an override feature that provides for a setting of either 60°F (42.2°C) or 90°F (72.2°C). Either of these two settings will override all in-car temperature control circuits to provide maximum cooling or heating conditions.

Usually, a microprocessor is located in the control head to input data to the programmer, based on operator-selected conditions. When the ignition switch is turned off, a memory circuit will remember the previous setting. These conditions will be restored the next time the ignition switch is turned on. If the battery is disconnected, however, the memory circuit is cleared and must be reprogrammed.

PROGRAMMER

The programmer, figure 20-10, receives electrical input signals from sensors and the main control panel. Based on all inputs, the programmer provides output signals to turn ON/OFF the compressor clutch, OPEN/CLOSE the heater water valve, determine blower speed, and position all MIX/BLEND mode doors.

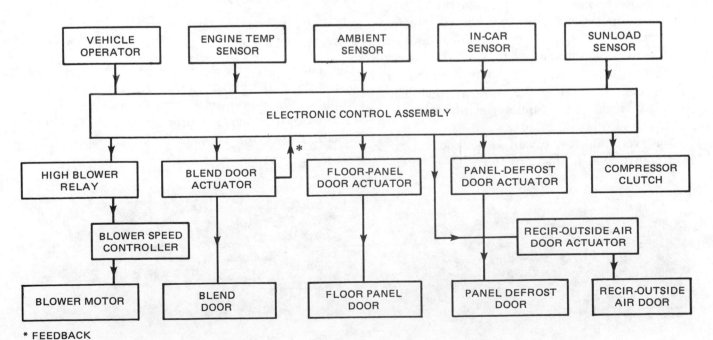

* FEEDBACK

Fig. 20-5 Typical flow chart for electronic temperature control system with five inputs.

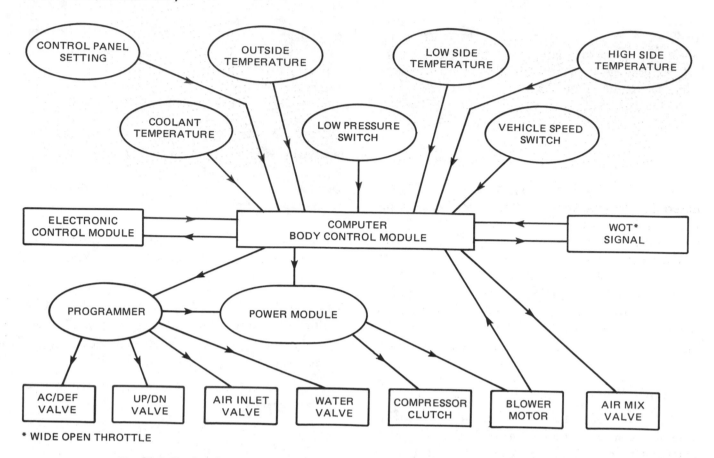

Fig. 20-6 Typical flow chart for electronic temperature control system with nine inputs.

BLOWER AND CLUTCH CONTROL

The blower and clutch control, figure 20-11, functions to convert low-current signals from the control panel to high-current feed to the blower motor. Blower speeds with this control are infinitely variable. The speed is controlled through a resistor strip on the temperature door actuator. The resistor strip, then, functions the same as a rheostat to input data to the control panel. The control panel, in turn, inputs the blower-speed signal to the blower control.

A power transistor circuit is included in the blower control which functions to engage the com-

pressor clutch circuit. The metal strip on which the transistor is mounted serves as a heat sink. This assembly is located in the blower airstream to aid in heat dissipation.

POWER MODULE

The power module, figure 20-12, controls the operation of the blower motor. The power module amplifies the blower-drive signal from the programmer; its output signal is proportional to its input signal. This provides variable blower speeds as

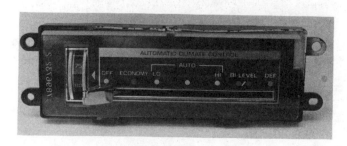

Fig. 20-7 Manual control panel.

Fig. 20-8 Push-button control panel.

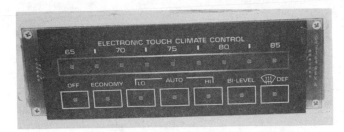

Fig. 20-9 Touch pad control panel.

determined by in-car conditions. If the in-car temperature is considerably higher than the selected temperature, in air conditioning, the blower will start at high speed and decrease to low speed as the in-car temperature is lowered.

Conversely, if the in-car temperature is considerably lower than the selected temperature, in heating, the blower will start at high speed and decrease to low speed as the in-car temperature rises.

CLUTCH DIODE

The clutch coil is an electromagnet with a strong magnetic field when current is applied. This magnetic field is constant as long as power is applied to the coil. When power is removed the magnetic field collapses and creates high-voltage *spikes*. These spikes are harmful to the computer and must be prevented.

A diode placed across the clutch coil, figure 20-13, provides a path to ground, holding the spikes to a safe level. This diode is usually taped inside the cluth coil connector, across the 12-volt

Fig. 20-11 A typical blower and clutch control.

lead and ground lead. A diode is checked with an analog ohmmeter in the following steps:

1. Carefully cut the tape to expose the diode leads.

2. Unplug the connector from the compressor clutch coil.

3. Disconnect the ground wire. Isolate this wire so it does not touch ground.

4. Touch the ohmmeter leads to the diode leads. Observe the ohmmeter needle.

5. Reverse the ohmmeter leads and repeat step 4. NOTE: In steps 4 and 5, the needle should indicate very high resistance in one step and little or no resistance in the other step. If the needle indicates very high resistance *or* little or no resistance in *both* steps, the diode is probably defective and should be replaced.

6. Replace the diode, if indicated defective.

7. Retape the diode and reconnect the ground wire.

8. Plug the connector into the clutch coil.

Fig. 20-10 A typical programmer.

Fig. 20-12 A typical power module.

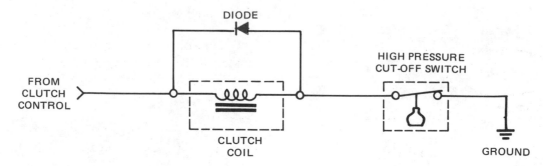

Fig. 20-13 A diode is placed across the clutch coil to reduce *spikes* as the clutch is cycled ON and OFF.

HIGH-SIDE TEMPERATURE SWITCH

The high-side temperature switch is located in the air-conditioning system liquid line between the condenser outlet and the orifice tube inlet, figure 20-14. Though it is a temperature-sensing device, it provides air-conditioner system pressure data to the processor. System temperature is determined by system pressure based on the temperature/pressure relationship of Refrigerant 12.

LOW-SIDE TEMPERATURE SWITCH

The low-side temperature switch is located in the air-conditioning system line between the orifice tube outlet and the evaporator inlet. Refer again to figure 20-14. Its purpose is to sense low-side refrigerant pressure and to provide this information to the processor.

HIGH-PRESSURE SWITCH

The high-pressure switch is normally closed (NC) and opens if air-conditioning system pressure exceeds 425–435 psig (2930–2953 kPa). It recloses when the system pressure drops to below 200 psig (1379 kPa). This switch provides for system safety if, for any reason, pressures exceed safe limits. Unlike the low-pressure switch, the high-pressure switch does not provide data to the processor. This switch is usually in-line with the compressor clutch circuit.

LOW-PRESSURE SWITCH

The low-pressure switch is located in the low side of the air-conditioning system, usually on the accumulator, figure 20-15. This normally closed (NC) switch opens when system low-side pressure drops below 2-8 psig (13.8–55.2 kPa). An open

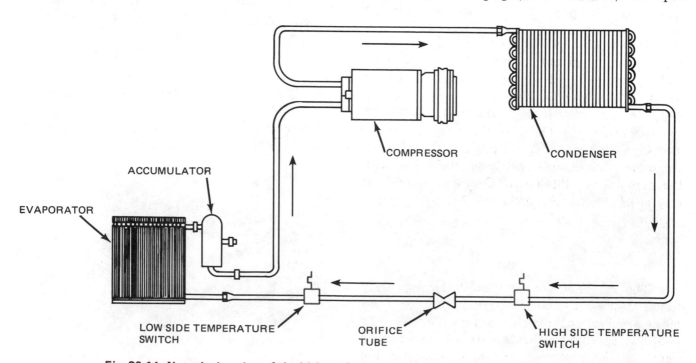

Fig. 20-14 Note the location of the high- and low- side temperature switch in the system.

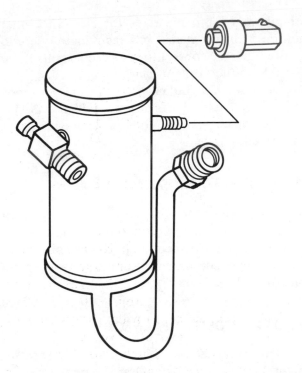

Fig. 20-15 The low-pressure switch is usually located on the accumulator.

low-pressure switch signals the processor to disengage the compressor clutch circuit to prevent compressor operation during low-pressure conditions. Low-pressure conditions may result due to a loss of refrigerant or a clogged orifice tube.

PRESSURE CYCLING SWITCH

The pressure cycling switch is found on some systems. It is used as a means of temperature control by opening and closing the electrical circuit to the compressor clutch coil. On cycling clutch systems, this switch usually opens at a low pressure of 25-26 psig (172.4-179.3 kPa) and closes at a high pressure of 46-48 psig (317.2-331 kPa). On some systems, this switch may be in-line with the compressor clutch coil. On other systems, it may send data to the processor to turn the compressor on and/or off.

SUNLOAD SENSOR

The sunload sensor, figure 20-16, is usually found atop the dashboard, adjacent to one of the radio speaker grilles. The sunload sensor is a photovoltaic diode that sends an appropriate signal to the processor to aid in regulating the in-car temperature.

OUTSIDE TEMPERATURE SENSOR

The outside temperature sensor is usually located just behind the radiator grille and in front of the condenser. Its purpose is to sense outside temperature conditions to provide data to the processor.

This sensor circuit has several programmed memory features to prevent false ambient temperature data input during periods of low-speed driving or when stopped, such as when waiting for a traffic signal.

IN-CAR TEMPERATURE SENSOR

The in-car temperature sensor, also called an in-vehicle sensor, figure 20-17, is located in a tubular device, called an *aspirator*. A small amount of in-car air is drawn through the aspirator across the in-car sensor to provide average in-car temperature data to the processor.

ASPIRATOR

The aspirator is a small duct system which is so designed that it causes a small amount of in-car air to pass through it, figure 20-18. The main airstream causes a low pressure (suction) at the inlet end of the aspirator. This causes in-car air to be drawn into the in-car sensor plenum. The in-car sensor, located in the plenum, is continuously exposed to average in-car air to monitor the in-car air temperature.

COOLANT TEMPERATURE SENSOR

The coolant temperature sensor is a thermistor that provides engine coolant temperature information to the processor. This sensor also provides input information to other on-board

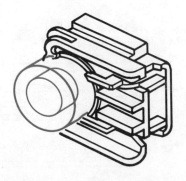

Fig. 20-16 A typical sunload sensor.

computers to provide data for fuel enrichment, ignition timing, exhaust gas recirculate operation, canister purge control, idle speed control, and closed loop fuel control.

A defective coolant temperature sensor will cause poor engine performance, which will probably be evident before poor air-conditioning performance is noticed.

VEHICLE SPEED SENSOR

The vehicle speed sensor is a pulse generator located at the transmission output shaft. It provides actual vehicle speed data to the processor as well as other subsystems, such as the electronic control module.

THROTTLE POSITION SENSOR

The throttle position sensor is actually a potentiometer with a voltage input from the processor. The processor, then, determines throttle position based on the return voltage signal. At the wide-open throttle (WOT) position the compressor clutch is disengaged to provide maximum power for acceleration. This device is often called the WOT sensor and is most often found on diesel engine-equipped vehicles.

Fig. 20-17   A typical in-car temperature sensor

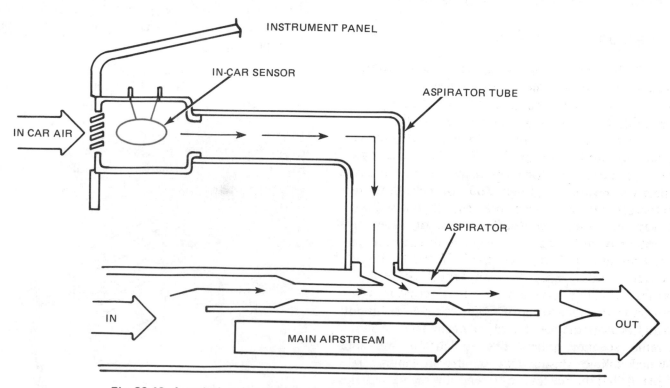

Fig. 20-18   A typical aspirator. Note the location of the in-car temperature sensor.

HEATER TURN-ON SWITCH

The heater turn-on switch is usually a bi-metallic snap-action switch found in the coolant stream of the engine. Its purpose is to prevent blower operation when engine coolant temperature is below 120–122°F (48.9–50°C), if heat is selected.

If cooling is selected, the programmer will override this switch to provide immediate blower operation, regardless of engine coolant temperature.

BRAKE BOOSTER VACUUM SWITCH

The brake booster vacuum switch is found on some cars. It is used to disengage the air-conditioning compressor when braking requires maximum effort. This switch is usually in-line with the compressor clutch electrical circuit and does not provide data to the processor.

POWER STEERING CUTOFF SWITCH

The power steering cutoff switch, found on some cars, is used to disengage the air-conditioning compressor when power steering requires maximum effort. This switch may be in-line with the compressor control relay and may not provide data to the programmer. On other applications, this switch is in the electronic control module which provides feedback data to the processor.

MODE ACTUATOR

Two types of mode actuators are used to position the mode doors: vacuum and electric. Vacuum-operated actuators, often called "pots" or "motors," are covered in Units 18 and 21.

Electric mode actuators, figures 20-19 and 20-20, have both drive and feedback circuitry. This provides the means for them to be stopped at any specified position through 360° of travel. Mode actuators are not reversible, and travel in one direction only. The feedback circuit provides constant data to the control panel relative to the position in which it is stopped. If the feedback circuit is interrupted through faulty or broken wiring or dirty connections, the actuator will continue to run. However, if the correct feedback signal is not received by the control panel within twenty seconds, power to the actuator will be turned off. If this occurs, on many systems an LED will flash on the control panel to warn the operator that there is a problem with the system.

Fig. 20-19 A typical electric mode actuator.

Fig 20-20 An electric mode actuator with cover removed.

Fig. 20-21 A typical electric water valve actuator.

WATER VALVE ACTUATOR

Two types of water valve actuators are available: vacuum and electric. See Unit 21 for vacuum-operated actuators.

The electric water valve actuator, figure 20-21, operates in a manner similar to the mode actuator. It differs only in that it is reversible and only travels 90°. Its purpose is to turn on and off the water valve. The water valve provides water to the heater core which is located in the air conditioning/heating duct system. Duct systems are covered in Unit 23.

SUMMARY

Many of the components of an automatic temperature control system are covered in this unit. Others are covered in Unit 21 and throughout this text. Because of the complexity of the automatic system and its number of variations, it is essential that manufacturers' specifications, manuals, and schematics be consulted for any specific year/model to be serviced.

Review

Select the appropriate answer from the choices given.

1. Technician A says that MOST electronic control circuits may be measured with an analog ohmmeter. Technician B says that ANY electronic control circuit may be measured with a digital ohmmeter.

   a. Technician A is correct.
   b. Technician B is correct.
   c. Both technicians are correct.
   d. Both technicians are wrong.

2. Technician A just checked a certain Ford with a code of "888." He says that this is a "no trouble" code and the customer's complaint is unfounded. Technician B agrees that this is a "no trouble" code and says that the problem may be other than microprocessor functions. Who is correct?

   a. Technician A
   b. Technician B
   c. Both A and B
   d. Both technicians are wrong.

3. Technician A says that the operator can select any temperature between 65°F (47.2°C) and 85°F (56.6°C). Technician B says that the select range is from 60°F (42.2°C) to 90°F (72.2°C).

   a. Technician A is correct.
   b. Technician B is correct.
   c. Both technicians are correct.
   d. Both technicians are wrong.

4. The clutch diode

   a. prevents unwanted "spikes."
   b. assures that 12 volts is supplied to the clutch coil.
   c. prevents reverse polarity.
   d. eliminates the magnetic field.

5. The high-pressure switch

   a. is normally open (NO) and closes at 430 psig (2965 kPa).
   b. is normally open (NO) and closes at 340 psig (2344 kPa).
   c. is normally closed (NC) and opens at 430 psig (2965 kPa).
   d. is normally closed (NC) and opens at 340 psig (2344 kPa).

UNIT 21:

Control Devices

Control devices to provide for an automatic or semiautomatic function are actuated directly or indirectly by lever, cable, or pressure (vacuum). Many controls also are actuated electrically. Often a combination control is used, such as a lever (dash) and electrical switch (on the device) with a cable linkage between the lever and the switch. In today's modern automobile, control devices are used to actuate door locks, deck lids, headlamp covers, windows, seats, antennas, and so on. In this text, however, the concern is only for those devices used to control air-conditioning and heating system functions.

HEATER CONTROL

The heater control valve may be located on the engine, on the fender well, near the heater core, or inside the heater case. In some systems, the control is actuated by a cable. However, for the automatic temperature system, the control is vacuum actuated. The operation of the control is governed by varying vacuum levels. A typical vacuum-operated hot water heater control valve is shown in figure 21-1. A typical cable-controlled water valve is shown in figure 21-2.

The cutaway view, in figure 21-3A, of a vacuum-operated water valve shows that when no vacuum is applied, the control valve is closed.

Fig. 21-1 Water valve

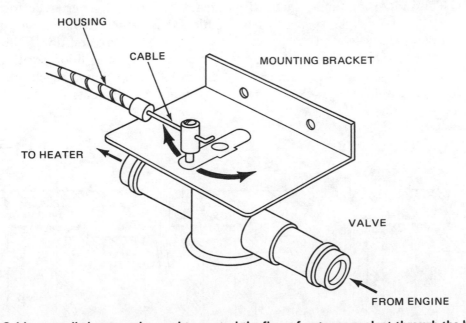

Fig. 21-2 Cable-controlled water valve used to control the flow of water or coolant through the heater core

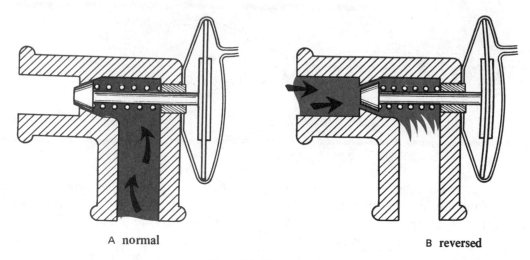

A normal   B reversed

Fig. 21-3 Water valve

The combined water pressure and spring pressure help to keep the valve in the closed position. Most valves have some provision to prevent them from being installed backwards. On some installations, however, accidental reversing of the hoses can occur. Figure 21-3B shows the effect that reversing the hoses has on the water circulation.

If it is assumed that no vacuum is applied to the control valve in figure 21-3B, then the pressure of the water affects the spring pressure and causes the valve to open. As a result, hot water is allowed to flow in the heater core. Actually, a pulsating effect is more likely to occur at automobile speeds in excess of 50 mph (80.5 km/h) (when water pressure is high). This condition has a marked effect on the operation of the temperature control.

In normal operation, the valve can be opened by varying degrees to control the water flow. Figure 21-4 shows the valve positions for no vacuum (A), a partial vacuum (B), and a full vacuum (C).

Since one of the primary functions of an automatic temperature control system is to provide for an in-car relative humidity of 45–50 percent, the hot-water valve is often opened slightly (cracked) to allow a small amount of engine coolant to enter the system. The heated air from the hot coolant will provide a great deal of humidity. Thus, this hot air is mixed with the cooler air from the passenger compartment, and through the air conditioner evaporator, to maintain the desired humidity level.

MODE DOORS

Vacuum-operated mode doors include the temperature deflector, diverter, defroster, outside-inside inlet, and heater/air-conditioner outlet doors.

For various conditions, there are a number of combinations of door positions. For example, in the air-conditioning cycle alone there are six different arrangements for the mode doors. There

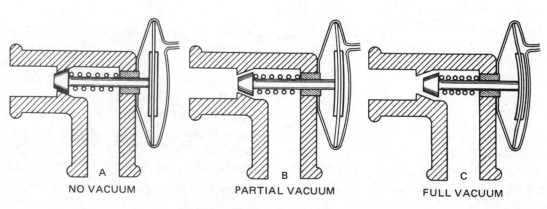

A   B   C
NO VACUUM   PARTIAL VACUUM   FULL VACUUM

Fig. 21-4 Water valve flow control

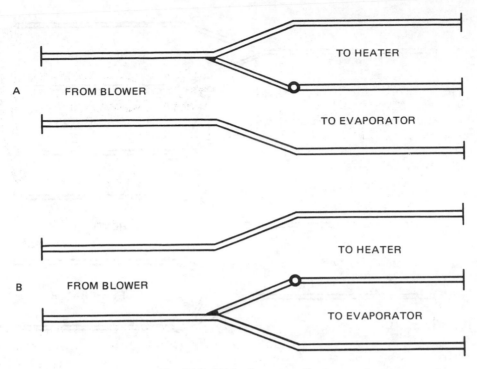

A   FROM BLOWER   TO HEATER   TO EVAPORATOR

B   FROM BLOWER   TO HEATER   TO EVAPORATOR

Fig. 21-5 Mode door operation

is a different arrangement for the normal and de-fog settings for each of three operating conditions: full outside, full recirculate, and modulated air conditioning.

Mode doors are used to divert the movement of air from one passage to another, as shown in figure 21-5. In figure 21-5A, the air is deflected into the air-conditioner core. In figure 21-5B, the air is diverted into the heater core.

Temperature Door

As indicated in the section on "Mode Doors," the temperature door regulates the air mixture. The position of the temperature mode door determines the temperature of the duct air in an automatic temperature control system. The temperature door is regulated by a vacuum motor, a temperature door actuator, or a servo.

VACUUM MOTORS

To bring about a change in conditions, the mode doors must be operated either manually or remotely. A cable is often used to control the door. However, for automatic temperature controls, a device known as a vacuum motor is used. This device is not a motor in the usual sense. It is a

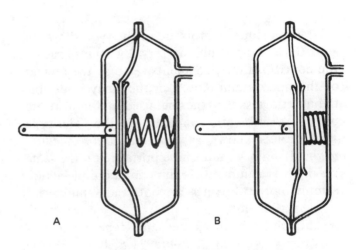

A   B

Fig. 21-6 Vacuum motor or pot

motor in the sense that it imparts motion. The vacuum motor is also known as a vacuum *pot*.

Figure 21-6 shows how a vacuum motor is used to operate the mode doors. In figure 21-6A the device is shown in the relaxed position. In figure 21-6B, it is in the applied position.

In the relaxed position, the spring keeps the arm extended. In the applied position, the vacuum overcomes the spring pressure and the arm is pulled to the IN position. The normal, or OFF, position of the vacuum motor is the relaxed position, figure 21-6A.

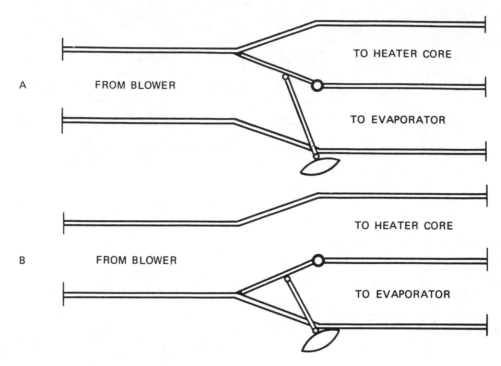

Fig. 21-7 Air diverter door with vacuum motor

Most vacuum motors are of the type shown in figure 21-6. Some units have two vacuum hose attachments. These attachments serve as tee fittings for another vacuum motor, or they may be double action fittings, such as the ones used for temperature control on automatic temperature units. This type of control is known as a *double-action vacuum motor*. If both vacuum hose ports are on the same side of the vacuum motor, it is not a double-action vacuum motor. Fittings on both sides indicate a double-action motor.

Figure 21-7 shows the same type of duct arrangements as given in figure 21-5, but with the addition of vacuum motors.

Air-conditioner and heater system duct systems with various mode door positions are covered in detail in Unit 23.

Double-Action Vacuum Motors

This type of vacuum motor, figure 21-8, has a double-action diaphragm which allows a vacuum to be applied to either side. The vacuum causes the control arm attached to the rubber diaphragm to be extended.

Some automatic temperature control units use a double-action vacuum motor which is known as a *temperature door actuator*, or TDA.

Fig. 21-8 Double-action vacuum motor

BLOWER CONTROL

The blower control permits the driver to select a high or low volume of airflow. Although the airflow setting results in less air noise, it is less likely to maintain comfort conditions within the passenger area of the vehicle. The high airflow setting is preferred for maximum benefit. In either range, however, the airflow varies automatically with the demand placed on the system by varying weather conditions. The high blower speed is obtained only when the servo is in the maximum air-conditioning position. This part of the operation of the system is electrically controlled, not vacuum controlled. The vacuum-controlled servo has electrical contacts (which complete various circuits) as does the vacuum switch section of the servo.

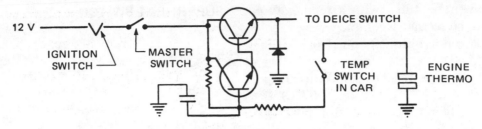

Fig. 21-9 Time-delay relay schematic

TIME-DELAY RELAY

The time-delay control unit is designed to prevent the heat cycle from coming on in the automatic unit until the engine coolant has reached a temperature of 110°F (43.34°C). The unit consists of two resistors, capacitors, and transistors. Figure 21-9 shows the time-delay circuit of the wiring diagram.

ELECTROVACUUM RELAY

The *electrovacuum relay* (EVR) contains a normally closed (NC) vacuum solenoid valve and a normally closed (NC) electrical relay. The purpose of the EVR is to prevent blower operation when the system is in the "heat" mode until engine coolant temperature reaches 115–120°F (46.1–48.8°C). When the coolant temperature is below this value, electrical contacts in the *engine temperature (sending) switch* (ETS) are closed. This grounds and completes the EVR circuit to open the ETR relay contacts. The ETR relay contacts, in series with the blower motor, interrupt current to the motor to open this circuit.

AMBIENT SWITCH

The *ambient switch,* figure 21-10, is an electrical switch actuated by changing ambient temperature. The ambient switch is used in many custom and automatic systems. (The student should not confuse the ambient switch with the ambient sensor.)

The ambient switch is located outside the engine area where it can sense the ambient temperature only. The actual switch location depends on its design. The switch is never mounted where it is possible to sense the engine heat.

If the master switch is pressed, the ambient switch will turn the air-conditioning compressor ON at 35°F (1.67°C). The switch turns the com-

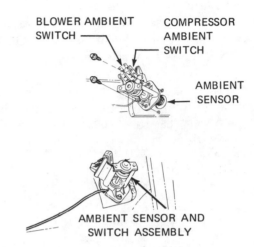

Fig. 21-10 Ambient sensor and switch assembly

pressor OFF if the ambient temperature falls to 25°F (–3.89°C).

Whenever the ambient temperature is in the range 64°F (17.78°C) and 55°F (12.78°C), the ambient switch bypasses the master control and the time-delay relay and allows the blowers to run regardless of the engine coolant temperature.

When the air-conditioning compressor or blower is operated at low ambient temperatures, the humidity of the incoming air is reduced by condensing the moisture from it. In this way, window fogging is prevented when an automobile is being operated during rainy, damp, or cool weather conditions.

THERMOSTATIC VACUUM VALVE

The thermostatic vacuum valve (TVV), figure 21-11, is a vacuum-control valve which is sensitive to temperature. The TVV is used only on late model automatic systems and is mounted where it can sense coolant temperature, such as on the side of the heater core. The TVV consists of a power element cylinder with a piston, vacuum parts, and spring.

The power element is filled with a temperature-sensitive compound so that when the engine is cold and the coolant is not warm, the inlet part of the TVV is blocked and the outlet part is vented. When the coolant temperature reaches a specified range, usually 100°F to 125°F (37.78°C to 51.67°C), the compound in the cylinder expands and moves the piston until vacuum flow starts.

In the automatic temperature control system, the vacuum flow proceeds from the selector vacuum disc switch to the program vacuum disc switch, the master switch, the vacuum diaphragm, and the outside-recirculate air-cooled diaphragm. On cold days, the TVV serves only as a time delay.

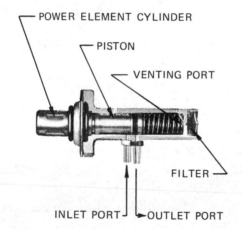

Fig. 21-11 Thermostatic vacuum valve (TVV)

SUPERHEAT SWITCH

The superheat switch is located in the rear head of some six-cylinder compressors. This device is a temperature/pressure-sensitive electrical switch which is normally in the open position, figure 21-12. The switch remains open during system high-temperature and high-pressure conditions or low-temperature and low-pressure conditions. The switch closes when the system experiences high-temperature and low-pressure conditions.

The high-temperature and low-pressure condition of the system is usually caused by a loss of refrigerant. This loss may result in compressor or system damage if the air-conditioning system remains in operation.

The superheat switch offers a failsafe method of stopping the compressor until the problem is corrected. When the superheat switch closes, a circuit is completed through a heater of the thermal fuse. The fuse blows, opens the clutch circuit, and stops the compressor.

The superheat switch was replaced in 1978 with a switch which is pressure-actuated only. The difference in appearance is that the late-model switch does not have the thermal sensing tube. It is important to note that the two switches are not interchangeable. Using the wrong switch can result in reduced voltage to the clutch, causing erratic clutch and compressor operation. This condition can lead to a loss of compressor oil and result in a seized (ruined) compressor.

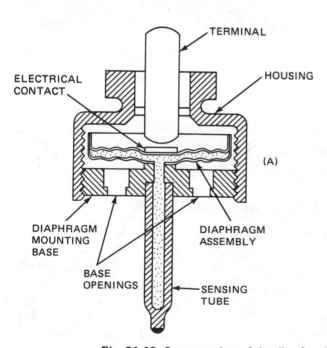

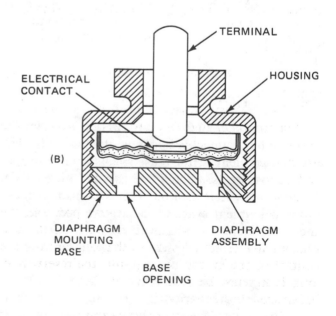

Fig. 21-12 Cutaway view of details of early model (A) and late model (B) superheat switch

THERMAL FUSE

The thermal fuse protects the compressor in the event of a refrigerant loss. As described previously, the fuse works with the superheat switch. The thermal fuse consists of a temperature-sensitive fuse and a wire-wound resistor (heater) mounted as one assembly, figure 21-13.

When the superheat switch closes, a ground is created in the clutch circuit. The same current that is supplied to the compressor now feeds through the thermal fuse heater to ground. As the heater warms, the fuse link reaches its melting point. The melting of the link causes the clutch circuit to open and the clutch action stops.

Because of the time required to provide sufficient heat to melt the fuse link, the link is not affected during short-term high-temperature and low-pressure conditions. In some circumstances, these conditions exist without affecting the operation of the system.

CHECK VALVES AND RELAYS

Vacuum systems normally have a vacuum check valve or check relay to prevent a vacuum loss during those periods when the engine manifold vacuum is less than the value required to operate a vacuum-actuated component.

In addition, most vacuum systems contain a vacuum reserve tank (which often resembles a large fruit juice can), figure 21-14. The check valve or check relay is usually located in the vacuum line between the reserve tank and the vacuum source.

Check Valve

The check valve, figure 21-15, is opened whenever the manifold vacuum is greater than the reserve vacuum. In other words, the check valve is opened by the normal engine vacuum. In this position, the check valve connects the source to the tank. The normal engine vacuum also opens the diaphragm and allows vacuum from the control to reach the vacuum motor. Whenever the manifold vacuum drops below the value of the reserve pressure, the check valve closes. When the valve closes, the diaphragm also closes and blocks the passage from the control to the motor. As a result, the reserve vacuum is not lost because it is not allowed to bleed back through the manifold.

The manifold vacuum drops during periods of acceleration and when the engine is stopped. The vacuum reserve is used both to operate the air-

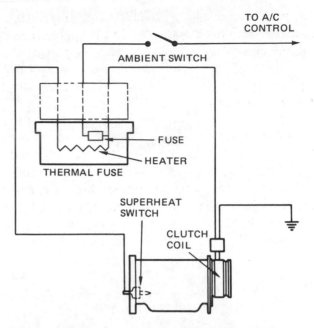

Fig. 21-13 Schematic of thermal fuse in the clutch circuit

Fig. 21-14 Vacuum reserve tanks resemble fruit juice cans

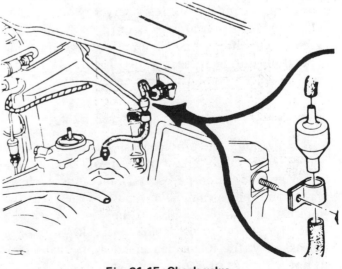

Fig. 21-15 Check valve

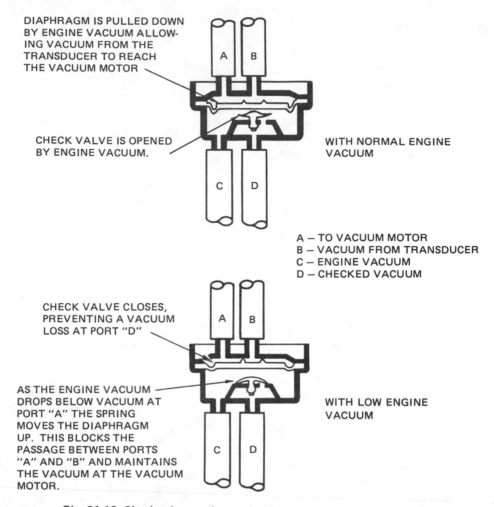

DIAPHRAGM IS PULLED DOWN
BY ENGINE VACUUM ALLOW-
ING VACUUM FROM THE
TRANSDUCER TO REACH
THE VACUUM MOTOR

CHECK VALVE IS OPENED
BY ENGINE VACUUM.

WITH NORMAL ENGINE
VACUUM

A – TO VACUUM MOTOR
B – VACUUM FROM TRANSDUCER
C – ENGINE VACUUM
D – CHECKED VACUUM

CHECK VALVE CLOSES,
PREVENTING A VACUUM
LOSS AT PORT "D"

AS THE ENGINE VACUUM
DROPS BELOW VACUUM AT
PORT "A" THE SPRING
MOVES THE DIAPHRAGM
UP. THIS BLOCKS THE
PASSAGE BETWEEN PORTS
"A" AND "B" AND MAINTAINS
THE VACUUM AT THE VACUUM
MOTOR.

WITH LOW ENGINE
VACUUM

Fig. 21-16 Check relay used to maintain vacuum at the vacuum motor

conditioning system vacuum components and other accessory equipment in the automobile, such as headlamp doors and door locks.

Check Relay

The vacuum check relay serves two purposes: (1) it prevents a vacuum loss during low manifold vacuum conditions, and (2) it prevents system mode operation during these periods. Figure 21-16 is a typical schematic of a vacuum check relay.

Servicing of Check Valves and Check Relays

In general, the problems associated with check valves and check relays consist of leaking diaphragms and improper seats. Since these check valves and relays cannot be repaired, they must be replaced as a unit assembly if they are found to be defective. Prior to replacing a check valve or a check relay, the technician must insure that a leak is not the result of a split or broken hose.

THERMOSTATIC VACUUM SWITCH

The *thermostatic vacuum switch* (TVS), figure 21-17, is not actually a part of the air-conditioner vacuum system. Its function and operation, however, is important to the air-conditioning technician. Its purpose is to help avoid engine overheating during prolonged idle periods at high ambient temperature when the air conditioner is operating. Actually, its operation is the same when the engine overheats even if the air conditioner is not operating. Without going into detail on theory about engine operation, the function of the TVS is to control vacuum advance of the distributor. This, in turn, relates to the advance of engine timing.

The TVS, located in the coolant passage of the thermostat housing, includes three vacuum hoses; one connects to the carburetor, one to the intake manifold, and one to the distributor advance mechanism, figure 21-18. Normal distributor vacuum provisions are off the carburetor throttle plate. The amount of vacuum applied to the advance

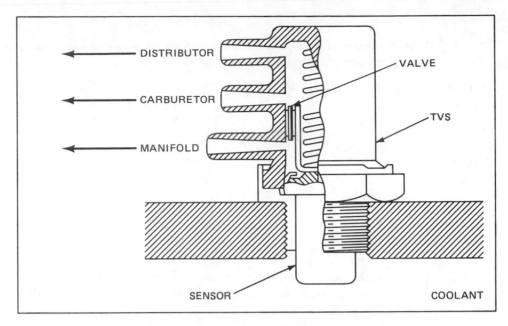

Fig. 21-17 Details of thermostatic vacuum switch (TVS)

from this source is proportional to engine speed. At curb idle speed there is little (or no) vacuum signal applied; thus, there is little (or no) vacuum advance.

At the same time, however, a greater vacuum source is available at the intake manifold. Should the engine coolant temperature exceed safe limits, usually about 225°F (107.2°), the thermal sensor of the TVS will shift the vacuum valve. This condition will provide full manifold vacuum to the distributor vacuum advance mechanism. This, in turn, advances engine timing and increases engine speed. At an increased speed, a greater volume of coolant will flow through the cooling system. Airflow through the radiator will also be increased. Greater coolant flow and increased airflow will result in a lower engine operating temperature. When the coolant temperature falls below the critical point, the vacuum valve will shift to its normal position. The engine speed will then return to normal idle conditions.

Knowledge of this often ignored and misunderstood device is important to the tune-up technician as well as to the air-conditioning technician. The primary reason for TVS failure is due to a binding or sticking of the vacuum valve. If stuck in the manifold to distributor position, the engine cannot

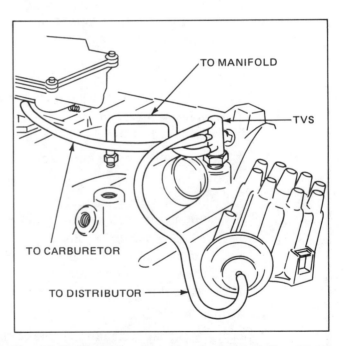

Fig. 21-18 Pictorial schematic of thermostatic vacuum switch (TVS) circuit

be tuned properly. If stuck in the carburetor to distributor position, overheating will occur, under certain conditions, with prolonged idle. A defective TVS must be replaced, since it is not repairable.

Review

Select the appropriate answer from the choices given.

1. What is most likely to happen if the heater control valve is installed backwards?
   a. The heater will not work.
   b. The heater will not turn on.
   c. The heater will not turn off.
   d. The valve will pulsate.

2. How is the operation of the POASTV controlled?
   a. By cable
   b. By vacuum
   c. By cable or vacuum, depending on application
   d. Automatically, by system pressure

3. What is the purpose of the thermostatic vacuum switch (TVS)?
   a. To prevent heater operation until the engine coolant has warmed up
   b. To prevent air-conditioner operation under low ambient conditions
   c. To shift carburetor to manifold vacuum when engine becomes overheated
   d. None of these answers is correct

4. Technician A says that in-car humidity is controlled by tempering cooled air with heated air from the heater core. Technician B says that in-car humidity is not important as long as the proper temperature is maintained.
   a. Technician A is correct.
   b. Technician B is correct.
   c. Both technicians are correct.
   d. Both technicians are wrong.

5. Technician A says that air-conditioning control devices are actuated by a lever and cable. Technician B says that they are actuated by a vacuum.
   a. Technician A is correct.
   b. Technician B is correct.
   c. Both technicians are correct.
   d. Both technicians are wrong.

6. A vacuum motor is also known as a vacuum
   a. pot.
   b. door.
   c. chamber.
   d. sensor.

7. A vacuum motor with vacuum fittings on both sides (two fittings) is known as
   a. a dual-range vacuum motor.
   b. a double-action vacuum motor.
   c. a universal vacuum motor.
   d. a heat/cool temperature door vacuum motor.

8. A time-delay relay
   a. prevents heat cycle until engine coolant reaches a predetermined temperature.
   b. prevents cool cycle until engine coolant reaches a predetermined temperature.
   c. delays program advance in automatic systems.
   d. delays "turn on" of systems until engine speed is adequate.

9. A thermal fuse is blown by action of the
   a. thermostatic vacuum valve (TVV).
   b. thermostatic vacuum relay (TVR).
   c. check relay.
   d. superheat switch.

10. Mode doors are used to
    a. provide heat to the passenger compartment.
    b. provide cool to the passenger compartment.
    c. provide a blend of heat/cool air to the passenger compartment.
    d. All are correct answers.

UNIT 22:

Engine Cooling System and Heater Circuits

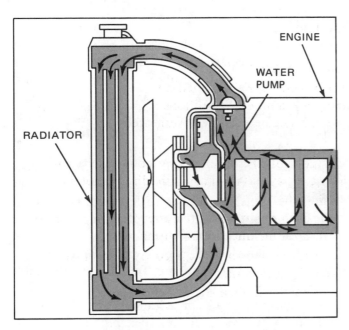

Fig. 22-1 Typical engine cooling system

Excessive automotive engine heat, a product of combustion, is transferred to and dissipated in the radiator. This is accomplished by two heat transfer principles known as *conduction* and *convection* (covered in Unit 5). The cooling system, when operating properly, maintains an operational design temperature for the engine and automatic transmission.

The cooling system functions by circulating a liquid coolant through the engine and the radiator, figure 22-1. Engine heat is picked up by the coolant by conduction, and is given up to the less hot outside air in the radiator by convection. Unlike air-conditioning systems, however, the coolant in the cooling system does not change in state during this process. It remains a liquid throughout the cooling system.

The semiclosed cooling system, figure 22-2, consists of four main parts: *radiator, water pump, pressure (radiator) cap,* and *thermostat.* Other essential parts include *water-pump pulley* and *belt(s),*

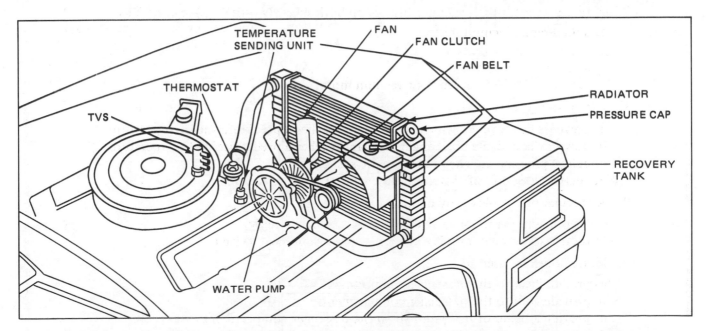

Fig. 22-2 Components of semiclosed cooling system. The heater core, control valve, and hoses are not shown.

fan, hoses, hose clamps, and engine water passages. Most late-model cars include a *thermostatic vacuum switch* (TVS, covered in Unit 21), and a *coolant recovery tank* with associated hoses. All cars also include a temperature *sending switch* and *dash gauge* or *lamps* (covered in Unit 17).

Actually, the cooling system is responsible for removing only about 35 percent of the total engine heat. With exhaust valve temperature as high as 4 500°F (2 482°C), the remaining unwanted heat is dissipated by the engine walls, heads, and pistons. A large percentage of heat also passes with exhaust gases through the exhaust system to the atmosphere.

RADIATORS

Radiators are constructed of either of two types of material: copper or aluminum. The re-

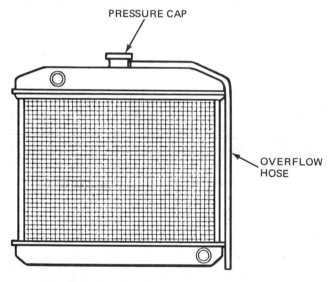

Fig. 22-3 Details of typical downflow radiator

ceiver and collector tanks of some late model radiators are constructed of a special high-temperature plastic. These tanks are held in place with clips onto the headers. A special gasket prevents leakage. Two basic styles of radiators are currently used: *downflow* and *crossflow.* In the downflow style, figure 22-3, coolant flow is from the top tank to the bottom tank. In the crossflow style, figure 22-4, flow is from one side to the other.

In this text, the first tank will be referred to as the *collector,* because it collects coolant from the engine. The second tank will be referred to as the *receiver* because it receives coolant after passing through the many tubes of the radiator *core.*

The collector usually contains a baffle plate to aid in even distribution of coolant through the core. The receiver, on automatic transmission equipped cars, contains a *transmission oil cooler,* figure 22-5. Some cars with a trailer-towing package have an external transmission cooler. In either case, the transmission cooler has little to do with the engine cooling system, except for adding a minor heat load to the coolant. Occasionally, the internal cooler develops a leak, which would be noticed by the presence of transmission fluid (oil) in the coolant and/or coolant in the transmission.

Two types of cores are used in automotive radiators: *cellular,* often called *honeycomb,* and *tubular.* The cellular core is fabricated by a process of soldering together thin, preformed sheets of metal, usually brass or copper, figure 22-6. The tubular core, figure 22-7, is constructed of small round or narrow oblong tubes that are soldered to *headers* of the collector and receiver.

Radiator cores are very fragile. The tube walls of the core are only a few thousandths of an

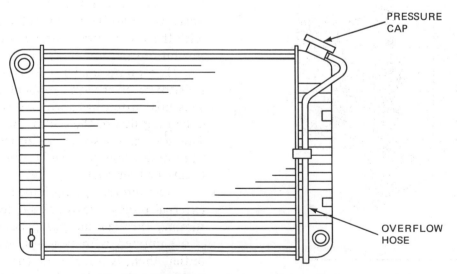

Fig. 22-4 Details of typical crossflow radiator

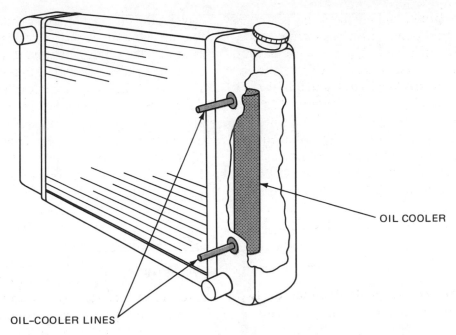

OIL COOLER

OIL-COOLER LINES

Fig. 22-5 Location of transmission oil cooler in radiator tank. Some heavy-duty package systems also have an external oil cooler.

Fig. 22-6 Typical cellular core radiator details

inch (millimeter) thick. Care must be taken when handling radiators to avoid costly damage.

Radiators develop leaks and/or become clogged. Whenever these situations occur, the radiators must be repaired. Repairs should be made only by those with the proper equipment and experience to do so.

WATER PUMP

A centrifugal-type water pump, figure 22-8, driven by a belt off the engine crankshaft, is used to pump coolant through the cooling system. At road speed, coolant may be circulated at a rate as great as 160–170 gallons (605–643 L) per minute with the water pump turning as fast as 4 500–5 000 revolutions per minute (r/min).

The pump inlet is connected to a *neck* on the radiator receiver with a rubber hose and two clamps. This hose often has a wire insert to prevent it from collapsing due to the suction of the pump impeller. The hose may also be preformed to fit a particular year-model engine, given in cubic-inch displacement (CID), or liters (L).

The internal pump impeller is attached to the external pulley provisions by means of a steel shaft running through the pump housing. This shaft is also equipped with bearings and seals. The pump outlet, then, is direct from the back side of the impeller into the engine block coolant passages.

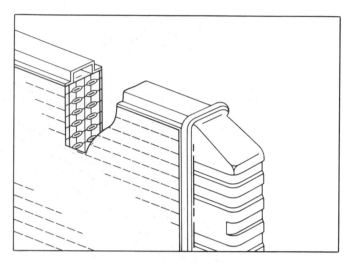

Fig. 22-7 Typical tubular core radiator details

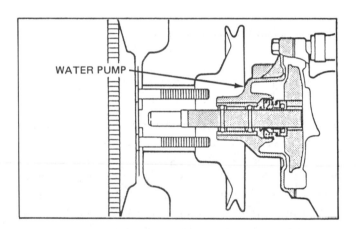

Fig. 22-8 Details of water (coolant) pump

The most common cause of water pump failure is due to leaks and/or worn bearings. Although kits are available for making repairs, it is generally advisable to replace defective pumps with new or factory-rebuilt units.

PRESSURE CAP

As is known, water boils at 212°F (100°C) at sea level atmospheric pressure. The boiling point of water, or any other coolant, is raised by increasing its pressure, figure 22-9. (See also Unit 6.) The boiling point is further increased if mixed with an ethylene glycol-type antifreeze (covered later in this unit).

Radiator pressure caps, figure 22-10, rated from 8 psi (55.1 kPa) to 17 psi (117.2 kPa) are used to increase the boiling point of cooling systems in order to maintain desired engine operating temperatures. Radiator caps are equipped with a pressure valve and a vacuum valve, figure 22-11. At the predetermined pressure rating of the cap, the pressure valve opens, under certain conditions, to expel excess coolant vapor and pressure to the atmosphere. This action prevents above-maximum cooling system pressure buildup.

When the engine is stopped for any length of time the cooling system will go from a positive to a negative pressure (vacuum). As this occurs, the vacuum valve will open to admit enough ambient air to raise cooling system pressure to atmospheric pressure.

A defective pressure valve may cause one of the cooling system components, such as a hose or radiator tank, to rupture due to excessive pressure buildup. A defective vacuum valve will result in below-atmospheric pressure in the cooling system (when cool) and may be noted by a collapse of the upper radiator hose.

Devices are available for testing radiator caps, following the procedures outlined in Section 3. As a rule of thumb, a pressure cap should be replaced with one of equal pressure rating when preventive maintenance is performed. It is important to note that a special aluminum cap is required on all aluminum radiators.

The effects of boiling points in relation to pressure are covered in Unit 6. The effects of boiling points with antifreeze-type solution and operation of pressure caps in a recovery system are covered later in this unit.

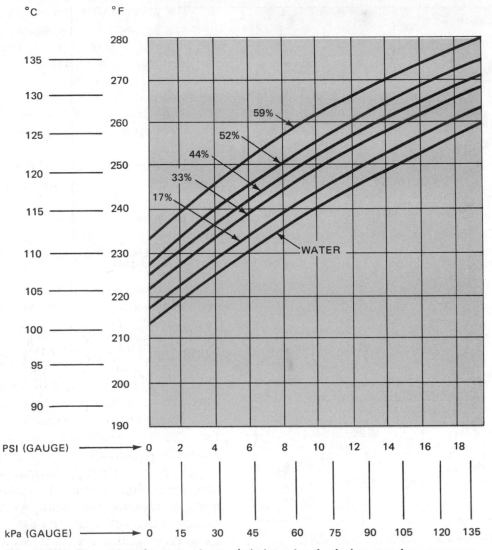

Fig. 22-9 Boiling point of water and water/ethylene glycol solution at various pressures

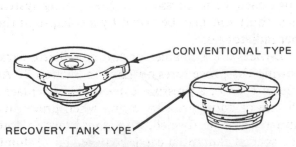

Fig. 22-10 Radiator pressure cap types

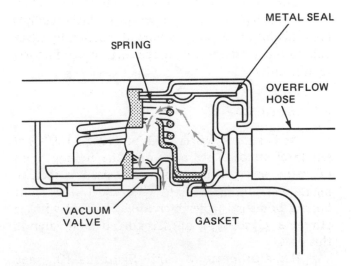

Fig. 22-11 Action of pressure cap while coolant is cooling (contracting)

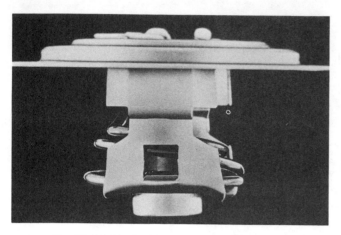

Fig. 22-12 Typical engine coolant thermostat

THERMOSTATS

The thermostat, figure 22-12, is located at the outlet of the engine coolant passage, usually under the return hose flange or *thermostat housing*. Engine coolant temperature, sensed by a sensing element, causes the normally closed (NC) thermostat to open at a predetermined temperature from 140°F (60°C) to 180°F (82.2°C).

Typically, a thermostat rated at 170°F (76.6°C) will start to open at its rated temperature and will be fully open at 195°F (90.5°C). A thermostat's opening and closing, figure 22-13, is gradual as the temperature of the coolant increases or decreases.

Two important facts regarding thermostats should be noted:

1. Thermostats are a design component of the engine cooling system and should not be omitted.
2. A thermostat will not affect maximum engine temperature, unless it is defective.

The purpose of a thermostat is to insure *minimum* engine operating temperature. This is particularly important if the car is often driven only for short distances. For example, if a thermostat rated at 180°F (82.2°C) is used, coolant will not circulate through the radiator until the coolant in the engine has reached this design temperature. The purpose of a thermostat, then, is to protect against engine *overcooling*.

A thermostat, unless defective, will not cause overheating. A thermostat rated at 180°F (82.2°C) is wide open at 205°F (96.1°C) and full coolant flow is provided through the cooling system. A thermostat rated at 160°F (71.1°C), wide open at 185°F (85°C), would provide no more or no less coolant flow.

Thermostats do fail, however. If failure occurs while in the closed position severe engine overheating will result. This may be noted by an extremely hot engine and a cool-to-warm radiator. If failure occurs while in the open position, a longer-than-normal warmup period may be noted by the "cold" dash lamp or temperature gauge.

PULLEY AND BELT

Two types of belt systems are now used to drive the air-conditioning compressor and other accessories: the *V* belt and the *serpentine* belt, also referred to as the V-groove belt. The V-belt system, shown in figure 22-14A, may have two or more belts driving the engine accessories. Figure 22-14B illustrates the serpentine belt. This is a single-belt system whereby one belt drives all of the accessories.

The pitch and width of belts in the V-belt system are important in that they must match

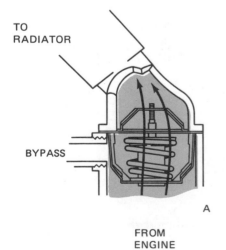

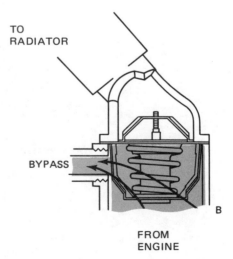

Fig. 22-13 Thermostat in (A) open position and (B) closed position

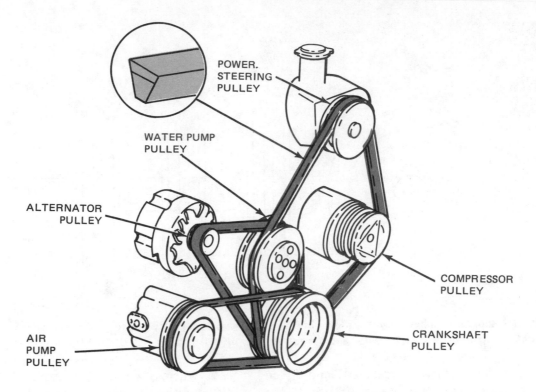

Fig. 22-14A Typical V-belt/pulley arrangement.

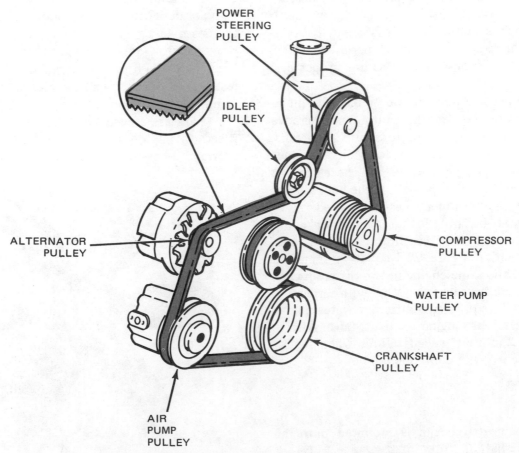

Fig. 22-14B Typical serpentine belt/pulley arrangement.

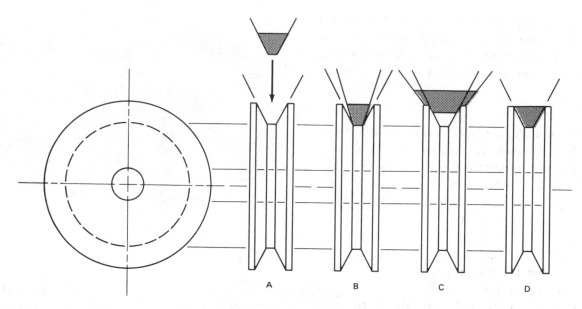

Fig. 22-15 Belt should fit pulley snugly as shown in A and D. The belt in pulley B is too narrow and has an improper pitch. The belt pulley C (exaggerated) is too wide and has an improper pitch.

those of the drive (engine crankshaft) and driven (engine accessories) pulleys, figure 22-15. If the compressor and/or alternator are driven with two belts, they should be replaced as a pair with a factory-matched set. This is true even though only one of the pair appears to be damaged. V-belts are tensioned in ft-lb (N·m), according to manufacturers' specifications. It is generally necessary to recheck after a "run-in" period of a few hundred miles (kilometers) to assure proper belt tensioning.

The serpentine belt must be replaced with an exact duplicate. Its length, width, and v-groove characteristics are important to assure proper fit. This system has a spring-loaded belt tensioner (idler pulley). It is therefore not necessary to manually tension this type belt. If the belt will not remain tight, the tensioner must be replaced.

It should be noted that the water pump pulley in figure 22-14A turns in the opposite direction from that in figure 22-14B. It is therefore possible that the same engine in two different cars, one with V-belt drive and the other with serpentine belt drive, will require two different water pumps and two different engine coolant fans. Always follow manufacturers' specifications when replacing these or any other components.

FAN

The engine-driven fan is mounted onto the water pump shaft in front of the pulley. Five- or six-blade fans are usually found on air-conditioned cars, whereas a four-blade fan is standard on non-air-conditioned cars. A six-blade fan is shown in figure 22-16. Fans may be made of steel, nylon, or fiberglass, and are precisely balanced to prevent water pump bearing and/or seal damage.

It should be noted that some engine-driven fans are designed to turn clockwise (cw), and some are designed to turn counterclockwise (ccw). For proper airflow, it is important that the replacement fan be suitable for the design. An improper fan will result in poor (or no) air circulation, and will cause engine overheating or failure.

Fans are especially required for idle- and low-speed driving to pull sufficient air through the radiator and across the engine to effect proper cooling.

Fig. 22-16 Six-blade, heavy-duty engine cooling fan

At road speeds, *ram air* would be sufficient for this purpose. To satisfy the needs for low-speed cooling and to reduce engine load at high speed, a *fan clutch, flexible fan,* or *electric fan* is often used.

FAN CLUTCH

A fan clutch, installed between the water pump pulley and fan, is sensitive to engine speed and underhood temperature. One type fan clutch, figure 22-17, uses a temperature-sensitive silicone fluid in lands and grooves. When the underhood temperature is below about 160°F (71.1°C) the fan clutch allows the fan to turn at water pump speed up to about 800 r/min. When above this temperature, the fan will turn at about the same speed as the water pump up to a maximum of about 2 600 r/min. It will not turn faster than 2 600 r/min regardless of how fast the water pump turns above that speed.

Note that fan clutches are not *omni-directional,* meaning they will not function properly in both directions. A replacement fan clutch, then, must be selected that will meet the requirements of the application, either clockwise (cw) or counterclockwise (ccw) rotation.

A defective fan clutch must be replaced since no provisions are made for repair. Failure is usually due to lockup, as noted by excessive noise, or fluid leak, which is noticeable by a tacky fluid at the clutch bearing area.

FLEXIBLE FANS

Flexible or *flex* fans, figure 22-18, have blades that are made of a material (metal, plastic, nylon,

Fig. 22-17 Typical fan clutch

or fiberglass) that will flex or change pitch based upon engine speed. As engine speed increases, the fan blade pitch decreases. The extreme pitch, at slower engine speeds, figure 22-19, provides maximum airflow to cool the engine and coolant.

At higher engine speeds the car is moving faster, and the need for fan-forced air is reduced. Engine and coolant air is provided by ram air produced by the forward motion of the car. The flex blades feather, reducing pitch, figure 22-20, which, in turn, saves engine power and reduces the noise level.

ELECTRIC FAN

In many late-model applications, to save power and reduce noise level, the conventional belt-driven, water-pump-mounted engine coolant fan has been replaced with an electrically driven fan, figure 22-21. This fan and motor are mounted to the radiator

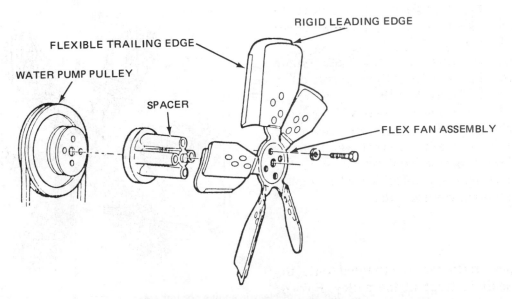

RIGID LEADING EDGE

FLEXIBLE TRAILING EDGE

WATER PUMP PULLEY

SPACER

FLEX FAN ASSEMBLY

Fig 22-18 Flexible fan details

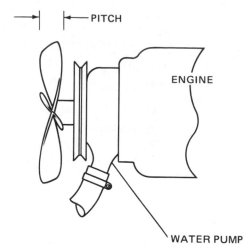

Fig. 22-19 Flex fan; extreme pitch at low speed

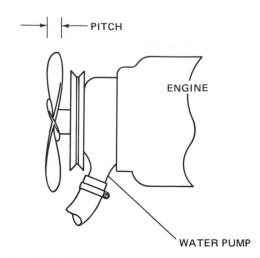

Fig. 22-20 Flex fan; reduced pitch at high speed

shroud, and are not connected mechanically or physically to the engine coolant (water) pump. The 12-volt, motor-driven fan is electrically controlled by either, or both, of two methods: an engine coolant temperature switch (thermostat) and/or the air conditioner select switch.

Following the schematic of figure 22-22, the cooling fan motor is connected to the 12-volt battery supply through a normally open (NO) set of contacts (points) in the cooling fan relay. Protection for this circuit is provided by a fusible link (F/L). During normal operation, with the air con-

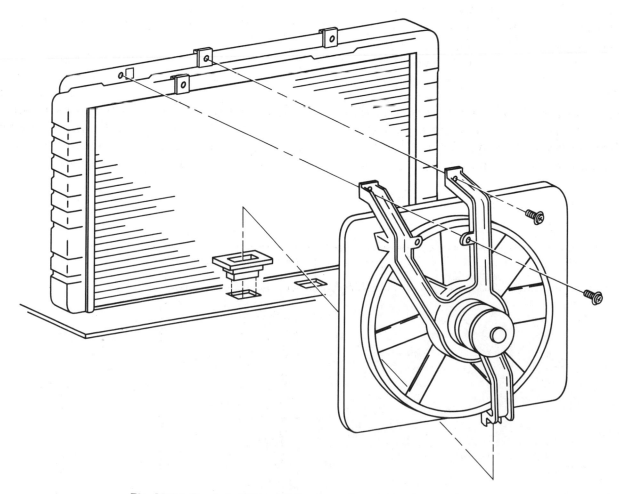

Fig. 22-21 Exploded view of electric engine cooling fan assembly

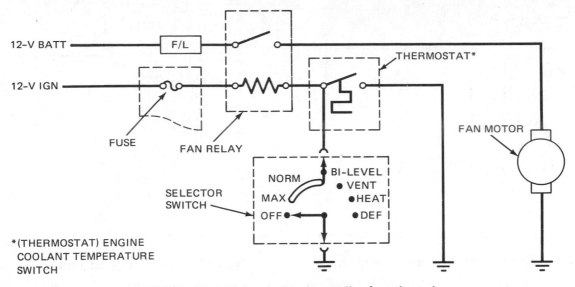

Fig. 22-22 Typical electrical engine cooling fan schematic

ditioner off and the engine coolant below a prede-termined temperature of approximately 215°F (102°C), the relay contacts are open and the fan motor does not operate.

Should the engine coolant temperature exceed approximately 230°F (110°C), the engine coolant temperature switch will close (figure 22-23) to energize the fan relay coil which, in turn, will close the relay contacts — assuming that the ignition switch is in the *run* position.

The 12-volt supply for the relay coil circuit is independent of the 12-volt supply for the fan motor circuit. The coil circuit is from the *run* terminal of the ignition switch, through a fuse in the fuse panel, and to ground through the relay coil and thermostat.

Should the air-conditioner select switch be turned to any *cool* position, figure 22-24, regardless of engine temperature, a circuit will be completed through the relay coil to ground through the select switch. This action will close the relay contacts to provide 12 volts to the fan motor. The fan will then operate as long as the air conditioner and ignition switches are *on*.

There are many variations of electric cooling fan operation. Some provide a *cool-down* period whereby the fan continues to operate after the engine has been stopped and the ignition switch is turned off. The fan stops only when the engine coolant falls to a predetermined safe temperature, usually about 210°F (99°C).

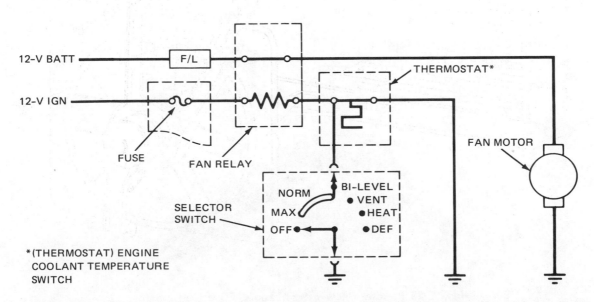

Fig. 22-23 When the thermostat is closed the relay will be energized, completing the circuit to the fan motor

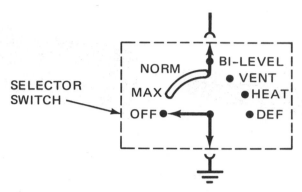

Fig. 22-24 Placing the selector switch in any *cool* position completes the fan relay coil circuit which, in turn, completes the fan motor circuit.

In some systems, the fan does not start when the air-conditioner select switch is turned on unless the system high side is above a predetermined high pressure. The fan does not run if the high side is below a predetermined pressure unless the engine coolant is above a predetermined safe temperature.

CAUTION: Some fans motors will start, and run, without warning even though the ignition switch may be in the OFF position. Extreme caution should therefore be exercised when working under the hood of a car equipped with an electric cooling fan.

Because of the variations of electric fan systems, manufacturers' schematics and specifications must be consulted for troubleshooting and repairing any particular year-model car.

HOSES AND CLAMPS

Radiators usually have two hoses: an upper hose and a lower hose. Radiator hoses are constructed of ozone- and oil-resistant reinforced synthetic rubber. Preformed lower hoses, figure 22-25, have a spiral tempered steel wire molded into them to prevent collapse due to suction of the water pump impeller. Upper hoses, not subject to this condition, usually do not have the wire. Unless the coolant has a rust retarder, such as ethylene glycol, and the cooling system is sound (free of leaks), this wire will rust away in a short period of time. (See "Coolant" later in this unit.)

Universal flexible hose, figure 22-26, with wire inserts are available. These hoses are usually used when preformed hoses are not available. Because of body and engine parts, hoses must often be critically routed. The flexible hose is not always so easily routed.

Many types of hose clamps are used. One very popular type replacement is the high-torque, worm-gear clamp with carbon steel screw and stainless steel band, figure 22-27. The important consideration is that the clamp be properly positioned at 90° to the hose and that it not be overtightened. Overtightening and/or mispositioning a hose clamp causes it to cut into the hose, often breaking the reinforcing fabric.

Fig. 22-25 Preformed lower radiator hose. Preformed upper radiator hoses are similar.

Fig. 22-26 Universal flexible hose

Fig. 22-27 Typical radiator hose clamps

COOLANT RECOVERY TANK

A coolant recovery tank is used to capture venting coolant and vapor from the radiator during the time the pressure valve of the radiator cap is open. When the vacuum valve of the cap opens, this same vented coolant is metered back into the cooling system. (See "Pressure Cap" earlier in this unit.)

The nonpressurized recovery tank, figure 22-28, has a capacity of about 0.5 gallon (1.8 L) and contains approximately one pint (0.47 L) of coolant when the cooling system is cold. Coolant level is checked, not by removing the radiator cap, but by noting coolant level in the recovery tank. It should be filled to the perimeters marked *cold, normal,* or *hot* on the side of the tank.

HEATER SYSTEM

The automotive heater system consists of two parts in addition to hoses and clamps. They are the

heater core and the *coolant flow valve.* The heater housing and duct are a part of the air-conditioning duct system, covered in Unit 23.

Heater Core

The heater core, figure 22-29, resembles a small radiator without a pressure cap. When the control valve is open, a small percentage of heated engine coolant is circulated through the heater core instead of the radiator core. This provides hot air inside the passenger compartment, when desired.

Leaks are common causes of heater problems. Leaks in a heater core are detected by an obvious loss of engine coolant and a wet front floor mat, usually on the passenger's side. These leaks are repaired by those qualified in radiator repair and service.

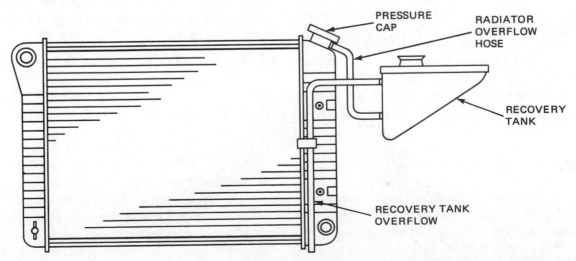

Fig. 22-28 Coolant recovery tank helps prevent loss of coolant due to contraction and expansion of fluid as the temperature changes

Fig. 22-29 Typical heater core

Fig. 22-30 Cable-operated heater control valve

Control Valve

The heater control valve may be either cable operated, figure 22-30, or vacuum controlled, figure 22-31. The amount of heated coolant allowed to enter the heater core, from 0 percent to 100 percent flow, is metered by the control valve. This depends upon the control selector cable position or the amount of vacuum signal applied.

Hoses and Clamps

Like radiator hoses, heater hoses are constructed of oil- and ozone-resistant synthetic rubber. These hoses, however, are smaller and somewhat more flexible than radiator hoses. Three popular sizes of heater hose are 1/2-inch, 5/8-inch, and 3/4-inch inside diameter.

Three hoses are usually associated with the heater system: one from the engine outlet to the control valve, one from the control valve to the heater core, and one from the heater core to the water pump inlet.

Hose clamps used on heater hoses are as previously described for radiator hoses, although smaller, figure 22-32.

ADDITIVES

Many additives, inhibitors, and "remedies" are available for use in the automotive cooling system. These include, but are not limited to, stop-leak, water pump lubricant, engine flush, and acid neutralizers. Extreme caution should be exercised when using any additive in the cooling system. Read

Fig. 22-31 Typical vacuum-controlled heater (coolant) shut-off valve

the label directions and precautions in order to *know* in advance the end results of any additive used. For example, *caustic solutions must never be used in aluminum radiators; alcohol-base "remedies" should never be used in any cooling system;* and so on.

If a cooling system is maintained in good order by a program of preventive maintenance (see "Summary"), additives and inhibitors should never be necessary. Only recommended ethylene glycol-base antifreeze-type solution should be added (covered next).

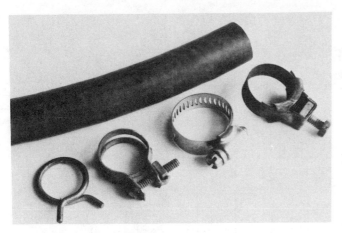

Fig. 22-32 Heater hose and common types of heater hose clamps

Fig. 22-33 Cooling system antifreeze and antiboil additive

ANTIFREEZE

Most manufacturers of automotive cooling systems recommend and specify ethylene glycol-base antifreeze, mixed with water, for cooling system protection. A 50–50 (%) mixture is recommended for year-round protection. Most manufacturers warn against the use of alcohol-base antifreeze solutions. Ethylene glycol and water coolant mixture is essential for three important reasons:

1. It lowers the freezing temperature point of the coolant.
2. It raises the boiling temperature point of the coolant.
3. It provides water pump lubrication and inhibits rust and corrosion.

The freezing temperature of water coolant, at ambient sea-level pressure, is 32°F (0°C). If one-third (33.3%) of the coolant is ethylene glycol and two-thirds (66.6%) is water, the freezing point is reduced to 0°F (−17.7°C). A half-and-half (50%) solution, easy to formulate, protects the cooling system to about −32°F (−35.5°C). Typical antifreeze and antiboil products are shown in figure 22-33.

The coolant should contain no less than 30% ethylene glycol, giving protection to 5°F (−15°C), and no more than 60%, giving protection to −62°F (−52.2°C). After 60%, protection is actually reduced. For example, 100% ethylene glycol will freeze at about −2°F (−18.8°C), figure 22-34. Protection should, of course, be to the lowest temperature expected. In warmer climate zones, protection is required for the benefits of antirust and anticorrosion inhibitors, as well as for water pump lubrication.

Ethylene glycol also increases the boiling point of the coolant. Water in a 15-psi (103.4-kPa) system boils at 250°F (121.1°C). A coolant of 50–50% mixture in the same system boils at about 265°F (129.4°C), a 15°F (8.3°C) advantage.

Most *permanent* antifreeze solutions are formulated to withstand two years of *normal* operation. A driver rarely experiences only normal operation in two years. Some manufacturers recommend changing the solution at intervals of 24 months or 24 000 miles (38 616 km), whereas others recommend every 12 months or 12 000 miles (19 308 km). Always follow label directions for adding or changing fluid.

SUMMARY

The cooling system, often neglected, is one of the most important systems of the car. If kept in good shape, and with routine preventive maintenance provided, the cooling system should give years of trouble-free service. The cost of maintenance every 12 000–15 000 miles (19 308–24 135 km), is more than offset by the cost of initial breakdown and consequent repairs. These repairs, incidentally, often result in expensive engine service. The preventive maintenance (PM) program should include the following procedures:

1. Test and/or replace thermostat and pressure cap.

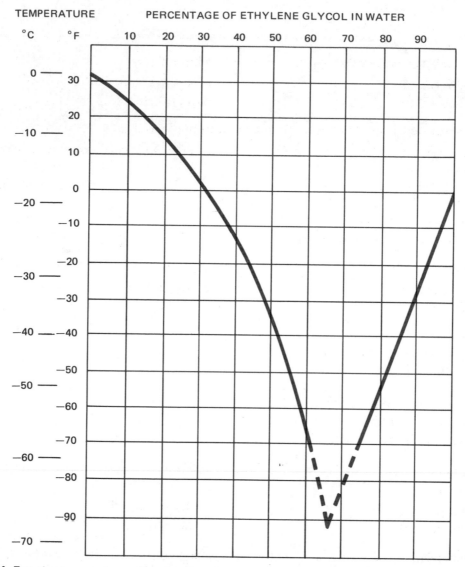

Fig. 22-34 Freezing temperature of coolant based on percentage of ethylene glycol solution in water

2. Inspect and/or replace radiator and heater hoses.
3. Pressure test the cooling system (see Service Procedures, Section 3).
4. Replace antifreeze solution.
5. Visually inspect water pump, heater valve, and belt(s). Replace belts that are frayed, glazed, or obviously damaged.

Design considerations of a typical cooling system provide for minimum sustained road speed operation of 90 mph (144.8 km/h) with an ambient temperature as high as 125°F (51.6°C), or 30 minutes of driving in congested stop-and-go traffic with an ambient temperature as high as 115°F (46.1°C) without overheating problems. These design considerations exceed the conditions one is likely to encounter in day-to-day driving. So, if the engine overheats, the problem must be found and corrected.

The life of an engine and a transmission that are habitually allowed to overheat is greatly reduced. The high-limit properties of lubricating oil in the engine and transmission require adequate and proper heat removal to preserve formulated lubricating characteristics.

In a word — *repair;* don't patch.

Review

1. Generally, maximum engine fan speed for a clutch fan is
   a. 800 r/min.
   b. 2 600 r/min.
   c. 3 500 r/min.
   d. 5 000 r/min.

2. A thermostat is used in the cooling system to prevent
   a. overheating.
   b. overcooling.
   c. Both answers a and b are correct.
   d. Neither answer a nor b is correct.

3. A 160°F (71.1°C) thermostat will fully open
   a. at its temperature rating.
   b. below its temperature rating.
   c. above its temperature rating.
   d. Thermostats do not open.

4. A cooling system removes about _____ of the heat generated by the engine.
   a. 25 percent
   b. 35 percent
   c. 45 percent
   d. 75 percent

5. Radiator design (coolant flow) is
   a. crossflow.
   b. downflow.
   c. either a or b.
   d. neither a nor b.

6. Radiator pressure caps are rated from _____ to _____.
   a. 6–15 psi (41.4–103.4 kPa)
   b. 8–17 psi (55.2–117.2 kPa)
   c. 10–19 psi (68.9–131 kPa)
   d. 12–21 psi (82.7–144.8 kPa)

7. Maximum concentration of an antifreeze solution, for system protection, should not exceed
   a. 30 percent.
   b. 40 percent.
   c. 50 percent.
   d. 60 percent.

8. Technician A says that a defective thermostat will cause overheating. Technician B says that a defective thermostat will result in overcooling.
   a. Technician A is correct.
   b. Technician B is correct.
   c. Both technicians are correct.
   d. Both technicians are wrong.

9. Technician A says that coolant loss may be reduced by the use of a coolant recovery system. Technician B says that coolant loss may be reduced by using an antifreeze solution.
   a. Technician A is correct.
   b. Technician B is correct.
   c. Both technicians are correct.
   d. Both technicians are wrong.

10. Cooling system pressure is increased by the use of
   a. a water pump.
   b. the fan clutch.
   c. a radiator cap.
   d. a thermostat.

UNIT 23:

Case/Duct Systems

The purpose of this unit is to provide for a basic understanding of the automotive heater/air-conditioner case/duct system. The system described in this unit, then, should be considered typical, and not as representative of any particular automotive case/duct system. An average automotive heater/air-conditioner case/duct system is shown in figure 23-1. At first glance, this system may seem to be a complicated maze of passages and doors. Actually, it is much simpler than it first appears.

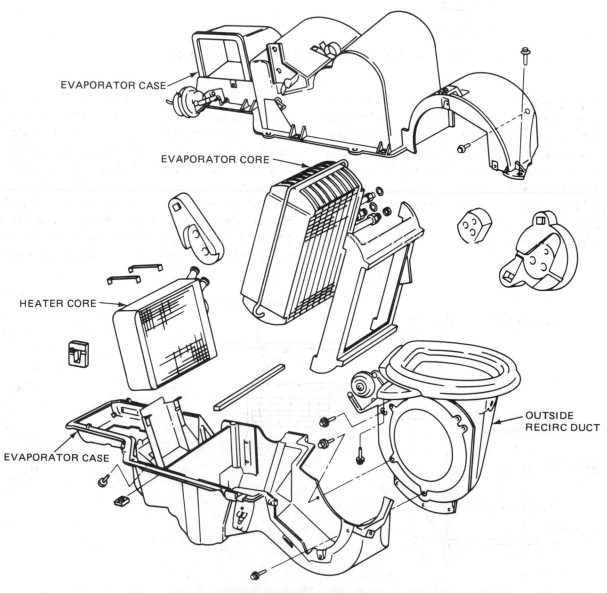

EVAPORATOR CASE

EVAPORATOR CORE

HEATER CORE

EVAPORATOR CASE

OUTSIDE RECIRC DUCT

Fig. 23-1 Exploded view of typical duct system

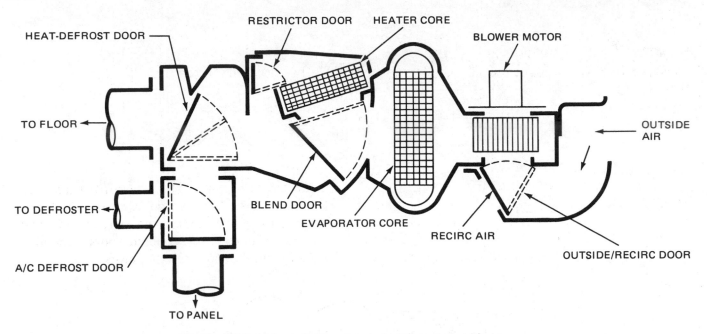

Fig. 23-2 Independent case system with upstream blower

The purpose of the system is twofold. It is used to house the heater core and the air-conditioner evaporator, and to direct the selected supply air through these components into the passenger compartment of the car. The supply air selected may be either fresh (outside) and/or recirculated (in-car) air, depending upon the system mode. After the air is heated and/or cooled, it is delivered to the floor outlet, dash panel outlets, and/or the defrost outlets.

Two types of case assemblies are used to house the heater core and air-conditioner evaporator: the independent case, and the split case. The independent case, used on compact and small cars, may have an upstream blower, figure 23-2, or a downstream blower, figure 23-3. An upstream integral blower, figure 23-4, or an independent blower, figure 23-5, is used on split case systems. The split case system, which is used on larger cars, is located on both sides of the engine firewall. The

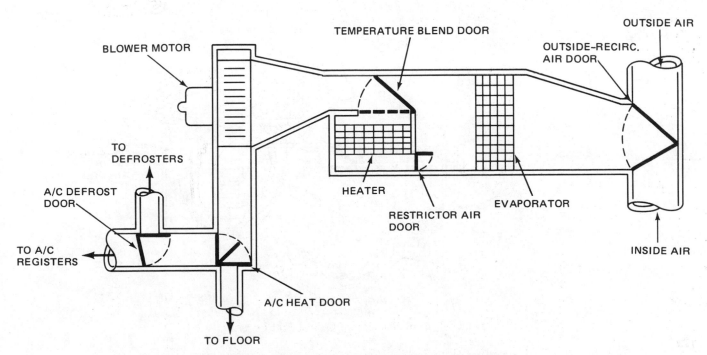

Fig. 23-3 Independent case system with downstream blower

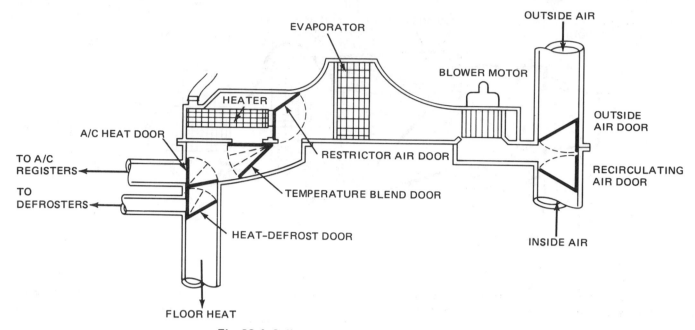

Fig. 23-4 Split case system with upstream blower

independent case system is usually located under the dash, on the inside of the firewall.

For simplicity of understanding, a typical hybrid case/duct system is illustrated in this unit. This system is divided into three sections, figure 23-6. For illustration, these sections are the air intake section, the heater core and air-conditioning evaporator (plenum) section, and the air distribution section. Each of these sections will be studied first individually, then as a complete system.

AIR INTAKE

The air intake or inlet section, figure 23-7, consists of a fresh (outside) air inlet, a recirculate (inside) air inlet, a fresh-recirculate air door, a blower with motor, and an air outlet. The fresh air inlet provides the system with fresh outside air supply; the recirculate air inlet provides recirculated in-car air supply.

The position of the vacuum motor operated fresh-recirculate door depends on the system mode.

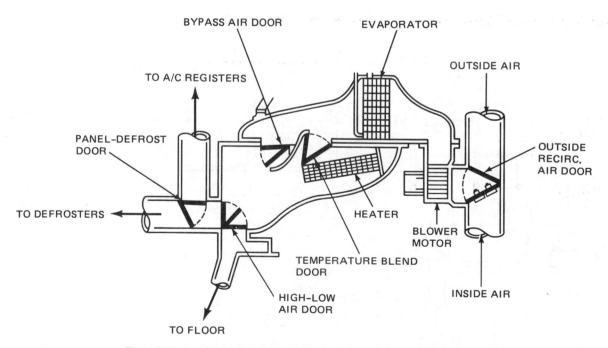

Fig. 23-5 Case/duct system with independent (downstream) blower

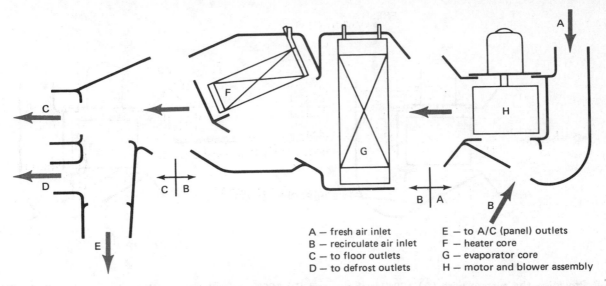

A — fresh air inlet
B — recirculate air inlet
C — to floor outlets
D — to defrost outlets

E — to A/C (panel) outlets
F — heater core
G — evaporator core
H — motor and blower assembly

Fig. 23-6 Case/duct system split into three sections for illustration. Section C is air distribution, Section B is heater core and evaporator plenum section, and Section A is the air intake.

For illustration, 100% fresh air is provided as shown in figure 23-8A, and 100% recirculated air is provided as shown in figure 23-8B. Actually, in all modes except maximum cooling (MAX A/C), the air supply is from the outside. In MAX A/C, the air supply is from the inside (recirculated). Even in the MAX A/C mode, some systems provide for up to 20% fresh air. This is to provide for a slightly positive in-car pressure.*

CORE SECTION

The core section, more appropriately called the *plenum* section, figure 23-9, is the center section of the duct system. It consists of the heater core, the air-conditioning evaporator, and a blend door. Airflow is from right to left in the illustration. The blend door, usually Bowden cable operated, provides full-range control of airflow either through or bypassing the heater core. All air passes through the air-conditioning evaporator. It is in this section that full-range temperature conditions are provided for in-car comfort. The following information describes how this is accomplished.

Heating

The heater water valve is open to allow hot engine coolant to flow through the heater core. Cool

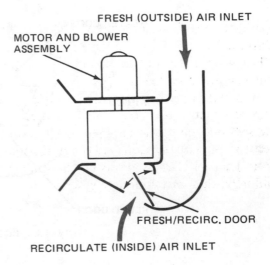

FRESH (OUTSIDE) AIR INLET

MOTOR AND BLOWER ASSEMBLY

FRESH/RECIRC. DOOR

RECIRCULATE (INSIDE) AIR INLET

Fig. 23-7 Air inlet section

outside fresh air is heated as it passes through the heater core. The air conditioner is not operational; therefore, it has no effect on the air temperature as the air first passes through the evaporator. The desired temperature level is achieved by the position of the blend door. This allows a percentage of the cool outside air to bypass the heater core to temper the heated air. The heated air and cool air are then blended in the plenum to provide the desired temperature level before passing on to the air distribution section.

*A slightly positive pressure inside the car prevents the entrance of dangerous exhaust gases which could produce a hazardous in-car atmosphere when all windows are tightly closed.

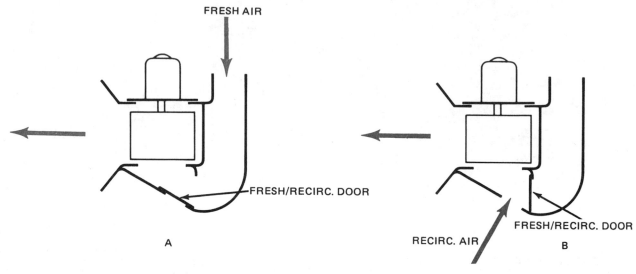

Fig. 23-8 Providing the system with (A) 100% fresh air, and (B) 100% recirculated air. Note the position of the FRESH/RECIRC. door.

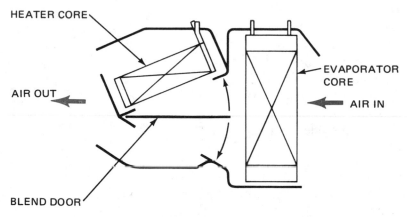

Fig. 23-9 Core section

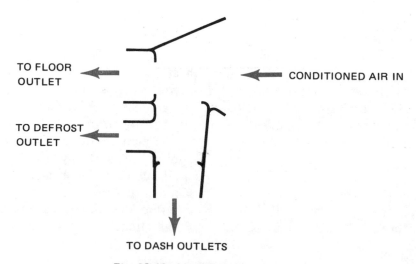

Fig. 23-10 Air distribution section

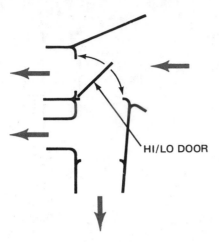

Fig. 23-11 Air distribution section illustrating the HI/LO diverter door

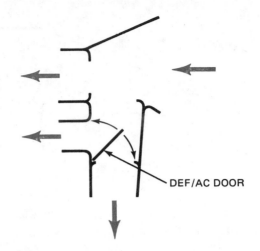

Fig. 23-12 Air distribution section illustrating the DEF/AC diverter door

Cooling

In maximum cooling (MAX A/C), recirculated air passes through the air-conditioner evaporator and is then directed back into the car. In other than MAX A/C, fresh outside air passes through the air-conditioning evaporator and is cooled before delivery into the car. The desired temperature level is achieved by the position of the blend door. The blend door allows a percentage of cooled air to pass through the heater core to be reheated. The cooled air passing through the evaporator and the reheated air passing through the heater core are blended in the plenum to provide the desired temperature level. This tempered air is then directed to the air distribution section.

DISTRIBUTION SECTION

The air distribution section, figure 23-10, directs conditioned air to be discharged to the floor outlets, the defrost outlets, or the dash panel outlets. Also, depending upon the position of the mode doors, conditioned air may be delivered to any combination of outlets. There are two mode (blend) doors in the air distribution section: the HI/LO door and the DEF/AC door. The HI/LO door, figure 23-11, provides 0–100% full-range conditioned air outlet control to the HI (dash) and LO (floor) outlets. The DEF/AC door, figure 23-12, provides conditioned air outlet control either to the defrost (windshield) outlets or to the dash panel outlets.

COMBINED CASE

The combined case/duct system provides full-range control of air circulation through the heater core and air-conditioner evaporator. Figure 23-13 illustrates 100% recirculated air through the air-

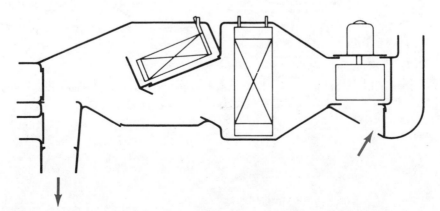

Fig. 23-13 Illustrating 100% recirculated air through the evaporator core to the dash air-conditioning outlets

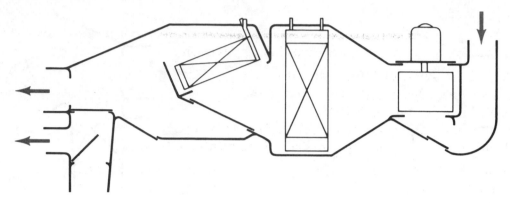

Fig. 23-14 Illustrating 100% fresh air through the heater core and out through the floor outlet. In the heating mode, although the air is also through the evaporator, there is no cooling effect since the compressor in this case would be OFF.

conditioner evaporator and out through the panel outlets. This may typically represent mode and blend door positions when maximum cooling (MAX A/C) is selected during high in-car ambient temperature conditions.

Figure 23-14 illustrates 100% fresh air circulation through the heater core and out through the floor outlets. This may typically represent the mode and blend door positions when heat is selected during low in-car ambient temperature conditions. A variation, figure 23-15, shows some of the heated air diverted to the defrost outlets. This would be the typical application to clear the windshield of fog or light icing conditions.

SUMMARY

There are many variations of mode and blend door positions, as well as many case/duct system designs. Some doors are vacuum operated, whereas others are Bowden cable operated. Some doors are either fully opened or fully closed; others are infinitely variable. Because of the many different types of systems and methods of control, it is necessary to consult a particular manufacturer's manual for specifications and testing procedures. The information given in this unit, then, must be considered typical, and not as representative of any particular case/duct system.

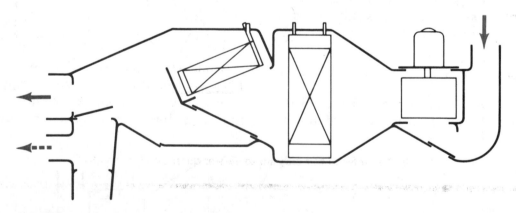

Fig. 23-15 By position of the HI/LO door and the DEF/AC door, a portion of the heated air is diverted to the defroster outlets.

Review

Select the appropriate answer from the choices given.

1. A fresh air supply of 100% is provided for
   a. all modes except MAX A/C.
   b. all modes except MAX HEAT.
   c. all modes, depending upon in-car ambient temperature.
   d. all modes, depending upon outside air ambient temperature.

2. Blend (mode) doors are found in _____ of the case/duct system.
   a. the first section   c. the third section
   b. the second section   d. all three sections

3. What component is shown as "A" in figure 23-16?
   a. Condenser   c. Evaporator
   b. Heater core   d. Blower motor

4. What component is shown as "B" in figure 23-16?
   a. HI/LO door   c. Blend door
   b. DEF/AC door   d. FRESH/RECIRC. door

5. The flow of air in the center section of figure 23-16 is from
   a. left to right.   c. left to right, then left.
   b. right to left.   d. right to left, then right.

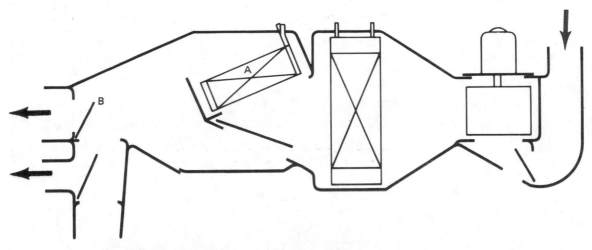

Fig. 23-16 Refer to this diagram to answer questions 3, 4, and 5.

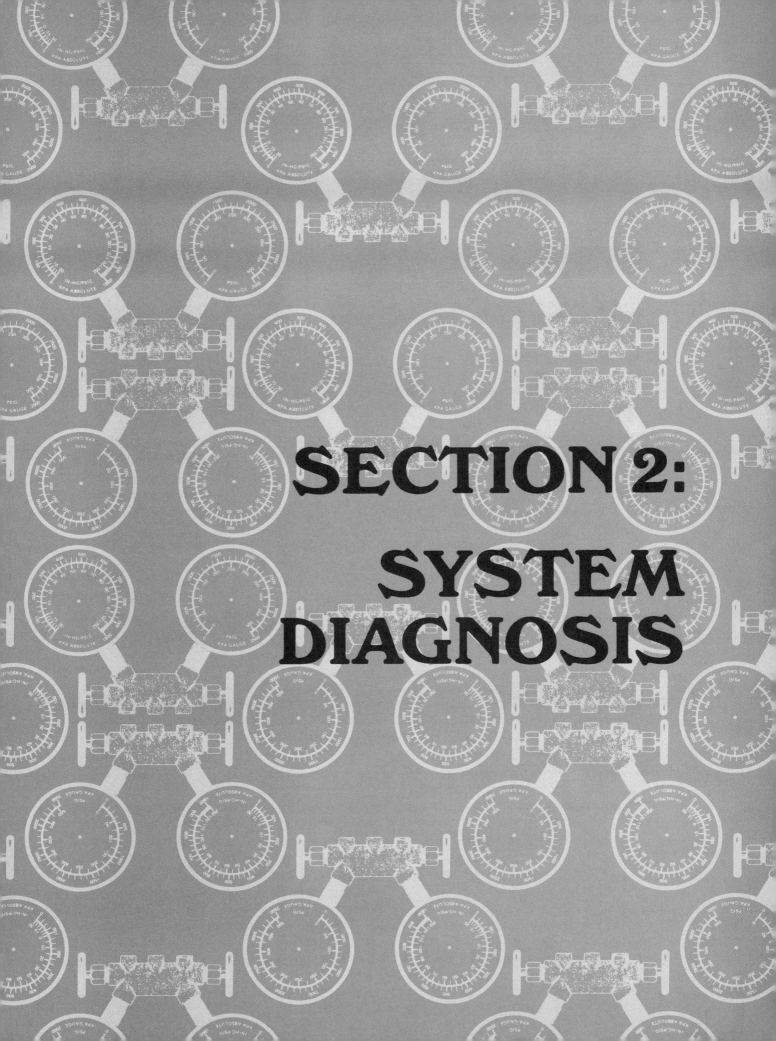

SECTION 2:

SYSTEM DIAGNOSIS

INTRODUCTION

An accurate diagnosis and determination of automotive air-conditioning system function and, more importantly, malfunction, depend largely upon the ability of the technician to interpret gauge pressure readings. The importance of a refrigeration technician's manifold and gauge set is often compared to that of a physician's stethoscope.

An improper gauge reading will relate to a specific problem. More than one problem may be associated with a particular gauge reading, however. A system operating normally will have a low-side gauge pressure reading that corresponds with the temperature of the liquid refrigerant as it becomes a vapor while removing heat in the evaporator. The high-side gauge readings should correspond with the temperature of the refrigerant vapor as it becomes a liquid while giving up its heat in the condenser. The use of a third gauge, in some systems, is to monitor the pressure of the refrigerant vapor as it enters the compressor. This compound gauge relates to the pressure drop in the system after the refrigerant has passed through the suction pressure control device.

Any deviation from normal gauge readings, other than slight, indicates a malfunction. This malfunction, if within the system, may be caused by a faulty control device, a restriction, or a defective component. It should be noted that improper mounting or location of components in a newly installed system may affect system performance. An overheated engine cooling system or an improperly tuned engine may also affect system performance, and will be noted as abnormal gauge readings.

Diagnosis of system malfunction is made easier with the knowledge that the low-side temperature (°F) and pressure (psig) are closely related. This is true of Refrigerant 12, and is easily determined in the English system of measure between 20 psig and 60 psig. The English temperature-pressure chart, figure SD-1, shows that there is only a slight variation between the temperature and pressure in this range.

It may, therefore, be correct to assume that for every pound (psig) pressure change in the low side that the temperature will correspondingly change by one degree (°F). For example, a pressure of 33.1 psig indicates (on the chart) an evaporating temperature of 36°F. A pressure increase of two pounds (2 psig) to 35.1 psig will result in a temperature increase of 2°F to 38°F.

This handy information does not, however, hold true in the metric system of measure. Unfortunately, there is no direct correlation between kilopascal (kPa) pressure, absolute or gauge, and Celsius (C) temperature. The metric temperature-pressure chart of figure SD-2 must be used when troubleshooting an air-conditioning system with gauges calibrated in metric units.

In either case, the actual temperature of the air after passing over the evaporator coil is several degrees warmer than that shown in the temperature-pressure charts. This is because of a temperature difference, called *Delta-T* (Δ_t), due to expected loss through the tubes and fins of the evaporator coil.

This section includes several exercises in gauge interpretations in both the English and metric scales. These exercises serve as an aid in the understanding of gauge pressure readings relating to system function and malfunction. Sixteen color plates are also included to serve as visual aids in determining system function. These plates may be keyed to appropriate diagnostic gauge sets, if desired.

ENGLISH TEMPERATURE-PRESSURE CHART

Low-Side Pressure psi		Temperature °F	High-Side Pressure psi		Temperature °F
Absolute	Gauge		Absolute	Gauge	
25.9	11.2	4	120	105	60
27	12.3	6	124	109	62
28.1	13.4	8	128	113	64
29.3	14.6	10	132	117	66
30.5	15.8	12	137	122	68
31.8	17.1	14	141	126	70
33	18.3	16	147	132	72
34.4	19.7	18	152	137	74
35.7	21	20	159	144	76
37.1	22.4	22	167	152	78
38.5	23.8	24	175	160	80
40	25.3	26	180	165	82
41.5	26.8	28	185	170	84
43.1	28.4	30	190	175	86
44.7	30	32	195	180	88
46.4	31.7	34	200	185	90
47.8	33.1	36	204	189	92
49.8	35.1	38	208	193	94
51.6	36.9	40	215	200	96
53.5	38.8	42	225	210	98
55.4	40.7	44	235	220	100
57.3	42.6	46	243	228	102
59.3	44.6	48	251	236	104

Fig. SD-1 English temperature-pressure chart

METRIC TEMPERATURE-PRESSURE CHART

Low-Side Pressure kPa		Temperature °C	High-Side Pressure kPa		Temperature °C
Absolute	Gauge		Absolute	Gauge	
175	74	−15	910	809	19
195	94	−13	942	831	20
210	109	−11	970	869	21
230	129	−9	1 010	909	22
245	144	−7	1 030	929	23
260	159	−5	1 070	969	24
280	179	−3	1 122	1 021	25
295	194	−1	1 175	1 074	26
308	207	0	1 210	1 109	27
320	219	1	1 245	1 144	28
340	239	3	1 275	1 174	29
363	262	5	1 308	1 207	30
385	284	7	1 340	1 239	31
420	319	9	1 375	1 274	32
437	336	11	1 390	1 289	33
480	379	13	1 405	1 304	34
510	409	16	1 446	1 345	35
540	439	18	1 515	1 414	36

Fig. SD-2 Metric temperature-pressure chart

Color Plates

The following sixteen color plates may be used as aids in determining system conditions in various functions and malfunctions. These plates illustrate the state of refrigerant in various parts of the system. In an air-conditioning system, the four states are: low-pressure liquid, high-pressure liquid, low-pressure vapor, and high-pressure vapor.

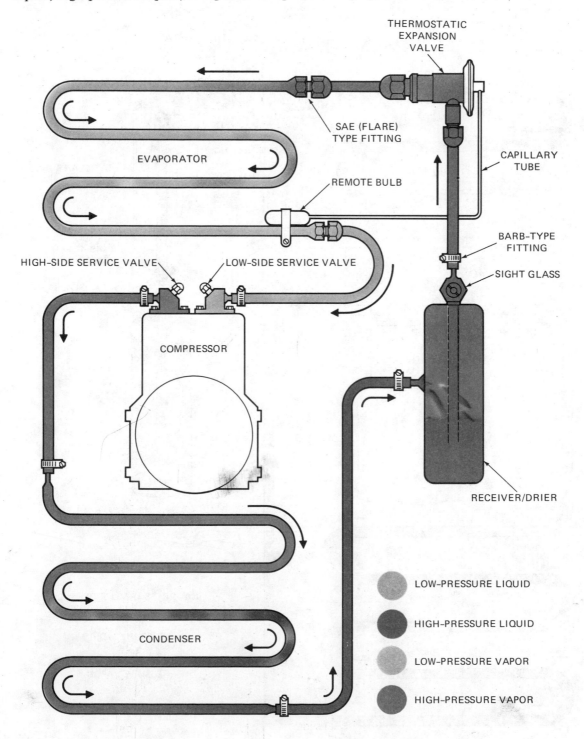

Plate 1. Normal system operation

Plates 1, 9, and 16 show normal system operation. As noted in these plates, refrigerant is low-pressure liquid from the metering device into the evaporator. In the evaporator the refrigerant changes to a low-pressure vapor while picking up heat. It is low-pressure vapor into the compressor where it is changed into a high-pressure vapor. This condition exists into the condenser where it changes to a high-pressure liquid while giving up its heat. The high-pressure liquid is then stored in the receiver/dehydrator where it is available to the metering device.

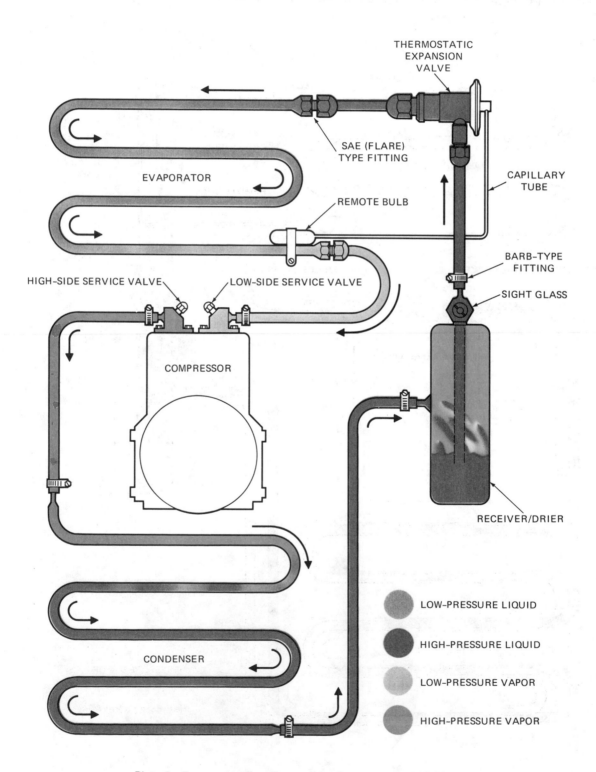

Plate 2. Evaporator flooding — defective expansion valve

Plates 2 and 8 show the condition of a flooded evaporator, whereas plates 3 and 11 show the condition of a starved evaporator. An undercharge of refrigerant is shown in plates 4 and 12, while an overcharge is shown in plates 5 and 13. Plates 6 and 14 show the effect of a defective compressor, such as bad valve plate(s); plates 7 and 15 show no compressor action, as would be the case with a defective clutch coil or broken drive belt.

In each of the plates, the refrigerant state or condition may be studied to determine the effect of malfunction. Additionally, if desired, the plates can be keyed to System Diagnosis assignments 1 through 16, as applicable.

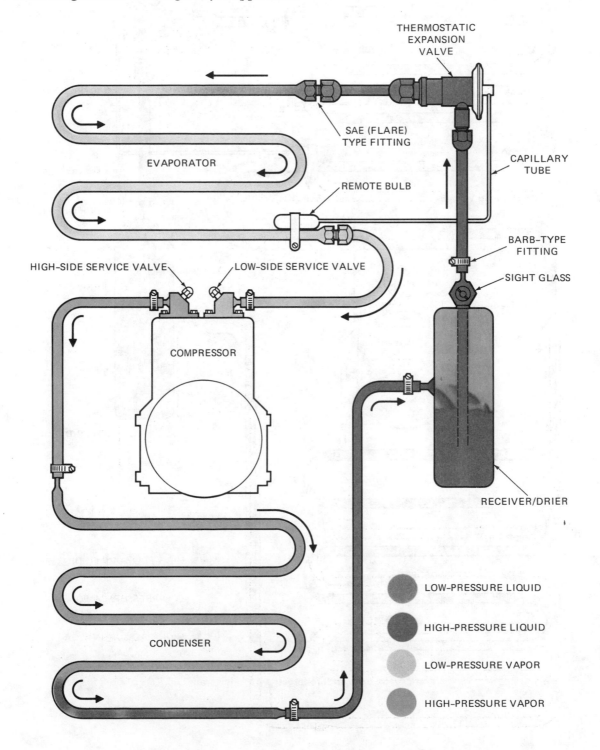

Plate 3. Evaporator starving — defective expansion valve

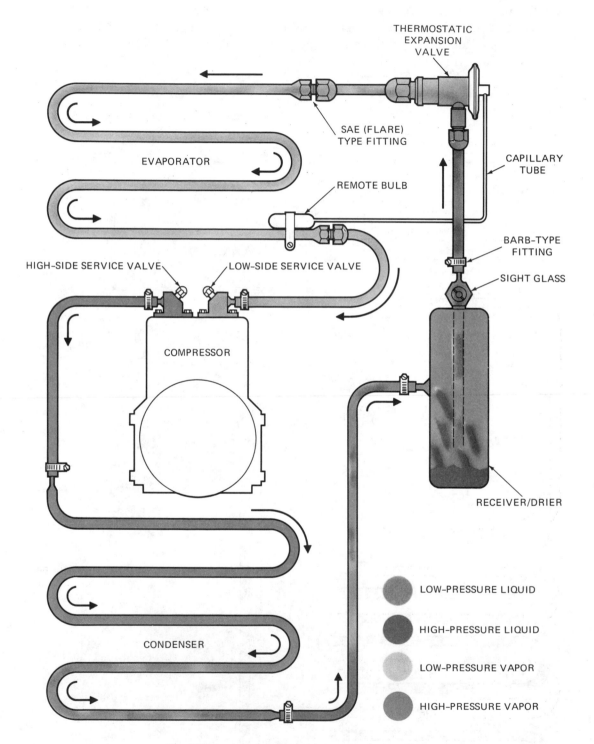

THERMOSTATIC
EXPANSION
VALVE

SAE (FLARE)
TYPE FITTING

EVAPORATOR

CAPILLARY
TUBE

REMOTE BULB

BARB-TYPE
FITTING

HIGH-SIDE SERVICE VALVE   LOW-SIDE SERVICE VALVE

SIGHT GLASS

COMPRESSOR

RECEIVER/DRIER

CONDENSER

LOW-PRESSURE LIQUID

HIGH-PRESSURE LIQUID

LOW-PRESSURE VAPOR

HIGH-PRESSURE VAPOR

Plate 4. System undercharged with refrigerant

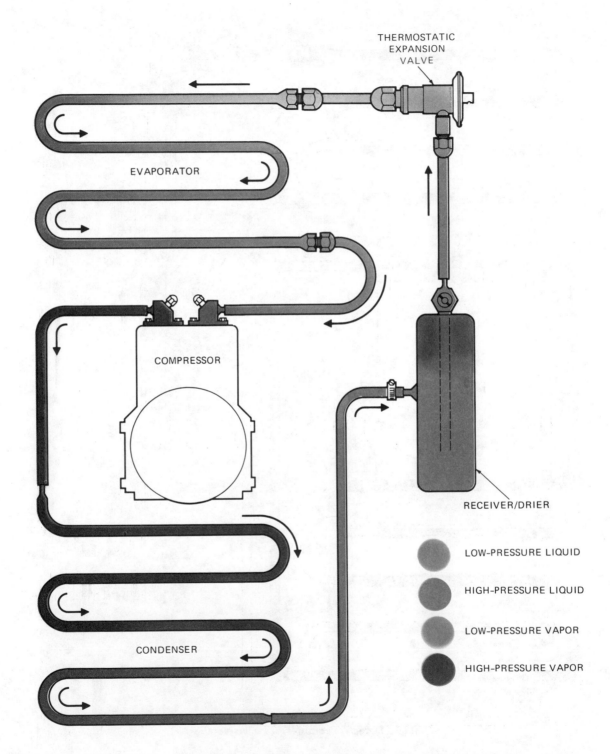

THERMOSTATIC
EXPANSION
VALVE

EVAPORATOR

COMPRESSOR

RECEIVER/DRIER

LOW-PRESSURE LIQUID

HIGH-PRESSURE LIQUID

LOW-PRESSURE VAPOR

HIGH-PRESSURE VAPOR

CONDENSER

Plate 5. Overcharge of refrigerant

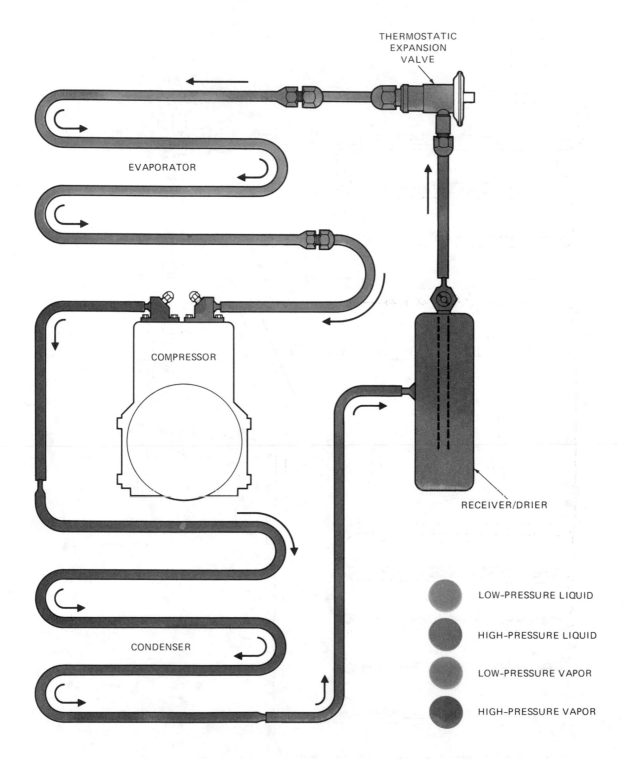

Plate 6. Defective compressor (valve plate)

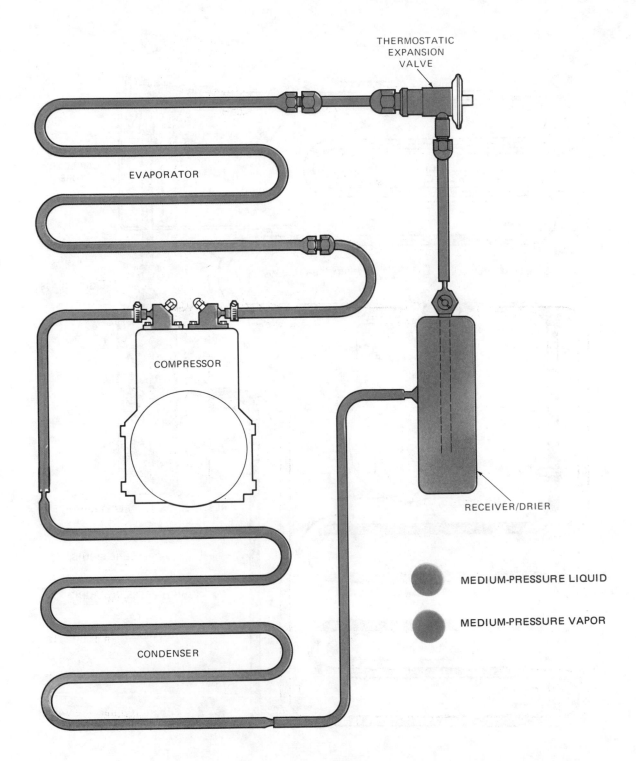

THERMOSTATIC
EXPANSION
VALVE

EVAPORATOR

COMPRESSOR

RECEIVER/DRIER

MEDIUM-PRESSURE LIQUID

MEDIUM-PRESSURE VAPOR

CONDENSER

Plate 7. No compressor action

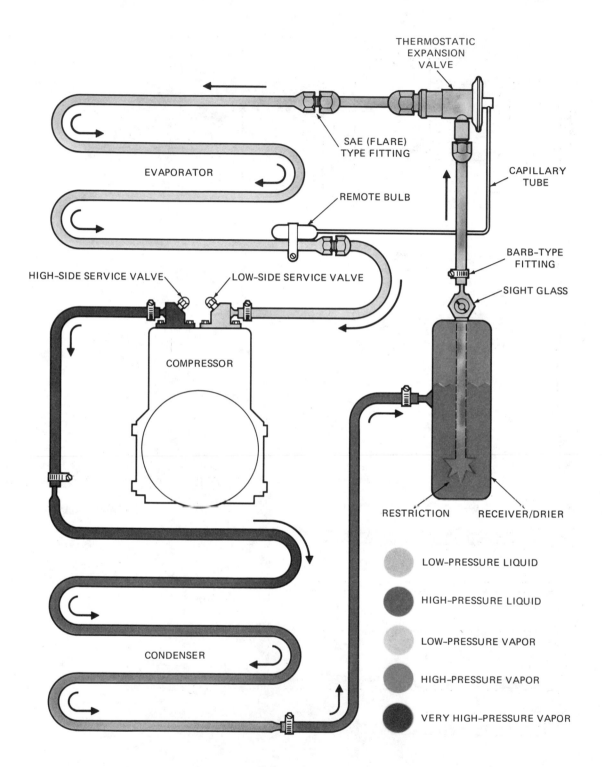

THERMOSTATIC
EXPANSION
VALVE

SAE (FLARE)
TYPE FITTING

EVAPORATOR

CAPILLARY
TUBE

REMOTE BULB

HIGH-SIDE SERVICE VALVE

LOW-SIDE SERVICE VALVE

BARB-TYPE
FITTING

SIGHT GLASS

COMPRESSOR

RESTRICTION   RECEIVER/DRIER

LOW-PRESSURE LIQUID

HIGH-PRESSURE LIQUID

LOW-PRESSURE VAPOR

CONDENSER

HIGH-PRESSURE VAPOR

VERY HIGH-PRESSURE VAPOR

Plate 8. Restriction in receiver/drier (at pickup tube inlet strainer)

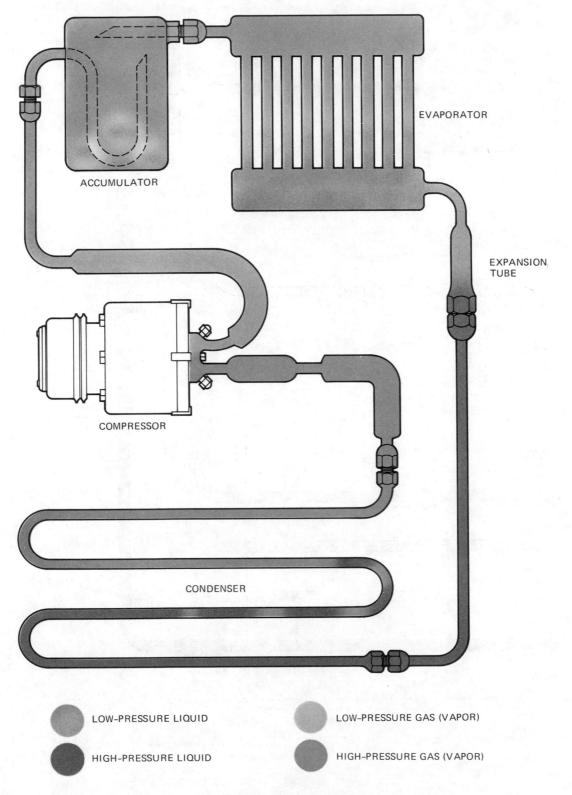

EVAPORATOR

ACCUMULATOR

EXPANSION TUBE

COMPRESSOR

CONDENSER

LOW-PRESSURE LIQUID

LOW-PRESSURE GAS (VAPOR)

HIGH-PRESSURE LIQUID

HIGH-PRESSURE GAS (VAPOR)

Plate 9. Normal operation

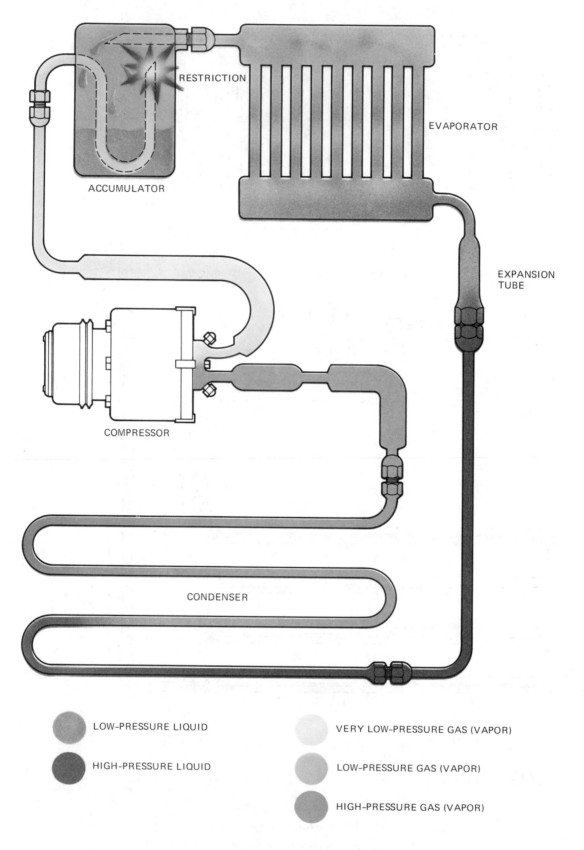

RESTRICTION

EVAPORATOR

ACCUMULATOR

EXPANSION
TUBE

COMPRESSOR

CONDENSER

LOW-PRESSURE LIQUID

HIGH-PRESSURE LIQUID

VERY LOW-PRESSURE GAS (VAPOR)

LOW-PRESSURE GAS (VAPOR)

HIGH-PRESSURE GAS (VAPOR)

Plate 10. Restriction in the accumulator

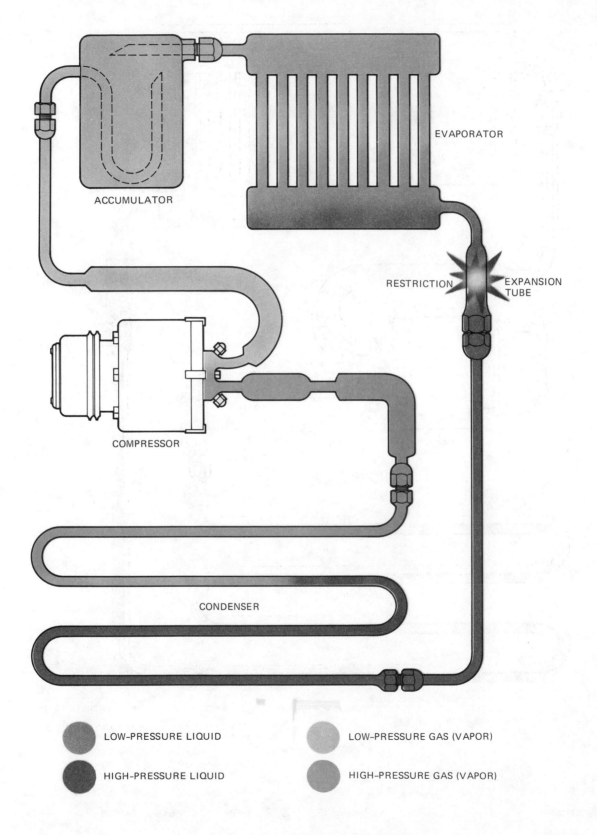

EVAPORATOR

ACCUMULATOR

RESTRICTION   EXPANSION TUBE

COMPRESSOR

CONDENSER

LOW-PRESSURE LIQUID

LOW-PRESSURE GAS (VAPOR)

HIGH-PRESSURE LIQUID

HIGH-PRESSURE GAS (VAPOR)

Plate 11. Restriction in the expansion tube

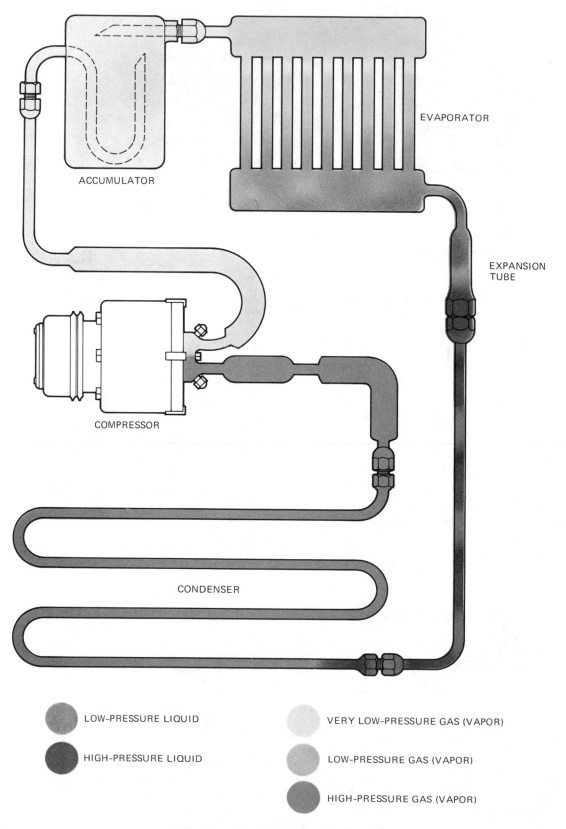

EVAPORATOR

ACCUMULATOR

EXPANSION
TUBE

COMPRESSOR

CONDENSER

LOW-PRESSURE LIQUID

HIGH-PRESSURE LIQUID

VERY LOW-PRESSURE GAS (VAPOR)

LOW-PRESSURE GAS (VAPOR)

HIGH-PRESSURE GAS (VAPOR)

Plate 12. Undercharge of refrigerant

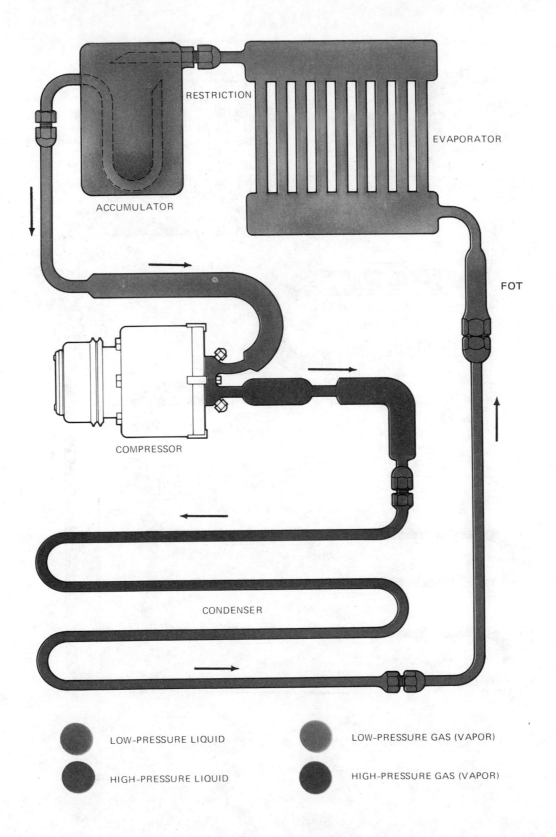

Plate 13. Overcharge of refrigerant

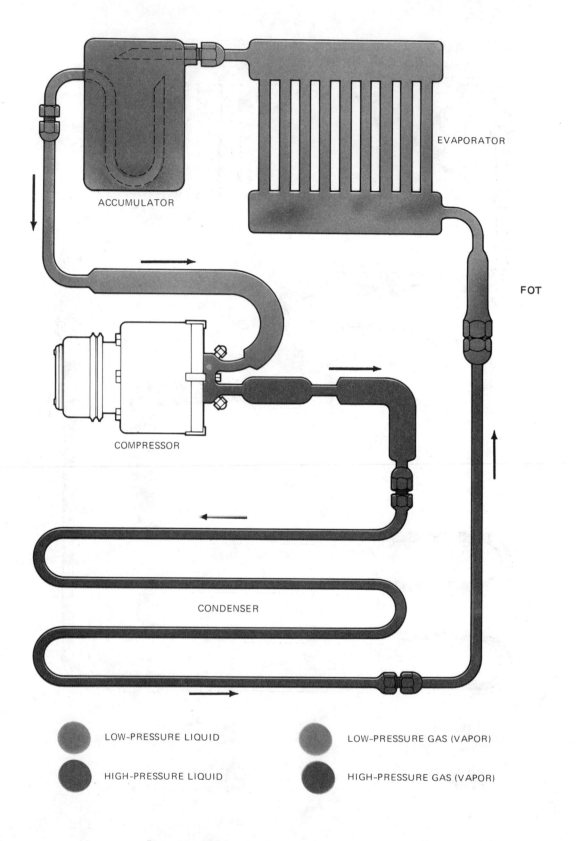

EVAPORATOR

ACCUMULATOR

FOT

COMPRESSOR

CONDENSER

LOW-PRESSURE LIQUID

LOW-PRESSURE GAS (VAPOR)

HIGH-PRESSURE LIQUID

HIGH-PRESSURE GAS (VAPOR)

Plate 14. Defective compressor (valve plate)

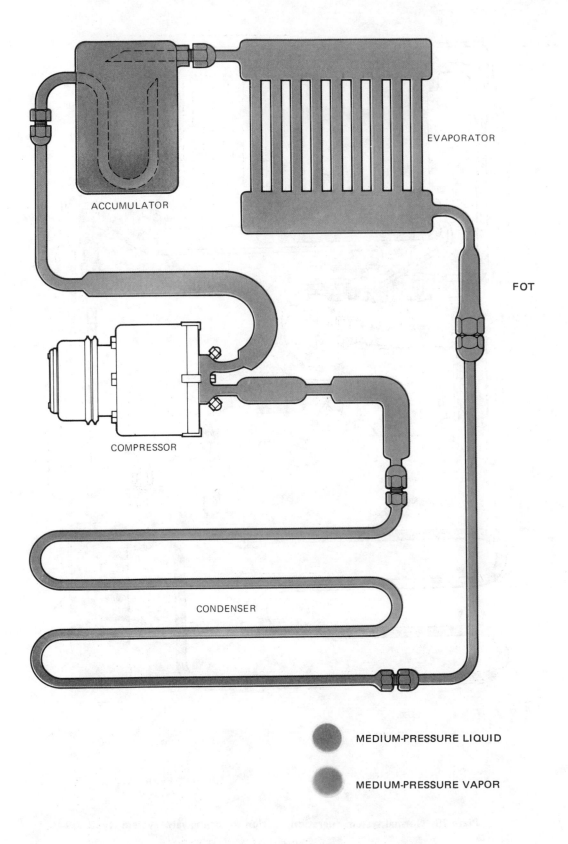

EVAPORATOR

ACCUMULATOR

FOT

COMPRESSOR

CONDENSER

● MEDIUM-PRESSURE LIQUID

● MEDIUM-PRESSURE VAPOR

Plate 15. No compressor action

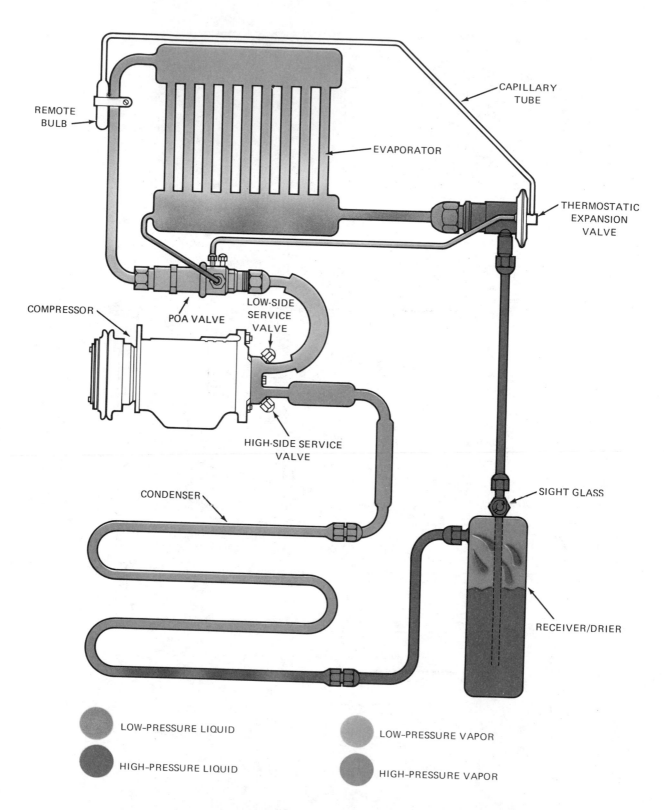

REMOTE
BULB

CAPILLARY
TUBE

EVAPORATOR

THERMOSTATIC
EXPANSION
VALVE

COMPRESSOR

POA VALVE

LOW-SIDE
SERVICE
VALVE

HIGH-SIDE SERVICE
VALVE

CONDENSER

SIGHT GLASS

RECEIVER/DRIER

LOW-PRESSURE LIQUID

LOW-PRESSURE VAPOR

HIGH-PRESSURE LIQUID

HIGH-PRESSURE VAPOR

Plate 16. Normal system operation, suction throttling valve system (typical)

Gauge Scales

The customary English pressures, pounds per square inch (psi), pounds per square inch gauge (psig), or pounds per square inch absolute (psia) all become kilopascal (kPa) in the metric system of pressure measurement. One psi (English) is equal to 6.895 kPa (metric). Conversely, one kPa (metric) is equal to 0.145 psi (English).

The English terms psi and psig reference zero pressure as atmospheric pressure. On gauges calibrated psi or psig, all pressures above atmospheric are scaled accordingly; psi or psig. All pressures below atmospheric are scaled in inches of mercury (inHg or "Hg).

The English term psia references zero pressure as absolute zero. All pressures above and below atmospheric pressure are scaled in psia. The chart of figure SD-3 compares psig, psia, kPa gauge, and kPa absolute.

The metric term kPa may reference zero pressure either as absolute or as atmospheric (gauge). The term must be qualified however. The expression *gauge* or *absolute* must be used as applicable. The kPa absolute scale references zero pressure as absolute zero. On this scale, sea-level atmospheric is 101.3 kPa absolute. This value is usually rounded off to 100 kPa. The kPa gauge scale, on the other hand, references atmospheric pressure as zero. (For comparison see the chart of figure SD-3.)

It must be noted, as discussed in Unit 2, the kilopascal is not used in negative terms. Therefore, compound gauges in the metric system of measure must be calibrated in absolute values. Pressure gauges, on the other hand, may be calibrated in either scale: absolute or atmospheric.

To provide experience in both atmospheric (gauge) and absolute values, the gauges in this section are scaled as follows.

COMPOUND GAUGE

The compound gauge, figure SD-4, includes both an English (30 "Hg to 120 psig) atmospheric (gauge) scale and a metric (0 to 900 kPa) absolute scale with retard to 250 psig and 1 800 kPa. The scale from 120 psig to 250 psig is referred to as *retard*. This means that pressures as high as 250 psig may be applied without affecting the accuracy of the gauge. English pressures below atmospheric

Pounds Per Square Inch		Kilopascal	
Gauge	Absolute*	Gauge*	Absolute*
30 "Hg	0	—	0
15 "Hg	7	—	51
0	15	0	101
15	30	103	205
30	45	207	308
45	60	310	412
60	75	414	515
75	90	517	618
100	115	690	791
150	165	1 034	1 136
200	215	1 379	1 480
250	265	1 724	1 825
300	315	2 069	2 170
400	415	2 758	2 859
500	515	3 448	3 549

*To nearest whole number

Fig. SD-3 Comparison of PSI gauge and absolute with KILOPASCAL gauge and absolute

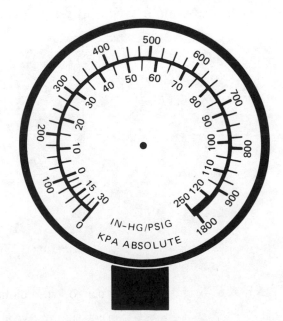

Fig. SD-4 Typical low-side (compound) gauge with English (gauge) and metric (absolute) scales

are given in inches of mercury ("Hg), whereas metric pressures are given in kilopascals absolute (kPa absolute). English pressures above atmospheric are given in pounds per square inch gauge (psig); metric pressures are given in kPa absolute.

The English scale below atmospheric pressure is calibrated in 5 "Hg divisions with 15 "Hg and 30 "Hg major divisions. Above atmospheric pressure major divisions are 10 psig through 120 psig. Minor divisions of the English scale are 5 psig.

Major divisions of the metric scale are 100 kPa from absolute with minor divisions of 25 kPa. The retard range of the metric scale is from 900 kPa to 1 800 kPa. There is no accuracy in the retard range of the gauge.

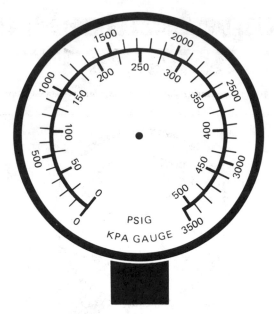

Fig. SD-5 Typical high-side (pressure) gauge with English (gauge) and metric (gauge) scales

PRESSURE GAUGE

The pressure gauge, figure SD-5, includes a psi or psig English scale and a kPa gauge metric scale. Both English and metric values are given using atmospheric pressure as zero reference.

The English scale major divisions are 50 psi with minor divisions of 25 psi. Major divisions of the metric scale are 500 kPa with minor divisions of 100 kPa.

CONVERSIONS

To convert the English psig scale to psia add 14.69, usually rounded off to 14.7 or 15, to the psig reading. To convert the metric gauge scale to absolute add 101.3, usually rounded off to 101 or 100, to the kPa gauge reading. To convert psig to kPa gauge multiply the psig reading by 6.895. The same multiplier may be used to convert psia to kPa absolute. To convert psig to kPa absolute first convert psig to psia, then apply the multiplier.

Temperature-Pressure Relationship 1

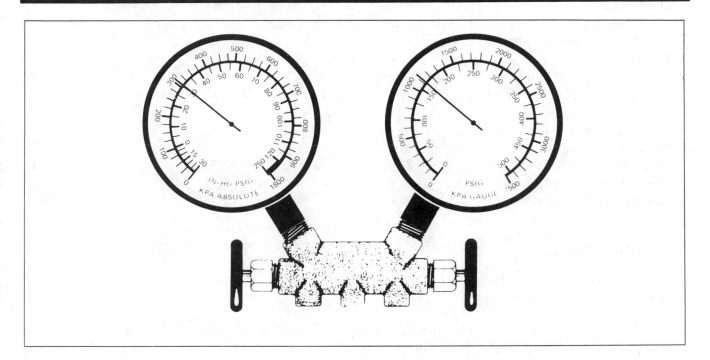

Consider all conditions normal in this problem. It is designed to familiarize the student with the similarities between temperature and pressure.

1. What approximate pressure is indicated on the low-side gauge?

   30 psig

   _____ kPa*

2. This pressure corresponds to an evaporator temperature of approximately

   32 °F

   _____ °C

3. What approximate pressure is indicated on the high-side gauge?

   160 psig

   _____ kPa*

4. This pressure corresponds to an ambient temperature of approximately

   80 °F

   _____ °C

   *absolute

Temperature-Pressure Relationship 2

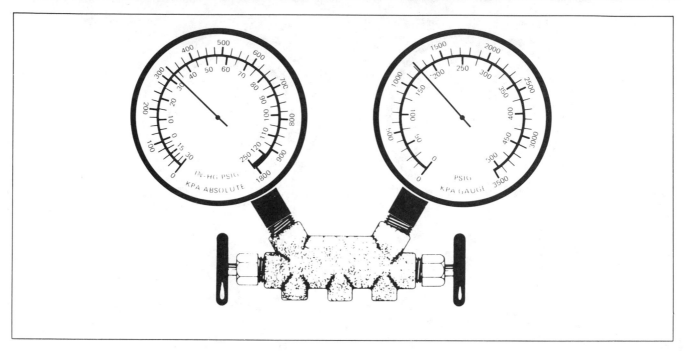

Consider all conditions normal in this problem. It is designed to familiarize the student with the similarities between temperature and pressure.

1. What approximate pressure is indicated on the low-side gauge? _____32_____ psig
   _____ kPa*

2. This pressure corresponds to an evaporator temperature of approximately _____34_____ °F
   _____ °C

3. What approximate pressure is indicated on the high-side gauge? _____175_____ psig
   _____ kPa*

4. This pressure corresponds to an ambient temperature of approximately _____86_____ °F
   _____ °C

*absolute

Temperature-Pressure Relationship 3

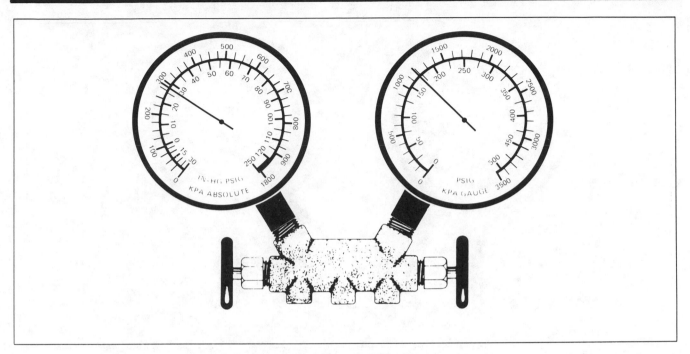

Consider all conditions normal in this problem. It is designed to familiarize the student with the similarities between temperature and pressure.

1. What approximate pressure is indicated on the low-side gauge? _____28_____ psig
   _____ kPa*

2. This pressure corresponds to an evaporator temperature of approximately _____30_____ °F
   _____ °C

3. What approximate pressure is indicated on the high-side gauge? _____170_____ psig
   _____ kPa*

4. This pressure corresponds to an ambient temperature of approximately _____84_____ °F
   _____ °C

*absolute

Temperature-Pressure Relationship 4

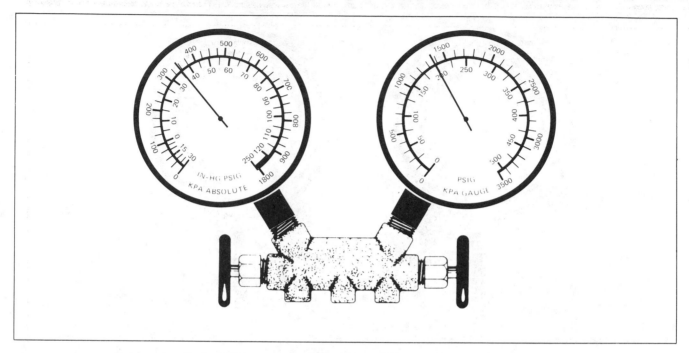

Consider all conditions normal in this problem. It is designed to familiarize the student with the similarities between temperature and pressure.

1. What approximate pressure is indicated on the low-side gauge? _____3,5_____ psig
   _____ kPa*

2. This pressure corresponds to an evaporator temperature of approximately _____37_____ °F
   _____ °C

3. What approximate pressure is indicated on the high-side gauge? _____200_____ psig
   _____ kPa*

4. This pressure corresponds to an ambient temperature of approximately _____96_____ °F
   _____ °C

*absolute

Temperature-Pressure Relationship 5

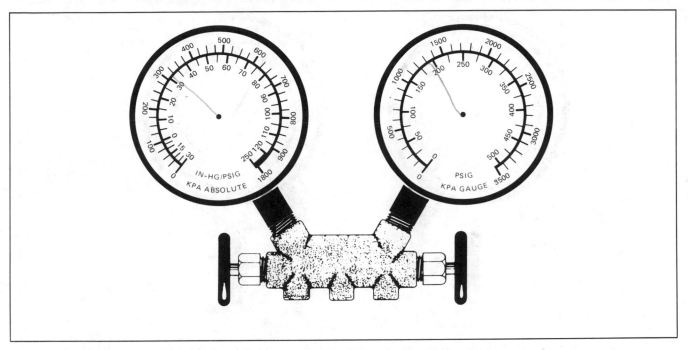

Consider all conditions normal in this problem. It is designed to familiarize the student with the similarities between temperature and pressure.

1. With an ambient temperature of 95°F (35°C), what is the normal head pressure? Indicate the pressure on the gauge in the diagram.

   _____197_____ psig
   _____ kPa

2. With an evaporator temperature of 33°F (0.5°C), what is the normal suction pressure? Indicate the pressure on the gauge in the diagram.

   _____31_____ psig
   _____ kPa*

   *Absolute

Temperature-Pressure Relationship 6

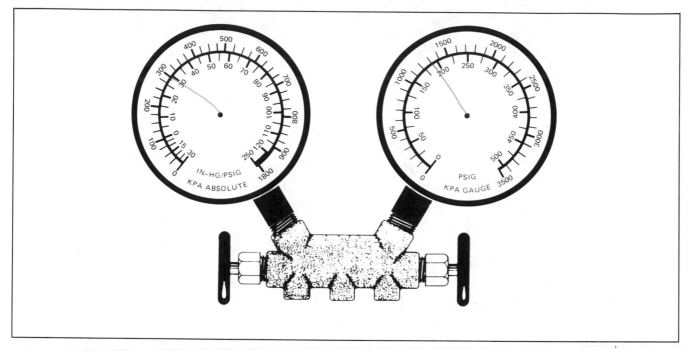

Consider all conditions normal. This problem is designed to familiarize the student with the similarities of temperature and pressure.

1. A head pressure of 185 psig (1 276 kPa) is normal at what ambient temperature? Show this pressure reading on the high-side gauge in the diagram.

   _____90_____ °F
   _____ °C

2. If the evaporator temperature is 31°F (−0.5°C) what is the low-side gauge reading? Show this pressure reading on the low-side gauge in the diagram.

   _____29_____ psig
   _____ kPa*

*Absolute

Temperature-Pressure Relationship 7

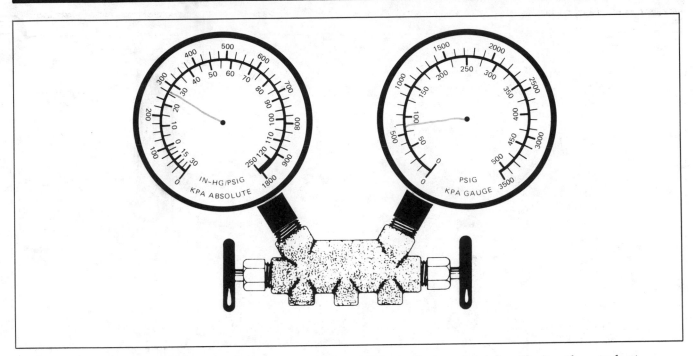

Consider all conditions normal. This problem is designed to familiarize the student with the similarities of temperature and pressure.

1. The ambient temperature is 100°F (37.8°C). What is the normal high-side pressure? Show the pressure reading on the gauge in the diagram.

_____58_____ psig

_____ kPa

2. The low-side gauge reads 26 psig (281 kPa absolute). What is the temperature of the refrigerant in the evaporator? Show this temperature reading on the low-side gauge in the diagram.

_____28_____ °F

_____ °C

Temperature-Pressure Relationship 8

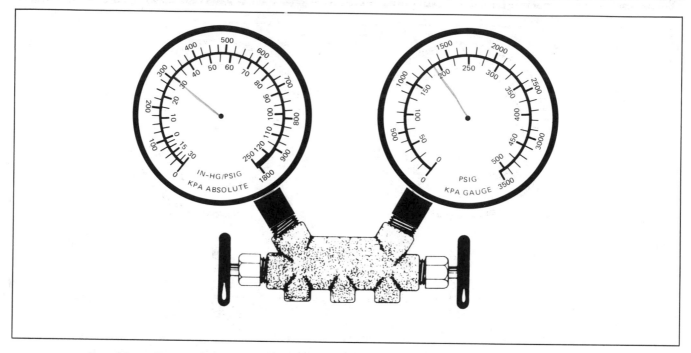

Consider all conditions normal. This problem is designed to familiarize the student with the similarities of temperature and pressure.

1. The high-side gauge reads 195 psi (1 345 kPa). Show this reading on the high-side gauge. What is the ambient temperature in this problem?

    _____95_____ °F
    _____ °C

2. The low-side gauge reads 30 psi (308 kPa absolute). Show this reading on the low-side gauge. What is the evaporator temperature in this problem?

    _____32_____ °F
    _____ °C

SYSTEM DIAGNOSIS 1:
The Compressor—Cycling Clutch TXV or FOT System

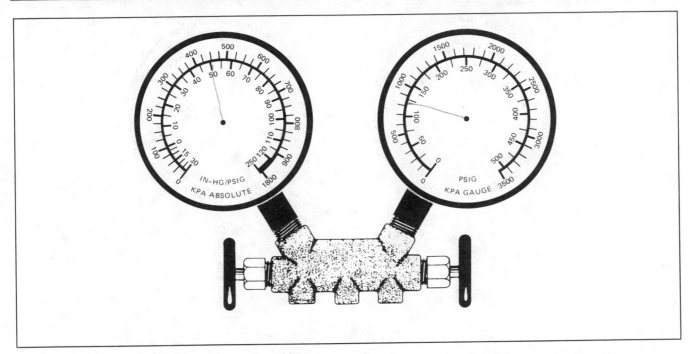

CONDITIONS

Ambient temperature: 90°F (32.2°C)
Low-side gauge: 50 psig (446 kPa absolute)
High-side gauge: 120 psi (827 kPa)

DIAGNOSIS

1. Show the high- and low-side readings on the gauges in the diagram.

2. What should the normal high-side reading be? _____185_____ psi
   _____ kPa

3. What is the evaporator temperature in this problem? _____52_____ °F
   _____ °C

4. A low-side reading of 50 psig (446 kPa absolute) is (high, low). _____HIGH_____

5. A high-side reading of 120 psi (827 kPa) is (high, low). _____LOW_____

6. This condition results in (good, poor, no) cooling from the evaporator. POOR/NO   _fan belt slipping_

7. An internal _____ of the compressor is indicated by these conditions. INTERNAL LEAK

8. To correct this condition, a new _____ and/or _____ must be installed. HEAD GASKET

9. This condition is generally caused by excessive _____. HEAD PRESSURE

SYSTEM DIAGNOSIS 2:
The Condenser—Cycling Clutch TXV or FOT System

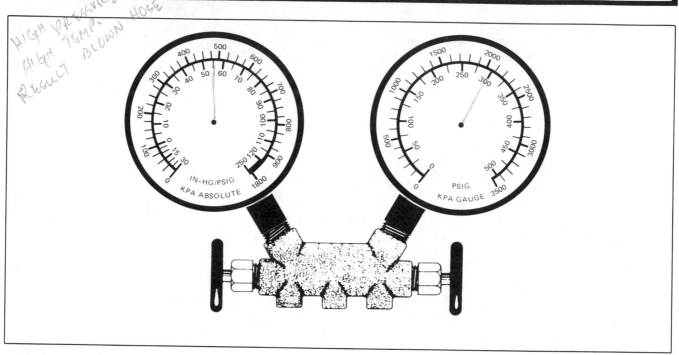

HIGH PRESSURE
HIGH TEMP.
RESULT BLOWN HOSE

CONDITIONS

Ambient Temperature: 95°F (35°C)
Low-side gauge: 55 psig (499 kPa absolute)
High-side gauge: 300 psi (2 069 kPa)

DIAGNOSIS

1. Show the high- and low-side gauge readings on the gauges in the diagram.

2. What should the normal high-side gauge reading be? ___195___ psi
   _____ kPa

3. What is the evaporator temperature in this problem? ___58___ °F
   _____ °C

4. A low-side reading of 55 psig (499 kPa absolute) is (high, low). ___HIGH___

5. A high-side pressure reading of 300 psi (2 069 kPa) is (high, low). ___HIGH___

6. This condition results in (good, poor, no) cooling from the evaporator. ___POOR / NO___

7. Give two conditions outside the air-conditioning system that can cause this pressure.
   PLUG CONDENSOR , FAN , COOLING SYSTEM

8. Give two conditions inside the air-conditioning system that can cause this pressure.
   OVER CHARGE , MOISTURE IN THE SYSTEM, pinch line
   TXV STOCK CLOSE

9. Give one type of damage that can occur by operating the air conditioner with this head pressure. BROKEN HEAD GASKET , LEAF VALVE , HOSES

SYSTEM DIAGNOSIS 3:
The Dehydrator—Cycling Clutch TXV System

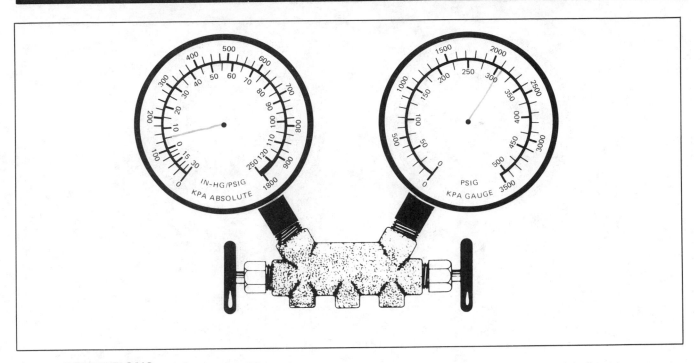

CONDITIONS

Ambient temperature: 100°F (37.8°C)
Low-side gauge: 5 psig (136 kPa absolute)
High-side gauge: 305 psi (2 103 kPa)

DIAGNOSIS

1. Show the high- and low-side gauge readings on the gauges in the diagram.

2. What should the normal high-side reading be? _____220_____ psi
   _____ kPa

3. What is the evaporator temperature in this problem? _____ °F
   Explain. _____ °C

   _____

4. A low-side reading of 5 psig (136 kPa absolute) is (high, low). _____LOW_____

5. A high-side reading of 305 psi (2 103 kPa) is (high, low). _____HIGH_____

6. This condition results in (good, poor, no) cooling from the evaporator. _____NO_____

7. A restriction at the _____ is indicated by these readings. _____

8. Frosting is likely to occur at the point of _____. _____RESTRICTION_____

9. How can this system be repaired? _REPLACE, EVACUATE, AND CHARGE_

SYSTEM DIAGNOSIS 4:
The Accumulator—Cycling Clutch FOT System

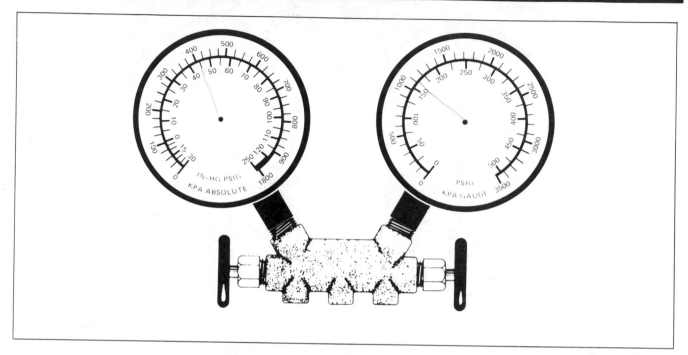

CONDITIONS

Low-side service valve located on accumulator
Ambient temperature: 95°F (35°C)
Low-side gauge: 45 psig (412 kPa absolute)
High-side gauge: 165 psig (1138 kPa)

DIAGNOSIS

1. Show the high- and low-side gauge readings on the gauges in the diagram.

2. What should the normal high-side reading be? _____196_____ psig
   _____ kPa

3. What is the evaporator temperature in this problem? Explain. _____47_____ °F
   _____ °C

   _____

4. A low-side reading of 45 psig (412 kPa absolute) is (high, normal, low). _____HIGH_____

5. A high-side reading of 165 psig (1138 kPa) is (high, normal, low). _____LOW_____

6. This condition results in (good, poor, no) cooling from the evaporator. _____POOR_____

7. A restriction in the _____ is indicated by these readings. _____ACCUMULATOR_____

8. Frosting is likely to occur at the point of _____. _____ACCUMULATOR_____

9. How can this system be repaired? _REPLACE ACCUMULATOR AND ORFICE TUBE, EVAC, RECHARGE_

SYSTEM DIAGNOSIS 5:
The Accumulator—Cycling Clutch FOT System

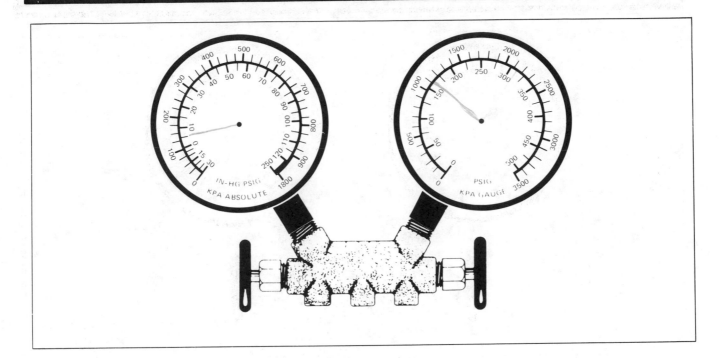

CONDITIONS

Low-side service valve located downstream of the accumulator
Ambient temperature: 95°F (35°C)
Low-side gauge: 5 psig (136 kPa absolute)
High-side gauge: 165 psig (1138 kPa)

DIAGNOSIS

1. Show the high- and low-side gauge readings.

2. What should the normal high-side reading be? _____ *196* _____ psig
   _____ kPa

3. What is the evaporator temperature in this problem? _____ °F
   Explain. _____ °C

   _____

4. A low-side reading of 5 psig (136 kPa absolute) is (high, _____ *LOW* _____
   normal, low).

5. A high-side reading of 165 psig (1138 kPa) is (high, nor- _____ *LOW* _____
   mal, low).

6. This condition results in (good, poor, no) cooling. _____ *NO* _____

7. A restriction in the _____ is indicated by these readings. _____ *ORFICE TUBE* _____

8. Frosting is likely to occur at the point of _____ . _____ *ORFICE TUBE* _____

9. How can this system be repaired? _____

   _____

SYSTEM DIAGNOSIS 6:
Thermostatic Expansion Valve
—Cycling Clutch TXV System

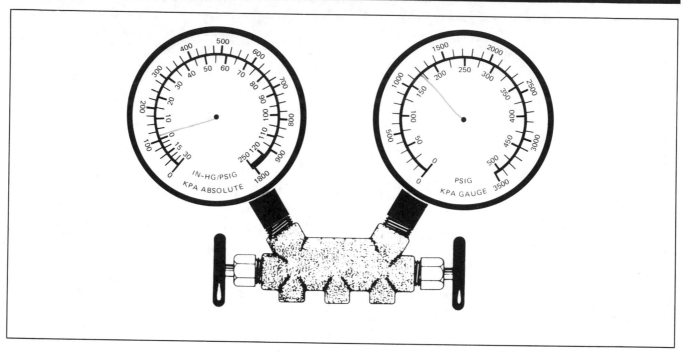

CONDITIONS

Ambient temperature: 95°F (35°C)
Low-side gauge: 2 psig (115 kPa absolute)
High-side gauge: 170 psi (1 172 kPa)

DIAGNOSIS

1. Show the high- and low-side manifold readings on the gauges in the diagram.

2. What should the normal high-side reading be? _____195_____ psi
   _____ kPa

3. What is the evaporator temperature in this problem? Explain. __AMBIENT__ °F
   _____ °C

4. A low-side reading of 2 psig (115 kPa absolute) is (high, normal, low). _____LOW_____

5. A high-side reading of 170 psi (1 172 kPa) is (high, normal, low). _____LOW_____

6. This condition results in (good, poor, no) cooling from the evaporator. _____NO_____

7. This condition indicates a (starved, flooded) evaporator due to a defective _____. _____STARVED_____

8. This condition is usually accompanied by frosting at the valve _____. _____TXV_____

9. How can this condition be corrected? __CHECK COMPRESSOR AND RECEIVER DRYER__

SYSTEM DIAGNOSIS 7:
Thermostatic Expansion Valve —Cycling Clutch TXV System

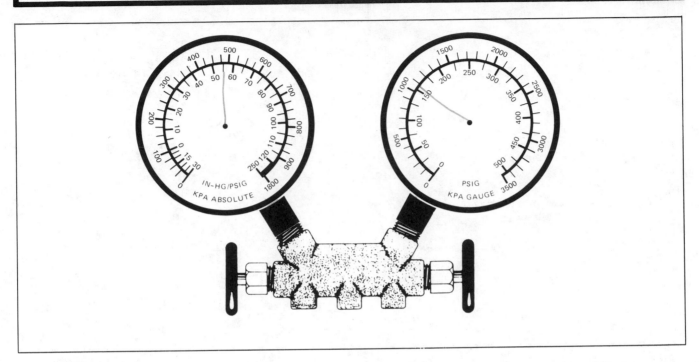

CONDITIONS
Ambient temperature: 95°F (35°C)
Low-side gauge: 55 psig (481 kPa absolute)
High-side gauge: 160 psi (1 103 kPa)

DIAGNOSIS

1. Show the high- and low-side manifold readings on the gauges in the diagram.

2. What should the normal high-side reading be? _____195_____ psi
   _____ kPa

3. What is the evaporator temperature in this problem? _____57_____ °F
   _____ °C

4. A low-side reading of 55 psig (481 kPa absolute) is (high, normal, low). _____HIGH+_____

5. A high-side reading of 160 psi (1 103 kPa) is (high, normal, low). _____LOW_____

6. This condition results in (good, poor, no) cooling from the evaporator. _____POOR_____

7. This condition indicates a (starved, flooded) evaporator due to a malfunctioning _____. _____FLOODED_____

8. List two possible causes for this malfunctioning. __TXV STUCK OPEN__
   _____
   _____

9. Can moisture in the system cause this system malfunction? Explain. ____NO____
   _____

217

SYSTEM DIAGNOSIS 8:
The Orifice Tube—Cycling Clutch FOT System

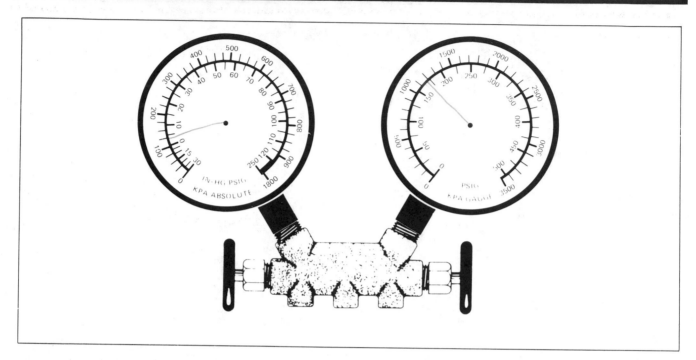

CONDITIONS

Ambient temperature: 95°F (35°C)
Low-side gauge: 3 psig (122 kPa absolute)
High-side gauge: 172 psig (1186 kPa)

DIAGNOSIS

1. Show the high- and low-side gauge readings.

2. What should the normal high-side reading be? _____195_____ psig
   _____ kPa

3. What is the evaporator temperature? _____95_____ °F
   Explain. _____ °C

4. A low-side reading of 3 psig (122 kPa absolute) is (high, normal, low). _____LOW_____

5. A high-side reading of 172 psig (1186 kPa) is (high, normal, low). _____LOW_____

6. This condition results in (good, poor, no) cooling. _____NO_____

7. This condition indicates a (starved, flooded) evaporator. _____STARVED_____

8. This condition indicates a clogged_____. _____ORFICE TUBE_____

9. This condition is usually accompanied by frosting at the _____. _____ORFICE TUBE_____

10. How can this condition be corrected? REPLACE THE RESTRICTION PART.

SYSTEM DIAGNOSIS 9:
The Thermostat—Cycling Clutch TXV or FOT System

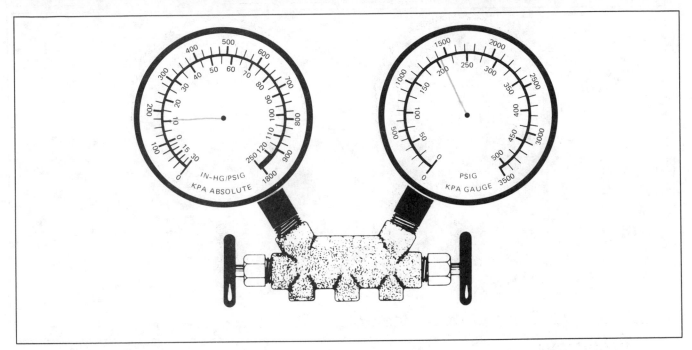

CONDITIONS
Ambient temperature: 97°F (36°C)
Low-side gauge: 10 psig (170 kPa absolute)
High-side gauge: 205 psi (1 413 kPa)

DIAGNOSIS

1. Show the high- and low-side gauge readings on the gauges in the diagram.

2. A high-side pressure of 205 psi (1 413 kPa) in this problem is (high, normal, low). _____NORMAL_____

3. A low-side pressure of 10 psig (170 kPa absolute) in this problem is (high, normal, low). _____LOW_____

4. What is the evaporator temperature in this problem? _____3_____ °F
   _____ °C

5. This condition results in (good, poor, no) cooling from the evaporator. _____NO_____

6. This condition can be accompanied by frosting of the _____EVAPORATOR_____, which blocks off airflow and results in poor _____.

7. List two possible causes of a malfunctioning thermostat that can result in this problem.
   CYCLING SWITCH IS OUT OF ADJUSTMENT, CAPALARY TUBE NOT SENSING.

8. How can the customer unintentionally cause this problem? _____

9. List two types of thermostats. BIMETALIC

10. Are all thermostats adjustable? NO

SYSTEM DIAGNOSIS 10:
The Thermostat—Cycling Clutch TXV or FOT System

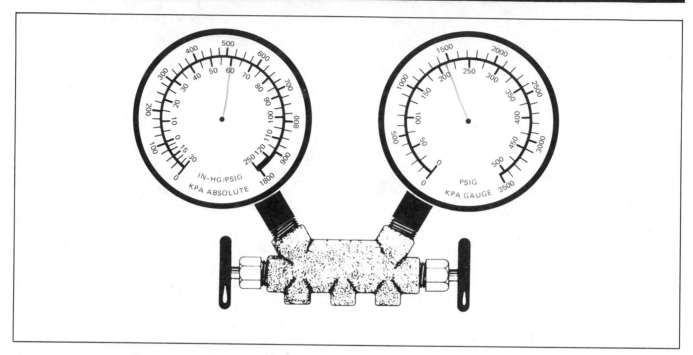

CONDITIONS

Ambient temperature: 98°F (36.7°C)
Low-side gauge: 60 psig (515 kPa absolute)
High-side gauge: 210 psi (1 448 kPa)

DIAGNOSIS

1. Show the high- and low-side gauge readings on the gauges in the diagram.

2. A high-side pressure of 210 psi (1 448 kPa) in this problem is (high, normal, low). _____

3. A low-side pressure of 60 psig (515 kPa absolute) in this problem is (high, normal, low). _____

4. What is the evaporator temperature? _____ °F
   _____ °C

5. This condition results in (good, poor, no) cooling from the evaporator. _____

6. Give two possible causes for this malfunction. _____
   _____
   _____

7. How can the customer unintentionally cause this problem? _____
   _____
   _____

8. Can all thermostats be adjusted? Explain. _____
   _____

SYSTEM DIAGNOSIS 11:
The System—Cycling Clutch TXV or FOT System

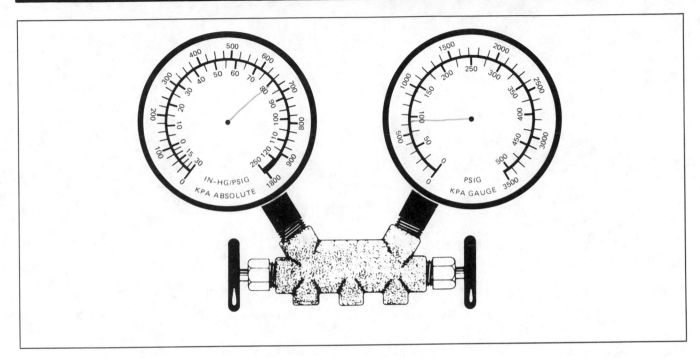

CONDITIONS

Ambient temperature: 90°F (32°C)
Low-side gauge: 80 psig (653 kPa absolute)
High-side gauge: 80 psi (552 kPa)

DIAGNOSIS

1. Show the high- and low-side gauge readings on the gauges
   in the diagram.

2. What should the normal high-side reading be?   _____185_____ psi
                                                    _____ kPa

3. The high side is (high, normal, low).   _____LOW_____

4. The low side is (high, normal, low).   _____HIGH_____

5. List three possible problems with this system.
   a. _CARS NOT ON_____
   b. _NO BELT_____
   c. _COMPRESSOR IS BAD_____

SYSTEM DIAGNOSIS 12:
The System—Cycling Clutch TXV or FOT System

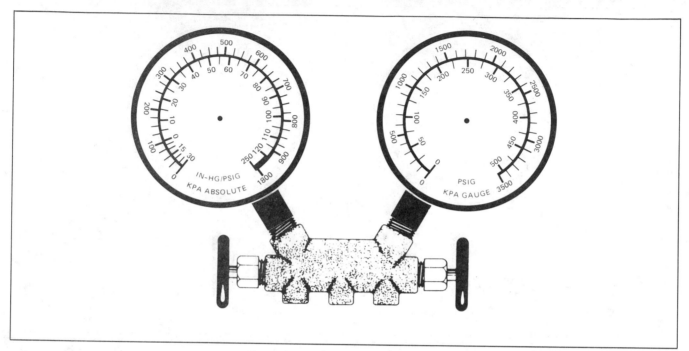

CONDITIONS

Ambient temperature: 80°F (27°C)
Low-side gauge: 20 psig (339 kPa absolute)
High-side gauge: 155 psi (1 069 kPa)

DIAGNOSIS

1. Show the high- and low-side gauge readings on the gauge set in the diagram.

2. The low-side gauge is (low, normal, high). _____

3. List four possible problems with this system.

   a. _____

   b. _____

   c. _____

   d. _____

SYSTEM DIAGNOSIS 13:
The System—Cycling Clutch TXV or FOT System

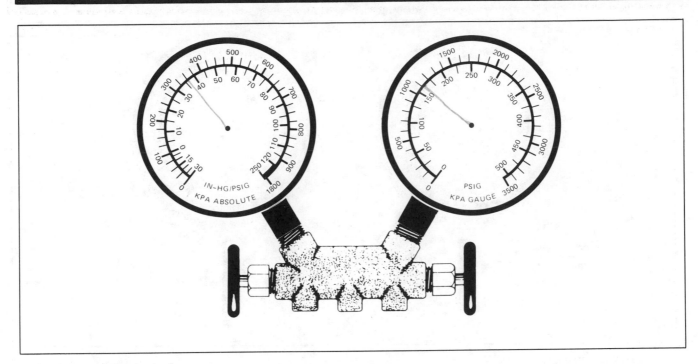

CONDITIONS

Ambient temperature: 83°F (28°C)
Low-side gauge: 37 psig (356 kPa absolute)
High-side gauge: 160 psi (1 103 kPa)

DIAGNOSIS

1. Show the gauge readings on the gauge set in the diagram.

2. What is the evaporator temperature in this problem? This
   temperature is (low, normal, high).

   _____39_____ °F
   _____ °C
   _____HIGH_____

3. List four possible causes for this malfunction.
   a. ___BELT SLIP_____
   b. ___CYCLING TOO FAST "SWITCH"_____
   c. ___POA VALVE_____
   d. ___BAD COMPRESSOR_____

SYSTEM DIAGNOSIS 14:
The System—Cycling Clutch TXV or FOT System

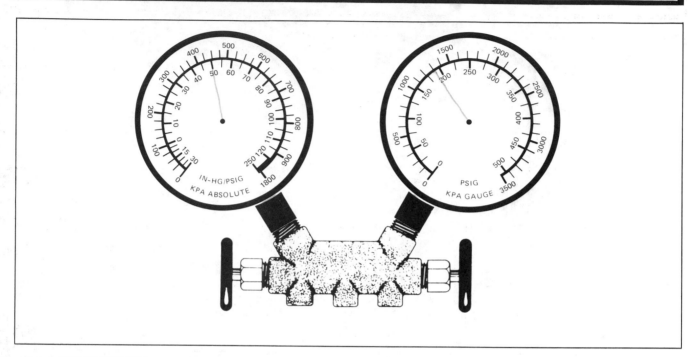

CONDITIONS

Ambient temperature: 90°F (32°C)
Low-side gauge: 50 psig (346 kPa absolute)
High-side gauge: 170 psi (1 172 kPa)

DIAGNOSIS

1. Show the gauge readings on the gauge set in the diagram.

2. The high-side pressure is (high, normal, low). _____ _LOW_

3. List four possible causes for this malfunction.
   a. _STV EKR POA_
   b. _COMPRESSOR BAD_
   c. _BELT SLIP_
   d. _CYCLING TOO FAST "SWITCH"_

SYSTEM DIAGNOSIS 15:
The System—Cycling Clutch TXV or FOT System

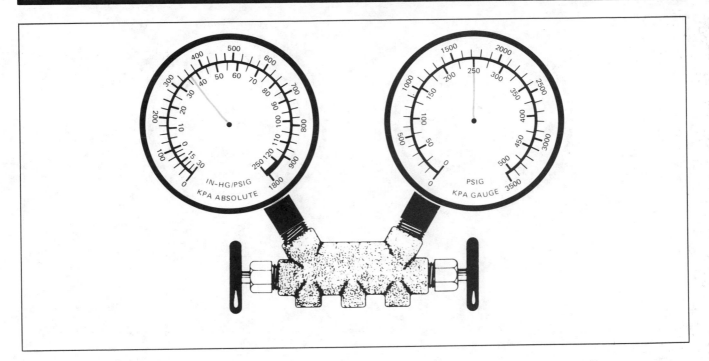

CONDITIONS

Ambient temperature: 95°F (35°C)
Low-side gauge: 37 psig (356 kPa absolute)
High-side gauge: 250 psi (1 724 kPa)

DIAGNOSIS

1. Show the gauge readings on the gauge set in the diagram.

2. The low-side gauge is (high, normal, low). _____ HIGH _____

3. The high-side gauge is (high, normal, low). _____ HIGH _____

4. List two possible causes for this malfunction.
   a. _OVER CHARGE_____
   b. _BAD FAN OR FAN CLUTCH " CONDENSER IS NOT GETTING COOL"_

5. An (undercharge, overcharge) of refrigerant can cause _____UNDERCHARGE_____
   this problem. _IF BOTH SIDE OF THE HOSES ARE HOT._

225

SYSTEM DIAGNOSIS 16:
The System—Cycling Clutch TXV or FOT System

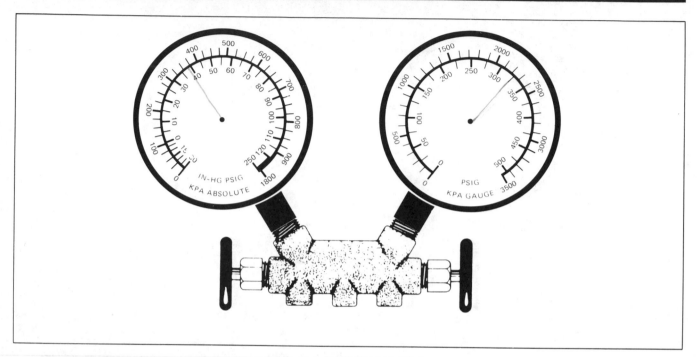

CONDITIONS

Ambient temperature: 96°F (36°C)
Low-side gauge: 39 psig (370 kPa absolute)
High-side gauge: 325 psi (2 241 kPa)

DIAGNOSIS

1. Show the gauge readings on the gauge set in the diagram.

2. List six possible causes of excessive head pressure.
   a. _Too much oil_
   b. _____
   c. _____
   d. _____
   e. _____
   f. _____

3. High head pressure is (always, not always) accompanied _Not always_
   by high suction pressure.

SECTION 3:
SERVICE PROCEDURES

INTRODUCTION

Servicing automotive air-conditioning and heating systems seems to become more complex each year. Basic theories do not change, but refrigerant and electrical control are redesigned or added from year to year. To add to the confusion, many domestic automotive manufacturers use metric fasteners (nuts and bolts) on some component and accessory assemblies. This means that both English and metric fasteners can now be found in the same automobile.

Many metric fasteners very closely resemble English fasteners, figure I-1, in size and appearance. Automotive service technicians must be extremely careful to avoid mixing these fasteners. English and metric fasteners *are not* interchangeable. For example, a metric 6.3 (6.3-mm) capscrew may replace, by design, an English 1/4-28 (1/4-in by 28 threads per inch) capscrew. Note, in the table of figure I-2 that the diameters differ by only 0.002 inch (0.05 mm), and the threads differ by only 2.6 per inch (1 per cm). There are 28 threads per inch (11 threads per cm) for a 1/4-28 capscrew, and 30.6 threads per inch (12 threads per cm) for a 6.3-mm capscrew.

Fig. I-1 Comparison of English 1/4-28 and metric 6.3-mm capscrew

English Series				Metric Series			
Size	Diameter		Threads Per Inch	Size	Diameter		Threads Per Inch (prox)
	in	mm			in	mm	
#8	0.164	4.165	32 or 36				
#10	0.190	4.636	24 or 32				
1/4	0.250	6.350	20 or 28	M6.3	0.248	6.299	25
				M7	0.275	6.985	25
5/16	0.312	7.924	18 or 24	M8	0.315	8.001	20 or 25
3/8	0.375	9.525	16 or 24				
				M10	0.393	9.982	17 or 20
7/16	0.437	11.099	14 or 20				
				M12	0.472	11.988	14.5 or 20
1/2	0.500	12.700	13 or 20				
9/16	0.562	14.274	12 or 18	M14	0.551	13.995	12.5 or 17
5/8	0.625	15.875	11 or 18				
				M16	0.630	16.002	12.5 or 17
				M18	0.700	17.780	10 or 17
3/4	0.750	19.050	10 or 16				
				M20	0.787	19.989	10 or 17
				M22	0.866	21.996	10 or 17
7/8	0.875	24.765	9 or 14				
				M24	0.945	24.003	8.5 or 12.5
1	1.000	25.400	8 or 14				
				M27	1.063	27.000	8.5 or 12.5

Fig. I-2 Comparison of English and metric series fasteners

These differences are small, but an English 1/4-28 nut on a metric 6.3 capscrew *will not* hold. Mismatching of fasteners can cause component damage and/or failure. *Such component failure can result in personal injury.*

The procedures given in this section are intended as typical. They are to be used as a guide only. Because of the great number of variations in automotive air-conditioning and heating systems, it would be impossible to include all specific and detailed information in this text. When specific or more detailed information is needed, the service technician should consult the appropriate manufacturer's service manual for that particular year-model automobile. Some general service manuals are now available that cover, in greater detail, most service procedures for automobiles of a specific year, make, and model. One such manual, covering the past ten years only, has little theory and is more than four inches (102 mm) thick.

The information in this section, then, is given only as a guide to enable the learning technician to perform many typical service procedures normally required. Proper service and repair procedures are vital to the safe, reliable, operation of the system. More importantly, proper service procedures and techniques are essential to provide personal safety to those performing the repair service.

SAFETY

It must be recognized that the skills and procedures of individuals performing the service work vary greatly. It is not possible to anticipate all conceivable ways or conditions under which service work may be performed. Therefore, it is impossible to provide precautions for every possible hazard that may result.

The following precautions are basic, and apply to any type of automotive service.

1. Wear safety glasses or goggles for eye protection when working under the hood of a car.

2. Set the parking brake. Place the gear selector in PARK if equipped with an automatic transmission, or in NEUTRAL if a manual transmission.

3. Unless required otherwise for the procedure, be sure that the ignition switch is in the OFF position.

4. Operate the engine, if required for the procedure, in a well-ventilated area.

5. Avoid loose clothing. Tie long hair securely behind the head. Remove rings, watches, and loose-hanging jewelry.

6. Keep clear of all moving parts when the engine is running.

7. Keep hands, clothing, tools, and test leads away from the cooling fan. Electric cooling fans may start without warning even when the ignition switch is in the OFF position.

8. Avoid contact with hot parts such as the radiator, exhaust manifold, and high-side refrigerant lines.

9. If in doubt, ASK; do not take chances.

> The technician must exercise extreme caution, and pay heed to every established safety practice, when performing these or any automotive air-conditioning service procedures.

SERVICE PROCEDURE 1:

Connecting the Manifold and Gauge Set into the System

This procedure can be used when it becomes necessary to install the manifold and gauge set on the air-conditioning system to perform any one of the many operational tests. This Service Procedure is given in two parts. Part I is used when installing a manifold and gauge set into a system equipped with three-way (hand shutoff) compressor service valves. Part II is used when installing a manifold and gauge set into a system equipped with Schrader-type service valves.

Safety glasses should be worn while working with a refrigerant. Remember, liquid refrigerant splashed in the eyes can cause blindness.

TOOLS

Manifold and gauge set equipped with compound and pressure gauges
Three service hoses with Schrader adapter pins
Service valve wrench
Suitable wrenches to remove the protective caps from the service ports
Suitable eye protection
Fender covers

PART I – PROCEDURE

Prepare the System

1. Place a fender cover on the car to avoid damage to the finish of the car.

2. Use a wrench of the correct size to remove the protective caps from the service valve stems. Some caps are made of light metal and can be removed by hand.

3. Using the correct wrench, remove the protective acorn caps from the service ports. *CAUTION: Remove the caps slowly to insure that no refrigerant leaks past the service valve.*

Connect the Manifold Gauge Service Hoses to the Compressor

1. Connect the low-side manifold hose to the suction side of the compressor.

2. Connect the high-side manifold hose to the discharge side of the compressor. Both of the connections (1 and 2) are to be fingertight.

3. Make sure the hand shutoff valves are closed on the manifold set before the next step.

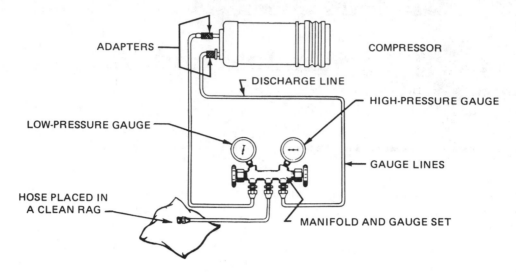

Fig. SP1-1 Typical manifold set connections

Purge the Service Hoses

1. Use a service valve wrench and rotate the suction-side service valve stem two or three turns clockwise.

2. Repeat the procedure in step 1 with the discharge service valve stem.

3. Purge the air from the low-side hose by cracking the low-side hand valve for a few seconds; then close the valve.

4. Repeat the procedure in step 3 with the high-side hand valve to purge the air from the high-side hose.

Prepare the System for Operational Tests

1. Start the motor and adjust the speed to about 1 250 r/min by adjusting the idle speed screw or the setting on the high cam.

2. Turn on the air conditioner and adjust all controls for maximum cold (with the blower on high speed).

3. If the motor is cold, allow sufficient time for the engine to warm up, between five and ten minutes.

4. Perform operational tests as required.

PART II — PROCEDURE

Prepare the System

1. Place a fender cover on the car to avoid damage to the finish of the car.

2. Using a wrench of the correct size to avoid damage, remove the protective acorn caps from the high- and low-side service ports. *CAUTION: Remove the caps slowly to insure that no refrigerant is leaking past a defective Schrader valve.*

Connect the Manifold Gauge Service Hoses

1. Service hoses must be equipped with a Schrader valve depressing pin. If the hoses are not so equipped, a suitable adapter must be used.

2. Make sure that the manifold hand shutoff valves are closed before the next step.

3. Connect the low-side manifold hose to the suction side of the system fingertight.

4. Connect the high-side manifold hose to the discharge side of the system fingertight.

    NOTE: The high-side fitting on most late model Ford and General Motors car lines is 3/16 inch. A special adapter must be used, connected to the manifold hose before connecting to the system.

Purge the Service Hoses

1. Purge the air from the low-side hose by cracking the low-side service valve on the manifold for a few seconds; then close the valve.

2. Repeat step 1 with the high-side manifold valve to purge the air from the high-side hose.

Prepare the System for Operational Tests

1. Start the engine and adjust the speed to about 1 250 r/min by adjusting the idle speed screw or the setting on the high cam.

2. Turn on the air conditioner and adjust all controls for maximum cooling (with the blower on high speed).

3. If the engine is cold, allow sufficient time for the engine to warm up, between five and ten minutes.

4. Perform operational tests as necessary.

Review

1. How is the low-side (suction) service valve identified?

2. Does a Schrader-type service valve have a front-seated position? Why or why not?

3. What is meant by "purging" air?

4. How tight should the hose connection be fastened to the service port? Why?

5. How is the hand shutoff-type compressor service valve "cracked"?

6. How is the Schrader-type service valve "back seated"?

7. Why is it important to wear safety glasses?

8. Which type service valve requires a service valve wrench?

9. Why should service valve protective caps be removed slowly?

10. Briefly, how are the manifold hoses purged of air?

SERVICE PROCEDURE 2:

Purging the Air-conditioning System

To *purge* an air-conditioning system is to remove all of the refrigerant from the system. This is usually necessary when a system component is to be serviced or replaced. This procedure outlines the steps to purge the refrigerant to the atmosphere, a common practice in most automotive shops. The Environmental Protection Agency (EPA) in recent years has criticized this practice, claiming that damaging contamination of the ionosphere is partly due to refrigerant "dumping." Some larger repair shops have installed refrigerant recovery systems which enable them to dry, clean, and reuse refrigerants purged from systems.

Adequate ventilation must be maintained during this operation. Do not discharge Refrigerant 12 near an open flame as toxic gas is formed.

TOOLS

Complete manifold and gauge set
Service valve wrench
Protective covers

Suitable hand wrenches
Eye goggles

PROCEDURE

Prepare System

1. Connect the manifold and gauge set into the system. Set all controls to the maximum cold position.

2. Set the engine speed to 1 000–1 200 r/min and operate for 10–15 minutes.

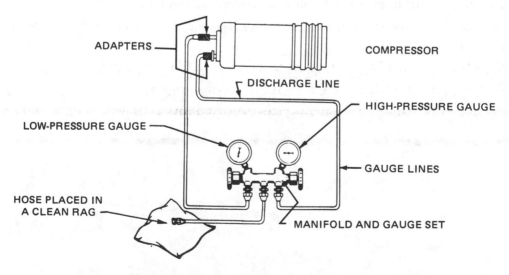

Fig. SP2-1 Manifold hookup to purge system

3. This procedure should be followed whenever possible to stabilize the system. However, certain system malfunctions can make this procedure impossible.

Purge Refrigerant from the System

1. Return the engine speed to normal to prevent dieseling. Shut off the engine.
2. Open the low- and high-side manifold valves slowly to allow refrigerant to bleed off through the center hose.
3. Open the hand valves only enough to bleed off the refrigerant. Rapid purging draws excessive oil from the system.
4. The center hose can be placed on a clean rag. If any refrigeration oil is pulled out of the system, it shows on the rag.

   NOTE: If it is apparent that a measurable amount of oil is being drawn from the system, place the center hose into a graduated container. The amount of oil drawn from the system must be replaced with clean, fresh oil, as outlined in the appropriate Service Procedure.

System Purged of Refrigerant

1. Both manifold gauges read zero when the system is purged.
2. Close the hand manifold valves when the refrigerant ceases to bleed off.
3. The system is now purged of refrigerant and can be opened for service as required.
4. Cap all openings and hoses to avoid the possibility of dirt or foreign matter entering the system.

Review

Briefly answer each of the following questions.

1. What is meant by purging the air-conditioning system?
2. What happens if Refrigerant 12 is discharged near an open flame?
3. After stabilizing the system, why is the engine speed returned to normal before the engine is shut off?
4. What is the result if a hand valve is opened all the way while purging?
5. How does one know when the system is purged of refrigerant?

SERVICE PROCEDURE 3:

Leak Testing the System

Three popular methods of leak detection are by soap bubbles, halide gas, or halogen electronic testing. This service procedure is given in three parts: Part I for soap bubble testing, Part II for halide gas testing, and Part III for halogen electronic testing.

The soap solution method of leak detection is often required when it is impossible or impractical to pinpoint the exact location of a leak using halide or halogen leak detectors. A commercially available solution, such as that shown in figure SP3-1, is more effective than a household solution. A good grade of sudsing liquid dishwashing detergent may be used, however, if a commercial solution is not available.

The halide leak detector is essentially a propane torch. This device, figure SP3-2, is the most popular form of leak detector insofar as the service technician is concerned because of its low initial cost and low upkeep. Other than propellant replacement, the only maintenance required is an occasional reactor plate replacement.

To check the sensitivity of the reactor plate, the pickup hose is passed over a recently opened (but empty) can of refrigerant. Alternatively, a service valve can be cracked open. The flame of the torch should be violet in color. If little or no color change occurs, the reactor plate must be replaced.

When leak testing, all joints and fittings should be free of oil. This precaution eliminates the possibility of a false reading caused by refrigerant absorbed in the oil. Cigarette smoke, purging of another unit nearby, and refrigerant vapors in the surrounding air can also give false readings on the detector.

A halide leak detector must only be used in a well-ventilated area. It must never be used in spaces where explosive gases are present. When refrigerant comes into contact with an open flame, toxic gases are formed. Never inhale the vapors or fumes from the halide leak detector — they can be poisnous.

Fig. SP3-1 Typical liquid leak detector

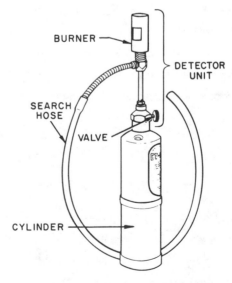

Fig. SP3-2 Leak detector (torch)

The halogen electronic leak detector is the most sensitive of all types of leak detectors. Some of these electronic detectors can sense a refrigerant leak as small as one-half ounce per year. The initial cost and upkeep are the controlling economic factors to be considered in purchasing electronic leak detectors. If a shop does a great deal of air-conditioner service, this type of leak detector can be of great value in detecting *impossible* leaks.

A halogen electronic leak detector must be used in a well-ventilated area only. It must never be used in spaces where explosive gases are present.

Fig. SP3-3 Leak detector

TOOLS

Service valve wrench
Suitable hand wrenches
Eye protection
Fender covers
Manifold and gauge set
Leak detector — soap, halide or halogen

PROCEDURE

Prepare the System (All Methods)

1. Connect the manifold and gauge set to the system.
2. Place the high- and low-side compressor service valves in the cracked position.
3. Place the high- and low-side manifold hand valves in the closed position.
4. Determine the presence of refrigerant in the system. A minimum value of 50 psig (348 kPa) is needed for leak detection.
5. If there is an insufficient charge of refrigerant in the system, continue with the next step, *Add Refrigerant for Leak Test Pressure*. If the charge is sufficient, omit the next step and proceed with the step, *Prepare the Leak Detector*.

Add Refrigerant for Leak Test Pressure (All Methods)

1. Open the high- and low-side hand valves to purge the hoses of air. Then close the valves.
2. Attach the center manifold hose to the refrigerant container.
3. Open the refrigerant container service valve.
4. Open the high-side manifold hand valve until a pressure of 50 psig (348 kPa) is reached on the low-side gauge. Then close the high-side hand valve.
5. Close the refrigerant container service valve and remove the hose.

Fig. SP3-4 Bubbles reveal point of leak when using soap solution

PART I — SOAP SOLUTION METHOD

Prepare the Leak Detector

1. Apply solution to all joints and/or suspected areas by:
   a. using dauber supplied with commercial solution.
   b. using small brush with household solution.

2. Leaks are exposed when a bubble forms, as shown in figure SP3-4.

3. Repair leak as outlined in "Repair System (All Methods)."

PART II — HALIDE GAS METHOD

Prepare the Leak Detector

1. Open the valve and light the gas. Adjust for a low flame; that is, one which burns about 1/2 inch above the reactor plate.

2. Allow the flame to burn until the copper reactor plate becomes cherry red in color.

3. Lower the flame until it is about 1/4 inch above or just even with the reactor plate.

Fig. SP3-5 Leak testing the condenser

Reaction of Halide Leak Detector in the Presence of Refrigerant

In the presence of refrigerant, a color change will occur in the flame above the reactor plate:

- Pale blue: no refrigerant loss
- Pale yellow at the edges of the flame: very small refrigerant loss
- Yellow: small amount of refrigerant loss
- Purplish-blue: large amount of refrigerant loss
- Violet: heavy amount of refrigerant loss; the volume may be great enough to extinguish the flame

Check for Leaks in the Air-conditioning System

1. Move the search hose under all of the joints and connections in the system. Check all seals and control devices.

2. Disconnect any vacuum hoses connected to the system. Check the vacuum hose ports for refrigerant vapors.

3. Repair leak as outlined in "Repair Service (All Methods)."

PART III — HALOGEN ELECTRONIC METHOD

Prepare the Leak Detector

NOTE: Follow the procedure as outlined in the manufacturer's instructions provided with the leak detector. Although the procedures may vary considerably for different leak detectors, the following steps can be used as a guide.

1. Turn the controls and the sensitivity knobs to off or zero.

2. Plug the leak detector into an approved voltage source and turn the switch on. Allow a warmup period of about five minutes (unless battery powered).

3. After the warmup period, place the probe at the reference leak and adjust the controls and sensitivity knob until the detector reacts. Remove the probe — the reaction should stop. If the reaction continues, the sensitivity adjustment is too high. If the reaction stops, the adjustment is adequate.

Check the System for Leaks

1. Move the search hose under all of the joints and connections. Check all seals and control devices.

2. Disconnect any vacuum hoses connected to the system. Check the vacuum hose ports for refrigerant vapor (indicating a control leak).

3. When a leak is located, the detector reacts as it does when placed by the reference leak.

4. Do not keep the probe in contact with refrigerant any longer than is necessary to locate the leak.

Never place the probe in a stream of refrigerant or where a severe leak is known to exist. The sensitive components of the leak detector can be damaged in this situation.

Repair System (All Methods)

1. After the leak is located, purge the system of refrigerant.

2. Repair the leak as indicated. Check the compressor oil as outlined in the appropriate Service Procedure.

3. Add oil and refrigerant. Recheck for leaks.

4. If no leaks are found, purge the system, evacuate, and charge the system as outlined in Service Procedures 2, 4, and 5.

5. Perform other service procedures as necessary.

Review

Briefly answer each of the following questions.

1. Technician A says that phosgene gas is formed when Refrigerant 12 comes into contact with an open flame. Technician B says that phosgene gas is formed when Refrigerant 12 comes into contact with a heated metal.
   a. Technician A is correct.
   b. Technician B is correct.
   c. Either technician may be correct.
   d. Both technicians are wrong.

2. What system pressure is usually required to detect a leak?

3. What is the color of the flame in the presence of a small leak?

4. What is the greatest advantage of the halogen leak detector?

5. What disadvantage may there be in the use of a halogen leak detector?

SERVICE PROCEDURE 4:

Evacuating the System

The air-conditioning system must be evacuated whenever the system is serviced to the extent that it is purged of refrigerant. Evacuation rids the system of all air and moisture that was allowed to enter the unit. At or near sea level, a good vacuum pump is one that can achieve a value of 29 inHg (3.4 kPa absolute) or better. For each 1 000 feet (305 meters) of elevation, the reading is about 1 inHg (3.4 kPa absolute) higher. For example, at 5 000 feet (1 524 meters) the vacuum reading is about 24 inHg (20.3 kPa absolute).

As the pressure in the air-conditioning system is lowered, the boiling temperature of the water (moisture) that is present in the system is also lowered. The water vapor can then be pulled out of the system. The table in figure SP4-1 illustrates the effectiveness of moisture removal for a given vacuum.

System Vacuum, inHg	Temperature, °F
27.99	100
28.89	80
29.40	60
29.71	40
29.82	20
29.88	0

Fig. SP4-1 Boiling point of water in a vacuum (English)

TOOLS

Service valve wrench
Hand wrenches
Fender covers
Manifold and gauge set
Vacuum pump or charging station

PROCEDURE

Prepare the System

1. Connect the manifold and gauge set to the system.

2. Place the high- and low-side compressor service valves in the cracked position.

3. Place the high- and low-side manifold hand valves in the closed position.

4. Remove the protective caps from the inlet and exhaust of the vacuum pump. Make sure the port cap is removed from the exhaust port to avoid damage to the vacuum pump.

5. Connect the center manifold hose to the inlet of the vacuum pump.

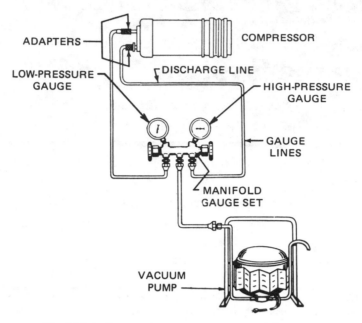

ADAPTERS

COMPRESSOR

LOW-PRESSURE
GAUGE

DISCHARGE LINE

HIGH-PRESSURE
GAUGE

GAUGE
LINES

MANIFOLD
GAUGE SET

VACUUM
PUMP

Fig. SP4-2 Connections for evacuation of system

Evacuate the System

1. Start the vacuum pump.

2. Open the low-side manifold hand valve and observe the compound gauge needle. The needle should be pulled down to indicate a slight vacuum.

3. After about five minutes, the compound gauge should indicate below 20 inHg (33.8 kPa absolute) and the high-side gauge needle should be slightly below the zero index of the gauge.

4. If the high-side needle does not drop below zero (unless restricted by a stop), system blockage is indicated.

5. If the system is blocked, discontinue the evacuation. Repair or remove the obstruction. If the system is clear, continue the evacuation.

6. Operate the pump for 15 minutes and observe the gauges. The system should be at a vacuum of 24–26 inHg (20.3–13.5 kPa absolute) minimum if there is no leak.

7. If the system is not down to 24–26 inHg, (20.3–13.5 kPa absolute) close the low-side hand valve and observe the compound gauge.

8. If the compound gauge needle rises, indicating a loss of vacuum, there is a leak which must be repaired before the evacuation is continued. Leak check the system as outlined in Service Procedure 3.

9. If no leak is evident, continue with the pumpdown.

Complete the Evacuation

1. Pump for a minimum of 30 minutes, longer if time permits.

2. After pumpdown, close the high- and low-side manifold hand valves. (The high-side valve can be opened after the system is checked for blockage.)

3. Shut off the vacuum pump, disconnect the manifold hose, and replace the protective caps.

Check the System for Irregularities

1. Note the compound gauge reading; it should be about 29 inHg (3.4 kPa absolute).

2. The compound gauge needle should not rise at a rate faster than 1 inch (3.4 kPa absolute) in five minutes.

3. If the system fails to meet this requirement, although not indicated previously, a partial charge must be installed and the system must be leak checked as outlined in Service Procedure 3.

4. After the leak is detected and repaired, the system must be purged of refrigerant and completely evacuated.

5. If the system holds the vacuum as specified, continue with the charging procedure (or other procedures as required).

Briefly answer each of the following questions.

1. What is the recommended minimum pumping requirement for a vacuum pump at sea level?

2. How is moisture removed from the system when the system is under a vacuum?

3. Can moisture normally be removed from a system under a vacuum of 27 inHg (10 kPa absolute)?

4. What is indicated if the system cannot be pumped down to a vacuum in 15 minutes?

5. What is the recommended minimum pumpdown time?

6. If the system is leak free, the vacuum rise after pumpdown should be no greater than 1 inHg per _____ minutes.

SERVICE PROCEDURE 5:

Charging the System

Three methods of charging an automotive air conditioning system are given in this service procedure; from pound cans with the system off (Part I), from pound cans with the system operating (Part II), and from a bulk source (Part III).

Containers of refrigerant are commonly called *pound cans,* but actually hold 14 ounces (396.9 g) of refrigerant. Pound cans are popular and are used in many shops, including shops with a large volume of business and those operating on a smaller scale.

The service technician must insure that only Refrigerant 12 is introduced into the air-conditioning system. To assist in identifying Refrigerant 12, the containers generally are painted white. For positive identification, however, the technician should check that the chemical name on the container is dichlorodifluoromethane (the symbol is CCl_2F_2).

CAUTION

Above 130°F (54.4°C), liquid refrigerant completely fills a container and hydrostatic pressure builds up rapidly with each degree of temperature added.

- Never heat a refrigerant container above 125°F (51.7°C). (It should never be necessary to heat a refrigerant container at all.)

- Never apply a direct flame to a refrigerant container or place an electric resistance heater close to the container.

- Do not abuse a refrigerant container.

- Use only approved wrenches to open and close the valves.

- Store the container in an upright position.

- Do not handle refrigerant without suitable eye protection and do not discharge refrigerant into an enclosed area having an open flame.

With the refrigerant can or tank inverted, vapor rises to the top of the container and liquid refrigerant is forced into the charging hoses. *Do not* invert the refrigerant container with low-side pressures in excess of 40 psig (377 kPa absolute). Regulating the valve on the container or the manifold hand valve insures a pressure of 40 psig (377 kPa absolute) or below. Liquid refrigerant entering the compressor low side can cause serious damage to internal parts such as pistons, reed valves, head, and head gaskets.

If the ambient temperature is lower than 80°F (26.7°C) do not invert the refrigerant container. The car engine and air-conditioning system should be at operating temperature.

TOOLS

Service valve wrench
Suitable hand wrenches
Eye protection
Fender covers

Manifold and gauge set
Can tap
Scales

MATERIAL

Refrigerant 12, as required.

PROCEDURE

Prepare the System (All Methods)

1. With both manifold hand valves in the closed position, connect the manifold and gauge set into the system.
2. Place the high- and low-side compressor service valves in the cracked position, if the unit is so equipped.
3. Place the system under a vacuum after an adequate pumpdown.

Install the Can Tap Valve on the Container of Refrigerant (Parts I and II)

1. The valve stem should be in the out, or counterclockwise, position.
2. Attach the valve to the can. Secure the locking nut, if the valve is so equipped.
3. Connect the center manifold hose to the can tap port.
4. Pierce the can by closing the can tap shutoff valve. Turn the valve stem all the way in the clockwise direction.

Purge the Line of Air (Parts I and II)

1. Once the can is pierced, back the can tap valve out as far as possible (turn in a counterclockwise direction).

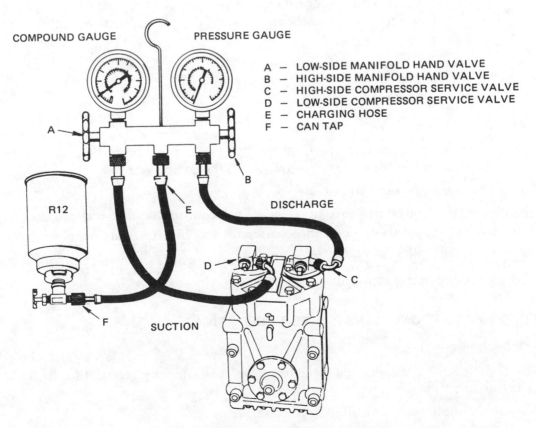

Fig. SP5-1 Charging the system with liquid

2. The center hose is now charged with refrigerant. *Do not crack* the high- or low-side hand valves.

3. Loosen the center hose connection at the manifold set until a hiss can be heard. Allow gases to escape for a few seconds, then retighten the connection.

4. The system is now purged and under a vacuum.

Check the System for Blockage (Parts I and II)

1. Open the high-side gauge manifold hand valve. Observe the low-side gauge pressure. Close the high-side hand valve.

2. If the low-side gauge does not move from the vacuum range into the pressure range, system blockage is indicated.

3. Correct the blockage, if indicated. Then evacuate and continue with the next operation.

PART I — USING POUND CANS (SYSTEM OFF)

Charge the System

1. Open the high-side gauge manifold hand valve.

2. Observe the low-side gauge pressure. If the gauge indication does not move from the vacuum range into the pressure range, system blockage is indicated.

3. If the system is blocked, correct the condition, evacuate, and continue with the procedure.

4. Invert the container and allow the liquid refrigerant to enter the system.

5. Tap the refrigerant container on the bottom. The can is empty if it gives a hollow ring.

6. Repeat this procedure with additional cans of refrigerant as required to charge the air conditioner completely. Refer to the manufacturer's specifications regarding the system capacity.

Complete the System Charge

1. Close the high-side manifold hand valve.

2. Remove the can tap from the center hose.

3. Rotate the compressor clutch by hand through two or three revolutions to insure that liquid refrigerant has not entered the low side of the compressor.

4. Start the engine and set it to fast idle.

5. Engage the clutch to start the compressor. Set all controls to maximum cooling.

6. Conduct a performance test, if indicated.

7. Back seat the compressor service valves. Remove the manifold gauge set from the system.

8. Replace all protective caps and covers.

PART II — USING POUND CANS (SYSTEM OPERATIONAL)

Charge the System

1. Start the engine and adjust the speed to about 1 250 r/min by turning the idle screw or the setting on the high cam.

2. Insure that both of the manifold hand valves are closed.

3. Adjust the controls for maximum cooling with the blower on high speed.

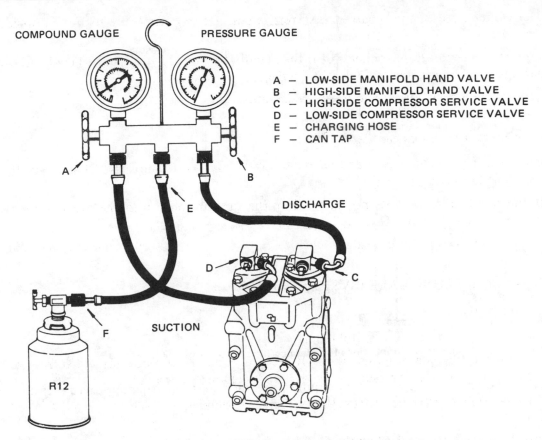

COMPOUND GAUGE   PRESSURE GAUGE

A — LOW-SIDE MANIFOLD HAND VALVE
B — HIGH-SIDE MANIFOLD HAND VALVE
C — HIGH-SIDE COMPRESSOR SERVICE VALVE
D — LOW-SIDE COMPRESSOR SERVICE VALVE
E — CHARGING HOSE
F — CAN TAP

DISCHARGE

SUCTION

R12

Fig. SP5-2 Charging the system with gas

4. Open the low-side gauge manifold hand valve to allow gaseous refrigerant to enter the system.

5. After the pressure on the low side drops below 40 psig (377 kPa absolute), the can should be inverted to allow more rapid removal of the refrigerant.

6. Tap the can on the bottom to determine if it is empty. An empty can will give a hollow ring.

7. Repeat this procedure with additional cans of refrigerant as required to charge the system completely. Refer to the manufacturer's specifications regarding the capacity of the system.

   NOTE: If the system capacity is not known, charge the unit until the sight glass is clear, then add another 1/4 pound (113 g) of refrigerant.

Complete the System Charge

1. Close the low-side manifold hand valve.

2. Remove the can tap from the center hose.

3. Conduct the performance test if indicated.

4. Back seat the compressor service valves and remove the manifold and gauge set.

5. Replace all protective caps and covers.

PART III — CHARGING FROM A BULK SOURCE

Shops that perform a large volume of air-conditioning service can obtain bulk refrigerant in 10-, 15-, 25-, 30-, 50-, and 145-pound (4.5-, 6.8-, 11.3-, 13.6-, 22.7-, and 65.8-kilogram)

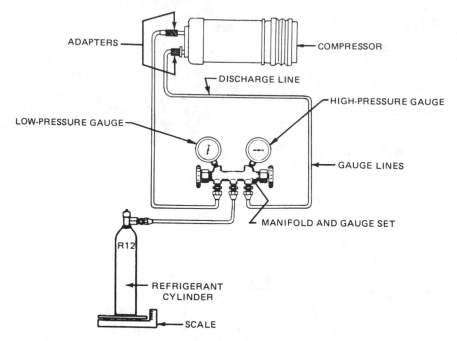

Fig. SP5-3 Connections for charging the system from a bulk source

cylinders. The use of bulk containers requires a set of scales, or other approved measuring device, to determine when the proper system charge is obtained.

Connect the Refrigerant Container and Purge the System

1. Connect the center manifold gauge hose to the refrigerant cylinder adapter.
2. Open the refrigerant cylinder hand valve.
3. Crack the center hose at the manifold gauge set for a few seconds to purge the hose of air.
4. The system is now purged and under a vacuum.

Check the System for Blockage

1. Do not start the engine at this time and do not turn the air conditioner on.
2. Open the high-side manifold hand valve. Observe the low-side gauge. Close the high-side hand valve.
3. System blockage is indicated if the low-side gauge needle does not move from the vacuum range into the pressure range.
4. If the system is blocked, correct the blockage, reevacuate the system, and continue with the procedure.

Charge the System

1. Insure that both the high- and low-side manifold hand valves are closed.
2. Start the engine and adjust the speed to about 1 250 r/min.
3. Adjust the air-conditioning controls for maximum cooling with the blower on high speed.
4. Keep the refrigerant cylinder in an upright position. Liquid refrigerant must not be allowed to enter the compressor since this can cause serious damage.

5. Open the low-side manifold hand valve and allow the gaseous refrigerant to enter the system.

6. Place the cylinder on a scale to insure that the refrigerant is measured properly. If the system capacity is not known, add refrigerant until it just passes the sight glass and then add four more ounces (113 g). The amount of refrigerant used can be determined by the scale reading. (Subtract the new scale reading from the original scale reading.)

Complete the System Charge

1. When the system is fully charged, close the low-side manifold hand valve.

2. Close the cylinder service valve and remove the hose from the adapter.

3. Conduct the performance tests or other tests as required.

4. Return the engine to its normal idle speed. Shut off the engine.

5. Back seat the compressor service valves and remove the manifold and gauge set.

6. Replace all protective caps and covers.

Review

Briefly answer each of the following questions.

1. What is the net weight of the contents of a "pound" can (in English and metrics)?

2. What is the proper name for Refrigerant 12? Underline one of the following.

   a. dichlorodifluoromethane   b. monochlordifluoromethane

3. What is the chemical symbol for Refrigerant 12? Underline one of the following.

   a. $CHC1F_2$ b. $CC1_2F_2$ c. CH_2Cl_2

4. Why is it important to be able to recognize the chemical name and symbol for Refrigerant 12?

5. Which side of the compressor is used to charge the system with liquid when the system is off?

SERVICE PROCEDURE 6:

Adding Dye or Trace Solution to the Air-conditioning System

A dye or trace solution can be introduced into an air-conditioning system to aid in pinpointing a small leak. The dye shows the exact location of a leak by depositing a colored film around the leak. Depending on the dye used, the film may be orange-red or yellow. Once the dye is introduced into the air-conditioning system, it remains until the system is cleaned. The trace solution or dye is formulated for use in air-conditioning systems and does not affect system operation in any way.

NOTE: Some refrigerant manufacturers produce refrigerants which include a red dye solution, figure SP6-1. This product is introduced into the system following the standard charging procedures as outlined in Service Procedure 5. This procedure is for adding dye solution which is not previously mixed with refrigerant, figure SP6-2.

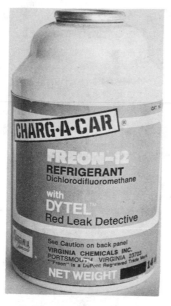

Fig. SP6-1 Typical "pound" can of Refrigerant 12 with a red dye additive. "Freon" and "Dytel" are trademarks of E.I. DuPont.

Fig. SP6-2 Typical dye solution which is compatible with Refrigerant 12

TOOLS

Manifold and gauge set
Copper tubing, 1/4" x 0.5'
Flare nuts, 1/4 inch (2)

Service valve wrench or Schrader adapter
Hand wrenches
Can tap

MATERIALS

Dye or trace solution, as required
Refrigerant 12

PROCEDURE

Prepare the System

1. Connect the manifold and gauge set to the system. If the system is charged with refrigerant, purge it from the system.

2. Construct a charging line using a six-inch (152-mm) piece of copper tubing and two flare nuts.

3. Remove the center hose from the manifold and connect the copper tubing (from step 2) to the center manifold connection.

4. Connect the dye solution to the copper tubing. Reconnect the center manifold hose to the dye solution.

5. Secure the other end of the center manifold hose (charging line) to a source of Refrigerant 12.

Add Dye to the System

1. Start the engine and operate it at idle speeds. Set the controls for maximum cooling.

2. Open the low-side manifold hand valve slowly and allow the trace dye to enter the system.

3. Charge the system to at least half capacity. Allow to operate for 15 minutes.

4. Shut off the air conditioner and the car engine.

Observe the System

1. Observe the hoses and fittings for signs of the dye solution. If no signs of a leak are evident, arrange to have the car available the following day for diagnosis and repair.

2. If one or more leaks is detected, make repairs as required. The dye solution can remain in the system without causing harm to the system.

Return the System to Normal Operation

1. Remove the manifold and gauge set.

2. Replace the protective caps.

Review

Select the appropriate answer from the choices given.

1. Dye trace solution has been introduced into the system. Technician A says that it will eventually fade out. Technician B says that it must be flushed out.

   a. Technician A is correct.
   b. Technician B is correct.
   c. Both technicians may be correct.
   d. Both technicians are wrong.

2. Technician A says that dye trace solution should not be used unless absolutely necessary because it does not mix well with refrigerant and oil. Technician B says it should not be used because it seriously affects system operation.

   a. Technician A is correct.
   b. Technician B is correct.
   c. Both technicians are correct.
   d. Both technicians are wrong.

3. Dye trace helps pinpoint a leak by leaving a(an)

   a. red film.
   b. orange film.
   c. yellow film.
   d. Any of these.

4. Dye solution is best used to pinpoint or detect

   a. a rapid leak.
   b. vacuum system problems.
   c. a slow leak.
   d. excessive moisture.

5. To remove the dye solution, it is necessary to

   a. discharge and recharge the system.
   b. discharge, evaculate, and recharge the system.
   c. discharge, clean, evacuate, and recharge the system.
   d. add neutralizer to the system.

SERVICE PROCEDURE 7:

Isolating the Compressor from the System

When a system has both high- and low-side compressor service valves, the compressor can be isolated from the system. The refrigerant can be retained in the system while the compressor is serviced. If a system uses a Schrader-type service port, the compressor cannot be isolated. In this situation, the compressor must be purged of refrigerant to perform any service procedures.

TOOLS

Service valve wrench
Hand wrenches
Eye protection

Fender covers
Manifold and gauge set

PROCEDURE

Prepare the System

1. With the manifold and gauge set connected into the system, set both hand valves in the closed position.
2. Set both compressor service valves in the cracked position.
3. Stabilize the system by running the car engine at about 1 200 r/min with the air-conditioner controls turned on maximum cooling for about 10 minutes.

Isolate the Compressor

1. Return the car engine to idle speed, about 500 r/min.
2. Close the low-side service valve until the low-side gauge reads 10 inHg (68 kPa absolute).
3. Turn off the car motor. Completely close (front seat) the low-side service valve.
4. Close the high-side service valve.
5. Open the low-side manifold hand valve and allow trapped refrigerant to escape.
6. Repeat step 5 with the high-side hand valve. Close both valves when the gauges read zero.
7. The compressor is now isolated and can be removed from the car if necessary.

   Service valves must be removed from the compressor. Do not attempt to remove the hoses.

Return the Compressor to the System

1. If the compressor was removed from the car, replace the service valve gaskets with new gaskets.

2. Purge the air from the compressor as follows:
   a. Open the high-side manifold hand valve.
   b. Crack the low-side compressor service valve until it is no longer in the front-seated position.
   c. The low-side refrigerant pressure forces air out of the compressor through the high-side manifold set.
   d. After a few seconds of purging, close the high-side manifold hand valve.
3. Midposition the low-side compressor service valve.
4. Midposition the high-side compressor service valve.

Continue the Performance Test

1. With the manifold and gauge set connected, check the refrigerant charge.
2. Add refrigerant as necessary.

Return the System to Service

1. Back seat the high- and low-side compressor service valves.
2. Remove the service hoses and replace the protective caps.

Review

Briefly answer each of the following questions.

1. Why is it desirable to isolate the compressor from the system?
2. Can all compressors be isolated from the air-conditioning system? Why?
3. When isolating the compressor, what is the recommended compressor speed?
4. After the compressor is isolated what is the pressure in the compressor?
5. Is it possible to isolate a compressor equipped with Schrader valves? Explain.

SERVICE PROCEDURE 8:

Performing a Volumetric Test of the Air-conditioning Compressor

The volumetric or compressor capacity test is performed to determine the condition of the discharge reed valves and the piston rings.

TOOLS

Manifold and gauge set
Test caps, 1/4 inch
Test cap, 1/2 inch

Test cap, 5/8 inch, or 3/4 inch (as applicable)
Service valve wrench
Hand wrenches

MATERIAL

Refrigerant for recharging the system, if necessary

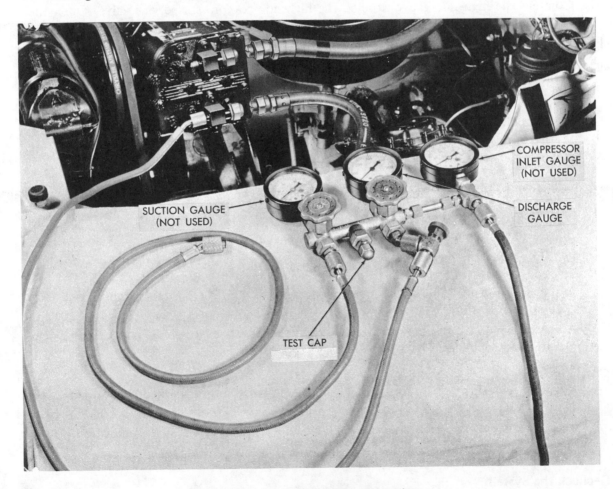

Fig. SP8-1 Volumetric test connections

PROCEDURE

Prepare the System for Volumetric Test

1. Attach the gauge and manifold set to the compressor, figure SP8-1.
2. Start the engine and adjust the speed to 1 000–1 200 r/min.
3. Adjust the controls for maximum cooling. Operate the system for about 10–15 minutes.
4. After 10–15 minutes, shut off all of the air-conditioning controls.
5. Return the engine speed to idle to prevent dieseling. Shut off the engine.
6. If the compressor is equipped with high- and low-side service valves, the compressor can be isolated, the valves removed, and another set of valves substituted for this test. If service valves are provided, follow the procedure outlined in Service Procedure 7.
7. If the compressor is equipped with Schrader-type service valves, the system must be purged of refrigerant. Follow the procedure outlined in Service Procedure 2.
8. When the system is purged of refrigerant, disconnect the high-side hose from the compressor outlet. Cap the hose end to prevent dirt and moisture from entering while the compressor check is being made. Repeat the procedure with the low-side hose.
9. If the compressor is isolated, remove the high- and low-side service valves and substitute other valves for this test.

   Do not remove the high- and low-side compressor hoses if the compressor is isolated.
10. Seal the compressor inlet fitting with the correct size of flare cap.
11. Connect the high-side gauge hose to the high-side compressor service valve. Open the high-side manifold hand valve.
12. Disconnect the low-side gauge hose from the compressor and the manifold.
13. Remove the center hose on the manifold and install a 1/4-inch test cap on the manifold fitting. The test cap is made by drilling a 1/4-inch acorn cap with a #71 drill to give an orifice of 0.026 inch.
14. If a Schrader-type valve is used, install an adapter to open the low side of the compressor to the atmosphere. If service valves are used, *both sides must be cracked or front seated.* The acorn nut must be removed from the low-side valve.

Perform the Volumetric or Capacity Test

1. Start the engine and allow it to idle at exactly 500 r/min.
2. Engage the clutch and operate the compressor as an air pump.

   NOTE: Never operate the air-conditioning compressor as an air pump for more than 15 seconds at a time. To do so can seriously damage the compressor because of improper lubrication. The manufacturer's warranty is void if compressor failure is due to a lack of lubrication.

   Air is drawn in at the compressor inlet and is pressurized to the center of the gauge manifold and the high-side gauge.
3. As soon as the maximum pressure is reached, turn off the compressor.
4. Read the high-side manifold gauge. The high-side gauge should read 180–200 psi (1 241–1 379 kPa).
5. If the reading is low, a faulty reed valve or a faulty valve plate gasket is indicated.
6. Make repairs as required. Follow the procedure outlined in this text.

Recheck the System

1. If necessary repairs are made, the compressor should be rechecked. Follow the procedure outlined.

Return the Compressor to Service

1. Remove all caps and plugs. Reconnect all lines and service valves.
2. If the system was purged, evacuate the system and recharge it as outlined previously.
3. If the compressor was isolated, purge the compressor of air as follows:
   a. Open the high-side manifold hand valve.
   b. Crack the compressor low-side service valve from the front-seated position.
   c. After a few seconds of purging, close the high-side manifold hand valve.
   d. Midposition the low- and high-side compressor service valves.

Continue the Performance Test

1. With the manifold gauge set connected, check the refrigerant charge.
2. Add refrigerant if necessary.

Return the System to Service

1. Back seat the high- and low-side compressor service valves.
2. Remove the service hoses and replace the protective caps.

Review

Briefly answer each of the following questions.

1. What is the purpose of the volumetric test?
2. To what specific parts of the air conditioner does the volumetric test apply?
3. At what speed should the compressor be run to hold the test?
4. What is the proper high-side gauge reading for the test?
5. If the high-side gauge reading is low, what malfunction is indicated?

SERVICE PROCEDURE 9:

Performance Testing the Air Conditioner

Humidity is an important factor in the temperature of the air delivered to the interior of the car. The service technician must understand the effect that humidity has on the performance of the system. When the humidity is high, the evaporator has a double function to perform. The evaporator must lower the air temperature as well as the temperature of the moisture carried in the air. The process of condensing the moisture in the air transfers a great deal of heat energy into the evaporator. As a result, the amount of heat that the evaporator can absorb from the air is reduced.

The evaporator capacity used to reduce the amount of moisture in the air is not wasted, however. Lowering the moisture content of the air entering the vehicle adds to the comfort of the passengers.

This procedure serves as a guide to the service procedures related to performance testing of the automobile air conditioner. The technician should refer to the manufacturer's service manuals for specific data.

TOOLS

Service valve wrench
Hand wrenches
Eye protection

Fender covers
Manifold and gauge set
Thermometer

PROCEDURE

Prepare the System

1. With the manifold and gauge set connected into the system, set both hand valves in the closed position.
2. Set the compressor high- and low-side service valves in the cracked position.
3. Run the engine at the high cam setting or adjust the idle screw to about 1 500–1 700 r/min.
4. Place the fan in front of the radiator to assist the ram airflow.
5. Turn on the air conditioner. Set all controls to maximum cooling.
6. Insert a thermometer in the air-conditioning duct as close as possible to the evaporator core. Set the blower on medium or low speed.

Visual Check of the Air Conditioner

1. The low-pressure gauge should be indicating within the range 20–30 psig (239–310 kPa absolute).
2. The high-side gauge should be within the specified range of 160–220 psig (1 103–1 517 kPa).
3. The discharge air temperature should be within the specified range of 40°F–50°F (4.4°C–10°C).

Inspect the High Side and Low Side of the System for Even Temperatures

1. Feel the hoses and components in the high side of the system to determine if the components are evenly heated.

   CAUTION: Certain system malfunctions cause the high-side components to become superheated to the point that a serious burn can result if care is not taken when handling these components.

2. Note the inlet and outlet temperatures of the drier assembly. Any change in the temperature indicates a clogged or defective drier.

3. All lines and components on the high side should be warm to the touch.

4. All lines and components on the low side of the system should be cool to the touch.

5. Note the condition of the thermostatic expansion valve. If the valve is frosted or cold on the inlet side, the valve may be defective.

Test the Thermostats and Control Devices

1. Refer to the service manual for the performance testing of the particular type of control device used.

2. Determine that the thermostat engages and disengages the clutch. There should be about a 12°F (6.7°C) temperature rise between the cutout and cut-in point of the thermostat.

3. Figures SP9-1A and SP9-1B are guides for determining the proper gauge readings and temperatures.

Ambient Air Temperature, °F	70	80	90	100	110
Average Compressor Head Pressure, psig	150–190	170–220	190–250	220–300	270–370
Average Evaporator Temperature, °F	38–45	39–47	40–50	42–55	45–60

Fig. SP9-1A (English)

Ambient Air Temperature, °C	21	27	32	38	43
Average Compressor Head Pressure, kPa	1 034–1 310	1 172–1 517	1 310–1 724	1 517–2 069	1 862–2 551
Average Evaporator Temperature, °C	3.3–7.2	3.9–8.3	4.4–10	5.5–12.8	7.2–15.6

Fig. SP9-1B (metric)

Ambient Temperature, °F	70			80			90			100		
Relative Humidity, %	50	60	90	50	60	90	40	50	60	20	40	50
Discharge Air Temperature, °F	40	41	42	42	43	47	41	44	49	43	49	55

Fig. SP9-2A (English)

Ambient Temperature, °C	21			27			32			38		
Relative Humidity, %	50	60	90	50	60	90	40	50	60	20	40	50
Discharge Air Temperature, °C	4.4	5	5.5	5.5	6.1	8.3	5	6.6	9.4	6.1	8.3	12.7

Fig. SP9-2B (metric)

4. The relative humidity at a particular temperature is a factor in the quality of the air as indicated by figures SP9-2A and SP9-2B. (These figures should be regarded as guides only.)

5. Complete the performance test as outlined in the manufacturer's service manual.

Return the System to Service

1. Return the engine speed to normal idle.

2. Back seat the high- and low-side compressor service valves.

3. Remove the service hoses and replace the protective caps.

Briefly answer each of the following questions.

1. What is the purpose of the performance test?

2. Does high humidity have an effect on the air-conditioning system? Explain.

3. At what speed should the engine run during the air-conditioning performance test?

4. What does a temperature change at the inlet and outlet of the drier indicate?

5. What does a temperature change from the inlet to the outlet of the expansion valve indicate?

SERVICE PROCEDURE 10:

Replacing the Compressor Shaft Oil Seal (York and Tecumseh Compressors)

This procedure can be followed when it is necessary to replace the compressor shaft oil seal. If the seal area can be serviced on the car, it is not necessary to remove the compressor from its mountings. If the engine fan or radiator clearance makes it impossible to remove the clutch for seal service, the compressor must be removed from the car.

TOOLS

Drive handle, 1/4 inch with 3/8-inch, 7/16-inch and 1/2-inch sockets
Open-end wrench, 3/4 inch
NC bolt, 5/8" x 2"
Screwdriver
Razor blade

MATERIALS

Ample supply of clean refrigeration oil
Seal assembly, including the seal plate, seal nose, and gasket(s)

PROCEDURE

Prepare the Compressor for Service

1. Isolate the compressor. Follow the procedure as outlined in Service Procedure 7.

2. If the seal cannot be serviced properly with the compressor mounted in the car, remove the compressor.

Fig. SP10-1 Typical shaft seal set

Fig. SP10-2 Using a 5/8-inch NC bolt to remove the clutch pulley from the York compressor

3. Using a 1/2-inch socket, remove the 7/16-inch Nyloc bolt from the compressor crankshaft at the clutch hub.

4. Using a 5/8-inch NC bolt, remove the clutch rotor. This bolt is inserted into the clutch hub at the point where the 7/16-inch Nyloc bolt was removed, Figure SP10-2.

5. If the fields of a stationary field clutch are mounted on the seal plate, remove the three retaining bolts and remove the fields.

Fig. SP10-3 Removing the Woodruff key before servicing the seal assembly

6. If the rotating fields and brushes are mounted on the seal plate, remove the brushes. Take care not to break the soft carbon brushes.

7. Clean the seal plate and all adjoining surfaces.

8. Remove the Woodruff key, figure SP10-3.

Remove the Seal Assembly

1. Remove the six (or remaining three) capscrews from the seal plate.

2. Gently pry the seal plate loose. Be careful not to nick or mar the crankcase mating surface or the compressor crankshaft, figure SP10-4.

    NOTE: The carbon ring on some models may stick to the seal plate when removed. Take care not to drop or damage this part.

3. Remove the seal nose assembly from the crankshaft by prying behind the seal. Be careful not to nick or mar the crankshaft, figure SP10-5.

4. With a razor blade, remove all gasket material from the crankcase mating surface.

5. Clean all foreign matter from the crankcase, crankshaft and all adjacent surfaces.

Fig. SP10-4 Remove the six capscrews and then remove the seal plate

Fig. SP10-5 Carefully remove the shaft seal assembly. Take care not to damage mating surfaces.

Install the New Seal Assembly

1. The Woodruff key must be removed from the crankshaft before attempting to install the new seal.

2. Soak the new seal and all gaskets in clean refrigeration oil for a few minutes. Apply ample oil to the crankshaft and mating parts.

3. Remove the carbon nose end from the shaft seal and slide the shaft seal on the crankshaft. If drive pins are located in the shaft shoulder, line up the notches in the shaft seal spring holder to engage. *If the new seal does not have notches, remove the drive pins.*

Fig. SP10-6 Coat the new seal assembly with clean refrigeration oil and carefully slide the assembly onto the compressor crankshaft

4. Install the seal nose, figure SP10-6. Flush the assembly with clean refrigeration oil.

Install the New Seal Plate

1. Use clean refrigeration oil to flush the seal plate and seal nose to remove any foreign particles.

2. *York Compressor:* Place the new seal plate and gasket(s) over the crankshaft; then move the seal back to the final operating position. Insert the original three (or six) capscrews and adjust them until they are fingertight.

   Tecumseh Compressor: Place the new seal plate and O-ring over the crankshaft and move the seal back to the final operating position. Insert the original three (or six) capscrews and tighten them until they are fingertight.

3. Rotate the compressor crankshaft to insure that there is no binding due to misalignment.

4. Check that there is an even clearance between the crankshaft and the seal plate all around.

5. Tighten all capscrews evenly to a torque of 10–12 ft-lb (13.6–16.3 N·m). Tighten the capscrews in a diagonally opposite sequence, figure SP10-7.

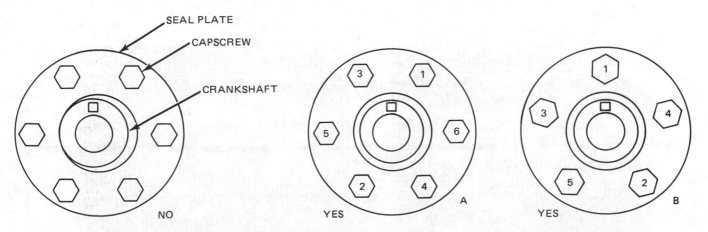

Fig. SP10-7 Before attempting to torque the capscrews in the seal plate, be sure that the plate is not off-center to the crankshaft as illustrated on the left. Note an almost even air gap between the seal plate and the crankshaft on the right. Torque the capscrews according to the sequence shown: A for six capscrew seal plate, and B for five capscrew seal plate.

Fig. SP10-8 Replacing the clutch field (coil)

Fig. SP10-9 Replacing the clutch rotor assembly and securing it with a Nyloc capscrew

Return the Compressor to Service

1. Replace the clutch field or brush assembly, figure SP10-8.
2. Replace the Woodruff key in the crankshaft.
3. Replace the clutch rotor and 5/16-inch Nyloc bolt, figure SP10-9.
4. If the compressor was removed from the car, replace the compressor, and provide new gaskets for the service valves.
5. Purge the air from the compressor as follows:
   a. Open the high-side manifold hand valve.
   b. Crack the low-side compressor service valve from the front-seated position.
   c. Low-side refrigerant pressure forces air out of the compressor through the high-side manifold hose.
   d. After a few seconds of purging, close the high-side manifold hand valve.
6. Midposition the high- and low-side compressor service valves.

Continue the Performance Test

1. Check the refrigerant charge. Add refrigerant if necessary.
2. Check the manifold gauge readings. Correct abnormal conditions if indicated.

Return the System to Service

1. Back seat the high- and low-side compressor service valves.
2. Remove the service hoses and replace the protective caps.

Review

Briefly answer each of the following questions.

1. Why is it necessary to isolate the compressor when servicing the compressor shaft seal?
2. What tool is used to remove the clutch rotor?
3. Why is the Woodruff key removed before replacing the new seal?
4. Which seal assembly used the O-ring only?
5. What is the torque of the seal plate?

SERVICE PROCEDURE 11:

Replacing the Compressor Shaft Seal (York Rotary VR4709 and VR4912)

When replacing the York rotary compressor shaft seal, it is advisable to remove the compressor from the car. If there is sufficient clearance, however, on-car seal replacement is possible. This procedure is given with the compressor removed from the car.

Special service tools are required. This procedure cannot be done without the proper tools. These tools are available from Draf Tool Company, Robinair Manufacturing Company, and others.

TOOLS

Internal snap ring plier
Holding fixture
Armature removal tool

Seal seat remover/replacer tool
Seal remover/replacer tool
1/4-inch, 12-pt socket w/handle

MATERIALS

Seal kit, as required
Refrigeration oil, 500 SUS viscosity
Clean shop rags

PROCEDURE

Prepare the Compressor

1. Place the compressor into the holding fixture, rotor end facing up. Secure with two thumbscrews.

2. Clamp the holding fixture securely in a sturdy vise.

Remove the Armature

1. Remove the #10 (10–32) screw from the center of the armature.

2. Install the long 10–24 screw into the hole where the screw was removed (step 1) until it bottoms, figure SP11-1.

   NOTE: This screw should be finger-tight only.

3. Install the armature removal tool using three thumbscrews.

Fig. SP11-1 Installing the armature plate removal tool

265

Fig. SP11-2 Armature plate removal

Fig. SP11-3 Removing the pulley retaining ring

4. Turn the puller bolt until the armature comes off the compressor shaft. The puller bolt must turn against the screw installed in step 2, as shown in figure SP11-2.

5. Remove the center bolt (installed in step 2).

Remove the Seal

1. Using the snap ring plier, remove the internal snap ring, figure SP11-3.

2. Thoroughly clean the internal seal bore of any dirt or foreign matter.

3. Insert the seal seat remover tool into bore. Rotate 1/4 turn and pull straight out, figure SP11-4.

4. Insert the seal removal tool into bore. Push in to compress and turn clockwise (cw) to engage the seal.

5. Pull straight out to remove the seal, figure SP11-5.

6. Recheck the bore to insure that it is clean and free of dirt or other foreign matter.

Install the Seal

1. Liberally coat the new shaft seal with oil.

2. Carefully engage the seal into the locking tangs of the seal remover tool.

3. Carefully slide the seal down the shaft. Rotate clockwise (cw) with a slight pressure until the seal is in place.

   NOTE: The seal *must* engage the flats on the compressor shaft.

4. Rotate the tool counterclockwise (ccw) to disengage it from the seal tangs. Remove the tool.

5. Coat the seal seat liberally with oil.

6. Grip the seal seat with the seal seat removal tool.

7. *Carefully* install the seal seat onto the compressor shaft and remove the tool.

Fig. SP11-4 Removing the seal seat

Fig. SP11-5 Removing the seal assembly

8. Using snap ring pliers, install the new snap ring.

9. Use the seal remover tool to push the snap ring and seal seat into the bore.

    NOTE: The snap ring *must* engage in the internal groove.

Replace the Armature

1. Insert the armature hub onto the compressor shaft spline.

2. Hand press the armature onto the compressor shaft, figure SP11-6.

    NOTE: Do not hammer or pound on the armature or end of the compressor shaft. To do so will cause severe damage to the compressor.

Fig. SP11-6 Installing the armature

3. Install the original 10–24 screw to secure the armature to the compressor shaft.

    NOTE: The armature-to-pulley air gap *must* be between 0.15 in (0.38 mm) and 0.050 in (1.3 mm) for proper clutch operation.

Return to Service

1. Rotate the armature several times to seat the new seal assembly.

2. Remove the compressor from the holding fixture.

Review

Briefly answer each of the following questions.

1. How does the armature replacement differ for the York rotary compressor as compared to other types of compressors?

2. Using a micrometer, what common item (matchbook cover, dime, and so forth) could be used as a gauge for setting the air gap?

SERVICE PROCEDURE 12:

Replacing the Compressor Shaft Oil Seal (Sankyo Compressors)

In general, when replacing the Sankyo compressor shaft oil seal, it is advisable to remove the compressor from the car. However, if there is sufficient room to permit access to the front of the compressor, the compressor shaft oil seal can be serviced on the car. This procedure is given with the compressor removed from the car.

TOOLS

NOTE: The tool part numbers given are Sankyo part numbers for special tools. These tools are also manufactured by Draf Tool Company and Robinair Manufacturing Company (under different part numbers, however).

Seal seat retainer tool (32419) Air gap gauge (32437)
Spanner wrench (32409) Socket wrench set
Clutch face puller (32416) Small hammer
Seal seat remover (32405) Screwdriver
Seal remover and installer (32425) Manifold and gauge set
O-ring remover (32406) Safety glasses
Seal protector (32426) Torque wrench
Clutch front plate installer (32436)

MATERIALS

Seal kit, as required Clean shop rag
Refrigeration oil Refrigerant 12, as required

PROCEDURE

Prepare the Compressor for Service

1. Purge the system of refrigerant as outlined in Service Procedure 2.

2. Remove the high- and low-side hoses from the compressor fittings. Plug the hoses and compressor fittings to prevent contaminants from entering the system or the compressor.

3. Loosen the compressor and/or idler pulley and remove the belt(s).

4. Remove the mounting hardware and lift the compressor from the engine compartment. Omit this step if there is sufficient clearance to service the seal without removing the compressor. The compressor must be tilted back and supported, however, to prevent damage to the refrigerant lines.

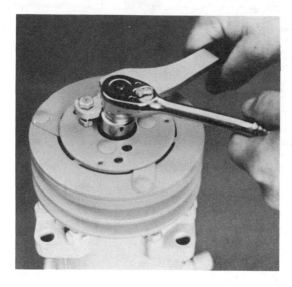

Fig. SP12-1 Removing the crankshaft hex nut

Fig. SP12-2 Removing the front clutch plate

Remove the Shaft Seal

1. Using a 3/4-inch hex socket and spanner wrench, figure SP12-1, remove the crankshaft hex nut.

2. Remove the clutch front plate, figure SP12-2, using the clutch front plate puller.

3. Remove the shaft key and spacer shims and set aside.

4. Using the snap ring pliers, figure SP12-3, remove the seal seat retaining snap ring.

Fig. SP12-3 Removing the seal seat retainer snap ring

5. Remove the seal seat, using the seal seat remover and installer, figure SP12-4.

6. Remove the seal, figure SP12-5, using the seal remover tool.

7. Remove the shaft seal seat O-ring, figure SP12-6, using the O-ring remover.

8. Discard all parts removed in steps 5, 6, and 7.

Fig. SP12-4 Removing the seal seat

Fig. SP12-5 Removing the seal

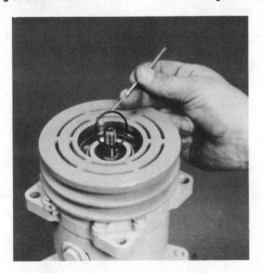

Fig. SP12-6 Removing the O-ring

Install the Shaft Seal

1. Clean the inner bore of the seal cavity by flushing it with clean refrigeration oil.

2. Coat the new seal parts with clean refrigeration oil. *Do not touch* the carbon ring face with the fingers. Normal body acids will etch the seal and cause early failure.

3. Install the new shaft seal seat O-ring. Make sure it is properly seated in the internal groove. Use the remover tool to position the O-ring properly.

4. Install the seal protector on the compressor crankshaft. Lubricate the part liberally with clean refrigeration oil.

5. Place the new shaft seal in the seal installer tool and carefully slide the shaft seal into place in the inner bore. Rotate the shaft seal clockwise (cw) until it seats on the compressor shaft flats.

Fig. SP12-7 Reinstalling the front clutch plate and checking the air gap

6. Rotate the tool counterclockwise (ccw) to remove the seal installer tool.

7. Remove the shaft seal protector.

8. Place the shaft seal seat on the remover/installer tool and carefully reinstall it in the compressor seal cavity.

9. Replace the seal seat retainer.

10. Reinstall the spacer shims and shaft key.

11. Position the clutch front plate on the compressor crankshaft.

12. Using the clutch front plate installer tool, a small hammer, and an air gap gauge, reinstall the front plate.

13. Draw down the front plate with the shaft nut. Use the air gap gauge for *go* at 0.016 in (0.4 mm) and *no-go* at 0.031 in (0.79 mm), figure SP12-7.

14. Using the torque wrench, tighten the shaft nut to a torque of 25–30 ft-lb (33.9–40.7 N·m).

Return the Compressor to Service

1. If the compressor was removed from the car, reinstall the compressor. Replace all bolts and braces. Tighten the bolts securely.

2. Replace the belt(s) and tighten to 90–100 ft-lb (122–135.6 N·m).

3. Remove the protective covers and reconnect the hoses to the compressor low- and high-side fittings. If these fittings are of the O-ring type, new O-rings must be installed.

4. Check the compressor oil level as outlined in the appropriate Service Procedures.

5. Evacuate the system as outlined in Service Procedure 4.

6. Charge the system as outlined in Service Procedure 5.

7. Operate the system for 10 to 15 minutes to *run-in* the new seal. Leak check the system as outlined in Service Procedure 3.

Review

Select the appropriate answer from the choices given.

1. A new shaft seal is seated on the compressor shaft flats by

   a. rotating the seal counterclockwise (ccw).
   b. rotating the seal clockwise (cw).
   c. rotating the seal back and forth.
   d. All of the above answers are correct.

2. Technician A says that the inner bore of the seal cavity is cleaned with a lint-free clean rag. Technician B says that it is cleaned with mineral spirits.

   a. Technician A is correct.
   b. Technician B is correct.
   c. Both technicians may be correct.
   d. Both technicians are wrong.

3. The compressor shaft nut should be tightened to

   a. 15–20 ft-lb (20.3–27.1 N·m).   c. 25–30 ft-lb (33.9–40.7 N·m).
   b. 20–25 ft-lb (27.1–33.9 N·m).   d. 30–35 ft-lb (40.7–47.5 N·m).

4. Technician A says that the shaft seal is rotated clockwise (cw) to seat it on the compressor shaft flats. Technician B says that it is rotated counterclockwise (ccw) to be seated.

   a. Technician A is correct.   c. Either technician may be correct.
   b. Technician B is correct.   d. Both technicians are wrong.

5. The compressor drive belt should be tensioned to

   a. 80–90 ft-lb (108.5–122 N·m).   c. 100–110 ft-lb (135.6–149.1 N·m).
   b. 90–100 ft-lb (122–135.6 N·m).   d. 110–120 ft-lb (149.1–162.7 N·m).

SERVICE PROCEDURE 13:

Replacing the Compressor Shaft Oil Seal (Chrysler Air-Temp)

This procedure can be used when it is necessary to replace the compressor shaft oil seal on a Chrysler Air-Temp unit. In general, the seal can be replaced without removing the compressor. The Air-Temp unit, using the York or Tecumseh compressor, is covered in Service Procedure 10.

TOOLS

Drive handle, 1/4 inch with 7/16-inch and 1/2-inch sockets
Open-end wrench, 3/4 inch

NC or NF bolt, 5/8″ x 2″
Screwdriver

MATERIALS

Ample supply of clean refrigeration oil
Seal assembly, including an O-ring gasket for the bearing housing
Stationary seat and gasket assembly
Rotating seal assembly

PROCEDURE

Prepare the Compressor for Service

1. If the compressor is equipped with both high- and low-side service valves, the compressor can be isolated. Follow the procedure outlined in Service Procedure 7.

2. If the compressor is not equipped with high- and low-side service valves, the system must be purged of refrigerant. Follow the procedure outlined in Service Procedure 2.

3. Using a 1/2-inch socket, remove the 7/16-inch bolt from the crankshaft. The bolt is located at the clutch hub.

4. Using a 5/8-inch NF or NC bolt, remove the clutch rotor. This bolt is inserted into the clutch hub at the point where the 7/16-inch bolt was removed.

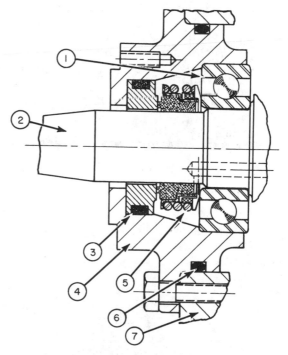

1 – CRANKSHAFT BEARING
2 – CRANKSHAFT
3 – STATIONARY SEAT AND GASKET
4 – BEARING HOUSING
5 – ROTATING SEAL ASSEMBLY
6 – O-RING GASKET
7 – CRANKCASE

Fig. SP13-1 Cutaway view of the Chrysler shaft oil seal

5. If the clutch is equipped with stationary fields, locate the three screws holding it to the seal housing. Remove the screws and the fields. If the unit is equipped with rotating fields, carefully remove the brush set by removing the two screws holding the set to the seal housing.

6. Clean the seal plate and all adjacent surfaces.

Remove the Old Seal Assembly

1. Remove the Woodruff key from the crankshaft.

2. Remove the bearing housing bolts.

3. Remove the bearing housing by inserting two screwdrivers in the slots provided and prying the housing from the crankcase, figure SP13-2.

4. Remove the bearing housing O-ring gasket and discard it.

5. Remove the stationary seat and gasket assembly from the bearing housing and discard it.

6. Remove the gas or shaft seal assembly from the crankshaft, using a small screwdriver. Discard this assembly. Take care not to nick or scratch the crankshaft. Either one of two types of interchangeable gas seals (cartridge or unitized) can be used. As a means of identifying the seals, the unitized type has a coil spring and the cartridge type has a wave spring, figure SP13-3.

7. Clean all foreign material from the bearing housing and crankshaft.

8. It may be necessary to polish these surfaces liberally with clean refrigeration oil.

Install New Seal Assembly

1. Lubricate the crankshaft, the bearing housing and all adjacent parts with clean refrigeration oil.

2. Dip the stationary seat and gasket assembly into clean refrigeration oil for a few minutes.

3. Install the stationary seat and gasket assembly into the bearing housing. Insure that it is fully seated. Do not damage the seal surface.

4. Place the bearing housing O-ring in the groove provided.

5. Dip the gas seal assembly into clean refrigeration oil for a few minutes.

6. Slide the gas seal assembly on the compressor crankshaft. Insure that the carbon nose of the seal assembly is facing outward.

Fig. SP13-2 Removing the crankshaft bearing housing

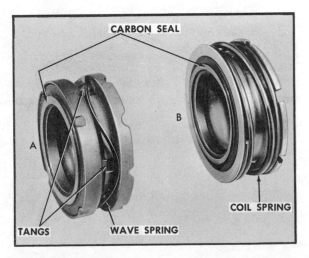

Fig. SP13-3 Gas seal identification (A) cartridge type (B) unitized type

7. Install the crankshaft bearing housing with the seal and O-ring in place, on the crankcase body. Replace the capscrews and draw them in uniformly.

8. Tighten the bearing housing capscrews to a torque of 10–13 ft-lb (13.6–17.6 N·m).

Return the Compressor to Service

1. Replace the Woodruff key. Replace the brush or field assembly.

2. Replace the clutch assembly and the 5/16-inch retaining bolt.

3. If equipped with service valves, purge the air from the compressor as follows:
    a. Open the high-side manifold hand valve.
    b. Crack the low-side compressor service valve from the front-seated position.
    c. The low-side refrigerant pressure forces air out of the compressor through the high-side manifold hose.
    d. After a few seconds of purging, close the high-side manifold hand valve.
    e. Midposition the high- and low-side compressor service valves.

4. If the unit is equipped with Schrader-type service valves, the unit must be evacuated. Follow the procedure outlined in Service Procedure 4.

Continue the Performance Test

1. If the system is equipped with compressor service valves, check for the proper refrigerant charge. Add refrigerant if necessary.

2. Check the manifold gauge readings. Correct any abnormal conditions indicated.

Return the System to Service

1. Back seat the high- and low-side compressor service valves.

2. Remove the service hoses and replace the protective caps.

Review

Briefly answer each of the following questions.

1. In general, what compressor(s) does Chrysler Air-Temp use?
2. What size wrench is used to remove the center bolt from the crankshaft?
3. Name the two types of fields which can be provided on the unit.
4. Which type of field does not use brushes?
5. What is the recommended torque of the bearing housing?

SERVICE PROCEDURE 14:

Replacing the Seal on Delco Air Compressors (Four-cyclinder)

Seal replacement on the General Motors Delco Air four-cylinder compressor is accomplished using a different procedure than is required for other types of compressors.

Careful handling of all seal parts is important. The carbon seal face and the steel seal seat must not be touched with the fingers because of the etching effect of the acid normally found on the fingers.

All four-cylinder compressors are equipped with Schrader-type service valves. Therefore, it is necessary to purge the system of refrigerant before servicing the seal assembly. This statement is true even if the procedure can be accomplished with the compressor mounted in the car.

TOOLS

Manifold and gauge set
Test fitting
Clutch hub holder
Set of hand wrenches
Installer snap ring plier
Seal seat remover/installer

O-ring installer
O-ring remover
Seal protector
Shaft seal seat remover/installer
Hub and drive plate remover/installer
Thinwall 9/16-inch socket with handle

MATERIALS

Clean refrigeration oil
Refrigerant 12

Service valve O-rings (2)
Compressor shaft seal kit

PROCEDURE

Prepare the Compressor for Service

1. The compressor and system must be purged of all refrigerant. Use the procedure outlined in Service Procedure 2.

2. If access to the compressor shaft seal is obstructed, remove the compressor from the car. The service valve should be removed from the rear of the compressor as a unit. Plug all hoses and service valve openings when removed. Attach the test fitting to the rear of the compressor.

Remove the Old Seal

1. Using a 9/16-inch thinwall socket wrench and clutch hub holding tool, remove the shaft nut, figure SP14-1.

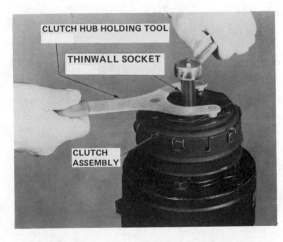

Fig. SP14-1 Removing the shaft locknut

277

2. Using a clutch hub and drive plate puller, remove this part, figure SP14-2.

3. Remove the shaft seal seat retainer ring using the snap ring pliers.

4. Remove the seal seat using a shaft seal seat remover.

5. Using the shaft seal remover, remove the shaft seal, figure SP14-3.

6. Using an O-ring remover (a wire with a hook on the end), remove the shaft seal seat O-ring. *Take care not to scratch the mating surfaces.*

Install the New Seal

NOTE: This procedure should be followed as given to avoid damage to the new seal assembly. For example, if the seal seat is installed backwards, it is almost impossible to remove it again to reinstall it properly.

1. Insure that the inner bore of the compressor is free of all foreign matter. Flush the area with clean refrigeration oil.

2. Place the seal seat O-ring on the installer tool and slide the O-ring into place, figure SP14-4. Remove the tool.

3. Coat the shaft seal liberally with refrigeration oil and place it on the shaft seal installer tool. Slide the shaft into place in the bore. Rotate the seal clockwise until it seats on the flats provided. Rotate the tool counterclockwise and remove it.

4. Place the shaft seal seat on the remover/installer tool, figure SP14-5. Slide the shaft seal seat into position and remove the tool.

5. Install the shaft seal seat snap ring. Note that the beveled edge of the snap ring must face the outside of the compressor.

6. Before replacing the clutch hub and drive plate, the seal should be checked for leaks.

Leak Test the Shaft Seal

1. With the test fitting in place, connect the manifold and gauge set to the test ports.

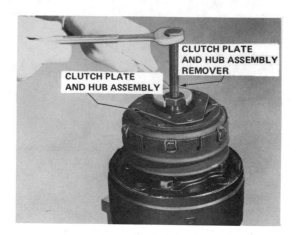

Fig. SP14-2 Removing the hub and drive plate assembly

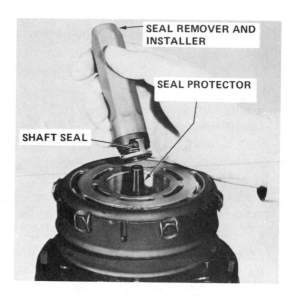

Fig. SP14-3 Removing the shaft seal assembly

Fig. SP14-4 Installing the seal seat O-ring

2. Tap a can of refrigerant and purge the lines of air. Open the high- and low-side manifold hand valves to allow the refrigerant pressure to enter the compressor.

3. With a leak detector, check the shaft seal area for escaping refrigerant. Refer to Service Procedure 3.

4. If a small leak is detected, rotate the crankshaft a few turns to seat the seal; then recheck the seal area for leaks. If the leak is heavy, or if it persists, the seal must be removed and checked for defects.

Replace the Clutch Hub and Drive Plate Assembly

1. Place the drive key into the clutch plate keyway, figure SP14-6. About 3/16 inch (4.8 mm) of the key should be allowed to protrude over the end of the keyway.

2. Align the key with the keyways of the drive plate and compressor crankshaft. Then slide the drive plate into position.

   NOTE: Take care not to force the drive key into the shaft seal. Occasional rotation of the drive plate during assembly insures that it is seated properly.

3. Using a hub and drive plate installer, press this part on the crankshaft. (Refer to the note following step 2 of this procedure.)

4. A clearance of 0.030 inch ±0.010 in (0.76 mm ± 0.25 mm) should exist between the drive plate and the rotor.

5. Replace the shaft nut.

Fig. SP14-5 Installing the shaft seal seat

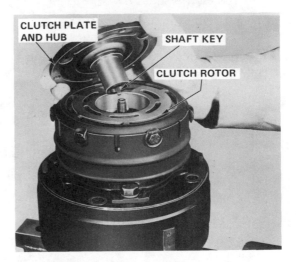

Fig. SP14-6 Drive plate key installed

Return the Compressor to Service

1. If the compressor was removed, return it to the car. Remove the test fittings and replace the service valves using new O-rings coated with clean refrigeration oil.

2. Evacuate the system as outlined in Service Procedure 4.

3. Charge the system as outlined in Service Procedure 5.

4. Return the compressor to service or continue the performance testing as necessary.

Review

Briefly answer the following questions.

1. In sequence, list the removal order of the following:
   a. Seal assembly
   b. Seal seat
   c. Retaining ring
   d. Seal seat O-ring

2. What wrench is used to remove the crankshaft nut from the compressor?

3. What part, if installed backwards, is almost impossible to remove?

4. What tool is used to remove the O-ring?

5. What should be used to coat O-rings before assembly?

SERVICE PROCEDURE 15:

Replacing the Seal on Delco Air Compressors, A-6 and DA-6 (Six-cylinder)

Special service tools are required to service the seal assembly on the Delco Air A-6 and DA-6 compressors. These tools are available from several suppliers, such as Kent-Moore and Robinair. Illustrations in this service procedure depict the A-6 compressor. Procedures, however, for the DA-6 compressor are basically the same.

Careful handling of the seal parts is important. There are two types of seal, steel and carbon, which require a different remover/installer. In either case, the carbon seal face and seal seat must not be touched with the fingers because of the etching effect of the acid normally found on the fingers.

TOOLS

Manifold and gauge set
Test fitting
Clutch hub holder
Set of hand wrenches
Internal snap ring plier
Seal seat remover/installer

O-ring installer
O-ring remover
Seal protector
Shaft seal seat remover/installer*
Hub and drive plate remover/installer
Thinwall 9/16-inch socket with handle

*Steel or ceramic seal, as required

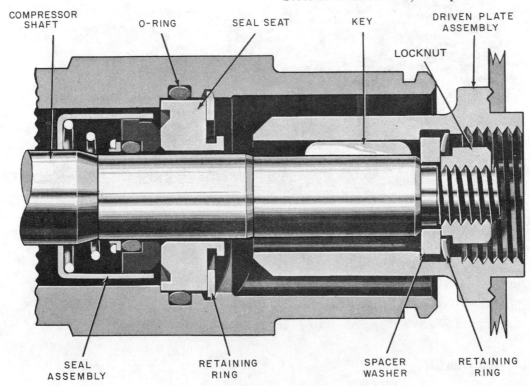

Fig. SP15-1 Compressor shaft and seal

MATERIALS

Clean refrigeration oil

Refrigerant 12

Service valve O-ring (2)

Compressor shaft seal kit

PROCEDURE

Prepare the Compressor for Service

1. The compressor and system must be purged of all refrigerant, following the procedure outlined in Service Procedure 2.

2. If access to the compressor shaft seal is obstructed, remove the compressor from the car. The service valve should be removed from the rear of the compressor as a unit. Plug all hoses and service valve openings when removed. Attach the test fitting to the rear of the compressor.

Remove the Old Seal

1. Using a 9/16-inch thinwall socket wrench and clutch hub holding tool, remove the shaft nut, figure SP15-2.

2. Using snap ring pliers, remove the clutch hub retainer ring.

3. Remove the spacer under the retainer ring.

4. Using a clutch hub and drive plate puller, remove this part, figure SP15-3.

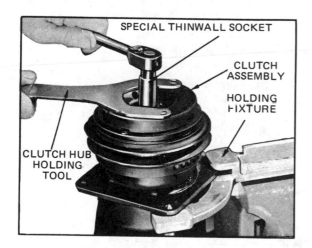

Fig. SP15-2 Removing the shaft locknut

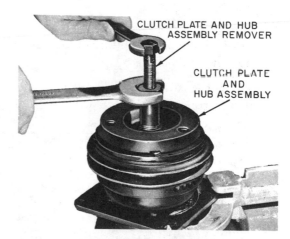

Fig. SP15-3 Removing the hub and drive plate assembly

5. Remove the shaft seal seat retainer ring using internal snap ring pliers, figure SP15-4.

6. Remove the seal seat using a shaft seal seat remover, figure SP15-5. (Use the appropriate tool.)

7. Using the shaft seal remover, remove the shaft seal, figure SP15-6.

8. Using an O-ring remover (a wire with a hook on the end), remove the shaft seal seat O-ring, figure SP15-7. *Take care not to scratch the mating surfaces.*

Install the New Seal

NOTE: This procedure should be followed as given to avoid damage to the new seal assembly. For example, if the seal seat is installed backwards, it is almost impossible to remove it again to reinstall it properly.

Fig. SP15-4 Removing the shaft seal retainer

Fig. SP15-5 Removing the seal seat

1. Insure that the inner bore of the compressor is free of all foreign matter. Flush the area with clean refrigeration oil.

2. Wet the seal seat O-ring with refrigerant oil and place it on the seal installer tool; slide the O-ring into place; then, remove the tool.

3. Coat the shaft seal liberally with refrigeration oil and place it on the shaft seal installer tool, figure SP15-8. Slide the shaft seal into place in the bore. Rotate the seal clockwise until it seats on the flats provided. Rotate the tool counterclockwise and remove it.

Fig. SP15-6 Removing the shaft seal assembly

4. Wet the shaft seal seat with refrigerant oil and place it on the remover/installer tool. Slide the shaft seal seat into position and remove the tool.

5. Install the shaft seal seat snap ring. Note that the beveled edge of the snap ring must face the outside of the compressor.

6. Before replacing the clutch hub and drive plate, the seal should be checked for leaks.

Leak Test the Shaft Seal

1. With the test fitting in place, connect the manifold and gauge set to the test ports.

Fig. SP15-7 Removing the seal seat O-ring

Fig. SP15-8 Installing the seal seat O-ring and the shaft seal

2. Tap a can of refrigerant and purge the lines of air. Open the high- and low-side manifold hand valves to allow the refrigerant pressure to enter the compressor.

3. With a leak detector, check the shaft seal area for escaping refrigerant. Refer to Service Procedure 3.

4. If a small leak is detected, rotate the crankshaft a few turns to seat the seal; then recheck the seal area for leaks. If the leak is heavy, or if it persists, the seal must be removed and checked for defects.

Replace the Clutch Hub and Drive Plate Assembly

1. Place the drive key into the crankshaft keyway, figure SP15-9. About 3/16 inch (4.8 mm) of the key should be allowed to protrude over the end of the keyway.

Fig. SP15-9 Drive plate key installed in keyway

2. Align the key with the keyways of the drive plate and compressor crankshaft. Then slide the drive plate into position.

NOTE: Take care not to force the drive key into the shaft seal. Occasional rotation of the drive plate during assembly insures that it is seated properly.

3. Using a hub and drive plate installer, press this part on the crankshaft, figure SP15-10. (Refer to the note following step 2 of this procedure.)

4. A clearance of 0.030 inch ±0.010 in (0.76 mm ± 0.25 mm) should exist between the drive plate and the rotor, figure SP15-11.

Fig. SP15-11 Checking the air gap

Fig. SP15-10 Installing the driven plate

5. Replace the spacer and clutch hub retainer ring. The retainer ring is installed using the snap ring plier.

6. Replace the shaft nut.

Return the Compressor to Service

1. If the compressor was removed, return it to the car. Remove the test fittings and replace the service valves using new O-rings coated with clean refrigeration oil.

2. Evacuate the system as outlined in Service Procedure 4.

3. Charge the system as outlined in Service Procedure 5.

4. Return the compressor to service or continue the performance testing as necessary.

Review

Briefly answer the following questions.

1. In sequence, list the removal order of the following:
   a. Drive plate assembly   c. Locknut
   b. Seal seat   d. Spacer washer

2. What tool is used to remove the internal snap rings?

3. How is the seal assembly engaged or seated onto the compressor shaft?

4. What tool is used to install the O-ring?

5. Why is it necessary to purge all refrigerant from the system to service the seal?

SERVICE PROCEDURE 16:

Replacing the Compressor Shaft Seal, Nippondenso (Includes Chrysler C-171 and Ford FS-6)

The Nippondenso compressor is also known as Chrysler's C-171 and Ford's FS-6 compressor. Seal replacement for this compressor is somewhat different from other compressors in that the front head assembly must first be removed.

This service procedure cannot be performed with the compressor on the car; it must first be removed from the engine.

TOOLS

Set of hand tools	Shaft protector
Hub remover	Shaft key remover
3-jaw puller	Seal seat remover
External snap ring plier	Seal seat installer
Bearing remover/pulley installer	Graduated measure

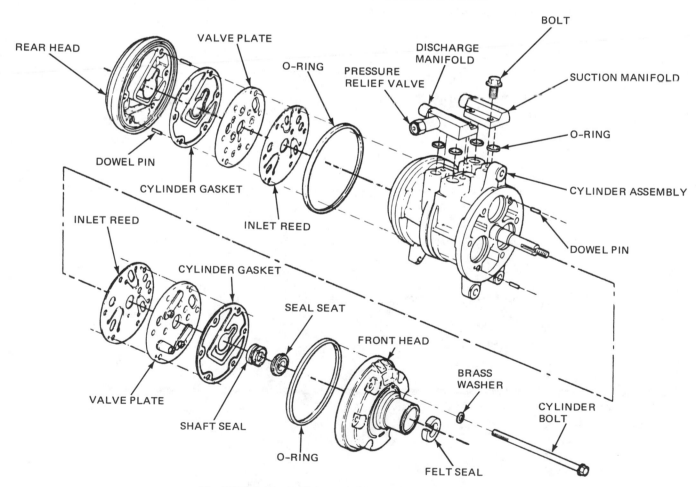

Fig. SP16-1 Exploded view of Nippondenso compressor

Hub replacer
Nonmagnetic feeler gauge set
Plastic hammer

Allen wrench set (metric)
Torque wrench

MATERIALS

Shaft seal kit
Refrigeration oil, as required
Mineral spirits

Brass washers (6) 10 mm, as required
Refrigerant 12, as required

PROCEDURE

Prepare the System

1. Purge the system of refrigerant as outlined in Service Procedure 2.

2. Remove the compressor assembly from the car engine.

3. Remove clutch and coil assemblies as outlined in Service Procedure 28.

4. Using the shaft key remover, remove the shaft key, figure SP16-2.

5. Remove the felt oil absorber and retainer from the front head cavity.

6. Clean the outside of the compressor with pure mineral spirits and air dry. Do not submerge the compressor into mineral spirits.

7. Drain the compressor oil into a graduated measure. See Service Procedure 22.

Fig. SP16-2 Removing crankshaft key

Remove the Seal

1. Remove the six through bolts from the front head. Use the proper tool; some require a 10-mm socket and others require a 6-mm Allen wrench.

2. Discard the six brass washers (if equipped) and retain the six bolts.

3. Gently tap the front head with a plastic hammer to free it from the compressor housing.

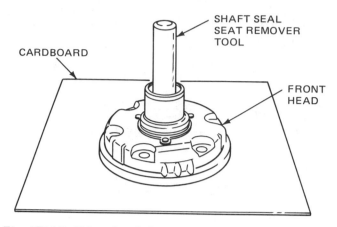

Fig. SP16-3 Using the shaft seal seat remover tool to remove the seal seat from the front head

Fig. SP16-4 Removing the shaft seal

4. Remove and discard the head to housing O-ring and the head to valve plate gasket.

5. Place the front head on a piece of soft material, such as cardboard, cavity side up.

6. Use the shaft seal seat remover to remove the seal seat, figure SP16-3.

7. Using both hands, remove the shaft seal cartridge, figure SP16-4.

Install the Seal

1. Liberally coat all seal parts, compressor shaft, head cavity, and gaskets with clean refrigeration oil.

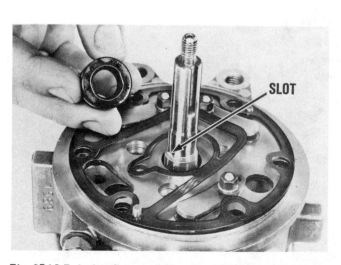

Fig. SP16-5 Index flat on shaft seal with slot on crankshaft

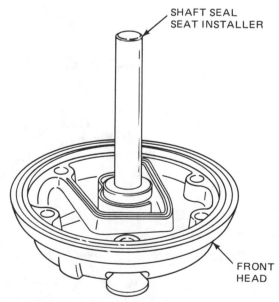

Fig. SP16-6 Install the shaft seal seat into the front head using the seal seat installer

2. Carefully install the shaft seal cartridge, figure SP16-5, making sure to index the shaft seal on the crankshaft slots.

3. Install the seal seat into the front head using the seal seat installer, figure SP16-6.

4. Install head to valve plate gasket over alignment pins in the compressor housing.

5. Install the head to housing O-ring.

6. Carefully slide head onto compressor housing insuring that the alignment pins engage in holes in the head.

7. Using six new brass washers (if required), install the six compressor through bolts.

8. Using a 10-mm socket or 6-mm Allen wrench, as required, tighten the bolts to a 260 lb-in (29.4 N·m) torque.

   NOTE: Use alternate pattern when torquing the bolts, figure SP16-7.

9. Replace the oil with clean refrigeration oil as outlined in Service Procedure 22.

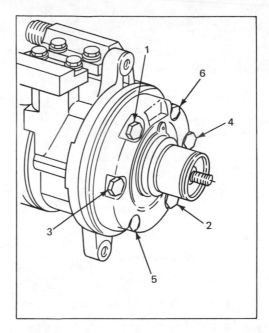

Fig. SP16-7 Use alternate pattern when torquing bolts. Torque sequence for tightening bolts is shown.

Return to Service

1. Install the crankshaft key, using a drift.

2. Align the ends of the felt and its retainer, figure SP16-8, and install into the head cavity. Be sure the felt and retainer are fully seated against the seal plate.

3. Replace the clutch and coil assemblies as outlined in Service Procedure 28.

4. Return compressor to car engine; install and tighten belt(s).

5. Leak test as outlined in Service Procedure 3.

6. Evacuate as outlined in Service Procedure 4.

7. Charge system as outlined in Service Procedure 5.

Fig. SP16-8 Align openings in felt and retainer

Review

Select the appropriate answer from the choices given.

1. Technician A says four through bolts hold the front head onto the Nippondenso compressor housing. Technician B says there are six through bolts. Which, if either, is correct?

   a. Technician A is correct.
   b. Technician B is correct.
   c. Either technician may be correct, depending on the compressor model.
   d. Both technicians are wrong; there are eight through bolts.

2. The wrench used to remove/replace the through bolts is the

   a. 10-mm hex socket.　　　　　　　c. Neither a nor b is correct.
   b. 6-mm Allen wrench.　　　　　　 d. Either a or b is correct.

3. The special tool used to remove the shaft seal cartridge is the

   a. shaft seal remover.　　　　　　 c. shaft seal seat remover.
   b. snap ring plier.　　　　　　　　d. A tool is not used.

4. Technician A says that the felt found in the front head cavity is used as an oil absorber. Technician B says that it is used as a sound absorber.

   a. Technician A is correct.
   b. Technician B is correct.
   c. Both technicians are correct.
   d. Both technicians are wrong.

5. The outside of the compressor is cleaned with

   a. mineral spirits.　　　　　　　　c. a clean dry cloth.
   b. gasoline.　　　　　　　　　　　d. dry air.

SERVICE PROCEDURE 17:

Checking the Compressor Oil Level (Air-Temp, Tecumseh, York Compressors)

This procedure is used when it is necessary to check the oil level in those Air-Temp, Tecumseh, and York compressors with high- and low-side compressor service valves. Compressors equipped with Schrader-type valves require that the refrigerant be purged from the system to check the oil level.

TOOLS

Service valve wrench
Hand wrenches
Eye protection

Fender covers
Manifold and gauge set
Oil dipstick

MATERIAL

Refrigeration oil

PROCEDURE

Prepare the System

1. The compressor must be isolated from the system. Follow the procedure outlined in this text.

Check the Oil Level

1. Remove the plug from the compressor body to gain access to the compressor crankcase.

2. Use the correct dipstick and measure the oil.

3. Compare the measurements with the chart, figure SP17-1, to determine the proper oil level.

4. Add refrigeration oil as necessary to bring the oil level to the proper height.

	York	Tecumseh	Air-Temp
Vertical	1 1/4 in (31.8 mm)	7/8 in (22.2 mm)	
Inclined	2 in (50.8 mm)	1 1/4 in (31.8 mm)	
Horizontal	7/8 in (22.2 mm)	1 1/8 in (28.6 mm)	
R.H. Mount			2 3/4 in (69.9 mm)
L.C. Mount			3 1/8 in (79.4 mm)

Fig. SP17-1 Oil level chart

Return the Compressor to the System

1. Replace the oil check plug.

2. If the oil check plug was removed from the compressor for more than five minutes, purge the air from the compressor as follows:
   a. Open the high-side manifold hand valve.
   b. Crack the low-side compressor service valve from the front-seated position.
   c. The low-side refrigerant pressure forces air out of the compressor through the high-side manifold set.
   d. After five seconds of purging, close the high-side manifold hand valve.

3. Midposition the low- and high-side compressor service valves.

Continue the Performance Test

1. With the manifold gauge set connected, check the refrigerant charge.

2. Add refrigerant if necessary.

3. Continue the performance testing as required, or return the unit to service.

Return the System to Service

1. Back seat the high- and low-side compressor service valves.

2. Remove the service hoses and replace the protective caps.

   NOTE: An oil dipstick, such as the one shown in figure 17-2, can be made from a piece of medium soft wire (such as a black coat hanger). A black wire should be used so that the oil level is readily visible on the dipstick.

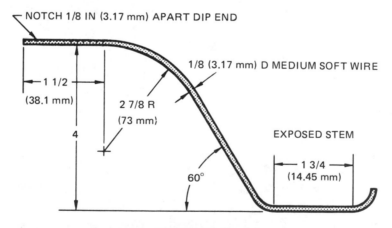

Fig. SP17-2 Oil dipstick

Review

Briefly answer each of the following questions.

1. Why must the compressor be isolated from the system?

2. What tool is used to measure the oil level?

3. Should air be purged from the compressor after the oil is checked?

4. Which compressor cannot be mounted in an inclined or horizontal position?

5. Can any good, clean refrigeration oil be used in compressors?

SERVICE PROCEDURE 18:

Checking the Compressor Oil Level (Sankyo Compressors)

The compressor oil level should be checked at the time of installation and after repairs are made when it is evident that there has been a loss of oil. The Sankyo compressor is factory charged with seven fluidounces (207 mL) of Suniso 5GS oil. Only this oil, or equivalent, should be added to the system.

The system must be purged of refrigerant before the oil level is checked. A special angle gauge and dipstick are used to check the oil level. The oil level chart, figure SP18-3, compares the oil level with the inclination angle of the compressor.

TOOLS

NOTE: The tool numbers given are Sankyo numbers.

Angle gauge (32448) Adjustable wrench
Dipstick (32447) Torque wrench
Manifold and gauge set

MATERIALS

Refrigeration oil, as required
Oil filler plug O-ring, as required

PROCEDURE

Prepare the System

1. Start the engine and run the air conditioner so that the compressor operates at idle speed for ten minutes.
2. Turn off the air conditioner and stop the engine.

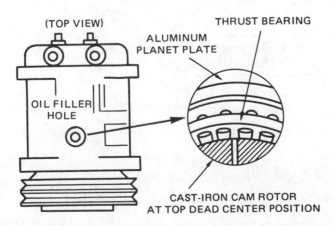

Fig. SP18-1 Position the rotor to top dead center (TDC)

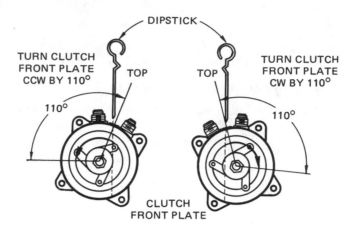

Fig. SP18-2 Rotate the clutch front plate

3. Purge the system of refrigerant, as outlined in Service Procedure 2. *Purge the system slowly to prevent a loss of oil.*

4. Position the angle gauge tool across the top flat surfaces of the two mounting ears.

5. Center the bubble and read the inclination angle.

6. Remove the oil filler plug. Rotate the clutch front plate to position the rotor at the top dead center (TDC), figure SP18-1.

7. Face the front of the compressor. If the compressor angle is to the right, rotate the clutch front plate counterclockwise (ccw) by 110°. If the compressor angle is to the left, rotate the plate clockwise (cw) by 110°, figure SP18-2.

Check the Oil Level

NOTE: The dipstick tool for this procedure is marked in eight increments. Each increment represents one ounce (29.57 milliliters) of oil.

1. Insert the dipstick until it reaches the stop position marked on the dipstick.

2. Remove the dipstick and count the number of increments of oil.

3. Compare the compressor angle and the number of increments with the table in figure SP18-3.

4. If necessary, add oil to bring the oil to the proper level. *Do not overfill.* Use only clean refrigeration oil of the proper grade.

Inclination Angle In Degrees	Acceptable Oil Level In Increments
0	6–10
10	7–11
20	8–12
30	9–13
40	10–14
50	11–16
60	12–17

Fig. SP18-3 Dipstick reading versus inclination angle

Return the System to Service

1. Check that the rubber O-ring is in place. Reinstall the oil filler plug. Tighten the plug to a torque of 8–9 ft-lb (10.8–12.2 N•m) (see step 3).

2. Leak test the system as outlined in Service Procedure 3.

3. If the oil filler plug leaks, *do not overtighten the plug*. Remove the plug and replace the O-ring (see step 1).

4. Evacuate the system as outlined in Service Procedure 4.

5. Remove the angle gauge tool from the compressor.

6. Charge the system as outlined in Service Procedure 5.

7. Return the system to service or conduct performance tests as required.

Review

Select the appropriate answer from the choices given.

1. What type of oil is recommended by the manufacturer for Sankyo compressors?

    a. Suniso 5GS
    b. Capella D

    c. Any good motor oil
    d. Any good refrigeration oil

2. If the oil filler plug leaks after being tightened to 8-9 ft-lb (10.8-12.2 N·m), how is the condition corrected? Technician A says to install a new O-ring and retorque to 9–10 ft-lb (12.2-13.6 N·m). Technician B says there is no need to install a new O-ring; just retorque to 9-10 ft-lb (12.2-13.6 N·m).

    a. Technician A is correct.
    b. Technician B is correct.

    c. Either technician may be correct.
    d. Both technicians are wrong.

3. The factory charge of oil in a new Sankyo compressor is

    a. 5 fluidounces (148 mL).
    b. 6 fluidounces (177 mL).

    c. 7 fluidounces (207 mL).
    d. 8 fluidounces (237 mL).

4. Which of the following need *not* be removed to check the oil level?

    a. Idler pulley or belt
    b. Clutch front plate
    c. Rotor
    d. None of these components need be removed.

5. Before checking the oil level, the rotor should be positioned to

    a. top dead center (TDC).
    b. bottom dead center (BDC).

    c. 110° counterclockwise (ccw).
    d. 110° clockwise (cw).

SERVICE PROCEDURE 19:

Checking and Adding Oil, Delco Air Four-cylinder Compressors (R-4)

The design of four-cylinder compressors requires a different oil checking procedure than the one used for other types of compressors. Four-cylinder compressors are factory charged with 5.50 to 6.50 fluidounces (163 to 192 mL) of 525 viscosity refrigeration oil.

In the four-cylinder compressor, it is not recommended that the oil level be checked as a matter of course. Generally, the compressor oil should be checked only where there is evidence of a major loss, such as that caused by a broken refrigeration line, a serious leak, or damage from a collision. The oil should also be checked if the compressor is to be repaired or replaced.

To check the compressor oil charge, the compressor must be removed from the car and drained. The oil is then measured. Whenever the oil is checked, the amount of oil drained from the compressor is noted. The old oil is then discarded.

In this procedure, it is assumed that the compressor is isolated or purged of refrigerant, and is removed from the car.

TOOLS

Set of hand tools   Graduated container(s)

MATERIALS

Refrigeration oil, as required   O-ring gaskets, as required

PROCEDURE

1. Clean the external surfaces of the compressor so that it is free of oil and grease.
2. Position the compressor with the shaft end up over a graduated container.
3. Drain the compressor. Allow it to drain for at least ten minutes. Measure and note the amount of oil removed, then discard the old oil.
4. Add new oil in the same amount as the oil drained.

   NOTE: If the replacement compressor is new, drain it as outlined in steps 2 and 3, then add new oil in the amount drained from the old compressor.

5. If a major component is also replaced, see the *Service Notes* for the addition of oil for the component.
6. If the loss of refrigerant occurs over an extended period of time, add three fluidounces (88.71 mL) of new oil. *Do not exceed a total of 6.5 ounces (192 mL) of oil.*

Service Notes

When the compressor is removed and drained, if it shows signs that foreign matter is present or that the oil contains chips or metallic particles, the system should be flushed. The receiver/dehydrator, desiccant, or accumulator (as applicable) should be replaced after the system is flushed. The compressor inlet and/or TXV inlet screens should be cleaned as well.

If the system is flushed, add a full six ounces (177 mL) of clean refrigeration oil to the four-cylinder compressor system.

With the exception of a system that is flushed, add oil as shown to any system that has had the following major components replaced.

COMPONENT	R-4 System
Accumulator	Replace with same amount of oil as drained, plus 3 oz (88.7 mL). If no oil is drained, add 2 oz (59.1 mL) to new accumulator.
Condenser	1 oz (29.6 mL)
Evaporator	2 oz (59.1 mL)
Receiver/dehydrator	1 oz (29.6 mL)

Disregard any loss of oil due to the changing of a line, hose, or muffler (unless the component contains a measurable amount of oil). If this is the case, add the same amount of clean refrigeration oil as measured in the component.

Review

Briefly answer each of the following questions.

1. What normal charge of oil is used in the Delco Air R-4 compressor?

2. How much oil must be added for the replacement of a condenser?

3. How much oil must be added for the replacement of the desiccant?

4. If the system is stabilized and four ounces (118 mL) of oil are removed, how much oil should be replaced in the R-4 compressor?

5. What grade of oil is used in the Delco Air R-4 compressor?

SERVICE PROCEDURE 20:

Checking and Adding Oil, Delco Air Six-cylinder Compressors (A-6 and DA-6)

The design of six-cylinder compressors requires a different oil checking procedure than the one used for other types of compressors. Six-cylinder compressors are fully charged at the factory; model A-6 with 11 ounces (325 mL); and model DA-6 with 8 ounces (237 mL) of 525 viscosity refrigeration oil.

In the six-cylinder compressor, it is not recommended that the oil level be checked as a matter of course. Generally, the compressor oil level should be checked only where there is evidence of a major loss, such as that caused by a broken refrigeration line, a serious leak, or damage from a collision. The oil should also be checked if the compressor is to be repaired or replaced.

To check the compressor oil charge, the compressor must be removed from the car and drained. The oil is then measured. Whenever the oil is checked, the amount of oil drained from the compressor is noted. The old oil is then discarded.

Some service procedures suggest that the model DA-6 compressor oil does not have to be measured. This compressor system oil is measured by removing and draining the accumulator only. In this procedure, it is assumed that the compressor is isolated, purged of refrigerant, and removed from the car.

TOOLS

Set of hand tools   Graduated container(s)

MATERIALS

Refrigeration oil, as required   O-ring gaskets, as required

PROCEDURE

Drain the Compressor

1. Clean the external surfaces of the compressor so that it is free of oil and grease.
2. Remove the oil drain plug located in the compressor oil sump, A-6 only.
3. Place the compressor in a horizontal position with the drain hole facing downward over a graduated container, A-6 only.
4. Place the compressor in a vertical position with the suction/discharge ports facing downward over a graduated container, DA-6 only.
5. Drain the compressor. Measure and note the amount of oil removed. Discard the old oil.

Add New Oil (System Stabilized)

NOTE: If the system is not stabilized before the compressor is removed from the car, as in the case of an inoperative compressor, omit this section. Instead, use the following procedure, "Add New Oil (System Not Stabilized)."

1. If the quantity of oil drained from the compressor is four ounces (118 mL) or more, add the same amount of new oil to the compressor.

2. If the quantity of oil drained from the compressor is less than four ounces (118 mL), add six ounces (177 mL) of new oil to the compressor.

3. If a major component of the system is also replaced, see "Service Notes" for the addition of oil for the component.

Add New Oil (System Not Stabilized)

NOTE: If the system is stabilized before the compressor is removed from the car, omit this section. Use the previous procedure, "Add New Oil (System Stabilized)."

1. If the quantity of oil removed is less than 4 ounces (118 mL) and the system shows no signs of a greater loss, add six ounces (177 mL) of new oil.

2. If the quantity of oil removed is greater than 4 ounces (118 mL) and the system shows no signs of a greater loss, add the same amount of new oil.

3. If a major component of the system is also replaced, see Service Notes for the addition of oil for the component.

4. If the compressor is replaced with a rebuilt unit, replace the oil in the amount as indicated in steps 1 or 2 and then add one more ounce (29.57 mL).

5. If a major component of the system is also replaced, see "Service Notes" for the addition of oil for the component.

Service Notes

When the compressor is removed and drained, if it shows signs that foreign matter is present or that the oil contains chips or metallic particles, the system should be flushed. The receiver/dehydrator, desiccant, or accumulator (as applicable) should be replaced after the system is flushed. The compressor inlet and/or TXV inlet screens should be cleaned as well.

If the system is flushed, add a full charge of clean refrigeration oil to the six-cylinder compressor system, as specified in the following chart.

With the exception of a system that is flushed, add oil as shown to any system that has had the following major components replaced.

COMPONENT	A-6 System	DA-6 System
Accumulator	Replace with same amount of oil drained, plus 3 oz (88.7 mL). If no oil was drained, add 3 oz (88.7 mL) for new accumulator.	Same
Compressor (if system was flushed)	11 oz (325 ML)	8 oz (237 mL)
Condenser	1 oz (29.6 mL)	Same
Evaporator	3 oz (88.7 mL)	2 oz (59.1 mL)

Disregard any loss of oil due to the changing of a line, hose, or muffler (unless the component contains a measurable amount of oil). If this is the case, add the same amount of clean refrigeration oil as measured in the component.

Review

Briefly answer each of the following questions.

1. What is the normal charge of oil used in the Delco Air A-6 compressor? In the DA-6 compressor?

2. What grade of oil is used in the Delco Air A-6 compressor? In the DA-6 compressor?

3. How much oil must be added for the replacement of an evaporator in the A-6 compressor system? In the DA-6 compressor system?

4. If it is impossible to stabilize a six-cylinder compressor system, and less than 1.5 ounces (44 mL) of oil are removed, how much oil should be replaced in the A-6 system? In the DA-6 system?

5. If the system is stabilized and four ounces (118 mL) of oil are removed, how much oil should be replaced in the A-6 compressor? In the DA-6 compressor?

SERVICE PROCEDURE 21:

Checking and Adding Oil, York Vane Rotary Compressor

The quantity of oil charge is not as critical in the York vane rotary compressor as it is in most other types. An overcharge of oil does not harm the compressor; an undercharge may cause a slight vane chatter though be sufficient for lubrication.

Normal oil charge is six to nine ounces (177 to 266 mL) depending upon system refrigerant capacity, as noted in the chart of figure SP21-2. The normal oil charge (level) in the compressor sump is two to four ounces (59 to 118 mL) regardless of the refrigerant charge.

This service procedure is given in two parts: Part I for checking the oil charge during system service (on the car), and Part II for bench checking the oil charge (off the car).

TOOLS

Socket wrench set
Oil dipstick
Graduated container

Manifold and gauge set
Vacuum pump

MATERIALS

Refrigeration oil, grade 500 SUS, as required
Refrigerant 12, as required
O-rings, as required

Fig. SP21-1 Cutaway view of York vane rotary compressor

System R-12 Charge		Oil Charge	
Pounds	Liters	oz	mL
2	0.946	6	177.4
3	1.419	7	207.0
4	1.892	8	236.6
5	2.365	9	266.2

Fig. SP21-2 Oil chart for York vane rotary compressor based on system refrigerant capacity

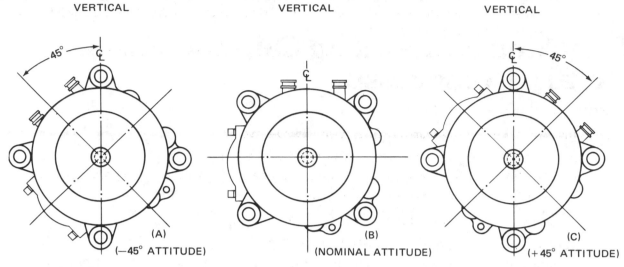

VERTICAL VERTICAL VERTICAL

45°

(A)
(−45° ATTITUDE)

(B)
(NOMINAL ATTITUDE)

(C)
(+45° ATTITUDE)

Fig. SP21-3 Adjust attitude of compressor so service valves are in vertical position as shown in B

PROCEDURE

PART I

Prepare the Compressor

1. Start and run the engine at idle speed for 10 minutes with the air-conditioning controls set for maximum cooling and medium fan speed.

2. Stop the engine. Slowly discharge the refrigerant (see Service Procedure 2).

   NOTE: Place the discharge hose into a graduated container to measure any oil lost while discharging the system.

3. Loosen the mounting hardware and belt(s) to adjust the attitude of the compressor, figure SP21-3, so that the service valves are vertical.

4. Remove the suction and discharge fittings. Discard the O-rings.

5. Rotate the compressor shaft, by hand, counterclockwise (ccw) five to ten turns.

Check Oil Level

1. Use the proper dipstick, figure SP21-4, to measure the oil level.

   NOTE: The oil level should be 2 to 4 ounces (59 to 118 mL).

Fig. SP21-4 Checking the oil level

2. If less than 2 ounces (59 mL), add oil to the correct level; if more than 2 ounces (59 mL), the oil level is considered adequate.

   NOTE: Oil may be added through the discharge port (stamped "D" on the compressor sump).

Return the Compressor to Service

1. Install suction and discharge fittings with new O-rings.

2. Replace belt(s) and reposition compressor to tension belts.

   NOTE: If using a belt tension gauge, proper tension is 80 pounds/strand for a dual belt or 100 to 120 pounds/strand for a single belt.

3. Evacuate the system as outlined in Service Procedure 4.

4. Charge the system as outlined in Service Procedure 5.

PART II

Part II assumes that the compressor is removed from the car for service. Part IIa is for checking the oil level in a compressor removed that is to be reinstalled. Part IIb is for adjusting the oil level in a new or replacement compressor.

Part IIa

1. Remove the oil drain plug and discard the O-ring.

2. Drain the oil into a graduated container. Drain oil from drain hole *and* suction and discharge ports.

   NOTE: If the amount of oil drained is less than 2 ounces (59 mL), replace with 2 ounces (59 mL); if more than 2 ounces (59 mL), replace with same amount as drained.

3. Replace oil (see note above). Oil may be added through the oil drain hole or the discharge port.

4. Replace oil drain plug with new O-ring.

Part IIb

1. Remove the oil drain plug from new or replacement compressor and discard O-ring.

2. Drain and discard oil. Drain from drain port *and* suction and discharge ports.

3. Remove the oil drain plug from the old compressor.

4. Drain oil into a graduated container. Drain oil from drain port *and* suction and discharge ports.

5. Add fresh oil to new compressor equal to that removed from old compressor if more than 2 ounces (59 mL). If less than 2 ounces (59 mL) is removed, add 2 ounces (59 mL).

   NOTE: Oil may be added to drain hole and/or discharge service port.

6. Replace oil plug with new O-ring.

Review

Select the appropriate answer from the choices given.

1. It is necessary to slowly discharge the refrigerant from the system in order to

   a. prevent the refrigerant from boiling.
   b. prevent the loss of oil.
   c. prevent moisture contamination.
   d. All of these

2. What is the normal oil charge if the refrigerant capacity is 4 pounds (1.81 kg)?

   a. 6 oz (177 mL)
   b. 7 oz (207 mL)
   c. 8 oz (237 mL)
   d. 9 oz (266 mL)

3. What grade oil is used in York's vane rotary compressor?

   a. 300 SAE
   b. 500 SAE
   c. 300 SUS
   d. 500 SUS

4. What is the normal sump level for on-the-car testing?

   a. 1 to 3 oz (29 to 89 mL)
   b. 2 to 4 oz (59 to 118 mL)
   c. 3 to 5 oz (89 to 148 mL)
   d. It depends upon the system refrigerant charge.

5. When bench checking oil, the oil is drained from

   a. the drain hole.
   b. the suction port.
   c. the discharge port.
   d. All of these are correct.

SERVICE PROCEDURE 22:

Checking and/or Adding Oil; Nippondenso Compressor (Includes Ford FS-6 and Chrysler C-171)

The Nippondenso compressor is factory charged with 13 ounces (384 mL) of 500 SUS (viscosity) refrigeration oil. It is not recommended that the oil level be checked as a matter of course unless there is evidence of a severe loss.

To check the oil level the compressor must be removed from the car. The oil is drained and measured. The amount of oil drained is noted then the oil is discarded.

The following procedure assumes that the compressor is removed from the car and that the suction and discharge service valves are removed from the compressor.

TOOLS

Graduated container

MATERIAL

Refrigeration oil, as required

PROCEDURE

Drain the Compressor

1. Drain the compressor oil through the suction and discharge service ports into a graduated container.
2. Rotate the crankshaft one revolution to insure that all oil is drained.
3. Note quality* and quantity** of oil drained.

   NOTE: *Inspect drained oil for brass or metallic particles which indicate a compressor failure.

   NOTE: **Record amount of oil removed, in ounces or milliliters.
4. Discard old oil.

Refill Compressor

1. Add oil, as follows:
   a. If the amount of oil drained was 3 ounces (89 mL) or more, add an equal amount of clean refrigeration oil.
   b. If the amount of oil drained was less than 3 ounces (89 mL), add 5 to 6 ounces (148 to 177 mL) of clean refrigeration oil.
2. If the compressor is to be replaced, drain all of the oil from the new or rebuilt compressor and replace oil as outlined in step 1 (a or b, as applicable).

   NOTE: Oil is added into the suction and/or discharge port(s). Rotate the compressor crankshaft at least five revolutions by hand after adding oil.

Review

1. When should the oil of a Nippondenso compressor be checked?

2. What is the difference in the words "quality" and "quantity" as used in step 3 of "Drain the Compressor"?

3. If the amount of oil drained from the compressor is 4 oz (118 mL), how much fresh oil should be used?

4. How is the oil added to the Nippondenso compressor?

5. What grade of oil is used in the Nippondenso compressor?

SERVICE PROCEDURE 23:

Servicing the Tecumseh HR-980 Compressor

The Tecumseh HR-980 compressor, used on some Ford car lines, requires special tools for servicing. Since the internal assembly is not accessible, service is limited to shaft seal and clutch repairs. The special tools required are available from Rotunda, Motorcraft, or Robinair.

This compressor is factory-charged with 8 oz (236.6 mL) of 500 viscosity refrigeration oil. In a balanced system, approximately 4 oz (118.3 mL) of oil will be found in the compressor, 3 oz (88.7 mL) in the evaporator, 1 oz (29.6 mL) in the condenser, and 1 oz (29.6 mL) in the accumulator.

This service procedure is in three parts; Part 1 for checking and adding oil, Part 2 for servicing the clutch, and Part 3 for replacing the seal.

TOOLS

Hub remover
Hub replacer
Seal protector
Pulley puller
Holding fixture
Spanner wrenches

Pulley/bearing replacer
Shaft protector
Pressure test fitting
Seal seat remover/replacer
Internal snap ring pliers
Small screwdriver

Shaft seal tool
O-ring guide
O-ring sleeve
O-ring replacer
O-ring remover

MATERIAL

Refrigeration oil
Refrigerant 12
Thread lock

Pulley bearing
Seal assembly

PROCEDURE

Part 1—CHECKING AND ADDING OIL

1. If replacing the compressor: Drain the new or rebuilt compressor and replace with 4 oz (118.3 mL) of clean refrigeration oil.

2. If replacing the evaporator: Add 3 oz (88.7 mL) of clean refrigeration oil to the new evaporator before installing.

3. If replacing the condenser: Add 1 oz (29.6 mL) of clean refrigeration oil to the new condenser before installing.

4. If replacing the accumulator: Drain the oil from the old accumulator, through pressure switch fitting, into a graduated container. Add the same amount of clean refrigeration oil to the new accumulator, plus 1 oz (29.6 mL). If no oil was drained from the old accumulator, add 1 oz (29.6 mL) of oil to the new accumulator.

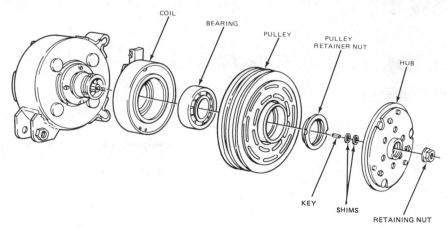

Fig. SP23-1 Exploded view of clutch and coil assembly

PART 2—CLUTCH SERVICE

Remove Clutch Assembly (Figure SP23-1)

1. Remove retaining nut.

2. Use the hub remover tool and remove the clutch hub from the compressor shaft, figure SP23-2. Remove and retain shim(s).

3. Using a spanner wrench, remove the clutch pulley retaining nut.

4. Remove the pulley and bearing assembly from the compressor. If the assembly cannot be removed by hand, use the shaft protector and pulley remover, figure SP23-3.

5. Remove the field coil from the compressor.

6. Clean the front of the compressor to remove any dirt and/or corrosion.

Replace Clutch Bearing

1. Place the pulley on the clutch pulley support, as shown in figure SP23-4.

2. Use the pulley replacer tool to drive out the bearing.

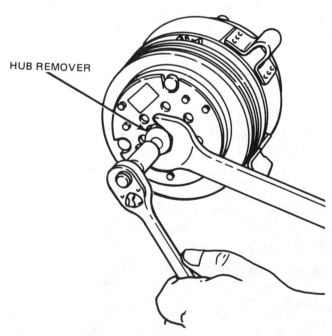

Fig. SP23-2 Use hub remover tool to remove clutch hub

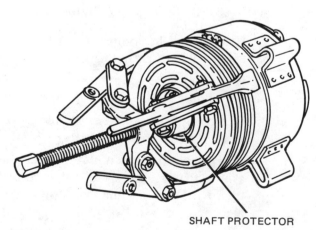

Fig. SP23-3 Use shaft protector and pulley remover to remove clutch pulley

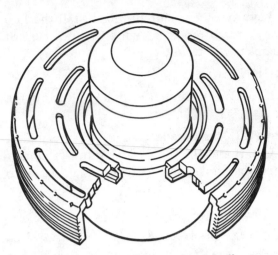

Fig. SP23-4 Place pulley on clutch pulley support

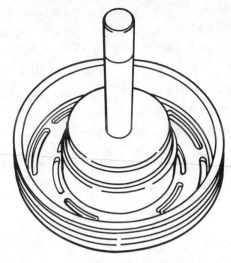

Fig. SP23-5 Seat bearing in pulley using tool

3. Turn the pulley over, flat side atop a clean board.

4. Position the new bearing in the bearing bore of the pulley and use the pulley bearing replacer to seat the bearing, figure SP23-5. Be sure that the bearing and bore are aligned.

5. Stake the new bearing. Use a blunt drift or punch at three equally spaced places inside the bore. Do not use the same places that were used to retain the old bearing.

Replace Pulley Assembly

1. Install the field coil. The slots of the coil should fit over the housing lugs. The electrical connector should be toward the top of the compressor.

2. Install the pulley and bearing assembly on the front of the compressor. If properly aligned, the assembly should slide on. If difficult, use pulley replacer and tap lightly with a plastic hammer. *Do not use unnecessary force.*

3. Apply a drop of thread lock to the threads of the pulley retainer nut.

4. Install the pulley retainer nut and tighten to 65-70 ft-lb (88-94 N·m) using spanner and torque wrenches.

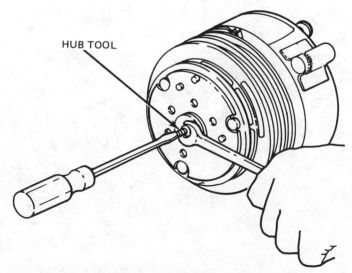

HUB TOOL

Fig. SP23-6 Use hub replacer tool to replace hub

5. Being sure that the key is aligned with the keyway of the clutch hub, install the hub and shim(s) onto the compressor shaft. Use the hub replacer, figure SP23-6. Do not drive the hub onto the shaft as compressor damage will result.

6. Install the nut and tighten to 10-14 ft-lb (14-18 N·m).

7. Check the air gap at three equally spaced intervals around the pulley. Record the measurements.

8. Rotate the compressor pulley one-half turn (180°) and repeat step 7. The smallest air gap permitted is between 0.021 in (0.53 mm) and 0.036 in (0.91 mm). If greater or less than these specifications, add or remove shims (step 5) to bring air gap into specifications.

PART 3—REPLACE SHAFT SEAL

Remove Seal (Figure SP23-7)

1. Remove the clutch and coil as outlined in Part 2.

2. Remove the key from the compressor shaft.

3. Carefully pry the dust shield from the compressor, using a small screwdriver, figure SP23-8. Take care not to damage the end of the compressor housing.

4. Remove the seal snap ring retainer, using the internal snap ring pliers.

5. Clean the inside of the seal cavity to prevent entry of foreign material when the seal is removed.

6. Insert the shaft seal seat tool and engage the seal. Tighten the outer sleeve to expand the tool in the seal seat, figure SP23-9.

7. Pull on the tool, while rotating it clockwise (cw), to remove the seal seat.

8. Use the O-ring remover and remove the O-ring, figure SP23-10.

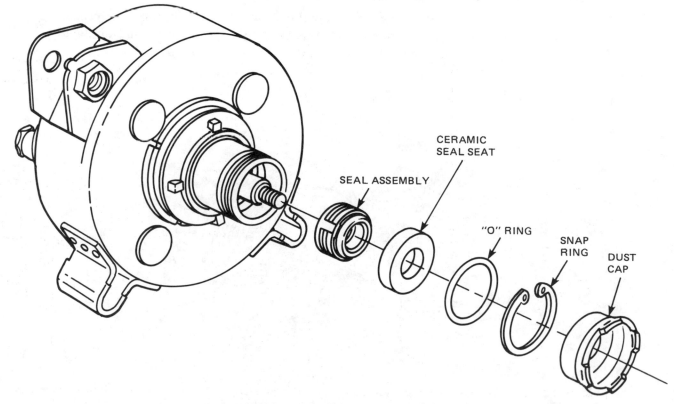

Fig. SP23-7 Exploded view of shaft seal assembly

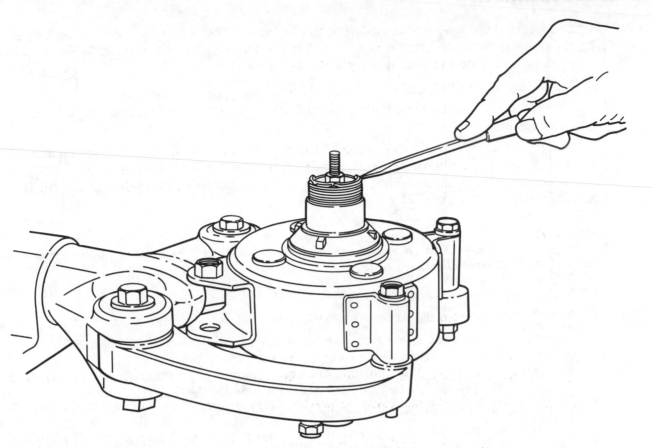

Fig. SP23-8 Use screwdriver to pry dust shield from seal cavity

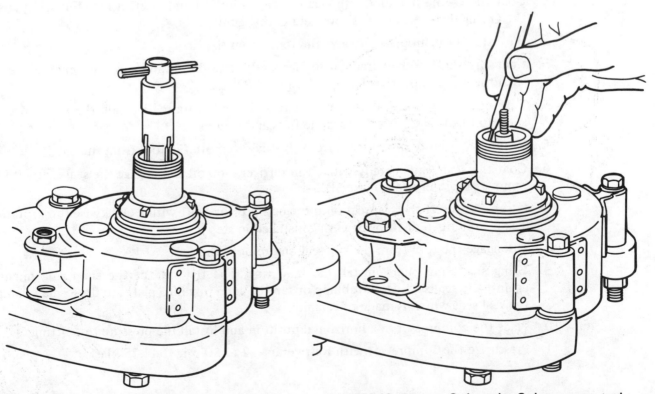

Fig. SP23-9 Insert shaft seal seat tool into seal cavity

Fig. SP23-10 Remove O-ring using O-ring remover tool

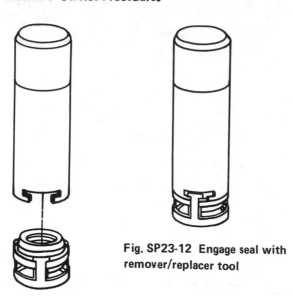

Fig. SP23-12 Engage seal with remover/replacer tool

Fig. SP23-11 Insert seal on remover/replacer tool

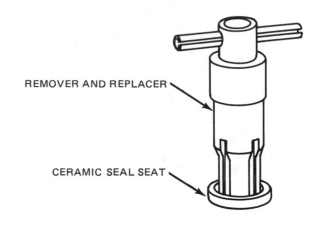

REMOVER AND REPLACER

CERAMIC SEAL SEAT

Fig. SP23-13 Engage seal seat with remover/replacer tool

9. Insert the seal assembly tool into the compressor. While forcing the tool downward, rotate it counterclockwise (ccw) to engage the tangs of the seal, figure SP23-11.

10. Pull the seal from the compressor and remove the seal from the tool.

11. Check the inside of the compressor to insure that all surfaces are free of nicks and burrs.

Install Seal

1. Coat the O-ring liberally with clean refrigeration oil and insert it into the cavity, using the O-ring installer, O-ring sleeve, and O-ring guide.

2. With the O-ring in place, remove the tools from the cavity.

3. Coat the shaft seal liberally with clean refrigeration oil and carefully engage the seal with the seal remover/replacer tool, figure SP23-12.

4. Carefully place the seal over the shaft and, while rotating it, slide the seal down the shaft until the assembly engages the flats and is in place.

5. Rotate the tool to disengage it from the seal. Remove the tool from the cavity.

6. Coat the seal seat liberally with clean refrigeration oil and engage the seal seat with the remover/replacer tool, figure SP23-13.

7. Carefully, insert the seal seat onto the compressor shaft with a clockwise (cw) rotation. Take care not to disturb the O-ring installed in step 1.

8. Disengage the tool from the seal seat and remove the tool.

9. Using snap ring pliers, install the snap ring. The flat side of the snap ring must be against the seal seat. Do not bump or tap the snap ring into place; to do so may damage the seal seat which is made of ceramic.

10. Place the compressor in a horizontal position and install the pressure test fitting.

11. Pressurize the compressor with Refrigerant 12 to 50 psig (344.75 kPa).

12. Leak test as outlined in Service Procedure 3. If the shaft seal leaks, temporarily install the shaft nut and rotate the compressor shaft several turns by hand.

13. Remove the nut. Release pressure and remove the test fitting.

14. Install the dust shield.

15. Replace the clutch and coil as outlined in Part 2.

Review

Select the appropriate answer from the choices given.

1. Technician A says that the air gap for the pulley should be 0.021 in (0.53 mm). Technician B says that the air gap should be 0.036 in (0.91 mm).

   a. Technician A is correct.
   b. Technician B is correct.
   c. Both technicians are correct.
   d. Both technicians are wrong.

2. Technician A says that the pulley and bearing assembly may be installed by hand. Technician B says that a pulley replacer may have to be used to tap it on with a plastic hammer.

   a. Technician A is correct.
   b. Technician B is correct.
   c. Both technicians are correct.
   d. Both technicians are wrong.

3. Technician A says that thread lock must be used on the pulley retainer nut. Technician B says that thread lock must be used on the hub retainer nut.

   a. Technician A is correct.
   b. Technician B is correct.
   c. Both technicians are correct.
   d. Both technicians are wrong.

4. The pulley retainer nut is torqued to

   a. 8-12 ft-lb (11-16 N·m).
   b. 10-14 ft-lb (14-18 N·m).
   c. 60-65 ft-lb (81-87 N·m).
   d. 65-70 ft-lb (88-94 N·m).

5. Approximately _____ of oil will be found in the compressor of a balanced system.

   a. 1 oz (29.6 mL)   c. 4 oz (118.3 mL)
   b. 3 oz (88.7 mL)   d. 8 oz (236.6 mL)

SERVICE PROCEDURE 24:

Servicing the Clutch Rotor and the Clutch Coil (Sankyo Compressors)

If ample clearance is provided in front of the compressor for clutch service, the compressor need not be removed from the car for this procedure. Additional tools and materials are required if the compressor is to be removed from the car (see Service Procedure 12).

TOOLS

NOTE: The tool part numbers are Sankyo part numbers.

Spanner wrench (32409)
Front plate puller (32416)
Snap ring pliers (32407 and 32417)
Pulley puller (32418)
Rotor installer (32435)
Front plate installer (32436)

Air gap gauge set (32437)
Torque wrench
Socket wrench set
Screwdriver
Soft hammer

MATERIALS

Front plate
Pulley

Bearing or field coil, as required

PROCEDURE

Removing the Clutch

1. Loosen the compressor and/or idler pulley and remove the belt(s).
2. Use a 3/4-in. hex socket and spanner wrench to remove the crankshaft hex nut (see figure SP12-1).
3. Remove the clutch front plate, using the clutch front plate puller (see figure SP12-2).
4. Using the snap ring pliers, remove the internal and external snap rings, figures SP24-1A and SP24-1B.

Fig. SP24-1A Removing the internal snap ring

Fig. SP24-1B Removing the external snap ring

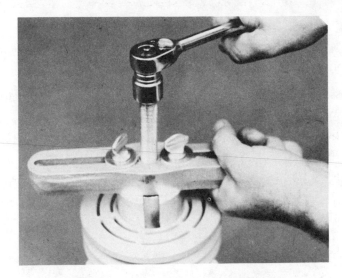

Fig. SP24-2 Removing the rotor assembly

5. Using the pulley puller, figure SP24-2, remove the rotor assembly.

6. If the clutch coil is to be replaced, remove the three retaining screws and the clutch field coil. Omit this step if the coil is not to be replaced.

Replace the Rotor Bearing

1. Using the snap ring pliers, remove the bearing retainer snap ring.

2. From the back (compressor) side of the rotor, knock out the bearing using the bearing remover tool and a soft hammer.

3. From the front (clutch face) side of the rotor, install the new bearing using the bearing installer tool and a soft hammer. Take care not to damage the bearing with hard blows of the hammer.

4. Reinstall the bearing retainer snap ring.

Replace the Clutch

1. Reinstall the field coil (or install a new field coil, if necessary) using the three retaining screws.

2. Align the rotor assembly squarely with the front compressor housing.

3. Using the rotor two-piece installer tools and a soft hammer, carefully drive the rotor into position until it seats on the bottom of the housing, figure SP24-3.

4. Reinstall the internal and external snap rings using the snap ring pliers.

5. Align the slot in the hub of the front plate squarely with the shaft key.

6. Drive the front plate on the shaft using the installer tool and a soft hammer. *Do not use unnecessary hard blows.*

7. Check the air gap with *go* and *no-go* gauges (see figure SP12-8).

8. Replace the shaft nut and tighten it to a torque of 25–30 ft-lb (33.9–40.7 N•m) using the torque wrench.

9. Replace the belt(s) and tighten to 90–110 ft-lb (122–149.1 N•m) tension.

Fig. SP24-3 Installing the rotor assembly

Review

Select the appropriate answer from the choices given.

1. The compressor shaft nut is removed by using a spanner wrench and

   a. a 3/4-in hex socket.
   b. a 3/4-in open end wrench.

   c. an adjustable wrench.
   d. a pair of pliers.

2. Technician A says that the clutch field coil is held in place with a snap ring. Technician B says that it is held in place with a locking nut.

   a. Technician A is correct.
   b. Technician B is correct.
   c. Either technician may be correct.
   d. Both technicians are wrong.

3. The bearing is installed by using a bearing installer tool and what other tool(s)? Technician A says that the other tool is a soft hammer. Technician B says that the other tool is snap ring pliers.

   a. Technician A is correct.
   b. Technician B is correct.
   c. Either technician may be correct.
   d. Both technicians are wrong.

4. During reassembly, which part should seat on the bottom of the compressor housing?

   a. The rotor
   b. The seal

   c. The clutch field coil
   d. The clutch bearing

5. Under which condition is it *necessary* to remove the compressor from the car for service?

   a. When there is time to do the job correctly.
   b. When the customer is watching.
   c. When there is ample clearance in front of the compressor for service.
   d. When there is not enough clearance in front of the compressor for service.

SERVICE PROCEDURE 25:

Servicing the Delco Air Four-cylinder Compressor Clutch

The General Motors Delco Air four-cylinder compressor clutch requires special tools for service. This procedure is given based on the use of the proper service tools.

It may be possible to perform this procedure without removing the compressor from the car if there is adequate work space in front of the compressor; only the drive belt(s) need to be removed. If service is to be performed on the car, the refrigerant need not be purged from the system.

TOOLS

Holding fixture (if compressor is removed from the car)
Socket set with 9/16-inch thinwall socket
7/16-inch 6-point box wrench
Prick punch, small
Cold chisel, small
Hammer
External snap ring plier
Rotor and bearing puller guide
Rotor and bearing puller
Rotor and bearing installer, with handle
Clutch hub holding tool
Clutch plate and hub remover
Clutch plate and hub installer
Nonmagnetic feeler gauge

MATERIALS

Clutch plate and hub assembly, as required
Rotor and bearing assembly, as required
Coil and housing assembly, as required
Bearing, as required

PROCEDURE

Removing the Clutch Plate and Hub Assembly

1. Using the clutch hub holding tool and a 9/16-inch thinwall socket, remove the retaining nut from the compressor shaft.

2. Using the clutch plate and hub assembly remover tool, remove the clutch plate and hub assembly.

3. If the shaft key is not removed in step 2, remove the shaft key.

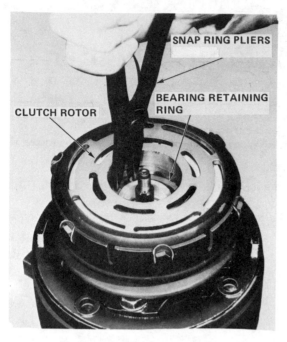

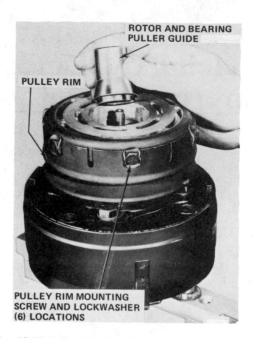

Fig. SP25-1 Removing the bearing retaining ring

Fig. SP25-2 Positioning the rotor and bearing puller guide

Clutch Rotor-Bearing and Coil-Pulley Rim Removal

1. Mark the location of the clutch coil terminals to insure proper reassembly.
2. Remove the rotor and bearing assembly retaining ring using the snap ring pliers, figure SP25-1.
3. Install the rotor bearing and puller guide over the end of the compressor shaft, figure SP25-2. *The guide should seat on the front head of the compressor.*
4. Using a puller, remove the clutch rotor and assembly parts, figure SP25-3.

Split the Clutch Rotor-Bearing and Coil-Pulley Rim

1. Using a cold chisel and hammer, bend the tabs of the six pulley rim mounting screw lockwashers flat, figure SP25-4.

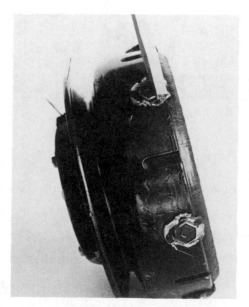

Fig. SP25-3 Removing the clutch rotor

Fig. SP25-4 Bending the locking tabs to allow removal of the capscrews

Fig. SP25-5 Separating the pulley rim from the rotor. The clutch coil is found in this assembly.

2. Using a 7/16-inch 6-point box wrench, loosen and remove all six screws.

3. Separate the pulley rim from the rotor, figure SP25-5.

Diagnosis

1. Visually check the coil for loose connections or cracked insulation.

2. Briefly, connect the coil to a 12-volt battery with an ammeter connected in series. If the coil draws more than 3.2 amperes at 12 volts it should be replaced.

3. Inspect the clutch plate and hub assembly. Check for signs of looseness between the plate and hub. See note following step 4.

4. Check the rotor and bearing assembly.

   NOTE: If the frictional surface of the clutch plate or rotor shows signs of warpage due to excessive heat, that part should be replaced. Slight scoring (see figure SP26-5) is normal; if either assembly is heavily scored, however, it should be replaced.

5. Check the bearing for signs of excessive noise, binding, or looseness. Replace the bearing if necessary.

Replacing the Bearing

1. Place the rotor and bearing assembly, split side down, atop two soft wood blocks, figure SP25-6.

2. Using the appropriate tool, with hammer, drive the bearing from the rotor, figure SP25-7. The bearing may also be removed with an arbor press.

3. Turn the rotor over with the frictional surface resting on a block of soft wood.

4. Using the appropriate tool, with hammer, drive the bearing into the rotor. To insure the alignment of the bearing outer surface into the rotor inner surface, the use of an arbor press, figure SP25-8, is recommended.

   NOTE: Insure that pressure is exerted on the outer bearing race during insertion. If pressure is exerted on the inner race, by either method of insertion, premature failure of the bearing will result.

Fig. SP25-6 Place the rotor atop two soft wood blocks

Fig. SP25-7 Driving the old bearing from the rotor

Fig. SP25-8 Pressing the new bearing into the rotor

Fig. SP25-9 Using a prick punch to stake the bearing into the rotor

Fig. SP25-10 Bend the tabs against the capscrews to prevent loosening during use

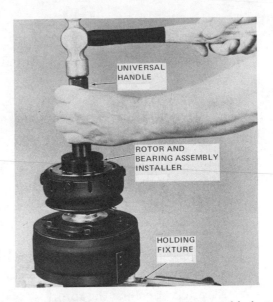

Fig. SP25-11 Using the rotor and bearing assembly installer

5. After the bearing is seated in the rotor, use a prick punch to stake it in place, figure SP25-9.

Reassemble the Clutch Rotor-Bearing and Coil-Pulley Rim

1. With the coil in place, join the pulley rim to the rotor.

2. Replace and/or tighten the six retaining screws using a 7/16-inch 6-point box wrench.

3. Using a cold chisel and hammer, bend the tabs of the six mounting screw lockwashers up against a flat of each of the screws (one tab for each screw), figure SP25-10.

Fig. SP25-12 Key, inserted into the keyway of the hub, should protrude 3/16 inch (4.7 mm)

Replace the Clutch Rotor-Bearing and Coil-Pulley Rim

1. Position the assembly on the front head of the compressor.

2. Using the rotor assembly installer with a universal handle, figure SP25-11, drive the assembly into place. *Before the assembly is fully seated, insure that the coil terminals are in the proper location and the three protrusions on the rear of the coil housing align with the locator holes in the front head.*

3. Install the retainer ring, using snap ring pliers.

Replace the Clutch Plate and Hub Assembly

1. Clean the frictional surfaces of the clutch plate and rotor, if necessary.

2. Insert the key into the slot (keyway) of the hub. *Do not insert the key into the compressor crankshaft slot (keyway).*

NOTE: The key should protrude about 3/16 inch (0.187 5 in or 4.7 mm) below the hub, figure SP25-12.

3. Place the clutch plate and hub assembly onto the compressor shaft by matching the key of the hub to the keyway of the shaft.

4. Using a clutch plate and hub installer, press this part on the crankshaft. *Do not hammer this part into position.*

5. Use a nonmagnetic feeler gauge to insure an air gap of 0.020 to 0.040 inch (0.508 to 1.016 mm) between the frictional surfaces.

6. Replace the shaft nut and torque to 8–12 ft-lb (10.8–16.3 N·m).

Review

Select the appropriate answer from the choices given.

1. The bearing is held into the rotor-bearing assembly by

   a. a snap ring.
   b. prick-punching the rotor.
   c. either a snap ring or prick-punching the rotor.
   d. both a snap ring and prick-punching the rotor.

2. How many bolts secure the pulley rim to the rotor?

   a. Two   c. Six
   b. Four   d. Eight

3. A hammer *should not* be used to

   a. remove a bearing.
   b. replace a bearing.
   c. replace the clutch rotor-bearing and coil-pulley rim.
   d. replace the clutch plate and hub assembly.

4. Technician A says that when installing the clutch rotor-bearing and coil-pulley rim one must insure that the coil terminals are in the proper location. Technician B says that one must insure that the three protrusions on the rear of the coil housing align with the locater holes in the front head.

   a. Technician A is correct.
   b. Technician B is correct.
   c. Both technicians are correct.
   d. Both technicians are wrong.

5. When the clutch coil is connected to a 12-volt battery with an ammeter in series, and the ammeter reads 0 amperes, the indication is that the coil is

   a. open.   c. suitable for use.
   b. shorted.   d. None of these answers is correct.

SERVICE PROCEDURE 26:

Servicing the Delco Air Six-cylinder Compressor Clutch (A-6)

This service procedure covers servicing the Delco Air model A-6 compressor clutch assembly. Procedures for servicing the Delco Air model DA-6 compressor clutch assembly are covered in Service Procedure 30.

This procedure may be performed without removing the compressor from the car if there is adequate work space in front of the compressor; only the drive belt(s) need be removed. Refrigerant need not be purged from the system if the clutch is serviced on the car.

Special service tools are required to service this compressor clutch. They are available from several sources, such as Robinair and Kent Moore. The following service procedure is based on the use of the proper service tools, and assumes that the compressor has been removed from the car.

TOOLS

Holding fixture (if the compressor
   is removed from the car)
Socket set with 9/16-inch thinwall
   socket
Adjustable wrench, 10 inch
Internal snap ring plier
External snap ring plier
Clutch hub holding tool

Hub and drive plate remover
Hub and drive plate installer
Pulley puller pilot
Pulley puller
Pulley bearing remover and installer,
   with handle
Small screwdriver
Nonmagnetic feeler gauge

MATERIALS

Hub and drive plate assembly, as
   required
Pulley and bearing assembly, as
   required
Coil and housing assembly, as
   required
Bearing, as required

PROCEDURE

Hub and Drive Plate Removal

1. Mount the compressor in a holding fixture and secure the fixture in a vise.

Fig. SP26-1 Removing the hub and drive plate assembly

Fig. SP26-2 Removing the pulley retaining ring

Fig. SP26-3 Removing the pulley

2. Using a drive plate holding tool and the 9/16-in thinwall socket, remove the locknut from the shaft.

3. Using the snap ring pliers, remove the clutch hub retaining ring. Remove the spacer under the ring.

4. Remove the hub and drive plate with the hub and drive plate remover tool, figure SP26-1.

Pulley and Bearing Assembly Removal

1. Using the snap ring pliers, remove the pulley and bearing snap ring retainer, figure SP26-2.

2. Place a puller pilot over the crankshaft. Using a pulley puller, remove the pulley, figure SP26-3.

    NOTE: The puller pilot must be in place. Placing the puller against the crankshaft will damage the internal assembly.

3. If the pulley bearing is to be replaced, use a sharp tool, such as a small screwdriver, to remove the wire retaining ring.

4. From the rear of the pulley, press or drive the bearing out.

Coil Housing Assembly

1. Scribe the location of the coil housing with relation to the compressor body to insure proper alignment during reassembly.

2. Using snap ring pliers, remove the coil housing retainer ring, figure SP26-4.

3. Lift off the coil housing assembly.

Fig. SP26-4 Removing the coil housing retainer ring

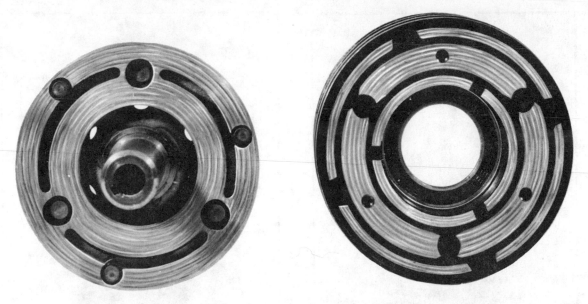

Fig. SP26-5 Scoring of the drive and driven plates is normal. Do not replace for this condition.

Diagnosis

1. Check the coil for loose connections or cracked insulation.

2. Briefly, connect the coil to a 12-volt battery with an ammeter in series. If the coil draws more than 3.2 amperes at 12 volts it should be replaced.

3. Inspect the hub and drive plate. Inspect for signs of looseness between the hub and drive plate. See note following step 4.

4. Check the pulley and bearing assembly.

    NOTE: If the frictional surface of the pulley or drive plate shows signs of warpage due to excessive heat, that part should be replaced. Slight scoring, figure SP26-5, is normal. If either assembly is heavily scored, it should be replaced.

5. Check the pulley bearing for signs of excessive noise, binding, or looseness. Replace the bearing if necessary.

Replace the Coil Housing

1. Note the original position of the coil housing by the scribe marks.
2. Slip the coil housing into place.
3. Replace the snap ring to secure the housing.

Replace the Pulley and the Bearing Assembly

1. Press the new bearing into the pulley, figure SP26-6, and replace the wire retaining ring (if bearing replacement is necessary).

2. Using the proper tool, figure SP26-7, press or drive the pulley and bearing assembly on the compressor front head.

3. Install the retainer snap ring.

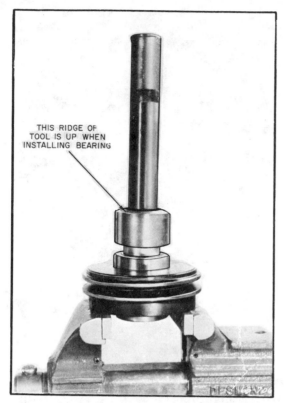

Fig. SP26-6 Installing the pulley and drive plate bearing

Fig. SP26-7 Installing the pulley and drive plate on the compressor

Replace the Hub and Drive Plate

1. Follow the procedures outlined in Service Procedure 15.

2. Turn the clutch hub by hand to insure that it (or the internal assembly) is not dragging or binding.

3. Spin the pulley to insure that it is not dragging or binding. It should turn freely.

Review

Select the appropriate answer from the choices given.

1. Technician A says that the clutch rotor bearing should be replaced if it is binding. Technician B says that it should be replaced if it is loose.

    a. Technician A is correct.
    b. Technician B is correct.
    c. Both technicians are correct.
    d. Both technicians are wrong.

2. Proper clearance between the clutch pulley and drive plate surfaces are

    a. 0.005 to 0.010 in (0.127 to 0.254 mm).
    b. 0.010 to 0.030 in (0.254 to 0.762 mm).
    c. 0.020 to 0.040 in (0.508 to 1.016 mm).
    d. 0.030 to 0.050 in (0.762 to 1.270 mm).

3. What tool is used to remove the pulley bearing retainer in order to remove the bearing from the pulley?

    a. Screwdriver or awl
    b. Internal snap ring plier
    c. External snap ring plier
    d. All answers are correct.

4. What is the maximum current draw to be expected when checking the clutch coil with an ammeter?

    a. 2.3 amperes
    b. 3.2 amperes
    c. 12 amperes
    d. None of these is correct.

5. When removing the pulley from the compressor

    a. a special puller must be used.
    b. a puller pilot must be in place.
    c. Both answers are correct.
    d. Neither answer is correct.

SERVICE PROCEDURE 27:

Servicing the York Vane Rotary Compressor Clutch

The York vane rotary clutch may be serviced on the car if there is adequate space in front of the compressor. Refrigerant need not be purged from the system if the compressor is serviced on the car.

There are two methods of removing the clutch pulley assembly. One method uses an internal groove in front of the pulley bearing; the other method uses three tapped holes in the face of the pulley plate. This procedure is given for the three threaded hole method, which requires fewer tools.

TOOLS

Holding fixture (if the compressor is removed from the car)
Socket set with Torx T-25 socket
Torque wrench, inch-pounds (newton-meters)
Armature assembly remover
Shaft pilot
Bearing driver head with handle
Internal snap ring plier
Hammer

MATERIALS

Armature plate assembly, as required
Pulley assembly, as required
Coil and housing assembly, as required
Bearing, as required

PROCEDURE

Armature Removal

1. Loosen bracket(s) and remove belt(s).

2. Remove the armature 10–24 x 1/2-inch retaining screw with a Torx T-25 socket and handle.

3. Remove the long 10–24 screw from the puller plate and screw it into the shaft until it bottoms, figure SP27-1.

Fig. SP27-1 Installing the armature plate removal tool

Fig. SP27-2 Armature plate removal

Fig. SP27-3 Removing the pulley retaining ring

4. Install the armature assembly removal tool on the 10–24 screw and secure with three thumb screws.

5. Turn the puller bolt against the screw until the armature assembly comes off, figure SP27-2.

   NOTE: Do not use screwdrivers to pry the armature assembly.

Pulley Assembly Removal

1. Remove the retaining ring, figure SP27-3, using internal snap ring pliers.

2. Place shaft pilot over compressor shaft (see note following step 4).

3. Install the puller on the pilot and thread the three screws into the pulley, figure SP27-4.

4. Turn the puller bolt against the pilot to remove the pulley.

   NOTE: Make sure the pilot is in place. Do not apply the pulling load to the compressor shaft; to do so may cause internal damage to the compressor.

Fig. SP27-4 Using the puller to remove pulley (rotor)

Coil Assembly Removal

1. Disconnect coil lead(s).

2. Remove the three 10–24 x 3/8-inch screws using a Torx T–25 socket with handle.

3. Remove coil assembly.

Fig. SP27-5 Coil assembly

Fig. SP27-6 Installing the pulley assembly

Coil Assembly Replacement

1. Set coil in place, figure SP27-5, and secure with three 10–24 x 3/8-inch Torx screws.

2. Torque screws to 30–50 inch-pounds (3.4–5.6 N·m).

3. Connect coil lead(s).

Pulley Assembly Replacement

1. Place shaft pilot onto compressor shaft. This is to align the bearing inner race with the compressor body.

2. Place the pulley installer tool on the assembly so the tool rests on the bearing inner race, figure SP27-6.

3. Tap on the tool to install the pulley, figure SP27-7.

4. Replace the snap ring and remove the pilot.

Fig. SP27-7 Installing the pulley assembly

Armature Plate Replacement

1. Insert the armature hub onto the compressor shaft spline.

2. Hand press the armature plate assembly onto the compressor shaft, figure SP27-8.

   NOTE: Do not hammer or pound the armature plate assembly into place; to do so will result in compressor internal damage.

3. Install the 10–24 x 1/2-inch Torx screw and torque it to 30–50 inch-pounds (3.4–5.6 N•m).

    NOTE: The plate to pulley air gap should be 0.015 to 0.050 inch (0.38 to 1.27 mm) for proper clutch operation.

Fig. SP27-8 Installing the armature

Review

Briefly, outline the procedure for replacing the armature and hub assembly.

SERVICE PROCEDURE 28:

Servicing the Nippondenso Compressor Clutch (Includes Chrysler C-171 and Ford FS-6)

The Nippondenso compressor is also known as the Chrysler C-171 and the Ford FS-6 compressor. This compressor may be equipped with either a Nippondenso or Warner clutch assembly. Though these two clutches are similar in appearance, their parts are not interchangeable. Complete clutch assemblies are, however, interchangeable on the Nippondenso compressor.

The apparent difference in the two clutches is that the Nippondenso pulley, figure SP28-1, has two, narrow single-row bearings which are held in place with a wire snap ring. The Warner clutch, figure SP28-2, has a single, wide double-row bearing which is staked or crimped in place.

Service procedures of the two clutches are similar. The same special tools are used for serving either clutch with one exception: the clutch pulley support, used for removing the bearing(s), differs between the Nippondenso and Warner clutch.

If there is sufficient space in front of the compressor, the clutch may be serviced on the car. If serviced on the car, the refrigerant need not be purged from the system. If the compressor is to be removed from the car for clutch service, the system must first be purged of refrigerant.

TOOLS

Set of hand tools
Hub remover
3-jaw puller
External snap ring plier
Bearing remover/pulley installer
Bearing installer
Hub replacer
Nonmagnetic feeler gauge set

Small screwdriver (if Nippondenso)
Clutch pulley support (for Warner or Nippondenso, as required)
Prick punch (if Warner)
Hammer, plastic
Shaft protector
Ammeter
Voltmeter

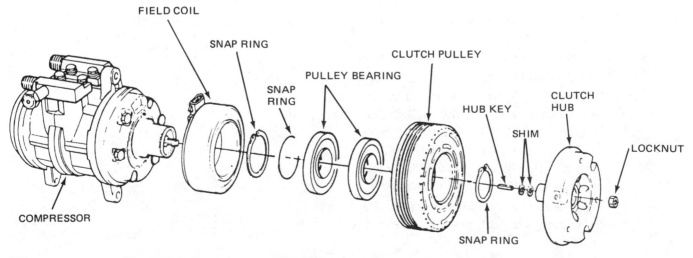

Fig. SP28-1 Exploded view of Nippondenso compressor with Nippondenso clutch

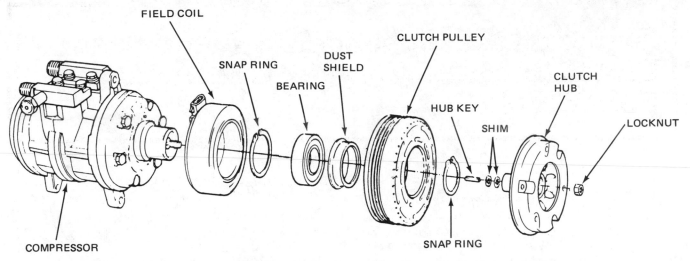

Fig. SP28-2 Exploded view of Nippondenso compressor with Warner clutch

MATERIALS

Clutch coil, as required
Bearing or bearings, as required
Refrigerant 12, as required

Pulley/bearing assembly, as required
Clutch hub, as required

PROCEDURE

Preparation

1. Loosen idler(s) and remove belt(s).

2. If there is insufficient room for service, remove the compressor from the engine. First purge the system of refrigerant, as outlined in Service Procedure 2.

Remove the Clutch

1. Remove the hub nut.

2. Use the hub remover and remove the clutch hub, figure SP28-3.

   NOTE: The shaft/hub key need not be removed. Take care not to lose the shim washer(s).

3. Use the snap ring plier to remove the pulley retainer snap ring.

4. With the shaft protector in place, figure SP28-4, remove the pulley and bearing assembly with the 3-jaw puller.

   NOTE: Make certain that the puller jaws are firmly and securely located behind the pulley to avoid damage.

5. Use the snap ring plier to remove the field coil retaining snap ring, figure SP28-5.

6. Note the location of the coil electrical connector and lift the field coil from the compressor.

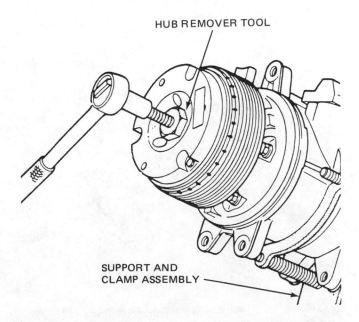

Fig. SP28-3 Using the hub remover tool to remove the clutch hub

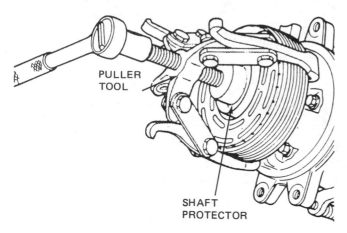

Fig. SP28-4 **Using a 3-jaw puller with shaft protector to remove pulley and bearing assembly**

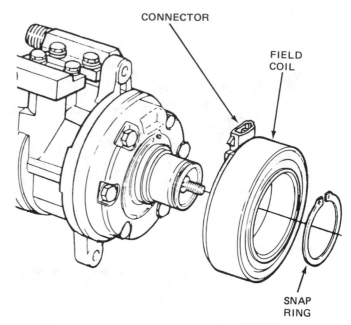

Fig. SP28-5 **Field coil is held in place with snap ring. Note location of connector and use snap ring plier to remove snap ring — then lift off field coil.**

Replace the Pulley Bearing

NOTE: If Nippondenso clutch, use a small screwdriver and remove the bearing retaining snap ring before proceeding.

1. Support the pulley with the proper clutch pulley support, figure SP28-6 (see introductory statements).

2. Drive out bearing(s) using hammer and bearing remover.

3. Lift out the dust shield and retainer or leave in place. Make sure the dust shield is in place *before* installing bearing.

4. Install new bearing(s) using the bearing installer and the hammer, figure SP28-7. Bearing(s) must be fully seated in the rotor.

5. Replace the wire snap ring if Nippondenso. If Warner, stake the bearing in place using the prick punch and the hammer.

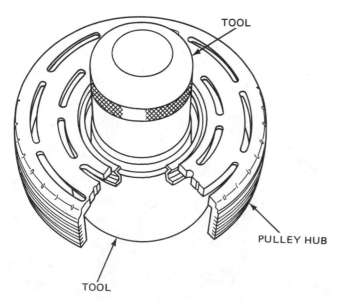

Fig. SP28-6 **With pulley supported, use tool to drive out pulley bearing**

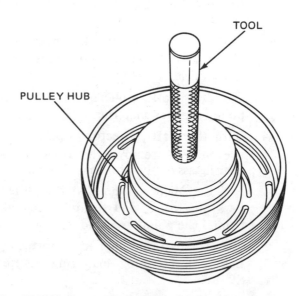

Fig. SP28-7 **Use bearing installer tool (and hammer) to drive new bearing into pulley hub**

Test the Clutch Coil

1. Hook up a 12-volt battery to the clutch coil with an ammeter in series and a voltmeter in parallel.

2. Record the voltage and amperage.

   NOTE: The clutch coil should draw approximately 60 volt-amperes (5 amperes at 12 volts).

3. Replace coil if
   a. the draw is in excess of 5 amperes, indicating turn-to-turn shorting.
   b. there is no draw (0 amperes), indicating an open coil. First insure that electrical connections are secure.

Install the Clutch

   NOTE: Before reassembly, clean all parts, including the pulley bearing surface and the compressor front head. These parts are cleaned with pure mineral spirits.

1. Install the field coil. Be sure the locator pin on the compressor engages with the hole in the clutch coil.

2. Install the snap ring. Be sure the bevel edge of the snap ring faces out.

3. Slip the rotor/bearing assembly squarely on the head. Using the bearing remover/pulley installer tool, *gently tap* the pulley on the head, figure SP28-8.

   NOTE: The pulley must be aligned and turn freely.

4. Install the rotor/bearing snap ring. The bevel edge of the snap ring must face out.

5. Install shim washers and/or be sure they are in place. Check shaft/hub key to insure proper seating.

6. Align the hub keyway with the key in the shaft. Press the hub onto the compressor shaft using the hub replacer tool, figure SP28-9. *Do not drive (hammer) the hub on; to do so will damage the compressor.*

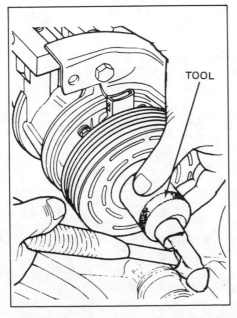

Fig. SP28-8 Gently *tap* the pulley onto the compressor head

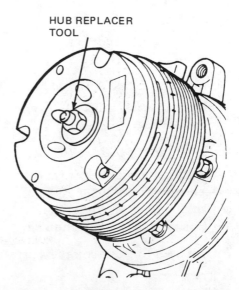

Fig. SP28-9 Press the hub onto the compressor shaft using the hub replacer tool only. *Do not drive or hammer hub onto the shaft.*

7. Using a nonmagnetic feeler gauge, check the air gap between hub and rotor, figure SP28-10.

   NOTE: Air gap should be 0.021–0.036 in (0.53–0.91 mm).

8. Turn the shaft (hub) one-half turn and recheck the air gap. Change the shim(s) as necessary to correct the air gap.

9. Install the locknut and tighten to 10–14 ft-lb (13.6–19.0 N·m).

10. Recheck the air gap. See steps 7 and 8.

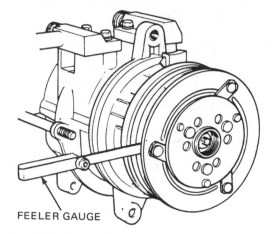

Fig. SP28-10 Check air gap between hub and rotor

Return the System to Service

1. If the compressor was removed from the car, reinstall the compressor.

2. Replace and tension belt(s).

   NOTE: Omit the following steps if the compressor was not removed from the car.

3. Leak test the system as outlined in Service Procedure 3.

4. Evacuate the system as outlined in Service Procedure 4.

5. Charge the system as outlined in Service Procedure 5.

Review

Select the appropriate answer from the choices given.

1. The Warner clutch bearing is held in place by

   a. a snap ring.
   b. staking.

   c. either a snap ring or staking.
   d. a bearing retainer.

2. Technician A says that a clutch coil with a current draw of 8 amperes at 12 volts indicates that it is shorted turn-to-turn. Technician B says that this is an indication that the clutch coil is shorted to ground.

   a. Technician A is correct.
   b. Technician B is correct.

   c. Either technician may be correct.
   d. Both technicians are wrong.

3. Air gap is measured with a

   a. magnetic feeler gauge.
   b. nonmagnetic feeler gauge.

   c. thin dime.
   d. thin screwdriver.

4. If the air gap is excessive (too wide), it may be corrected by

   a. reducing the number of shims.
   b. increasing the number of shims.
   c. tightening the shaft locknut.
   d. repositioning the shaft/hub key.

5. What is used to clean compressor parts?

   a. Dry air
   b. Clean rag(s)

   c. Gasoline
   d. Mineral spirits

SERVICE PROCEDURE 29:

Adjusting the Thermostat (Cycling Clutch Units)

The thermostat controls the evaporator temperature by cycling the clutch. The thermostat is preset at the factory. Different altitudes and humidity conditions can require that the thermostat be checked and occasionally adjusted to local conditions. This procedure deals with the thermostat adjustment. It should be noted that some thermostats have no provisions for adjustment.

TOOLS

Service thermometer
Manifold and gauge set
Hand wrenches

Service valve wrench
Small screwdriver

PROCEDURE

Prepare the System for Service

1. Connect the manifold and gauge set into the system.
2. Start the engine and set it to run at 1 200–1 500 r/min. Set the air-conditioning controls for maximum cooling.
3. Operate the system for 5–10 minutes with the core thermometer inserted into the evaporator at or near the thermostatic expansion valve.

   Insure that the evaporator does not have blowers mounted in the front of the unit.

4. Check the sight glass to insure that there is a full charge of refrigerant.

Check the Thermostat Operation

1. Turn the thermostat to the full on, or clockwise, position.
2. Turn the blowers to low or medium speeds.
3. Observe the manifold compound gauge: the reading should be in the 14-psig to 26-psig (96.5 to 179 kPa) range after the system is operated for 5–10 minutes.
4. Observe the manifold pressure or the high-side gauge. The high-side pressure should compare approximately with the temperature-pressure chart, figure SP29-1A or SP29-1B.
5. Compare the low-pressure gauge readings with the core thermometer readings against the temperature-pressure relationship chart. The thermometer should read from 15°F to 35°F (–9°C to 1.7°C), allowing for a temperature rise due to wall loss in the evaporator coil tubing.

Check the Thermostat Cutout and Cut-in Points

NOTE: For the proper thermostat operation, a dealer service manual should be consulted. However, the following steps can be used as a guide.

Temperature-Pressure Relationship Chart (English)			
Low Side		**High Side**	
Evaporator Temperature, °F	Evaporator Pressure, psi	Condenser Pressure, psi	Ambient Temperature, °F
5	11.8	72	40
10	14.7	86	50
15	17.1	105	60
20	21.1	126	70
22	22.5	140	75
24	23.9	160	80
26	25.4	185	90
28	26.9	195	95
30	28.4	220	100
32	30.0	240	105
34	31.7	260	110
38	35.1	290	120
40	36.9	305	125

Fig. SP29-1A

1. The thermostat should cut out when the thermometer indicates 24°F to 26°F (−4.4°C to −3.3°C).

2. The thermostat should cut back in when the thermometer indicates 36°F to 38°F (2.2°C to 3.3°C).

3. The manifold compound gauge should show a pressure rise of about 26–32 psig (179–221 kPa) between the cutout and cut-in points.

4. Check the thermostat operation three or four times to insure consistent operation.

Temperature-Pressure Relationship Chart (Metric)				
Low Side			**High Side**	
Evaporator Temperature, °C	Evaporator Pressure		Condenser Pressure, kPa Gauge	Ambient Temperature, °C
	kPa Absolute	kPa Gauge		
−15	175.3	73.9	495	4.3
−12	202.6	101.3	595	10.0
− 9	219.2	117.9	725	15.5
− 6.6	246.8	145.5	870	21.1
− 5.5	256.4	155.1	965	23.9
− 4.4	266.1	164.8	1 100	26.7
− 3.3	276.4	175.1	1 275	32.2
− 2.2	286.8	185.5	1 345	35.0
− 1.1	297.1	195.8	1 515	37.8
0	308.1	206.8	1 655	40.6
+ 1.1	319.9	218.6	1 790	43.3
+ 2.2	331.6	230.3	1 895	46.1
+ 3.3	343.3	242.0	2 000	48.9
+ 4.4	355.7	254.4	2 105	51.7

Fig. SP29-1B

ADJUST THE THERMOSTAT

1. Locate and gain access to the thermostat assembly.

2. Find the adjusting screw (located behind an access cover).

   NOTE: The design of some evaporators requires the thermostat to be removed from the case before access is gained to the adjusting screw.

3. Rotate the adjusting screw in a counterclockwise direction to lower the temperature by delaying the point opening. Conversely, a clockwise rotation of the screw increases the temperature. See figure SP29-2.

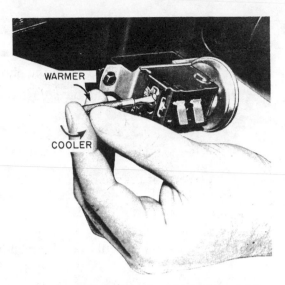

Fig. SP29-2 Thermostatic switch adjustment

4. Check the operation of the thermostat for the newly adjusted cycle of operation. If the operation is determined to be correct, check the thermostat three or four times to insure consistent operation.

5. If the cycle of operation is inconsistent or cannot be adjusted, the thermostat must be replaced.

Return the System to Service

1. Return the engine to the normal idle speed. Turn off the engine.

2. Replace the thermostat access door and replace the thermostat in the evaporator case. Replace other parts that were removed to permit access to the thermostat.

3. *Remove the thermometer.*

4. Back seat the compressor service valves and remove the manifold and gauge set. Replace the protective covers and caps.

Review

Select the appropriate answer from the choices given.

1. The thermostat should be adjusted to cut out when the evaporator thermometer indicates

    a. 24°F–26°F (–4.44°C to –3.33°C).   c. 26°F–32°F (–3.33°C to 0°C).
    b. 36°F–38°F (2.22°C to 3.33°C).   d. 34°F–36°F (1.11°C to 2.22°C).

2. What temperature rise range (cutout to cut-in) allows the proper defrost?

    a. 6°F (3.33°C)   c. 12°F (6.67°C)
    b. 9°F (5°C)   d. 15°F (8.33°C)

3. What precaution should be observed before inserting the thermometer into the evaporator core?

    a. The air-conditioning controls should be at maximum cooling.
    b. The engine should be running 5–10 minutes at fast idle.
    c. Insure that the evaporator does not have blowers mounted in front of the unit.
    d. All of these are precautions to be taken.

4. What is the head pressure at an ambient temperature of 95°F (35°C) if the system is operating properly? (Refer to figure SP29-1A or SP29-1B).

    a. 185 psig (1 275.6 kPa)   c. 220 psig (1 516.9 kPa)
    b. 195 psig (1 344.5 kPa)   d. 240 psig (1 654.8 kPa)

5. Between cutout and cut-in of the thermostat, what pressure increase should be noted on the low-side manifold gauge?

    a. 16–22 psig (110–152 kPa)   c. 26–32 psig (179–221 kPa)
    b. 22–26 psig (152–179 kPa)   d. 32–36 psig (221–248 kPa)

SERVICE PROCEDURE 30:

Servicing the Delco Air DA-6 Compressor

Like many other compressors, the Delco Air DA-6 compressor requires special tools for servicing. These tools are available from several sources, such as Kent Moore and Robinair. Unlike the A-6 compressor, the internal assembly of the DA-6 is not serviceable except to replace the O-ring.

This service procedure is given in six parts. Part 1 for Clutch Service, Part 2 Compressor Shaft Seal Service (covered in Service Procedure 15), Part 3 Rear Head Service, Part 4 Front Head Service, Part 5 Compressor Cylinder and Shaft Assembly, and Part 6 Center Cylinder Seal.

TOOLS

Snap ring pliers
Puller bar
Bearing remover
Bearing installer
Pressure test connector
Support block
Hub/drive plate remover/installer
Bearing staking tool
Shaft seal protector
Puller pilot
Clutch coil puller legs
Clutch hub holding tool
5/16-inch drill rod
Nonmagnetic feeler gauge set

Driver handle
Forcing screw
O-ring remover
O-ring installer
Seal seat remover/installer
Cylinder alignment rods
Pulley/bearing assembly installer
Pulley puller
Shaft nut socket w/handle
Clutch coil installer adapter
Compressor holding fixture
Open end wrench set
Plastic hammer
Ball peen hammer

MATERIAL

Refrigerant 12
Refrigeration oil
O-ring(s)
Valve plate(s)

Seal assembly
Clutch bearing
Head gasket(s)
Piston/cylinder assembly

PROCEDURE

PART 1—CLUTCH SERVICE

Remove Clutch

1. Clamp the compressor into an appropriate holding fixture.
2. Hold the clutch hub with the clutch hub holding tool and remove the shaft nut, figure SP30-1.

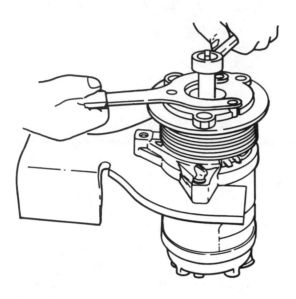

Fig. SP30-1 Remove the shaft nut while holding the clutch hub

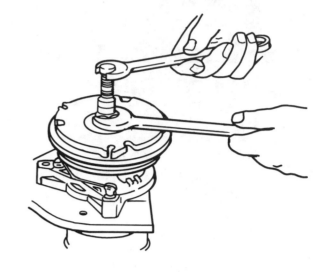

Fig. SP30-2 Remove the clutch hub

3. Use the clutch plate and hub installer/remover tool to remove the clutch hub, figure SP30-2.

4. Remove the shaft key and set aside for reassembly.

5. Use the snap ring pliers to remove the rotor snap ring, figure SP30-3.

6. Use the pulley rotor and bearing guide over the compressor shaft and insert the puller in the rotor slots to remove the rotor, figure SP30-4.

Remove Clutch Coil

1. Mark the clutch coil terminal location on the compressor front head for ease in reassembly.

2. Install the puller pilot on the front head.

3. Install the puller and tighten the forcing screw against the pilot to remove the clutch coil, figure SP30-5.

Fig. SP30-3 Use snap ring pliers to remove the snap ring

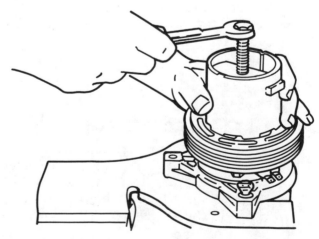

Fig. SP30-4 Remove the rotor using the rotor remover tool

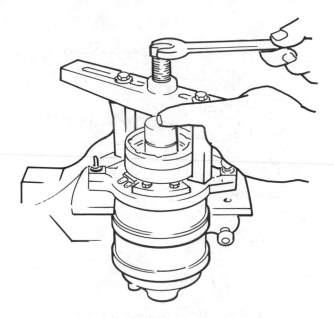

Fig. SP30-5 Remove the clutch coil

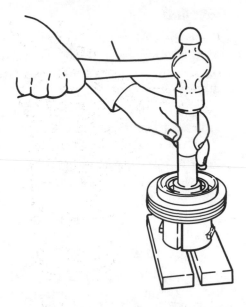

Fig. SP30-6 Place the puller atop a solid flat surface and, using the rotor bearing remover tool, drive the bearing out of the rotor.

Replace Bearing

1. Attach the rotor and bearing puller tool (less forcing screw) to the rotor. Place the puller atop a solid flat surface, figure SP30-6.

2. With the rotor bearing remover tool and universal handle, drive the bearing out of the rotor hub.

3. Remove the rotor and bearing puller tool from the rotor.

4. Place the rotor on the support block, figure SP30-7, to support the rotor during bearing installation.

5. Align the bearing with the hub bore. Using the puller and bearing installer tool, drive the bearing fully into the hub.

6. Position the bearing staking guide and staking pin tool, figure SP30-8, in the hub bore.

7. Strike the staking pin with a hammer. Form three stakes 120° apart. The staked metal should not touch the outer race of the bearing. *Take care not to damage the bearing during staking procedure.*

8. Remove staking tools and support block.

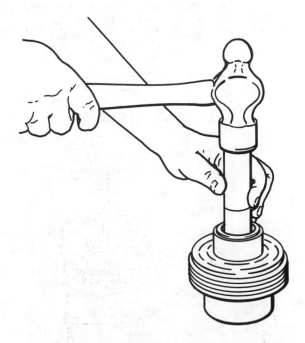

Fig. SP30-7 Place the rotor on the support block and, using the bearing installer tool, drive the bearing fully into the rotor

Replace Clutch Coil

1. Place the clutch coil on the front head of the compressor. Note the location of the electrical terminals as marked during removal of the coil.

2. Assemble the clutch coil installer, puller crossbar, and bolts atop the clutch coil, as shown in figure SP30-8.

3. Turn the forcing screw of the crossbar to force the clutch coil onto the front head of the compressor. Make sure that the clutch coil and clutch coil installer tool remain *in-line* during this procedure.

4. After the clutch coil is fully seated, use a 1/8-inch punch and stake the front head at 120° intervals to hold the coil in proper position.

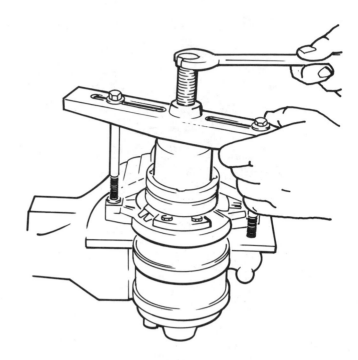

Fig. SP30-8 Assemble the clutch coil installer

Replace Clutch

1. Position the rotor and bearing assembly on the front head.

2. Assemble the puller pilot, crossbar and bolts atop the rotor and bearing assembly, as shown in figure SP30-9.

3. Tighten the forcing screw to force the rotor and bearing assembly onto the compressor front head. Make sure that the assembly stays *in-line* during this procedure.

4. Use the snap ring pliers to install the rotor and bearing assembly retainer snap ring (see figure SP30-3).

5. Install the shaft key into the hub key groove. The key should protrude about 1/8 inch (3.2 mm) out of the keyway.

6. Align the shaft key with the shaft keyway and position the clutch plate and hub assembly onto the compressor shaft.

7. Install the drive plate installer and bearing onto the clutch plate and hub assembly, figure SP30-10. The forcing tip of the installer must be flat or the end of the shaft/axial plate assembly will be damaged.

8. Using wrenches, as shown, force the clutch plate and hub assembly onto the compressor shaft. Remove the tool from time-to-time to insure that the key is still in place in the keyway. The key should be even with or slightly above the clutch hub when the hub is fully seated.

9. Using nonmagnetic feeler gauges, check the air gap. The air gap should be between 0.015 in (0.38 mm) and 0.025 in (0.64 mm).

10. Install the shaft nut and torque it to 8-16 ft-lb (11-22 N·m).

PART 2—COMPRESSOR SHAFT SEAL SERVICE

See Service Procedure 15.

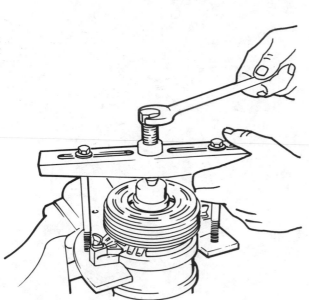

Fig. SP30-9 Assemble the puller pilot, crossbar, and bolts atop the rotor and bearing assembly

Fig. SP30-10 Install the clutch plate and hub assembly

PART 3—REAR HEAD SERVICE

Remove Head

1. Drain the oil from the compressor into a graduated container. Note the quantity drained and discard oil.

2. Remove the clutch and coil assembly as outlined in Part 1 of this service procedure.

3. Mark the location and note the alignment of the front head, cylinder assembly, and rear head, figure SP30-11. This is important to insure proper reassembly.

4. Remove the six compressor through bolts and gaskets. Discard the gaskets.

5. With a plastic hammer and wooden block, tap around the edge of the rear head to disengage it from the cylinder assembly, figure SP30-12.

6. Separate the rear head, head gasket, valve plates and O-ring. Discard the gasket and O-ring.

7. Inspect the head and valve plates. Discard any that are found to be defective.

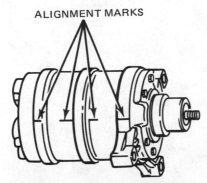

ALIGNMENT MARKS

Fig. SP30-11 Mark the location of the front head, cylinder assembly, and rear head to insure proper reassembly

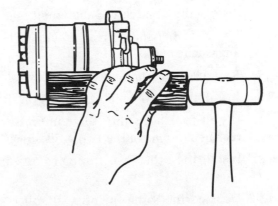

Fig. SP30-12 Disengage the rear head from the cylinder assembly

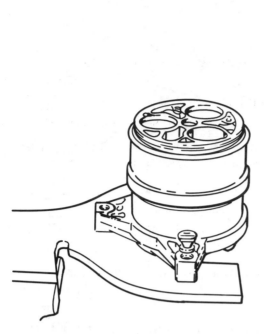

Fig. SP30-13 Secure the front head and cylinder assembly in the holding fixture

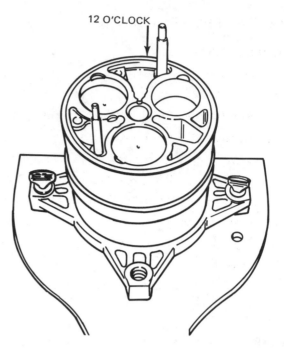

Fig. SP30-14 Install two guide pins in the front head and cylinder assembly

Replace Head

1. Secure the front head and cylinder assembly in the holding fixture, figure SP30-13.

2. Install two guide pins in the front head and cylinder assembly, as shown in figure SP30-14. Insert the guide pins with the small diameter end *up* as shown.

3. Liberally lubricate a new O-ring with clean refrigeration oil. Install the O-ring in the rear cylinder O-ring groove.

4. Install the suction reed valve plate over the guide pins.

5. Install the discharge valve plate over the guide pins. Check for proper position of the valve plates.

6. Install the rear head gasket over the guide pins. Be sure that it is in the proper position.

7. Carefully, install the rear head over the guide pins. The alignment mark on the rear head should match the alignment mark on the cylinder assembly.

8. Using both hands, press down on the rear head to force it over the O-ring. Recheck alignment marks.

9. Remove the compressor from the holding fixture and place it on the workbench.

10. Install new through bolt gaskets on the six through bolts.

11. Install four bolts into the compressor. After all four bolts have been threaded into the rear head, remove the two guide pins.

12. Install the other two through bolts and alternately torque all six to 72-84 in-lb (8-10 N·m).

13. Replace the same quantity of oil as was removed. Use only 525 viscosity clean refrigeration oil.

14. Replace the clutch and coil assembly as outlined in Part 1.

PART 4— FRONT HEAD SERVICE

Remove Head

1. Drain the compressor oil into a graduated container. Note the quantity of oil removed and discard the oil.

2. Remove the clutch and coil assembly as outlined in Part 1.

3. Remove the compressor shaft seal assembly as outlined in Service Procedure 15.

4. Mark the location and note the alignment of the front head, cylinder assembly, and rear head, figure SP30-11. This step is important to insure proper reassembly.

5. Remove the six through bolts and discard washers.

6. Using a plastic hammer, tap the front head to disengage it from the cylinder assembly.

7. Remove the front head, valve plates, O-ring, and head gasket. Discard the O-ring and head gasket.

8. Inspect the head and valve plates. Discard any that are found to be defective.

Replace Head

1. Rest the rear head and cylinder assembly on the support block, figure SP30-15.

2. Install two guide pins into the rear head and cylinder assembly. Insert the guide pins with the small diameter *down* as shown.

3. Liberally lubricate the new O-ring with clean refrigeration oil and install the O-ring in the front cylinder O-ring groove.

4. Install the suction reed valve plate over the guide pins.

5. Install the discharge valve plate over the guide pins. Check for proper position of valve plates before proceeding.

6. Install the front head gasket over the guide pins.

7. Note the position of the alignment marks and carefully install the front head over the guide pins.

8. Using both hands, press down on the front head to force it over the O-ring. Recheck the alignment marks to insure proper alignment of the compressor assembly.

9. Install new gaskets on all six through bolts.

10. Install four through bolts into the compressor. After all four bolts have been threaded into the rear head, remove the two guide pins.

11. Install the other two through bolts and alternately torque all six bolts to 72–84 in-lb (8-10 N·m)

12. Install the new shaft seal as outlined in Service Procedure 15.

13. Replace the same quantity of oil as was removed. Use only clean 525 viscosity refrigeration oil.

14. Replace the clutch and coil assembly as outlined in Part 1.

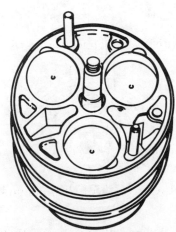

Fig. SP30-15 Rest rear head and cylinder assembly on support block

PART 5—COMPRESSOR CYLINDER ASSEMBLY

Remove Assembly

1. Follow steps 1 through 6 of Part 3, "Remove Head," to remove the rear head assembly.

2. Follow steps 3, 5, and 6 of Part 4, "Remove Head," to remove the front head assembly.
   NOTE: if removal was to replace the assembly center seal, refer to Part 6 for procedure and reassembly. If removal was to replace the assembly, proceed with "Replace Assembly."

Replace Assembly

1. Set rear head on support block and insert two guide pins, figure SP30-16. Install the rear head gasket in the proper position.

2. Install the rear discharge valve plate over the guide pins. Check for proper positioning of the valve plate.

3. Install the rear suction valve plate over the guide pins. Check to insure the proper positioning of the valve plates.

4. Lubricate the rear head O-ring liberally with clean refrigeration oil and install the O-ring in the rear cylinder O-ring groove.

5. Carefully lower the cylinder assembly over the guide pins to the rear head.

6. Using both hands, press the cylinder and shaft assembly down into the rear head.

7. Follow steps 3 through 14 of Part 4, "Replace Head," to replace the front head assemblies.

PART 6—CENTER CYLINDER SEAL

Remove Seal

1. Follow steps 1 through 6 of Part 3, "Remove Head," to remove the rear head assembly.

2. Follow steps 3, 5, and 6 of Part 4, "Remove Head," to remove the front head assembly.

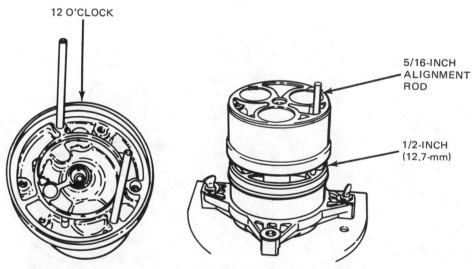

Fig. SP30-16 Set rear head on support block with two guide pins

Fig. SP30-17 Separate the two cylinder halves no more than 1/2 inch (12.7 mm)

3. Using a wooden block and plastic hammer, figure SP30-17, tap around the rear cylinder half to separate the two cylinder sections. Do not separate the sections more than one-half inch (12.7 mm).

   NOTE: Depending on the position of the pistons, one may be pulled out of the cylinder bore when the halves are separated. This piston should reenter the cylinder bore in-line with no damage to the piston or ring during step 10. Make no attempt at this time to reinsert the piston.

4. Remove and discard the center cylinder assembly O-ring.

5. Check to be sure that the small O-ring between the two cylinder halves is in place. It may stick to the front half or be in the rear half recess. It need not be replaced unless it is missing.

Replace Seal

1. Secure the front head in the holding fixture, figure SP30-18.

2. Carefully insert the cylinder and shaft assembly into the front head, shaft end *down*.

3. Lubricate the center O-ring with clean refrigeration oil and position it at the center cylinder O-ring groove.

4. With the discharge crossover O-ring in place (see step 5), insert a piece of 5/16-inch drill rod through the discharge crossover passage in both cylinder halves. This will insure proper alignment for step 10.

5. Using both hands, carefully press the cylinder halves together.

6. Remove the drill rod.

7. Reassemble the rear head, valve plates, gasket, and O-ring, following the procedures given in Part 3, "Replace Head."

8. Install the clutch coil as outlined in Part 1, "Replace Clutch Coil."

9. Install the clutch assembly as outlined in Part 1, "Replace Clutch."

Fig. SP30-18 Secure the front head in the holding fixture

Review

Select the appropriate answer from the choices given.

1. The bearing is staked into the clutch hub at
   - a. 45° intervals.
   - b. 90° intervals.
   - c. 120° intervals.
   - d. 180° intervals.

2. The shaft to the hub key should protrude about _____ out of the keyway.
   - a. 1/16 inch (1.6 mm)
   - b. 3/32 inch (2.4 mm)
   - c. 1/8 inch (3.2 mm)
   - d. 5/32 inch (4 mm)

3. Technician A says that an air gap of 0.020 inch (0.51 mm) is proper for the clutch. Technician B says that an air gap of 0.030 inch (0.76 mm) is proper for the clutch.
   - a. Technician A is correct.
   - b. Technician B is correct.
   - c. Either technician may be correct.
   - d. Both technicians are wrong.

4. The center cylinder assembly is separated no more than _____ in order to replace the center O-ring seal.
   - a. 1/4 inch (6.35 mm)
   - b. 3/8 inch (9.53 mm)
   - c. 1/2 inch (12.7 mm)
   - d. 3/4 inch (19.05 mm)

5. What are the torque requirements of the six through bolts?
   - a. 8-16 ft-lb (11-22 N·m)
   - b. 8-16 in-lb (0.9-1.8 N·m)
   - c. 72-84 ft-lb (97-113 N·m)
   - d. 72-84 in-lb (8-10 N·m)

SERVICE PROCEDURE 31:

Servicing the Delco Air V-5 Compressor

The Delco Air V-5 compressor requires special service tools for repairs. Like the DA-6 compressor, the V-5 compressor internal assembly is not serviceable.

This service procedure is given in five parts. Part 1, "Clutch Service" (covered in Service Procedure 30), Part 2, "Compressor Shaft Seal Service," Part 3, "Rear Head Service," Part 4, "Front Head Service," and Part 5, "Control Valve Service."

TOOLS

Same as for Service Procedure 30

MATERIAL

Same as for Service Procedure 30

PROCEDURE

PART 1—CLUTCH SERVICE

Remove Clutch

1. Follow the procedures outlined in Service Procedure 30, Part 1, "Remove Clutch," steps 1 through 6.

Remove Clutch Coil

1. Follow the procedures outlined in Service Procedure 30, Part 1, "Remove Clutch Coil," steps 1 through 3.

Replace Bearing

1. Follow the procedures outlined in Service Procedure 30, Part 1, "Replace Bearing," steps 1 through 8.

Replace Clutch Coil

1. Follow the procedures outlined in Service Procedure 30, Part 1, "Replace Clutch Coil," steps 1 through 4.

Replace Clutch

1. Follow the procedures outlined in Service Procedure 30, Part 1, "Replace Clutch," steps 1 through 10.

PART 2—SHAFT SEAL SERVICE

Remove Seal

1. Remove the clutch hub as outlined in Service Procedure 30, Part 1, "Remove Clutch," steps 1 through 3. It is not necessary to remove the clutch rotor for seal service.

2. Remove the shaft key and set aside for reassembly.

3. Clean the inside of the seal cavity to prevent any dirt or foreign matter from entering the compressor when the seal is removed.

4. Engage the knurled tangs of the seal seat remover and installer tool into the seal by turning the tool clockwise (cw).

5. With a rotary motion, remove the seal from the cavity, figure SP31-1.

6. Remove the O-ring from the seal cavity using the O-ring remover tool.

7. Clean and check the seal cavity for nicks and/or burrs.

Replace Seal

1. Lubricate the new O-ring with clean refrigeration oil and attach it to the O-ring installer.

2. Install the O-ring into the seal cavity. The lower recess is for the O-ring seal.

3. Rotate the tool to seat the O-ring into its recess and remove the installer tool.

4. Lubricate the new seal with clean refrigeration oil and attach it to the seal remover/installer tool.

5. Install the seal protector, figure SP31-2, in the seal and place over the compressor shaft.

6. Push seal into place with a rotary motion.

7. Using snap ring pliers, install the new snap ring to retain the seal. Use the sleeve from the remover/installer to press on the snap ring until it snaps into its groove.

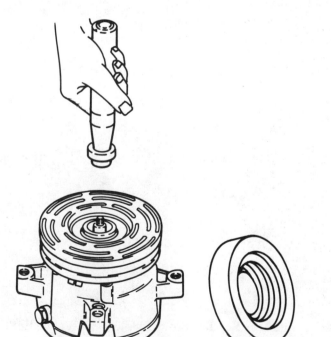

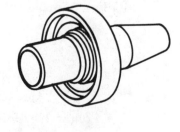

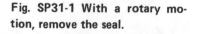

Fig. SP31-1 With a rotary motion, remove the seal.

Fig. SP31-2 Install the seal protector in the seal

8. With a clean, lint-free cloth, remove the excess oil from the seal cavity.

9. Replace the clutch hub by following the procedures outlined in Service Procedure 30, Part 1, "Replace Clutch," steps 5 through 10.

PART 3—REAR HEAD SERVICE

Remove Head

1. Follow the procedures outlined in Service Procedure 30, Part 3, "Remove Head," steps 1 through 7.

Replace Head

1. Place the rear head on a clean, flat surface with the control valve facing the 6 o'clock position, figure SP31-3.

2. Insert the guide pins in the mounting holes at 5 and 11 o'clock positions, small end facing *down.*

3. Install the discharge valve plate over the guide pins.
   NOTE: The elongated hole should be at the upper left (11 o'clock) guide pin, figure SP31-4.

Fig. SP31-3 Place the rear head on a flat surface with control valve facing 6 o'clock

Fig. SP31-4 Insert assembly guide pin at 11 o'clock

4. Install the suction valve plate over the guide pins. (See note for step 3.)

5. Remove the 5 o'clock guide pin before proceeding.

6. Lubricate the new O-ring with clean refrigeration oil and install it in the cylinder O-ring groove.

7. Carefully install the front head and cylinder assembly over the guide pin.
   NOTE: Locate the relief boss for the compressor guide pin at the 6 o'clock position.

8. Using both hands, press the front head and cylinder assembly down and into the rear head.

9. Add the new gaskets to the six through bolts. Install five bolts into the assembly.

10. Insure that three or four through bolts are securely screwed into the rear head. Then, remove the 11 o'clock guide pin.

11. Insert the other through bolt and torque all bolts to 72-84 in-lb (8-10 N·n).

12. Leak check the assembly. Attach the pressure testing connector and pressurize the compressor to 50 psig (344.8 kPa) with Refrigerant 12. Check the front and rear O-rings, shaft seal, and through bolt gaskets.

13. Depressurize the compressor and remove the testing connector.

14. Install the clutch coil following the procedures outlined in Service Procedure 30, Part 1, "Replace Clutch Coil," steps 1 through 4.

15. Install the clutch, following the procedures outlined in Service Procedure 30, Part 1, "Replace Clutch," steps 1 through 10.

16. Replace oil with the same quantity as was removed.

PART 4—FRONT HEAD SERVICE

Remove Head

1. Follow the procedures in Service Procedure 30, Part 4, "Remove Head," steps 1 and 2.

2. Remove the seal assembly following the procedures given in this service procedure, Part 2, "Remove Seal," steps 1 through 7.

3. Follow the procedures in Service Procedure 30, Part 4, "Remove Head," steps 4 through 8.
   NOTE: In step 7, note the sequence of assembly of the thrust washer(s) and bearing.

Replace Head

1. Place the rear head and cylinder assembly on the support ring tool with the control valve facing 6 o'clock.

2. Install an assembly guide pin at 11 o'clock, small end *down,* figure SP31-4.

3. Lubricate the new O-ring with clean refrigeration oil and place it in the cylinder O-ring groove.

4. Install the thrust washer(s) and bearing in the same order as removed.

5. Carefully install the front head over the guide pin.

6. Using both hands, press the front head assembly down over the O-ring on the cylinder assembly.

7. Add the new gaskets to the six through bolts. Install five bolts into the assembly.

8. Insure that three or four bolts are securely screwed into the rear head. Then, remove the 11 o'clock guide pin.

9. Insert the other through bolt and torque all bolts to 72-84 in-lb (8-10 N·m).

10. Follow the procedures outlined in this service procedure, Part 2, "Replace Seal," steps 1 through 8, to replace the seal assembly.

11. Follow the procedures outlined in this service procedure, Part 3, "Replace Head," steps 12 through 16.

PART 5—CONTROL VALVE SERVICE

Remove Valve

1. Use snap ring pliers to remove the control valve retaining ring.

2. Remove the control valve assembly.

Install Valve

1. Lubricate O-ring(s) with clean refrigeration oil.

2. Use thumb pressure to push the control valve into the compressor.

3. Use the snap ring pliers to install the snap ring. Be sure that the snap ring is properly seated in the ring groove.

Review

Select the appropriate answer from the choices given.

1. There are _____ through bolts in the V-5 compressor.

   a. two
   b. four
   c. six
   d. eight

2. When assembling the head(s), the control valve faces

   a. 11 o'clock.
   b. 12 o'clock.
   c. 5 o'clock.
   d. 6 o'clock.

3. When leak testing, the compressor is pressurized to

   a. 30 psig (206.8 kPa).
   b. 40 psig (275.8 kPa).
   c. 50 psig (344.7 kPa).
   d. 60 psig (413.7 kPa).

4. Technician A says that replacement oil should equal the amount removed, *less* 1 oz (29.57 mL). Technician B says that the replacement oil should equal the amount removed, *plus* 1 oz (29.57 mL).

   a. Technician A is correct.
   b. Technician B is correct.
   c. Either technician may be correct.
   d. Both technicians are wrong.

5. Technician A says that, when fully seated, the shaft key should be even with the hub. Technician B says that it may protrude slightly above the hub.

   a. Technician A is correct.
   b. Technician B is correct.
   c. Either technician may be correct.
   d. Both technicians are wrong.

SERVICE PROCEDURE 32:

Testing the Performance of the Valves-in-receiver (VIR)

The valves-in-receiver (VIR), also known as the evaporator equalizer valves-in-receiver (EEVIR), replaces the thermostatic expansion valve, receiver/drier, and the POA valve by combining these components into one assembly. Each component, however, functions in the same manner as in other systems. This procedure can be used to determine which part, if any, of the VIR or EEVIR is defective.

TOOLS

Manifold and gauge set   Thermometer

PROCEDURE

Prepare the System for Test

1. Connect the compound manifold gauge to the service port of the VIR or EEVIR.
2. Connect the high-side manifold gauge to the high-side service port.
3. Start the engine and adjust the engine speed to 2 000 r/min.
4. With the hood open, fully open all of the windows.
5. Set the controls for maximum cooling with the blower on high.

Conduct the Test

1. Note the delivery air temperature by placing the thermometer in the right air duct.
2. Note the evaporator pressure as observed on the compound gauge.
3. If the head pressure is not normal, check for conditions which can cause an abnormal pressure reading.
4. Note the condition of the refrigerant in the sight glass.

   NOTE: Some VIRs have a moisture-indicating sight glass. A *dry* system is indicated by a blue color, a *wet* system by pink, and a *saturated* system by white. If either pink or white, the drier desiccant bag assembly should be replaced. See Service Procedure 35.
5. Compare the observations with the chart given in figure SP32-1.

Return the System to Service

1. Decrease the engine speed to normal idle to prevent dieseling.
2. Turn off all of the air-conditioning controls.
3. Stop the engine.
4. Remove the manifold and gauge set and replace the protective covers.

EVAPORATOR PRESSURE	SIGHT GLASS	AIR DELIVERY	PROBABLE SYSTEM DEFECT	NOTE
28–30 psig (193–207 kPa)	CLEAR	40°–50°F (4.4°–10°C)	NORMAL	
LOW	CLEAR	WARMER	TXV	1 & 2
HIGH	CLEAR	WARMER	POA	
NORMAL-LOW	CLEAR	COLDER	POA	1, 3 & 4
HIGH	CLOUDY	WARMER	POA	1
NORMAL-LOW	CLOUDY	WARMER	LOW CHARGE	1
NORMAL-LOW	CLOUDY	WARMER	DRIER RESTRICTED	1

1. Can cause the superheat to close and blow the thermal fuse link in the compressor clutch circuit.
2. Turn the system off to warm up and equalize the system. Repeat the test. If the system performs properly on the second test, the system probably contains excess moisture. Replace the desiccant (Service Procedure 35).
3. The evaporator can become clogged with ice, thus resticting the airflow.
4. The system can go into a low pressure (or vacuum) when the blower is disconnected.

Fig. SP32-1

Review

Select the appropriate answer from the choices given.

1. The valves-in-receiver replaces
   a. the TXV.
   b. the receiver.
   c. the POA valve.
   d. All of these

2. According to the chart in figure SP32-1, an evaporator pressure of 35 psig (241 kPa) and a cloudy sight glass can indicate a defective
   a. TXV.
   b. receiver pickup tube.
   c. POA valve.
   d. All of these

3. The normal air delivery temperature should be
   a. 30° to 40°F (–1.1° to 4.4°C).
   b. 35° to 45°F (1.7° to 7.2°C).
   c. 40° to 50°F (4.4° to 10°C).
   d. 45° to 55°F (7.2° to 12.8°C).

4. The thermometer is used to check the
   a. evaporator core temperature.
   b. condenser temperature.
   c. air delivery temperature.
   d. ambient air temperature.

5. Excess moisture in the system causes the
   a. expansion valve to freeze.
   b. receiver pickup tube screen to freeze.
   c. POA valve to freeze.
   d. condenser to freeze.

SERVICE PROCEDURE 33:

Testing the Performance of the Thermostatic Expansion Valve

It must be noted that it is not always possible to test the thermostatic expansion valve (TXV or TEV) in the car. Suction pressure regulators and/or pressure switches often prevent valid testing. If this is the case the TXV may be removed from the car for bench testing as oulined in Part II of this procedure. Part I is given for those TXVs that can be tested in the car. If it is necessary to remove the TXV from the car, follow the procedures given in Service Procedure 49.

TOOLS

Manifold and gauge set*
Set of hand tools*
Coupler, 1/4-in FF**
Tee, 1/4-in MF**
Test cap, 1/4-in FF (drilled 0.026)**
Adapter, TXV inlet x 1/4-in MF**
Adapter, TXV outlet x 1/4-in MF**
Adapter, TXV equalizer x 1/4-in MF**

*For Parts I and II
**For Part II only

MATERIALS

Container of ice and water
Container of 125°F (52°C) water
Salt
Refrigerant 12*

*NOTE: A constant source of pressure at 70 psig (483 kPa) is required to perform the bench test. A cylinder of R-12 will supply this pressure only at an ambient above approximately 70°F (21°C). Other suitable pressure sources include dry air, carbon dioxide, or dry nitrogen. *These are dangerously high pressure materials. They must have suitable pressure regulating valves to reduce the pressure to a safe level.*

PART I — PROCEDURE

This procedure is given with the thermostatic expansion valve in the car.

Prepare the System

1. Attach the manifold and gauge set as outlined in Service Procedure 1.
2. Start the engine and adjust the engine speed to 1 000–1 200 r/min.

3. Adjust all air-conditioning controls to maximum (MAX) cooling.

4. Operate the system for 10–15 minutes.

Test the TXV

NOTE: Follow steps 1 through 5 for abnormally low low-side gauge readings or steps 6 through 8 for abnormally high low-side gauge readings.

1. Observe the low-side gauge reading. If abnormally low, place a warm (125°F or 52°C) rag around the TXV body.

2. Observe the low-side gauge. If the pressure rises to normal, or near normal, moisture in the system is indicated (see the following note). If the pressure does not rise, proceed with step 3.

   NOTE: To correct moisture in the system, replace the receiver/drier or desiccant. Evacuate, charge, and retest the system. See the appropriate Service Procedures.

3. Remove the TXV remote bulb from the evaporator outlet and warm it in the hand or in a warm (125°F or 52°C) rag.

4. Observe the low-side gauge pressure. If the pressure rises, the remote bulb was probably improperly placed (see the following note). If the pressure does not rise, proceed with step 5.

   NOTE: To correct the rise in pressure, reposition the remote bulb, insulate, and retest the system.

5. If the low-side gauge reading is abnormally low and steps 1 through 4 do not correct the problem, remove the TXV from the system for bench testing (see Part II).

   NOTE: Observe the inlet screen when removing the TXV. If it is clogged, the receiver/drier or desiccant must be replaced after servicing and/or cleaning the TXV.

6. If the low-side gauge reading (step 1) is abnormally high, remove the remote bulb from the evaporator outlet and place it in an ice-water bath.

   NOTE: Rock salt added to the ice water will lower the temperature to 32°F (0°C).

7. If the pressure falls to normal, or near normal, the problem may be:
   a. a lack of insulation at the remote bulb. Reinsulate the area and retest.
   b. an improperly placed remote bulb. Reposition the remote bulb and retest.

8. If the pressure does not fall to normal or near normal, remove the TXV and bench test as outlined in Part II of this procedure.

Conclude the Test

1. Turn off all air-conditioning controls.

2. Reduce the engine speed to idle and stop the engine.

3. Remove the manifold and gauge set as outlined in Service Procedure 1.

PART II – PROCEDURE

This procedure is given with the thermostatic expansion valve removed from the system. See Service Procedure 49.

Prepare the Thermostatic Expansion Valve for Test

1. Close the high- and low-side manifold hand valves.

2. Remove the low-side service hose at the manifold.

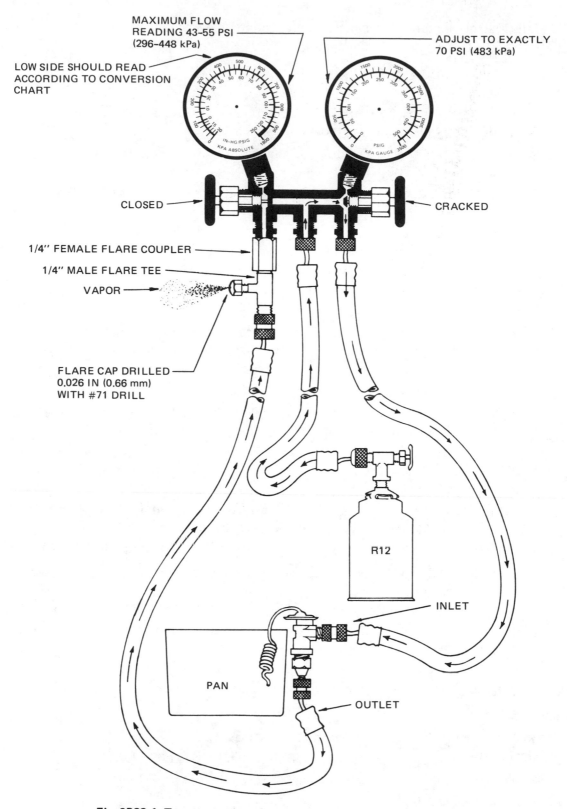

MAXIMUM FLOW
READING 43-55 PSI
(296-448 kPa)

LOW SIDE SHOULD READ
ACCORDING TO CONVERSION
CHART

ADJUST TO EXACTLY
70 PSI (483 kPa)

CLOSED

CRACKED

1/4" FEMALE FLARE COUPLER

1/4" MALE FLARE TEE

VAPOR

FLARE CAP DRILLED
0.026 IN (0.66 mm)
WITH #71 DRILL

R12

INLET

PAN

OUTLET

Fig. SP33-1 Test connections for the internally equalized valve

3. Install a 1/4-in female flare coupler to the low-side manifold.

4. Install a 1/4-in male flare tee to the flare coupler at the low side.

5. Reinstall the low-side manifold hose to the 1/4-in flare tee.

6. Install a 1/4-in test cap, drilled to 0.026 in (0.66 mm), to the 1/4-in tee.

7. Install the TXV inlet x 1/4-in MF adapter to the inlet of the TXV.

8. Install the TXV outlet x 1/4-in MF adapter to the outlet of the TXV.

9. Fasten the low-side manifold hose to the expansion valve outlet.

10. Fasten the high-side manifold hose to the expansion valve inlet.

11. Install a can tap on the can of R-12.

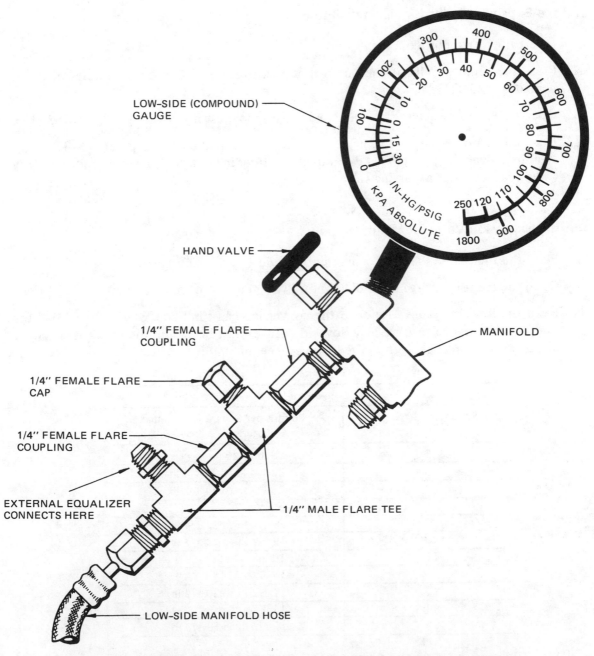

Fig. SP33-2 Modified version of Fig. SP33-1 for use with externally equalized valves

12. Pierce the can and back the piercing tap out to release the pressure to the manifold.

13. Fill an insulated container with cracked ice and add water. Use a thermometer to indicate exactly when the temperature is 32°F (0°C). If necessary, add salt and stir the mixture.

14. Heat the water in a second container until it reaches 125°F (52°C).

NOTE: The diagram for the thermostatic expansion valve test connections, figure SP33-1, is for an internally equalized thermostatic expansion valve only. If an externally equalized expansion valve is to be tested, another fitting must be added *before* the test cap, figure SP33-2. The external equalizer is connected to this fitting. If an externally equalized expansion valve is to be tested, the following additional tools are required: one 1/4-in female flare coupler and one 1/4-in male flare tee.

Test the Expansion Valve for Maximum Flow

1. Invert the refrigerant container.

2. Place the remote bulb of the thermostatic expansion valve into a container of water heated to 125°F (52°C).

3. Open the high-side gauge manifold hand valve and adjust it to exactly 70 psig (483 kPa).

4. Read the low-side gauge. The maximum flow test should be 43–55 psig (296–379 kPa). Readings over 55 psig (379 kPa) indicate a flooding valve. A reading under 43 psig (296 kPa) indicates a starving valve.

Test the Expansion Valve for Minimum Flow

1. Place the thermal bulb into a container of liquid at 32°F (0°C).

2. Open the high-side gauge manifold hand valve and adjust it to exactly 70 psig (483 kPa).

3. Read the low-side gauge. Refer to the conversion chart in figure SP33-3 or SP33-4 for the proper low-side reading. The low-side gauge must be within the limits as specified in the conversion chart if the valve is to pass the minimum flow test.

Conversion Chart	
Superheat Setting °F	Pounds per Square Inch Gauge Refrigerant 12 Pressure
5	23 lb to 26 lb
6	22 1/4 lb to 25 1/4 lb
7	21 1/2 lb to 24 1/2 lb
8	21 lb to 24 lb
9	20 1/4 lb to 23 1/4 lb
10	19 1/2 lb to 22 1/2 lb
11	19 lb to 22 lb
12	18 lb to 21 lb
13	17 1/2 lb to 20 1/2 lb
14	17 lb to 20 lb
15	15 1/2 lb to 18 1/2 lb

Fig. SP33-3 Conversion chart for TXV testing (English)

Superheat Setting °C	Kilopascals (Gauge) Refrigerant 12 Pressure
2.8	158.6–179.3
3.3	153.4–174.1
3.9	148.2–168.9
4.4	144.8–165.5
5.0	139.6–160.3
5.6	134.5–155.1
6.1	131.0–151.7
6.7	124.1–144.8
7.2	120.7–141.3
7.8	117.2–137.9
8.3	106.9–127.6

Fig. SP33-4 Conversion chart for TXV testing (metric). For absolute kPa, add 101.4 to pressure indicated.

NOTE: The valve superheat settings corresponding to the valve outlet pressure readings are for Refrigerant 12 expansion valves only.

Cleaning the Expansion Valve

NOTE: If the expansion valve fails to pass either or both of the tests previously given, valve cleaning can be attempted. Otherwise, a new valve must be used. Although each valve is different in structure, the following steps can be used as a guide.

1. Remove the diaphragm, the capillary, and the remote bulb assembly.

2. Remove the superheat adjusting screw. Count the number of turns required to remove the screw. Knowing the number of turns aids in relocating the proper position when reassembling the valve.

3. Remove the superheat spring and the valve seat. Remove the valve and push rod(s).

4. Clean the valve and all parts in *clean* mineral spirits. Let the parts drain and then blow them dry.

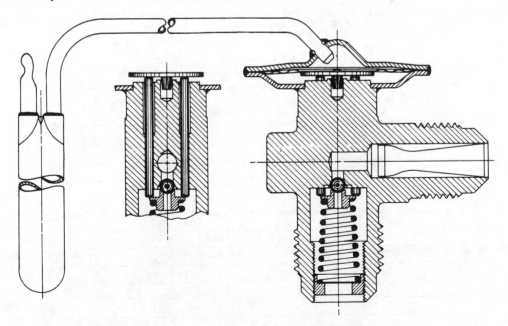

Fig. SP33-5 Cross section of the thermostatic expansion valve

5. Reverse steps 1–4 and reassemble the valve.

6. Check the expansion valve for maximum and minimum flow as outlined in this procedure.

7. If the valve fails to pass the maximum/minimum flow test, attempt to adjust the super-heat spring setting.

8. If the valve fails the test repeatedly, a new valve must be installed. No further repair is possible.

Review

Briefly answer each of the following questions.

1. What pressure source must be available for this test?

2. Why is a minimum flow test conducted?

3. Why is a maximum flow test conducted?

4. What should the minimum flow be?

5. What should the maximum flow be?

6. Can all expansion valves be cleaned?

7. Name two types of thermostatic expansion valves.

8. What cleaning agent is recommended?

9. What size of test cap is used in this test?

10. How is an externally equalized valve tested?

11. In figure SP33-6, name as many as possible of the component parts of the thermostatic expansion valve.

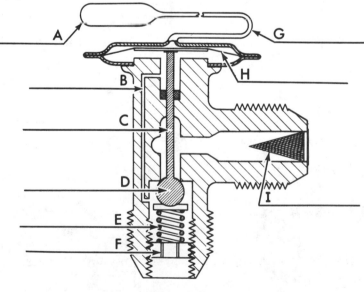

Fig. SP33-6

SERVICE PROCEDURE 34:

Testing and/or Replacing the Fixed Orifice Tube (FOT)

The fixed orifice tube (FOT) is also known as an expansion tube or, more simply, as an orifice tube. This device is used on systems referred to as CCOT or CCFOT which are the abbreviations for cycling clutch orifice tube or cycling clutch fixed orifice tube.

It must be noted that not all orifice tubes are of the same size. For example, the orifice tube used on 1981 Ford car lines has a slightly smaller diameter than orifice tubes used by Ford in prior years. Though the same service tool may be used to remove and replace either size, the orifice tubes are not interchangeable. When replacing the orifice tube, it is most important that the correct replacement be used.

Some car lines have a nonaccessible orifice tube in the liquid line. Its exact location, anywhere between the condenser outlet and evaporator inlet, is determined by a circular depression or three indented notches in the metal portion of the liquid line. An orifice tube replacement kit is used to replace this type orifice tube and 2 1/2 inches (63.5 mm) of the metal liquid line.

Testing the fixed orifice tube is reasonably simple. There are only two basic problems that one may find: moisture in the system freezing at the orifice tube, or a clogged tube.

This service procedure is given in three parts. Part 1 covers testing the FOT, Part 2 covers replacing the accessible FOT, and Part 3 covers replacing the nonaccessible FOT.

TOOLS

Manifold and gauge set
Open end wrench set
Tubing cutter

FOT remover/installer
Clean shop rags

MATERIALS

Orifice tube, as required
Accumulator, as required

Refrigerant 12, as required
Refrigeration oil, as required

PROCEDURE

PART 1—TESTING THE FOT

Prepare the System

1. Attach the manifold and gauge set as outlined in Service Procedure 1.

2. Start the engine and adjust the speed to 1 000–1 200 r/min.

3. Adjust all air-conditioning controls to maximum (MAX) cooling.

4. Operate the system for 10–15 minutes.

5. Observe the low-side gauge. An abnormally low low-side gauge reading indicates that the orifice tube is not metering a sufficient amount of refrigerant into the evaporator.

Test the Orifice Tube

NOTE: It may be necessary to bypass the low-pressure switch to prevent clutch cycling on CCOT systems. Bypass the switch only long enough to perform the test. The following steps are to determine if the problem is caused by moisture or by a restriction.

1. Place a warm rag 125°F (52°C) around the fixed orifice tube.

2. Observe the low-side gauge. If the pressure rises to normal, or near normal, moisture in the system is indicated.

3. If moisture is found in the system, the accumulator must be replaced as outlined in Service Procedure 49. If moisture is not indicated, the orifice tube is probably clogged. Follow the procedure outlined in Part II of this procedure.

PART 2—SERVICING THE ACCESSIBLE FOT

Remove the Fixed Orifice Tube

1. Purge the system of refrigerant as outlined in Service Procedure 2.

2. Using the proper open end wrenches, remove the liquid line connection at the inlet of the evaporator to expose the FOT.

3. Pour a small quantity of clean refrigeration oil into the FOT well to lubricate the seals.

4. Insert the FOT removal tool, figure SP34-1, onto the FOT.

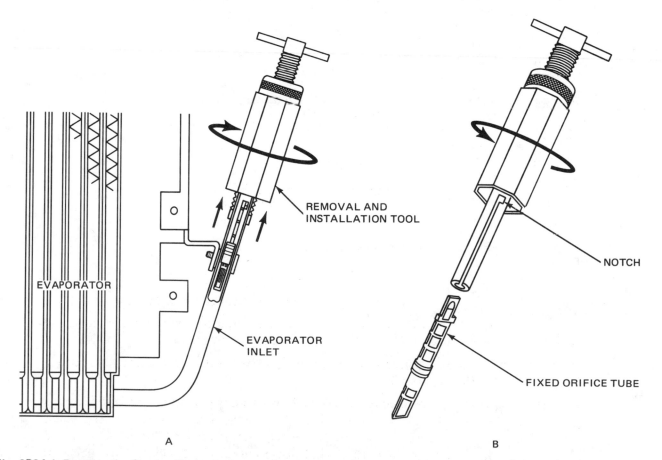

Fig. SP34-1 Remove the fixed orifice tube by turning the outer sleeve only. *Do not turn the handle. The handle is turned only enough to engage the notch of the tool onto the fixed orifice tube, detail B.*

5. Turn the T-handle of the tool *only enough* to engage the tool onto the tabs of the FOT—slightly clockwise (cw).

6. Hold the T-handle and turn the outer sleeve or spool clockwise (cw) to remove the FOT. *Do not turn the T-handle.*

   NOTE: Sometimes the FOT will break during removal. If this happens, proceed with step 7. If not, proceed with "Install the Fixed Orifice Tube." A second tool, known as an *extractor*, is used to remove a broken orifice tube.

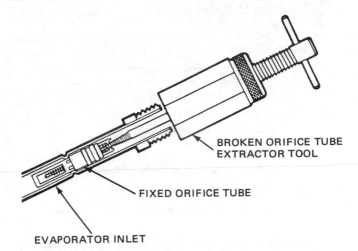

Fig. SP34-2 Using an extractor tool to remove a broken fixed orifice tube

7. Insert the extractor into the well and turn the T-handle clockwise (cw) until the threaded portion of the tool is securely inserted into the brass portion of the broken FOT, figure SP34-2.

8. Pull the tool. The broken FOT should slide out.

   NOTE: The brass tube may pull out of the plastic body. If this happens, remove the brass tube from the puller and reinsert the puller into the plastic body. Repeat steps 7 and 8.

Install the Fixed Orifice Tube

1. Coat the new FOT liberally with clean refrigeration oil.

2. Place the FOT into the evaporator well and push it in until it stops against the evaporator tube inlet dimples.

3. Install a new O-ring and replace the liquid line.

4. Replace the accumulator as outlined in Service Procedure 49.

PART 3—SERVICING THE NONACCESSIBLE FOT

Remove the FOT

1. Purge the system following the procedures outlined in Service Procedure 2.

2. Remove the liquid line from the car. Note how the liquid line was routed so it can be replaced in the same manner.

3. Locate the orifice tube. A circular depression, figure SP34-3, or three notches identify the outlet side of the orifice tube.

4. Use a sharp tube cutter to remove a 2 1/2 inch (63.5 mm) section of the liquid line, as shown in figure SP34-4. Allow at least 1 inch (25.4 mm) of exposed tube at any bend.
   NOTE: Do not use excessive pressure on the feed screw of the tube cutter to avoid distorting the liquid line. A hacksaw should not be used. If a hacksaw must be used; however, flush both pieces of the liquid line to remove all contaminants, such as metal chips.

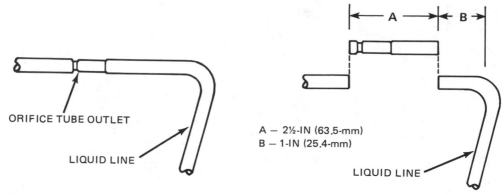

ORIFICE TUBE OUTLET

LIQUID LINE

Fig. SP34-3 Locating the orifice tube

A — 2½-IN (63.5-mm)
B — 1-IN (25.4-mm)

LIQUID LINE

Fig. SP34-4 Cut out old orifice tube

Replace the FOT

1. Slide a compression nut onto each section of the liquid line.
2. Slide a compression ring onto each section of the liquid line with the taper portion toward the compression nut.
3. Lubricate the two O-rings with clean refrigeration oil and slide one onto each section of the liquid line.
4. Attach the orifice tube housing, with the orifice tube inside, to the two sections of the liquid line. Hand tighten both compression nuts. Note the flow direction indicated by the arrows, figure SP34-5. The flow should be *toward* the evaporator.
5. Hold the orifice tube housing in a vise to tighten the compression nuts. Insure that the hose bends are in the same configuration as when removed for ease in replacing the liquid line.
6. Tighten each compression nut to 65-70 ft-lb (87-94 N·m) torque.

Return the System to Service, Parts 2 or 3

1. Leak test the system as outlined in Service Procedure 3.
2. Evacuate the system as outlined in Service Procedure 4.
3. Charge the system as outlined in Service Procedure 5.
4. Repeat or continue performance testing.

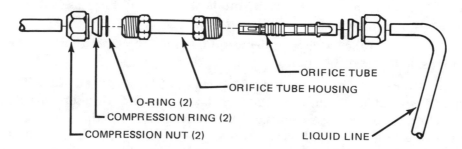

ORIFICE TUBE

ORIFICE TUBE HOUSING

O-RING (2)

COMPRESSION RING (2)

COMPRESSION NUT (2)

LIQUID LINE

Fig. SP34-5 Exploded view of new orifice tube assembly

Review

Select the appropriate answer from the choices given.

1. Another name for the fixed orifice tube is

   a. expansion tube.
   b. metering tube.

   c. vacuum tube.
   d. flow tube.

2. The accumulator should be replaced if

   a. there is moisture in the system.
   b. the fixed orifice tube is clogged.
   c. there is moisture in the system or the FOT is clogged.
   d. The accumulator need not be replaced when servicing the FOT.

3. When removing the accessible orifice tube,

   a. the T-handle is turned.
   b. the outer sleeve is turned.
   c. both the T-handle and the outer sleeve are turned.
   d. neither the T-handle nor the outer sleeve is turned.

4. All orifice tubes are of the same size.

   a. True

   b. False

5. The same tool may be used to remove all orifice tubes unless they are broken.

   a. True

   b. False

SERVICE PROCEDURE 35:

Rebuilding the Valves-in-receiver (VIR)

The valves-in-receiver (VIR), also known as the evaporator equalizer valves in receiver (EEVIR), should be removed from the car if it is necessary to rebuild the assembly (see Service Procedure 49). However, the sight glass, the liquid line valve core, and the evaporator gauge valve core can be easily replaced without removing the assembly from the car.

It should be noted that some car lines have a moisture-indicating sight glass. A *dry* system is indicated by a blue color, whereas *wet* and *saturated* systems are indicated by pink and white, respectively. If either pink or white, the VIR (EEVIR) assembly should be rebuilt and the drier desiccant bag replaced.

The following procedure is given in three parts: Part I deals with sight glass replacement; Part II covers the replacement of either (or both) of the valve cores; and Part III covers the rebuilding of the assembly.

Kent Moore tool numbers are given in the illustrations. Only three special tools are required for all VIR service: the valve core remover, the pickup tube installer, and the valve capsule remover.

TOOLS

Screwdrivers
Open end wrenches
Allen wrench, 7/16 in

Valve core remover
Pickup tube installer
Valve capsule remover

MATERIALS

Set of O-rings
Refrigeration oil

Cleaning solvent
Any parts that are determined to be defective

PART I, SIGHT GLASS — PROCEDURE

Preparation

1. Purge the system of refrigerant as outlined in Service Procedure 2.

2. Remove the sight glass retaining nut using the 7/16 in Allen wrench, figure SP35-1.

Remove the Sight Glass

1. Place a finger over the sight glass to hold it in place.

2. Slightly pressurize the system with refrigerant vapor.

Fig. SP35-1 Location of the valves-in-receiver (VIR) sight glass

SIGHT GLASS
RETAINING NUT

3. Shift the finger pressure on the sight glass from side to side until the sight glass is free of the opening. The system pressure (as applied in step 2) should force the glass from the opening.

4. Discard the sight glass O-ring, thrust washer, and nut. Inspect the sight glass. If it is damaged, discard the sight glass.

Install the Sight Glass

1. Coat the new O-ring, nylon thrust washer, and sight glass retaining nut with refrigeration oil.

2. Install the parts in the cavity in the opposite order from that in which they were removed.

3. Tighten the retaining nut to a torque of 20–25 in-lb (2.3–2.8 N·m).

Return the System to Service

1. Evacuate the system as outlined in Service Procedure 4.

2. Leak check the system as outlined in Service Procedure 3.

3. Charge the system as outlined in Service Procedure 5.

PART II, VALVE CORE(S) — PROCEDURE

Preparation

1. Purge the system of refrigerant as outlined in Service Procedure 2.

2. Determine if one or both of the valve cores must be replaced.

Remove the Valve Core

1. Remove the protective cap from the evaporator gauge valve core and/or the liquid bleed line from the bleed valve fitting of the VIR.

2. Using a numbered tool, remove either (or both) of the valve cores.

3. Discard the core(s) removed.

Install the Valve Core(s)

1. Note the different colors of the cores. The evaporator gauge core is blue and the oill bleed line valve core is gold or red.

2. Using the numbered tool, figure SP35-2, install the valve core(s).

3. When the core just begins to tighten, note the location of the tool handle and turn it an additional 180° (half turn). This provides a torque of about 24–36 in-oz (0.17–0.25 N·m).

Fig. SP35-2 Location of the valves-in-receiver (VIR) valve core

Return the System to Service

1. Replace the oil bleed line. Tighten the fitting but do not overtighten it.

2. Evacuate the system as outlined in Service Procedure 4.

3. Leak check the system as outlined in Service Procedure 3.

4. Charge the system as outlined in Service Procedure 5.

PART III, REBUILDING THE VIR ASSEMBLY — PROCEDURE

Preparation

1. Purge the system of refrigerant as outlined in Service Procedure 2.

2. While purging, clean the exterior surface of the VIR.

3. Disconnect the oil bleed line.

4. Disconnect the inlet and outlet hoses (from the compressor and the condenser).

5. Disconnect the inlet and outlet lines from the evaporator.

6. Discard all O-rings.

7. Remove the mounting clamp(s) and lift the VIR from the car.

Disassembly of the VIR

1. Note the location of the parts shown in figure SP35-3.

2. Loosen the six receiver shell-to-valve housing retaining screws. Turn the screws approximately three turns. *Do not* completely remove the screws until instructed to do so in step 5.

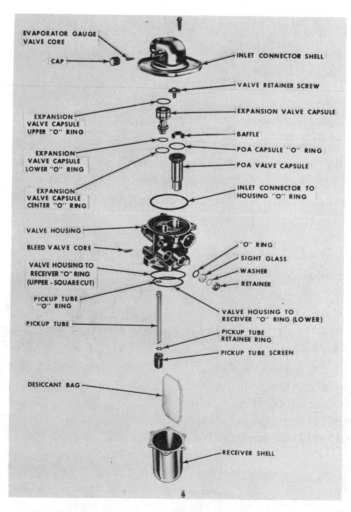

Fig. SP35-3 Exploded view of the valves-in-receiver (VIR)

3. Hold the VIR valve housing and push on the lower end of the receiver shell. This should break the seal between the shell and the housing.

4. If step 4 does not break the seal, *carefully* pry between the receiver shell mounting flange and the valve housing. Take care not to mar or scratch the mating surfaces.

5. Remove the six retaining screws (loosened in step 2).

6. Lower the receiver shell to clear the pickup tube and screen. Keep the assembly in an upright position, figure SP35-4.

7. Remove and discard the bag of desiccant.

8. Drain, measure, and discard any oil found in the receiver. Note the amount of oil drained.

9. Remove, but do not discard, the pickup tube filter screen.

10. Remove the four inlet connector shell-to-valve housing screws.

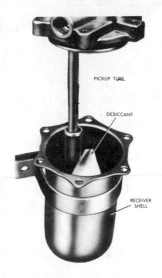

Fig. SP35-4 Location of the pickup tube and desiccant inside the receiver

11. Carefully slip the inlet connector shell off the valve housing. Do not scratch the mating surfaces.

12. Loosen both valve capsule retaining screws about 3/16 in (4.8 mm). *Do not* remove the screws entirely until instructed to do so in step 17.

13. Attach the valve capsule remover tool to the tapered groove projection on the expansion valve capsule as shown in figure SP35-5.

14. Position the tool over one of the screws (step 12) and press down on the handle to loosen the expansion valve capsule.

15. Insert the opposite side of the valve capsule remover tool under the STV baffle. The edge of the tool must clear the edge of the capsule, figure SP35-6.

16. Taking care not to damage the valve housing O-ring groove area, press down on the handle to loosen the STV capsule.

17. With both capsules loose, remove both retaining screws (step 12).

18. Remove the expansion valve and the STV capsules from the valve housing.

19. Remove and discard all O-rings and/or gaskets.

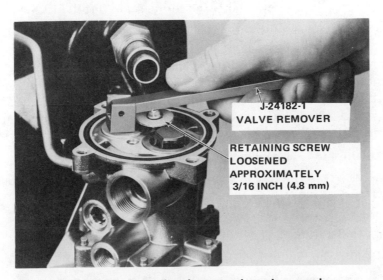

Fig. SP35-5 Removing the expansion valve capsule

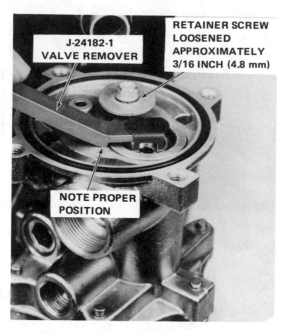

Fig. SP35-6 Removing the STV capsule

Cleaning and Inspection

1. Clean all parts in a good solvent, such as stoddard or kerosene. Trichlorethylene or naphtha, however, are the preferred solvents.

2. Carefully inspect all parts for nicks, scratches, or any other flaws.

3. Place all of the parts to be reassembled (except the desiccant bag) into a container of clean refrigeration oil.

4. Check the pickup tube filter screen to insure that it is clear of any contaminants.

Reassembly of the VIR

1. Reassemble the VIR components in the reverse order of their disassembly.

2. The capsule retaining screws should be tightened to a torque of 5–7 ft-lb (6.8–9.5 N•m).

3. The inlet connector shell screws should be torqued to 10 ft-lb (13.5 N•m).

4. The pickup tube screen must be in place before the receiver shell is replaced. In addition:
   a. place a new bag of desiccant into the shell, and
   b. replace the oil using the quantity noted when the old oil was removed. If less than one ounce (29.57 mL) of oil was removed, replace one ounce (29.57 mL). If more than one ounce (29.57 mL) was removed, replace with the same amount. *Use new, clean refrigeration oil.*

5. The receiver shell screws should be torqued to 10 ft-lb (13.5 N•m).

6. Check the work area. If there are any parts such as O-rings on the bench, they may have been left out of the VIR assembly.

Return the System to Service

1. Place the VIR into the mounting clamp(s).

2. Using new O-rings, connect the inlet and outlet lines (from the evaporator).

3. Using new O-rings, connect the inlet and outlet hoses (from the compressor and the condenser).

4. Using a new O-ring, reconnect the oil bleed line.

5. Evacuate the system as outlined in Service Procedure 4.

6. Leak check the system as outlined in Service Procedure 3.

7. Charge the system as outlined in Service Procedure 5.

8. Retest the operation of the VIR as outlined in Service Procedure 32.

Review

Select the appropriate answer from the choices given.

1. Special tools are required for the removal of the

   a. VIR.
   b. STV capsule.
   c. sight glass.
   d. pickup tube screen.

2. If the amount of oil removed from the receiver shell is 3/4 ounce (22 mL), it should be replaced with

   a. 1/2 ounce (14.8 mL).
   b. 3/4 ounce (22 mL).
   c. 1 ounce (29.57 mL).
   d. 1 3/4 ounces (51.6 mL).

3. When replacing the oil bleed valve it should be

   a. snug, then turned 90°.
   b. snug, then turned 180°.
   c. snug, then turned 270°.
   d. snug, then turned 360°.

4. The evaporator gauge valve core is

   a. blue.
   b. red.
   c. gold.
   d. green.

5. The procedure for letting all of the refrigerant out of a system is called

   a. evacuation.
   b. charging.
   c. purging.
   d. leak down.

SERVICE PROCEDURE 36:

Installing Mount and Drive Assemblies

The mount and drive assembly covered in this procedure is designed for several specific Chrysler automobile models, namely those with a slant six-cylinder engine, with or without power steering.

No attempt should be made to install this mount and drive kit on other automobile models. Each kit is designed for a particular engine. The installation instructions included with each kit must be followed exactly to avoid costly mistakes. Measure all bolts to insure that they are as specified. Check all hoses to insure that they do not rub against moving parts, such as pulleys and the accelerator linkage.

These installation procedures are for a typical mount and drive package.

TOOLS

Complete set of mechanic's hand tools, including
pullers, screwdrivers, and hose clamp pliers

MATERIALS

Mount and drive kit, as required
Permatex
Belts or hoses to replace defective parts

PROCEDURE

1. Drain the radiator. Disconnect the water hoses and the transmission fluid cooling lines. Unfasten the radiator mounting screws and carefully remove the radiator from the engine compartment.

2. Remove the engine fan, fan spacer, and water pump pulley. Discard the original fan spacer.

3. Always clean the face of the crankshaft pulley thoroughly before installing the drive pulley. Remove the bolts retaining the crankshaft pulley, and, if the car is equipped with power steering, remove and discard the power steering pulley only. Install the drive pulley, using three 5/16" x 1" NC bolts with lockwashers, and one 3/4" x 2 1/4" NF bolt with lockwasher.

4. IMPORTANT: *The fuel filter line must be modified on some models to facilitiate compressor mount/drive clearance.*
   a. Unfasten the fuel filter line clamp from the water pump housing.
   b. Remove the original fuel line tubing and the union fitting located between the carburetor and the filter bowl.
   c. Cut the tubing so that the original union fitting can be removed and reinstalled against the flanged end of the 5/16" x 6 1/2" copper fuel line.

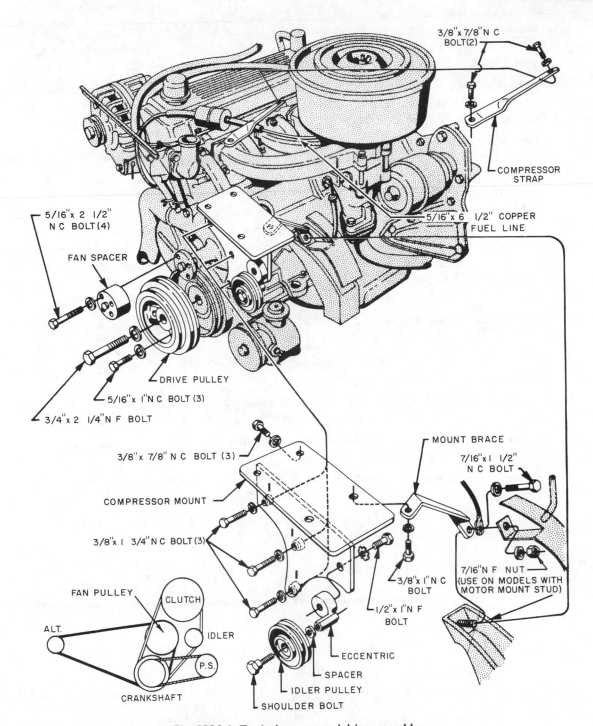

3/8"x 7/8" N C
BOLT(2)

COMPRESSOR
STRAP

5/16"x 6 1/2" COPPER
FUEL LINE

5/16"x 2 1/2"
N C BOLT(4)

FAN SPACER

DRIVE PULLEY

5/16"x 1"N C BOLT (3)

3/4"x 2 1/4"N F BOLT

3/8"x 7/8"N C BOLT (3)

COMPRESSOR MOUNT

3/8"x 1 3/4"N C BOLT(3)

MOUNT BRACE

7/16"x1 1/2"
N C BOLT

3/8"x 1"N C
BOLT

1/2"x 1"N F
BOLT

7/16"N F NUT
(USE ON MODELS WITH
MOTOR MOUNT STUD)

FAN PULLEY

CLUTCH

IDLER

P.S.

ALT.

CRANKSHAFT

ECCENTRIC

SPACER

IDLER PULLEY

SHOULDER BOLT

Fig. SP36-1 Typical mount and drive assembly

 d. Fasten the new tubing and union fitting to the carburetor.

 e. Bend the long fuel line, with the filter bowl, up and over the valve cover (as shown on the engine schematic, figure SP36-1).

 f. Bend the new copper line as required and then insert the tubing into the filter bowl hose.

 g. Use the original clamp and tighten it securely around the tubing.

5. Remove the bolts from the engine as indicated on the schematic. Hold the mount in the approximate position with relation to the engine to identify the exact bolts to be removed.

6. Loosely install the compressor mount on the engine, using three 3/8" x 1 3/4" NC bolts with lockwashers. Insert the bolts through the three front vertical mounting holes and welded spacers into the water pump housing.

7. Install the clutch coil and clutch on the compressor. Loosely install the compressor and clutch to the mount, using three 3/8" x 7/8" NC bolts with lockwashers. Install the bolts in the compressor through the two forward and one left rear top plate holes.

8. Loosely install the compressor strap and mounting brace.
   a. Compressor Strap: insert a 3/8" x 7/8" NC bolt with lockwasher through the flat strap end into the engine head. A second 3/8" x 7/8" NC bolt with lockwasher is inserted through the opposite strap end into the compressor side.
   b. Mounting Brace: insert into the engine block a 7/16" x 1 1/2" NC bolt with lock-washer through the battery ground wire (power steering models only), the welded ear of the brace, and the motor mount bracket. On models equipped with a motor mount stud, fasten the brace with a 7/16-in NF nut and lockwasher. Then insert a 3/8" x 1" NC bolt with lockwasher through the upper brace and remaining top plate hole into the compressor.

9. All assembly bolts and/or nuts should be uniformly tightened to prevent strain or misalignment.

10. Install the eccentric and idler assembly to the front vertical, using a 1/2" x 1" NF bolt with starwasher.

11. Insert a 1 5/8-in fan spacer between the original fan and pulley. Install this assembly using four 5/16" x 2 1/2" NC bolts. Tighten the bolts securely.

12. Thread all drive belts as shown on the schematic. Adjust and tighten each belt as required to obtain the proper belt tension.

13. Replace the radiator, connect the water hoses, and connect the transmission fluid cooling lines. Add coolant.

NOTE: Both the mount and the drive pulley must be furnished by the same company to insure alignment of the belt(s).

Review

Briefly answer each of the following questions.

1. List three precautions to be observed when installing a mount and drive assembly.
2. Are mount and drive assemblies interchangeable?
3. Why is it necessary to remove the radiator?
4. Why is it stated that the drive pulley and compressor mount must be furnished by the same company?
5. What can happen if the idler pulley is not in line with the compressor clutch and the drive pulley?
6. What is the purpose of the fan spacer?
7. Explain the answer given for question 2.
8. How is the compressor driven from the engine?

SERVICE PROCEDURE 37:

Installing the Evaporator Assembly, Condenser, Hoses, and Hardware

After the mount and drive assembly is installed according to Service Procedure 36, the other components of the air conditioner can be installed. The components may be installed in any order — as long as the receiver/drier is installed last (to prevent the possibility of excess moisture and foreign matter from entering the system as other components are installed.)

Custom air-conditioner units are available for most year/model automobiles. Each type of unit requires a different installation procedure. For example, the installation of some units requires that parts of the fresh air or heater system ducts be removed so that the air-conditioning ducts can be connected into the system. For other units, the radio, lighter, and even the glove box are relocated to permit the installation.

Although this procedure is not intended for a particular installation, it can serve as a guide to the DOs and DON'Ts of installing an aftermarket air conditioner.

TOOLS

Compete set of mechanic's hand tools
Electric drill with drill set

Hole saw, 2-in
Manifold and gauge set

MATERIALS

Automotive air conditioner
Installation package

Clean refrigeration oil
Refrigerant 12

PROCEDURE

Preparation

1. Carefully unpack the air conditioner and the installation package.

2. Check the contents against the packing slip to insure that the following major parts are included:

   - Compressor
   - Condenser
   - Receiver/drier
   - Thermostatic expansion valve
   - Liquid line hose (drier to evaporator)
   - Suction line hose (evaporator to compressor)
   - Clutch coil or brush set
   - Clutch rotor assembly
   - Evaporator case with blower assembly
   - Hardware package
   - Discharge line hose (compressor to condenser)
   - High-pressure liquid line (condenser to drier)

3. Lay out all of the parts on a workbench and check for damage.

4. Read the installation information provided with the unit.

Mount the Evaporator

1. Remove those parts designated for the evaporator installation in the installation sheet provided with the unit.

2. Hold the evaporator in position and note the location of all of the mounting hardware.

3. After insuring that there are no electrical wires, cables, or other hoses on the reverse side of the panel where the evaporator installation is to be made, drill the holes for the mounting hardware.

4. Note where the hoses are to pass through the firewall and the floorboard (for the condensate hose).

5. Again, after insuring that there are no electrical wires, cables, brake or gas lines behind the panels:
    a. Drill a 2-in hole through the firewall for the refrigeration hoses.
    b. Drill a 1/2-in hole through the floorboard for the condensate hose.

    NOTE: There may be two condensate hoses. As a result, two holes must be drilled. *Take care not to drill into the transmission housing.*

6. Install the suction hose to the evaporator outlet fitting as follows:
    a. If flare-type fittings are used on the suction hose, use refrigeration oil on the fittings. Using two wrenches, install and tighten the hose. Caution: do not overtighten the fittings.
    b. If the suction hose has a barb-type fitting, use refrigeration oil on the fittings. Then place a clamp over the hose and push the hose into the fitting. Tighten the clamp, but take care not to overtighten the clamp on the hose.

7. With the expansion valve secured to the evaporator core, install the liquid line to the TXV inlet, according to the procedures outlined in step 6.

8. Slide the condensate hose(s) to the provisions of the evaporator case.

9. Pass the hose(s) through the firewall hole drilled previously. The hose(s) must not interfere with cables, electrical wiring, or any mechanical linkages under the dash. Reroute the hoses if necessary to avoid any interference.

10. Place the evaporator assembly into position and secure it to the hardware (steps 2 and 3).

11. Pass the condensate hose(s) through the floorboard hole(s) drilled previously.

Mount the Condenser

1. Remove those parts designated for the condenser assembly in the installation sheet provided with the unit.

2. Position the condenser and note the location of the mounting hardware.

3. After insuring that there is no interference with the hood latch cables, headlamp linkage or vacuum lines (if the car is so equipped), battery box, battery, radiator, or electrical wires, drill the holes for the condenser mounting hardware.

4. Install the hot gas discharge hose to the top fitting of the condenser as follows:
    a. If the hose has a flare-type fitting, use refrigeration oil on the fittings. Using two wrenches, install and tighten the hose. Do not overtighten the hose fitting.
    b. If the hose has a barb-type fitting, use refrigeration oil on the fitting, place a clamp over the hose, and push the hose on the fitting. Tighten the clamp, but do not overtighten it on the hose.

5. Install the high-pressure hose to the bottom fitting of the condenser using the procedure outlined in step 4.

6. If necessary, drill a 2-in diameter hole so that the hoses can be passed through the panel to the engine side of the radiator. There must be no obstructions on the other side of the panel. In many cases, holes or slots are provided and drilling is not necessary.

7. Pass both hoses through the panel. The hoses must not interfere with any of the components given in step 3. Reroute the hoses if necessary.

8. Secure the condenser to the mounting hardware installed in steps 2 and 3. The condenser must be at least one inch (25.4 mm) in front of the radiator.

Mount the Compressor

1. Mount the compressor to the mount assembly (installed in Service Procedure 36).

2. Locate and secure the compressor mounting braces as required (see the illustration in Service Procedure 36).

3. Insure that all bolts are installed in the compressor to hold it securely to the engine. Do not cross thread any of the bolts. Tighten the bolts securely, but do not overtighten them.

4. Install the clutch coil or brush set on the compressor.

5. Install the clutch rotor (pulley) assembly on the crankshaft. Use only the Nyloc capscrew provided.

6. Spin the rotor to insure that it rotates freely. If a scraping or grinding noise is noted, remove the rotor to determine the problem. Correct and reinstall the rotor.

7. Check the alignment of the clutch rotor with the crankshaft drive pulley.

8. If the rotor is not aligned, check that the compressor and compressor mount are installed properly. Correct the mountings as necessary.

9. Install and tighten the drive belt, but do not overtighten the belt.

10. Check for belt alignment. If the belt is not aligned properly, the belt cannot stay on the pulley during operation. Correct the belt alignment as necessary.

Mount the Receiver/Drier

1. Check the length of the liquid line and high-pressure hoses to determine the approximate location of the receiver/drier.

2. After determining the location, drill holes for the receiver/drier mounting hardware. Do not drill into the receiver tank. Also, insure that the other side of the panel is unobstructed before drilling the holes.

3. Mount the drier with its hardware. Do not remove the protective covers from the drier at this time. The drier should be mounted in a position that is as close to vertical as possible.

Connect the Hoses into the System

Refer also to Service Procedure 38, "Servicing Refrigerant Hoses and Fittings."

1. Remove the protective covers from the suction line and the inlet service valve of the compressor.

2. Using refrigeration oil on the hose fitting, connect the hoses as follows:
    a. If the hose has a flare-type fitting, use two wrenches to tighten it. Do not overtighten the fitting.
    b. If the hose has a barb-type fitting, slip the clamp over the hose and slide the hose on the fitting. Tighten the clamp, but be careful not to overtighten it.

3. Repeat steps 1 and 2 with the hot gas discharge hose (compressor to condenser).

4. Repeat steps 1 and 2 with both hoses to the receiver/drier. See notes A and B.

    NOTE A: Determine the direction of flow through the receiver/drier. The flow direction is generally indicated by an arrow or the word IN.. The flow is toward the TXV. Do not reverse the receiver/drier.

    NOTE B: Work quickly. Do not allow foreign matter or airborne moisture to enter the system.

Leak Test the System

1. Follow Service Procedure 3 and leak test the system.

2. If a leak is found in one of the hose connections, retighten the connection. See step 3 following.

3. Do not overtighten the hose connection. If the leak persists, follow either step 3a or step 3b.
    a. If the hose has a flare-type fitting, remove the hose and check for a defective flare or foreign matter in the fitting. Use more refrigeration oil on the fitting. Reinstall the fitting and tighten it.
    b. If the hose has a barb-type fitting, remove the hose and cut off about one inch (25.4 mm). Use refrigeration oil on the fitting and reinstall it. Tighten the clamp around the hose.

Evacuate the System

1. Evacuate the system according to the procedures outlined in Service Procedure 4.

2. The system can be evacuated while the electrical connections are being made.

Electrical Connections

1. Locate the accessory (ACC) terminal (either on the fuse block or in back of the ignition switch).

2. Connect a No. 10 or No. 12 wire to the accessory terminal and evaporator master switch control. Check to be sure that the circuit is protected by a fuse or circuit breaker.

3. Connect the clutch lead wire from the evaporator thermostat to the clutch coil or brush set. Make sure that the wire does not touch the manifold or any mechanical linkages. Reroute the wire if necessary.

4. For a separate assembly, connect the blower motor lead wire(s) to the evaporator blower control.

Cleanup

1. Replace the protective covers, floor mat, or any other panels removed from the installation.

2. Using tie-down clamps, secure the hoses to prevent them from interfering with:
   - any moving parts, such as cables and linkages,
   - the battery and battery box (battery fumes are harmful to the inner braid of refrigeration hoses),
   - any heat-laden components, such as the engine and manifold.

Charge the System

1. Remove the vacuum pump as outlined in Service Procedure 4.
2. Charge the system as outlined in Service Procedure 5.
3. The system should now be ready for use.

Review

Select the appropriate answer from the choices given.

1. The receiver/drier is connected into the system

   a. first.
   b. last.

   c. at any time.
   d. before the condenser.

2. The hot gas discharge hose is connected between the

   a. compressor and the condenser.
   b. evaporator and the compressor.

   c. condenser and the receiver/drier.
   d. receiver/drier and the evaporator (TXV).

3. Technician A says that the compressor drive belt(s) can jump off the pulleys due to high head pressure. Technician B says that the belt(s) can jump off if the pulleys are improperly aligned.

   a. Technician A is correct.
   b. Technician B is correct.
   c. Either technician may be correct.
   d. Both technicians are wrong.

4. The minimum clearance between the radiator and condenser is

   a. one inch (25.4 mm).
   b. one and a half inches (38 mm).

   c. two inches (50.8 mm).
   d. two and a half inches (63.5 mm).

5. The clutch lead wire is connected from the clutch coil or brush set to the

   a. master control.
   b. fan control.

   c. accessory (ACC) terminal.
   d. thermostat.

SERVICE PROCEDURE 38:

Servicing Refrigerant Hoses and Fittings

Many types of connectors are used to join refrigerant hoses to the various components of the air-conditioning system. Some of these connectors are: male and female SAE flare (figure SP38-1), male and female upset flange, commonly called O-ring (figure SP38-2), male and female spring lock (figure SP38-3), and male barb (figure SP38-4).

This procedure is given in five parts: Part I for installing an insert (barb) fitting, Part II for repairing a hose using an insert fitting, Part III for repairing a damaged "factory" fitting, Part IV for servicing spring lock fittings, and Part V for O-ring service.

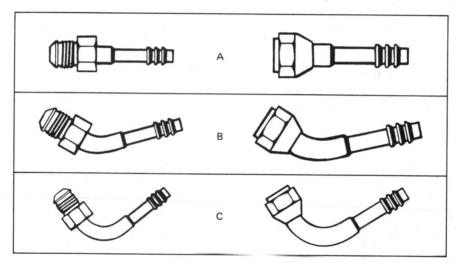

Fig. SP38-1 Male (left) and female (right) SAE flare fittings: (A) Straight, (B) 45° elbow, and (C) 90° elbow

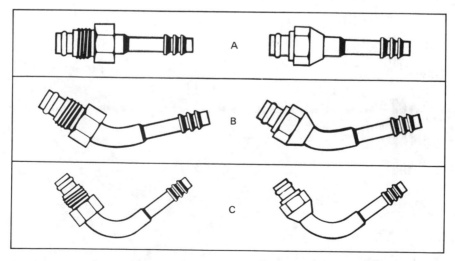

Fig. SP38-2 Male (left) and female (right) O-ring fittings: (A) Straight, (B) 45° elbow, and (C) 90° elbow

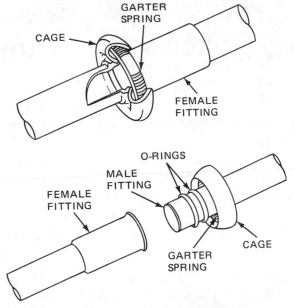

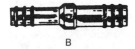

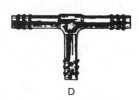

Fig. SP38-3 Details of spring lock (garter) connector

Fig. SP38-4 Male barb fittings: (A) straight, (B) straight reducing, (C) 90° elbow, and (D) Tee or branch

TOOLS

Hacksaw with 32 teeth-per-inch (TPI) blade
Pliers
Razor blade (single edge)
Screwdriver
Spring lock tool
Open end or flare nut wrench set

MATERIALS

Hose, if required
Fitting(s), as required
O-rings, as required

Clean refrigeration oil
Geared hose clamps

PROCEDURE

PART I – INSERT BARB FITTING

Prepare the Hose

1. a. Measure and mark the required length of replacement hose, or
    b. Determine how much hose must be cut ahead of the damaged fitting.

2. Use a single-edge razor blade and cut the hose.

    NOTE: Single-edge razor blades are available at most cleaning supply houses or hardware stores.

3. Trim the end of the hose to be used to insure that the cut is at right angle (square), figure SP38-5.

Insert the Fitting

1. Apply clean refrigeration oil to the inside of the hose to be used.

2. Insure that the fitting is free of all nicks and burrs.

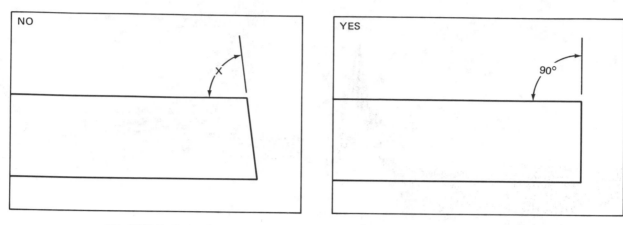

Fig. SP38-5 Cut and trim hose at right angle (90°) for best fit on barb-type fitting

3. Coat the fitting liberally with clean refrigeration oil.

4. Slip the insert fitting into the refrigeration hose in one constant, deliberate motion.

5. Install the hose clamp and tighten it to a torque of 30 ft-lb (40.6 N·m).

   NOTE: The hose clamp should be placed at the approximate location of the fitting barb closest to the nut end of the fitting, figure SP38-6.

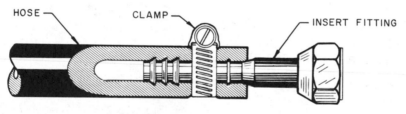

Fig. SP38-6 Insert fitting detail

PART II – HOSE REPAIR USING INSERT FITTING

Prepare the Hose

1. Determine how much of the damaged hose must be cut out and mark hose.

2. Use a single-edge razor blade and cut the hose. Remove the damaged section.

3. Trim the ends of the hose to insure that the cut is at right angle.

Insert the Fitting

1. Apply clean refrigeration oil to the inside of the hoses to be joined.

2. Coat the splice fitting liberally with clean refrigeration oil.

3. Slip the fitting into the hoses in one constant, deliberate motion.

4. Install the hose clamps and tighten to 30 ft-lb (40.6 N·m).

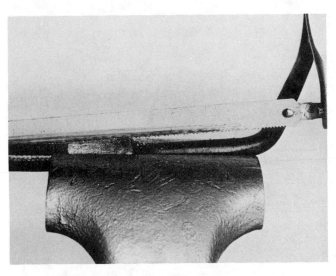

Fig. SP38-7 Using a hacksaw to cut through the ferrule to remove the hose from the fitting

Fig. SP38-8 Using pliers to "peel" off the ferrule

PART III — REPAIRING A DAMAGED "FACTORY" FITTING

Prepare the Hose

1. Remove the hose from the car and place the damaged fitting securely in a vise or other holding device.

2. Use a hacksaw and cut through the ferrule as shown in figure SP38-7.

3. Use pliers to "peel" off the ferrule, figure SP38-8.

4. Slice the hose end, figure SP38-9, with a single-edge razor blade and remove the hose.

5. Cut off the damaged end of the hose, figure SP38-10.

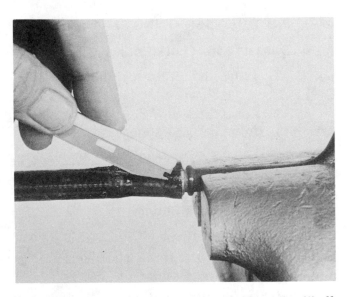

Fig. SP38-9 Slice the hose end with a blade and "peel" off the fitting

Rejoin the Hose

1. Apply clean refrigeration oil to the inside of the hose.

2. Coat the fitting liberally with clean refrigeration oil.

3. Slip the hose onto the fitting with one constant, deliberate motion.

4. Install a hose clamp and tighten to 30 ft-lb (40.6 N•m).

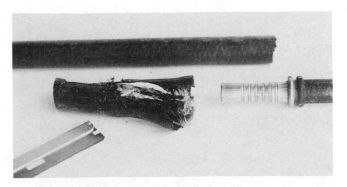

Fig. SP38-10 Cut off the damaged end of the hose

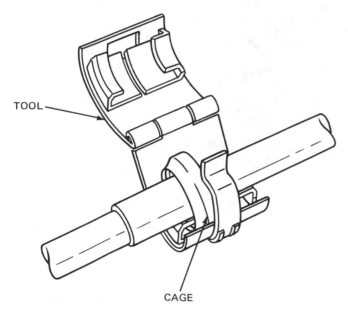

Fig. SP38-11 Installing special tool to disconnect spring lock connector

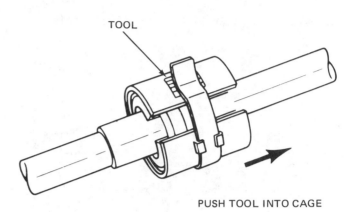

PUSH TOOL INTO CAGE

Fig. SP38-12 After closing, push tool into the cage to release fitting from garter spring

PART IV — SERVICING SPRING LOCK FITTINGS

Separate Spring Lock Fittings

1. Install the special tool onto the coupling so it can enter the cage to release the garter spring, figure SP38-11.

2. Close the tool, figure SP38-12, and push it into the cage to release the female fitting from the garter spring.

3. Pull the male and female coupling fittings apart, figure SP38-13.

4. Remove the tool from the now disconnected spring lock coupling, figure SP38-14.

Join Spring Lock Fittings

1. Lubricate two new O-rings with clean refrigeration oil and install them on the male fitting.

   NOTE: The O-ring material is of a special composition and size. To avoid leaks, use the proper O-rings.

2. Insert the male fitting into the female fitting and push together to join.

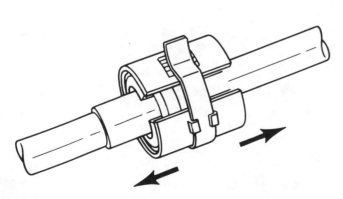

Fig. SP38-13 Pull the coupling apart

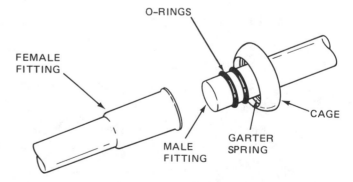

Fig. SP38-14 Separated male and female fittings with tool removed

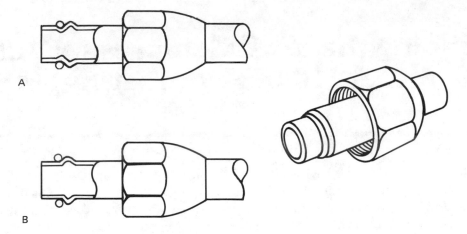

Fig. SP38-15 Captive (A) and standard (B) O-ring fittings

PART V — SERVICING O-RINGS

O-rings are replaced whenever a component fitting is removed. They do not usually leak if not disturbed. On occasion, however, an O-ring may be found to be leaking and must be replaced.

If it becomes necessary to replace an O-ring, one should be aware of the two different types of O-ring fittings: captive and standard, figure SP38-15. When replacing O-rings it is important to use the proper O-ring for the fitting. The inside diameter (ID) of the two types is slightly different.

Review

Briefly answer each of the following questions.

1. How can an insert fitting be used to repair a damaged hose?
2. What is the recommended torque for tightening a hose clamp?
3. What lubricant is used on hoses and fittings?
4. Which type fitting does not require a hose clamp?
5. What is another name for an upset flange fitting?

SERVICE PROCEDURE 39:

Rebuilding the York Compressor A206, A209, and A210 (Reciprocating) Models

This procedure can be followed when it is necessary to completely tear down a York compressor for repair.* Some compressor models will vary slightly from this procedure.

All York compressors are similar in appearance. However, the year and model of the compressor must be identified when it is necessary to replace parts. Refer to the appropriate manufacturer's instruction manuals and service data.

The procedure for rebuilding the York compressor is given in five parts:

- Shaft seal assembly servicing
- Head and valve plate servicing
- Servicing pistons and connecting rods
- Servicing crankshafts and main bearings
- Oil pump assembly

TOOLS

One set of 1/4-in drive sockets,
   to 9/16 in
Hard rubber hammer
Small screwdriver
Needlenose pliers

Snap ring pliers
Single-edge razor blades
Piston ring compressor
Allen wrench set
Torque wrench (ft-lb and in-lb)

Fig. SP39-1 York compressor

*The text and diagrams, in part, are reprinted with permission from the York Corporation.

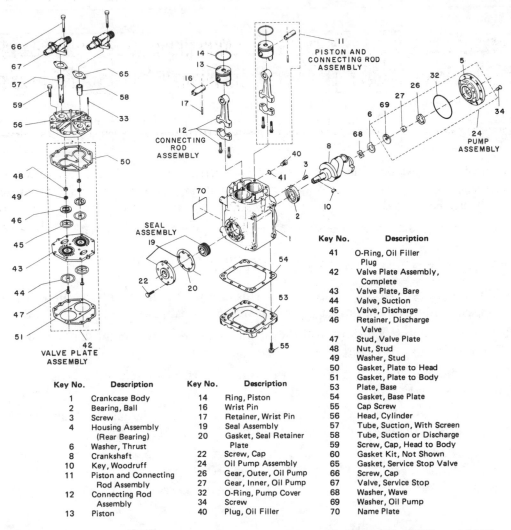

Key No.   Description

Key No.	Description
41	O-Ring, Oil Filler Plug
42	Valve Plate Assembly, Complete
43	Valve Plate, Bare
44	Valve, Suction
45	Valve, Discharge
46	Retainer, Discharge Valve
47	Stud, Valve Plate
48	Nut, Stud
49	Washer, Stud
50	Gasket, Plate to Head
51	Gasket, Plate to Body
53	Plate, Base
54	Gasket, Base Plate
55	Cap Screw
56	Head, Cylinder
57	Tube, Suction, With Screen
58	Tube, Suction or Discharge
59	Screw, Cap, Head to Body
60	Gasket Kit, Not Shown
65	Gasket, Service Stop Valve
66	Screw, Cap
67	Valve, Service Stop
68	Washer, Wave
69	Washer, Oil Pump
70	Name Plate

Key No.	Description	Key No.	Description
1	Crankcase Body	14	Ring, Piston
2	Bearing, Ball	16	Wrist Pin
3	Screw	17	Retainer, Wrist Pin
4	Housing Assembly (Rear Bearing)	19	Seal Assembly
6	Washer, Thrust	20	Gasket, Seal Retainer Plate
8	Crankshaft	22	Screw, Cap
10	Key, Woodruff	24	Oil Pump Assembly
11	Piston and Connecting Rod Assembly	26	Gear, Outer, Oil Pump
12	Connecting Rod Assembly	27	Gear, Inner, Oil Pump
		32	O-Ring, Pump Cover
13	Piston	34	Screw
		40	Plug, Oil Filler

Fig. SP39-2 Exploded view of typical York compressors, Models A206, A209, and A210

MATERIALS

Ample supply of clean refrigeration oil
Gasket set
Seal assembly
Replacements for defective parts, as necessary

OIL CHARGE

Positions (See Note)		Oil Level					
		Minimum		Normal Running		Initial Charge	
Mount	Range	Dipstick Depth	Fractional Pints	Dipstick Depth	Fractional Pints	Dipstick Depth	Fractional Pints
Vertical	90°–70°	7/8″	3/8 Pt	1-1/4″	1/2 Pt	1-3/8″	5/8 Pt
Inclined	50°–15°	1-5/8″	1/3 Pt	2″	3/8 Pt	2-3/4″	5/8 Pt
Horizontal	10°–0°	3/4″	1/4 Pt	7/8″	1/4 Pt	1-5/8″	5/8 Pt

Oil Type: Suniso #5, Texaco Capella E, or equivalent.

NOTE: The compressor can be inclined to any angle between vertical and 90 degrees either right or left. Oil level – minimum and maximum.

Fig. SP39-3 Oil charge for York reciprocating compressors (English)

Positions (See Note)		Oil Level					
Mount	Range	Minimum		Normal Running		Initial Charge	
		Dipstick Depth	Milliliters	Dipstick Depth	Milliliters	Dipstick Depth	Milliliters
Vertical	90°-70°	22.2 mm	177 mL	31.7 mm	237 mL	34.9 mm	296 mL
Inclined	50°-15°	41.3 mm	157 mL	50.8 mm	177 mL	69.8 mm	296 mL
Horizontal	10°-0°	19.0 mm	118 mL	22.2 mm	118 mL	41.3 mm	296 mL

Oil Type: Suniso #5, Texaco Capella E, or equivalent.

NOTE: The compressor can be inclined to any angle between vertical and 90 degrees either right or left. Oil level – minimum and maximum.

Fig. SP39-4 Oil charge for York reciprocating compressors (metric)

SHAFT SEAL ASSEMBLY SERVICING PROCEDURE

NOTE: A seal assembly kit is required. This kit includes the front seal plate, seal nose, spring assembly, and the gasket O-ring for the front seal plate.

1. Remove the clutch and Woodruff key from the compressor crankshaft. Use a 5/8-in NC bolt to remove the clutch to avoid damage.

2. Remove the clutch coil if it is seal-plate mounted. If the clutch coil is boss mounted, it is not necessary to remove it for seal servicing.

3. Remove the seal plate capscrews and gently pry the seal plate loose. Take care not to scratch the flat sealing surfaces or the polished shaft surfaces.

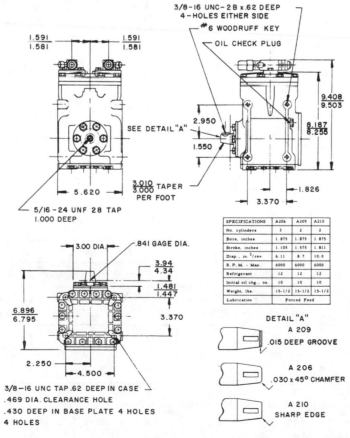

Fig. SP39-5 The York compressor: dimensions and specifications

4. Remove the shaft seal from the shaft by prying behind the drive ring. The drive ring is the portion of the seal assembly farthest back on the shaft. Take care not to scratch the crankshaft.

5. Clean all parts and surfaces of all foreign material and of gasket or O-ring material.

6. Place the new seal assembly and gaskets in clean refrigeration oil.

7. Inspect all mounting surfaces for nicks and burrs. Coat all surfaces with clean refrigeration oil.

8. Place the seal plate gasket(s) or O-ring in position on the seal housing face (it is necessary to insert the O-ring into the compressor crankcase).

9. Push the seal assembly, less the carbon ring if it is free, over the end of the crankshaft with the carbon ring retainer facing out. Now place the carbon ring into the seal assembly with the polished surface facing out. The indentations in the outside edge of the carbon ring must engage the tangs in the retainer. Install the seal plate.

10. Insert the capscrews and tighten them until they are fingertight. There must be equal clearance between the crankshaft and the seal plate.

11. Tighten all of the capscrews in sequence so that the capscrews diagonally opposite from one another are evenly drawn to a torque of 13–17 ft-lb (17.6–23.0 N·m).

HEAD AND VALVE PLATE SERVICING PROCEDURE

NOTE: A valve plate kit is required. This kit includes the valve plate, discharge valves, suction valves, valve retainer parts, valve plate and cylinder head gasket, and service valve gaskets.

1. Remove the capscrews from the flange-type service valves. Note that these four capscrews are longer than the remaining head capscrews. If the valves are of the Rotolock type, remove the valves by loosening the hex nuts which are a part of the Rotolock valve assembly.

2. Remove the remaining capscrews and washers in the head. Then remove the valve plate and head from the cylinder by prying or tapping under the ears which extend from the valve plate. Since the head is made of aluminum, care must be taken not to damage it.

3. Remove all foreign material and gaskets from the head and compressor crankcase. Do not mar or scratch any of the mating surfaces.

4. Do not disassemble the valves. The reed valves and valve plate are an assembly and are not serviced separately.

5. Apply a thin coat of refrigeration oil to all gaskets and surfaces.

6. Place a valve plate gasket over the compressor crankcase so that the dowel pins go through the dowel pin holes in the gasket.

7. Place the valve plate assembly in position over the gasket. Check that the discharge valves face up to avoid piston damage (the smaller of the two reed valves is the discharge valve). Position the assembly over the dowel pins.

8. Place the head gasket over the valve plate so that the dowel pins pass through the holes provided in the gasket.

9. Place the head on the cylinder head gasket so the dowel pins line up with the holes in the head.

10. Insert all capscrews through the head, valve plate, and gaskets. Tighten the capscrews fingertight.

11. Insert the discharge tube and the suction screen through the head and push them into place.

12. Lay the service valve gaskets in place and install the service valves on the proper side. Insert the capscrews to hold the service valves in place. Tighten the capscrews finger-tight.

13. Tighten the head and service valve capscrews to a torque of 14 to 18 ft-lb (18.9–24.4 N•m).

14. Tighten the inside service valve capscrews first. Then tighten the outside service valve capscrews. Tighten the remaining head capscrews in a sequence so that the capscrews diagonally opposite one another are evenly drawn to the specified torque. Retorque the capscrews after two hours.

PROCEDURE FOR SERVICING PISTONS AND CONNECTING RODS

The following parts are required for this procedure:

Piston and connecting rod assembly, including the rod, cap, screws, piston, piston rings, piston pins, pin retainers, gasket kit and oil charge.

1. Remove the head and valve plate assembly according to the previous precedure (steps 1 and 2).

2. Drain the oil and remove the baseplate.

3. Remove the damaged piston assembly by removing the capscrews holding the rod cap in place.

4. If the connecting rod(s) are to be reused, match and mark the rod, cap, and crankshaft throw. Marking these parts before the connecting rod bolts are removed insures that the parts can be reinstalled properly.

5. Clean all gasket material and foreign material from the crankcase, baseplate, valve plate, and head.

6. Insert the new piston(s) assembly through the top of the compressor.

    NOTE: The wrist pin roll pin must be positioned toward the center of the compressor. If the roll pin is positioned toward the outside of the compressor, it can contact the crankshaft when the piston is at the bottom of its stroke.

7. Install the connecting rod caps. Install the connecting rod cap bolts and torque them to 90 to 100 in-lb (10.2–11.3 N•m).

8. Replace the bottom plate and gasket. Replace the capscrews and tighten them until they are fingertight. Then continue tightening the capscrews in a sequence such that capscrews diagonally opposite one another are evenly drawn to a torque of 11 to 14 ft-lb (14.9–18.9 N•m).

9. Replace the valve plate and head assembly. Follow steps 5 through 14 as outlined in the previous procedure.

10. Replace oil as necessary to bring it to the proper level.

PROCEDURE FOR SERVICING THE CRANKSHAFT AND MAIN BEARINGS

The following parts are required for this procedure:

Crankshaft and/or main bearing or rear bearing, as required
Gasket kit and oil charge
Seal assembly kit

The rear main bearing is a bronze-sleeve bearing with a steel outer shell. This bearing is a press fit in the bearing cavity in the rear bearing cover plate. The rear bearing and the cover plate are replaced as an assembly.

The seal end main bearing is a ball-type bearing. It is mounted in the bearing recess machined in the inside wall of the crankcase. The bearing is a shrink fit; that is, it is inserted in the recess after the crankcase is heated in an oven at 150° to 300°F (65.6° to 148.9°C).

The inner race of the bearing is a press fit on the crankshaft.

When replacing the crankshaft, the seal end main bearing should also be replaced because the existing bearing may be damaged in dismantling the assembly.

1. Remove the crankcase base and drain the oil.

2. Mark the rod caps, rods, and crankshaft throw to insure proper reinstallation. Remove the rod caps.

3. Remove the compressor shaft seal and the rear bearing housing.

4. Remove the head and valve plate assembly. Remove the piston and rod assemblies.

5. Use a clean solvent and wash the crankcase to remove all foreign matter. Blow dry.

6. Heat the *complete* crankshaft-crankcase assembly in an oven to 300°F (148.9°C). Avoid localized heating since this can crack the assembly.

7. At 300°F (148.9°C) the crankshaft and ball bearing assembly can be removed from the crankcase with little applied pressure.

8. If the crankshaft is to be reused, remove the bearing.

9. Press the new bearing on the crankshaft by exerting pressure on the inner race only.

10. Again heat the crankcase to 300°F (148.9°C) in an oven. Slide the crankshaft and bearing assembly into place. Using the opening in the bottom of the crankcase as a point of entry, place the bearing in the recess. If necessary, apply force to the outer race to be sure that it is seated in the bottom of the recess.

    NOTE: On one side of the bearing, the faces of the inner and outer races are flush. On the other side, the face of the inner race is recessed since the races are not of the same width. Figure SP39-6 shows the proper positioning of the races in the crankcase. Allow the crankcase to cool and insert the crankshaft through the rear bearing cover plate opening. Guide the flywheel end through the inner race of the ball bearing.

11. Position the crankcase so that it is completely supported on the inner race of the bearing. Press the shaft into place until the cheek of the shaft contacts the inner bearing race.

12. Replace the rear bearing O-ring and assembly. Torque the mounting screws to 7-10 ft-lb (9.5-13.5 N·m).

13. Replace the pistons in the proper position and replace the rod caps. Torque the hardware to 90-100 in-lb (10.2-11.3 N·m).

14. Replace the seal, baseplate, valve plate, and head assembly as outlined previously.

OIL PUMP ASSEMBLY

The part required for this procedure is the oil pump assembly including the housing, gears, spacers, washers, and O-ring.

1. Place the compressor so that it is resting on the baseplate and the

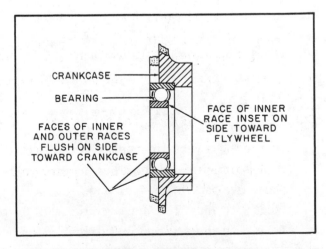

Fig. SP39-6 Position of races

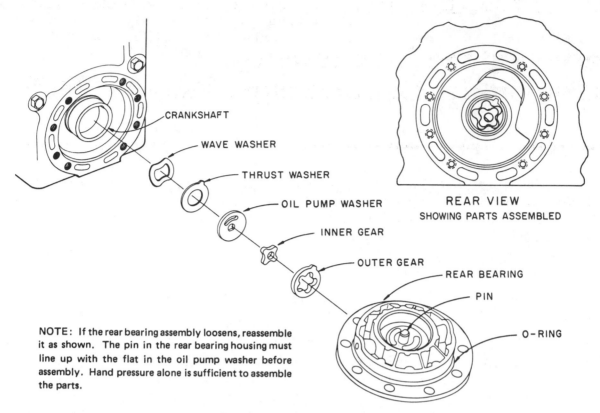

REAR VIEW
SHOWING PARTS ASSEMBLED

NOTE: If the rear bearing assembly loosens, reassemble it as shown. The pin in the rear bearing housing must line up with the flat in the oil pump washer before assembly. Hand pressure alone is sufficient to assemble the parts.

Fig. SP39-7 Oil pump assembly

front of the crankshaft. Insert the wave washer in the crankshaft cavity and then place the thrust washer on top of the wave washer. The tang of the thrust washer must be in the drive slot of the crankshaft.

2. Place the oil pump washer in the cavity with the kidney-shaped slot toward the top head of the compressor and the half-circle slot offcenter toward the left side.

3. Place the outer gear in the cavity with the tang of this gear in the drive slot of the crankshaft. Then place the inner gear within the outer gear. Position the inner gear so that the hole through the gear is aligned with the half circle of the oil pump washer.

4. Insert the rear bearing housing with the pin in the housing aligned with the hole in the inner gear.

5. With the bearing housing partially inserted in the compressor, rotate the housing slightly to the right and left until the parts slide into position.

6. Insert the rear bearing housing completely and rotate it slowly to the proper position. Take care not to damage the O-ring.

7. Insert the screws and tighten them to a torque of 7–10 ft-lb (9.5–13.5 N·m).

Review

Briefly answer each of the following questions.

1. How is the rear bearing replaced?
2. How is the shrink fit front bearing removed from the crankcase?
3. Name five parts of the oil pump.
4. What parts must be removed to replace a piston assembly?
5. What parts must be removed to replace the oil pump?

SERVICE PROCEDURE 40:

Servicing the Nippondenso Ten-cylinder Compressor, Model 10P15

The Nippondenso 6- and 10-cylinder compressors are similar in appearance. The Nippondenso 6-cylinder compressor is covered in Service Procedures 22, 28, and 43. Unlike the 6-cylinder compressors, the 10-cylinder model shaft seal may be serviced without removing the front head.

Service to the 10-cylinder compressor is limited to the clutch and shaft seal. It is not advisable to attempt internal repairs.

TOOLS

Pulley and bearing remover/replacer
Clutch plate holder or strap wrench
Hydraulic press (if replacing bearing)
Nonmetallic feeler gage set
Thrust plate remover/replacer
Thrust seal remover/replacer
Pulley bearing replacer

Pulley support
Shaft key remover
Pressure plate remover
Snap ring pliers
Socket wrench set
Open end wrench set
Plastic hammer

MATERIAL

Refrigerant 12
Refrigeration oil

Clutch bearing
Shaft seal kit

PROCEDURE

Procedures are given in two parts: Part I for clutch service, and Part II for seal service.

PART I – CLUTCH SERVICE

Remove Clutch

1. While holding the clutch plate with a strap wrench or clutch plate holding tool, remove the shaft nut with a 12-mm socket and handle.

2. Use the clutch plate remover, figure SP40-1, to remove the clutch plate.

3. Remove the clutch plate shim(s) and set them aside for later reassembly.

4. Use the snap ring pliers, figure SP40-2, to remove the pulley retaining snap ring.

5. Use the plastic hammer, figure SP40-3, to tap the pulley off the compressor. Take care not to damage the pulley.

6. Remove the clutch coil ground wire from the compressor.

7. Use the snap ring pliers to remove the clutch coil retaining snap ring.

8. Lift the coil from the compressor.

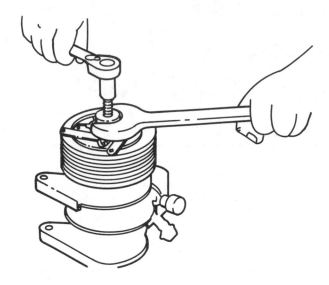

Fig. SP40-1 Use clutch plate remover to remove clutch plate

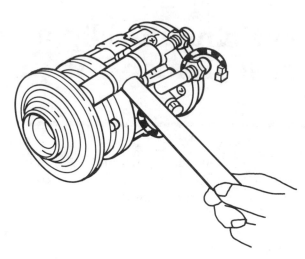

Fig. SP40-3 Use plastic hammer to tap pulley off the compressor

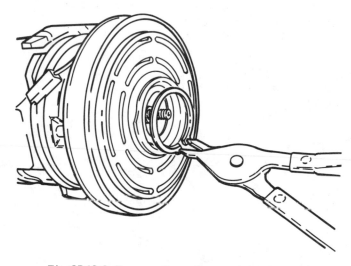

Fig. SP40-2 Remove the pulley retaining snap ring

Replace Bearing

1. Assemble the pulley with the pulley support and bearing remover on a hydraulic press, as shown in figure SP40-4. Make sure that the tools and the pulley are *in-line*.

2. Press the bearing from the pulley rotor. Discard the bearing.

3. Assemble the pulley with the pulley support, the bearing replacer tool, and the new bearing, as shown in figure SP40-5. Make certain that the tools, the pulley, and the bearing are *in-line*.

4. Carefully press the bearing into the pulley.

Replace Clutch Assembly

1. Place the clutch coil into position and secure it with a snap ring. Be sure that the snap ring is seated.

2. Replace the clutch coil ground wire.

3. Use the plastic hammer to gently tap the pulley onto the compressor. Take care not to damage the pulley.

4. Replace the pulley snap ring. Make sure it is fully seated.

5. Replace the clutch plate shim(s).

6. Replace the clutch plate.

7. Use a nonmetallic feeler gauge and check the clutch plate clearance. Clearance should be 0.016 inch (4 mm) to 0.028 inch (7 mm). If necessary, add or subtract shim(s) to obtain the proper clearance.

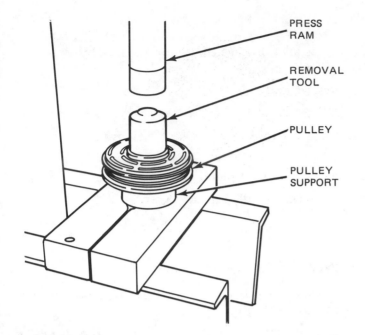

Fig. SP40-4 Use a hydraulic press to remove pulley bearing

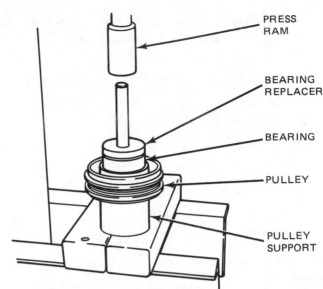

Fig. SP40-5 Use a hydraulic press to replace pulley bearing

8. Replace the compressor shaft nut and torque to 10-14 ft-lb (13.6-19.0 N·m).

9. Recheck the air gap. Adjust it if necessary. See step 7.

PART II – SHAFT SEAL SERVICE

Remove Seal

1. Remove the clutch and coil assembly as outlined in Part I.

2. Remove the felt seal from the seal cavity.

3. Using the O-ring pliers, remove the thrust plate snap ring.

4. Use the shaft key remover, figure SP40-6, to remove the shaft key. Set the key aside for reuse.

5. Insert the shaft thrust plate remover/installer into the seal cavity to engage the thrust plate.

6. Hold down on the holder ring and pull out on the T-handle to remove the thrust plate. Discard the thrust plate.

7. Insert the shaft thrust seal remover/installer into the seal cavity and engage the shaft thrust seal. Press against the seal while turning the tool clockwise (cw).

8. Pull the tool out of the seal cavity to remove the seal. Discard the shaft thrust seal.

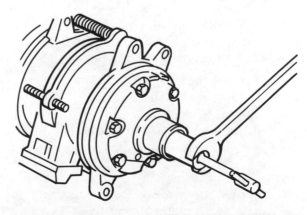

Fig. SP40-6 Use the shaft key remover to remove shaft key

Replace Seal

1. Install the new seal on the thrust seal remover/installer. Engage the seal to the tool by turning the tool or seal clockwise (cw) while applying pressure.

2. Coat the seal and seal cavity liberally with clean refrigeration oil.

3. Insert the seal into the seal cavity until it is fully seated.

4. Rotate the tool counterclockwise (ccw) to release the tool from the seal. Remove the tool from the seal cavity.

5. Use the thrust plate remover/installer to install the new thrust plate.

6. Replace the thrust plate snap ring. Be sure the snap ring is fully seated.

7. Replace the felt seal.

8. Replace the shaft key.

9. Replace the clutch and coil assembly, as outlined in Part I of this procedure.

Select the appropriate answer from the choices given.

1. Technician A says that the 10-cylinder compressor seal service is the same as for the 6-cylinder seal service. Technician B says that the seal service procedures may be the same, but different tools are required.

   a. Technician A is correct.
   b. Technician B is correct.
   c. Either technician may be correct.
   d. Both technicians are wrong.

2. The clutch rotor (pulley) is removed

   a. by hand.
   b. by using a plastic hammer.
   c. by using a puller.
   d. Any of these is correct.

3. The air gap between the pulley and the plate should be torqued

   a. 8-12 ft-lb (10.8-16.1 N·m).
   b. 10-14 ft-lb (13.6-19.0 N·m).
   c. 12-16 ft-lb (16.1-21.5 N·m).
   d. 14-18 ft-lb (19.0-24.2 N·m).

4. The air gap between the pulley and the plate is adjusted by

   a. using shims.
   b. torquing the shaft nut.
   c. a snap ring.
   d. The air gap need not be adjusted.

5. Not counting snap ring(s), how many parts are there to the shaft seal assembly?

   a. one   c. three
   b. two   d. four

SERVICE PROCEDURE 41:

Rebuilding Tecumseh Compressors, Model HG500, HG850, and HG1000

This procedure is recommended when it is necessary to tear down a Tecumseh compressor for overhaul.* To aid the service technician, the procedure is given in seven parts:

- Valve Plate Replacement
- Seal Assembly Replacement
- Rear Bearing Installation
- Front Bearing Installation
- Crankshaft Installation
- Connecting Rod Installation
- Piston Assembly Installation

The compressor models covered in this procedure are made of cast iron with aluminum connecting rods and pistons. Ball-type main bearings are used. Lubrication is accomplished by differential pressure; thus, an oil pump is not required.

TOOLS

Set of 1/4-in drive sockets,
   to 9/16 in
Hard rubber hammer
Small screwdrivers
Needlenose pliers

Snap ring pliers
Single-edge razor blades
Piston ring compressor
Allen wrench set
Torque wrench

MATERIALS

Ample supply of clean refrigeration oil
Gasket set
Seal assembly
Replacements for defective parts, as necessary

OIL CHARGE

Compressor Position	Oil Height (inch)	Oil Height (mm)	Remarks
Vertical	1 5/16	33.3	Factory charge of 11 fl oz (325 mL)
Horizontal	1 9/16	39.7	Factory charge of 11 fl oz (325 mL)
Vertical	7/8	22.2	Minimum recommended height*
Vertical	1 1/16	27.0	Maximum recommended height*
Horizontal	7/8	22.2	Minimum recommended height*
Horizontal	1 1/8	28.6	Maximum recommended height*
*After connection to system and run			

Oil charge for Tecumseh compressors

*Text and diagrams reprinted with the permission of Tecumseh Products Company.

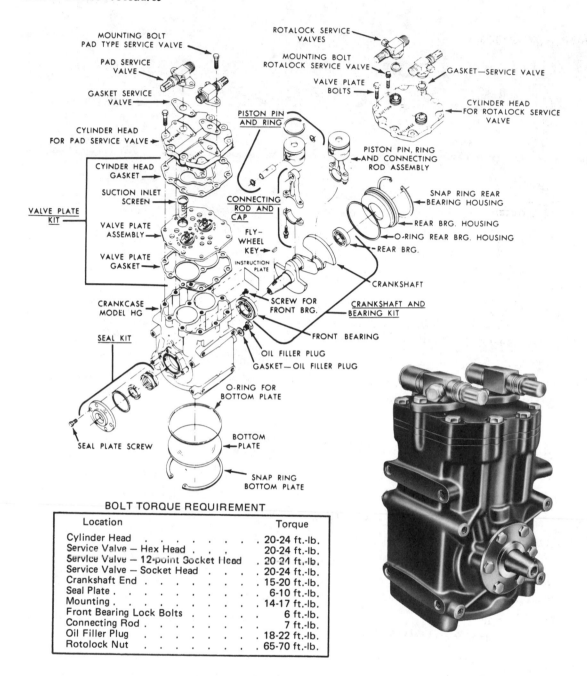

BOLT TORQUE REQUIREMENT

Location	Torque
Cylinder Head	20-24 ft.-lb.
Service Valve — Hex Head	20-24 ft.-lb.
Service Valve — 12-point Socket Head	20-24 ft.-lb.
Service Valve — Socket Head . . .	20-24 ft.-lb.
Crankshaft End	15-20 ft.-lb.
Seal Plate	6-10 ft.-lb.
Mounting	14-17 ft.-lb.
Front Bearing Lock Bolts	6 ft.-lb.
Connecting Rod	7 ft.-lb.
Oil Filler Plug	18-22 ft.-lb.
Rotolock Nut	65-70 ft.-lb.

COMPRESSOR SPECIFICATIONS

Model	Bore	Stroke	No. Cyl.	Disp. Cu. In.	Max. rpm	Refr.	Factory Oil Charge Oz.	Suction Valve	Discharge Valve	Weight* Net	Weight* Ship.
HG500	1 7/8	1 7/8	1	5.18	6000	R-12	8	5/8	1/2	19.5 lb.	20 lb.
HG850	1 7/8	1 35/64	2	8.54	6000	R-12	11	5/8	1/2	24 lb.	24 1/2 lb.
HG1000	1 7/8	1 7/8	2	10.35	6000	R-12	11	5/8	1/2	24 lb.	24 1/2 lb.

Fig. SP41-1 Exploded view and parts assembly kit for Tecumseh Models HG500, HG850, and HG1000 automotive compressors

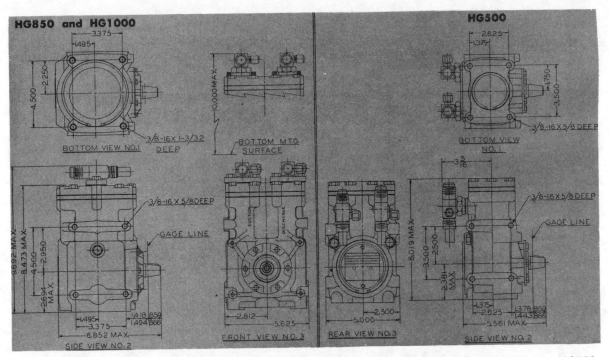

Fig. SP41-2 Comparison of compressors. Note the location of the service valves on the Model HG500 compressor.

VALVE PLATE REPLACEMENT PROCEDURE

The part required for this procedure is a valve plate kit which includes the valve plate, discharge valves, suction valves, valve retainer parts, valve plate, and cylinder head gaskets.

1. Isolate the compressor from the system.

2. Remove all bolts from the cylinder head.

3. Remove the valve plate and the cylinder head assembly from the crankcase by tapping against the side of the valve plate. Do not tap the cylinder head or crankcase body since these parts can be damaged.

4. Remove the valve plate from the cylinder head by holding the cylinder head and tapping against the side of the valve plate.

5. Remove all gasket material, dirt, and other foreign material from the surface of the cylinder head and cylinder face. Take care not to scratch or nick the mating surfaces.

6. Place the new valve plate gasket over the crankcase cylinder face. Make sure the gasket is dry.

7. Place the new valve plate assembly over the valve plate gasket so that the letter S stamped on the valve plate is visible and on the same side as the word *Suction* on the front of the crankcase. Place the valve plate assembly so that the mounting holes are aligned with those of the valve plate gasket and cylinder face.

8. Check that the suction inlet screen is clean. Insert the screen into the counterbore of the valve plate.

9. Locate the new cylinder head gasket over the valve plate so that the largest opening (circle) is over the top of the screen and the other circular holes line up with the holes in the valve plate. Keep the cylinder head gasket dry.

10. Place the cylinder head over the head gasket so that the side of the head with the word *Suction* is on the same side as the word *Suction* on the front of the crankcase.

11. Insert eight or twelve bolts as required through the cylinder head and valve plates. Tighten the bolts fingertight. Then torque the bolts in sequence so that the bolts diagonally opposite one another are evenly drawn to a torque of 20–24 ft-lb (27–32.5 N•m).

12. Mount the service valves:
    a. *Rotolock type.* Connect the service valves to the correct ports and tighten the valves to a torque of 65–70 ft-lb (88–95 N•m). Use new gaskets.
    b. *Pad base type.* Use a new service valve gasket and insert the valve mounting bolts through it. Locate the valve over the correct service valve ports. Tighten the bolts to a torque of 20–24 ft-lb (27–32.5 N•m).

13. After a period of about two hours from the time of assembly, retorque the cylinder head and pad-type service valves.

SEAL ASSEMBLY REPLACEMENT PROCEDURE

The parts required for this procedure are included in the seal assembly kit: the front seal plate, seal nose, spring assembly, and O-ring for the front seal plate.

1. Isolate the compressor from the system.

2. Wash and clean the seal plate and the adjoining surfaces to remove dirt and foreign matter.

3. Remove the seal plate nose assembly by removing the six bolts in the plate. Gently pry the plate loose. Take care not to scratch the crankcase mating surfaces.

4. Remove the carbon nose and spring assembly from the shaft by prying behind the drive ring. The drive ring is that portion of the seal assembly farthest away on the shaft. When prying the seal assembly from the shaft, do not scratch the crankshaft. If the rubber seal around the shaft does not come out with the carbon nose and spring assembly, remove it with needlenose pliers on the edge of the grommet.

5. Remove all gasket material, dirt, and other foreign matter from the crankcase mating surfaces, the exposed crankshaft, and adjacent surfaces.

6. Remove the new shaft seal washer in the bellows seal assembly. Coat the exposed surface of the crankshaft with clean refrigeration oil. Dip the new bellows seal assembly and shaft seal washer in clean refrigeration oil. Place the bellows seal assembly over the shaft. The end which holds the shaft seal washer is to go on last. Using the hand, push the bellows seal assembly on the crankshaft to a position beyond the taper of the shaft.

7. Assemble the shaft seal washer in the bellows seal assembly. Check to insure that the bellows seal assembly and shaft are free from dirt and foreign material. Assemble the seal washer so that the raised rim is away from the bellows seal assembly. The notches in the washer are to line up with the nibs in the bellows seal assembly. Cover the exposed surface of the shaft seal washer with clean refrigeration oil.

8. Insert the new O-ring in the crankcase mating surface for the seal plate.

9. Place the new front seal plate over the shaft. Line up the mounting holes. Place the hands on each side of the front seal plate and push it against the crankcase. Insert the six capscrews and tighten them evenly. Tighten the capscrews in a circular sequence at 9–12 ft-lb (12.2–16.3 N•m).

PROCEDURE FOR THE REAR BEARING INSTALLATION

The parts required for this procedure are as follows:

Rear bearing   Oil charge, as specified
Gasket kit

1. Isolate the compressor and remove it from the system.

2. Remove all dirt and foreign matter from the rear and base cover plates and adjoining surfaces.

3. Remove the oil filler plug and drain the crankcase of oil.

4. With the appropriate snap ring pliers, remove the snap ring which secures the rear bearing housing in position. Remove the end plate.

5. Remove the rear O-ring and discard it.

6. Remove the rear bearing by using two offset screwdrivers with their ends inserted diametrically apart under the inner edge of the bearing outer race. Pry evenly on both sides to lift the rear bearing.

7. Remove the baseplate by turning the compressor upside down. Then, using the appropriate snap ring pliers, remove the snap ring holding the bottom cover in place. Remove the cover.

8. Remove the O-ring and discard it.

9. Clean all of the exposed parts and surfaces with solvent. Drain the parts and blow dry.

10. Support the compressor on the drive end of the shaft. Place the new bearing over the end of the crankshaft. Press on the bearing until the inner race rests against the shaft shoulder. CAUTION: *Press on the inner race of the bearing only.*

11. Insert the new O-ring into the counterbored hole provided for the rear bearing cover plate. The O-ring must be seated at the bottom of the bore and against its sides.

12. Check that the rear bearing housing is properly aligned and positioned on top of the bearing. Then press the bearing housing into the compressor crankcase counterbore until it is inserted to its full depth. Insert the snap ring.

13. Insert the new O-ring into the crankcase base groove. With the bracket of the baseplate on the outside, position the baseplate in the base counterbore. Insert the snap ring. By tapping with a hammer or pressing with the hand on the base, the snap ring will enter the crankcase groove.

14. Place the compressor in the upright position. Charge the compressor with the proper amount of oil. Oil is added until the charge is 11 ounces (325 mL) or the oil level is 1 5/16 in (33.3 mm) on a dipstick.

FRONT BEARING INSTALLATION PROCEDURE

The parts required for this procedure are as follows:

Front bearing	Gasket kit
Seal kit	Oil charge, as required

1. Remove the shaft seal assembly following steps 1 through 5 of "Seal Assembly Replacement Procedure."

2. Remove the rear bearing housing following steps 1 through 5 of "Procedure for the Rear Bearing Installation."

3. Remove the cylinder head and valve plate by following steps 2 through 5 of "Valve Plate Replacement Procedure."

4. Remove the baseplate by turning the compressor upside down. Then, using a snap ring plier, remove the snap ring holding the bottom cover in place. Remove the cover.

5. Remove and discard the O-ring.

6. Identify the rod caps and rods to insure that they can be reassembled in the same position. Remove the two rod caps by removing the four screws holding them.

7. Push the connecting rod/piston assemblies out of the crankcase.

8. Support the crankcase from the rear and gently tap the front of the crankshaft with a rubber or fiber mallet until the crankshaft moves out of the front bearing.

9. Remove the crankshaft and rear bearing from the compressor.

10. From the rear of the compressor, remove the two bolts that hold the front bearing in place. Remove the front bearing by placing a wood or metal rod against the front end of the bearing inner race and gently tapping the rod.

11. Clean all parts with solvent. Drain the parts and blow dry.

12. Install the new front bearing in the crankcase by placing the properly aligned bearing in the counterbore. Press or gently tap the outer race of the bearing until it is inserted to the full depth of the bore.

13. Install the two bolts holding the bearing in place. Torque the bolts to 6 ft-lb (8.1 N·m).

14. Insert the crankshaft in the front bearing assembly. Align the crankshaft and press or gently tap on the rear end of the crankshaft until it moves the full length of the bearing journal and bottoms.

15. Insert the piston and the connecting rod assembly (less the rod cap) into the cylinder bore. The assembly is to be positioned so that the connecting rod bearings are aligned with the crankshaft journals.

16. Using a piston ring compressor, collapse the ring against the piston and complete the installation of the piston and rod assembly in the cylinder bore.

17. Position the connecting rod bearings around the crankshaft journals. Locate the connecting rod caps in the proper positions over the journals. The parts must be mated properly.

18. Insert the screws and torque them to 9–11 ft-lb (12.2–14.9 N·m).

19. Rotate the crankshaft several times to insure that the connecting rod does not bind.

20. Install the rear bearing, bearing housing, and cover plate as outlined in the "Rear Bearing Installation Procedure," steps 11 and 12.

21. Install the new seal assembly as outlined in the "Seal Assembly Replacement," steps 5 through 9.

22. Install the baseplate by inserting the new O-ring in the counterbore. Position the baseplate (with the bracket to the outside) and press it into the counterbore. Insert the snap ring.

CRANKSHAFT INSTALLATION PROCEDURE

The parts required for this procedure are as follows:

Crankshaft kit   Seal kit
Gasket kit

1. Perform the "Front Bearing Installation Procedure," steps 1 through 9.

2. Install the new rear bearing on the new crankshaft by pressing or tapping on the inner race of the bearing.

3. Perform the "Front Bearing Installation Procedure," steps 14 through 22.

CONNECTING ROD INSTALLATION PROCEDURE

The parts required for this procedure are as follows:

Connecting rod and cap assembly   Oil charge
Gasket kit

1. Isolate the compressor from the system.

2. Remove all dirt and foreign material from the compressor. Pay particular attention to the area around the base and the head.

3. To remove the baseplate, first turn the compressor upside down. Then, using the appropriate snap ring pliers, remove the snap ring holding the bottom cover in place. Remove the cover.

4. Drain the oil from the compressor and discard it. Flush the exposed parts with solvent. Drain the parts and blow dry.

5. Identify the rod caps and rods to insure that they are replaced in the proper positions. Remove the two rod caps by removing the four screws holding them. If only one rod is to be replaced, remove only that rod cap.

6. Remove the valve plate and head. Follow the procedure outlined in the "Valve Plate Replacement Procedure," steps 2 through 5.

7. Remove the piston and connecting rod assembly by pressing them out through the top of the crankcase.

8. Using snap ring pliers, remove the piston pin snap ring.

9. Push the piston pin out so as to clear one side of the piston and connecting rod bearing. Remove the connecting rod.

10. Clean all foreign material from the parts to be reused.

11. Remove the cap from the new connecting rod assembly to be installed. Note the relative positions of the parts so that they can be reassembled properly.

12. Place the new connecting rods in the pistons and push on the piston pin until it rests against the installed snap ring.

13. Reinstall the snap ring in the piston.

14. Insert the piston and connecting rod assembly (less the cap) into the cylinder bore. Position the assembly so that the connecting rod bearings are aligned with the crankshaft journals.

15. Collapse the ring against the piston with a piston ring compressor and complete the installation of the piston assembly into the cylinder bore.

16. Locate the connecting rod caps in the proper position over the journals. The parts must be mated properly.

17. Insert the screws and torque them to 9–11 ft-lb (12.2–14.9 N•m).

18. Rotate the crankshaft several times to insure that the connecting rods do not bind.

19. Insert the new O-ring in the crankcase base groove. With the bracket to the outside, position the baseplate in the groove. Insert the snap ring. Tap or press on the base so that the snap ring enters the crankcase groove.

20. Replace the valve plate and head assembly by performing the procedure outlined in the "Valve Plate Replacement Procedure," steps 6 through 13.

PISTON ASSEMBLY INSTALLATION PROCEDURE

The parts required for this procedure are as follows:

Piston   Gasket kit
Pin and ring assembly kit   Oil charge

1. Perform the "Connecting Rod Installation Procedure," steps 1 through 11.

2. Select the correct piston, pin, and ring assembly. A 0.020-in (0.5-mm) oversize can be identified by a figure 2 stamped on the piston top.

3. Perform the "Connecting Rod Installation Procedure," steps 12 through 20.

Review

Select the appropriate answer from the choices given.

1. What is the normal factory charge of oil in the Tecumseh compressor?

   a. 10 oz (295 mL)   c. 12 oz (355 mL)
   b. 11 oz (325 mL)   d. 14 oz (414 mL)

2. What is the recommended torque of the valve plate and head bolts?

   a. 18–22 ft-lb (24.4–29.8 N•m)   c. 22–26 ft-lb (29.8–35.2 N•m)
   b. 20–24 ft-lb (27.1–32.5 N•m)   d. 24–28 ft-lb (32.5–37.9 N•m)

3. In which position can the Tecumseh compressor *not* be mounted for operation?

   a. Vertical   c. Horizontal, left
   b. Inverted (upside down)   d. Horizontal, right

4. How many capscrews hold the seal plate assembly in place?

   a. Two   c. Six
   b. Four   d. Eight

5. What special tool is used to insert (install) a piston assembly?

   a. Inserter tool   c. Feeler gauge set
   b. Ring expander   d. Ring compressor

SERVICE PROCEDURE 42:

Rebuilding the Sankyo Compressor

Rebuilding the Sankyo compressor is limited to replacing the shaft oil seal (Service Procedure 12), servicing the clutch (Service Procedure 24), and repairing the rear head and/or valve plate, as outlined in this service procedure. The proper oil level of the Sankyo compressor is checked following Service Procedure 18. This procedure, then, may be used if it is determined that the valve plate, rear head, or valve plate gaskets are defective.

TOOLS

Gasket scraper
Torque wrench
Socket wrench set with a 13-mm socket

Manifold and gauge set
Soft hammer

MATERIALS

Valve plate and/or gasket set, as required
Refrigerant

Refrigeration oil
Clean shop rags

PROCEDURE

Prepare the Compressor for Service

1. Purge the system of refrigerant as outlined in Service Procedure 2.
2. Remove the low-side and high-side hoses from the compressor fittings. Plug the hoses and compressor fittings to avoid contamination.
3. Loosen the compressor and/or idler pulley and remove the belt(s).
4. Remove the mounting hardware and lift the compressor from the engine.

Remove the Valve Plate Assembly

1. Remove the five screws from the cylinder head using a 13-mm hex socket wrench.

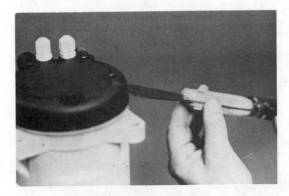

Fig. SP42-1 Removing the rear head

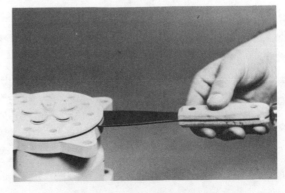

Fig. SP42-2 Removing the valve plate

2. Remove the head and valve plate assembly from the cylinder block by tapping lightly with a soft hammer on the gasket scraper which is placed between the valve plate and the cylinder head, figure SP42-1.

3. To remove the valve plate, insert the gasket scraper between the valve plate and the cylinder block, figure SP42-2. *Do not damage the mating surfaces.*

4. Carefully remove all gasket material, figure SP42-3, from the mating surfaces. *Do not nick or scratch the surfaces.*

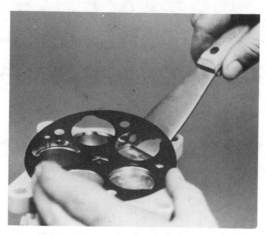

Fig. SP42-3 Removing the gasket material

Install the Valve Plate Assembly

1. Apply a thin coat of clean refrigeration oil to all gaskets and mating surfaces.

2. Install the valve plate gasket on the cylinder block. The alignment pin insures that the gasket is installed properly.

3. Place the valve plate into position. The alignment pin must pass through the pin hole in the valve plate.

4. Install the head gasket on the valve plate. Check for the proper alignment of the gasket.

5. Reinstall the cylinder head and check for the proper alignment.

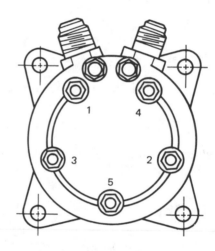

Fig. SP42-4 Rear head torque sequence

6. Install the five hex head screws and tighten them to a snug fit.

7. Tighten the five screws to a torque of 22–25 ft-lb (29.8–33.8 N•m). Tighten the screws in the sequence shown in figure SP42-4. *Do not undertighten or overtighten the screws.*

8. Add 1 or 2 ounces (29.5 or 59 mL) of oil to the compressor to compensate for any loss that occurs as a result of this repair.

Return the Compressor to Service

1. Return the compressor to the car in its original position. Replace all bolts and braces. Tighten the bolts securely.

2. Replace the belt(s) and tighten them to a tension of 90–110 in-lb (10.2–12.4 N•m).

3. Remove the plugs and replace the compressor low-side and high-side hoses. Use new O-rings if O-ring type fittings are provided.

4. Check the compressor oil level as outlined in Service Procedure 18. Omit steps 1 and 2 under the heading "Prepare the System."

5. Leak check the system as outlined in Service Procedure 3.

6. Evacuate the system as outlined in Service Procedure 4.

7. Charge the system as outlined in Service Procedure 5.

8. Return the compressor to service or conduct the performance test, as necessary.

Review

Select the appropriate answer from the choices given.

1. The valve plate and cylinder head screws should be torqued to

   a. 20–23 ft-lb (27.1–31.2 N•m).   c. 30–33 ft-lb (40.6–44.7 N•m).
   b. 22–25 ft-lb (29.8–33.8 N•m).   d. 32–35 ft-lb (43.4–47.4 N•m).

2. How much oil should be added to compensate for any loss as a result of repairs as outlined in this procedure?

   a. 1–2 ounces (29.57–59 mL).   c. No oil need be added.
   b. 3–4 ounces (89–118 mL).   d. All of the oil should be replaced.

3. Which of the tools used in this procedure is, in your opinion, a metric tool (not a standard U.S. tool)?

   a. The torque wrench (ft-lb)   c. The gasket scraper
   b. The soft hammer   d. The 13-mm socket

4. Technician A says that gasket material must be *carefully* removed from mating surfaces to insure that the surfaces are not nicked or scratched. Technician B says that old gasket material is removed to insure proper sealing of the new gasket.

   a. Technician A is correct.
   b. Technician B is correct.
   c. Either technician may be correct.
   d. Both technicians are wrong.

5. Which of the following gauge pressure readings best indicates a defective valve plate or gasket?

   a. High suction pressure with low head pressure.
   b. Low suction pressure with high head pressure.
   c. Low suction pressure with low head pressure.
   d. High suction pressure with high head pressure.

Rebuilding the Nippondenso Compressor (Includes Chrysler C-171 and Ford FS-6)

Rebuilding the Nippondenso compressor, also known as Chrysler's C-171 and Ford's FS-6, is limited to the following: Clutch Service, as covered in Service Procedure 28; Seal Service, as covered in Service Procedure 16; Checking and/or Adding Oil, as covered in Service Procedure 22; and Replacing Valve Plates and/or O-rings and Gaskets, as covered in this service procedure.

The compressor must be removed from the car for this service procedure.

TOOLS

Set of hand tools	Plastic hammer
Hub remover	Shaft protector
3-jaw puller	Shaft key remover
External snap ring plier	Graduated measure
Bearing remover/installer	Allen wrench set (metric)
Hub replacer	Torque wrench
Nonmagnetic feeler gauge	Valve plate remover

Also, if seal assembly is to be replaced:

Seal seat remover	Seal seat installer

MATERIALS

O-ring set
Gasket set
Refrigeration oil, as required
Pure mineral spirits
Refrigerant 12, as required
Parts, as required

PROCEDURE

Preparation for Service

1. Purge the system of refrigerant as outlined in Service Procedure 2.

2. Remove the compressor assembly from the car engine.

3. Remove the clutch and clutch coil assemblies as outlined in Service Procedure 28.

4. Using the shaft key remover, remove the shaft key, figure SP43-1.

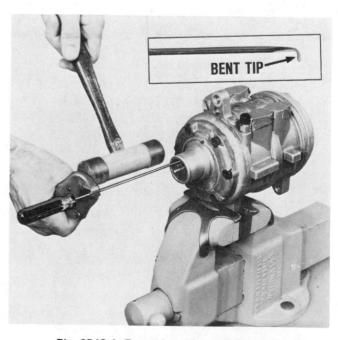

Fig. SP43-1 Removing the crankshaft key

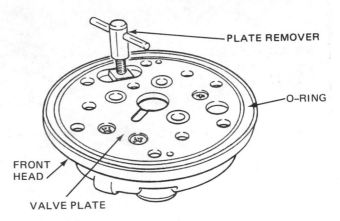

Fig. SP43-3 Use special tool to remove valve plate from the head

Fig. SP43-2 Removing the shaft seal

5. Remove the felt oil absorber and retainer from the front head cavity.

6. Clean the outside of the compressor with pure mineral spirits and air dry. Do not submerge the compressor into mineral spirits.

7. Drain the compressor oil into a graduated measure. See Service Procedure 22.

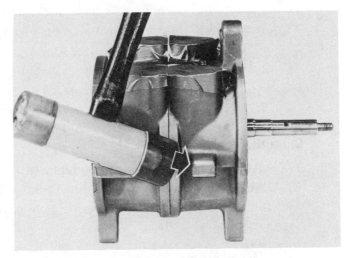

Fig. SP43-4 Separating the front and rear housings

Open the Compressor

1. Remove the six through bolts from the front head of the compressor. Use the proper tool; some require a 10-mm hex socket while others require a 6-mm Allen wrench.

2. Discard the six brass washers, if equipped. Retain the six through bolts for reassembly.

3. Gently tap the front head with a plastic hammer to free it from the compressor housing.

4. Remove and discard the head to housing O-ring and the head to valve plate gasket.
   NOTE: If replacing the seal assembly, proceed with step 5. If not, proceed with step 7.

5. Place the front head on a piece of soft material, such as cardboard, cavity side up.

6. Use the shaft seal seat remover to remove the seal seat.

7. Using both hands, remove the shaft seal cartridge, figure SP43-2.

8. Tap the rear head with a plastic hammer and remove the head.

9. Discard the head to housing O-ring.

10. Remove the valve plate from the head using the valve plate remover, figure SP43-3.

11. Discard head to valve plate gasket.

12. Tap on the compressor body lugs, figure SP43-4, to separate the front and rear housings.
    NOTE: Separate no more than one inch (25.4 mm), figure SP43-5.

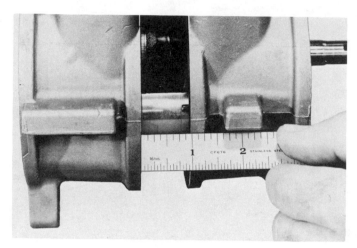

Fig. SP43-5 Separate the housings no more than one inch (25.4 mm)

Inspection

1. Inspect both suction valve plates for damage.
2. Inspect both discharge valve plates for damage.
   NOTE: Replace any valve plate found to be damaged.
3. Inspect all mating surfaces for nicks and/or burrs.
4. Inspect for brass or metallic material in the compressor piston bores or body.
   NOTE: If brass or metallic material is found, replace the compressor.

Close the Compressor

1. Liberally coat all O-rings and gaskets with clean refrigeration oil.
2. Position the front-to-rear housing O-ring and slide the two housings together.
3. Install the rear head to the valve plate gasket. Install the discharge valve plate and the suction valve plate.
   NOTE: Make sure the gaskets and valve plates are aligned with the alignment pins in the rear head.
4. Install the rear head O-ring and mount the rear head/valve plate assembly to the compressor housing. The rear head alignment pins must engage in corresponding holes in the compressor housing.
5. Position the compressor on the rear head and install the suction valve plate, the discharge valve plate, and the head to valve plate gasket.
   NOTE: Make sure the valve plates and gasket are aligned with the alignment pins in the compressor housing.
6. Install the compressor shaft seal cartridge, figure SP43-6, making sure to index the shaft seal on the crankshaft slots.
   NOTE: If the seal seat was removed, proceed with step 7. If not, proceed with step 8.

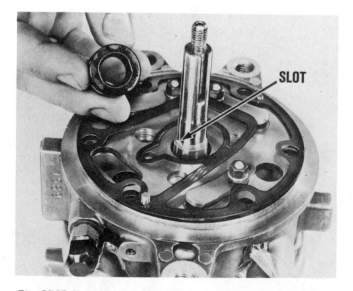

Fig. SP43-6 Index flat on shaft seal with slot on crankshaft

7. Install the seal seat into the front head using the seal seat installer (refer to figure SP16-6).

8. Install the front head to housing O-ring and carefully slide the head onto the compressor body.

9. Using six new brass washers, if required, install the six compressor through bolts.

10. Using a 10-mm hex socket or 9-mm Allen wrench socket, as required, tighten the bolts to 260 in-lb (29 N•m). Use alternate pattern, figure SP43-7, when tightening bolts.

11. Replace oil as outlined in Service Procedure 22.

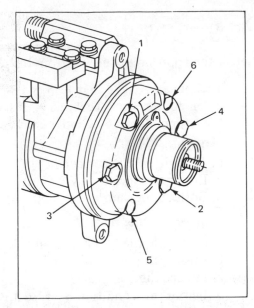

Fig. SP43-7 Use alternate pattern when torquing bolts. Torque sequence for tightening bolts is shown.

Return to Service

1. Using a drift, install the crankshaft key.

2. Align the ends of the felt and its retainer and install into the head cavity. Be sure the felt and retainer are fully seated against the seal plate.

3. Replace the clutch and coil assemblies as outlined in Service Procedure 28.

   NOTE: Before installing the compressor on the car, check for sticking and/or binding conditions, as follows.

4. Insert the socket wrench with torque handle into the shaft locknut and turn clockwise (cw). The suction and discharge service valves should be removed for this test.

5. Note the torque required to turn the compressor crankshaft. The maximum torque required should be 7 ft-lb (9.5 N•m).

   NOTE: If a greater torque is required, determine the cause and correct it before proceeding. If 7 ft-lb (9.5 N•m) or less is required, proceed with step 6.

6. Return the compressor to the car engine. Install and tighten belt(s).

7. Leak test the system as outlined in Service Procedure 3.

8. Evacuate the system as outlined in Service Procedure 4.

9. Charge the system as outlined in Service Procedure 5.

Review

Select the appropriate answer from the choices given.

1. Technician A says that Ford's FS-6 compressor is the same as the Nippondenso 6-cylinder compressor. Technician B says that Chrysler's C-171 compressor is the same as the Nippondenso 6-cylinder compressor.

   a. Technician A is correct.
   b. Technician B is correct.
   c. Either technician may be correct.
   d. Both technicians are wrong.

2. If brass or other metallic material is found in the piston bores or body,

   a. dismantle the two halves and clean thoroughly.
   b. flush with pure mineral spirits; do not dismantle.
   c. replace the compressor.
   d. Ignore this condition because it is to be expected.

3. What maximum torque should be required to turn the compressor crankshaft?

   a. 5 ft-lb (6.8 N•m)   c. 7 ft-lb (9.5 N•m)
   b. 6 ft-lb (8.1 N•m)   d. 8 ft-lb (10.8 N•m)

4. Technician A says that front and rear housings should not be separated more than 1 1/4 inch (31.75 mm). Technician B says it should not be separated more than 1 1/2 inch.

   a. Technician A is correct.
   b. Technician B is correct.
   c. Either technician may be correct.
   d. Both technicians are wrong.

5. What precaution(s) is/are required when installing the compressor shaft seal cartridge?

   a. Liberally coat the seal assembly with clean refrigeration oil.
   b. Insure that the seal assembly is installed with mating side away from the valve plate.
   c. Make sure to index the shaft seal on the crankshaft slots.
   d. All of these

SERVICE PROCEDURE 44:

Pressure Testing the Engine Cooling System

Engine cooling system performance often affects air-conditioning system performance. An important consideration for proper cooling system performance is a leakproof system. If coolant must be added frequently, a leak is indicated and should be repaired.

Many leaks are not easily detected without the use of a cooling system pressure tester. It is best to leak test the system when the coolant is cold. Slight coolant leaks, when striking a hot engine surface, evaporate before being detected. When using the pressure tester, the engine should *not* be running.

The following procedure is given in two parts: Part I for testing the pressure cap, and Part II for testing the cooling system.

TOOLS

Cooling system pressure tester

MATERIALS

Heater hose(s)	Radiator hose(s)	Gasket(s)
Hose clamps(s)	Radiator or heater core	Radiator cap

PROCEDURE

PART I – TESTING THE PRESSURE CAP

1. *To avoid injury,* make sure that the engine is cool and the cooling system is not pressurized. Remove the pressure cap.

2. Inspect the mating surfaces. Inspect the rubber gaskets of the pressure cap.

3. Install the pressure cap adapter on the pressure tester, figure SP44-1.

4. Insure that all seating surfaces of the adapter and pressure cap are clean. The lever should be in the *closed* position of safety-type pressure caps.

5. Wet the rubber gasket in water (H_2O) and install the pressure cap on the tester, figure SP44-2. Make sure that the locking ears of the cap stop on the adapter cams.

6. Hold the tester with the gauge facing you and operate the pump until the needle reaches its highest point.

7. Stop pumping and observe the needle.

   A. If the needle is below the rated range of the pressure cap, replace the cap.

   B. If the needle is above the rated range of the pressure cap, replace the cap.

   C. If the needle falls rapidly, replace the pressure cap.

   NOTE: The needle should remain in the proper range for at least 30 seconds. If in doubt, replace the cap.

8. Remove the cap and the adapter from the tester.

Fig. SP44-1 Install pressure cap adapter on pressure tester

Fig. SP44-2 Install pressure cap on adapter

PART II – TEST THE COOLING SYSTEM

1. The radiator cap is removed as described in Part I; the engine is not running.

2. Insure that the engine coolant is at the proper level in the radiator.

3. Wipe out the inside of the filler neck and examine the lower inside sealing seat for nicks, debris and/or solder bumps.

4. Inspect the overflow tube to insure that it is not restricted.

5. Inspect the cams on the outside of the filler neck. Carefully reform cams that are bent. Take care not to break the solder joint between the radiator tank and the filler neck.

6. Attach the pressure tester to the filler neck, figure SP44-3. Carefully, press down on it, rotating it clockwise (cw) until the lock ears are fully engaged to the stop lugs of the filler neck. *Do not force.*

    NOTE: A spacer washer may have to be used on some one inch (25.4 mm) deep necks such as are found on many import cars.

7. For the following procedures, refer to current published specifications to determine the proper cooling system operating pressures for the vehicle being tested. These specifications may also be found in the Owner's Manual for the vehicle.

8. Operate the pump until the needle on the gauge reaches the arrow just beyond the end of the color band for the specific system pressure range, figure SP44-4.

9. Observe the gauge needle; proceed as required:

    A. Needle is Steady
        a. If the needle holds steady for two minutes, there are no serious leaks.
        b. Using a flashlight, examine all gaskets and hose connections for seepage.
        c. If any leaks are found, correct as necessary.

Fig. SP44-3 Install pressure tester on radiator filler neck

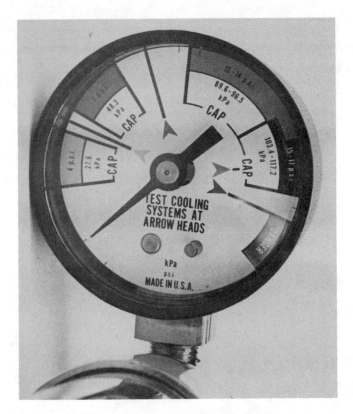

Fig. SP44-4 Operate pump until needle reaches the arrow just beyond the end of the color band

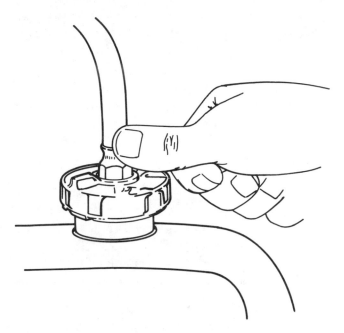

Fig. SP44-5 Use thumb to release pressure

B. Needle Drops Slowly

    a. If the needle drops slowly, a slight leak or seepage is indicated.
    b. Using a flashlight, examine the radiator, heater core, gaskets, and hose connections.
    c. Correct any leak(s) found, as necessary.
    d. Recheck the system. Repeat this procedure starting at step 2.

C. Needle Drops Rapidly

    a. An indication of a serious leak.
    b. Examine the radiator, heater core, gaskets, and hose connections.
    c. Correct all leak(s) found, as necessary.

    NOTE: If no leaks are found externally, the cooling system may be leaking into the transmission cooler or into the engine. Follow the procedures outlined in the appropriate service manuals for further leak testing.

    d. Recheck the system. Repeat this procedure starting at step 2.

10. Remove the tester from the radiator filler neck by first pressing the tester stem to one side, figure SP44-5, to release system pressure.

SUMMARY

The cooling system should be sound at all times. Even a slight leak will require periodic replenishing of coolant. A sound system should not require the addition of coolant between annual service.

Review

Select the appropriate answer from the choices given.

1. Technician A says that an automatic transmission oil cooler leak may be detected using a pressure system tester. Technician B says that a heater core leak may be detected by using a pressure system tester.

   a. Technician A is correct.
   b. Technician B is correct.
   c. Either technician may be correct.
   d. Both technicians are wrong.

2. Technician A says that a 14-psi (96.5-kPa) pressure cap that opens at 14 psi (96.5 kPa), and holds that pressure for at least 30 seconds, is acceptable. Technician B says that a 14-psi (96.5-kPa) pressure cap that opens at 17 psi (117.2 kPa), and does not fall below 14-psi (96.5 kPa) in 30 seconds, is acceptable.

   a. Technician A is correct.
   b. Technician B is correct.
   c. Either technician may be correct.
   d. Both technicians are wrong.

3. Before connecting the pressure tester to the radiator filler neck

   a. wipe out the inside of the filler neck.
   b. inspect the sealing seat.
   c. inspect the overflow tube.
   d. All of these are correct answers.

4. A pressure cap rated at 16 psi (110.3 kPa) should open at

   a. 13-15 psi (89.6-103.4 kPa).
   b. 14-16 psi (96.5-110.3 kPa).
   c. 15-17 psi (103.4-117.2 kPa).
   d. 16-18 psi (110.3-124.1 kPa).

5. Replace the pressure cap if, while testing,

   a. the needle stops above its rated capacity.
   b. the needle stops below its rated capacity.
   c. the needle falls rapidly.
   d. All of these are correct answers.

SERVICE PROCEDURE 45:

Rebuilding the Delco Air Four-cylinder Compressor, Model R-4 (Includes Internal Assembly)

Rebuilding the General Motors Delco Air four-cylinder compressor is considered to be a major service operation.* The compressor must be removed from the car and placed on a clean workbench, preferably one that is covered with a clean piece of white paper.

When the service technician works on the internal assembly of a compressor, it is very important that cleanliness and organized work habits be observed. An adequate supply of parts must be maintained for servicing four-cylinder compressors. Some of the more important parts to be stocked include:

Bearings, shaft, thrust, and pulley   Gasket set; O-ring gaskets
Suction reed valves   Retainer rings, all sizes
Discharge reed valves   Seals

The following procedures are based on the use of the proper service tools and on the condition that an adequate stock of service parts is at hand. The procedure is given in two parts: Part I for general compressor rebuilding, and Part II for rebuilding the internal assembly.

The special service tools required are available from the Draf Tool Company, Kent-Moore Tool Company, or from most automotive air-conditioning supply parts houses. The following list serves as a guide to the tool requirements.

TOOLS

Nonmagnetic feeler gauge set
Compressor holding fixture
Pulley puller
Socket wrench set
Pulley bearing remover and installer
Pressure test connector
Wrenches, pliers, screwdrivers
Torque wrench, in-lb and ft-lb
Snap ring pliers, internal and external
Compressing fixture(s)
Clutch hub holder
Hub and drive plate remover and installer
O-ring installer

MATERIALS

Overhaul gasket set   Shaft seal set
Refrigeration oil   Other parts, as required

*Some of the illustrations and charts in this procedure are used by permission of Cadillac Motor Car Division, Buick Motor Division, and Oldsmobile Division of General Motors Corporation, as well as other divisions.

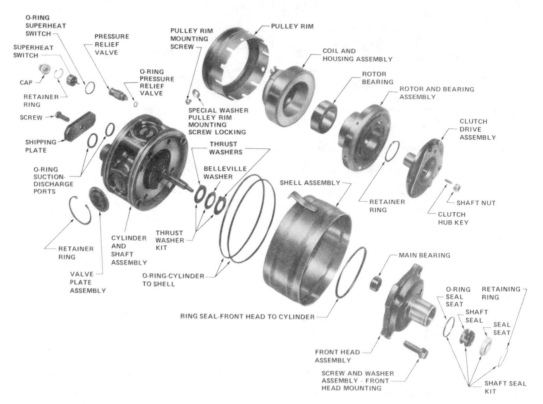

Fig. SP45-1 Exploded view of four-cylinder General Motors compressor

PROCEDURE, PART I

Hub Assembly and Seal Assembly Removal

1. Follow the procedures as outlined in Service Procedure 14.

2. Mount the compressor with the front side up in a holding fixture. Secure the fixture in a vise.

Clutch Rotor-Bearing and Coil-Pulley Rim Removal

1. Mark the location of the clutch coil terminals to insure proper reassembly.

2. Remove the rotor and bearing assembly retaining ring using the snap ring pliers, figure SP45-2.

3. Install the rotor bearing and puller guide over the end of the compressor shaft, figure SP45-3. *The guide should seat on the front head of the compressor.*

4. Using a puller, remove the clutch rotor and assembly parts, figure SP45-4.

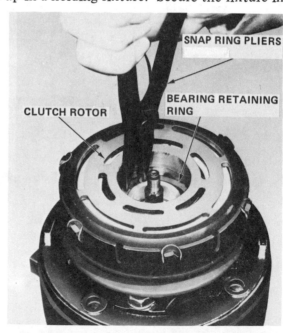

Fig. SP45-2 Removing bearing retaining ring

Fig. SP45-3 Positioning the rotor and bearing puller guide

Fig. SP45-4 Removing the clutch rotor

Front Head and Main Bearing Removal

1. Remove the four front head mounting screws, figure SP45-5.

2. Carefully lift off the front head. Remove and discard the front head seal ring.

   NOTE: At this point the main bearing, front seal ring, Belleville washers, and thrust washers may be serviced.

Remove the Internal Assembly from the Shell

1. Pry the shell retaining strap from the cylinder, figure SP45-6. Position the strap so that it clears the cylinder as the shell is removed.

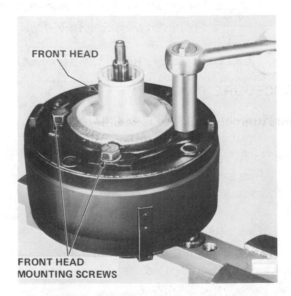

Fig. SP45-5 Removing the front head screws

2. Reposition the holding fixture, as shown in figure SP45-7. Install the puller bolts and tighten them until they are fingertight against the compressor cylinder and the fixture protrusions contact the compressor shell. *The step protrusions must pass both sides of the cylinder to avoid damage before the procedure can be continued.*

3. Alternately tighten each bolt one-quarter turn to push the shell free of the O-rings. *The compressor must be at room temperature for this procedure.*

   NOTE: If one bolt (step 3) seems to require more force than the other, immediately turn the other to bring the screw threading sequence into step. *Do not turn the bolts any more than is necessary to remove the shell.*

4. Remove the shell. Remove and reverse the holding fixture to secure the internal assembly.

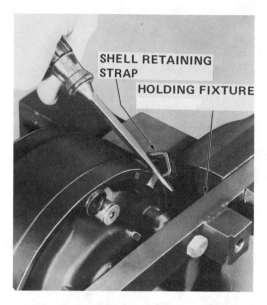

Fig. SP45-6 Prying the shell retaining strap

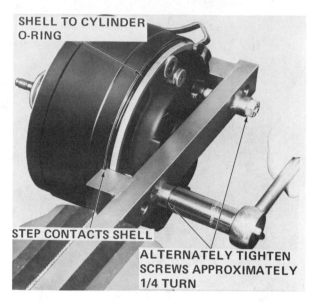

Fig. SP45-7 Removing internal assembly from shell

Diagnosis

1. If major damage is obvious, the compressor must be replaced. Compressor rebuilding is limited to main bearing and valve plate replacement. These procedures are outlined in Part II.

2. Discard all O-rings. Replace with new O-rings.

3. Examine the Belleville washers and the thrust washers. If scored or damaged, replace the washers as a set.

4. Inspect the seal and seat for damage of any kind. A new seal is suggested whenever a compressor is rebuilt.

5. Check the pulley and bearing assembly. If the frictional surface shows signs of warpage due to excessive heat, the pulley should be replaced. Slight scoring is normal. If the assembly is heavily scored, it should be replaced.

6. Check the pulley bearing for signs of excessive noise or looseness. Replace the bearing if necessary.

7. Inspect the hub and drive plate. Refer to comments of step 5.

Replace the Internal Assembly

1. With the internal assembly in a holding fixture, dip the front and rear O-rings in refrigeration oil and slide them over the assembly into the grooves provided. Do not damage the O-rings during the assembly.

2. Place the shell on the assembly and rotate the retaining strap to its original position.

3. Attach the shell installing fixture, figure SP45-8. Align the step projections of the fixture to contact the shell evenly on both sides.

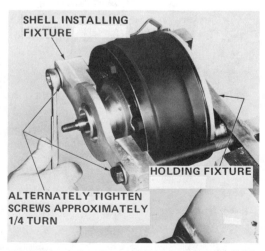

Fig. SP45-8 Using the shell installing fixture for reassembly

4. Push the shell as close to the O-ring as possible by hand and check for alignment. Tighten the screws fingertight.

5. Alternately tighten the screws one-quarter turn to push the shell over the O-rings and back against the stop flange.

    NOTE: If one screw (step 5) seems to require more force than the other, immediately turn the other screw to bring the screw threading sequence into step. *Do not force or overtighten the screws.*

6. Bend the shell retaining strap into place by gently tapping it with a hammer.

Replace the Front Head and Main Bearing

1. Make sure that the front seal ring and the Belleville thrust washer set are in place.

2. Place the front head in position. Secure the head with four hex head mounting screws.

3. Tighten the screws to a torque of 18–22 ft-lb (24.4–29.8 N•m).

Replace the Clutch Rotor-Bearing and Coil-Pulley Rim

1. Position the assembly on the front head of the compressor.

2. Using the rotor assembly installer with a universal handle, figure SP45-9, drive the assembly into place. *Before the assembly is fully seated, insure that the coil terminals are in the proper location and the three protrusions on the rear of the coil housing align with the locator holes in the front head.*

3. Install the retainer ring, using snap ring pliers.

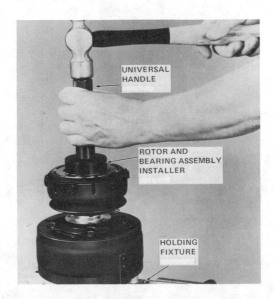

Fig. SP45-9 Using the rotor and bearing assembly installer

Replace the Hub Assembly and the Seal Assembly

1. Follow the procedures outlined in Service Procedure 14.

Leak Test the Compressor

1. Follow the procedures outlined in Service Procedure 14.

2. If either internal O-ring leaks, the assembly must be disassembled to determine the cause and correct the leak.

3. If no leaks are found, continue with the next procedure.

Return the Compressor to Service

1. Refill the compressor with 525 viscosity refrigeration oil. If the compressor is being returned to the car, refill it with the same amount of oil that was drained and recorded earlier. If the compressor is being returned to stock, refill it with six ounces (177 mL) of oil.

2. Return the compressor to stock or service.

PROCEDURE, PART II

NOTE: Servicing the internal assembly of the four-cylinder compressor is limited to replacement of the main bearing, thrust and Belleville washers, and the valve plates. If the internal assembly has sustained major damage, it is necessary to replace the compressor as an assembly. If repair of the internal assembly is considered worthwhile, proceed as follows.

Replace the Main Bearing

1. Remove the front head and main bearing assembly from the compressor as outlined in Part I.

2. Place the front head assembly on two blocks, figure SP45-10. Using the bearing remover and the hammer, drive the bearing out of the front head.

3. Place the front head with the neck end down on a flat, solid surface of the workbench.

4. Align the new bearing using the bearing installer, figure SP45-11, squarely with the bearing bore.

5. Drive the bearing into place with a hammer. *The bearing installer must seat against the front head to insure the proper clearance depth.*

6. Reassemble the front head to the compressor as outlined in Part I.

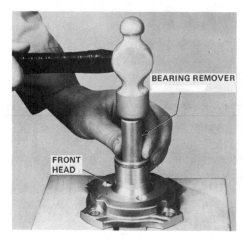

Fig. SP45-10 Removing the bearing from the front head

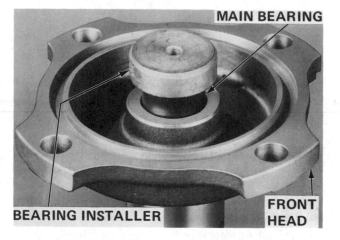

Fig. SP45-11 Installing the new bearing in the front head

Replace the Thrust and Belleville Washers

1. Remove the front head and bearing assembly from the compressor as outlined in Part I.

2. Remove the washers (two thrust washers and one Belleville washer) from the compressor shaft. Note the assembled position of the washers.

3. Install the new washer set as follows:
    a. install the thrust washer with the tang pointing up.
    b. install the Belleville washer with the high center of the washer pointing up.
    c. install the second thrust washer with the tang pointing down.
    d. lubricate the assembly liberally with clean refrigeration oil.

4. Reassemble the front head to the compressor as outlined in Part I.

Replace the Valve Plate(s)

1. Remove the internal assembly from the shell as outlined in Part I.

2. Using snap ring pliers, remove the valve plate retaining ring(s), as shown in figure SP45-12.

3. Lift out the valve plate(s) from the bore.

4. Inspect the top of the pistons for damage. Seriously damaged pistons mean that the compressor must be replaced. If the pistons are not damaged, proceed with step 5.

5. Replace the damaged valve plates.

6. Replace the retaining rings using the snap ring pliers.

7. Reassemble the internal assembly with the compressor shell as outlined in Part I.

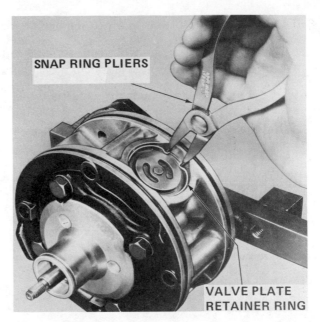

SNAP RING PLIERS

VALVE PLATE RETAINER RING

Fig. SP45-12 Removing the valve plate retaining ring

Review

Briefly answer each of the following questions.

1. What internal parts may be replaced (internal assembly)?

2. What is the clearance between the hub assembly and the rotor assembly?

    a. _____ in   b. _____ mm

3. The front head bolts should be torqued to:

    a. _____ ft-lb   b. _____ N•m

4. Under what conditions should the hub and/or rotor be replaced?

5. What is considered to be an important factor in rebuilding the compressor, aside from having the proper tools?

6. Technician A says that the Delco Air R-4 compressor has thrust washer(s) in the internal assembly. Technician B says that this compressor has Belleville washer(s) in the internal assembly.

    a. Technician A is correct.
    b. Technician B is correct
    c. Both technicians are correct.
    d. Both technicians are wrong.

CONTINUED

7. What is an important point to remember when replacing the main bearing?

8. List the steps in the procedure for replacing a valve plate in an internal assembly of a four-cylinder compressor.

9. Technician A says that refrigeration oil having a viscosity rating of 500 must be used in the R-4 compressor. Technician B says that the viscosity rating is not important as long as the oil is designated for refrigeration service.

    a. Technician A is correct.
    b. Technician B is correct
    c. Both technicians are correct.
    d. Both technicians are wrong.

10. How is the clutch coil properly seated onto the compressor?

SERVICE PROCEDURE 46:

Rebuilding the Delco Air Six-cylinder Compressor, Model A-6 (Includes Internal Assembly)

Rebuilding the General Motors Delco Air six-cylinder A-6 compressor is considered to be a major service operation.* The compressor must be removed from the car and placed on a clean workbench, preferably one that is covered with a clean piece of white paper.

When the service technician works on the internal assembly of a compressor, it is very important that cleanliness and organized work habits be observed.

An adequate service parts stock must be maintained for servicing six-cylinder compressors. Some of the more important parts to be stocked are as follows:

- Piston drive balls
- Shoe discs, ten sizes
- Thrust races, fourteen sizes
- Pistons and piston rings
- Bearings: shaft, thrust, and pulley
- Oil pickup tube

- Suction reed valves
- Discharge reed valves
- Gasket set; O-ring gaskets
- Retainer rings, all sizes
- Discharge crossover tube
- Oil pump gears: drive and driven

The following procedures are based on the use of the proper service tools and on the condition that an adequate stock of service parts is at hand. Part I gives the procedure for rebuilding a six-cylinder compressor and Part II gives the procedure for rebuilding the internal assembly.

The special service tools required are available from the Draf Tool Company and Kent-Moore Tool Company, or from an air-conditioning supply house. The following list serves as a guide to the tool requirements. However, all of the tools may not be necessary for a particular operation. The list also includes all tools suggested by equipment manufacturers as being essential for proper compressor service.

TOOLS

Nonmagnetic feeler gauge set
Compressor holding fixture(s)
Pulley puller
Socket wrench set with 9/16-in thinwall socket
Pulley bearing remover and installer
Oil pickup tube remover
Pressure test connector
Parts tray
Wrenches, pliers, screwdrivers
Torque wrench, in-lb and ft-lb

Snap ring pliers, internal and external
Compressing fixture(s)
Clutch hub holder
Hub and drive plate remover and installer
Internal assembly support block
Needle bearing installer
Suction crossover seal installer
O-ring installer
Micrometer
Dial indicator
Spring tension scale

MATERIALS

Overhaul gasket set
Refrigeration oil

Shaft seal set
Other parts, as required

*Some of the illustrations and charts in this procedure are used by permission of Cadillac Motor Car Division, Buick Motor Division, and Oldsmobile Division of General Motors Corporation, as well as other divisions.

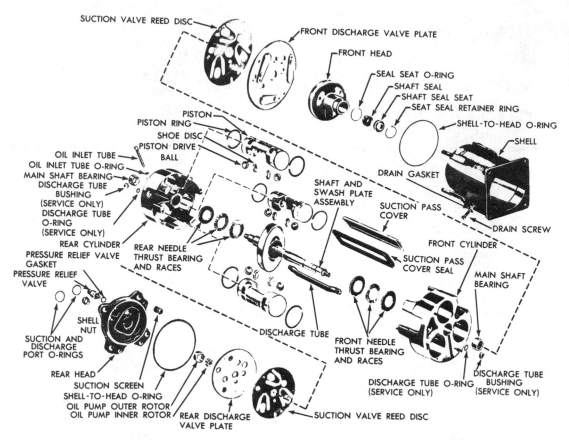

Fig. SP46-1 Exploded view of General Motors six-cylinder compressor

PROCEDURE, PART I

Hub and Drive Plate Removal

1. Mount the compressor in a holding fixture and secure the fixture in a vise.

2. Using a drive plate holding tool and the 9/16-in thinwall socket, remove the locknut from the shaft.

3. Using the snap ring pliers, remove the clutch hub retaining ring. Remove the spacer under the ring.

4. Remove the hub and drive plate with the hub and drive plate remover tool, figure SP46-2.

Fig. SP46-2 Removing the hub and drive plate assembly

Pulley and Bearing Assembly Removal

1. Using the snap ring pliers, remove the pulley and bearing snap ring retainer, figure SP46-3.

2. Place a puller pilot over the crankshaft. Using a pulley puller, remove the pulley, figure SP46-4.

   NOTE: The puller pilot must be in place. Placing the puller against the crankshaft will damage the internal assembly.

Fig. SP46-3 Removing the pulley retaining ring

3. If the pulley bearing is to be replaced, use a sharp tool, such as a small screwdriver, to remove the wire retaining ring.

4. From the rear of the pulley, press or drive the bearing out.

Coil Housing Assembly

1. Scribe the location of the coil housing with relation to the compressor body to insure proper alignment during reassembly.

2. Using snap ring pliers, remove the coil housing retainer ring, figure SP46-5.

3. Lift off the coil housing assembly.

Remove the Shaft Seal Assembly

1. Follow the procedures outlined in Service Procedure 15.

Rear Head, Oil Pump, and Valve Plate Removal

1. Remove the oil sump plug. Remove the compressor from the holding fixture and drain the oil from the compressor into a graduated container.

2. After noting the quantity of oil drained, discard the oil.

Fig. SP46-4 Removing the pulley

Fig. SP46-5 Removing the coil housing retainer ring

Fig. SP46-6 Rear head removal

3. Return the compressor to the holding fixture with the rear head up.

4. Remove the four nuts from the shell studs. Remove the rear head, figure SP46-6. *Take care not to scratch or nick the Teflon surface.*

5. Remove the oil pump drive and driven gears. Set the gears aside in their original position to insure proper reassembly.

6. Remove the rear head-to-shell O-ring and discard.

7. Using two screwdrivers, figure SP46-7, carefully pry up the rear discharge valve plate assembly. Lift out the valve plate assembly.

8. Carefully lift out the suction reed valve.

Remove the Internal Mechanism from the Shell

1. Remove the oil inlet tube and O-ring with the oil inlet tube remover, figure SP46-8. *To avoid damage to the tube and shell do not omit this step.*

2. Carefully remove the compressor assembly from the holding fixture and lay it on its side.

3. Gently tap the front head casting with a soft hammer to slide the internal assembly and head out of the shell.

   Do not attempt to remove the internal assembly without removing the front head with it to avoid serious damage to the Teflon surface.

4. Place the internal assembly and the front head on the support block, figure SP46-9.

5. Carefully remove the front head. *Use extreme caution to prevent damage to the Teflon-coated surface of the front head.*

6. Remove the discharge and suction valve plates from the internal assembly.

7. Remove and discard the front O-ring gasket.

Fig. SP46-7 Removing the rear discharge valve plate

Fig. SP46-8 Removing the oil inlet tube and O-ring

Fig. SP46-9 Remove the internal assembly (held on support block) with the front head

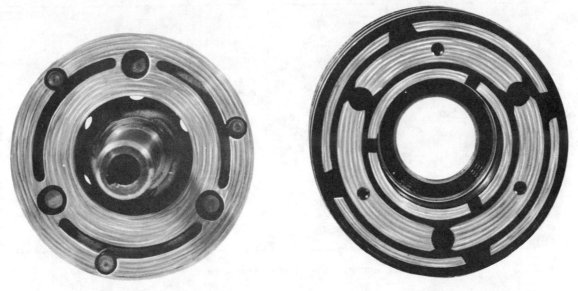

Fig. SP46-10 Scoring of the drive and driven plates is normal. Do not replace for this condition.

Diagnosis

1. If necessary, replace the six-cylinder internal assembly. Otherwise, rebuild the assembly following the procedures outlined in Part II.

2. Examine the front and rear discharge and suction valve plates for damaged or broken valves. Replace any valves that are damaged.

3. Examine the Teflon surfaces on the front and rear heads. If damaged, nicked, or scratched, the head must be replaced.

4. Examine the suction screen in the rear head. If the screen is clogged or damaged, clean or replace it.

5. Examine the oil pump gears. If either gear shows signs of damage or wear, replace both gears.

6. Inspect the seal and seal seat for damage of any kind. If damage is noted, replace the seal assembly.

   NOTE: A new seal is suggested when the compressor is rebuilt.

7. Check the coil for loose connections or cracked insulation. If the coil is checked with an ammeter, the reading should be no more than 3.2 amperes at 12 volts.

8. Check the pulley and bearing assembly. If the frictional surface of the pulley shows signs of warpage due to excessive heat, the pulley should be replaced. Slight scoring, figure SP46-10, is normal. If the assembly is heavily scored, it should be replaced.

9. Check the pulley bearing for signs of excessive noise or looseness. Replace if necessary.

10. Inspect the hub and drive plate. Refer to the comments of step 8.

Replace the Internal Mechanism

1. Place the internal mechanism, oil pump end down, in the support block.

2. Place the suction valve plate and then the discharge valve plate in place over the dowel pins.

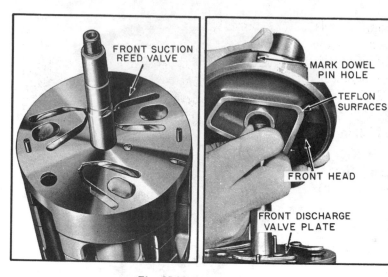
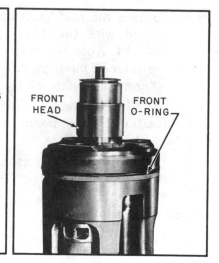

Fig. SP46-11 Installing the front reed valve, head, and O-ring

3. Carefully locate the front head in place over the dowel pins, figure SP46-11. *Take care not to damage the Teflon surface.*

4. Place the front O-ring in position. This O-ring is properly located between the head and discharge valve.

5. Locate the oil pickup tube hole with the center of the shell, figure SP46-12. Slide the shell over the internal assembly.

6. Gently tap the shell in place with a soft hammer. *Do not pinch or distort the O-ring.*

Install the Rear Head Assembly

1. Hold the internal mechanism securely in the shell and invert the assembly. Place the assembly with the front end down in the holding fixture. Secure the fixture in a vise.

2. Insure that the internal mechanism is in the proper position and drop the oil pickup tube in place, figure SP46-13. Some units are equipped with an O-ring. If so equipped, make sure the O-ring is in place.

3. Install the suction valve plate and the discharge valve plate in their proper positions.

4. Install the oil pump gears. Install the rear O-ring gasket.

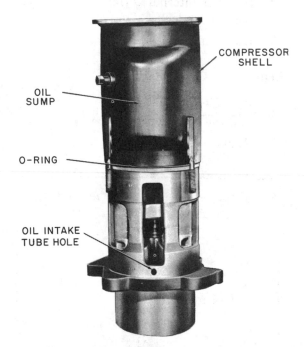

Fig. SP46-12 Replace the shell over the internal assembly

Fig. SP46-13 Installing the oil intake (pickup) tube

5. Position the rear head casting so it is aligned with the dowel pins, figure SP46-14. *Note the position in which the outer oil pump gear must be placed to prevent damage to the Teflon surface of the head.*

6. Position the oil pump and slide the rear head into place.

7. Install the four hex nuts and torque them to 19–23 ft-lb (25.7–31.1 N•m).

Fig. SP46-14 Installing the rear head

Install the Seal Assembly

1. Follow the procedures outlined in Service Procedure 15.

Leak Test the Compressor

1. Follow the procedures outlined in Service Procedure 15.

2. If either internal O-ring leaks, the assembly must be disassembled to find the cause and correct the leak.

3. If no leaks are found, continue with the next procedure.

Replace the Coil Housing

1. Note the original position of the coil housing by the scribe marks.

2. Slip the coil housing into place.

3. Replace the snap ring to secure the housing.

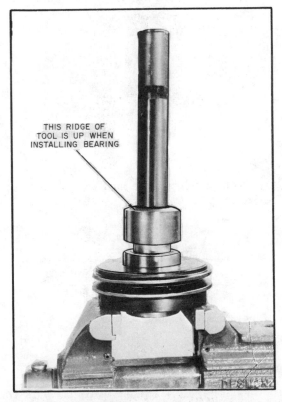

THIS RIDGE OF TOOL IS UP WHEN INSTALLING BEARING

Fig. SP46-15 Installing the pulley and drive plate bearing

Fig. SP46-16 Installing the pulley and drive plate on the compressor

Replace the Pulley and the Bearing Assembly

1. Press the new bearing into the pulley, figure SP46-15, and replace the wire retaining ring (if bearing replacement is necessary).

2. Using the proper tool, figure SP46-16, press or drive the pulley and bearing assembly on the compressor front head.

3. Install the retainer snap ring.

Replace the Hub and Drive Plate

1. Follow the procedures outlined in Service Procedure 15.

2. Turn the clutch hub by hand to insure that it (or the internal assembly) is not dragging or binding.

3. Spin the pulley to insure that it is not dragging or binding. It should turn freely.

Return the Compressor to Service

1. Refill the compressor with 525 viscosity refrigeration oil. If the compressor is being returned to the car, refill it with the same amount of oil that was drained and recorded earlier. If the compressor is being returned to stock, refill it with ten ounces (295 mL) of oil.

2. Return the compressor to stock or service as applicable.

PROCEDURE, PART II

NOTE: If the internal assembly, as shown in figure SP46-17, has sustained major damage, due possibly to the loss of refrigerant and oil, it may be necessary to replace the complete internal assembly rather than replacing individual parts. If further disassembly is considered worthwhile, proceed as follows.

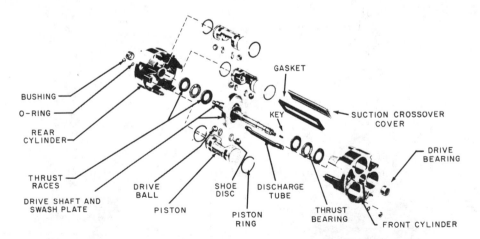

Fig. SP46-17 Exploded view of the internal assembly

Separate the Cylinder Halves

1. To insure that the components are reassembled in their original positions, mark the pistons and the cylinder bores with a prick punch.

Do not mark or punch mark a machined surface.

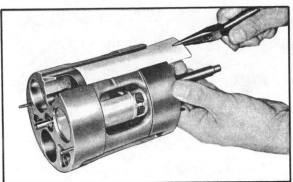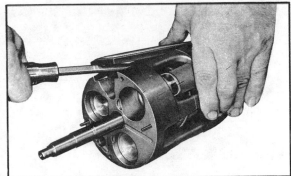

Fig. SP46-18 Removing the suction crossover cover

2. Remove the suction crossover cover, figure SP46-18.

3. Use the discharge remover tool to drive the discharge tube out of the cylinder. Drive the discharge tube toward the rear of the assembly.

4. Position the crankshaft so that the low part of the wobble plate is under the crossover tube toward the rear of the cylinder assembly.

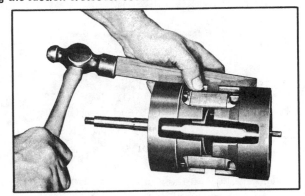

Fig. SP46-19 Separating the cylinder halves

5. Drive the cylinder halves apart and free them from the dowel pins and the discharge crossover. Use a fiber or wooden block and a hammer in this operation. Do not hit the internal assembly with a steel hammer, figure SP46-19.

6. Carefully remove the rear half of the cylinder from the pistons and set the front cylinder half (including the internal parts) into the holding fixture.

7. Push up on the shaft. One at a time, remove the pistons, balls, and shoes.

8. Remove the rings, balls, and shoes from the pistons. Note the notch at one end of the piston which identifies the front end of the piston, figure SP46-21.

9. Replace the pistons, rings, and balls into their proper positions in the parts tray, figure SP46-22.

10. Lay the ball shoes aside.

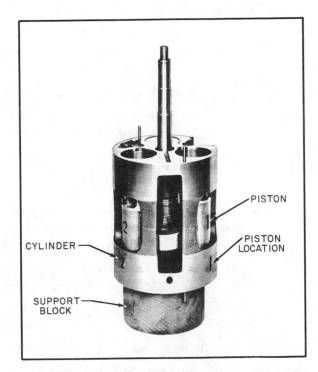

Fig. SP46-20 Piston and cylinder bores numbered

11. Remove the thrust washer and bearing combination from the rear half of the cylinder and place them in their proper positions in the parts tray.

12. Remove the shaft and wobble plate from the front half of the cylinder.

13. Remove the thrust washer and bearing combination from the front half of the cylinder. Place the parts in their proper positions in the parts tray.

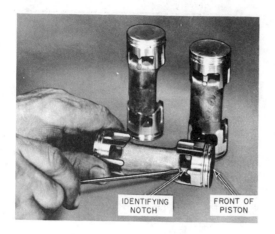

Fig. SP46-21 Piston identification

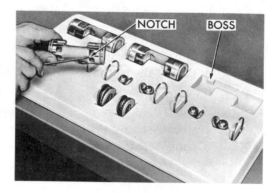

Fig. SP46-22 Parts tray

14. If it is determined that the front and/or rear main bearing must be replaced, use the main bearing tool to drive the bearings from the cylinder halves. If the bearings are not to be replaced, do not remove them.

Inspection and Diagnosis

1. Examine the front and rear thrust washers and bearings. Keep them in the proper position to insure that they can be reassembled correctly. If any or all of these parts shows signs of wear or damage, discard all of them. Otherwise, return them to the parts tray.

2. If the thrust washers and bearings are to be replaced, place two new thrust bearings and four new *zero* thrust races in the parts tray.

3. Examine the rings. For any that are damaged or broken, place new rings in the parts tray.

4. Examine all of the balls. If any are damaged, place new balls in the parts tray.

5. Examine all pistons for chips or cracks. Examine the ball sockets for damage. For those parts found to be damaged, place new ones in the parts tray.

6. Add a zero ball shoe to each front piston ball in the parts tray. If zero ball shoes are not used, select ball shoes of 0.017 in (0.43 mm). The method of obtaining the correct ball shoe size is covered at the end of this procedure.

7. Examine the shaft and the wobble plate. If either part shows signs of damage, both parts must be replaced as an assembly.

8. Examine both cylinder halves. Note that each half is identified with a number stamped into the casting. This identification insures that the halves can be perfectly mated and aligned. If either half is damaged, both must be replaced.

9. Wash all of the parts in a good cleaner, such as clean mineral spirits. Blow the parts dry.

Preparation for Gauging

1. Place the front half of the compression fixture in the holding fixture.

2. Place the front head in the fixture. Note that the front head is not drilled for the oil pickup tube.

3. From the parts tray, select the front thrust washers and bearing and install them on the front cylinder half.

4. Slide the long end of the shaft through the washers, bearing, and front cylinder half.

5. Place the rear thrust washers and bearing into place at the rear of the shaft.

6. Do not install piston rings for the gauging operation.

7. Place a ball and a zero ball shoe in the front part of the piston, figure SP46-23.

   NOTE: Zero ball shoes are usually 0.017 in (0.43 mm). The dimension of the ball shoe can be obtained by measuring the thickness of the shoes removed from compressors.

8. Place a ball in the rear of the piston. Clean lubricant helps to hold the balls in their sockets.

9. Slide this assembly on the wobble plate and slip the front of the piston into the cylinder bore.

   NOTE: The front of the piston is identified with a notch.

10. Repeat steps 7, 8, and 9 with the other two pistons.

11. Install the four compression fixture vertical bolts and tighten them.

12. Align the rear cylinder half with the dowel pins and slide it into place.

13. Install the rear half of the compression fixture. Install the nuts and tighten them to a torque of 19–23 ft-lb (25.7–31.1 N•m).

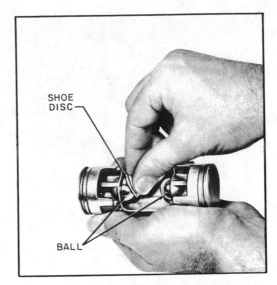

Fig. SP46-23 Zero shoe and ball at front of piston

Gauging Procedures

NOTE: All gauging procedures are to be performed using undamaged feeler gauges and a spring or dial scale of known calibration. Coat the feeler gauges with clean refrigeration oil.

1. Start with the number one piston. Insert a feeler gauge between the ball and wobble plate, figure SP46-24. The gauge should require a pull of 4–8 ounces (113–227 g) for removal. If less than 4 oz (113 g) of pull are required, increase the thickness of the stock. If more than 8 oz (227 g) of pull are required, use a thinner stock.

2. Make a note of the thickness of the stock required to cause a pull of 4–8 oz (113–227 g).

3. Rotate the shaft 120 degrees and recheck the number one cylinder. Make a note of the thickness of the stock required to cause a pull of 4–8 oz (113–127 g) to remove the stock in this position.

4. Rotate the shaft another 120 degrees and repeat the procedure. Note the stock thickness.

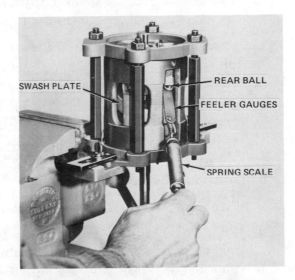

Fig. SP46-24 Checking clearance between the rear ball and the wobble plate

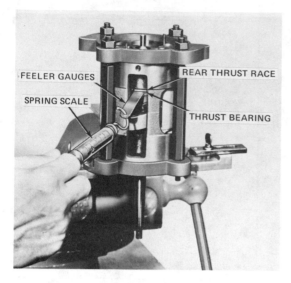

Fig. SP46-25 Checking clearance between the rear thrust bearing and the outer thrust race

SHOE CHART

SERVICE *PART NUMBER	IDENTIFICATION NO. STAMPED ON SHOE
6557000	0
6556180	18
6556190	19
6556200	20
6556210	21

*The last three digits indicate the identification number on the shoes.

THRUST BEARING RACE CHART

Service *Part Number	Thickness Dimension (Inches)	Identification No. Stamped on Race
6556000	0.092 0	0
6556060	0.097 0	6
6556070	0.098 0	7
6556080	0.099 0	8
6556090	0.100 0	9
6556100	0.101 0	10
6556110	0.102 0	11
6556120	0.103 0	12

*The last three digits indicate the identification number on the race.

Fig. SP46-26

5. Repeat steps 1, 2, 3, and 4 with pistons two and three.

6. If new thrust bearings and races are used, proceed with step 7. If the old bearings and races are used, go to step 8.

7. Place a feeler gauge between the thrust bearing and the upper rear thrust race, figure SP46-25. To remove the gauge, a pull of 4–8 oz (113–127 g) should be indicated on the scale. Note the thickness of the gauge.

8. Insure that all pistons are gauged and identified.

Dismantle the Assembly

1. Remove the nuts and the rear ring from the compression fitting.

2. Remove the internal assembly and lay it flat on the bench.

3. Carefully drive the cylinder halves apart, using a fiber or wooden block and a hammer.

4. Place the front cylinder half (including its internal parts) in the holding fixture.

5. Carefully remove the pistons and place them in their proper positions in the parts tray. The pistons will include the balls and ball shoes.

6. It is not necessary to remove the thrust races or bearings.

7. If the original thrust races and bearings are used, disregard this step. If new zero races are used, remove the rear zero race and select a race corresponding to the feeler gauge reading. (If the feeler gauge reading was 0.009 5 in (0.24 mm), use a thrust race stamped 9 1/2; if the gauge was 0.011 in (0.28 mm), use a race stamped 11.) Substitute this race for the zero race removed.

8. Place a rear ball shoe in the parts tray to correspond to the smallest of the three readings obtained when the clearance between the ball and plate is checked, figure SP46-27.

   EXAMPLE: If the readings on piston one are 0.019 in (0.483 mm), 0.019 5 in (0.495 mm), and 0.019 in (0.483 mm), use a shoe marked 19; if the readings are 0.022 in (0.559 mm), 0.021 in (0.533 mm), and 0.022 in (0.559 mm), use a shoe marked 21.

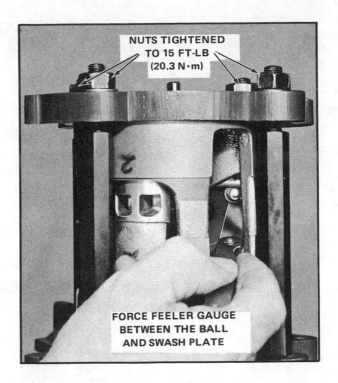

Fig. SP46-27 Checking the drive ball-to-swash plate clearance

NUTS TIGHTENED TO 15 FT-LB (20.3 N·m)

FORCE FEELER GAUGE BETWEEN THE BALL AND SWASH PLATE

9. Assemble the rings on the pistons. The scraper groove is assembled toward the center of the piston.

10. Insure that all parts are clean and free of all foreign matter. All parts must be in their proper positions in the parts tray.

Assemble the Internal Assembly

1. Rotate the wobble plate so that the high point is above the number one cylinder bore.

2. Place a ball in each end of the piston. Place the zero ball shoe at the front end of the piston and a selected ball shoe at the rear of the piston.

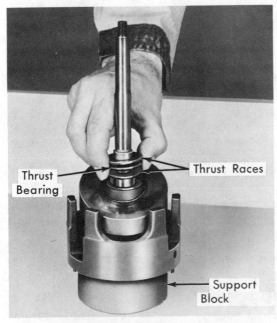

Thrust Bearing

Thrust Races

Support Block

Fig. SP46-28 Front thrust races and bearing

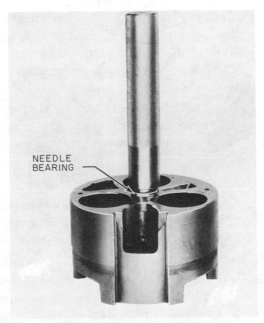

NEEDLE BEARING

Fig. SP46-29 Installing the drive shaft bearing

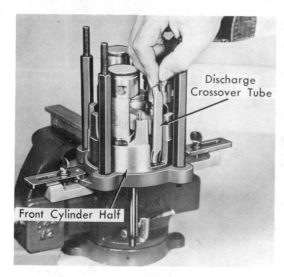

Fig. SP46-30 Installing the service discharge crossover tube

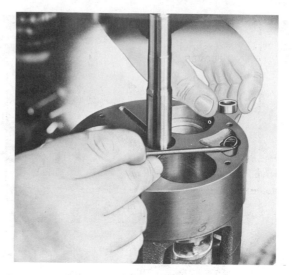

Fig. SP46-31 Installing the service discharge crossover parts

NOTE: The balls and shoes can be held in place using a thin coat of clean petroleum jelly.

3. Locate the ball shoes on the wobble plate. Carefully compress the front ring and place the piston in the front half of the cylinder.

4. Repeat steps 1, 2, and 3 with pistons two and three.

5. Place the discharge crossover tube in the front cylinder half, figure SP46-30. The flattened portion of this tube must face the inside of the compressor to allow clearance for the wobble plate.

6. Carefully place the rear cylinder half in position and insert the pistons into the bores one by one. Compress the rings on each piston to ease them into the bores.

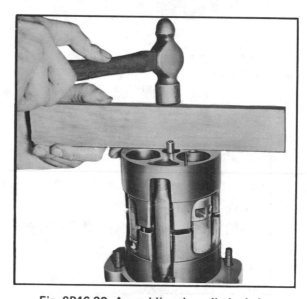

Fig. SP46-32 Assembling the cylinder halves

7. When all of the parts are aligned properly, tap the assembly with a wooden block and hammer to seat the rear cylinder half over the dowel pins, figure SP46-32. If necessary, clamp the assembly in the compression fixture to drive the halves together completely.

8. Install the rear portion of the compression fixture and tighten the nuts to a torque of 19–23 ft-lb (25.7–31.1 N•m).

9. Lubricate the internal mechanism generously with clean refrigeration oil.

10. Check for free operation by rotating the crankshaft. If there is any binding or if tight spots are felt, these conditions must be corrected.

11. Remove the internal assembly from the compression fixture and lay it on a flat surface.

12. Install the suction crossover cover, figure SP46-33 or SP46-34. If the cover is equipped with a gasket, use a piece of flat spring steel 0.015 in to 0.020 in (0.38 to 0.51 mm) thick as a shoehorn to press the gasket in place. This shoehorn is a part of the regular compressor tool assortment for early model compressors.

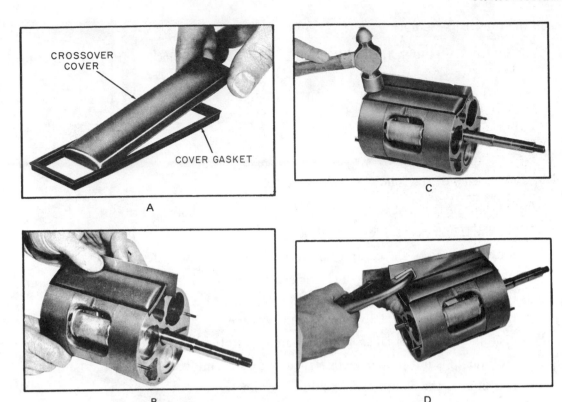

A

B

C

D

Fig. SP46-33 Installing the suction crossover and gasket assembly

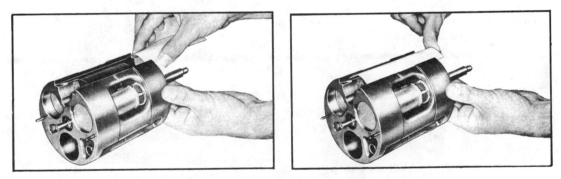

Fig. SP46-34 Installing the suction crossover cover

Fig. SP46-35 The internal mechanism

Install the Internal Assembly

1. The internal assembly, figure SP46-35, is now ready for placement in the compressor shell.

2. Follow the procedures outlined in Part I.

Review

Briefly answer each of the following questions.

1. What tool or instrument is used to separate the cylinder halves of the internal assembly?
2. What is the thickness of a zero ball shoe?
3. Toward which end of the compressor does the notch in the piston rest?
4. If a pull of six ounces (170 g) is sufficient to remove an 0.018-in (0.457-mm) shim on all three checks, what ball shoe should be used?
5. What is the purpose of the discharge crossover tube?
6. What is done if the internal assembly is damaged to the point that repair is not practical?
7. If the oil pump is not properly positioned during assembly, what part will be damaged?
8. The rear nuts of the compressor should be torqued to:

   a. _____ ft-lb   b. _____ N·m

9. When installing the internal assembly into the shell, where must the oil pickup tube hole be located?
10. Aside from having the proper tools, what is considered to be an important factor in rebuilding the compressor?

SERVICE PROCEDURE 47:

Troubleshooting the Air-conditioning System

This procedure is given as a quick reference to enable the service technician to isolate many of the conditions that can cause improper air-conditioning system operation or noise. This procedure is given in four parts to outline the basic four typical customer complaints.

- Part I covers a noisy system. It suggests causes of noise and how to correct the problem.

- Part II covers intermittent cooling which is used as an aid to troubleshoot the customer complaint, "Sometimes it works; sometimes it does not." Suggested causes and corrections are given.

- "It just is not cool enough," a common customer complaint, is covered in Part III. Causes of insufficient cooling and the suggested remedies are given.

- "It does not cool at all," the easiest to diagnose, is covered in Part IV. Possible causes and corrections are given for this complaint.

It should be noted that air-conditioning problems may often be caused by, or may cause, cooling system problems. Conversely, cooling system problems may be caused by, or may cause, air-conditioning system problems. Therefore, it is necessary to work also with Service Procedure 48, "Troubleshooting the Heater/Cooling System," while using this procedure.

TOOLS

As required

MATERIALS

As required

PROCEDURE, PART I

NOISY SYSTEM

Possible Cause	Possible Correction
Loose electrical connection causing "clutch chatter"	Tighten or repair the connection, as necessary.
Defective clutch coil	Replace the clutch coil.
Defective clutch	Replace the clutch.
Defective clutch bearing(s)	Replace the clutch bearing(s).
Loose belt(s)	Tighten the belt(s). Do not overtighten.
Broken belt (if two-belt drive)	Replace both belts as a pair.
Worn or frayed belt(s)	Replace belt(s).
Loose compressor mount	Tighten the compressor mount.
Loose compressor brace(s)	Tighten the compressor brace(s).

Broken compressor mount	Repair or replace the compressor mount.
Broken compressor brace(s)	Repair or replace the compressor brace(s).
Blower fan rubbing against case	Adjust or reposition the blower fan.
Defective blower motor	Replace the blower motor.
Idler pulley bearing(s) defective	Replace the idler pulley assembly or bearing(s), as applicable.

NOISY COMPRESSOR

Overcharge of refrigerant	Purge the system until the charge is correct or recharge the system.
Undercharge of refrigerant	Locate and repair the leak. Recharge the system.
Overcharge of oil	Remove excess oil or replace the oil.
Undercharge of oil	Locate and repair the leak. Replace the oil to the proper level.
Moisture in the system	Purge the system, replace the drier, and evacuate and recharge the system.
Defective compressor	Repair or replace the compressor.

PROCEDURE, PART II

SYSTEM COOLS INTERMITTENTLY

Possible Cause	Possible Correction
Defective circuit breaker	Replace the circuit breaker.
Circuit breaker trips on overload	Correct the problem: short circuit or excessive current draw.
Loose wiring	Repair or replace the wiring.
Defective blower speed control	Replace the control (switch).
Defective blower speed resistors	Replace the resistor block.
Defective blower motor	Replace the blower motor.
Defective clutch coil	Replace the clutch coil.
Loose belt(s)	Tighten the belt(s). Do not overtighten.
Defective clutch brush set	Replace the brush set.
Loose ground connection at blower	Tighten or repair the ground connection.
Loose ground connection at clutch coil	Tighten or repair the ground connection.
Loose ground connection at clutch brush set	Tighten or repair the ground connection.
Clutch slipping; low voltage	Determine the cause and correct it.
Clutch slipping; excessive wear	Replace worn clutch part(s).
Thermostat improperly adjusted	Adjust the thermostat.
Defective thermostat	Replace the thermostat.
Defective low-pressure control	Replace the low-pressure control.
Defective high-pressure control	Replace the high-pressure control.
Defective suction pressure regulator	Replace the suction pressure regulator.
Moisture in the system	Purge the system, replace the drier, and evacuate and recharge the system.

PROCEDURE, PART III

INSUFFICIENT COOLING

Possible Cause

Possible Correction

Blower motor "sluggish" (runs slow)

Check for loose connections. If none, replace the motor.

Clutch slipping; low voltage

Determine the cause and correct it.

Clutch slipping; excessive wear

Replace worn clutch part(s).

Clutch cycles too often

Adjust or replace the thermostat. Replace the low-pressure control.

Defective thermostat

Replace the thermostat.

Defective low-pressure control

Replace the low-pressure control.

Defective suction pressure regulator

Replace the suction pressure regulator.

Insufficient airflow from evaporator

Clean the evaporator and/or repair sticking or binding "blend" doors.

Insufficient airflow over condenser (also see cooling system troubles)

Clean the condenser and/or correct the cooling system problem(s).

Partially clogged screen in receiver-drier.

Replace the receiver-drier.

Partially clogged screen in expansion valve

Clean the screen and replace the drier.

Partially clogged screen in fixed orifice tube

Clean the screen and replace the accumulator

Partially clogged screen in inlet of compressor

Clean the screen, determine the cause, and correct as necessary.

Thermostatic expansion valve remote bulb loose

Clean the contact area and tighten the remote bulb. Wrap with cork tape.

No insulation on TXV remote bulb

Insulate the remote bulb with cork tape.

Moisture in system

Purge the system, replace the drier, and evacuate and recharge the system.

Air in system

Purge the system. Evacuate and recharge the system.

Excess refrigerant in system

Purge the system until correct or purge and recharge the system.

Excess oil in system

Drain oil to the proper level or change the oil.

Partially clogged accumulator

Replace the accumulator.

Partially clogged receiver-drier

Replace the receiver-drier.

Defective thermostatic expansion valve

Replace the thermostatic expansion valve.

Undercharge of refrigerant

Repair the leak, and evacuate and charge the system.

Cooling system problem

See "Troubleshooting the Heater/Cooling System," Service Procedure 48.

PROCEDURE, PART IV

NO COOLING

Possible Cause

Possible Correction

Blown fuse

Correct the problem, if any, and replace the fuse.

Defective circuit breaker

Correct the problem, if any, and replace the circuit breaker.

Broken electrical wire

Repair or replace the wire.

Disconnected electrical wire	Reconnect the wire.
Corroded electrical wire (high-resistance connection)	Clean and reconnect or replace the connector.
Defective clutch coil	Replace the clutch coil.
Defective or worn clutch brush set	Replace the brush set.
Defective blower motor	Replace the blower motor.
Defective thermostat	Replace the thermostat.
Defective low-pressure control	Replace the low-pressure control.
Loose compressor drive belt(s)	Tighten the belt(s). Do not overtighten.
Broken drive belt(s)	Replace the belt(s).
Defective compressor suction valve plate(s)	Replace the suction valve plate(s) and gasket(s).
Defective compressor discharge valve plate(s)	Replace the discharge valve plate(s) and gasket(s).
Blown compressor head or valve plate gasket(s)	Replace head and valve plate gasket(s).
Defective compressor	Rebuild the compressor or replace with a new or rebuilt compressor.
Undercharge or no charge of R-12:	Locate and repair the leak.
a. Compressor shaft seal leaking	Replace the shaft seal and gasket set.
b. Defective hose (leaking R-12)	Replace the defective hose.
c. Fusible plug leaking R-12	Replace the fusible plug (do not repair).
d. Refrigerant leak in system	Locate and correct the leak, as required.
Plugged (clogged) line or hose	Clean or replace the line or hose.
Clogged inlet screen in expansion valve	Clean the screen and replace the drier.
Defective thermostatic expansion valve	Replace expansion valve.
Clogged expansion tube	Clean or replace the expansion tube. Replace the accumulator.
Clogged screen in receiver-drier	Replace the receiver-drier.
Excessive moisture in system	Replace the drier, and evacuate and charge the system.
Clogged screen in accumulator	Replace the accumulator.
Defective suction pressure control	Repair or replace the control.

Review

Select the appropriate answer from the choices given.

1. Which of the following is more likely to be a cause of all four of the customer complaints?

   a. Blown fuse
   b. Loose belt(s)

   c. Overcharge of refrigerant
   d. Defective thermostat

2. Technician A says that worn clutch parts may cause the clutch to slip. Technician B says that low voltage to the clutch coil may cause the clutch to slip.

   a. Technician A is correct.
   b. Technician B is correct
   c. Both technicians are correct.
   d. Both technicians are wrong.

3. Technician A says that an overcharge of refrigerant may cause the compressor to be noisy. Technician B says that an overcharge of oil may cause the compressor to be noisy.

   a. Technician A is correct.
   b. Technician B is correct
   c. Both technicians are correct.
   d. Both technicians are wrong.

4. Which of the following may not be adjusted, but must be replaced?

   a. Thermostat
   b. Low-pressure control

   c. Thermostatic expansion valve
   d. Clutch

5. How is the drier (desiccant) replaced in a CCOT or CCFOT system?

   a. By replacing the receiver
   b. By replacing the accumulator

   c. By replacing the bag of desiccant
   d. By replacing the VIR

SERVICE PROCEDURE 48:

Troubleshooting the Heater/Cooling System

This procedure is given as a quick reference to enable the service technician to isolate many of the conditions that can cause improper engine cooling system and/or heater operation. This procedure is given in three parts: Part I, engine overcooling, Part II, engine overheating, and Part III, loss of coolant. The customer's probable complaint would be for an overheating condition. If the problem is due to a loss of coolant, the customer may complain that coolant or water must be added frequently.

It should be noted that cooling system problems are often caused by, or may cause, air-conditioning system problems. Conversely, air-conditioning problems may be caused by, or may cause, cooling system problems. Therefore, it is necessary to work also with Service Procedure 47, "Troubleshooting the Air-Conditioning System," while using this procedure.

TOOLS

As required

MATERIALS

As required

PROCEDURE, PART I

ENGINE OVERCOOLING

Possible Cause	Possible Correction
Thermostat missing	Install a thermostat and replace the gasket.
Thermostat defective	Replace the thermostat and gasket.
*Defective temperature sending unit	Replace the sending unit.
*Dash gauge (if equipped) defective	Replace the dash gauge.
*Broken or disconnected wire (if dash gauge unit)	Repair or replace the wire.
*Grounded or shorted "cold" indicator wire (if equipped with "cold" lamp)	Repair or replace the wire.

*Symptoms indicating overcooling though engine temperature may be within safe limits.

PROCEDURE, PART II

ENGINE OVERHEATING

Possible Cause	Possible Correction
Collapsed radiator hose	Replace the hose.
Coolant leak	See "Loss of Coolant," Part III.

450

Defective water pump	Replace the water pump and gasket.
Loose fan belt(s)	Tighten the fan belt(s). Do not overtighten.
Defective fan belt(s)	Replace the fan belt(s).
Broken belt (if two-belt drive)	Replace both belts as a pair.
Fan bent or damaged	Replace the fan. Do not straighten.
Fan broken	Replace the fan.
Defective fan clutch	Replace the fan clutch.
Exterior of radiator dirty	Clean the radiator.
Dirty "bug" screen	Clean or remove the screen.
Damaged radiator	Repair or replace the radiator.
Engine improperly timed	Have the engine timed.
Engine out of tune	Have the engine tuned up.
*Temperature sending unit defective	Replace the sending unit.
*Dash gauge (if equipped) defective	Replace the dash gauge.
*Grounded or shorted wire (if dash gauge unit)	Repair or replace the wire.
*Grounded or shorted "hot" indicator wire (if indicator lamp equipped)	Repair or replace the wire.

*Symptoms indicating overheating though engine temperature may be within safe limits.

PROCEDURE, PART III

LOSS OF COOLANT

Possible Cause   **Possible Correction**

Ruptured (leaking) radiator hose	Replace the radiator hose.
Ruptured (leaking) heater hose	Replace the heater hose.
Loose hose clamp	Replace and/or tighten the hose clamp.
Leaking radiator (external)	Have the radiator repaired.
Leaking transmission cooler (internal)	Have the radiator repaired.
Leaking water pump shaft seal	Replace the water pump and gaskets.
Leaking gasket(s)	Replace the gaskets, as required.
Leaking core plug(s)	Replace all core plugs.
Loose engine head(s)	Torque the head(s) to specifications.
Warped head(s)	Have the head(s) milled flat or replace the heads. Install new gaskets and torque to specifications.
Excessive coolant	Adjust the coolant level. May install coolant recovery tank.
Defective radiator pressure cap	Replace the cap.
Incorrect pressure cap	Replace with the proper cap.
Defective thermostat	Replace the thermostat and gasket.
Incorrect thermostat	Replace with proper thermostat.
Rust in system	Have the cooling system cleaned.
Radiator internally clogged	Have the radiator cleaned.
Heater core leaking	Repair or replace the heater core.
Heater shut-off valve leaking	Replace the shut-off valve.

Review

Select the appropriate answer from the choices given.

1. What is one possible cause of engine overcooling and engine overheating?

   a. Loose fan belt(s)
   b. Engine out of tune
   c. Defective fan clutch
   d. Defective thermostat

2. Assume that the temperature gauge (dash) indicates HOT but the engine coolant is in the proper range. The problem may be

   a. a grounded or shorted wire, sending unit to dash gauge.
   b. the engine is improperly timed.
   c. a defective thermostat.
   d. a collapsed radiator hose.

3. Assume that the temperature indicator (lamp) indicates COLD but the engine coolant is in the proper range. The problem may be

   a. a missing thermostat.
   b. a defective fan clutch.
   c. a defective fan belt (or belts).
   d. a defective temperature sending unit.

4. Which of the following would *not* result in a loss of coolant?

   a. Thermostat missing
   b. Defective radiator pressure cap
   c. Internal leak in transmission cooler
   d. Warped head(s)

5. Technician A says that air-conditioning system problems can cause cooling system problems. Technican B says that cooling system problems can cause air-conditioning system problems.

   a. Technician A is correct.
   b. Technician B is correct.
   c. Both technicians are correct.
   d. Both technicians are wrong.

SERVICE PROCEDURE 49:

Replacing Air-conditioning Components

The following procedures are typical for step-by-step replacement of air-conditioning system components. For specific replacement details, refer to the shop service manual for the particular year/model of the unit.

TOOLS

Manifold and gauge set
Vacuum pump

Hand tools, as required

MATERIALS

Refrigeration oil
Gaskets and/or O-rings

Components, as required

PROCEDURE

Preparation

1. Purge the system of refrigerant. See Service Procedure 2.
2. Disconnect the battery (ground cable).
3. Locate the component that is to be removed for repair or replacement.
4. Remove the necessary access panel(s) or other hardware to gain access to the component.

Remove the Component

1. For a thermostatic expansion valve:
   a. Remove the insulation tape and clamp to free the remote bulb.
   b. Disconnect the external equalizer, if the TXV is so equipped.
   c. Remove the liquid line from the inlet of the TXV.
   d. Remove the evaporator inlet fitting from the outlet of the TXV.
   e. Remove the holding clamp (if provided on the TXV) and carefully lift the TXV from the evaporator. Do not damage the remote bulb or capillary tube.
2. For an expansion tube: See Service Procedure 34.
3. For an accumulator:
   a. Remove the accumulator inlet fitting.
   b. Remove the accumulator outlet fitting.
   c. Remove the bracket attaching screw and remove the accumulator from the car.
4. For a compressor:
   a. Remove the inlet and outlet hoses or the service valves from the compressor.
   b. Remove the clutch lead wire. Loosen and remove the belt(s).
   c. Remove the mounting bolts from the compressor brackets and braces and lift the compressor from the car.

5. For a condenser:
   a. Remove the inlet and outlet hoses.
   b. Remove the mounting hardware and lift the condenser from the car.
6. For an evaporator:
   a. Aftermarket (add on) unit:
      1. Remove the inlet hose from the TXV.
      2. Remove the suction line from the evaporator.
      3. Disconnect the electrical lead wire(s).
      4. Remove the mounting hardware and lift the evaporator from the car.
   b. Factory-installed unit:
      1. Remove the inlet hose from the TXV (or VIR, if the automobile is equipped with this device).
      2. Remove the outlet hose from the evaporator, STV, POA, or VIR, as equipped.
      3. Remove the mechanical linkage or vacuum line(s) from the evaporator controls, as equipped.
      4. Remove the mounting bolts and hardware from the evaporator housing.
      5. Carefully lift the evaporator assembly from the car. Do not force the assembly.
7. For a receiver/drier:
   a. Remove the low-pressure switch wire, if the unit is so equipped.
   b. Remove the inlet and outlet hoses from the drier.
   c. Remove the mounting hardware and lift the receiver/drier from the car.
   d. Remove the low-pressure switch from the drier, if the unit is so equipped.
8. For an ETR, EPR, or POEPR valve:
   a. If an ETR valve is used, disconnect the electrical wire.
   b. Remove the two bolts holding the suction service valve to the compressor.
   c. Remove the suction service valve and gasket.
   d. Remove the valve from the compressor cavity.
9. For an STV or POA valve:
   a. Remove the TXV external equalizer from the valve assembly.
   b. Remove the oil bleed line from the valve assembly.
   c. Remove the cable- or vacuum-controlled line(s) or hose(s), if the unit is so equipped.
   d. Remove the valve inlet (evaporator outlet) line from the assembly.
   e. Remove the valve outlet (suction line) hose.
   f. Remove the mounting clamp and lift the assembly from the car.
10. For a VIR:
   a. Disconnect the oil bleed line.
   b. Disconnect the inlet and outlet hoses (from the compressor and the condenser).
   c. Disconnect the inlet and outlet lines (from the evaporator).
   d. Remove the mounting clamp and lift the assembly from the car.
11. For a superheat switch:
   a. Remove the wire from the switch.
   b. Remove the internal snap ring.
   c. Using two screwdrivers, remove the switch.
   d. Remove and discard the O-ring.

Component Replacement

1. Use new gaskets and/or O-rings when replacing a component.
2. Coat all components liberally with clean refrigeration oil before reassembly.
3. For reassembly, reverse the removal procedure.

Return the System to Service

1. Replace any access panels, clamps, or other hardware previously removed.
2. Reconnect the battery ground cable.
3. Evacuate the system as outlined in Service Procedure 4.
4. Charge the system as outlined in Service Procedure 5.

Review

Select the appropriate answer from the choices given.

1. Before installation, all gaskets and O-rings should be coated with

   a. Permatex.
   b. refrigerant.
   c. form-a-gasket.
   d. refrigeration oil.

2. The hot gas discharge hose runs from the

   a. condenser to the drier.
   b. drier to the TXV.
   c. evaporator to the compressor.
   d. compressor to the condenser.

3. On which of the following is an external equalizer *not* found?

   a. Accumulator
   b. Expansion valve
   c. Suction throttling valve
   d. POA valve

4. Technician A says that desiccant is found in the receiver/drier. Technician B says that desiccant is found in the accumulator.

   a. Technician A is correct.
   b. Technician B is correct.
   c. Both technicians are correct.
   d. Both technicians are wrong.

5. The expansion tube is located at or before the

   a. evaporator inlet.
   b. evaporator outlet.
   c. VIR inlet.
   d. POA outlet.

SERVICE PROCEDURE 50:

Component Replacement, Heating/Engine Cooling System

The following procedures are typical for replacement of engine cooling system and heater components. For specific details, refer to the manufacturer's shop service manuals for the particular year/model car being serviced.

TOOLS

Hand tools, as required   Special tools, as required

MATERIALS

Components, as required

PROCEDURE

Preparation

1. Insure that the engine is cool and the cooling system is not pressurized.
2. Open the radiator drain provision and drain the cooling system.

   NOTE: If the coolant is to be reused, drain it into a clean container.

3. Locate the component that is to be removed.
4. Remove the necessary fasteners, panels, wiring or hardware to gain access to the component.

   NOTE: Disconnect the battery ground cable if working under the dash.

Remove the Component

1. For a temperature sending unit:

   a. Disconnect the wire(s) from the sending unit.
   b. Using the proper wrench, remove the sending unit. This is usually a special wrench.

   NOTE: It is not always necessary to drain the cooling system to replace the temperature sending unit.

2. For a heater control valve:

   a. Remove the cable linkage or vacuum hose(s) from the control valve.
   b. Loosen the hose clamps and remove the hoses from the control valve.
   c. Remove the heater control.
   d. Inspect the hose ends removed. If hard or split, cut 0.5 inch (12.7 mm) from damaged ends.

3. For heater hose(s):

   NOTE: It is good practice to replace *all* heater hoses if one is found to be defective.

   a. Remove the hose clamps from both ends of the hose.
   b. Remove the hose. Do not use unnecessary force when removing the hose end from the heater core.

4. For radiator hose(s):

 NOTE: It is good practice to replace *both* radiator hoses if one is found to be defective.

 a. Remove the hose clamps from both ends of the hose.

 b. Remove the hose. Do not use unnecessary force when removing the hose end from the radiator.

5. For a thermostat:

 a. Remove the bolts holding the thermostat housing onto the engine. It is not necessary to remove the radiator hose from the housing.

 b. Lift off the thermostat housing.

 NOTE: Observe pellet-side down position of the thermostat to insure proper replacement. Do not reinstall the thermostat backward.

 c. Lift out the thermostat.

 d. Clean all old gasket material from the thermostat housing and engine mating surfaces.

6. For a radiator:

 a. If fan is shroud equipped, remove the attachments and slide the shroud toward the engine.

 b. Carefully remove the upper and lower radiator hoses from the radiator.

 c. Remove the transmission cooler lines (if automatic transmission equipped) from the radiator. Plug the lines to prevent transmission fluid loss.

 d. Remove the radiator attaching bolts and brackets.

 e. Carefully lift out the radiator.

 NOTE: Take care not to damage the delicate fins of the radiator when removing.

7. For a heater core:

 NOTE: It is often necessary to follow the manufacturer's service manual procedures for heater core service.

 a. Remove the access panel(s) or the split heater/air-conditioning case to gain access to the heater core.

 b. Remove the heater coolant hoses.

 c. Remove the cable and/or vacuum control lines (if equipped).

 d. Remove the heater core securing brackets and/or clamps.

 e. Lift the core from the case. Do not use force. Take care not to damage the fins of the heater core when removing.

8. For a water pump:

 NOTE: It is often necessary to remove such accessories as the power-steering pump, the air-conditioning compressor, the alternator, the air pump, and so forth, to gain access to the water pump. If necessary, refer to the specific manufacturer's service manuals.

 a. Remove the radiator as outlined in procedure 6 if it is necessary to gain access to the water pump.

 b. Loosen and remove all belts.

 c. Remove the fan and fan/clutch assembly and water pump pulley.

 d. Remove accessories as necessary to gain access to the water pump bolts.

 e. Remove the lower radiator hose from the water pump.

 f. Remove the bypass hose, if equipped.

 g. Remove the bolts securing the water pump to the engine.

 NOTE: For reassembly, note the length of the bolts removed. All of the bolts may not be of the same length.

 h. Tap the water pump lightly to remove it from the engine, if necessary.

 i. Clean old gasket material from all surfaces.

Component Replacement

1. Inspect all components removed, such as hoses, clamps, housings, and so forth. Replace any that are found to be defective.

2. Use new gaskets where gaskets are required.

3. For reassembly, reverse the removal procedure.

Return to Service

1. Replace any access panels, clamps, or hardware previously removed.

2. Reconnect the battery ground cable, if previously disconnected.

3. Replace the coolant or install new coolant.

4. Check the cooling system for leaks.

Review

Briefly answer each of the following questions.

1. Which of the following may be replaced without draining the coolant from the system?

    a. Radiator cap

    b. Water pump pulley

    c. Temperature sending unit

    d. All answers are correct.

2. Which of the following may require a special tool for replacement?

    a. Thermostat

    b. Heater control valve

    c. Temperature sending unit

    d. All answers are correct.

3. What precaution is given when removing a radiator?

4. What precaution is given when removing the water pump bolts?

5. What should one observe when removing a thermostat?

GLOSSARY

Absolute Pressure: pressure measured from absolute zero instead of normal atmospheric pressure.

Absolute Temperature: temperature measured on the Rankine and Kelvin thermometers calibrated from absolute zero. The freezing point of water on the Rankine Scale is 492°R (273°K).

Absolute Zero: the complete absence of heat, believed to be –459.67°F (–273.15°C). This is shown as 0° on the Rankine and Kelvin temperature scales.

A/C: abbreviation for air conditioning or air conditioner.

Accumulator: a tank located in the tailpipe to receive the refrigerant that leaves the evaporator. This device is constructed to insure that no liquid refrigerant enters the compressor.

Accumulator-Dehydrator: an accumulator that includes a desiccant. See "Accumulator" and "Desiccant."

Air Conditioner: a device used in the control of the temperature, humidity, cleanness, and movement of air.

Air Conditioning: the control of the temperature, humidity, cleanness, and movement of air.

Air Door: a door in the duct system that controls the flow of air in the air conditioner and/or heater.

Air Inlet Valve: a movable door in the plenum blower assembly that permits the selection of outside air or inside air for both heating and cooling systems.

Air Outlet Valve: a movable door in the plenum blower assembly that directs airflow into the heater core or into the ductwork that leads to the evaporator.

Air Pollution: see "Pollution."

Ambient Air: air surrounding an object.

Ambient Air Temperature: see "Ambient Temperature."

Ambient Compressor Switch: an electrical switch that energizes the compressor clutch when the outside air temperature is 47°F (8.3°C), or above. Similarly, the switch turns off the compressor when the air temperature drops below 32°F (0°C).

Ambient Sensor: a thermistor used in automatic temperature control units to sense ambient temperature. Also see "Thermistor."

Ambient Switch: a switch used to control compressor operation by turning it on or off. The switch is regulated by ambient temperature.

Ambient Temperature: temperature of the surrounding air. In air-conditioning work, this term refers to the outside air temperature.

Ammeter: a meter used to determine the current draw, in amperes, of a circuit or component.

Ampere: a measure of current.

Amplifier: a device used in automatic temperature control units to provide an output voltage that is in proportion to the input voltage from the sensors.

Analog: continuous physical variables, such as voltage or rotation, as opposed to "Digital."

Annealed Copper: copper that has been heat treated to render it workable; commonly used in refrigeration systems.

Antifreeze: a commercially available additive solution used to increase the boiling temperature and reduce the freezing temperature of engine coolant. A solution of 50% water and 50% antifreeze is suggested for year-round protection.

Aspirator: a device that uses suction to move air, accomplished by a differential in air pressure.

A.T.C.: abbreviation for automatic temperature control.

Atmosphere: air.

Atmospheric Pollution: see "Pollution."

Atmospheric Pressure: air pressure at a given altitude. At sea level, atmospheric pressure is 14.696 psia (101.329 kPa absolute).

Atom: the smallest possible particle of matter.

Auto: abbreviation for automatic or automobile.

Auto Control: see "Automatic Control."

Automatic: a self-regulating system or device which adjusts to variables of a predetermined condition.

Automatic Control: a thermostatic dial on the instrument panel that can be set at a comfortable temperature level to control the flow of air automatically.

Automatic Temperature Control: the name of an air-conditioner control system designed to maintain an in-car temperature and humidity level automatically at a preset level or condition.

Auxiliary Seal: a seal mounted outside the seal housing to prevent refrigeration oil from entering the clutch assembly.

Axial: pertaining to an axis; a pivot point.

Back Idler: a pulley that tightens the drive belt; the pulley rides on the back or flat side of the belt.

Back Seat (Service Valve): turning the valve stem to the left (ccw) as far as possible back seats the valve. The valve outlet to the system is open and the service port is closed.

Bellows: an accordion-type chamber which expands or contracts with temperature changes to create a mechanical controlling action such as in a thermostatic expansion valve.

Belt: see "V-belt," "V-groove belt," "Serpentine belt."

Belt Dressing: a prepared spray solution formulated for use on automotive belts to reduce or eliminate belt noise. Not recommended for serpentine belts.

Bimetal: see "Bimetallic."

Bimetallic: two dissimilar metals fused together; these metals expand (or contract) at different temperatures to cause a bending effect. Bimetallic elements are used in temperature sensing controls.

Bimetallic Sensor: a sensor using a bimetallic strip or coil.

Bimetallic Thermostat: a thermostat that uses bimetallic strips instead of a bellows for making or breaking contact points.

Bleeding: slowly releasing pressure in the air-conditioning system by drawing off some liquid or gas.

Blend Air Door: a door in the duct system that controls temperature by blending heated and cooled air.

Blend Airstream: that part of a duct system where heated and cooled air are blended to accomplish the desired output temperature.

Blend Door: see "Blend Air Door."

Blower: see "Squirrel-Cage Blower."

Blower Circuit: all of the electrical components required for blower speed control.

Blower Fan: see "Squirrel-Cage Blower" or "Fan."

Blower Motor: see "Motor."

Blower Motor Relay: see "Blower Relay."

Blower Relay: an electrical device used to control the function or speed of a blower motor.

Blower Resistor: see "Resistor."

Blower Switch: a dash-mounted device that allows the operator to turn the blower motor on/off and/or control its speed.

Boiling Point: the temperature at which a liquid changes to a vapor.

Bore: a compressor cylinder, or any cylindrical hole. The "bore" size is the inside diameter of the hole.

Bowden Cable: a wire cable inside a metal or rubber housing used to regulate a valve or control from a remote place.

Brazing: a high-temperature metal joining process that is satisfactory for units with relatively high internal pressures.

British Thermal Unit (Btu): a measure of heat energy; one Btu is the amount of heat necessary to raise one pound of water one degree Fahrenheit.

Btu: abbreviation for British thermal unit.

Bypass Control Valve: see "Hot Gas Bypass Valve."

Calorie: the smallest measure of heat energy. One calorie is the amount of heat energy required to raise one gram of water one degree Celsius. There are 252 calories in one Btu.

Cam: an off-center member of a turning shaft. A lobe.

Can Tap: a device used to pierce, dispense, and seal small cans of refrigerant.

Can Valve: see "Can Tap."

Capacitor: an electrical device for accumulating and holding a charge of electricity.

Capacity: refrigeration produced, measured in tons or Btu per hour.

Capillary: a small tube with a calibrated length and inside diameter used as a metering device.

Capillary Attraction: the ability of tubular bodies to draw up a fluid.

Capillary Tube: a tube with a calibrated inside diameter and length used to control the flow of refrigerant. In automotive air-conditioning systems, the tube connecting the remote bulb to the expansion valve or to the thermostat is called the capillary tube.

Carbon Monoxide: a hazardous byproduct of burned gasoline. It is odorless and colorless, therefore not easily detected. *Inhalation of carbon monoxide (CO) can be fatal.*

Carbonyl Chlorofluoride: a toxic byproduct of Refrigerant 12 if allowed to come into contact with an open flame or heated metal. The fumes of carbonyl chlorofluoride (COClF) should be avoided.

Carbonyl Fluoride: a toxic byproduct of Refrigerant 12 if allowed to come into contact with an open flame or heated metal. The fumes of carbonyl fluoride (COF_2) should be avoided.

CCFOT: abbreviation for cycling clutch fixed orifice tube.

CCOT: abbreviation for cycling clutch orifice tube.

Celsius: a metric temperature scale using the freezing point of water as zero. The boiling point of water is 100°C (212°F English).

Center-Mount Components: the installation in a heating and air-conditioning system whereby the evaporator is mounted in the center of the firewall on the engine side and the heater core is mounted directly to the rear in the passenger compartment.

Centigrade: a term often used to indicate "Celsius." A term not used in the SI metric system. See "Celsius."

Centimeter: a unit of measure in the SI metric system. One centimeter is equal to 0.393 7 inch in English measure.

CFM: also cfm. Abbreviation for cubic feet per minute.

Change of State: rearrangement of the molecular structure of matter as it changes between any two of the three physical states: solid, liquid, or gas.

Charge: a specific amount of refrigerant or oil by volume or weight.

Charging: the act of placing a charge of refrigerant or oil into the air-conditioning system.

Charging Cylinder: a container with a visual indicator for use where a critical, or exact, amount of refrigerant must be measured.

Charging Hose: a hose with a small diameter constructed to withstand high pressures; the hose is located between the unit and the manifold set.

Charging Station: a unit containing a manifold and gauge set, charging cylinder, vacuum pump, and leak detector. This unit is used to service air conditioners.

Check Relay: see "Check Valve Relay."

Check Valve: a device located in the liquid line or inlet to the drier. The valve prevents liquid refrigerant from flowing the opposite way when the unit is shut off.

Check Valve Relay: an electrical switch to control a solenoid-operated check valve.

Chemical Instability: an undesirable condition caused by the presence of contaminants in the refrigeration system.

CID: abbreviation for cubic-inch displacement.

Circuit Breaker: a bimetallic device used instead of a fuse to protect a circuit.

Clean: see "Purge" and "Flush."

Clutch: a coupling device which transfers torque from a driving to a driven member when desired.

Clutch Armature: that part of the clutch attached to the compressor crankshaft that is pulled in when engaged.

Clutch Coil: see "Clutch Field."

Clutch Field: consists of many windings of wire and is fastened to the front of the compressor. Current applied to the field sets up a magnetic field that pulls the armature in to engage the clutch.

Clutch Plate: see "Clutch Armature."

Clutch Rotor: that portion of the clutch in which the belt rides. The rotor is freewheeling until the clutch is engaged. On some clutches the field is found in the rotor and the electrical connection is made by the use of brushes.

cm: abbreviation for centimeter.

CO: chemical symbol for carbon monoxide.

Cold: the absence of heat.

Comb: see "Condenser Comb."

Combination Valve: used on some Ford car lines, an H-valve having a suction throttling valve and expansion valve combined.

Comfort: a pleasing and enjoyable environment; the removal of excessive heat, moisture, dust, and pollen from the air.

Comfortron: another name for an automatic temperature control.

Complete Circuit: a circuit without interruption in which electrical current may travel to and from the battery.

Compound Gauge: a gauge that registers both pressure and vacuum (above and below atmospheric pressure); used on the low side of the systems.

Compressor: a component of the refrigeration system that pumps refrigerant and increases the pressure of the refrigerant vapor.

Compressor Discharge Pressure Switch: a pressure-operated electrical switch that opens the compressor clutch circuit during high-pressure conditions.

Compressor Displacement: a value obtained by multiplying the displacement of the compressor cylinder or cylinders by a given r/min, usually the average engine speed of 30 mph, or 1 750 r/min.

Compressor Protection Switch: an electrical switch installed in the rear head of some compressors to stop the compressor in the event of a loss of refrigerant.

Compressor Shaft Seal: an assembly consisting of springs, snap rings, O-rings, shaft seal, seal sets, and gasket. The shaft seal is mounted on the compressor crankshaft and permits the shaft to be turned without a loss of refrigerant or oil.

Condensate: water taken from the air; the water forms on the exterior surface of the evaporator.

Condensation: the process of changing a vapor to a liquid.

Condenser: the component of a refrigeration system in which refrigerant vapor is changed to a liquid by the removal of heat.

Condenser Comb: a comb-like device used to straighten the fins on the evaporator or condenser.

Condenser Temperature: the temperature at which compressed gas in the condenser changes from a gas to a liquid.

Condensing Pressure: head pressure as read from the gauge at the high-side service valve; the pressure from the discharge side of the compressor to the condenser.

Conditioned Air: air that is cool, dry, and clean.

Conduction: the transmission of heat through a solid.

Conduction of Heat: the ability of a substance to conduct heat.

Contaminants: anything other than refrigerant and refrigeration oil in the system.

Control Head: the master controls (such as temperature and fan speed) which the driver uses to select the desired system condition.

Convection: the transfer of heat by the circulation of a vapor or liquid.

Cool Pack: a tradename used by Harrison Radiator Division of General Motors to describe their hang-on or underdash (aftermarket) air-conditioning systems.

Coolant: water or a mixture of water and antifreeze used in the cooling system to carry away unwanted engine heat.

Coolant Recovery Tank: see "Expansion Tank."

Coolant Thermostat: see "Thermostat."

Cooling Coil: see "Evaporator."

Cooling System: all of the components that are required to remove heat from the engine. These include the engine water jackets, water pump, radiator, thermostat, pressure cap, and connecting hoses.

Core: the coolant passages and fins of a radiator or heater found between the two header tanks.

Core Hole Plug: see "Core Plug."

Core Plug: commonly known as a "freeze plug," the core plug is a metal cup-shaped disc which is inserted into the engine block to seal holes which were provided to remove casting sand when the block was cast.

Corrosion: the decomposition of metal; caused by a chemical action, usually acid.

Crankcase: see "Sump."

Crankshaft: that part of a reciprocating compressor on which the wobble plate or connecting rods are attached to provide for an up-down or to-fro piston action.

Crankshaft Seal: see "Compressor Crankshaft Seal."

Crossflow Radiator: a radiator in which the coolant flow is from one side to the other, as opposed to a "Vertical Flow Radiator."

Cubic Feet Per Minute: the quantity of air or fluid that will pass a given point in one minute.

Cubic-inch Displacement: the cylinder volume of a compressor as the piston moves from the bottom of its stroke to the top of its stroke, in cubic inches.

Current Draw: the amount of current required to operate an electrical device.

Custom System: a deluxe automotive air-conditioning system that uses both inside and outside air.

Cutoff Switch: an electrical switch which is pressure or temperature operated. The switch is used to interrupt the compressor clutch circuit during certain low- or high-pressure conditions.

Cycle: an event, from start to finish. Also, see "Refrigeration Cycle."

Cycling Clutch: a clutch that is turned on/off to control temperature.

Cycling Clutch Fixed Orifice Tube: an air-conditioning system having a fixed orifice tube (expansion tube) in which the air temperature is controlled by starting and stopping the compressor with a thermostat or pressure control. See "CCFOT."

Cycling Clutch FOT: see "Cycling Clutch Fixed Orifice Tube."

Cycling Clutch Orifice Tube: see "Cycling Clutch Fixed Orifice Tube."

Cycling Clutch System: an air-conditioning system in which the air temperature is controlled by starting and stopping the compressor with a thermostat or pressure control.

Cylinder: a circular tubelike opening in a compressor block or casting in which the piston moves up and down or back and forth; a circular drum used to store refrigerant.

Declutching Fan: an engine cooling fan mounted on the water pump. A temperature sensitive device is provided to govern or limit terminal speed.

Defogger: that part of the heater system designed to clear the windshield of fog haze under certain conditions.

Defrost Door: a small door within the duct system to divert a portion of the delivery air to the windshield.

Defroster: that part of the heater system designed to clear heavy frost or light ice from the inside or outside of the windshield.

Defroster Door: see "Defrost Door."

Dehumidify: to remove water vapor from the air.

Dehydrate: see "Purge" and "Evacuate."

Dehydrator: see "Filter Drier."

Dehydrator Filter: see "Filter Drier."

Deice Switch: a switch used to control the compressor operation to prevent evaporator freezeup.

Delay Relay: see "Time-delay relay."

Density: the weight or mass of a gas, liquid, or solid.

Deoxidized: a tubing or metal surface that is free of oxide formations, which are caused by the action of air or other chemicals.

Depressurize: see "Discharge."

Desiccant: a drying agent used in refrigeration systems to remove excess moisture.

Design Working Pressure: the maximum allowable working pressure for which a specific system component is designed to work safely.

Dew Point: the point where air becomes 100% saturated with moisture at a given temperature.

Diagnosis: the procedure followed to locate the cause of a malfunction.

Diaphragm: a rubber-like piston or bellows assembly which divides the inner and outer chambers of back-pressure-regulated air-conditioning control devices.

Dichlorodifluoromethane: see "Refrigerant 12."

Digital: of or pertaining to digits. Generally refers to a meter, such as an ammeter, that displays numbers as opposed to "Analog."

Diode: an electrical check valve. Current flows only in one direction through a diode.

Discharge: bleeding some or all of the refrigerant from a system by opening a valve or connection and permitting the refrigerant to escape slowly.

Discharge Air: conditioned air as it passes through the outlets and enters the passenger compartment.

Discharge Line: connects the compressor outlet to the condenser inlet.

Discharge Pressure: pressure of the refrigerant being discharged from the compressor; also known as the high-side pressure.

Discharge Pressure Switch: see "Compressor Discharge Pressure Switch."

Discharge Side: that portion of the refrigeration system under high pressure, extending from the compressor outlet to the thermostatic expansion valve inlet.

Discharge Valve: see "High-Side Service Valve."

Displacement: in automotive air conditioning, this term refers to the compressor stroke X-bore.

Distributor: a device used to divide the flow of liquid refrigerant between parallel paths in an evaporator.

Double Flare: a flare on the end of a piece of copper tubing or other soft metal; the tubing is folded over to form a double face.

Downflow Radiator: a radiator in which the coolant flow is from the top tank to the bottom tank, as opposed to a "Crossflow Radiator."

Downstream Blower: a blower arranged in the duct system so as to pull air through the heater and/or air-conditioner core(s).

Drier: a device containing desiccant; a drier is placed in the liquid line to absorb moisture in the system.

Drip Pan: a shallow pan, located under the evaporator core, used to catch condensation. A drain hose is fastened to the drip pan and extends to the outside to carry off the condensate.

Drive Pulley: a pulley attached to the crankshaft of an automobile; this pulley drives the compressor clutch pulley through the use of a belt or belts.

Drying Agent: see "Desiccant."

Duct: a tube or passage used to provide a means to transfer air or liquid from one point or place to another.

EEVIR: abbreviation for evaporator equalizer valves-in-receiver. see "Valves-in-Receiver."

Electromagnet: a temporary magnet created by passing electrical current through a coil of wire. A clutch coil is a good example of an electromagnet.

Electromagnetic Field: the magnetic force created by an electromagnet.

Electronic Leak Detector: an electrically (ac or dc) powered leak detector that emits an audible and/or visual signal when its sensor is passed over a refrigerant leak.

Engine Cooling System: see "Cooling System."

Engine Idle Compensator: a thermostatically controlled device on the carburetor which prevents stalling during prolonged hot weather periods while the air conditioner is operated.

Engine Thermal Switch: an electrical switch designed to delay the operation of the system in cool weather to allow time for the engine coolant to warm up.

Engine Thermostat: a temperature sensitive mechanical device found at the coolant outlet of an engine which expands (opens) or contracts (closes) to control the amount of coolant allowed to leave the engine, based on its temperature.

EPR: see "Evaporator Pressure Regulator."

Equalizer Line: a small-bore line used to provide a balance of pressure from one point to another, as in a thermostatic expansion valve.

Ethylene Glycol: see "Antifreeze."

ETR: see "Evaporator Temperature Regulator."

Evacuate: to create a vacuum within a system to remove all trace of air and moisture.

Evaporation: the process of changing from a liquid to a vapor.

Evaporator: the component of an air-conditioning system that conditions the air.

Evaporator Control Valve: can refer to any of the several types of evaporator suction pressure control valves or devices that are used to regulate the evaporator temperature by controlling the evaporator pressure.

Evaporator Core: the tube and fin assembly located inside the evaporator housing. The refrigerant fluid picks up heat in the evaporator core when it changes into a vapor.

Evaporator Equalizer Valves-in-Receiver: see "Valves-in-Receiver."

Evaporator Housing: the cabinet, or case, that contains the evaporator core. Often, the diverter doors, duct outlets, and blower mounting arrangement are found on the housing.

Evaporator Pressure Regulator: a back-pressure-regulated temperature control device used by Chrysler products.

Evaporator Temperature Regulator: a temperature-regulated device used by Chrysler Air-Temp to control the evaporator pressure.

Expansion: the increase in volume of a gas or a liquid as it becomes heated.

Expansion Plug: see "Core Plug."

Expansion Tank: an auxiliary tank, usually connected to the inlet tank or a radiator, which provides additional storage space for heated coolant. Often called a coolant recovery tank.

Expansion Tube: a metering device, used at the inlet of some evaporators, to control the flow of liquid refrigerant into the evaporator core.

Expansion Valve: see "Thermostatic Expansion Valve."

External Equalizer: see "Equalizer Line."

Fahrenheit: an English thermometer scale using 32° as the freezing point of water, and the boiling point of water as 212°F.

Fan: a device having two or more blades attached to the shaft of a motor. The fan is mounted in the evaporator and causes air to pass over the evaporator. A fan is also a device having four or more blades, mounted on the water pump, which cause air to pass through the radiator and condenser.

Fast Flushing: the use of a special machine to clean the cooling system by circulating a cleaning solution.

Feeler Gauge: see "Nonmagnetic Feeler Gauge."

Field: a coil with many turns of wire located behind the clutch rotor. Current passing through this coil sets up a magnetic field and causes the clutch to engage.

Field Coil: see "Clutch Field" or "Electromagnet."

Filter: a device used with the drier or as a separate unit to remove foreign material from the refrigerant.

Filter Drier: a device having a filter to remove foreign material from the refrigerant and a desiccant to remove moisture from the refrigerant.

Fin Comb: see "Condenser Comb."

Fins: thin metal strips in an evaporator, condenser, or radiator found around the tubes to aid in heat transfer.

Fitz-All: a can tap designed to be used on screw top and flat top disposable refrigerant cans.

Fixed Orifice Tube: a refrigerant metering device, used at the inlet of evaporators, to control the flow of liquid refrigerant allowed to enter the evaporator. See "FOT."

Flare: a flange or cone-shaped end applied to a piece of tubing to provide a means of fastening to a fitting.

Flash Gas: gas resulting from the instantaneous evaporation of refrigerant in a pressure-reducing device such as an expansion valve or a fixed orifice tube.

Flooding: a condition caused by too much liquid refrigerant being metered into the evaporator.

Fluid: a liquid, free of gas or vapor.

Fluorocarbon: pertains to a group of refrigerants; R-12, for example, is a fluorocarbon.

Flush: to remove solid particles such as metal flakes or dirt. Refrigerant passages are purged with refrigerant.

Flux: a substance used in the joining of metals when heat is applied to promote the fusion of metals.

Foaming: the formation of a froth of oil and refrigerant due to the rapid boiling out of the refrigerant dissolved in the oil when the pressure is suddenly reduced.

Foot-pound: a unit of energy required to raise one pound a distance of one foot.

Forced Air: air that is moved mechanically such as by a fan or blower.

FOT: abbreviation for fixed orifice tube. See "Fixed Orifice Tube."

Freeze Plug: see "Core Plug."

Freeze Protection: controlling evaporator temperature so that moisture on its surface does not freeze and block the airflow.

Freezeup: failure of a unit to operate properly due to the formation of ice at the expansion valve.

Freezing Point: the temperature at which a given liquid solidifies. Water freezes at 32°F (0°C); this value is its freezing point.

Freon: registered trademark of E.I. Dupont.

Freon 12: see "Refrigerant 12."

Front Idler: a groove pulley used in automotive air conditioning as a means of tightening the drive belt. The belt rides in the pulley groove(s).

Front-of-Dash Components: the installation of heating and air-conditioning components which are mounted on the firewall in the engine compartment.

Front Seat: closing of the compressor service valves by turning them as far as possible in the clockwise direction.

Front Seating: closing off the line leaving the compressor open to the service port fitting. This allows service to the compressor without purging the entire system. *Never* operate the system with the valves front seated.

Frosting Back: the appearance of frost on the tailpipe and suction line extending back as far as the compressor.

Ft-Lb: abbreviation for foot pound.

Functional Test: see "Performance Test."

Fuse: an electrical device used to protect a circuit against accidental overload or unit malfunction.

Fusible Link: a type of fuse made of a special wire which melts to open a circuit when current draw is excessive.

Fusion: the act of melting.

Gas: a vapor having no particles or droplets of liquid.

Gasket: a thin layer of material or composition that is placed between two machined surfaces to provide a leakproof seal between them.

Gauge Manifold: see "Manifold."

Gauge Set: two or more instruments attached to a manifold and used for measuring or testing pressure.

Genetron 12: registered trademark of Allied Chemicals Company (Refrigerant 12).

Gram: a unit of measure in the metric system. One gram is equal to 0.035 3 ounce in the English system.

Halide Leak Detector: a device consisting of a tank of acetylene gas, a stove, chimney, and search hose used to detect leaks by visual means.

Halogen Leak Detector: see "Electronic Leak Detector."

Head: that part of a compressor that covers the valve plates and separates the high side from the low side.

Header Tanks: the top and bottom tanks (downflow) or side tanks (crossflow) of a radiator. The tanks in which coolant is accumulated or received.

Headliner: that part of the automobile interior overhead or covering the roof inside. Some early air conditioners had ductwork in the headliner.

Head Pressure: pressure of the refrigerant from the discharge reed valve through the lines and condenser to the expansion valve orifice.

Heat: energy; any temperature above absolute zero.

Heat Exchanger: an apparatus in which heat is transferred from one fluid to another, on the principle that heat moves to an object with less heat.

Heat Intensity: the measurement of heat concentration with a thermometer.

Heat of Respiration: the heat given off by ripening vegetables or fruits in the conversion of starches and sugars.

Heat Quantity: the amount of heat as measured on a thermometer. See "British Thermal Unit."

Heat Radiation: the transmission of heat from one substance to another while passing through, but not heating, intervening substances.

Heat Transmission: any flow of heat.

Heater Core: a water-to-air heat exchanger which provides heat for the passenger compartment.

Heater Hose: rubber or composition lines used to move heated coolant to the heater and back to the cooling system.

Heater Valve: a manual or automatic valve in the heater hose used to open (start) or close (stop) coolant flow to the heater core.

Heliarc: the act of joing two pieces of aluminum or stainless steel using a high-frequency electric weld and an inert gas, such as argon. This weld is made electrically while the inert gas is fed around the weld. This gas prevents oxidation by keeping the surrounding air away from the metals being welded.

Hg: chemical symbol for mercury (used to identify a vacuum).

High Head: a term used when the head (high-side) pressure of the system is excessive.

High Heat Load: refers to the maximum amount of heat that can be absorbed by R-12 as it passes through the evaporator.

High-load Condition: those instances when the air conditioner must operate continuously at its maximum capacity to provide the cool air required.

High-pressure Control: see "High-pressure Cutoff Switch."

High-pressure Cutoff Switch: an electrical switch that is activated by a predetermined high pressure. The switch opens a circuit during high-pressure periods.

High-pressure Lines: the lines from the compressor outlet to the expansion valve inlet; these lines carry high-pressure liquid and gas.

High-pressure Relief Valve: a mechanical device designed so that it releases the extreme high pressures of the system to the atmosphere.

High-pressure Switch: see "High-pressure Cutoff Switch."

High-pressure Vapor Line: see "Discharge Line."

High Side: see "Discharge Side."

High-side Pressure: see "Discharge Pressure."

High-side Service Valve: a device located on the discharge side of the compressor; this valve permits the service technician to check the high-side pressures and perform other necessary operations.

High Suction: the low-side pressure is higher than normal due to a malfunction of the system.

High Vacuum: a vacuum below 500 microns (0.009 6 psia or 0.66 kPa).

High-vacuum Pump: a two-stage vacuum pump that has the capability of pulling below 500 microns (0.009 6 psia or 0.66 kPa). Many vacuum pumps can pull to 25 microns (0.005 psia or 0.003 kPa).

Hot Gas: the condition of the refrigerant as it leaves the compressor until it gives up its heat and condenses.

Hot Gas Bypass Line: the line that connects the hot gas bypass valve outlet to the evaporator outlet. Metered hot gas flows through this line.

Hot Gas Bypass Valve: a device used to meter hot gas back to the evaporator through the bypass line to prevent condensate from freezing on the core.

Hot Gas Defrosting: the use of high-pressure gas in the evaporator to remove frost.

Humidify: to add moisture to the atmosphere. To increase the relative humidity.

Humidity: see "Moisture."

H-Valve: an expansion valve with all parts contained within used on some Chrysler and Ford car lines.

Hydrochloric Acid: a corrosive acid produced when water and R-12 are mixed as within an automotive air-conditioning system.

Hydrolizing Action: the corrosive action within the air-conditioning system induced by a weak solution of hydrochloric acid formed by excessive moisture chemically reacting with the refrigerant.

Hydrometer: a device used to measure the specific gravity of the coolant to determine its freezing temperature.

Ice Melting Capacity: refrigerant equal to the latent heat of fusion of a stated weight of ice at 144 Btu per pound.

ID: also id. Abbreviation for inside diameter.

Ideal Humidity: a relative humidity of 45% to 50%.

Ideal Temperature: temperature from 68° to 72°F (20° to 22.2°C).

Idler: a pulley device that keeps the belt whip out of the drive belt of an automotive air conditioner. The idler is used as a means of tightening the belt.

Idler Eccentric: a device used with the idler pulley as a means of tightening the belt.

Impeller: a rotating member with fins or blades used to move liquid. The rotating part of a water pump, for example.

In-car Sensor: a thermistor used in automatic temperature control units for sensing the in-car temperature. Also, see "Thermistor."

Inches of Mercury: an English unit of measure when referring to a vacuum; abbreviated inHg.

Inch-pound: a unit of energy required to raise one pound a distance of one inch; abbreviated in-lb.

In-duct Sensor: a thermistor used in automatic temperature control units for sensing the in-duct return air temperature. Also, see "Thermistor."

In-Lb: abbreviation for inch-pounds.

Inside Diameter: the measure across the inside walls of a tube or pipe at its widest point.

Insulate: to isolate or seal off with a nonconductor.

Insulation Tape: tape (either rubber or cork) that is used to wrap refrigeration hoses and lines to prevent condensate drip.

In-vehicle Sensor: see "In-car Sensor."

Isotron 12: a trademark of Penn Salt Company (Refrigerant 12).

Junction: a point where two or more components, such as electrical wires or vacuum hoses, are joined.

Junction Block: a device on which two or more junctions may be found.

Kelvin: a thermometer scale using 273°K as the freezing point of water. Absolute zero is the beginning of this temperature scale: 0°K.

Kilogram: a unit of measure in the metric system. One kilogram is equal to 2.205 pounds in the English system.

Kilopascal: a unit of measure in the metric system. One kilopascal is equal to 0.145 pound per square inch (psi) in the English system.

Kilopascal Absolute: see "kPa Absolute."

Kinetic: refers to motion.

kPa: abbreviation for kilopascal.

kPa Absolute: a metric unit of measure for pressure measured from absolute zero.

kPa Gauge: a metric unit of measure for pressure measured from atmospheric or sea-level pressure.

Latent Heat: the amount of heat required to cause a change of state of a substance without changing its temperature.

Latent Heat of Condensation: the quantity of heat given off while changing a substance from a vapor to a liquid.

Latent Heat of Evaporation: the quantity of heat required to change a liquid into a vapor without raising the temperature of the vapor above that of the original liquid.

Latent Heat of Fusion: the amount of heat that must be removed from a liquid to cause it to change to a solid without causing a change of temperature.

Latent Heat of Vaporization: see "Latent Heat of Evaporation."

Leak Detector: see "Halide Leak Detector" or "Halogen Leak Detector."

LED: abbreviation for light emitting diode.

Light-emitting Diode: a diode that emits a light when current passes through it. LEDs are available in many colors, such as red, green, and yellow. See "Diode."

Liquefier: same as condenser. See "Condenser."

Liquid: a column of fluid without gas pockets or solids.

Liquid Line: the line connecting the drier outlet with the expansion valve inlet. The line from the condenser outlet to the drier inlet is sometimes called a liquid line.

Liter: a metric unit of measure. One liter is equal to 0.264 2 gallon in the English system.

Load: the required rate of heat removed in a given time.

Low-head Pressure: the high-side pressure is lower than normal due to a malfunction of the system.

Low Pressure: usually refers to system pressure below normal; less than expected for a given condition.

Low-pressure Control: see "Low-pressure Cutoff Switch."

Low-pressure Cutoff Switch: an electrical switch that is activated by a predetermined low pressure. This switch opens a circuit during certain low-pressure periods.

Low-pressure Line: see "Suction Line."

Low-pressure Side: see "Suction Side."

Low-pressure Switch: see "Low-pressure Cutoff Switch."

Low-pressure Vapor Line: see "Suction Line."

Low Side: see "Suction Side."

Low-side Service Valve: a device located on the suction side of the compressor which allows the service technician to check low-side pressures or perform other necessary service operations.

Low-suction Pressure: pressure lower than normal in the suction side of the system due to a malfunction of the unit.

Low Voltage: usually refers to voltage below normal; less than expected for a given condition.

Lubricant: a lubricating material such as grease or oil; see "Refrigeration Oil."

Magnetic Clutch: a coupling device used to turn the compressor on and off electrically.

Manifold: a device equipped with a hand shutoff valve. Gauges are connected to the manifold for use in system testing and servicing.

Manifold Gauge: a calibrated instrument used to measure pressures in the system.

Manifold Gauge Set: a manifold complete with gauges and charging hoses.

Manifold Vacuum: an unregulated vacuum source at the intake manifold of an engine. See "Vacuum."

Mean Altitude: 900 feet (274.3 m) is used as the mean, or average, altitude by engineers.

Melting Point: the temperature above which a material cannot exist as a solid at a given pressure.

Mercury: see "Hg."

Meter: to regulate the flow of a fluid or gas. Also, a unit of measure in the metric system. One meter is equal to 39.37 inches in the English system.

Metering Device: any device that meters or regulates the flow of a liquid or vapor. See "Thermostatic Expansion Valve," "Fixed Orifice Tube," and "Expansion Tube."

Micron: a unit of measure; 1 000 microns = 1 mm = 0.039 37 in.

Milliliter: a unit of metric measure. One milliliter is equal to 0.033 8 liquid ounce in the English system.

Millimeter: a metric unit of measure; 1 millimeter = 1/1 000 meter = 0.039 37 inch.

Mineral Spirits: a petroleum distillate that is suitable for use as a solvent.

mm: abbreviation for millimeter.

Mobil Gel: a trade name. See "Desiccant."

Mobil Sorbead: a drying agent. See "Desiccant."

Modulated Vacuum: a vacuum signal that is regulated to a particular level. See "Vacuum."

Moisture: droplets of water in the air; humidity, dampness or wetness.

Molecular Sieve: a drying agent. See "Desiccant."

Monochlorodifluoromethane: see "Refrigerant 22."

Motor: an electrical device which produces a continuous turning motion. A motor is used to propel a fan blade or a blower wheel.

Mount and Drive: pulleys, mounting plates, belts, and fittings necessary to mount a compressor and clutch assembly on an engine.

Muffler: a hollow tubular device used in the discharge line of some air conditioners to minimize the compressor noise transmitted to the inside of the car. Some units use a muffler on the low side as well.

Newton-meter: a unit of measure in the metric system. One newton-meter is equal to 0.737 ft-lb or 8.844 in-lb.

Nichrome Wire: wire made of an alloy of nickel (Ni) and chromium (Cr) that withstands high temperatures. Used for dropping resistors in blower speed controls.

N·m: abbreviation for newton-meter.

Nonmagnetic Feeler Gauge: thin strip(s) of metal of calibrated thickness made of nonferrous metals to check air gap of components that may have a magnetic field.

OD: also, od. Abbreviation for outside diameter.

Ohmmeter: an electrical instrument used to measure the resistance, in ohms, of a circuit or component.

Oil: an organic chemical used as a lubricant. A specially formulated oil is used in air-conditioning systems.

Oil Bleed Line: an external line that usually bypasses an expansion valve, evaporator pressure regulator, or bypass valve to insure positive oil return to the compressor at high compressor speeds and under a low charge or clogged system condition.

Oil Bleed Passage: internal orifice that bypasses an expansion valve, evaporator pressure regulator, or bypass valve to insure a positive oil return to the compressor.

Oil Injection Cylinder: a special cylinder that may be used to inject a measured amount of refrigeration oil into the system.

Oil Injector: see "Oil Injection Cylinder."

Operational Test: see "Performance Test."

Orifice Tube: see "Expansion Tube" or "Fixed Orifice Tube."

O-ring: a synthetic rubber gasket with a round (O-shaped) cross section.

Outside Diameter: the measure across the outside walls of a tube or pipe at its widest point.

Overcharge: indicates that too much refrigerant or refrigeration oil is added to the system.

Oxidize: the formation of a crust on certain metals due to the reaction of the metal, heat, and oxygen.

Ozone: a form of oxygen, O_3.

Ozone Depletion: the reduction of the ozone layer due to contamination, such as by the release of refrigerants into the atmosphere. See "Ozone Layer."

Ozone Layer: also called Ozonosphere. A layer at a height of about 20 miles (32 kilometers) having a high concentration of ozone.

Package Tray: shelf behind the rear seat in a sedan. Trunk-mounted air-conditioner units use ducts through the package tray as the intake and outlets of the unit.

Parts per Million: the unit used to measure the amount of moisture in refrigerant. The maximum (desirable) moisture content is ten parts of moisture to one million parts of refrigerant, or 10 ppm.

Performance Test: readings of the temperature and pressure under controlled conditions to determine if an air-conditioning system is operating at full efficiency.

Phosgene Gas: a highly toxic gas, carbonyl chloride ($COCl_2$). Until recently, it was believed that phosgene gas was produced when R-12 came into contact with heated metal or an open flame. It is now known that little or none of this gas is produced in this manner.

Photovoltaic Diode: a device having a junction of two dissimilar metals that produces an electrical signal proportional to the amount of light that strikes it.

Pickup Tube: a tube extending from the outlet of the receiver almost to the bottom of the tank to insure that 100% liquid is supplied to the liquid line or metering device.

Pilot-operated Evaporator Pressure Regulator: an EPR valve that is regulated by an internal pilot valve pressure.

Piston: a cylindrical part that moves up and down or back and forth in a compressor cylinder.

Plenum: see "Plenum Chamber."

Plenum Blower Assembly: located on the engine side of the firewall, this assembly contains air ducts, air valves, and a blower that permits the selection of air from the outside or inside of the car and directs it to the evaporator or to the heater core if desired.

Plenum Chamber: an area, filled with air at a pressure that is slightly higher than the surrounding air pressure, such as the chamber just before the blower motor.

POASTV: see "Positive Absolute Suction Throttling Valve."

POA Valve: see "Positive Absolute Suction Throttling Valve."

POEPR: the abbreviation for pilot-operated evaporator pressure regulator.

Pollen: an irritant to those who suffer from hay fever or other allergies. The fine, yellowish powder from the anthers of flowers.

Positive Absolute Suction Throttling Valve: a suction throttling valve used by Delco Air. This valve has a bronze bellows under a nearly perfect vacuum which is not affected by atmospheric pressure.

Potentiometer: see "Rheostat."

Pounds Per Square Inch Absolute: pressure which is not compensated or adjusted for altitude or other variables.

Power Servo: a servo unit used in automatic temperature control which is operated by a vacuum or an electrical signal.

PPM: also, ppm. Abbreviation for "Parts Per Million."

Pressure: force per unit of area; the pressure of refrigerant is measured in pounds per square inch.

Pressure Cap: a radiator cap which increases the pressure of the cooling system and allows higher operating temperatures.

Pressure Drop: the difference in pressure between any two points; a pressure drop may be caused by a restriction or friction.

Pressure Line: although all refrigerant lines are under pressure, the term "pressure line" refers to the discharge line. See "Discharge Line."

Pressure Sensing Line: see "Remote Bulb."

Pressure Switch: an electrical switch that is actuated by a predetermined low or high pressure. A pressure switch is generally used for system protection.

Pressure Tester: a device used to pressure test the cooling system and pressure cap to insure that the systems are not leaking under pressure.

Prestone 12: a tradename of the Union Carbon and Carbide Chemical Company (Refrigerant 12).

Primary Seal: a seal between the compressor shaft seal and the shaft to prevent the leakage of refrigerant and oil.

Programmer: that part of an automatic temperature control system that controls the blower speed, air mix doors, and vacuum diaphragms.

Propane: a flammable gas used in the halide leak detector.

Psi: abbreviation for pounds per square inch.

Psia: abbreviation for pounds per square inch absolute.

Psig: abbreviation for pounds per square inch gauge.

Psychrometer: see "Sling Psychrometer."

Pulley: a flat wheel with a V-groove machined around the outer edge; when attached to the drive and driven members, the pulley provides a means of driving the compressor.

Pump: the compressor. Also refers to the vacuum pump.

Pumpdown: see "Evacuate."

Purge: to remove moisture and/or air from a system or a component by flushing with a dry gas refrigerant to remove all refrigerant from a system.

Quick Coupler: a coupler that allows hoses to be quickly connected and/or disconnected. Most shop air hoses, for example, are equipped with quick couplers.

R-12: abbreviation for Refrigerant 12.

Radial Compressor: a space-saving compressor used on small cars.

Radiation: the transfer of heat without heating the medium through which it is transmitted.

Radiator: a coolant to air heat exchanger. The device that removes heat from coolant passing through it.

Radiator Cap: see "Pressure Cap."

Radiator Core: see "Core."

Radiator Hose: rubber or synthetic tubes used to carry coolant from the engine to the radiator and from the radiator to the engine.

Radiator Pressure Cap: see "Pressure Cap."

Radiator Pressure Test: see "Pressure Test."

Ram Air: air that is forced through the radiator and condenser coils by the movement of the vehicle or the action of the fan.

Ranco Control: a tradename used when referring to a thermostat. See "Thermostat."

Rankine: a thermometer scale for which the freezing point of water is 492°R. Absolute zero is the beginning of this thermometer scale.

Receiver: a container for the storage of liquid refrigerant.

Receiver/Dehydrator: a combination container for the storage of liquid refrigerant and a desiccant.

Receiver/Drier: see "Receiver/Dehydrator."

Reciprocating Compressor: an air-conditioning compressor in which the pistons move up and down or back and forth.

Recovery Tank: see "Expansion Tank."

Red Dye Trace Solution: the dye shows the exact location of a leak in the air-conditioning system by depositing a colored film around the leak.

Reed Valves: thin leaves of steel located in the valve plate of automotive compressors; these leaves act as suction and discharge valves. The suction valve is located on the bottom of the valve plate and the discharge valve is on top.

Refrigerant: the chemical compound used in a refrigeration system to produce the desired cooling.

Refrigerant 12: the refrigerant used in automotive air conditioners, as well as other air-conditioning and refrigeration systems. The chemical name of Refrigerant 12 is dichlorodifluoromethane. The chemical symbol is CCl_2F_2.

Refrigerant 22: a refrigerant used in some early automotive applications. Refrigeration 22 is not used today for automotive air conditioning because of high pressures. However, R-22 is a popular refrigerant for domestic and commercial air-conditioning and refrigeration systems. The chemical name and symbol of this refrigerant are: monochlorodifluoromethane and $CHClF_2$.

Refrigeration: the removal of heat by mechanical means.

Refrigeration Cycle: the complete cycle of the refrigerant back to the starting point, evidenced by temperature and pressure changes.

Refrigeration Oil: highly refined oil free from all contaminants, such as sulfur, moisture, and tars.

Relative Humidity: the actual moisture content of the air in relation to the total moisture that the air can hold at a given temperature.

Relay: an electrical switch device that is activated by a low-current source and controls a high-current device.

Remote Bulb: a sensing device connected to the expansion valve by a capillary tube. This device senses the tailpipe temperature and transmits pressure to the expansion valve for its proper operation.

Remote Sensing Bulb: see "Remote Bulb."

Resistance: the property of a substance that impedes current and results in the dissipation of power in the form of heat.

Resistor: a voltage dropping device, usually wire wound, which provides a means of controlling fan speeds.

Restriction: a blockage in the air-conditioning system caused by a pinched or crimped line, foreign matter, or moisture freezeup.

Restrictor: an insert fitting or device used to control the flow of refrigerant or refrigeration oil.

Reverse Flush: a method of cleaning an engine and/or radiator by flushing in a direction opposite of normal coolant flow, under pressure.

Revolutions Per Minute: the number of times a moving member rotates through 360° in one minute.

Rheostat: a wire-wound variable resistor used to control blower motor speeds.

R/min: also, r/min. Abbreviation for revolutions per minute.

Room Temperature: with reference to the temperature range of 68°F (20°C) to 72°F (22.2°C).

Rotary Vacuum Valve: that part of a vacuum control that is used to divert a vacuum signal for operation of doors, switches, and/or valves.

Rotor: the rotating or freewheeling portion of a clutch; the belt sides on the rotor.

RPM: also, rpm. Abbreviation for "Revolutions Per Minute."

Saddlebag: air chambers or openings in the left and right front corners of the car body between the kickpads and the exterior of the car. The evaporator is sometimes located in the right saddle bag.

Safety Glasses: eyeglasses with shatterproof lenses worn for eye protection.

Safety Goggles: goggles worn over eyeglasses for eye protection.

Saturated Desiccant: a desiccant that contains all of the moisture it can hold at a given temperature.

Saturated Drier: see "Saturated Desiccant."

Saturated Point: the point at which matter must change state at any given temperature and pressure.

Saturated Temperature: the boiling point of a refrigerant at a particular pressure.

Saturated Vapor: saturation indicates that the space holds as much vapor as possible. No further vaporization is possible at this particular temperature.

Schrader Valve: a spring-loaded valve similar to a tire valve. The Schrader valve is located inside the service valve fitting and is used on some control devices to hold refrigerant in the system. Special adapters must be used with the gauge hose to allow access to the system.

Screen: a metal mesh located in the receiver, expansion valve, and compressor inlet to prevent particles of dirt from circulating through the system.

Sending Unit: that part of a temperature or pressure warning device that triggers or transmits a warning signal to the dash gauge or lamps.

Sensible Heat: heat that causes a change in the temperature of a substance, but does not change the state of the substance.

Sensor: a temperature-sensitive unit such as a remote bulb or thermistor. See "Remote Bulb" and "Thermistor."

Serpentine: curving or winding.

Serpentine Belt: a flat or V-groove belt that winds through all of the engine accessories to drive them off the crankshaft pulley.

Service Port: fitting found on the service valves and some control devices; the manifold set hoses are connected to this fitting.

Service Valve: see "High-side (Low-side) Service Valve."

Shaft Seal: see "Compressor Shaft Seal."

Short Cycling: can be caused by poor air circulation or a maladjusted thermostat. The unit runs for very short periods.

Side Dash Components: the installation of heating and air-conditioning components which has the evaporator mounted on the curb side of the firewall in the engine compartment and the heater core in back, in the passenger compartment.

Sight Glass: a window in the liquid line or in the top of the drier; this window is used to observe the liquid refrigerant flow.

Silica Gel: a drying agent used in many automotive air conditioners because of its ability to absorb large quantities of water.

Silver Solder: an alloy containing from 5% to 45% silver. Silver solder melts at 1 120°F (604°C) and flows at 1 145°F (618°C). Ideal material for use in refrigeration service.

Sling Psychrometer: a device using two matched mercury-filled thermometers to obtain the relative humidity reading.

Slugging: the return of liquid refrigerant or oil to the compressor.

Soft Solder 50/50: a metallic alloy of 50% tin and 50% lead; used to repair or join ferrous metal parts for temperatures up to 250°F (121°C). Not recommended for refrigeration service.

Soft Solder 95/5: a metallic alloy of 95% tin and 5% antimony; used to repair or join ferrous metal parts for temperatures below 350°F (176°C). Often used for refrigeration service.

Solder: a metallic alloy used to unite metals.

Solenoid Valve: an electromagnetic valve controlled remotely by electrically energizing and deenergizing a coil.

Solid: a state of matter that is not liquid and is not a gas or vapor.

Sorbead: a desiccant.

Specific Heat: the quantity of heat required to change one pound of a substance by one degree Fahrenheit.

Specifications: service information and procedures provided by the manufacturer that must be followed in order for the system to operate properly.

Squirrel Cage: a blower case designed for use with the squirrel-cage blower.

Squirrel-Cage Blower: a blower wheel designed to provide a large volume of air with a minimum of noise. The blower is more compact than the fan and air can be directed more efficiently.

Standard Ton: see "Ton."

Stethoscope: an instrument used to convey sounds of the engine to the ear of the technician.

Strainer: see "Screen."

Stroke: the distance a piston travels from its lowest point to its highest point.

STV: see "Suction Throttling Valve."

Subcooler: a section of liquid line used to insure that only liquid refrigerant is delivered to the expansion valve. This line may be a part of the condenser or may be placed in the drip pan of the evaporator.

Substance: any form of matter.

Suction Line: the line connecting the evaporator outlet to the compressor inlet.

Suction Line Regulator: see "Suction Throttling Valve" or "Evaporator Pressure Regulator."

Suction Pressure: compressor inlet pressure. Reflects the pressure of the system on the low side.

Suction Service Valve: see "Low-side Service Valve."

Suction Side: that portion of the refrigeration system under low pressure; the suction side extends from the expansion device to the compressor inlet.

Suction Throttling Valve: a back-pressure-regulated device that prevents the freezeup of the evaporator core.

Suction Throttling Valve-POA: see "Positive Absolute Suction Throttling Valve."

Sump: the bottom part of the compressor that contains oil for lubrication of the moving parts of the compressor. Not all compressors have a sump.

Sun Load: heat intensity and/or light intensity produced by the sun.

Sun-load sensor: a device that senses heat and/or light intensity. See "Photovoltaic Diode."

Super Heat: adding heat intensity to a gas after the complete evaporation of a liquid.

Superheated Vapor: vapor at a temperature higher than its boiling point for a given pressure.

Superheat Switch: an electrical switch activated by an abnormal temperature-pressure condition (a superheated vapor); used for system protection.

Swaging: a means of shaping soft tubing so that two pieces of the same size of tubing can be joined without the use of a fitting. The inside diameter of one tube is increased to accept the outside diameter of the other tube.

Swash Plate Compressor: a compressor in which the pistons are driven by an offset (swash) plate affixed to the main shaft, such as the Delco Air six-cylinder compressor.

Sweat: the use of a soft solder to join two pieces of tubing or fittings using heat.

Sweat Fitting: a fitting designed to be used in sweating.

Sweeping: see "Purge."

System: all of the components and lines that make up an air-conditioning system.

Tailpipe: the outlet pipe from the evaporator to the compressor. See "Suction Line."

Tank: see "Header Tank" and "Expansion Tank."

Taps All Valve: see "Fitz-All Valve."

Temperature: heat intensity measured on a thermometer.

Temperature Gauge: a dash-mounted device that indicates engine temperature.

Temperature Indicator: see "Temperature Gauge." May also be COLD and HOT lamps to warn of overcooling or overheating of engine coolant.

Temperature-regulated Valve: see "Hot Gas Bypass Valve."

Temperature Sending Unit: see "Sending Unit."

Temperature Sensing Bulb: see "Remote Bulb."

TEV: abbreviation for thermostatic expansion valve.

Thermal: of, caused by, or pertaining to heat.

Thermal Delay Fuse: a device used with the "Compressor Protection Switch" which heats and blows a fuse to stop compressor action during abnormal operation.

Thermal Fuse: a temperature-sensitive fuse link designed so that it melts at a certain temperature and opens a circuit.

Thermal Limiter: an electrical or mechanical device used to control the intensity or quantity of heat.

Thermistor: a temperature-sensing resistor that has the ability to change values with changing temperature.

Thermostat: a device used to cycle the clutch to control the rate of refrigerant flow as a means of temperature control. The driver has control over the temperature desired.

Thermostatic Clutch Control: see "Thermostat."

Thermostatic Expansion Valve: the component of a refrigeration system that regulates the rate of flow of refrigerant into the evaporator as governed by the action of the remote bulb sensing tailpipe temperatures.

Thermostatic Switch: see "Thermostat."

Throttling Valve: see "Suction Throttling Valve" and "Evaporator Pressure Regulator."

Time-delay Relay: an electrical switch device that provides a time delay before closing (or opening).

Tinning: coating two surfaces to be joined with solder.

Ton of Refrigeration: the effect of melting one ton of ice in 24 hours. One ton equals cooling 12 000 Btu per hour.

Torque: a turning force; for example, the force required to seal a connection; measured in (English) foot-pounds (ft-lb) or inch-pounds (in-lb); (metric) newton-meters (N·m).

Torque Wrench: a wrench calibrated in a manner to determine torque, in in-lb or ft-lb (N·m) of a bolt or nut.

Total Heat Load: The amount of heat to be removed or added, based on all conditions.

Trace: a colored dye (suitable for use in a refrigeration system) introduced to the system to detect leaks.

Transducer: a vacuum valve used to transfer the electrical signal from the amplifier into a vacuum signal. This vacuum signal regulates the power servo unit in automatic temperature control units.

Trunk Unit: an automotive air-conditioning evaporator that mounts in the trunk compartment and is ducted through the package tray.

TXV: abbreviation for thermostatic expansion valve.

Ucon: a tradename for refrigerant.

Undercharge: a system that is short of refrigerant; this condition results in improper cooling.

Unloading Solenoid: an electrically controlled valve for operating the throttling valve or bypass valve in some applications.

Upstream Blower: a blower arranged in the duct system so as to push air through the heater and/or air-conditioner core(s).

Vacuum: any pressure below atmospheric pressure.

Vacuum Check Relay: a mechanical air-operated device that checks (closes off) a vacuum line to a pot whenever the manifold vacuum pressure falls below the applied vacuum pressure.

Vacuum Check Valve: an air-operated mechanical device that checks (closes) a vacuum line to the vacuum reserve tank whenever the manifold vacuum pressure falls below the reserve vacuum pressure.

Vacuum Hose: see "Vacuum Line."

Vacuum Line: a rubber tube used to transmit a vacuum reading from one to another.

Vacuum Motor: a device designed to provide mechanical control by the use of a vacuum.

Vacuum Pot: see "Vacuum Motor."

Vacuum Power Unit: a device for operating the doors and valves of an air conditioner using a vacuum as a source of power.

Vacuum Programmer: a device with a bleed valve which changes vacuum pressure by bleeding more or less air thereby controlling the vacuum signal.

Vacuum Pump: a mechanical device used to evacuate the refrigeration system to rid it of excess moisture and air.

Vacuum Reserve Tank: a container that is used to store reserve (engine) vacuum pressure.

Vacuum Tank: see "Vacuum Reserve Tank."

Valve Plate: a plate containing suction and/or discharge valves located under the compressor heads.

Valves-in-receiver (VIR): an assembly containing the expansion valve, suction throttling valve, desiccant, and receiver.

Vapor: see "Gas."

Vapor Lines: lines that are used to carry refrigerant gas or vapor.

Variable Displacement: to change the displacement of a compressor by changing the stroke of the piston(s).

V-belt: a rubber-like continuous loop placed between the engine crankshaft pulley and accessories to transfer rotary motion of the crankshaft to the accessories.

Ventilation: the act of supplying fresh air to an enclosed space, such as the inside of an automobile.

Venturi: a tubelike device that contains a restriction to create a negative pressure.

Vertical Flow Radiator: see "Downflow Radiator."

V-Groove Belt: see "Serpentine Belt."

VIR: abbreviation for "valves-in-receiver."

Viscosity: the thickness of a liquid or its resistance to flow.

Volatile Liquid: a liquid that evaporates readily to become a vapor.

Volt: a unit of measure of electrical force.

Voltmeter: a device used to measure volt(s).

V-pulley: used in automotive applications to drive the accessories, such as a water pump, generator, alternator, power steering, and air-conditioner compressor.

Water Control Valve: a mechanically operated or vacuum-operated shutoff valve that stops the flow of hot water to the heater.

Water Pump: a device, usually belt driven, that provides a means of circulating coolant through the engine and cooling system.

Water Valve: see "Water Control Valve."

Wobble Plate Compressor: see "Swash Plate Compressor."

Woodruff Key: an index key that prevents a pulley from turning on a shaft.

Zener Diode: a diode with properties that prevent current flow up to a given voltage and allow current flow above a given voltage.

INDEX